Lecture Notes in Computer Science 14029

Founding Editors

Gerhard Goos
Juris Hartmanis

The series Lecture Notes in Computer Science (LNCS), including its subseries Lecture Notes in Artificial Intelligence (LNAI) and Lecture Notes in Bioinformatics (LNBI), has established itself as a medium for the publication of new developments in computer science and information technology research, teaching, and education.

LNCS enjoys close cooperation with the computer science R & D community, the series counts many renowned academics among its volume editors and paper authors, and collaborates with prestigious societies. Its mission is to serve this international community by providing an invaluable service, mainly focused on the publication of conference and workshop proceedings and postproceedings. LNCS commenced publication in 1973.

Vincent G. Duffy
Editor

Digital Human Modeling and Applications in Health, Safety, Ergonomics and Risk Management

14th International Conference, DHM 2023
Held as Part of the 25th HCI International Conference, HCII 2023
Copenhagen, Denmark, July 23–28, 2023
Proceedings, Part II

 Springer

Editor
Vincent G. Duffy
Purdue University
West Lafayette, IN, USA

ISSN 0302-9743   ISSN 1611-3349 (electronic)
Lecture Notes in Computer Science
ISBN 978-3-031-35747-3   ISBN 978-3-031-35748-0 (eBook)
https://doi.org/10.1007/978-3-031-35748-0

This Springer imprint is published by the registered company Springer Nature Switzerland AG
The registered company address is: Gewerbestrasse 11, 6330 Cham, Switzerland

Foreword

Human-computer interaction (HCI) is acquiring an ever-increasing scientific and industrial importance, as well as having more impact on people's everyday lives, as an ever-growing number of human activities are progressively moving from the physical to the digital world. This process, which has been ongoing for some time now, was further accelerated during the acute period of the COVID-19 pandemic. The HCI International (HCII) conference series, held annually, aims to respond to the compelling need to advance the exchange of knowledge and research and development efforts on the human aspects of design and use of computing systems.

The 25th International Conference on Human-Computer Interaction, HCI International 2023 (HCII 2023), was held in the emerging post-pandemic era as a 'hybrid' event at the AC Bella Sky Hotel and Bella Center, Copenhagen, Denmark, during July 23–28, 2023. It incorporated the 21 thematic areas and affiliated conferences listed below.

A total of 7472 individuals from academia, research institutes, industry, and government agencies from 85 countries submitted contributions, and 1578 papers and 396 posters were included in the volumes of the proceedings that were published just before the start of the conference, these are listed below. The contributions thoroughly cover the entire field of human-computer interaction, addressing major advances in knowledge and effective use of computers in a variety of application areas. These papers provide academics, researchers, engineers, scientists, practitioners and students with state-of-the-art information on the most recent advances in HCI.

The HCI International (HCII) conference also offers the option of presenting 'Late Breaking Work', and this applies both for papers and posters, with corresponding volumes of proceedings that will be published after the conference. Full papers will be included in the 'HCII 2023 - Late Breaking Work - Papers' volumes of the proceedings to be published in the Springer LNCS series, while 'Poster Extended Abstracts' will be included as short research papers in the 'HCII 2023 - Late Breaking Work - Posters' volumes to be published in the Springer CCIS series.

I would like to thank the Program Board Chairs and the members of the Program Boards of all thematic areas and affiliated conferences for their contribution towards the high scientific quality and overall success of the HCI International 2023 conference. Their manifold support in terms of paper reviewing (single-blind review process, with a minimum of two reviews per submission), session organization and their willingness to act as goodwill ambassadors for the conference is most highly appreciated.

This conference would not have been possible without the continuous and unwavering support and advice of Gavriel Salvendy, founder, General Chair Emeritus, and Scientific Advisor. For his outstanding efforts, I would like to express my sincere appreciation to Abbas Moallem, Communications Chair and Editor of HCI International News.

July 2023   Constantine Stephanidis

HCI International 2023 Thematic Areas and Affiliated Conferences

Thematic Areas

- HCI: Human-Computer Interaction
- HIMI: Human Interface and the Management of Information

Affiliated Conferences

- EPCE: 20th International Conference on Engineering Psychology and Cognitive Ergonomics
- AC: 17th International Conference on Augmented Cognition
- UAHCI: 17th International Conference on Universal Access in Human-Computer Interaction
- CCD: 15th International Conference on Cross-Cultural Design
- SCSM: 15th International Conference on Social Computing and Social Media
- VAMR: 15th International Conference on Virtual, Augmented and Mixed Reality
- DHM: 14th International Conference on Digital Human Modeling and Applications in Health, Safety, Ergonomics and Risk Management
- DUXU: 12th International Conference on Design, User Experience and Usability
- C&C: 11th International Conference on Culture and Computing
- DAPI: 11th International Conference on Distributed, Ambient and Pervasive Interactions
- HCIBGO: 10th International Conference on HCI in Business, Government and Organizations
- LCT: 10th International Conference on Learning and Collaboration Technologies
- ITAP: 9th International Conference on Human Aspects of IT for the Aged Population
- AIS: 5th International Conference on Adaptive Instructional Systems
- HCI-CPT: 5th International Conference on HCI for Cybersecurity, Privacy and Trust
- HCI-Games: 5th International Conference on HCI in Games
- MobiTAS: 5th International Conference on HCI in Mobility, Transport and Automotive Systems
- AI-HCI: 4th International Conference on Artificial Intelligence in HCI
- MOBILE: 4th International Conference on Design, Operation and Evaluation of Mobile Communications

List of Conference Proceedings Volumes Appearing Before the Conference

1. LNCS 14011, Human-Computer Interaction: Part I, edited by Masaaki Kurosu and Ayako Hashizume
2. LNCS 14012, Human-Computer Interaction: Part II, edited by Masaaki Kurosu and Ayako Hashizume
3. LNCS 14013, Human-Computer Interaction: Part III, edited by Masaaki Kurosu and Ayako Hashizume
4. LNCS 14014, Human-Computer Interaction: Part IV, edited by Masaaki Kurosu and Ayako Hashizume
5. LNCS 14015, Human Interface and the Management of Information: Part I, edited by Hirohiko Mori and Yumi Asahi
6. LNCS 14016, Human Interface and the Management of Information: Part II, edited by Hirohiko Mori and Yumi Asahi
7. LNAI 14017, Engineering Psychology and Cognitive Ergonomics: Part I, edited by Don Harris and Wen-Chin Li
8. LNAI 14018, Engineering Psychology and Cognitive Ergonomics: Part II, edited by Don Harris and Wen-Chin Li
9. LNAI 14019, Augmented Cognition, edited by Dylan D. Schmorrow and Cali M. Fidopiastis
10. LNCS 14020, Universal Access in Human-Computer Interaction: Part I, edited by Margherita Antona and Constantine Stephanidis
11. LNCS 14021, Universal Access in Human-Computer Interaction: Part II, edited by Margherita Antona and Constantine Stephanidis
12. LNCS 14022, Cross-Cultural Design: Part I, edited by Pei-Luen Patrick Rau
13. LNCS 14023, Cross-Cultural Design: Part II, edited by Pei-Luen Patrick Rau
14. LNCS 14024, Cross-Cultural Design: Part III, edited by Pei-Luen Patrick Rau
15. LNCS 14025, Social Computing and Social Media: Part I, edited by Adela Coman and Simona Vasilache
16. LNCS 14026, Social Computing and Social Media: Part II, edited by Adela Coman and Simona Vasilache
17. LNCS 14027, Virtual, Augmented and Mixed Reality, edited by Jessie Y. C. Chen and Gino Fragomeni
18. LNCS 14028, Digital Human Modeling and Applications in Health, Safety, Ergonomics and Risk Management: Part I, edited by Vincent G. Duffy
19. LNCS 14029, Digital Human Modeling and Applications in Health, Safety, Ergonomics and Risk Management: Part II, edited by Vincent G. Duffy
20. LNCS 14030, Design, User Experience, and Usability: Part I, edited by Aaron Marcus, Elizabeth Rosenzweig and Marcelo Soares
21. LNCS 14031, Design, User Experience, and Usability: Part II, edited by Aaron Marcus, Elizabeth Rosenzweig and Marcelo Soares

22. LNCS 14032, Design, User Experience, and Usability: Part III, edited by Aaron Marcus, Elizabeth Rosenzweig and Marcelo Soares
23. LNCS 14033, Design, User Experience, and Usability: Part IV, edited by Aaron Marcus, Elizabeth Rosenzweig and Marcelo Soares
24. LNCS 14034, Design, User Experience, and Usability: Part V, edited by Aaron Marcus, Elizabeth Rosenzweig and Marcelo Soares
25. LNCS 14035, Culture and Computing, edited by Matthias Rauterberg
26. LNCS 14036, Distributed, Ambient and Pervasive Interactions: Part I, edited by Norbert Streitz and Shin'ichi Konomi
27. LNCS 14037, Distributed, Ambient and Pervasive Interactions: Part II, edited by Norbert Streitz and Shin'ichi Konomi
28. LNCS 14038, HCI in Business, Government and Organizations: Part I, edited by Fiona Fui-Hoon Nah and Keng Siau
29. LNCS 14039, HCI in Business, Government and Organizations: Part II, edited by Fiona Fui-Hoon Nah and Keng Siau
30. LNCS 14040, Learning and Collaboration Technologies: Part I, edited by Panayiotis Zaphiris and Andri Ioannou
31. LNCS 14041, Learning and Collaboration Technologies: Part II, edited by Panayiotis Zaphiris and Andri Ioannou
32. LNCS 14042, Human Aspects of IT for the Aged Population: Part I, edited by Qin Gao and Jia Zhou
33. LNCS 14043, Human Aspects of IT for the Aged Population: Part II, edited by Qin Gao and Jia Zhou
34. LNCS 14044, Adaptive Instructional Systems, edited by Robert A. Sottilare and Jessica Schwarz
35. LNCS 14045, HCI for Cybersecurity, Privacy and Trust, edited by Abbas Moallem
36. LNCS 14046, HCI in Games: Part I, edited by Xiaowen Fang
37. LNCS 14047, HCI in Games: Part II, edited by Xiaowen Fang
38. LNCS 14048, HCI in Mobility, Transport and Automotive Systems: Part I, edited by Heidi Krömker
39. LNCS 14049, HCI in Mobility, Transport and Automotive Systems: Part II, edited by Heidi Krömker
40. LNAI 14050, Artificial Intelligence in HCI: Part I, edited by Helmut Degen and Stavroula Ntoa
41. LNAI 14051, Artificial Intelligence in HCI: Part II, edited by Helmut Degen and Stavroula Ntoa
42. LNCS 14052, Design, Operation and Evaluation of Mobile Communications, edited by Gavriel Salvendy and June Wei
43. CCIS 1832, HCI International 2023 Posters - Part I, edited by Constantine Stephanidis, Margherita Antona, Stavroula Ntoa and Gavriel Salvendy
44. CCIS 1833, HCI International 2023 Posters - Part II, edited by Constantine Stephanidis, Margherita Antona, Stavroula Ntoa and Gavriel Salvendy
45. CCIS 1834, HCI International 2023 Posters - Part III, edited by Constantine Stephanidis, Margherita Antona, Stavroula Ntoa and Gavriel Salvendy
46. CCIS 1835, HCI International 2023 Posters - Part IV, edited by Constantine Stephanidis, Margherita Antona, Stavroula Ntoa and Gavriel Salvendy

47. CCIS 1836, HCI International 2023 Posters - Part V, edited by Constantine Stephanidis, Margherita Antona, Stavroula Ntoa and Gavriel Salvendy

https://2023.hci.international/proceedings

Preface

Software representations of humans, including aspects of anthropometry, biometrics, motion capture and prediction, as well as cognition modeling, are known as Digital Human Models (DHM), and are widely used in a variety of complex application domains where it is important to foresee and simulate human behavior, performance, safety, health and comfort. Automation depicting human emotion, social interaction and functional capabilities can also be modeled to support and assist in predicting human response in real-world settings. Such domains include medical and nursing applications, work, education and learning, ergonomics and design, as well as safety and risk management.

The 14th Digital Human Modeling & Applications in Health, Safety, Ergonomics & Risk Management (DHM) Conference, an affiliated conference of the HCI International Conference 2023, encouraged papers from academics, researchers, industry and professionals, on a broad range of theoretical and applied issues related to Digital Human Modeling and its applications.

The research papers contributed to this year's volumes span across different fields that fall within the scope of the DHM Conference. The study of DHM issues in various application domains has yielded works emphasizing human factors and ergonomics based on human models, novel approaches in healthcare, and the application of Artificial Intelligence in medicine. Applications of interest are shown across many industries. Job design and productivity, robotics and intelligent systems are among the human-technology modeling and results reporting efforts this year.

Two volumes of the HCII 2023 proceedings are dedicated to this year's edition of the DHM Conference. The first volume focuses on topics related to human factors and ergonomics, job design and human productivity, as well as interaction with robots and exoskeletons. The second volume focuses on topics related to digital health, IoT and AI in medicine and healthcare, as well as modeling complex human behavior and phenomena.

Papers of these volumes are included for publication after a minimum of two single–blind reviews from the members of the DHM Program Board or, in some cases, from members of the Program Boards of other affiliated conferences. I would like to thank all of them for their invaluable contribution, support and efforts.

July 2023   Vincent G. Duffy

14th International Conference on Digital Human Modeling and Applications in Health, Safety, Ergonomics and Risk Management (DHM 2023)

Program Board Chair: **Vincent G. Duffy,** *Purdue University, USA*

- Karthik Adapa, *UNC-Chapel Hill, USA*
- Giuseppe Andreoni, *Politecnico di Milano, Italy*
- Mária Babicsné Horváth, *Budapest University of Technology and Economics, Hungary*
- Angelos Barmpoutis, *University of Florida, USA*
- André Calero Valdez, *University of Lübeck, Germany*
- Yaqin Cao, *Anhui Polytechnic University, P.R. China*
- Damien Chablat, *CNRS/LS2N, France*
- Anirban Chowdhury, *NMIMS University, India*
- H. Onan Demirel, *Oregon State University, USA*
- Yi Ding, Anhui *Polytechnic University, P.R. China*
- Manish K. Dixit, *Texas A&M University, USA*
- Lucia Donatelli, *Saarland University, Germany*
- Martin Fleischer, *Technical University of Munich, Germany*
- Martin Fränzle, *Oldenburg University, Germany*
- RongRong Fu, *East China University of Science and Technology, P.R. China*
- Afzal Godil, *NIST, USA*
- Wenbin Guo, U*niversity of Florida, USA*
- Jaana Hallamaa, *University of Helsinki, Finland*
- Sogand Hasanzadeh, *Purdue University, USA*
- Nicola Helfer, *KAN - Commission for Occupational Health and Safety and Standardization, Germany*
- Sandy Ingram, *University of Applied Sciences of Western Switzerland, Switzerland*
- Genett Isabel Jimenez Delgado, *Institucíon Universitaria de Barranquilla IUB, Colombia*
- Taina Kalliokoski, *University of Helsinki, Finland*
- Sougata Karmakar, *Indian Institute of Technology Guwahati, India*
- Najmeh Khalili-Mahani, *Concordia University, Canada*
- Steffi Kohl, *Zuyd University of Applied Sciences, The Netherlands*
- Nicola Francesco Lopomo, *Università degli Studi di Brescia, Italy*
- Alexander Mehler, *Goethe University Frankfurt, Germany*
- Manivannan Muniyandi, *IIT Madras, India*
- Peter Nickel, *Institute for Occupational Safety and Health of the German Social Accident Insurance (IFA), Germany*
- Miguel Ortiz-Barrios, *Universidad de la Costa CUC, Colombia*
- Thaneswer Patel, *North Eastern Regional Institute of Science and Technology, India*
- Manikam Pillay, *RESMEERTS, Australia*

- James Pustejovsky, *Brandeis University, USA*
- Qing-Xing Qu, *Northeastern University, P.R. China*
- Caterina Rizzi, *University of Bergamo, Italy*
- Deep Seth, *Mahindra University, India*
- Thitirat Siriborvornratanakul, *National Institute of Development Administration, Thailand*
- Beatriz Sousa Santos, *University of Aveiro, Portugal*
- Debadutta Subudhi, *IIT Madras, India*
- Youchao Sun, *Nanjing University of Aeronautics and Astronautics, P.R. China*
- Zhengtang Tan, *Hunan Normal University, P.R. China*
- Leonor Teixeira, *University of Aveiro, Portugal*
- Renran Tian, *IUPUI, USA*
- Joseph Timoney, *Maynooth University, Ireland*
- Alexander Trende, *German Aerospace Center (DLR), Germany*
- Dustin van der Haar, *University of Johannesburg, South Africa*
- Kuan Yew Wong, *Universiti Teknologi Malaysia, Malaysia*
- Shuping Xiong, *Korea Advanced Institute of Science and Technology, South Korea*
- James Yang, *Texas Tech University, USA*
- Azeema Yaseen, *Maynooth University, Ireland*
- Yulin Zhao, *Guangdong University of Technology, P.R. China*

The full list with the Program Board Chairs and the members of the Program Boards of all thematic areas and affiliated conferences of HCII2023 is available online at:

http://www.hci.international/board-members-2023.php

HCI International 2024 Conference

The 26th International Conference on Human-Computer Interaction, HCI International 2024, will be held jointly with the affiliated conferences at the Washington Hilton Hotel, Washington, DC, USA, June 29 – July 4, 2024. It will cover a broad spectrum of themes related to Human-Computer Interaction, including theoretical issues, methods, tools, processes, and case studies in HCI design, as well as novel interaction techniques, interfaces, and applications. The proceedings will be published by Springer. More information will be made available on the conference website: http://2024.hci.international/.

General Chair
Prof. Constantine Stephanidis
University of Crete and ICS-FORTH
Heraklion, Crete, Greece
Email: general_chair@hcii2024.org

https://2024.hci.international/

Contents – Part II

Digital Health

Computational Support to Apply Eladeb Auto-Evaluation in Multiple
Platforms 3
 Adriano Mendes Borges, Walbert Cunha Monteiro,
 Vinicius Favacho Queiroz, Kelly Vale Pinheiro,
 Thiago Augusto Soares de Sousa, and Bianchi Serique Meiguins

Let's Start Tomorrow - Bridging the Intention Behavior Gap Using Fitness
Apps 20
 Laura Burbach, Rachel Ganser, Luisa Vervier, Martina Ziefle,
 and André Calero Valdez

A Study on the Service Design of Self-health Management for Adolescents
with Asthma Based on Persuasive Technology 38
 Zhe Hu and Yi Li

Demystifying the Role of Digital Leadership in the Healthcare Industry:
A Systematic Review Towards the Development of a Digital Leadership
Framework in the Healthcare Industry 49
 Muzammil Hussain, Isra Sarfraz, and Abhishek Sharma

Promote or Restrict? A Co-design Practice of a Palliative Care Information
Management System in China 65
 Yue Jiang, Jing Chen, Qi Chen, and Long Liu

Motivation Enhancement Design for Individual Exercise Habits Based
on Multimodal Physiological Signals 77
 Xiangyu Liu, Di Zhang, Jiayuan Lu, Bin Shi, Lv Ding, Yingjie Huang,
 Ke Miao, and Hao Tang

Designing Relational AI-Powered Digital Health Coaching for Chronic
Disease Prevention and Management 88
 Yunmin Oh, Kika Arias, Lisa Auster-Gussman, and Sarah Graham

A Hybrid Multi-criteria Framework for Evaluating the Performance
of Clinical Labs During the Covid-19 Pandemic 104
 Miguel Ortiz-Barrios, Andrea Espeleta-Aris, Genett Jiménez-Delgado,
 Helder Jose Celani-De Souza, Jonas Santana-de Oliveira,
 Alexandros Konios, Leonardo Campis-Freyle,
 and Eduardo Navarro-Jimenez

The Role of Social Networks When Using Digital Health Interventions
for Multimorbidity 123
  Sara Polak, Cora van Leeuwen, Myriam Sillevis Smitt, Julie Doyle,
  Suzanne Cullen-Smith, and An Jacobs

Applying the Trajectories Conceptual Framework: A Case Study of an IoT
Health Data Monitoring Application 138
  Elizabeth Reisher, Soundarya Jonnalagadda, and Ann Fruhling

Multidimensional Data Integration and Analysis for Youth Health Care
During the Covid-19 Pandemic 154
  Jianlun Wu, Yaping Ye, Yuxi Li, Ruichen Cong, Yishan Bian,
  Yuerong Chen, Kiichi Tago, Shoji Nishimura, Atsushi Ogihara,
  and Qun Jin

Design for Shoulder and Neck Pain Based on Yoga Asanas Practice 169
  Yeqi Wu, Ziyan Dong, Xinran Liu, Xiang Wu, Tianfeng Xu, Xiangyu Liu,
  and Li Xu

Proposal for Family Health Management Service Based on Personal
Medical and Lifelog Data, and Genetic Information 185
  Jae Sun Yi and Mingyeong Kim

An Interactive Design Solution for Sleep Persuasion Based on Health Risk
Visualization 197
  Kaiqiao Zheng, Jing Luo, and Yuqing Yan

Comparison of Physiological Responses to Stroop Word Color Test
and IAPS Stimulation 211
  Sayyedjavad Ziaratnia, Peeraya Sripian, Tipporn Laohakangvalvit,
  and Midori Sugaya

IoT and AI in Medicine and Healthcare

Artificial Intelligence for Clinical Intensive Care in the Hospital:
Opportunities and Challenges 225
  Kirsten Brukamp

Proposal of a Prototype Wireless Network Based on IoT that Allows
the Monitoring of Vital Signs of Patients 236
  Leonel Hernandez, Aji Prasetya, Jainer Enrique Molina-Romero,
  Leonardo Campis, Jose Ruiz Ariza, Hugo Hernández Palma,
  and Emilse María Vásquez Avendaño

Mel Frequency Cepstral Coefficients and Support Vector Machines
for Cough Detection 250
Mpho Mashika and Dustin van der Haar

Multi-stakeholder Approach for Designing an AI Model to Predict
Treatment Adherence 260
Beatriz Merino-Barbancho, Peña Arroyo, Miguel Rujas,
Ana Cipric, Nicholas Ciccone, Francisco Lupiáñez-Villanueva,
Ana Roca-Umbert Würth, Frans Folkvord, María Fernanda Cabrera,
María Teresa Arredondo, and Giuseppe Fico

Using Lean Six Sigma and Discrete-Event Simulation to Reduce Patient
Waiting Time Before Sample Collection: A Clinical Lab Case Study 272
Miguel Ortiz-Barrios, Matías García-Constantino,
Zahiry Castro-Camargo, Cindy Charris-Maldonado,
Sulay Escorcia-Charris, Gisell Sierra-Urbina,
Estefany Molinares-Ramirez, Alina Torres-Mercado,
Armando Pérez-Aguilar, and Pedro López-Meza

A Hybrid Fuzzy MCDM Approach to Identify the Intervention Priority
Level of Covid-19 Patients in the Emergency Department: A Case Study 284
Armando Perez-Aguilar, Miguel Ortiz-Barrios, Pablo Pancardo,
and Fernando Orrante-Weber-Burque

Generation of Consistent Slip, Trip and Fall Kinematic Data via Instability
Detection and Recovery Performance Analysis for Use in Machine
Learning Algorithms for (Near) Fall Detection 298
Moritz Schneider, Anika Weber, Mirko Kaufmann, Annette Kluge,
Ulrich Hartmann, Kiros Karamanidis, and Rolf Ellegast

Safe Environments to Understand Medical AI - Designing a Diabetes
Simulation Interface for Users of Automated Insulin Delivery 306
Tim Schrills, Marthe Gruner, Heiko Peuscher, and Thomas Franke

Advanced Artificial Intelligence Methods for Medical Applications 329
Thitirat Siriborvornratanakul

Automated Nystagmus Parameter Determination: Differentiating
Nystagmic from Voluntary Eye-Movements 341
Alexander Walther, Julian Striegl, Claudia Loitsch,
Sebastian Pannasch, and Gerhard Weber

Modeling Complex Human Behavior and Phenomena

Disaster Mitigation Education Through the Use of the InaRISK Personal
Application in Indonesia   357
   Afisa, Achmad Nurmandi, Misran, and Dimas Subekti

Using Agent-Based Modeling to Understand Complex Social Phenomena
- A Curriculum Approach   368
   André Calero Valdez, Johannes Nakayama, Luisa Vervier,
   Hendrik Nunner, and Martina Ziefle

Policy-Based Reinforcement Learning for Assortative Matching in Human
Behavior Modeling   378
   Ou Deng and Qun Jin

The Influence of Background Color and Font Size of Mobile Payment
App Interface on Elderly User Experience   392
   Hongyu Du, Weilin Liu, Peicheng Wang, Xiang Sun, and Wenping Zhang

A Roadmap for Technological Innovation in Multimodal Communication
Research   402
   Alina Gregori, Federica Amici, Ingmar Brilmayer, Aleksandra Ćwiek,
   Lennart Fritzsche, Susanne Fuchs, Alexander Henlein,
   Oliver Herbort, Frank Kügler, Jens Lemanski, Katja Liebal,
   Andy Lücking, Alexander Mehler, Kim Tien Nguyen, Wim Pouw,
   Pilar Prieto, Patrick Louis Rohrer, Paula G. Sánchez-Ramón,
   Martin Schulte-Rüther, Petra B. Schumacher, Stefan R. Schweinberger,
   Volker Struckmeier, Patrick C. Trettenbrein, and Celina I. von Eiff

News Articles on Social Media: Showing Balanced Content Adds More
Credibility Than Trust Badges or User Ratings   439
   Patrick Halbach, Laura Burbach, Martina Ziefle,
   and André Calero Valdez

Semantic Scene Builder: Towards a Context Sensitive Text-to-3D Scene
Framework   461
   Alexander Henlein, Attila Kett, Daniel Baumartz, Giuseppe Abrami,
   Alexander Mehler, Johannes Bastian, Yannic Blecher,
   David Budgenhagen, Roman Christof, Tim-Oliver Ewald,
   Tim Fauerbach, Patrick Masny, Julian Mende, Paul Schnüre,
   and Marc Viel

A Digital Human Emotion Modeling Application Using Metaverse
Technology in the Post-COVID-19 Era   480
   Chutisant Kerdvibulvech

Bibliometric Analysis and Systematic Literature Review on Data
Visualization 490
    Byeongmok Kim, Yonggab Kim, and Vincent G. Duffy

A Modular Framework for Modelling and Verification of Activities
in Ambient Intelligent Systems 503
    *Alexandros Konios, Yasir Imtiaz Khan, Matias Garcia-Constantino,
and Irvin Hussein Lopez-Nava*

An Analysis and Review of Maintenance-Related Commercial Aviation
Accidents and Incidents 531
    *Neelakshi Majumdar, Divya Bhargava, Tracy El Khoury,
Karen Marais, and Vincent G. Duffy*

Analysis of Human Factors and Resilience Competences in ASRS Data
Using Natural Language Processing 548
    Mako Ono and Miwa Nakanishi

Non-immersive vs. Immersive: The Difference in Empathy, User
Engagement, and User Experience When Simulating the Daily Life
of Rheumatoid Arthritis Patients 562
    *Alexicia Richardson, Cheryl D. Seals, Kimberly B. Garza,
Gary Hawkins, Sathish Akula, Sean Kim, Adam Biggs, Lily McGuckin,
Ravindra Joshi, and Majdi Lusta*

Trend Analysis on Experience Evaluation of Intelligent Automobile
Cockpit Based on Bibliometrics 576
    Lei Wu and Qinqin Sheng

Intelligent Human-Computer Interaction Interface: A Bibliometric
Analysis of 2010–2022 590
    Yi Zhang, Yaqin Cao, Yu Liu, and Xiangjun Hu

Author Index 605

Contents – Part I

Human Factors and Ergonomics

Simulation of Cable Driven Elbow Exosuit in Matlab 3
Sreejan Alapati, Deep Seth, and Yannick Aoustin

Experimental Research on Ergonomics Evaluation of HMDs 14
Kai An, Xu Wu, Chongchong Miao, Lin Ding, and Guoqiang Sun

A Platform for Long-Term Analysis and Reporting of Sitting Posture 24
*Rafael de Pinho André, Almir Fonseca, Kayo Yokoyama, Lucas Westfal,
Luis Laguardia, and Marcelo de Souza*

Design and Development of a Novel Wearable System for Assessing
the Biomechanical and Psychological Risk of the Healthcare Worker 35
*Carla Dei, Giulia Stevanoni, Emilia Biffi, Fabio Storm,
Nicola Francesco Lopomo, Paolo Perego, and Giuseppe Andreoni*

The Impact of Smart Glasses on Commissioning Efficiency Depends
on the Display Device Used 48
*Daniel Friemert, Martin Laun, Christopher Braun, Nicolai Leuthner,
Rolf Ellegast, Christoph Schiefer, Volker Harth, Claudia Terschüren,
Kiros Karamanidis, and Ulrich Hartmann*

Digital Twin Modelling for Human-Centered Ergonomic Design 58
*Micah Wilson George, Nandini Gaikwad, Vincent G. Duffy,
and Allen G. Greenwood*

Wearables and Mixed Reality in Applied Ergonomics: A Literature Review 70
Xiyun Hu, Runlin Duan, Ziyi Liu, and Vincent G. Duffy

Enhancing Ergonomic Design Process with Digital Human Models
for Improved Driver Comfort in Space Environment 87
*Md Tariqul Islam, Kamelia Sepanloo, Ronak Velluvakkandy,
Andre Luebke, and Vincent G. Duffy*

Improving Facility Layout Using an Ergonomics and Simulation-Based
Approach 102
Krittika J. Iyer, Nandini Narula, Marlyn Binu, and Vincent G. Duffy

A Smart Sensor Suit (SSS) to Assess Cognitive and Physical Fatigue
with Machine Learning 120
   Ashish Jaiswal, Mohammad Zaki Zadeh, Aref Hebri,
   Ashwin Ramesh Babu, and Fillia Makedon

Application of Ramsis Digital Human Modeling to Human Factors in Space ... 135
   Kevin Jin, Mackenzie Richards, and Kevin Lee

Ergonomics Research of Domestic Vehicle Cab Central Control System
Based on Entropy Method 147
   Qingchen Li and Yongxin Wu

Investigating the Time Dependency of Elbow Flexion Angle Variations
in Real and Virtual Grabbing Tasks Using Statistical Parametric Mapping 162
   Nils Mayat, Stella Adam, Mahmood Alkawarit, Anika Weber,
   Jan P. Vox, Krzysztof Izdebski, Thomas Schüler, Karen Insa Wolf,
   and Daniel Friemert

An Experimental Study of the Psychological Effects of Vision Loss
for Practical Application to Windowless Cockpits 175
   Yuki Mekata, Nagisa Hashimoto, and Miwa Nakanishi

Human Factors in Interface Design of Electronic Control Systems
for Mechanical Equipment in Stage and Studio Automation 184
   Peter Nickel

Quantitative Characterization of Upper Limb Intensity and Symmetry
of Use in Healthcare Workers Using Wrist-Worn Accelerometers 194
   Micaela Porta, Giulia Casu, Bruno Leban, and Massimiliano Pau

Human Ergonomic Assessment Within "Industry 5.0" Workplace: Do
Standard Observational Methods Correlate with Kinematic-Based Index
in Reaching Tasks? 205
   Emilia Scalona, Doriana De Marco, Pietro Avanzini,
   Maddalena Fabbri Destro, Giuseppe Andreoni,
   and Nicola Francesco Lopomo

Challenges for Standardized Ergonomic Assessments by Digital Human
Modeling 215
   Kerstin Schmidt, Paul Schmidt, and Anna Schlenz

Assessing Ergonomics on IPS IMMA Family of Manikins 242
   Manuela Vargas, Maria Pia Cavatorta, Valerio Cibrario,
   Enrica Bosani, and Meike Schaub

Improving Ergonomic Training Using Augmented Reality Feedback 256
Diego Vicente, Mario Schwarz, and Gerrit Meixner

BGHW Warehouse Simulation – Virtual Reality Supports Prevention
of Slip, Trip and Fall (STF) Accidents 276
Christoph Wetzel, Andy Lungfiel, and Peter Nickel

The Low Back Fatigue Research Based on Controlled Sedentary Driving
Tasks 290
*Xiang Wu, Tianfeng Xu, Yeqi Wu, Ziyan Dong, Xinran Liu, Xiangyu Liu,
and Li Xu*

An Experimental Study of the Comfort of Stroke Rehabilitation Gloves
Based on ANSYS 303
Yanmin Xue, Liangliang Shi, Qing Liu, and Suihuai Yu

Job Design and Human Productivity

Development and Evaluation of a Knowledge-Based Cyber-Physical
Production System to Support Industrial Set-Up Processes Considering
Ergonomic and User-Centered Aspects 317
*Nils Darwin Abele, Sven Hoffmann,
Aparecido Fabiano Pinatti De Carvalho, Marcus Schweitzer,
Volker Wulf, and Karsten Kluth*

Evaluating Domain-Independent Small Talk Conversations to Improve
Clinical Communication Interaction for Human and Machine 330
*Chloe Aguilar, Muhammad Amith, Lu Tang, Jane Hamilton,
Lara S. Savas, Danniel Rhee, Tazrin Khan, and Cui Tao*

The Impacts of Covid-19 Pandemic on Nursing Workflow in a Medical ICU ... 344
*Vitor de Oliveira Vargas, Jung Hyup Kim, Alireza Kasaie Sharifi,
and Laurel Despins*

Human Factors in Manufacturing: A Systematic Literature Review 355
Fabio Garofalo and Passawit Puangseree

Pre-defined Emergencies on Demand: Simulation-Based Analysis
of Information Processing in Emergency Dispatching 368
Marthe Gruner, Tim Schrills, and Thomas Franke

Design Requirements for Working with Mobile Smart devices—a Scoping
Review 383
Germaine Haase, Kristin Gilbert, and Ulrike Pietrzyk

Implementation of Lean Six Sigma to Improve the Quality and Productivity
in Textile Sector: A Case Study 395
  Genett Jiménez-Delgado, Iván Quintero-Ariza, Jeremy Romero-Gómez,
  Carlos Montero-Bula, Edgar Rojas-Castro, Gilberto Santos,
  José Carlos Sá, Luz Londoño-Lara, Hugo Hernández-Palma,
  and Leonardo Campis-Freyle

Simulation-Based Training in the Manufacturing Industry: A Suggested
Quick Assessment 413
  Tiantian Li and Kevin J. Kaufman-Ortiz

Analysis of Work-Flow Design Related to Aspects of Productivity
and Ergonomics 429
  Sindhu Meenakshi and Santhosh Kumar Balasankar

Quality of Experience and Mental Energy Use of Cobot Workers
in Manufacturing Enterprises 444
  Fabio Alexander Storm, Luca Negri, Claudia Carissoli,
  Alberto Peña Fernández, Carla Dei, Marta Bassi, Daniel Berckmans,
  and Antonella Delle Fave

Something Old, Something New, Something Inspired by Deep Blue?:
A Scoping Review on the Digital Transformation of Office and Knowledge
Work from the Perspective of OSH 459
  Patricia Tegtmeier, Jan Terhoeven, and Sascha Wischniewski

Description of Sequential Risky Decision-Making Choices
in Human-Machine Teams Using Eye-Tracking and Decision Tree 478
  Wei Xiong, Chen Wang, and Liang Ma

Interacting with Robots and Exoskeletons

Introduction of a Cobot as Intermittent Haptic Contact Interfaces in Virtual
Reality 497
  V. K Guda, S. Mugisha, C. Chevallereau, and D. Chablat

The Efficiency of Augmented Pointing with and Without Speech
in a Collaborative Virtual Environment 510
  Oliver Herbort and Lisa-Marie Krause

Does the Form of Attachment Have an Impact on Occupational Thermal
Comfort? A Study on the Spinal Exoskeleton 525
  Yang Liu, Yanmin Xue, Chang Ge, Yihui Zhou, and Wen Yan

A Multimodal Data Model for Simulation-Based Learning
with Va.Si.Li-Lab 539
  Alexander Mehler, Mevlüt Bagci, Alexander Henlein,
  Giuseppe Abrami, Christian Spiekermann, Patrick Schrottenbacher,
  Maxim Konca, Andy Lücking, Juliane Engel, Marc Quintino,
  Jakob Schreiber, Kevin Saukel, and Olga Zlatkin-Troitschanskaia

TWINMED T-SHIRT, a Smart Wearable System for ECG and EMG
Monitoring for Rehabilitation with Exoskeletons 566
  Paolo Perego, Roberto Sironi, Emanuele Gruppioni,
  and Giuseppe Andreoni

Evaluating Multimodal Behavior Schemas with VoxWorld 578
  Christopher Tam, Richard Brutti, Kenneth Lai, and James Pustejovsky

Robust Motion Recognition Using Gesture Phase Annotation 592
  Hannah VanderHoeven, Nathaniel Blanchard, and Nikhil Krishnaswamy

Short Intervention of Self-study-Videos in a Safety Engineering Learning
Arrangement: An Investigation of Effects on Learning Performance
and Motivation 609
  Julia Waldorf, Florian Hafner, Marina Bier, Nina Hanning,
  Lucia Maletz, Carolin Frank, and Anke Kahl

An AI-Based Action Detection UAV System to Improve Firefighter Safety 632
  Hong Wang, Yuan Feng, Xu Huang, and Wenbin Guo

The Effect of Transparency on Human-Exoskeleton Interaction 642
  Yilin Wang, Jing Qiu, Hong Cheng, Xiuying Hu, Peng Xu,
  Jingming Hou, and Hongqin Xie

Author Index 653

Digital Health

Computational Support to Apply Eladeb Auto-Evaluation in Multiple Platforms

Adriano Mendes Borges[1]📧, Walbert Cunha Monteiro[1](✉)📧,
Vinicius Favacho Queiroz[1]📧, Kelly Vale Pinheiro[2]📧,
Thiago Augusto Soares de Sousa[1]📧, and Bianchi Serique Meiguins[1]📧

[1] Federal University of Pará, Rua Augusto Corrêa, 01, Guamá, Belém,
PA 66075-110, Brazil
`ppgcc@ufpa.br, walbertcm@gmail.com`

[2] Abrigo Especial Calabriano, Av. Senador Lemos, 1431, Telegráfo, Belém,
PA 66113-000, Brazil
`abrigocalabriano@pobresservos.org.br`
`https://ppgcc.propesp.ufpa.br`

Abstract. Assessing the difficulties and needs of psychiatric patients is the first step in an intervention process. A self-assessment instrument called (ELADEB) was developed to quantitatively measure the difficulties and needs of psychiatric patients and draw individualized clinical profiles for use in patient care. The instrument is familiar, but it is not easy to find free computer versions. This paper aims to present computer versions of the ELADEB instrument in the WEB/Desktop, Augmented Reality (AR), and Virtual Reality (VR) versions capable of creating standard or customized self-assessment scenarios with media content more familiar to the patient (images, animations, and videos) and also the result of usability evaluations applied to the software developed. Some motivations include the remote use of the tool to avoid patients being unattended in a scenario of isolation or geographical distance, the possibility of using new environments such as AR and VR, and the increase in patient engagement thanks to the personalization of the self-assessment. Finally, the results of this work can provide greater access to the ELADEB tool, especially remotely, due to the more familiar and dynamic content and thus improve patient engagement in the self-assessment process. For future works, new versions should be made available to minimize the difficulties found in the usability tests, evaluations with more specialists in the application domain should be carried out to later evaluate with another audience.

Keywords: ELADEB · Usability Assessment · WEB Application · Augmented Reality · Virtual Reality

---

Federal University of Pará.

V. G. Duffy (Ed.): HCII 2023, LNCS 14029, pp. 3–19, 2023.
https://doi.org/10.1007/978-3-031-35748-0_1

1 Introduction

The public health crisis generated by the pandemic of COVID-19 has impacted people's lives in many countries, causing negative consequences for the psychosocial and mental issues of the population [7]. The World Health Organization (WHO) declares that the pandemic has promoted an increase in cases of depression, suicide, self-mutilation, increased loneliness, anxiety, insomnia, and harmful use of alcohol and drugs [10–12].

Patients affected by such adversities may have diverse diagnostic profiles, symptoms, cognitive dysfunctions, skill deficits, social problems, and barriers to receiving adequate treatment, such as prejudice, time, lack of available services, inability to pay for services, geographical limitations, or social isolation [3,8,9].

Assessing patients' difficulties and needs is the first step in establishing an intervention process. This assessment identifies priorities to be addressed, assisting professionals in determining intervention strategies, treatment choices, and goals [13,17].

Researchers have developed a self-assessment instrument for identifying the difficulties and needs of psychiatric patients who need to be more verbal and are reluctant to use classical questionnaires. The instrument is called Echelles Lausannoises d'Auto-Evaluation des Difficultés Et des Besoins (ELADEB). It is widely used in French-speaking countries such as Switzerland, France, and Canada and can be used in different clinical contexts [6,13]. The instrument has methods to identify and quantitatively measure the areas of life in which patients with psychosocial problems encounter difficulties. The instrument application process uses manual methods and depends on the interaction between a healthcare professional and the patient [13].

The self-assessment instrument is available via the internet through a kit for printing, containing: instruction manual, a set of 20 cards (representing areas of life), sets of labels, and a spreadsheet for quantification of results and determination of the profile of difficulties and needs of the patient [2]. Figure 1 presents some elements of the ELADEB kit.

Fig. 1. Set of cards and labels used in ELADEB. Adapted from [2].

Thus, this paper aims to present computer versions of the ELADEB instrument for WEB/Desktop, Augmented Reality (AR), and Virtual Reality (VR) platforms using standard content of the methodology or customizable (images, animations, and videos more familiar to the patient), and evaluate the usability of the systems based on Ergonomic Inspections [4], and Cognitive Walkthrough technique [14] from two expert evaluators in the field of computing and one expert in the application domain.

The contributions of this work will provide access to the ELADEB tool, especially remotely, improve the engagement of the assisted patient in the self-assessment process due to the personalized content (more familiar and dynamic to the patient), provide new environments (AR and VR) for application of the self-assessment instrument, and propose improvements in the interface design.

The results show that the prototypes developed are functional and usable remotely for WEB/Desktop, AR, and VR platforms. The first phase of usability evaluations identified criteria and subcriteria with a higher and lower degree of conformity and proposals for improvements in the interfaces suggested.

2 Digital Self-assessment Instrument ELADEB

This section presents the characteristics of the applications developed. Figure 2 displays an overview of the system architecture and the elements that compose it.

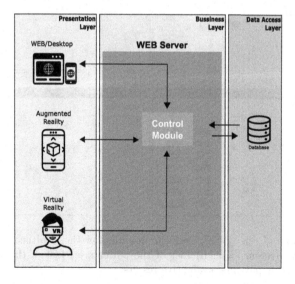

Fig. 2. Overview of the multilayer architecture applied to the ELADEB system.

The presentation layer enables user interaction with the system interfaces. The components of the interfaces are implemented using the WEB/Desktop, AR, and VR platforms. The business layer implements and processes the application's business logic through rules and data passed between components. The data layer has objects responsible for performing data access and persistence logic.

All modules allow you to apply assessments with standardized or customizable elements (images, animations, and videos). Only the WEB/Desktop module permits the healthcare professional to create assessment scenarios for the patient.

2.1 WEB/Desktop Module

Accessible from a computer or mobile device (smartphone or tablet) connected to the internet, the patient can perform the self-assessment procedure of difficulties and needs. The health professional will manage: patients, patient assessment scenarios, and the results of the assessments.

Figure 3 presents system interfaces for healthcare professional user requirements. Figure 4 and Fig. 5 show system interfaces for patient user requirements.

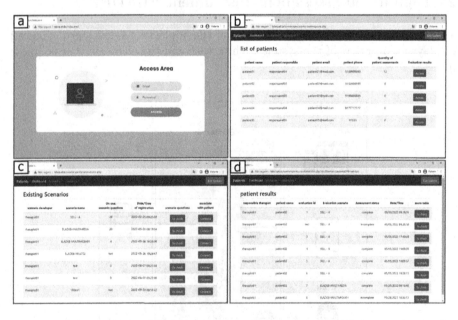

Fig. 3. Interfaces of the WEB/Desktop module for the healthcare professional's requirements. a) System login; b) List of the patients. c) List of the evaluative scenarios; d) List of the patients' evaluative results.

Fig. 4. WEB/Desktop module interfaces for patient requirements. a) Select assessment. b)Instructions on the assessment process.

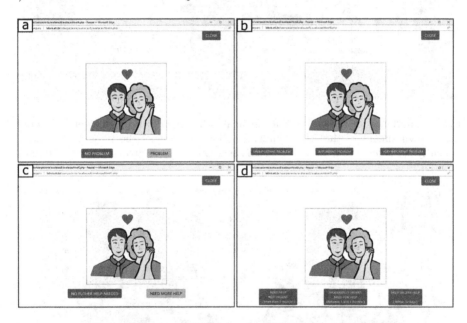

Fig. 5. WEB/Desktop module interfaces for patient user assessment using standardized elements. a) Difficulty assessment, b) Quantification of the degree of difficulty, c) Needs assessment, d) Quantification of the degree of need. Adapted from [2].

2.2   Augmented Reality Module

Available through mobile devices (smartphones or tablets), it combines standardized or customized virtual objects from assessment of difficulties and needs to the real-world environment. Figure 6 and Fig. 7 present the interactive environment of the AR module.

Fig. 6. Interfaces for patient user assessment using standardized elements. a) Interactive environment of the AR module; b) Quantification of the patient's degree of difficulty; c) Selection of needs; d) Quantification of the degree of needs. Adapted from [2].

Fig. 7. Show the interface with a customizable element for quantifying the intensity of difficulties.

2.3   Virtual Reality Module

Accessible from specialized equipment (virtual reality glasses) or less immersive equipment (monitor), it allows the patient to perform assessments of difficulties and needs in an immersive and interactive environment. In this module, senses such as stereoscopic have stimulated vision. Figure 8 and 9 show interfaces of the VR module for the patient user.

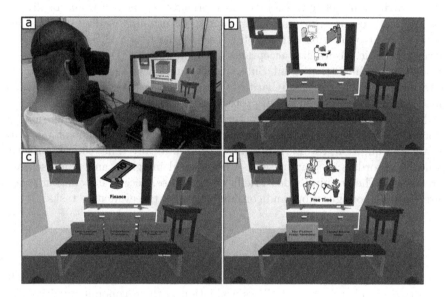

Fig. 8. Interfaces using standardized elements. a) Interaction between the user and the VR module. b) Interface for assessing difficulties. c) Interface for quantifying the degree of difficulties. d) Interface for assessing needs. Adapted from [2].

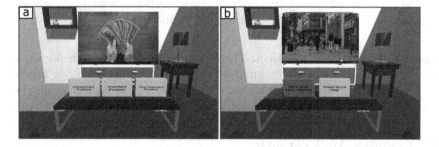

Fig. 9. Interactive VR module environment for assessing difficulties and needs with personalized elements (video). a) Quantification of the degree of difficulty. b) Needs assessment.

3   Methodology

3.1   Participant Profile and Testing Procedures

Three volunteers participated in the evaluations, two men and one woman between 25 and 50 years old, and they were invited via email. Two are developers and know usability evaluation techniques, and one is an occupational therapist with experience in the problem domain.

The invitation sent to the volunteers informed that the test would be divided into two features, an ergonomic evaluation and a usability evaluation. The procedures would be carried out remotely due to the new SARS-CoV- 2 Coronavirus pandemic. To confirm acceptance of the invitation, the participant should respond to the invitation email. Subsequently, items were sent to carry out the tests, including, The Free and Clarified Consent Term - (FCCT), Training video, and Manual for access and use of prototypes.

The Free and Clarified Consent Term presented objectives and information about the participation of the volunteer, the autonomy to accept or refuse to answer any question, to interrupt data collection at any time, the risks related to health disorders or physical and psychological integrity, and non-disclosure agreements. The training video briefly presents use, access, installation procedures, system configuration, and considerations for the evaluative tasks.

3.2   Ergonomic Inspection

An inspection technique via checklist was applied based on the criteria of Scapin and Bastien [5]. According to [15], the technique presents eight criteria, subdivided into 18 subcriteria, and allows evaluation of the ergonomic qualities that an interface presents.

For this research, a checklist implemented through the ErgoList [1] tool was used. It has 194 questions based on the ergonomic criteria of Scapin and Bastien [5]. The checklist allows the evaluator to mark the points that present: conformity, non-conformity, and those that are not applicable.

Ergonomic Inspection Session. The average duration for each inspection session was three hours and thirty minutes per evaluator. Each evaluator answered the questions individually. The answers were collected through an online form and made available later for discussion and data summarization.

3.3   Cognitive WalkThrough

The purpose of this method is to evaluate product usage scenarios based on tasks. The evaluator goes through a sequence of actions necessary to complete the task, identifying and discussing the cognitive path the user will take to complete the task [14,16].

In the cognitive journey, four questions are applied to identify whether the user will succeed in the flow phase. Three questions are asked before each step of the task and one at the end. According to [14], the questions are: 1) Will users try to achieve the correct outcome?; 2) Will users notice that the correct action is available?; 3) Will users associate the correct action with the outcome they are trying to achieve? 4) After the action is performed, will users see that progress is made toward the goal?

The results were collected through online forms and stored for analysis and identification of the success or failure of the evaluative task. If any step of the task contains failures, the entire cycle of the task will be marked as failed by the evaluator.

Test Scenario. The standardized evaluation cycle of a psychiatric patient's difficulties and needs to the WEB/Desktop, AR, and VR modules has been used as a test scenario. A set of tasks and subtasks associated with the scenario was applied to carry out the cognitive path.

- User tasks in the WEB/Desktop module
  - Access the system at www.labvis.eti.br
  - Log in to the system.
  - Select standardized assessment.
    * Click on the performance evaluation button.
    * View assessment instructions, click the continue button.
  - Carry out an assessment of difficulties.
    * View cards, click the NO PROBLEM button or PROBLEM button.
    * View shutdown instructions, click the Finish button.
  - Carry out an assessment of the degree of difficulties.
    * View assessment instructions, click the Proceed button
    * View cards, click the UNIMPORTANT PROBLEM, or IMPORTANT PROBLEM, or VERY IMPORTANT PROBLEM button.
    * View shutdown instructions, click the Finish button.
  - Carry out a needs assessment.
    * View assessment instructions, click the Proceed button.
    * View cards, click the NO FURTHER HELP NEEDED button or NEED MORE HELP button.
    * View shutdown instructions, click the Finish button.
  - Carry out an assessment of the degree of needs.
    * View assessment instructions, click the Proceed button.
    * View cards and click the NEED HELP NOT URGENT button. or MODERATELY URGENT NEED FOR HELP button, or NEED URGENT HELP button.
    * View shutdown instructions, click the Finish button.

- User tasks through the RA module
  - Access the system.
  - Select standardized assessment.
    * Click on the performance evaluation button.
    * View assessment instructions, click the continue button.

- Carry out an assessment of difficulties.
  * View cards, click the NO PROBLEM button or PROBLEM button.
  * View shutdown instructions, click the Finish button.
- Carry out an assessment of the degree of difficulties.
  * View assessment instructions, click the Proceed button
  * View cards, click the UNIMPORTANT PROBLEM, or IMPORTANT PROBLEM, or VERY IMPORTANT PROBLEM button.
  * View shutdown instructions, click the Finish button.
- Carry out a needs assessment.
  * View assessment instructions, click the Proceed button.
  * View cards, click the NO FURTHER HELP NEEDED button or NEED MORE HELP button.
  * View shutdown instructions, click the Finish button.
- Carry out an assessment of the degree of needs.
  * View assessment instructions, click the Proceed button.
  * View cards and click the NEED HELP NOT URGENT button. or MODERATELY URGENT NEED FOR HELP button, or NEED URGENT HELP button.
  * View shutdown instructions, click the Finish button.

- User tasks through the VR module.
  - Access the system.
  - Select standardized assessment.
    * Click on the performance evaluation button.
    * View assessment instructions, click the continue button.
  - Carry out an assessment of difficulties.
    * View cards, click the NO PROBLEM button or PROBLEM button.
    * View shutdown instructions, click the Finish button.
  - Carry out an assessment of the degree of difficulties.
    * View assessment instructions, click the Proceed button
    * View cards, click the UNIMPORTANT PROBLEM, or IMPORTANT PROBLEM, or VERY IMPORTANT PROBLEM button.
    * View shutdown instructions, click the Finish button.
  - Carry out a needs assessment.
    * View assessment instructions, click the Proceed button.
    * View cards, click the NO FURTHER HELP NEEDED button or NEED MORE HELP button.
    * View shutdown instructions, click the Finish button.
  - Carry out an assessment of the degree of needs.
    * View assessment instructions, click the Proceed button.
    * View cards and click the NEED HELP NOT URGENT button. or MODERATELY URGENT NEED FOR HELP button, or NEED URGENT HELP button.
    * View shutdown instructions, click the Finish button.

Test Session. The evaluation sessions lasted an average of 10 to 15 min for each evaluator. The participants flowed through the proposed tasks, answered a set of questions, and identified success or failure in completing the task. The data collected in the sessions has been classified as task performance data: completion time and completion status (completed successfully, completed with difficulty, failure). Subsequently, the group synthesized the collected data and proposed improvements in the design of the interfaces.

4 Results

This section presents the results from ergonomic inspections and usability evaluations.

4.1 Ergonomic Inspection Results

WEB/Desktop Module. Figure 10 shows the results of the ergonomic inspection from the subcriteria with the highest and lowest conformity rates.

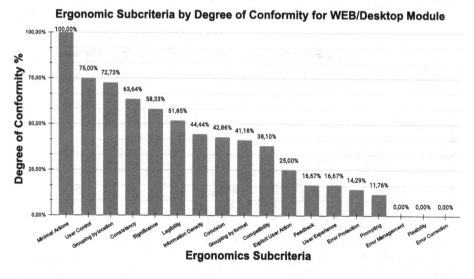

Fig. 10. Percentage of conformity from ergonomic subcriteria for the WEB/Desktop module.

The criteria with the highest conformity rate are:

– Minimal Actions: (100%), it concerns the number of actions necessary to perform the task: limit the number of steps.
– User Control: (75%), allows the user to control the processing of actions (interrupt, cancel, pause, or continue);

- Grouping by location: (72,73%), refers to the relative placement of items, whether they belong or not to a class or indicate distinctions between different classes or items of the same class.
- Consistency: (63,64%), refers to how the interface design choices (codes, names, formats, procedures) are kept identical in the same or different contexts.
- Significance: (58,33%), it concerns the adequacy between the object, the information presented or requested, and it is reference in terms of a semantic relationship. Short expressive terms may cause driving problems.
- Legibility: (51,85%), it concerns the lexical characteristics of the information presented (brightness, contrast, font size, spacing), which may make it difficult or easier to read.

The subcriteria: error correction (allows correction of errors), error management (information about the nature of the error committed), and flexibility (ability to react according to the context and according to the needs and influenced by the user) obtained a 0% conformity rate.

Augmented Reality Module. Figure 11 shows the results of the ergonomic inspection from the subcriteria with the highest and lowest conformity rates.

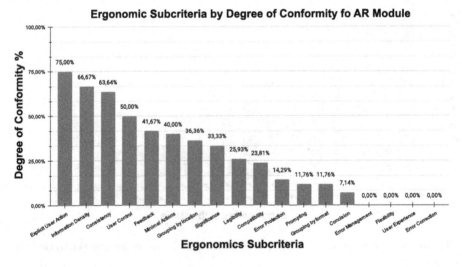

Fig. 11. Percentage of conformity from ergonomic subcriteria for the AR module.

The criteria with the highest conformity rate are:

- Explicit User Action: (75.00%), refers to the processing of actions requested by the user;

- Information Density (66.67%), perceptive and cognitive point of view in relation to the entire set of information presented to users.
- Consistency (63.64%), refers to how the interface design choices (codes, naming, formats, procedures) are maintained in similar contexts and are different when applied to different contexts.
- User Control: (50.00%), allows the user to control the processing of actions (interrupt, cancel, pause, or continue);

The subcriteria: error correction (allowing errors to be corrected), user experience (means available to prevent or reduce errors and to recover from them when they occur), flexibility (ability to react according to the context and according to the user's needs and preferences), and error management (information about the nature of the committed error), obtained a 0% conformity rate.

Virtual Reality Module. Figure 12 shows the results of the ergonomic inspection from the subcriteria with the highest and lowest conformity rates.

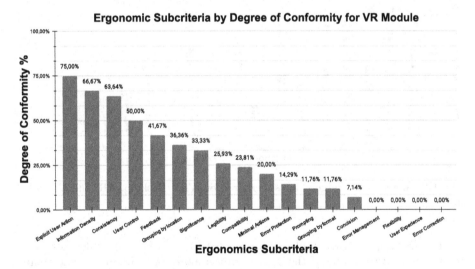

Fig. 12. Percentage of conformity from ergonomic subcriteria for the VR module.

- Explicit Action:(75.00%), refers to the processing of actions requested by the user;
- Information Density (66.67%), perceptive and cognitive point of view **in relation** to the entire set of information presented to users.
- Consistency (63.64%), refers to how the interface design choices (codes, naming, formats, procedures) are maintained in similar contexts and are different when applied to different contexts.

– User Control (50.00%), allows the user to control the processing of actions (interrupt, cancel, pause, or continue);

The subcriteria: error correction (allowing errors to be corrected), user experience (means available to prevent or reduce errors and to recover from them when they occur), flexibility (ability to react according to the context and according to the user's needs and preferences), and error management (information about the nature of the committed error) obtained a 0% conformity rate.

Comparison Between Modules. The comparison of the ergonomic subcriteria for the modules: Desktop/WEB, AR, and VR are shows in Fig. 13, and the following results are identified.

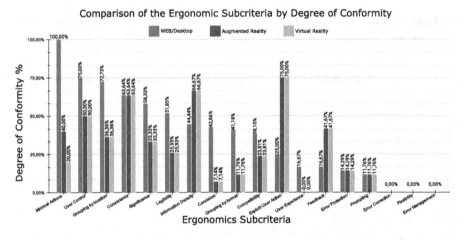

Fig. 13. Comparison of ergonomic subcriteria for WEB/Desktop, AR, and VR modules.

The Desktop/WEB module, compared with AR and VR modules, obtained more conformity in nine of the 18 subcriteria analyzed. The nine highest subcriteria are minimum actions, user controls, grouping by location, meanings, readability, conciseness, grouping by format, compatibility, and user experience.

The Desktop/Web, AR, and VR modules show equal ergonomic conformity for the following subcriteria: consistency, error protection, and prompting.

The AR module has a higher degree of conformity than the VR module in the subcriteria minimum actions. The comparison between the AR and VR modules had a higher degree of conformity than the WEB/Desktop module in the subcriteria: explicit actions, information density, and feedback.

All modules have a 0% conformity rate for the error management, flexibility, and error correction subcriteria. In addition, the AR and VR modules show 0% conformity for the user experience subcriterion.

4.2   Cognitive Walkthrough Usability Evaluation Results

The result of the usability evaluation using the Cognitive Walkthrough technique is presented in Table 1. All tasks and subtasks were completed within the estimated average time.

Table 1. List of tasks applied in the Cognitive Walkthrough evaluation.

Task	WEB/Desktop	Augmented Reality	Virtual Reality
Select standardized assessment	Success	Success	Success
Carry out an assessment of difficulties	Success	Success	Success
Carry out an assessment of the degree of difficulties	Success	Success	Success
Carry out a needs assessment	Success	Success	Success
Carry out an assessment of the degree of needs	Success	Success	Success

5   Recommendations

Based on the usability problems identified in the interfaces, are proposed improvements to increase efficiency, effectiveness, and user satisfaction:

- Create objects to provide supplementary information identifying allowed actions and user locations during the task execution cycle.
- Graphically identify the progress of the evaluation;
- Develop elements to customize the environment according to the particularities of the user;
- Improve the mechanisms to assist in error handling, information about the nature of the error committed, and the permission of error correction.

6   Conclusion

This study presented the digital implementation of the ELADEB self-assessment instrument in WEB/Desktop, AR, and VR platforms, by standardized or customizable elements (images, animations, and videos). It presented an ergonomic and usability evaluation for the prototypes and identified usability and ergonomic problems of the interfaces. There were no problems of an impeding nature for completing the tasks proposed in the evaluations, and recommendations for a better design were reported for maximizing ease of learning, memorization, productivity, and user satisfaction.

7 Future Works

For future works, we intend to conduct new evaluations to prove the improvement of the interfaces, identify and apply new usability evaluations to a more extensive set of users, apply usability evaluations to users with particular characteristics and needs, and use new custom evaluation scenarios and other evaluative methods to identify positive user experiences.

References

1. Site da Usabilidade - Ergolist. https://github.com/usabilidade/usabilidade.github.io
2. ANFE: Kit ELADEB (2022). https://anfe.fr/product/kit-eladeb-2/
3. Baños, R.M., Herrero, R., Vara, M.D.: What is the current and future status of digital mental health interventions? Span. J. Psychol. **25**, E5 (2022)
4. Bastien, C., Scapin, D.: Ergonomic criteria for the evaluation of human-computer interfaces. Technical report, RT-0156, INRIA, June 1993. https://hal.inria.fr/inria-00070012
5. Bastien, C., Scapin, D.: Ergonomic criteria for the evaluation of human-computer interfaces. Ph.D. thesis, Inria (1993)
6. Bellier-Teichmann, T., Golay, P., Bonsack, C., Pomini, V.: Patients' needs for care in public mental health: unity and diversity of self-assessed needs for care. Front. Public Health **4**, 22 (2016). https://www.frontiersin.org/articles/10.3389/fpubh.2016.00022
7. Gallegos, M., et al.: Covid-19: psychosocial impact and mental health in Latin America. Fractal Revista de Psicologia **33**(3), 226–232 (2021). https://doi.org/10.22409/1984-0292/v33i3/51234
8. Henderson, C., Evans-Lacko, S., Thornicroft, G.: Mental illness stigma, help seeking, and public health programs. Am. J. Pub. Health **103**(5), 777–780 (2013)
9. Kumar, A., Nayar, K.R.: Covid 19 and its mental health consequences. J. Ment. Health **30**(1), 1–2 (2021). pMID: 32339041. https://doi.org/10.1080/09638237.2020.1757052
10. OPAS: Transtornos mentais - OPAS/OMS – organização pan-americana da saúde (2023). https://www.paho.org/pt/topicos/transtornos-mentais
11. World Health Organization: Mental health and psychosocial considerations during the COVID-19 outbreak, 18 March 2020
12. World Health Organization: Technical Advisory Group on the mental health impacts of COVID-19 in the WHO European Region briefing: Mental health impacts of COVID-19 across the European Region and associated opportunities for action
13. Pomini, V., Golay, P., Reymond, C.: Assessment of psychiatric patients' difficulties and needs. The Lausanne ELADEB scales. L'Information Psychiatrique **84**(10), 895–902 (2008)
14. Salazar, K.: Evaluate interface learnability with cognitive walkthroughs, February 2022. https://www.nngroup.com/articles/cognitive-walkthroughs/

15. Scapin, D.L., Bastien, J.M.C.: Ergonomic criteria for evaluating the ergonomic quality of interactive systems. Behav. Inf. Technol. **16**(4–5), 220–231 (1997). https://doi.org/10.1080/014492997119806
16. Stanton, N.A.: Human factors and ergonomics methods. In: Handbook of Human Factors and Ergonomics Methods, pp. 27–38. CRC Press (2004)
17. Thyloth, M., Singh, H., Subramanian, V., et al.: Increasing burden of mental illnesses across the globe: current status. Indian J. Soc. Psychiatry **32**(3), 254 (2016)

Let's Start Tomorrow - Bridging the Intention Behavior Gap Using Fitness Apps

Laura Burbach[1]([✉])[ID], Rachel Ganser[1], Luisa Vervier[1][ID], Martina Ziefle[1][ID],
and André Calero Valdez[2][ID]

[1] RWTH Aachen University, Aachen, Germany
burbach@comm.rwth-aachen.de
[2] University of Lübeck, Lübeck, Germany

Abstract. The intention-behavior gap is a well-known phenomenon in health behavior research. Individuals often intend to engage in healthy behaviors but fail to act. Fitness apps have emerged as a promising tool to bridge this gap and promote physical activity. This study aimed to understand the acceptance factors relevant to intending to use fitness apps (UTAUT2) and factors that prevent people from using fitness apps. By shedding light on behavioral-related factors such as organizational and motivational challenges, social inclusion, and volitional factors, this study contributes to explaining and bridging the intention-behavior gap. An online survey was conducted with a sample size of n = 100. Participants were asked about their fitness app usage, motivation for using fitness apps, and barriers preventing them from using them. The results showed that while hedonic motivation and habit influence users' intention to use fitness apps, performance expectancy influences the intention to use a fitness app for non-users. Further, the results showed no influence of behavioral-related factors on the intention to use fitness apps but on sport behavior. The study's findings offer implications for research and actionable guidelines for promoting physical activity and overcoming the intention-behavior gap.

Keywords: Fitness Apps · Acceptance · Intention Behaviour Gap · Volition

1 Introduction

"Let's start tomorrow" refers to people's tendency to delay taking action on their intentions, such as using a fitness app. Even though the desire to lead a healthy life is familiar to many. In addition to a genetic predisposition, general lifestyle significantly impacts health. Diet, exercise, relaxation, and sleep are four pillars that positively influence life [7]. Regular physical activity is crucial for maintaining good health and well-being. Despite the well-known benefits of exercise, many people struggle to engage in physical activity consistently. Based on the most recent study results of the WHO 40 % of the German population

© The Author(s), under exclusive license to Springer Nature Switzerland AG 2023
V. G. Duffy (Ed.): HCII 2023, LNCS 14029, pp. 20–37, 2023.
https://doi.org/10.1007/978-3-031-35748-0_2

lacks exercise. This results in dramatic health consequences such as back problems, cardiac disease, obesity, diabetes, depression, and dementia, among other diseases [20]. The rising number of diseases, demographic change, and the shortage of skilled healthcare professionals represent an enormous challenge for the healthcare system [19].

Fortunately, the rise of digitization has brought new opportunities to promote physical activity. Fitness apps are popular digital tools that people can use to track their exercise and monitor their progress toward their fitness goals. These apps can motivate individuals to engage in physical activity and improve their health and well-being. Tracking and analyzing personal data using fitness apps has increased in the last decade. The so-called *quantified-self movement* is one of the factors driving people's interest in using fitness health apps [18]. In addition, people, in general, are increasingly interested in taking an active role in their own healthcare [23].

However, the usage of fitness apps is still evolving, and usage is relatively low. Moreover, even intending to do sports with the help of a fitness app does not automatically lead to taking actual action to change behavior [28]. People may encounter various obstacles that prevent them from acting on that intention to do sports. For example, they may lack motivation, feel overwhelmed, or encounter technical difficulties with the app.

Therefore, this study was examined to understand the acceptance-relevant factors of intending to use fitness apps and factors that prevent people from using fitness apps. By shedding light on behavioral-related factors such as organizational and motivational challenges, social inclusion as well as volitional factors, this study contributes to explaining and thus bridging the intention-behavior gap. The study's findings offer implications for research as well as actionable guidelines on promoting physical activity and overcoming the intention-behavior gap.

2   Related Work

In the following the value of fitness apps, the empirical approach to measure acceptance as well as behavioral related factors that might be seen as obstacles to using fitness apps is described.

2.1   Value of Fitness-Apps

Fitness apps, belonging to the broader category of eHealth and known as mobile health apps (mHealth app), are software applications designed to help individuals track and manage their physical fitness and well-being through digital devices such as smartphones, tablets, or wearable devices [36]. These apps typically include features such as tracking physical activity, monitoring food intake, providing customized exercise plans, and offering community support.

Fitness apps have taken on new meaning and importance during the COVID-19 pandemic. With gyms and fitness studios closed or operating at reduced capacity in many areas, people have had to find alternative ways to stay active and maintain their fitness routines. Fitness apps have provided a convenient and accessible option for individuals to exercise at home or outdoors while following social distancing guidelines [29].

Moreover, fitness apps can contribute to the achievement of the third Sustainable Development Goal to ensure health and well-being for all by promoting physical activity, healthy behaviors, and providing education and resources for good health [29]. Thus, the value of fitness apps is high, especially regarding the convenient fact that they are accessible for free or at a low cost for everyone who owns a smartphone.

Even though the advantages of fitness apps are outstanding, there is often an intention-behavior gap which means that people fail to translate their positive intentions to use a fitness app into action [12]. For this reason, this study aims to reveal the factors that prevent people from doing physical exercise with fitness apps.

2.2 Measuring Acceptance of Fitness Apps

Acceptance of fitness apps can be defined as the degree to which a person is willing to use and engage with the app. There have been several models developed to understand the factors that influence acceptance. Most of these models are based on the Theory of Reasoned Action (TRA) proposed by Fishbein and Ajzen in 1977 [13]. The TRA has been the foundation for subsequent acceptance models and suggests that actual behavior is the immediate predictor of technology use based on behavioral or usage intention. This intention is determined by attitude towards the behavior and social norms.

The Unified Theory of Acceptance and Use of Technology (UTAUT) was developed as a successor to the Technology Acceptance Model (TAM) models, with a focus on predicting adoption in the work context [32]. However, with the increased use of technology outside the work context, UTAUT and its extension UTAUT2, have provided a model for investigating acceptance in commercial and other contexts, such as the digital health sector. The model includes seven constructs: performance expectancy, effort expectancy, social influence, facilitating conditions, hedonic motivation, price value, and habit.

Performance expectancy refers to the degree to which users believe that using the technology will improve their performance. Effort expectancy refers to the ease of use of the technology. Social influence refers to the degree to which users perceive that others expect them to use the technology. Facilitating conditions refer to the availability of resources to support the use of technology. Hedonic motivation refers to the pleasure and enjoyment users derive from using technology. Price value refers to the perceived value of the technology in relation to its cost. Finally, habit refers to the automatic and repetitive use of technology.

Several studies have used the UTAUT2 model to measure the acceptance of fitness apps. Performance expectancy, effort expectancy, social influence, and hedonic motivation were significant predictors of users' intentions to use fitness apps [3,17].

Since UTAUT2 provides a useful framework for understanding the factors that influence the acceptance and use of fitness apps, it was chosen as a basic model in this study.

2.3 Approaching the Intention Behavior Gap

The intention-behavior gap refers to the discrepancy between an individual's intentions to engage in a behavior, and their actual behavior [27]. In other words, it is failing to act on one's intentions.

There are several theoretical approaches to understanding the intention-behavior gap, including the Theory of Planned Behavior [1] and the Health Action Process Approach [26]. Both models propose that behavior is the result of a combination of intention, which is influenced by attitudes, subjective norms, and perceived behavioral control, and actual behavior, which is influenced by environmental and personal factors.

In addition, several empirical studies have identified various factors that contribute to the intention-behavior gap in the context of health-related behaviors.

One major factor is usability. If the app is difficult to use or does not provide a clear and easy-to-understand interface, users may abandon the app or not use it as frequently as intended.

Furthermore, organizational factors such as workplace policies and social support have been shown to influence individuals' ability to act on their intentions [22]. Motivational challenges, such as low self-efficacy and lack of intrinsic motivation, have also been identified as significant barriers to behavior change [30].

Social inclusion, or the degree to which an individual feels connected to a social group, has been found to impact the intention-behavior gap in various ways. For example, individuals who feel socially excluded may be less motivated to engage in healthy behaviors [16].

Finally, volition, or an individual's ability to self-regulate their behavior, has been identified as a critical factor in the intention-behavior gap. For example, individuals who lack self-control may struggle to follow through on their intentions to engage in healthy behaviors [25].

Overall, the intention-behavior gap is a complex phenomenon that is influenced by a variety of factors. This study intends to bridge the intention behavior gap by examining behavior-related factors such as organizational and motivational challenges, social inclusion, and volitional factors.

3 Empirical Approach and Logic of Procedure

To get insights into the factors that are acceptance relevant and, moreover, to understand the intention-behavior gap by shedding light on behavioral-related factors, we conducted an online survey as part of a bachelor thesis at RWTH Aachen University in the summer of 2021. The participants took part voluntarily and were not compensated. The sample, procedure, and results are briefly outlined below. The following research questions guided the study:

1. What are acceptance-relevant factors that describe the intention to use a fitness app?
2. In how far do these acceptance relevant factors differ regarding users and non-users of fitness apps?
3. To what extent do behavioral-related factors (organizational, motivational challenges, social inclusion, and volitional factors) coupled with the acceptance-related factors (UTAUT2) contribute to the intention to use a fitness app?
4. Do behavioral-related factors (organizational, motivational challenges, social inclusion, volitional factors) differ between fitness app users and non-users?

Figure 1 overviews the proposed research model underlying this study.

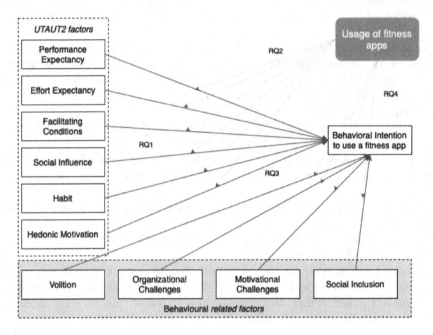

Fig. 1. Proposed research model: RQ: research question; UTAUT2: unified theory of acceptance and use of technology 2.

3.1 Evaluation Measures

The online survey consisted of four parts. The constructs used in the survey with their respective sources can be seen in Table 1.

Demographic Data. In the first part, demographic data such as age, gender, marital status, school qualifications, occupation and whether children lived in the household were queried.

Table 1. Constructs used in the questionnaire with their respective sources.

Constructs	Subconstructs	Source upon which the construct was based
UTAUT2[a] constructs	Performance expectancy	Venkatesh et al. [4]
	Effort expectancy	
	Social Influence	
	Facilitating Conditions	
	Hedonic motivation	
	Habit	
	Behavioral intention	
Organizational Challenges	N/A[b]	Brown et al., 1999 [6]
Motivational Challenges	N/A[b]	Brown et al., 1999 [6]
Social inclusion	N/A[b]	Brown et al., 1999 [6]
Volition[c]	N/A[b]	Elsborg et al., 2017 [10]

[a]UTAUT2: unified theory of acceptance and use of technology 2.
[b]N/A: not applicable; the construct did not have any subconstructs.
[c]: German validation by Pfeffer et al. [21]

Sport Behavior, App Usage and Hurdles. The second part comprises the actual sport behavior which was explored retrospectively with three foci: the commitment to planned sports (*Have you exercised every time you set out to do so in the last three weeks?*) and the quality (*Are you satisfied with the amount of exercise you have done in the last three weeks?*) which could be indicated on a five-point Likert scale and quantity (*How often have you exercised on average in the last three weeks?* could be answered from *once a week* to *daily* seven gradations in the possible answers.

Respondents were also asked whether they owned a smartphone, tablet, or wearable device, whether they had installed a fitness app, whether and how long they had been using fitness apps, and - in case they had installed one - which app they use.

They were also asked what they use an app for or can imagine using it for *to create workout plans, regular reminders to exercise, monitoring of vital signs (heartbeat, sleep...), competition with friends and other people, tracking and sharing distances run, progress monitoring/statistics, calorie tracking, social exchange with other athletes* or other functions that could be typed in as free text. Furthermore, experienced hurdles were asked which have prevented one from doing sports in the past few weeks (*retrospective barriers*), such as: *too many work and university appointments, too many leisure dates, health problems, ffinding people with whom to train together, motivational issues* or other hurdles that could be entered as free text. All items were examined on a five-point Likert scale between "do not agree at all" to "agree completely".

Theory of Planned Behavior and UTAUT2 Factors. The third part comprised the intention to do sport based on the Theory of Planned Behavior. For this purpose, as suggested by Ajzen [2], the instrumental and experimental aspects, the subjective norm, the perceived behavioral control and the intention were presented on five-point Likert scales. For the instrumental and experiential aspects, it should be indicated whether more physical activity would be rather bad or good and rather pleasant or unpleasant. The subjective norm was indicated by *Most of the people I care about like it when I exercise.* Perceived behavioral control was queried with the statements *I am confident that I can do sport* and *Doing sport is my decision.* For intention, respondents were asked whether it was more likely or less likely that they would plan to do sport.

The general attitude towards fitness apps was asked by scales adopted by Vervier [35] based on Venkatesh's UTAUT2 model [32]. The Performance Expectancy indicates whether a fitness app brings a personal benefit. Here, for example, the question was asked to what extent the statement that a fitness app is useful in everyday life was agreed upon. The effort expectancy asks how difficult it is for the user to use a fitness app, i.e. the ease of use, indicating, for example, whether the handling of such apps is clear and understandable. Social influence measures whether significant others have an influence on the willingness to use fitness apps through questions like to what extent people whose opinion is valued think that one should use those. The facilitating conditions show whether the necessary prerequisites and knowledge are available to use fitness apps. This means, among other things, whether you have a smartphone or tablet that runs such an app or whether you have the necessary knowledge to use an app. The hedonic motivation in the use of fitness apps measures whether the use of an app is perceived as pleasant and entertaining. Regarding the habit of using fitness apps, respondents were asked whether the use had already become a habit, whether one could still do without such an app, and whether one needed this app. Price Value was not included in the study. Behavioral Intention measures whether the intention is to continue using a fitness app or whether it is intended to be integrated into everyday life.

Behavioral Related Factors. The fourth part consists of social, organizational, and motivational challenges as well as volitional factors which are anticipated to explain overcoming hurdles to use a fitness app. All items are shown in Table 2.

Items referring to the volitional factors were taken over completely from [21], but the proposed four-point Likert scale was transformed to a five-point Likert scale in order to have coherent five-point scales with the same classification in all questionnaire items. Table 1 gives an overview of the constructs used in the questionnaire with their respective sources.

In the following, the methodological approach is outlined.

3.2   Structural Equation Modeling (SEM)

Structural equation modeling (SEM) is used to understand cause-and-effect relationships in empirical data. SEMs can be used to confirm theories, for which covariance-based SEMs are used, while variance-based partial least squares SEMs

Table 2. Behavioral related constructs with corresponding items and respective sources.

N.[a]	Scale item: I can imagine, that a fitness app can help me	from [6] N.[a]
	social inclusion	
1	...exercise on my own	o.c.[b]
2	...to adapt my behavior to that of my friends	9
3	...ask others for help when I need it	60
4	...to be like the people around me	44
5	...motivate myself to exercise by sharing with my friends	o.c.[b]
6	...find a group to do sports together	o.c.[b]
	organizational challenges	
1	...set aside time in my schedule for exercise.	o.c.[b]
2	...be less easily distracted from my plans	6
3	...find a routine	24
4	...stick to a plan that works well	27
5	...make plans to help me reach my goals	40
6	...set goals and monitor my progress.	42.
	Motivational challenges	
1	...reward myself for progress on my goals	7
2	...follow through with things once I set my mind to do them	20
3	...look for possible solutions as soon as I see a problem or challenge	32
4	...strengthen my willpower	34
5	...resist temptations	41
6	...stick to rules no matter what	48

[a]N.: Number
[b]o.c.: own consideration

are used for exploratory purposes [8]. Using both techniques, two kinds of effects can be investigated: The measurement model considers the relationships between observed and latent variables and the structural model considers the relationships between the latent variables.

In the first step (measurement model), the latent factors are calculated from the manifest, observed variables. These calculated latent factors give the analyzed variance of the manifest indicators adjusted for measurement errors. In the second step (structural model), it can be considered how the latent independent variables (or exogenous variables) influence the latent dependent variables (or endogenous variables). As input variables, the exogenous variables are at the beginning of the model, they are not influenced by other variables. In contrast, the endogenous variables are influenced by other variables in the model. It is possible that some variables within structural equation modeling are simultaneously dependent and independent. By using structural equation modeling, it is possible to investigate whether one variable directly influences another variable or whether the relationship between the two variables is mediated by another variable [8,15].

3.3 Assessment of Quality

We followed the guideline by Hair et al. [14] to check for the quality of the measurement model (Table 3).

Table 3. Dispersion and reliability of *UTAUT2* constructs and *behavioral related* factors

	Mean	SD	Reliability (Cronbachs α)	Quantity items
Performance Expectancy	3.09	0.92	$\alpha = .884$	6
Effort Expectancy	4.05	0.77	$\alpha = .899$	4
Facilitating Conditions	4.65	0.55	$\alpha = .698$	2
Social Influence	2.30	0.90	$\alpha = .912$	3
Habit	2.27	0.98	$\alpha = .827$	3
Hedonic Motivation	3.25	0.83	$\alpha = .912$	2
Behavioral Intention	2.86	1.19	$\alpha = .927$	3
Organizational Challenges	3.60	0.79	$\alpha = .889$	6
Motivational Challenges	2.76	0.81	$\alpha = .834$	6
Social Inclusion	2.64	0.87	$\alpha = .843$	6
Volitional Factors	3.36	1.11	$\alpha = .934$	18
Intention to exercise (tpb)	1.95	0.57	$\alpha = .781$	3

*S*D: standard deviation

4 Results

After a short introduction of our sample, we present the actual results of our study answering the four research questions.

4.1 Sample

Table 4 shows the demographic characteristics of the sample separately for users and non-users of fitness apps. In total 100 surveys were fully completed consisting of 64 % female and 34 % male participants (2 %diverse) between 17 and 77 (*mean* = 28.35, *SD* = 13.96) years. Overall, the sample is well-educated. 37% have high school diploma, 29 % a university degree and 7% intermediate maturity.

Participants' Sports Behavior/Intention to Do Sports. In the last three weeks, most participants exercised once a week (47%). Also, many participants exercised two (20%) or three times (21%) a week and only a few participants (11%) exercised more often (4–6x) or daily (1%).

Fitness app users ($N = 55$) exercised more often in the last three weeks ($MW = 3.45$, $SD = 1.27$) than non-users ($N = 45$, $MW = 2.73$, $SD = 1.28$) and are more satisfied (users: $MW = 2.89$, $SD = 1.34$, non-users: $MW = 2.20$, $SD = 1.16$) with how frequently they did sports.

Table 4. Demographic characteristics of the sample comparing users and non-user of fitness apps (n = 100).

Characteristic	Users ($n = 55$)	Non-users ($n = 45$)
Age (years), mean(SD)	28.24 (12.72)	28.49 (13.40)
Gender, n(%)		
Women	31	31
Men	20	16
Diverse	2	0
Education level		
intermediate maturity	7	3
high school diploma	32	32
university degree	19	10

SD: standard deviation

Attitude Towards App Usage. 52% of the participants use a fitness app such as Fitbit, Samsung Health, and Komoot. Respondents currently use fitness apps most for *progress monitoring or statistics* (56%), or can imagine using a fitness app for this purpose. Also, many respondents use an app for *regular reminders to exercise* (48%) and for *tracking and sharing distances run* (47%). 37% use fitness apps *to create workout plans*. 36% *monitor vital signs* (such as heartbeat, sleep, etc.). 24% stated to use the app for *a competition with friends and other people*, 21% *to track calories* and 6% for *social exchange with other athletes*.

Hurdles Experienced. For the participants, *motivation issues* were the biggest barrier to exercising in the last three weeks ($M = 3.66$, $SD = 1.32$). In addition, *too many work and university appointments* prevented the participants from exercising ($M = 3.39$, $SD = 1.35$). In comparison *leisure dates* ($M = 2.75$, $SD = 1.20$), *health problems* ($M = 2.84$, $SD = 1.43$) and *finding people with whom to train together* ($M = 2.56$, $SD = 1.43$) represented lower barriers for participants to exercise.

4.2 Acceptance Relevant Factors

Regarding the first question about what are acceptance-relevant factors that describe the intention to use a fitness app the following results were found: a structural-equation model analyzing the influence of the *UTAUT2* factors on *behavioral intention to use fitness apps* explained 58% of the variance of *app usage* (R^2 : 0.583). *Enjoyment when using the app* (0.407, $p < .001$) leads participants most strongly to indicate app use in the future. Besides, *performance expectancy* (0.282, $p = .001$) and *habit* (0.208, $p = .004$) result in a higher *behavioral intention to use fitness apps*. In contrast, *facilitating conditions* (0.130, $p = .134$), *effort expectancy* (0.013, $p = .870$), and *social influence* (0.049, $p = .533$) do not influence *fitness app use* in our sample.

The f^2 test for *app use fun* was 0.203. Cronbach's alpha, rhoA, composite reliability, and mean extracted variance were all sufficiently good.

4.3   Acceptance Relevant Factors of Users and Non-users

In a second structural-equation model, we compared users and non-users of fitness apps (see Fig. 2) considering the influence of the *UTAUT2* factors on the *behavioral intention to use a fitness app*. The construct *habit* drops out for the non-users since they do not have it yet. The model explains about 43% variance for non-users and about 73% variance of users of fitness apps.

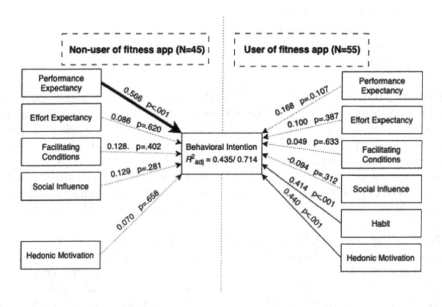

Fig. 2. Influence of *UTAUT2* factors on *behavioral intention to use fitness apps* contrasting users and non-users of fitness apps. (significance based on bootstrapping; n = 100). adj: adjusted.

For non-users of fitness apps only *performance expectancy* (0.566, $p < .001$, $f^2 = 0.333$) strongly influences how strong they *intend to use a fitness app*. For users of fitness apps, *hedonic motivation* (0.440, $p < .001$, $f^2 = 0.410$) and *habit* (0.414, $p < .001$, $f^2 = 0.370$) lead to a higher *behavioral intention to use a fitness app*.

4.4 Acceptance Explained by UTAUT2 and Behavioral Related Factors

Using another structural-equation model ($n = 100$), we analyzed whether *behavioral related* factors (*volition, organizational challenges, motivational challenges, social inclusion*) influence the *intention to use a fitness app* in addition to the *UTAUT2* factors. The model explained around 60% ($n = 100, R^2_{adj} = 0.605$) of the variance. Next to *performance expectancy, hedonic motivation* and *habit*, we found a significant influence of *organizational challenges* ($0.172, p = .041$) on *intention to use a fitness app*, but according to the f^2-test only the effect of *hedonic motivation* was big enough for the sample ($0.373, p < .001, f^2 = 0.184$).

Zooming in to the group of users of fitness apps, another structural-equation model explained 70% of the variance of the *intention to use a fitness app* ($n = 55, R^2_{adj} = 0.704$). As could be seen for the overall sample, *hedonic motivation* and *habit* significantly lead to a higher *intention to use fitness apps*, but the model showed no significant influences of the *behavioral related* factors ($p_s > .05$).

Considering the non-users of fitness apps, a structural-equation model explained 47% of the variance of the *intention to use a fitness app* ($n = 45, R^2_{adj} = 0.472$). Again, as could be shown for the overall sample, only the *performance expectancy*, but no *behavioral related* factors influenced the *intention to use a fitness app* ($p_s > .05$).

4.5 Bridging the Intention Behavior Gap

Another structural-equation model (see Fig. 3) explained 39% ($n = 55, R^2adj = 0.385$) of the variance of *sports behavior in the past*.

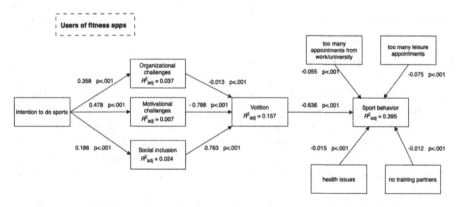

Fig. 3. Structural model from *intention to do sports* to *sport behavior retrospective* (significance based on bootstrapping; n = 55). adj: adjusted.

The results revealed that *intention to do sport* significantly influences *motivational challenges* ($0.478, p < .001, f^2 = 0.297$). In turn, *motivational challenges* ($-0.768, p < .001, f^2 = 0.185$) and *social inclusion* ($-0.763, p < .001,$

$f^2 = 0.263$) significantly influence *volition*. *organizational challenges* also showed an significant influence on *volition*, but the f^2 was too low for the sample (0.013, $p < .001$, $f^2 = 0.006$). *Volition* in turn, significantly influences *sport behavior* (-0.636, $p < .001$, $f^2 = 0.612$). The *external barriers* showed a significant influence on the *sport behavior*, but the f^2-values were too low for the sample ($f^2s < 0.009$).

We also calculated a structural-equation model from the *intention to do sports* to *sport behavior* for the non-users of fitness apps (see Fig. 4).

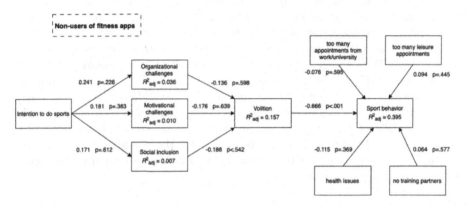

Fig. 4. Structural model from *intention to do sports* to *sport behavior retrospective* (significance based on bootstrapping; n = 45). adj: adjusted.

The model explains 40% of the variance of *sport behavior*. In this model, only *volition* significantly influences *sport behavior* (-0.666, $p < .001$, $f^2 = 0.728$)

5   Discussion and Guidelines

Acceptance relevant factors of using a fitness app We designed this study aiming to better understand which acceptance factors motivate or prevent users and non-users of fitness apps from doing sports using an app. A further aim of this study was to investigate whether individuals behave according to an intention-behavior gap and if so, how this can be overcome. The intention-behavior gap exists, when individuals indicate that they want to exercise (more), but then fail to put this into practice.

As a base to understand what motivates individuals (users and non-users) to use fitness apps, we applied the established technology acceptance model UTAUT2 [4] and added behavioral related factors (organizational challenges, motivational challenges, social inclusion, volitional factors) to the model.

In our study, the UTAUT2 model could explain 58% of the variance in the intention to use fitness apps. From the original validated UTAUT2 model, we identified only three constructs that influence the intention to use fitness apps.

Without distinguishing between user groups, enjoyment when using a fitness app predicts the use of fitness apps most strongly. Besides, performance expectancy and habit (only users) contribute to the intention to use fitness apps. The construct effort expectancy is modeled as a main aspect in other established acceptance models (for example [11,31]), but showed no significant influence on acceptance in our study.

Considering the user groups, our results show, that different factors motivate non-users and users of fitness apps to start using/ continue using a fitness app. Individuals, that are users of fitness apps, are already one step ahead of non-users in that they have at least some experience in using the app. If they have fun while using a fitness app, it motivates them to use the app (further). In addition, the use of the app also becomes a habit for some users reinforcing its further usage. In contrast, non-users would most likely start using a fitness app if they expect it to be useful. Exemplary, an app can help people in taking care of their health in daily life.

Influence of Behavioral Related Factors. We considered whether behavioral-related factors can add value to the UTAUT2 factors in explaining the intention to use a fitness app. The results showed, that the behavioral related factors, that we considered in this study, did not contribute to the explanation of the fitness app use. Thus, further factors adding to the UTAUT2 factors exist, that we did not take into account. Mirroring, that the app-related acceptance factors can strongly lead to a higher intention to use fitness apps and to exercise.

Intention-Behavior-Gap. When participants plan to do sports (often) but in reality do no or very little sports, their behavior corresponds to an intention-behavior-gap. Whether an intention-behavior gap exists depends not on the frequency of doing sports but whether humans do sports when they plan to. Therefore, we considered which factors influenced whether participants did sport in the past when they planned to exercise.

We assume that the participants are then dissatisfied with their (sports-) behavior. Considering, whether participants show an intention-behavior-gap, the individuals considered, are rather sportive. Supporting our assumption, fitness app users exercise more often and are more satisfied with the sports they do than non-users. Nevertheless, an intention-behavior gap has been shown, as more than half of the considered individuals did not do sports (always), when they planned to exercise. An individual with a generally higher intention to do sports is also more motivated to use an app to overcome motivational challenges. Also, individuals that can better imagine that the app can help overcome motivational challenges and lead to better social inclusion perceive less volition. This result is in line with results of [16] that being socially excluded demotivates individuals in healthy behaviors. In turn, individuals with a higher volition (users and non-users) did less often sports when they planned to do sports. This result reflects the results of [25] a lack of self-control leads individuals to struggle to follow through on their intentions to engage in healthy behaviors. The volition of individuals is obviously an important adjusting screw if individuals are to be motivated to do more sport.

Guidelines. The findings of our study offer implications for research and actionable guidelines for promoting physical activity and overcoming the intention-behavior gap: In trying to overcome the intention-behavior gap and motivate individuals to exercise more, fitness apps can be of great help. Differences between users and non-users of fitness apps must be taken into account. For example, a fitness app must be designed for users in such a way that users enjoy using it. It should also be easy for them to integrate the app into their everyday lives so that a habit is established that users will ideally want to stick with in the long term. In contrast, non-users must first be motivated to use a fitness app. Here it is important to emphasize the benefits of the app for potential users.

5.1 Limitations and Future Research

Our study provides interesting insights to understand why individuals use fitness apps and what motivates them to overcome the intention-behavior gap. Nevertheless, with a revised survey in the future, more questions and our questions in more detail can be answered. In further studies, larger samples would allow us to make representative statements for all users and non-users respectively potential users of fitness apps. Besides, in our study, we asked non-users about anticipated attitudes toward fitness apps. In future studies, hands-on experience is needed to evaluate real attitudes and not only anticipated ones. Our study asked how much exercise was done in the last three weeks. Instead, it would be interesting to conduct a long-term study where behavior can be observed. Not only the difference between users and non-users [9] is important when investigating the acceptance of technology, but also different fitness apps can have an influence on the intention to do sports using an app. In addition, our sample is rather young and educated and was acquired via social contacts. Since the health topic is very important for everyone, it is recommendable to include a wide age range in further studies.

Equally, only healthy persons were regarded, but it is important to include sick people as well. Not only do sick people have different challenges when using fitness apps compared to healthy people, but fitness apps also offer them more options. Thus, by using fitness apps, they can try not only to maintain their health status but also to improve it if necessary. Likewise, fitness apps can enable mobility-impaired individuals to perform exercises at home under guidance.

There are factors that were not considered in this study but which do have a major impact on the intention to use a fitness app. One major factor is privacy concern: Users may be hesitant to use fitness apps that require access to personal information or location data, due to concerns about data privacy and security [33,34]. Furthermore, trust is also an important factor which could be found in several studies [5,24]. Future studies on the intention behavior gap should therefore consider these factors for a more holistic explanation.

5.2 Conclusion

Fitness apps vary in their ability to overcome different challenges that constitute the intention-behavior gap. People who have trouble finding time in their schedule to exercise, or do not have a plan for how to achieve their athletic goals are most likely to use fitness apps to exercise more. Fitness apps are less suited to address social and motivational challenges. Motivationally experienced challenges have a large impact on volition, which in turn has a large impact on whether one is satisfied with the amount of exercise done. In the future, we will investigate which app features can better assist with social and motivational challenges and are more accepted to influence volition and thus behavior. We will also investigate what other options besides fitness apps exist to overcome individual barriers. Finally, we will investigate how different options can be combined, leading more people to overcome their intention-behavior gap.

References

1. Ajzen, I.: The theory of planned behavior. Organ. Behav. Hum. Decis. Process. **50**(2), 179–211 (1991)
2. Ajzen, I.: Constructing a Theory of Planned Behavior Questionnaire, p. 8 (2013)
3. Barbosa, H.F., García-Fernández, J., Pedragosa, V., Cepeda-Carrion, G.: The use of fitness centre apps and its relation to customer satisfaction: a UTAUT2 perspective. Int. J. Sports Market. Sponsorship (2021, ahead-of-print)
4. Batucan, G.B., Gonzales, G.G., Balbuena, M.G., Pasaol, K.R.B., Seno, D.N., Gonzales, R.R.: An extended UTAUT model to explain factors affecting online learning system amidst Covid-19 pandemic: the case of a developing economy. Front. Artif. Intell. **5** (2022). https://doi.org/10.3389/frai.2022.768831. https://www.frontiersin.org/articles/10.3389/frai.2022.768831
5. Beldad, A.D., Hegner, S.M.: Expanding the technology acceptance model with the inclusion of trust, social influence, and health valuation to determine the predictors of German users' willingness to continue using a fitness app: a structural equation modeling approach. Int. J. Hum. Comput. Interact. **34**(9), 882–893 (2018)
6. Brown, J.M., Miller, W.R., Lawendowski, L.A.: The self-regulation questionnaire. In: Innovations in Clinical Practice: A Source Book, vol. 17, pp. 281–292. Professional Resource Press/Professional Resource Exchange, Sarasota, FL, US (1999)
7. Chatterjee, R.: The 4 Pillar Plan: How to Relax, Eat Move and Sleep Your Way to a Longer Healthier Life. Penguin, UK (2017)
8. Davcik, N.S.: The use and misuse of structural equation modeling in management research: a review and critique. J. Adv. Manage. Res. **11**(1), 47–81 (2014). https://doi.org/10.1108/JAMR-07-2013-0043
9. Sezgin, E., Yildirim, S.Ö., Yildirim, S.: Intention vs. perception: understanding the differences in physicians' attitudes toward mobile health applications. In: Sezgin, E., Yildirim, S., Yildirim, S.Ö., Sumuer, E. (eds.) Current and Emerging mHealth Technologies, pp. 153–166. Springer, Cham (2018). https://doi.org/10.1007/978-3-319-73135-3_10
10. Elsborg, P., Wikman, J.M., Nielsen, G., Tolver, A., Elbe, A.M.: Development and initial validation of the volition in exercise questionnaire (VEQ). Meas. Phys. Educ. Exerc. Sci. **21**(2), 57–68 (2017). https://doi.org/10.1080/1091367X.2016.1251436

11. Davis, F.D., Davis, F.: Perceived usefulness, perceived ease of use, and user acceptance of information technology. MIS Q. **13**(3), 319–340 (1989). https://doi.org/10.2307/249008
12. Feng, W., Tu, R., Hsieh, P.: CAN gamification increases consumers' engagement in fitness apps? The moderating role of commensurability of the game elements. J. Retail. Consum. Serv. **57**, 102229 (2020). https://doi.org/10.1016/j.jretconser.2020.102229. https://linkinghub.elsevier.com/retrieve/pii/S0969698918306428
13. Fishbein, M., Ajzen, I.: Belief, Attitude, Intention, and Behavior: An Introduction to Theory and Research (1977)
14. Hair, J.F., Risher, J.J., Sarstedt, M., Ringle, C.M.: When to use and how to report the results of PLS-SEM. Eur. Bus. Rev. **31**(1), 2–24 (2019). https://doi.org/10.1108/EBR-11-2018-0203. https://www.emerald.com/insight/content/doi/10.1108/EBR-11-2018-0203/full/html
15. Iacobucci, D.: Everything you always wanted to know about SEM (Structural Equations Modeling) but were afraid to ask. J. Consum. Psychol. **19**(4), 673–680 (2009). https://doi.org/10.1016/j.jcps.2009.09.002
16. Jetten, J., Haslam, C., Alexander, S.H.: The Social Cure: Identity, Health and Well-Being. Psychology Press (2012)
17. Kim, B., Lee, E.: What factors affect a user's intention to use fitness applications? The moderating effect of health status: a cross-sectional study. Inquiry J. Health Care Organ. Provision Financing **59**, 00469580221095826 (2022)
18. Lupton, D.: Quantifying the body: monitoring and measuring health in the age of mHealth technologies. Crit. Public Health **23**(4), 393–403 (2013)
19. World Health Organization: The world health report 2006: working together for health. World Health Organization (2006)
20. World Health Organization: Global status report on physical activity 2022: executive summary (2022)
21. Pfeffer, I., Elsborg, P., Elbe, A.M.: Validation of the German-language version of the Volition in Exercise Questionnaire (VEQ-D). German J. Exerc. Sport Res. **50**(1), 102–113 (2020). https://doi.org/10.1007/s12662-019-00632-y. http://link.springer.com/10.1007/s12662-019-00632-y
22. Rhodes, R.E., Dickau, L.: Experimental evidence for the intention-behavior relationship in the physical activity domain: a meta-analysis. Health Psychol. **31**(6), 724 (2012)
23. Rutz, M., Kühn, D., Dierks, M.L.: Kapitel 5. gesundheits-apps und prävention. Chancen und Risiken von Gesundheits-Apps (CHARISMHA); Albrecht, U.-V. (Hrsg.), Ed (2016)
24. Schomakers, E.M., Lidynia, C., Vervier, L.S., Calero Valdez, A., Ziefle, M.: Applying an extended UTAUT2 model to explain user acceptance of lifestyle and therapy mobile health apps: survey study. JMIR Mhealth Uhealth **10**(1), e27095 (2022)
25. Schröder, T., Haug, M., Gewald, H.: The difference between motivation and volition matters!-a qualitative study on mobile health application adoption. In: ECIS (2021)
26. Schwarzer, R.: Modeling health behavior change: how to predict and modify the adoption and maintenance of health behaviors. Appl. Psychol. **57**(1), 1–29 (2008)
27. Sheeran, P., Conner, M., Norman, P.: Can the theory of planned behavior explain patterns of health behavior change? Health Psychol. **20**(1), 12–19 (2001). https://doi.org/10.1037/0278-6133.20.1.12. http://doi.apa.org/getdoi.cfm?doi=10.1037/0278-6133.20.1.12

28. Sniehotta, F.F., Scholz, U., Schwarzer, R.: Bridging the intention-behaviour gap: planning, self-efficacy, and action control in the adoption and maintenance of physical exercise. Psychol. Health **20**(2), 143–160 (2005). https://doi.org/10.1080/08870440512331317670. http://www.tandfonline.com/doi/abs/10.1080/08870440512331317670

29. Soulé, B., Marchant, G., Verchère, R.: Sport and fitness app uses: a review of humanities and social science perspectives. Eur. J. Sport Soc. **19**(2), 170–189 (2022)

30. Teixeira, P.J., Carraça, E.V., Markland, D., Silva, M.N., Ryan, R.M.: Exercise, physical activity, and self-determination theory: a systematic review. Int. J. Behav. Nutr. Phys. Act. **9**(1), 1–30 (2012)

31. Venkatesh, V., Morris, M.G., Davis, G.B., Davis, F.D.: User acceptance of information technology: toward a unified view. MIS Q. **27**(3), 425 (2003). https://doi.org/10.2307/30036540. https://www.jstor.org/stable/10.2307/30036540

32. Venkatesh, V., Thong, J.Y.L., Xu, X.: Consumer acceptance and use of information technology: extending the unified theory of acceptance and use of technology. MIS Q. **36**(1), 157 (2012). https://doi.org/10.2307/41410412. http://www.jstor.org/stable/10.2307/41410412

33. Vervier, L., Valdez, A.C., Ziefle, M.: "Attitude"-mhealth apps and users' insights: an empirical approach to understand the antecedents of attitudes towards mhealth applications. In: ICT4AWE, pp. 213–221 (2019)

34. Vervier, L., Ziefle, M.: A meta-analytical view on the acceptance of mhealth apps. In: ICT4AWE, pp. 322–329 (2022)

35. Vervier, L.S.: Akzeptanz, Nutzerdiversität und Design digitaler Informations- und Kommunikationstechnologien im Gesundheitswesen, September 2021. https://www.apprimus-verlag.de/akzeptanz-nutzerdiversitat-und-design-digitaler-informations-und-kommunikationstechnologien-im-gesundheitswesen.html

36. Yoganathan, D., Kajanan, S.: Persuasive technology for smartphone fitness apps. In: PACIS, p. 185. Citeseer (2013)

A Study on the Service Design of Self-health Management for Adolescents with Asthma Based on Persuasive Technology

Zhe Hu[1,2] and Yi Li[1,2](✉)

[1] School of Design, Hunan University, Changsha, China
2012171@hnu.edu.cn
[2] Yuelushan, Changsha 410082, Hunan, China

Abstract. Based on persuasion theory to solve the existing problems in the process of self-health management of adolescent asthma patients and build a more effective asthma self-health management service system. Firstly, research methods such as observation method and in-depth interview methods are used to obtain the potential needs of users, and through the analysis of the behavior of adolescent asthma patients, the persuasion design problems existing in the current asthma self-health management process are extracted, and then the corresponding persuasion design strategies are formulated to guide the design of the asthma self-health management service system by combining the theory and analysis tools of service design. Based on the research results of self-health management for adolescent asthma patients, the corresponding persuasion service design strategies are proposed in three aspects: enhancing user motivation, enhancing user ability, and giving user behavior trigger points. Finally, the persuasion design strategy was applied to the design practice of an asthma self-health management service system, and the feasibility of the persuasion service design strategy was initially verified.

Keywords: Asthma · Persuasive technology · Self-health management · Service design

1 Introduction

Subsequent paragraphs, however, are indented. The WHO predicts that the number of people with asthma will increase to 400 million worldwide by 2025 [1] while studies show that only 44.9% of Chinese patients meet the asthma control criteria defined by GINA (Global INitiative for Asthma) Asthma is a chronic respiratory disease requiring long-term, standardized, and individualized self-management. Asthma control rates are low due to complex medication regimens, recurrent asthma conditions, and poor patient compliance [2].To solve this problem, the study proposes a non-medical means of design intervention, that is, based on persuasive technology and service design concept, through in-depth research, insight analysis of the behavior problems of service recipients, combined with the behavior change strategy of persuasive technology, the construction of

V. G. Duffy (Ed.): HCII 2023, LNCS 14029, pp. 38–48, 2023.
https://doi.org/10.1007/978-3-031-35748-0_3

a persuasion service method for self-health management of adolescent asthma, and the design of an asthma self-health management system of "equipment + application + service" to promote more conscious and spontaneous participation of patients in self-health management, improve the compliance and effectiveness of treatment of asthma patients, so that asthma can be well controlled.

2 Persuasive Design Theory

A deeper understanding of the mechanisms and drivers of behavior formation is key and fundamental to effectively influence and motivating behavior change [3], for this purpose, scholars in the fields of psychology and economics have conducted a lot of relevant research, among which, the persuasive design and FBM (Fogg behavior model) behavior model proposed by Fogg have received more attention in recent years. Persuasive design refers to the use of persuasive technology in design to intervene in users' behavior and change their behavioral habits or thoughts to achieve certain persuasive goals. The FBM behavior model in persuasive design provides insights into users' behavioral characteristics in three dimensions: motivation, ability, and trigger, and explains in detail why persuasive behavior occurs [4, 5] (see Fig. 1). Based on the FBM behavioral model theory, the asthma self-management service system needs to create positive motivation for users, enhance their ability to perform, and add triggers for the occurrence of user behaviors to motivate users to perform self-health management behaviors. Introducing persuasive design into the asthma self-health management service system to guide patients' behavior and thus improve the effectiveness of the self-health management system.

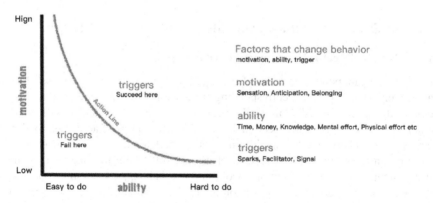

Fig. 1. Fogg behavior model for persuasive design (Adapted from Fogg [4]).

Persuasion design can be applied to numerous domains that need to encourage the participation of target users, such as educational learning [6] and electronic entertainment [7]. Recent developments in mobile Internet technology have expanded the application of persuasion technology in health management, and constructing persuasion strategies, will have a positive impact on both the user's health and society [8]. In this study, we will use the FBM behavioral model of persuasion design to analyze the health behaviors of adolescent asthma patients to construct appropriate persuasion design strategies for asthma self-health management service system design.

The study follows the research methodology of "Obtaining behavioral information - Insight into behavioral needs - Developing persuasion strategies - Outputting design solutions" (see Fig. 2), to provide new ideas for the design of self-health management for asthma patients. Firstly, we used questionnaires, user interviews, user profiles, and other qualitative and quantitative research methods to obtain behavioral information on adolescent asthma patients, and analyzed the data information to extract the current user experience problems in the process of self-health management. To address the problems of self-health management, according to the theory of the FBM behavior model, and also combined with the theory and analysis tools of service design, corresponding persuasive service design strategies are proposed in three aspects of enhancing user behavior motivation, enhancing user behavior ability, and increasing user behavior trigger mechanism, respectively, to guide the design of asthma self-health management service system.

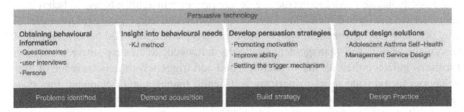

Fig. 2. Research method.

3   Analysis of User Behavior of Adolescent Asthma Patients

3.1   Asthma Self-health Management User Research

To explore the pain points and needs of adolescent patients in the process of self-health management and to propose corresponding persuasion strategies and service design methods, the study adopted an in-depth interview method and conducted in-depth discussions with sixteen relevant users, including different groups of adolescent patients, their family members and doctors. The interviews started with the daily management of asthma and explored various aspects of asthma self-health management, such as self-examination of health conditions, work and rest habits, medication use, and attitude toward health management. Based on the feedback obtained from the interviews, we sorted out the ways for patients to acquire knowledge and develop the ability of self-health management and summarized the contact points that are more in line with patients' psychological expectations.

3.2   Analysis of Asthma Self-health Management Behavior

In this study, the KJ method was used to organize and classify the scattered problems obtained from the interview and research. First, as much information as possible about the relevant self-health management problem points was organized and collected, and the summarized problem items were made into cards and categorized according to the degree of similarity between each problem item to obtain a preliminary table of patients' self-health management problems, which was divided into three categories in total: lack of motivation, lack of ability and lack of triggers. The following Table 1 gives a summary of the self-health management problem.

Table 1. Patient self-health management problem

Problem Category	Problem Description
lack of motivation	Lack of communication partners Lack of recognition and encouragement Not aware of the importance of self-health management Lack of awareness and confidence in self-health management Negative emotions during long-term treatment
lack of ability	Difficulty in adhering to management behaviors and poor execution Unable to discern their health status Not knowing how to promote healthy behaviors Unclear asthma allergens, leading to irritation Lack of access to learning about self-health management Broad medical advice and lack of guidance on specific behaviors Lack of knowledge of medication/monitoring/application Complex and cumbersome procedures for regular follow-up visits
lack of triggers	Forgetting to implement the plan that was made Not self-testing/medicating on time

4 Persuasive Service Design Strategies for Asthma Self-management

4.1 Enhancing User Behavior Motivation

When motivation is high, users can do difficult tasks, but once motivation subsides, then users will only do simple tasks. From the perspective of enhancing motivation for self-health management in adolescents with asthma, inform strategy, reward strategy, and identification strategy can be adopted, see Table 2.

Informe Strategy. Given the reality that adolescent asthma patients are less aware of self-health management, the first step is to improve the knowledge of adolescent patients about asthma disease management, the more knowledge they have, the more they will pay attention to the management of their disease, and the higher their willingness and motivation to participate in self-health management. Health education for asthma patients can be positive, by showing successful cases to enhance users' confidence in the results of behavior change and raise patients' "hope", thus achieving the purpose of increasing

Table 2. Persuasion Strategies and Design.

Persuasion Strategies	Persuasive Design
Inform	Send asthma health information
Reward	Earn medals/points and redeem prizes
Identification	Build a community of doctors/patients

patients' motivation; at the same time, it can also be persuasive by conveying a negative sense of "fear" to keep patients alert to the onset of their condition, thereby increasing motivation for health management and promoting behavior change.

Reward Strategy. Adolescent asthma patients need to control their condition through regular medication and self-examinations. Patients suffer from both physical and psychological stress during long-term treatment and are prone to negative emotions. The periodic health management of patients is quantified, and when the condition shows a stable trend, patients are given certain medals or point rewards to increase their sense of achievement and also increase the fun of the health management process, thus enhancing patients' motivation to persist in the long term.

Identification Strategy. Often, people will behave differently than usual to increase social identification. Specifically, when patients are supervised by others, they generally behave in a manner consistent with the expectations of the supervisor. Especially for adolescent patients, it is necessary not only to monitor their condition but also to pay attention to whether the patient implements actions according to the established health management plan. In addition to the supervision of adolescent patients by their guardians, it is also possible to facilitate communication among patients by building a patient communication community and achieving mutual supervision and encouragement through punch card recording, thus helping patients with health management.

4.2 Enhancing User Behavior Ability

There are two ways to improve patients' self-health management ability. One is to improve users' ability, that is, when patients perform a certain behavior, users think it is simple and effective in the process of performing the behavior. The second is to reduce the difficulty of user behavior implementation so that patients feel it is simple and controllable in expectation. To improve the self-health management ability of adolescents with asthma, objective refinement strategy, information simplification strategy, and fast access strategy can be used, as shown in Table 3.

Refine Objectives Strategy. User research results show that many adolescent patients have low execution of self-health management behaviors, and by refining health management tasks, patients' ability to self-manage their health can be enhanced. Refinement

Table 3. Persuasion Strategies and Design.

Persuasion Strategies	Persuasive Design
Objective refinement	Quantification of cyclical management tasks
Information simplification	More understandable information presentation
Fast access	Online doctor-patient communication platform

of goals is to break down large goals into simple individual tasks, thus enhancing the execution of behaviors. In asthma self-health management, a step-by-step persuasive strategy that combines the actual situation of the patient to develop a corresponding monthly and daily plan health management program for the patient can avoid making the patient give up in the process of action by becoming intimidated.

Information Simplification Strategy. Information simplification means that the presentation of information is delivered to users in an easy-to-understand way so that they can better understand the content and translate it into action. Visual feedback is given to patients on the effectiveness of their long-term self-health management. By setting up task progress bars, patients are given a clearer picture of the completion of their health management tasks, which in turn motivates patients to have confidence in their health management.

Fast Access Strategy. Asthma patients need to visit hospitals regularly for follow-up and long-term customized treatment, which is a complicated process, and this problem can be solved by building an accessible communication platform. Relying on Internet technology to analyze patients' self-examination results, give scientific health interventions, regularly track patients' health status and make corresponding health improvement plans, and register for medical appointments through online methods to reduce the difficulties for patients to go to hospitals so that patients can change their lives more actively and have their health effectively managed.

4.3 Set User Behavior Triggers

The process of target behavior execution is an important part of asthma self-management. In different scenarios, users have different motivations and abilities, and adding trigger points at key moments will prompt the target behavior. In the design of self-health management for adolescent asthma, the corresponding persuasion design strategies are reminder strategy and feedback strategy, see Table 4.

Reminder Strategy. That is, the user is urged to perform health management by setting a regular alarm clock. Although health management for asthma patients is multi-dimensional, the core is the management of self-examination and medication, and the

Table 4. Persuasion Strategies and Design.

Persuasion Strategies	Persuasive Design
Reminder	Quantification of cyclical management tasks
Feedback	Online doctor-patient communication platform

reminder strategy will work at the point where users need to manage. Teenage patients spend most of their time at school, so providing personalized reminders based on the user's work schedule and behavioral habits will have a more effective persuasive effect.

Feedback Strategy. By providing users with the right feedback at the right time, it can make them aware of the correctness of their behavior, thus inspiring enthusiasm and promoting higher frequency and longer-term adherence to management behaviors by patients. Distinguish between completed and uncompleted tasks, and when users persist in completing health management tasks, create a completion feedback interface that sends encouraging messages to give users a greater sense of accomplishment and thus successfully implement behavioral persuasion.

5 Design Practice Based on Persuasion Strategies

Based on the persuasive service design strategy proposed above, the asthma self-health management service system is constructed. Through the functions of health status self-examination, medication reminder, exercise control, health monitoring, outdoor environment inquiry, remote consultation, and communication, we help patients improve their self-management and develop good living habits to truly achieve the effect of asthma self-health management.

5.1 Asthma Self-management Smart Product Design

For the design of medical products for asthma self-management, two key products with high utilization rates in the treatment process were selected, namely nebulizer inhaler and peak flow meter (see Fig. 3). The nebulizer can nebulize the medication so that it can directly enter the lungs, which has an obvious effect on the treatment of asthma. Considering the persuasive strategy of rapid access, the nebulizer is designed in the form of a wearable device watch, which is not only convenient for adolescents to carry around but also monitors the physiological signals of the patient, which is easy for the patient's family to view. It also reminds adolescent patients to take their medication through the beeping or vibration of the watch, thus improving the compliance of patients to take their medication. The purpose of the peak flow meter is to determine the patient's respiratory disease condition through expiratory volume, and this data can be used to develop the patient's rehabilitation plan. When in use, the test data will be displayed on the screen, and patients can get real-time feedback on their health status by observing the data on the screen. At the same time, the intelligent peak flow meter is connected to the cell phone server, which can automatically obtain the user's usage behavior detection data and carry out data recording and processing.

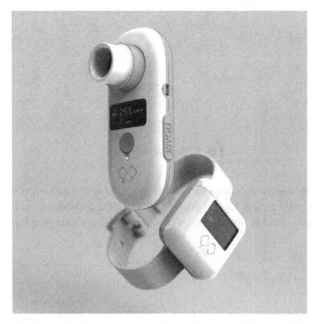

Fig. 3. Medical Product Design for Asthma Self-Management.

5.2 Asthma Self-management Persuasion Service Design

The service blueprint reflects the operation process of the asthma self-management service system, by finding the touch points in the system and intervening in the persuasive design tools, we achieve a truly effective health management design. The service blueprint depicts in detail the service system and service flow of asthma self-health management in health status self-examination, medication reminder, and other related medical product experiences as well as online health monitoring, outdoor environment inquiry, remote consultation and communication. The interaction demarcation line, visual demarcation line, and internal interaction line divide the service system behavior into four parts: user behavior, front-end behavior, back-end behavior, and support process, involving different stakeholders including patients, patients' families, doctors, and merchants [9]. The service blueprint provides an accurate depiction of the asthma self-management service system visually (see Fig. 4).

An important aspect in the construction of the asthma self-management service system is the software application design, the core of which is to provide a platform for users to develop self-management plans, self-check health status, remote consultations, and environmental status inquiries. Information architecture, as a tool for information

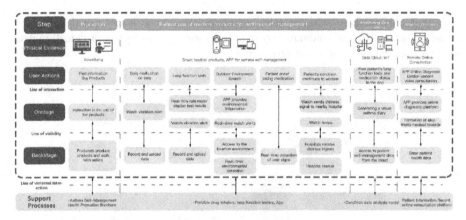

Fig. 4. Service blueprint.

organization, can integrate various functional modules in the asthma self-management application and build a clear logical framework [10], the asthma self-management user interface is mainly divided into the hospital side and patient side (see Fig. 5).

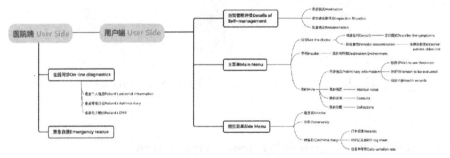

Fig. 5. Information architecture.

The Hospital Side. The hospital side is mainly divided into the online consultation module and the emergency relief module. In the online consultation module, doctors can regularly conduct remote online video consultations with patients, and can also view data such as patients' personal information, asthma diaries, and electronic cases to help doctors make a diagnosis. The emergency rescue module allows the hospital to rescue the patient as soon as possible when the patient sends an emergency call for help.

The Patient Side. The patient side consists of a self-management module, online consultation module, query module, user center module, and community module. The self-management module includes the patient's medication record, pulmonary function monitoring record, and physiological data such as heart rate and blood pressure, so that the guardian can monitor the patient in real-time, and at the same time, the guardian can set the time and frequency reminders related to the self-management content according to the actual needs of the patient, and can also view the trend forecast chart of the condition after the periodic use. The online consultation module includes a quick question function and a stage review function. The quick question is mainly for patients to describe their questions for doubtful problems or symptoms and then be answered by professional medical personnel; the stage review is a video online consultation with individual primary care doctors to meet the needs of asthma patients who need regular review. The query module facilitates users to inquire about the air and environmental conditions of their destinations to avoid asthma attacks due to environmental-induced factors. The user center module contains the user's electronic medical history, consultation information, and condition management diary. The main purpose of the community module is to provide a channel for asthma patients to communicate with other asthma patients, to learn from the experience of others in self-management, and to serve as an incentive for patients to persevere. In addition to this, it also includes authoritatively released scientific articles and knowledge mini-classes to enhance patients' knowledge of the condition. The application interface of the hospital side and patient side is shown in Fig. 6.

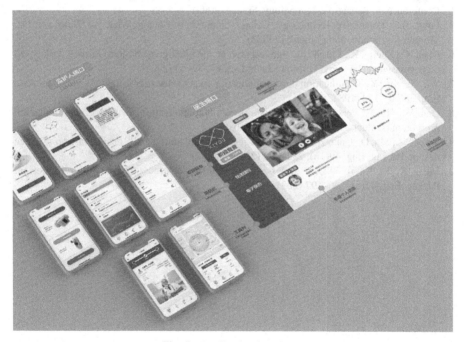

Fig. 6. Application interfaces.

6   Conclusion

Using the theoretical tools and methods of persuasive technology and service design to analyze the behavior of adolescent asthma patients in self-health management, the behavioral characteristics of users and their needs in behavior execution can be clarified, so that more reasonable and efficient service models for changing user behavior and user attitudes can be developed. It is hoped that through these methods, we can find the conditions that drive the generation of behaviors for adolescent asthma patients and obtain a continuous quality experience, and promote the positive development of the self-health management service system.

References

1. Tang, S., Jiang, X., Deng, L.: Design strategy of asthma mobile medical application based on context awareness. Packag. Eng. **40**(14), 242–246 (2019)
2. Wang, Y., Sun, A., Te, R.: Evaluation of the skill, adherence, and effectiveness of medication in asthma patients from a pharmacist perspective. China Pharm. **33**(13), 1642–1646+1659(2022)
3. Yu, Z., Xiao, Y., Li, J.: Design of systematic research framework for household energy saving through behavior modification in smart cities from multidiscipline perspectives. Ecol. Econ. **37**(05), 222–227 (2021)
4. Fogg, B.J.: A behavior model for persuasive design. In: Proceeding of the 4th International Conference on Persuasive Technology, France (2009)
5. Fogg, B.J.: Persuasive Technology: Using Computers to Change What We Think and Do. Morgan Kaufmann, San Francisco (2003)
6. Chen, C., Zheng, K., Liu, X.: Design research on the intelligent children learning desk based on persuasive technology. Furniture Inter. Des. **07**, 59–63 (2021)
7. Wu, X., Xin, X.: Gamification design application to persuade user behavior change. Packag. Eng. **38**(20), 194–198 (2017)
8. Gan, W., Hu, F.: Persuasion mechanism design and application research on mobile health promotion product. Art Des. **09**, 68–69 (2016)
9. Wang, M., Ma, D., Qian, H.: "Same Road" personalized tourism APP design based on service design. Packag. Eng. **40**(16), 232–238 (2019)
10. Meng, K., Li, K., Yu, Q.: The APP design of healthy diet structure based on service design. Packag. Eng. **42**(8), 190–197 (2021)

Demystifying the Role of Digital Leadership in the Healthcare Industry: A Systematic Review Towards the Development of a Digital Leadership Framework in the Healthcare Industry

Muzammil Hussain[✉] ⓘ, Isra Sarfraz ⓘ, and Abhishek Sharma ⓘ

Swinburne University of Technology, Victoria, Australia
{muzammilhussain,isarfraz}@swin.edu.au

Abstract. The healthcare industry has observed several changes in its operations over the past decades due to continuous innovation and new technologies. To combat the challenges of the digital world, digital leadership has become a necessity of the industry. Due to the growing significance of digital leadership across the globe, researchers are trying to understand what digital leadership entails and how today's leaders can be transformed into digital leaders to be successful in today's highly technology-driven world. Despite its growing importance, the healthcare industry has been slow in the adaptation of digital leadership along with the gap in research present. The current study aims to focus on the development of a digital leadership framework specific to the healthcare industry by conducting a systematic literature review. To address the purpose of this study, three databases – Google Scholar, EBSCO Host and Scopus were searched to retrieve 821 relevant articles. After the considerable screening, 47 articles were chosen for inclusion in the current review. From the review of literature, 37 attributes required by digital leaders in the healthcare industry were identified, which were grouped around six themes. The themes identified include leadership and learning, working with others, using technology, understanding informatics, research and innovation, and digital analytics. Implications and future research directions are also discussed.

Keywords: Digital Leadership · Healthcare · Digital Workforce · Digital Leadership Framework

1 Introduction

The pandemic has changed our life in various ways and has affected the workforce to adopt new techniques. The COVID-19 pushed labour from the physical environment to the digital environment, such as virtual teams and teleworking groups, which have become heavily IT-dependent. The healthcare industry around the globe was under the most pressure as it was at the forefront to deal with the challenges imposed by the pandemic. However, a significant advantage that the healthcare system had during this

V. G. Duffy (Ed.): HCII 2023, LNCS 14029, pp. 49–64, 2023.
https://doi.org/10.1007/978-3-031-35748-0_4

pandemic (compared to past pandemics) was the availability of advanced technologies in the highly connected world. Moreover, the industry was quick in the adaptation of technology with innovative solutions, for example, the widespread use of telehealth system instead of face-to-face consultation, the deployment of 'the hospital in the home' system and digital triage before hospital visits (Lai et al. 2020).

Even before the pandemic, the introduction of artificial intelligence and IoT technologies paved the way for organisations and operational processes to undergo transformations (Jahmunah et al. 2021, Yousif et al. 2021, Siddiqui et al. 2021). These transformations are most visible in the healthcare industry, where technologies such as wearable sensors, remote health monitoring, bed management, and contact tracing techniques are used to monitor patients and provide care efficiently (Sharma 2021, Javaid and Khan 2021, De Morais Barroca Filho et al. 2021, Jena et al. 2021). For the efficient deployment of these transformations to bring significant changes to the healthcare industry, it is vital to address the need for digital leaders who can demonstrate the ability to handle technologies such as cloud computing, artificial intelligence, big data, the internet of things, and blockchain while efficiently leading the industry towards success (Gun and Aslan 2022, Eberl and Drews 2021, Drury et al. 2018, Karippur and Balaramachandran 2022).

Digital leaders require a vibrant combination of approach, behaviour and skills that facilitates change and bring cultural enhancement to the healthcare industry by employing relevant technology (Damayanti and Mirfani 2020). The World Health Organisation (WHO) has also significantly emphasised the implementation of digital health practises and its universal health coverage as its Sustainability Development Goal 3 (Drury et al. 2018, Organization 2021). Studies have indicated that digital leaders should be trained in health information systems, user-centred design and information technology, decision support systems, knowledge management, and data analytics to manage digital data transformations in the healthcare industries effectively (Farrell and Sood 2020, Gun and Aslan 2022, Drury et al. 2018).

Despite the importance of digital leadership (DL) in the healthcare industry, its definition and the elements that influence effective digital leadership attributes remain ambiguous, preventing the creation of a digital leadership framework in the healthcare industry. To fill this gap, the current research conducts a systematic literature review to identify the appropriate leadership traits and practices that contribute to establishing a digital leadership framework in the healthcare industry. In particular, this study aims to address the following question: what is the structure and components of digital leadership particularly relevant to the healthcare industry?

2   Background

Big Data, machine learning software, and robotics are recent AI technologies used to monitor, identify, and quantify risks and advantages in the healthcare sector (Duan et al. 2022). The healthcare industry largely relies on medical data and analytics to improve processes and make the administration of medical services easier. Further, the volume and scope of leadership in healthcare have grown dramatically in recent years. For instance, physicians, healthcare professionals, researchers, and patients collaborate virtually to have consultations and discuss medical reports or data gathered via different mediums. Moreover, these mediums or sources include health tracking devices, electronic health records, data from medical imaging, and data from other monitoring devices (Liu et al. 2020).

In this context, digital technology can capture data, process it, perform dynamic analyses, and produce conclusions that can be used successfully for medical intervention (Comito et al. 2020). This role is often carried out using machine learning algorithms, aided by data storage and processing capability (Charan et al. 2018; Woo et al. 2021). Patient behaviour patterns, for example, may be possible to establish reasonable predictions by daily observations of medical data. As a result, the role of digital leadership may provide recommendations for diagnosis, medical intervention, therapeutic insights, and strategies for mitigating health deterioration and supporting proactive strategies to prevent patients' health from worsening, thereby improving patient outcomes at various stages of diagnosis and investigations and prescription use.

Technologically based healthcare institutions are now investigating the role of digital leadership (DL) to enhance technologically based practices (Zhou et al. 2021; Mary et al. 2020) and minimise operational costs (Zhou et al. 2021). Furthermore, DL potentially aids medical professionals and patients to make educated treatment decisions by offering thorough information on several treatment options (Deng et al. 2019). To respond to intense market competition and thrive, healthcare organisations' need to acquire new technological based competencies. In order to take advantage of digital technology, adapt to new skills, and boost efficiency, organisations require leaders who exhibit modern leadership attributes. Currently, digital leadership has taken a vital role and has become one of the essential determinants of any organisation's success. However, the primary functions of digital leaders should not be seen in this context as broad use of programmes in the company or data entry. Instead, digital leadership is an ongoing process that encompasses technology use, adaption, and development. One of the industries seeing the most rapid technological transformation is health care. Health technologies and information systems come to the fore increasingly with each new technology developed. The rapid technological changes (above discussed) in healthcare services emphasis the strategic importance of DL in this sector.

In order to fully understand the role of DL in the healthcare sector, there is a need to call for future research on both the practical and theoretical aspects (Chen et al. 2020; Johnson et al. 2022). There are interesting evolving insights of DL, such as innovative visionary, networking intelligence, digital intelligence (Klein 2020), ability to perform data-driven analysis instead of subjective analysis (Tutar and Guler 2022), outcomes-driven, advanced information and data literacy, collaboration through digital technologies, creating digital content (Alanazi 2022) and protect the privacy of patient data (Zhou et al. 2021). Furthermore, machine learning and expert systems use raw data acquired from patients and hospitals. However, while collecting these data, ethical considerations should be considered (Liu et al. 2020; Shaban-Nejad et al. 2021). The norms of technology development and health applications must be established to optimally use AI technology in medical care.

3 Literature Review

We are currently living in a period of constant change because of the invasion of digital technology, which is causing a shift in how the market and enterprises work in general (Karippur and Balaramachandran 2022, Eberl and Drews 2021). On the other hand, organisations in the public and private sectors have been forced to adopt advanced technology and its applications (Gun and Aslan 2022, Matarazzo et al. 2021, Kraus et al. 2021). This process has typically involved the digital transformation of large business operations, influencing processes, goods, services, organisation structures, and representations.

The notion of "Digital Transformation" encompasses digital innovation at various levels, including technology, procedures, organisational elements, particularly business model disruption, and society (Kraus et al. 2021). Several notions have been offered to identify "Digital Transformation" (e.g., digitalisation, digitation). While they are frequently used interchangeably in the literature, researchers constantly attempt to define their boundaries to avoid overlaps (Gun and Aslan 2022).

As a result of this, consistently developing innovative solutions has recently been identified as the organisation's core competency. The significance of an organisational leader in terms of its role in the process of innovation and development is becoming more critical in the present age. Leaders must comprehend the terminology of "digital" and recognise its importance in business. Furthermore, it is ensured that digital leaders not only develop digitally innovative business strategies but effectively implement them, leading to exceptional business performance.

3.1 Notion of Digital Leadership

According to recent studies, digital leaders are thought to be capable of managing digital transformation strategies in an organisation in order to generate innovation. Besides this, several researchers have developed various definitions of digital leadership at the organisational and individual levels, and the digital leader influences the individual in ways such as people management. More precisely, Eberl and Drews (2021) defined digital leadership as:

> "a complex construct aiming for a customer-centred, digitally enabled, leading-edge business model by (a) transforming the role, skills, and style of the digital leader, (b) realising a digital organisation, including governance, vision, values, structure, culture, and decision processes, and (c) adjusting people management, virtual teams, knowledge, and communication and collaboration on the individual level".

Furthermore, Abbu et al. (2020) stated:

> "Digital Leadership is a fast, cross-hierarchical, team-oriented, and cooperative approach, with a strong focus on innovation. The personal competence of the leader, their mindset as well as their ability to apply new methods and instruments are critical dimensions for digital leaders".

In general, it is likely that the best leadership approach in the digital age is a combination of leadership approaches. However, this requires a broad set of leadership strategies and digital skills. The simplest but least radical digital changes occur within pure zones, and the most complex digital transformations occur at the framework's apex, which captures the three overlapping leadership approaches (Warner and Wäger 2019). In addition to this, several researchers state that implementing transactional, transformational, and other leadership approaches can lead to successful results in implementing large-scale digital transformation strategies (Eberl and Drews 2021, Karippur and Balaramachandran, 2022). As a result, it can be implied that digital leadership is a combination of leadership approaches, which, when implemented, can kick off a disruptive, large-scale digital transformation process.

In today's dynamic and technology-driven corporate world, the fundamental capabilities of a digital leader are increasingly important. Further, Gun and Aslan (2022) and Băeşu and Bejinaru (2020) stated that a digital leader should have several characteristics such as (a) Digital literacy, (b) Learning agility, (c) Mental agility, (d) Data-driven, (e) Cultural diversity, (f) Collaborative, (g) Rapid adaptivity, (h) Customer focused. While the given capabilities of digital leaders have been increasingly in demand in various sectors, their implications towards health organisations to direct people by using digital platforms in managing the COVID-19 outbreak is an example of digital leadership in healthcare sectors. As a result, the upcoming sub-sections provide deeper insights into the appropriate leadership attributes and practices that contribute to developing a digital leadership framework in the healthcare industry.

3.2 Digital Leadership in Healthcare Industries

Globally, businesses are becoming increasingly digital. The health sector, like all other sectors, is being transformed in accordance with new digital organisational structures. As digital transformations occur in a radical and fast-paced manner, firms that miss the digitalisation trend today will be slower, less agile, and less competitive than digital pioneers in the future. Moreover, the recent Covid-19 pandemic has created a unique scenario for digital transformation in the domain of health, with innovative technology targeted at irreversibly transforming the provision of medical services in the future years (See Fig. 1) (Acharya and Sharma 2022, Sharma 2021, Sharma et al. 2022, Yousif et al. 2021, Javaid and Khan 2021).

Furthermore, due to the Covid-19 pandemic, those in managerial positions in healthcare organisations are expected to be digital leaders with innovative, adaptable, and technologically savvy skill sets. Even though digital leadership is a relatively new concept, it has received little attention in the healthcare sector. Fewer studies have stated that digital leaders in healthcare sectors should be capable of managing (a) health information systems and technologies, (b) user-centred design and citizen-driven informatics, (c) decision support, knowledge management, and actionable data analytics, and (d) strategy implementation and organisational change (Farrell and Sood 2020, Gun and Aslan 2022, McKeever and Brown 2019, Pundzicne et al. 2022, Fernández-Luque et al. 2021, Rotaru and Edelhauser 2021, Hermes et al. 2020). Hence, based on the above notions, it is anticipated that digital leadership, in conjunction with technological innovation, will aid in developing and continuously improving healthcare industries (See Fig. 2).

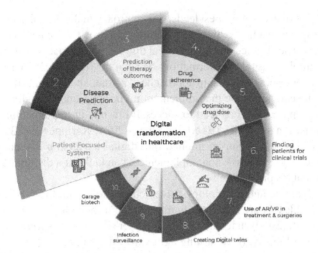

Fig. 1. Digital Transformation in Healthcare Industries. Source-Rotaru and Edelhauser (2021)

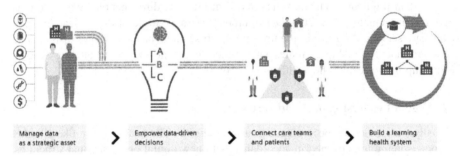

Fig. 2. Digital Leadership Empowering Healthcare Industries. Source-Rotaru and Edelhauser (2021)

4 Methodology

Healthcare professionals are now working in an environment that is dynamic and complex; however, they are not provided with formal training or prepared to deal with the challenges of delivering care online. A systematic literature review was conducted to address this study's purpose. Data on digital leadership and its implementation in the healthcare sector was collected from Google Scholar, Scopus and Web of Science. A Boolean search with the search terms 'digital leadership', 'digital leaders' and 'healthcare industry' was carried out. The peer-reviewed articles published in the last five years in English language were included in this review. Reference lists of the articles were also scrutinised to maximise the number of data sources. This resulted in 821 articles in total from all three databases. Articles were screened in three stages to examine their relevance to the current study. The articles were first screened based on their titles, followed by screening abstracts, and finally, full texts of the articles were searched. Articles discussing the required digital leadership skills and attributes were included in the review.

As a result of screening, 47 articles were identified for inclusion in the systematic review. The following figure summarises the systematic search and selection process (Fig. 3).

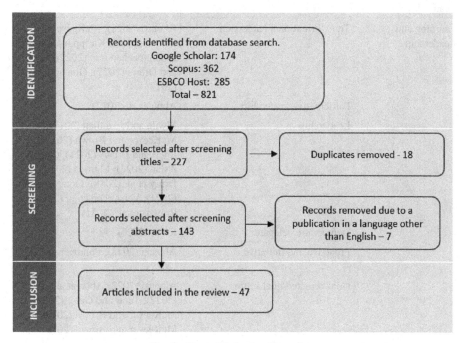

Fig. 3. Record Selection Procedure

5   Findings

Based on the articles reviewed, several themes relevant to digital leadership were identified. The review results identified 37 attributes required by a successful digital leader in the healthcare industry, which were categorised into six themes. Key themes include learning and leadership, working with others, using technology, understanding informatics, research and innovation, and digital analytics. Understanding these themes and sub-themes enables us to understand better the notion of digital leadership in the healthcare sector. A summary of the key themes, sub-themes and references is presented in Table 1 below.

Table 1. Themes and Sub-themes of Digital Leadership Attributes Identified from Literature

Themes of Digital Leadership	Sub-themes	References
Learning and Leadership	Transformational leadership	Alanazi (2022); McKeever and Brown (2019); Karippur and Balaramachandran (2022); Eberl and Drews (2021); Gun and Aslan (2022)
	Participative leadership	Abbu et al. (2022)
	Leadership	Mwita and Joanthan (2019); McKeever and Brown (2019); Eberl and Drews (2021); Gun and Aslan (2022); Martins (2019); Drury et al. (2018); Organization (2021); VonAchen et al. (2021); Roberts et al. (2021)
	Democratic delegate	Klein (2020)
	Proactive and initiative	Alanazi (2022); Pundziene et al. (2022)
	Goal-oriented/goal setting	Alanazi (2022);Abbu et al. (2022); Tutar and Guler (2022); McKeever and Brown (2019); McKeever and Brown (2019)
	Visionary	Tutar and Guler (2022); Magesa and Jonathan (2022); Pundziene et al. (2022); Karippur and Balaramachandran (2022)
	Knowledge sharing	Abbu et al. (2022); Klein (2020); MAS et al. (2020); McKeever and Brown (2019); Eberl and Drews (2021)
	Lifelong learner	Klein (2020); Orero-Blat et al. (2022)
	Enthusiastic	Magesa and Jonathan (2022)
Working with others	Delegating	Alanazi (2022); Mwita and Joanthan (2019); Fernández-Luque et al. (2021); MAS et al. (2020)
	Building consensus	Alanazi (2022); Mwita and Joanthan (2019); Magesa and Jonathan (2022)

(continued)

Table 1. (*continued*)

Themes of Digital Leadership	Sub-themes	References
	Team player and collaborative	Alanazi (2022);Rotaru and Edelhauser (2021); Fernández-Luque et al. (2021); MAS et al. (2020); Pundziene et al. (2022); McKeever and Brown (2019); Karippur and Balaramachandran (2022); Eberl and Drews (2021); Gun and Aslan (2022)
	Interpersonal and communication skills	Alanazi (2022); Orero-Blat et al. (2022); Magesa and Jonathan (2022); Fernández-Luque et al. (2021); MAS et al. (2020); McKeever and Brown (2019)
	Influencing/Inspiring/motivating	Abbu et al. (2022); Klein (2020); Mwita and Joanthan (2019); Magesa and Jonathan (2022); Karippur and Balaramachandran (2022); Eberl and Drews (2021)
	Digital collaboration	Tutar and Guler (2022); Orero-Blat et al. (2022); Rotaru and Edelhauser (2021); Pundziene et al. (2022); Karippur and Balaramachandran (2022); Eberl and Drews (2021); Gun and Aslan (2022); Drury et al. (2018); Eden et al. (2019); Papavasiliou et al. (2021); Malik et al. (2022); Rachh (2021)
	Social intelligence/people skills	Alanazi (2022); Abbu et al. (2022); Klein (2020); Fernández-Luque et al. (2021); MAS et al. (2020); Martins (2019); Papavasiliou et al. (2021); Kwiatkowska and Skórzewska-Amberg (2019)
	Mentorship	Mwita and Joanthan (2019); Magesa and Jonathan (2022); McKeever and Brown (2019); Eberl and Drews (2021)

(*continued*)

Table 1. (*continued*)

Themes of Digital Leadership	Sub-themes	References
	Ethical	Klein (2020)
Using technology	Willing to adopt change	Abbu et al. (2022); Klein (2020); Gun and Aslan (2022)
	Innovative	Alanazi (2022); Abbu et al. (2022); Fernández-Luque et al. (2021); Pundziene et al. (2022); Gun and Aslan (2022); Martins (2019); Ratta et al. (2019); Holterman et al. (2022); Malik et al. (2022)
	Digital literacy	Abbu et al. (2022); Tutar and Guler (2022); Klein (2020); Orero-Blat et al. (2022); Magesa and Jonathan (2022); Hermes et al. (2020); Rotaru and Edelhauser (2021); Fernández-Luque et al. (2021); Gun and Aslan (2022); Martins (2019); Drury et al. (2018); Organization (2021); Papavasiliou et al. (2021); Rachh (2021)
	Creating digital content	Tutar and Guler (2022); Rotaru and Edelhauser (2021); Gun and Aslan (2022); Organization (2021)
	Creating a digital culture	Tutar and Guler (2022); Rotaru and Edelhauser (2021); Gun and Aslan (2022); Organization (2021)
	Digital talent scout	Klein (2020); Hermes et al. (2020); Rotaru and Edelhauser (2021)
Understanding informatics	Ethical awareness	Orero-Blat et al. (2022); Karippur and Balaramachandran (2022); Organization (2021)

(*continued*)

Table 1. (*continued*)

Themes of Digital Leadership	Sub-themes	References
	Data focused	Abbu et al. (2022); Tutar and Guler (2022); Hermes et al. (2020); Rotaru and Edelhauser (2021); Pundziene et al. (2022); Karippur and Balaramachandran (2022); Gun and Aslan (2022); Martins (2019); Organization (2021)
	Information management	Orero-Blat et al. (2022); Rotaru and Edelhauser (2021); Pundziene et al. (2022); Gun and Aslan (2022); Drury et al. (2018)
Research and innovation	Critical thinking	Alanazi (2022); Orero-Blat et al. (2022); Eppley et al. (2021)
	Ability to use visual analytics	Abbu et al. (2022); Hermes et al. (2020); Rotaru and Edelhauser (2021); Fernández-Luque et al. (2021); Karippur and Balaramachandran (2022); Drury et al. (2018); Organization (2021)
	Attention to detail	Alanazi (2022); Fernández-Luque et al. (2021)
	Problem-solving using digital technologies	Tutar and Guler (2022);Orero-Blat et al. (2022); Fernández-Luque et al. (2021); Karippur and Balaramachandran (2022)
	Creative	Orero-Blat et al. (2022); Klein (2020); Eppley et al. (2021); Hermes et al. (2020); Rotaru and Edelhauser (2021); Fernández-Luque et al. (2021); Pundziene et al. (2022); Karippur and Balaramachandran (2022); Drury et al. (2018)
Digital Analytics	Ethical AI	Abbu et al. (2022); Hermes et al. (2020); Karippur and Balaramachandran (2022)

(*continued*)

Table 1. (*continued*)

Themes of Digital Leadership	Sub-themes	References
	Data security and Governance	Rotaru and Edelhauser (2021); Fernández-Luque et al. (2021); Karippur and Balaramachandran (2022); Eberl and Drews (2021), Gun and Aslan (2022); Organization (2021); Malik et al. (2022); Fuqua et al. (2020)
	Safe and Sustainable Use	Fernández-Luque et al. (2021); Rotaru and Edelhauser (2021); Organization (2021)
	Cyber security planning	Karippur and Balaramachandran (2022); Organization (2021); Malik et al. (2022)

A digital leadership framework specific to the healthcare industry is developed based on these themes. The framework highlights the significant attributes that enable a digital leader to perform in today's technology-intensive healthcare industry and the outcomes of implementing digital leadership that aligns with the requirements of sustainable operations. Theme 1 – 'Leadership and Learning' focuses on the qualities required by the digital leader to lead in the health care industry while staying abreast with the latest information and knowledge. The focus of theme 2 – 'Working with Others' is on the ability of the digital leader to work with peers, upper management, and subordinates in an efficient manner. Theme 3 – 'Using Technology' informs the ability of the digital leader to utilise and exploit technology at its best to perform the duties of a digital leader. Theme 4 – 'Understanding Informatics' deals with the ability of the digital leader to process and store data in an ethical manner while protecting the patients' identity and personal information. Theme 5 – 'Research and Innovation' focus on exploring new technologies to solve problems and find creative solutions while using visual analytics for easier understanding of information by all parties. Theme 6 – 'Digital Analytics' emphasises the presence of digital analytical skills required to combat the risks of cybercrime while keeping sustainability of data at the forefront. Figure 4 below presents the framework for digital leadership in the healthcare industry.

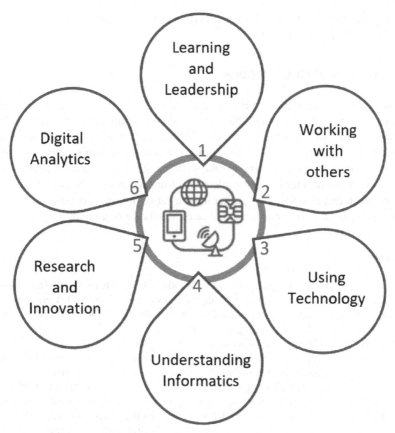

Fig. 4. Digital Leadership Framework for Healthcare Industry

6 Conclusion and Implications

Leadership is a social influence process that has entered a digital epoch that demands an interdisciplinary lens to view the phenomena in the recent era (Banks et al. 2022). However, there are several implications of digital leadership in the healthcare sector as well as in general organisational processes. First, the Covid-19 era heightened the need for remote interactions, showing how the use of technology shapes the behaviours of the digital workforce. Second, digital leadership is not a theoretically mature concept yet; however, it provides further support for the use of artificial intelligence and big data for digital transformation in the healthcare sector, such as blockchain technology. Third, in the current age of the advanced medical field, the majority of medical procedures and equipment are IT based, such as robotics.

Furthermore, the role of digital leadership has become more important than ever to design effective policies focusing patients' safety while using IT based procedures and apparatus. Therefore, ambidextrous organisational design (capacity of keeping both ends) is becoming popular where leaders are adopting digital and traditional forms of leadership aspects. Fourth, digital leadership can cultivate vision, and digital capabilities among both leaders and followers.

7   Future Research Directions

The concept of digital leadership is emerging; it is essential to conduct future studies to advance theoretical conceptualisation and explore relevant characteristics of digital leadership. As the current paper is a systematic literature review, there is an opportunity to develop the measurement scale for digital leadership for future empirical studies. Different aspects of digital leadership and adoption stages, based on a questionnaire, might assist leaders in determining their level of IT understanding and virtual leadership. Future research can also focus on evaluating the set of digital leadership determinants and their impacts on the overall performance of healthcare organisations.

References

Abbu, H., Mugge, P., Gudergan, G., Hoeborn, G., Kwiatkowski, A.: Measuring the Human dimensions of digital leadership for successful digital transformation: digital leaders can use the authors' digital leadership scale to assess their own readiness and ability to accelerate digital transformation. Res. Technol. Manag. **65**, 39–49 (2022)

Abbu, H., Mugge, P., Gudergan, G., Kwiatkowski, A.: Digital leadership-character and competency differentiates digitally mature organisations. In: 2020 IEEE International Conference on Engineering, Technology and Innovation (ICE/ITMC), pp. 1–9. IEEE (2020)

Acharya, N., Sharma, A.: Demarcating the privacy issues of Aarogya Setu app in Covid-19 pandemic in India: an exploration into contact tracing mobile applications from elaboration likelihood model. In: Moallem, A. (eds.) HCI for Cybersecurity, Privacy and Trust. HCII 2022. Lecture Notes in Computer Science, vol. 13333, pp. 457–468. Springer, Cham (2022). https://doi.org/10.1007/978-3-031-05563-8_28

Alanazi, A.T.: Digital leadership: attributes of modern healthcare leaders. Cureus **14**(2), e21969 (2022)

Băeşu, C., Bejinaru, R.: Knowledge management strategies for leadership in the digital business environment. Proc. Int. Conf. Bus. Excellence **14**, 646–656 (2020)

Charan, S., Khan, M.J., Khurshid, K.: Breast cancer detection in mammograms using convolutional neural network. In: The International Conference on Computing, Mathematics and Engineering Technologies, pp. 1–5 (2018)

Comito, C., Falcone, D., Forestiero, A.: Current trends and practices in smar health monitoring and clinical decision support. In: IEEE International Conference on Bioinformatics and Biomedicine, pp. 2577–2584 (2020)

Damayanti, F.P., Mirfani, A.M.: An analysis of digital leadership in the pandemic covid-19 ERA. In: 4th International Conference on Research of Educational Administration and Management, ICREAM 2020, pp. 156–159. Atlantis Press (2021)

De Morais Barroca Filho, I., Aquino, G., Malaquias, R.S., Girão, G., Melo, S.R.M.: An IoT-based healthcare platform for patients in ICU beds during the Covid-19 outbreak. IEEE Access **9**, 27262–27277 (2021)

Zhou, R., Zhang, X., Wang, X., Yang, G., Guizani, N., Du, X.: Efficient and traceable patient health data search system for hospital management in smart cities. IEEE IoT J. **8**(8), 6425–6436 (2021)

Drury, P., Roth, S., Jones, T., Stahl, M., Medeiros, D.: Guidance for investing in digital health (2018)

Duan, L., Street, W.N., Xu, E.: Healthcare information systems: data mining methods in the creation of a clinical recommender system. Enterp. Inf. Syst. **5**, 169–181 (2011)

Eberl, J.K., Drews, P.: Digital leadership – mountain or molehill? A literature review. In: Ahlemann, F., Schütte, R., Stieglitz, S. (eds.) WI 2021. LNISO, vol. 48, pp. 223–237. Springer, Cham (2021). https://doi.org/10.1007/978-3-030-86800-0_17

Eden, R., Burton-Jones, A., Casey, V., Draheim, M.: Digital transformation requires workforce transformation. MIS Q. Exec. **18**(1), 1–17 (2019)

Eppley, H.B., Zhou, W., Wilson, G.A., Toscani, M., York, J.M.: Using lean startup to discover customers in the mHealth industry: current landscape and challenges. J. Commercial Biotechnol. **26**, 25–38 (2021)

Farrell, D., Sood, H.: The NHS Digital Academy–learning from the past to look ahead. Fut. Healthc. J. **7**, 185 (2020)

Fernández-Luque, A.-M., Ramírez-Montoya, M.-S., Cordón-García, J.-A.: Training in digital competencies for health professionals: systematic mapping (2015–2019). Profesional de la Información **30**, e300213 (2021)

Fuqua, R., Aronson, E., Gritzmacher, D.: A case of bad behavior and a whistleblower label: how to handle the situation. J. Leadersh. Account. Ethics **17**(3), 30–32 (2020)

Gun, İ., Aslan, Ö.: Digital leadership in healthcare organization. In: HEALTH SCIENCES Current Researches and New Tends, vol. 50 (2022)

Hermes, S., Riasanow, T., Clemons, E.K., Böhm, M., Krcmar, H.: The digital transformation of the healthcare industry: exploring the rise of emerging platform ecosystems and their influence on the role of patients. Bus. Res. **13**(3), 1033–1069 (2020). https://doi.org/10.1007/s40685-020-00125-x

Holterman, S., Hettinga, M., Buskens, E., Lahr, M.: Factors influencing procurement of digital healthcare: a case study in Dutch district nursing. Int. J. Health Policy Manag. **11**(9), 1883–1893 (2022)

Jahmunah, V., et al.: Future IoT tools for COVID-19 contact tracing and prediction: a review of the state-of-the-science. Int. J. Imaging Syst. Technol. **31**, 455–471 (2021)

Javaid, M., Khan, I.H.: Internet of Things (IoT) enabled healthcare helps to take the challenges of Covid-19 pandemic. J. Oral Biol. Craniofac. Res. **11**, 209–214 (2021)

Jena, K.K., Bhoi, S.K., Prasad, M., Puthal, D.: A fuzzy rule-based efficient hospital bed management approach for coronavirus disease-19 infected patients. Neural Comput. Appl. **34**, 11361–11382 (2021). https://doi.org/10.1007/s00521-021-05719-y

Karippur, N.K., Balaramachandran, P.R.: Antecedents of effective digital leadership of enterprises in Asia Pacific. Australas. J. Inf. Syst. **26**, 1–35 (2022)

Klein, M.: Leadership characteristics in the era of digital transformation. Bus. Manage. Stud. Int. J. **8**(1), 883–902 (2020)

Kraus, S., Schiavone, F., Pluzhnikova, A., Invernizzi, A.C.: Digital transformation in healthcare: analysing the current state-of-research. J. Bus. Res. **123**, 557–567 (2021)

Kwiatkowska, E.M., Skórzewska-Amberg, M.: Digitalisation of healthcare and the problem of digital exclusion. Central Eur. Manage. J. **27**, 48–63 (2019)

Lai, L., et al.: Digital triage novel strategies for population health management in response to the COVID-19 pandemic. Healthcare **8**, 100493 (2020)

Liu, J., Ma, J., Li, J., Huang, M., Sadiq, N., Ai, Y.: Robust watermarking algorithm for medical volume data in internet of medical things. IEEE Access **8**, 93939–93961 (2020)

Malik, H., Chaudhary, G., Srivastava, S.: Digital transformation through advances in artificial intelligence and machine learning. J. Intell. Fuzzy Syst. **42**(2), 615–622 (2022)

Magesa, M.M., Jonathan, J.: Conceptualising digital leadership characteristics for successful digital transformation: the case of Tanzania. Inf. Technol. Dev. **28**, 777–796 (2022)

Martins, H.: Digital transformation and digital leadership. Healthc. Inf. Res. **25**, 350–351 (2019)

Wain, M.J., Handel, D.A., Williford, K., Stewart, K.: Field report: transitioning from physician to hospital leader: a competency based model. Phys. Leadersh. J. **7**, 32–35 (2020)

Matarazzo, M., Penco, L., Profumo, G., Quaglia, R.: Digital transformation and customer value creation in made in Italy SMEs: a dynamic capabilities perspective. J. Bus. Res. **123**, 642–656 (2021)

Mckeever, J., Brown, T.: What are the client, organisational and employee-related outcomes of high quality leadership in the allied health professions?: a scoping review. Asia Pac. J. Health Manage. **14**, 19–30 (2019)

Mwita, M.M., Joanthan, J.: Digital leadership for digital transformation. Electron. Sci. J. **10**, 2082–2677 (2019)

Orero-Blat, M., Jordán, H.D.J., Palacios-Marqués, D.: A literature review of causal relationships in 21st century skills and digital leadership. Int. J. Serv. Oper. Inf. **12**, 1–12 (2022)

Papavasiliou, S., Reaiche, C., Papavasiliou, S.: Digital health and patient-centred care: a digital systems view. Syst. Res. Behav. Sci. **38**(2), 231–245 (2021)

Pundziene, A., Gutmann, T., Schlichtner, M., Teece, D.J.: Value impedance and dynamic capabilities: the case of MedTech Incumbent-Born digital healthcare platforms. Calif. Manage. Rev. **64**, 108–134 (2022)

Rachh, A.: A study of future opportunities and challenges in digital healthcare sector: cyber security vs. crimes in digital healthcare sector. Asia Pac. J. Health Manage. **16**(3), 7–15 (2021)

Ratta, P., Kaur, A., Sharma, S., Shabaz, M., Dhiman, G.: Application of blockchain and internet of things in healthcare and medical sector: applications, challenges, and future perspectives. J. Food Qual. **2021**, 1–20 (2021)

Roberts, B.H., Damiano, L.A., Graham, B.S., Rogers, E.W., Coots, N.V.: A case study in fostering a learning culture in the context of COVID-19. Phys. Leadersh. J. **8**(3), 53–57 (2021)

Rotaru, N., Edelhauser, E.: The impact of digital transformation on health service management. Ann. Univ. Petroşani Econ. **21**, 13–20 (2021)

Sharma, A.: The role of IoT in the fight against covid-19 to restructure the economy. In: Stephanidis, C., Duffy, V.G., Krömker, H., Fui-Hoon Nah, F., Siau, K., Salvendy, G., Wei, J. (eds.) HCII 2021. LNCS, vol. 13097, pp. 140–156. Springer, Cham (2021). https://doi.org/10.1007/978-3-030-90966-6_11

Sharma, A., Hewege, C., Perera, C.: Exploration of privacy, ethical and regulatory concerns related to COVID-19 vaccine passport implementation. In: Moallem, A. (eds.) HCI for Cybersecurity, Privacy and Trust. HCII 2022. Lecture Notes in Computer Science, vol. 13333, pp. 480–491. Springer, Cham (2022). https://doi.org/10.1007/978-3-031-05563-8_30

Siddiqui, S., Shakir, M.Z., Khan, A.A., Dey, I.: Internet of Things (IoT) enabled architecture for social distancing during pandemic. Front. Commun. Netw. **2**, 6 (2021)

Tutar, H., Guler, S.: Digital leadership as a requirement for the new business ecosystem: a conceptual review. Çankırı Karatekin Üniversitesi İktisadi ve İdari Bilimler Fakültesi Dergisi **12**, 323–349 (2022)

Warner, K.S., Wäger, M.: Building dynamic capabilities for digital transformation: an ongoing process of strategic renewal. Long Range Plan. **52**, 326–349 (2019)

Woo, Y., Andres, P.T.C., Jeong, H., Shin, C.: Classification of diabetic walking through machine learning: survey targeting senior citizens. In: The International Conference on Artificial Intelligence in Information and Communication, pp. 435–437 (2021)

Yousif, M., Hewage, C., Nawaf, L.: IoT technologies during and beyond COVID-19: a comprehensive review. Fut. Internet **13**, 105 (2021)

Promote or Restrict? A Co-design Practice of a Palliative Care Information Management System in China

Yue Jiang[1] (ID), Jing Chen[1], Qi Chen[2], and Long Liu[1(✉)]

[1] Tongji University, Shanghai 200082, China
{yue.jiang,tegobao,liulong}@tongji.edu.cn
[2] Shanghai Linfen Community Health Service Center, Shanghai 200040, China

Abstract. Palliative care is a multidisciplinary clinical practice focusing on the relief of suffering, psychosocial support, and closure near the end of life. However, unique palliative care challenges require a more agile, effective, and intelligent management method. This article explores how to design, develop, evaluate (1st test and 2nd test), and iterate a whole course information management system for palliative care (named Multidisciplinary Life Care System, MLS), under the guidance of a medical innovation frame (Eagle Model), a medical co-design methodology (MeX), usability scales (SUS and HUS), based on the practice in Linfen Community Health Service Center, Shanghai, China. The iteration by co-design was arranged between two tests, to longitudinally demonstrate the impact of it. The results show: (1) Users with different educational backgrounds significantly differ in the usability feedback after co-design (F = 5.887, p < 0.05). (2) The total usability score is negatively correlated with HUS (1st test: r = -0.664, p < 0.01) (2nd test: r = -0.454, p < 0.05). (3) Users' perception of technical support (t = 2.918, p < 0.01) and consistency of the system (t = 2.389, p < 0.05) have been observably improved after co-design. (4) There is no statistically significant change in the total SUS score (t = 1.356, p > 0.05) or HUS score (t = 0.561, p > 0.05) after co-design.

Keywords: Palliative Care · Co-design · Information Management System · Usability · Community Health Center

1 Introduction

Currently, the world is facing severe challenges with the coming of an aging society [1, 2]. How to care for terminal patients with serious or life-threatening illnesses is becoming increasingly essential and urgent. Palliative care is a multidisciplinary clinical practice focusing on the relief of suffering, psychosocial support, and closure near the end of life [3–5]. It meets both the needs of patients and their families. As early as 1994, the palliative care department was included in the list of diagnosis and treatment subjects of China's medical institutions [6]. In December 2000, the National Health Commission of China (NHCC) stipulated that urban community health service centers can provide palliative care [7]. In May 2019, NHCC released the list of the second batch of pilots of palliative care, in which Shanghai is the only province-level city selected [8]. Currently, palliative care has become a critical part of the national healthcare system in China, especially at the community level [9–12]. This article is also going to discuss this topic in a community health service center in Shanghai, China.

However, palliative care has the unique challenge in contrast with other medical areas. Patients often have various physical, psychological, social, and spiritual problems that require a diverse team of professionals to work collaboratively to care for them [5]. This complicated user peculiarity calls for the emergence of a more agile, effective, and intelligent information management system. And this system should ideally have features such as the process digitalization, data management, staff coordination, and scientific research support [13].

So, what is the path of creating such an information management system for palliative care? We believe the answer to this question has been hidden as the distributed collective intelligence in palliative care stakeholders already [14–17]. Therefore, in this research, we tried methods that can make more use of the collective intelligence of caregivers, designers, engineers, and even patients [13, 18], to co-design a innovative palliative care information management system. Here, "co-design" refers to those activities in that designers and people who are not trained in design work together and integrate their creativity in the design development process [14, 19]. Frequently, the co-design activities are in the form of workshops/meetings/focus groups, sometimes with specific toolkits/processes/environments [20–22]. Moreover, co-design activities in the medical area are called "medical co-design" in this article [23, 24].

This research is based on a practical project at Linfen Community Health Service Center in Shanghai, China. And the information management system for palliative care we designed and developed is named Multidisciplinary Life Care System (MLS), which was put into use in early 2022.

To better reveal the impact of medical co-design, this article plans a longitudinal study with two stages via the same evaluation methods: (1) In the first stage, a prototype of MLS was developed referring to the universal Chinese Hospital Information System (HIS), considering the functionality only by the collaboration of organizers and participators (users, engineers). After running for two weeks, we conducted a system usability evaluation (1st test) involving all the users in Linfen via System Usability Scale (SUS) and Heuristic Usability Scale (HUS). (2) In the second stage, based on the evaluation results, we iterated the prototype into an officially online system by bringing in professional designers and palliative care experts as supporters, with the additional consideration of user experience. The main co-design activities were agile meetings held once per month in Linfen, where all the organizers, participators, and supporters discussed the pain points and proposed a next-step iteration scheme through a set of medical co-design tools from MeX. After running for nine months, we conducted the second-time system usability evaluation (2nd test), involving all the same users via the same scales.

2 Design and Development

Towards the unique challenge of palliative care, we explore how to handle a variety of users' needs and construct, evaluate, and iterate a whole course information management system for it (named Multidisciplinary Life Care System, MLS), based on the practice in Linfen Community Health Service Center, Shanghai, China. The design and development process are structured under the guidance of the Eagle Model and the medical co-design methodology MeX.

2.1 Methods of Design and Development

Eagle Model. This design process follows the Eagle Model proposed by the authors before. Eagle Model is a comprehensive model to describe the structure and factors of medical design and can instruct the preliminary medical designers better to start their work (see Fig. 1). It is composed of the principal medical axis in the center line as the "body", with the technology axis on the left and the human axis on the right as the "wings". Each line is constructed by four layers, from basic to applied, service, and product factors. [25].

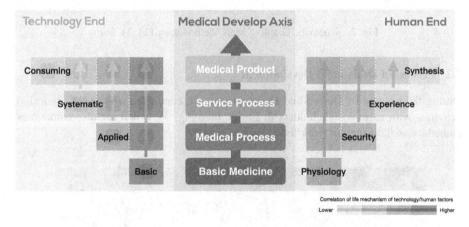

Fig. 1. Schematic Graph of the Eagle Model [25].

MeX Methodology. MeX (Media-supported Service System Model for Medical Co-design) is a methodology to provide a media-support service system for medical co-design (see Fig. 2). It introduces the Malezik Communication System Model and Symbolic Interaction Theory into medical co-design, integrates the information flow of all parties with distributed media touchpoints, and fully uses the reaction force of different levels of media on people to improve the co-design effect. MeX divides medical stakeholders into three parties: the organizer, the participator, and the supporter. [23, 24, 26].

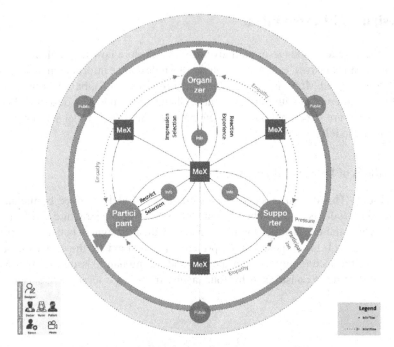

Fig. 2. Schematic Graph of MeX Methodology [23, 24, 26]

2.2 Process of Design and Development

During the process of Design and Development, we conducted a series of co-design activities with various stakeholders in Linfen (see Fig. 3), which are also sometimes embedded in their regular workflow.

Fig. 3. Photos of medical co-design in Linfen

2.3   Results of Design and Development

The information management system for palliative care we designed and developed is named Multidisciplinary Life Care System (MLS), which was put into use in early 2022.

MLS was developed with a certain degree of referring to the Chinese Hospital Information System (HIS) [27, 28], which is commonly used in many health institutes in China. It includes two modes, C/S and App, and provides platform support for modern hospitals to build a comprehensive system that integrates back-office control, internal management, and mobile services. The system's frame and UI (only in the Chinese version) are shown in Fig. 4 and Fig. 5.

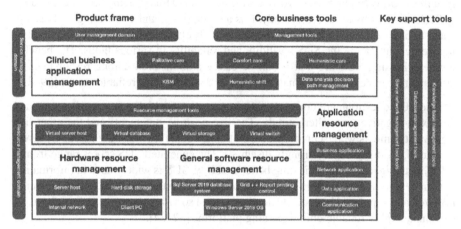

Fig. 4. The frame of the MLS system

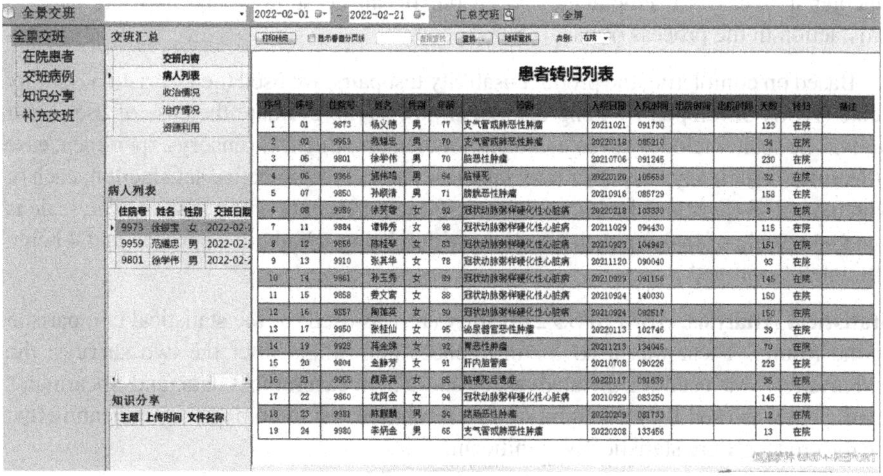

Fig. 5. The UI of the MLS system (only in the Chinses version)

3   Evaluation

To give us a more objective view of the overall system feedback, we conducted a system usability evaluation (1st test) involving all the users in Linfen via System Usability Scale (SUS) and Heuristic Usability Scale (HUS) before the co-design phase. Furthermore, we re-surveyed the same group of people after co-design using the same scales (2nd test).

3.1   Method of Evaluation

System Usability Scale (SUS).   To assess the usability of this system, the System Usability Scale (SUS) was used in this study. It is a valid, rapid, and cost-saving tool used in many studies in different contexts. Its flexibility and popularity have led to studies exploring and demonstrating the SUS's validity and reliability in various fields. The benefits of research using SUS are that it can be easily administered among respondents or participants, can be used with small samples, and still produce reliable results [29–32].

The SUS questionnaire consists of 10 items, one of which has a positive tone and the next a negative tone, alternatingly. The five positive statements and the other five negative statements were scored on a 5-point Likert scale (5 - strongly agree, 4 - agree, 3 - neutral, 2 - disagree, 1 - strongly disagree). The generated SUS scores range from 0 to 100, with higher scores indicating better usability. SUS is widely used in information systems research, especially in evaluating interactive systems with the rise of learning mediated and supported by tools, technologies, and software systems. SUS is also used to evaluate highly reliable online learning platforms [32–34].

Heuristic Usability Scale (HUS).   Ease of use is an essential parameter of product performance, which refers to whether the product is easy for users to use and learn, whether it is easy to remember, and so on. It can be summarized as users' overall satisfaction in the process of use. [35–37].

Based on completing the product usability test pairs, we used the Heuristic Usability Scale (HUS) developed by Peng Xiaoyuan [38, 39] to evaluate the ease of use in our study. The scale includes seven evaluation indicators: fluency, sensory experience, ease of learning, efficiency, less error rate, fault tolerance, and subjective satisfaction, each of which has 1–3 questions based on the specific requirements of the system. The scale is rated on a scale of 0–4 for each question, with 0 being wholly disapproved and 4 being ultimately approved.

Statistical Analysis.   IBM SPSS 21.0 software was used for the statistical comparison of the results. T-test was used for differences before and after the two surveys; the variance test was used for the analysis of one-way measurement data, and Spearman's coefficient was used for evaluation of the correlation test, with $p < 0.05$ indicating that the differences were statistically significant.

3.2 Sample Collection

The population of this study was all employees working in Linfen and using the system, which was 20 people in total when we conducted the evaluations. Their average working years were 10 years, and their average age was 34.

3.3 Results of Evaluation

According to the evaluation results, we claim that: (1) There was no difference between various users in the 1st test. Nonetheless, variance tests show that users with different educational backgrounds significantly differ in the usability feedback after co-design ($F = 5.887$, $p < 0.05$). (2) Correlation tests in both scales show that the total usability score is negatively correlated with HUS (1st test: $r = -0.664$, $p < 0.01$) (2nd test: $r = -0.454$, $p < 0.05$). (3) Users' perception of technical support ($t = 2.918$, $p < 0.01$) and consistency of the system ($t = 2.389$, $p < 0.05$) have been observably improved after co-design. (4) However, there is no statistically significant change in the total SUS score ($t = 1.356$, $p > 0.05$) or HUS score ($t = 0.561$, $p > 0.05$) after co-design.

There is no statistically significant change in the total SUS score ($t = 1.356$, $p > 0.05$) or HUS score ($t = 0.561$, $p > 0.05$) after co-design. Users' perception of technical support ($t = 2.918$, $p < 0.01$) and consistency of the system ($t = 2.389$, $p < 0.05$) have been observably improved after co-design (Tables 1 and 2).

Table 1. T-test analysis results of pre-test and post-test in SUS.

SUS items	Subgroups (mean ± standard deviation)		t	p
	Pre-test	Post-test		
I think that I would like to use this product frequently	3.20 ± 0.77	3.00 ± 0.79	0.745	0.462
I found the product unnecessarily complex	1.27 ± 0.96	1.00 ± 0.92	0.834	0.410
I thought the product was easy to use	2.67 ± 0.82	2.75 ± 1.02	−0.260	0.797
I think I would need the support of a technical person to use this product	1.93 ± 1.03	1.00 ± 0.86	2.918	0.006**
I found the various functions in the product were well integrated	2.20 ± 0.68	2.65 ± 0.99	−1.598	0.120
I thought there was too much inconsistency in this product	2.67 ± 0.72	1.90 ± 1.07	2.389	0.023*
I imagine that most people would learn to use this product very quickly	2.60 ± 0.91	2.65 ± 1.14	−0.140	0.890
I found the product very awkward to use	2.33 ± 0.72	2.05 ± 1.00	0.929	0.359
I felt very confident using the product	2.47 ± 0.74	2.60 ± 0.88	−0.472	0.640
I needed to learn many things before I could get going with this product	2.00 ± 0.85	1.50 ± 0.89	1.682	0.102
The total score of SUS	**58.33 ± 13.65**	**52.75 ± 9.52**	**1.356**	**0.188**

* $p < 0.05$ ** $p < 0.01$

Table 2. T-test analysis results of pre-test and post-test in HUS.

HUS items	Subgroups (mean ± standard deviation)		t	p
	Pre-test	Post-test		
Does the system run smoothly?	2.47 ± 0.74	2.65 ± 0.93	−0.626	0.536
How is the visual effect of the system?	3.13 ± 0.52	2.55 ± 0.89	2.441	0.020*
How is the physical interaction of the system?	2.87 ± 0.83	2.55 ± 0.83	1.118	0.272
Is the experience process dizzying?	2.07 ± 1.10	2.25 ± 1.02	−0.509	0.614
Is the system easy to start?	2.53 ± 1.19	2.45 ± 0.94	0.231	0.818
Is the system easy to learn to use?	2.53 ± 0.92	2.60 ± 1.05	−0.197	0.845
How is the efficiency of the system interface interaction?	2.87 ± 1.19	2.65 ± 0.93	0.605	0.549
How is the efficiency of the system function?	2.67 ± 0.98	2.50 ± 0.95	0.509	0.614
Is the system easy to operate by mistake?	2.73 ± 1.03	2.65 ± 0.81	0.267	0.791
Is there any error in the interactive function of the system?	2.67 ± 0.82	2.75 ± 0.91	−0.280	0.781
Is the system easy to recover from misuse or error?	2.60 ± 0.83	2.75 ± 0.91	−0.501	0.620
Are you satisfied with the system's scene layout and environment design?	3.20 ± 0.86	2.50 ± 0.89	2.336	0.026*
Are you satisfied with the interface design and interaction design of the system?	3.07 ± 1.10	2.35 ± 0.88	2.148	0.039*
The total score of HUS	**37.87 ± 9.21**	**35.90 ± 10.98**	**0.561**	**0.579**

* $p < 0.05$ ** $p < 0.01$

Correlation tests in both scales show that the total usability score is negatively correlated with HUS (1st test: r = −0.664, p < 0.01) (2nd test: r = −0.454, p < 0.05) (Table 3).

Table 3. SUS and HUS correlation in pre-test and post-test (Spearman)

	Pre-test	SUS	HUS
Pre-test	SUS	–	−0.664(0.007**)
	HUS	−0.664(0.007**)	–
Post-test	SUS	–	−0.454(0.044*)
	HUS	−0.454(0.044*)	–

* $p < 0.05$ ** $p < 0.01$

There was no difference between various users in the 1st test. Nonetheless, variance tests show that users with different educational backgrounds significantly differ in the usability feedback after co-design (F = 5.887, p < 0.05) (Table 4).

Table 4. ANOVA results (Educational level in post-test)

	F	p
S9	3.740	0.045*
SUS	5.887	0.011*
HUS	2.289	0.132

* $p < 0.05$

4 Discussion and Conclusion

4.1 Relevance of Co-design and Usability

The research results respectively show that:

(1) Factors influencing user perceptions, such as their educational backgrounds, still need to be considered. During the operation and iteration of this system, users with higher educational backgrounds may have higher participation, think more deeply, and then produce higher demands, which causes a phenomenon that the longer they have used for, the lower the usability satisfaction is. Moreover, they gradually clarify their needs in the co-design process, thus bringing higher requirements for the system.
(2) The system meets all the users' needs in Linfen and has a good performance in usability to some extent. Moreover, the iteration of the system user interface results in the improvement of the system's usability. In addition, the results show that ease of use and usability are closely related, which means improving usability can dramatically enhance the performance of the user experience.
(3) The medical co-design methodology MeX, which involves different stakeholders in the design, development, evaluation, and iteration process, can improve the usability of certain aspects of the information management system for palliative care.
(4) The design and development of a medical information system in China is still in a relatively passive situation, because of the policy, regulation, finance, and resources, which remains challenging to achieve the anticipated design goals even by the medical co-design methodology. These essential issues need to be further studied to achieve a more high-quality design more effectively within these limits or break through them.

4.2 Limitation

This article has three main limitations in research as follows:

(1) This study has only conducted a short co-design design, and further program iterations and system improvements are needed.

(2) Although all users were included in this study as test subjects, the sample size is still tiny. In the future, our research group will expand the use of the system and try to promote it in several new hospitals.
(3) In the further works, this study will adopt a more targeted evaluation method to evaluate the system's usability for the users' whole usage cycle.

Acknowledgments. The authors would like to acknowledge the financial support of the 2022 Tongji University First-class Interdisciplinary Innovation Design and Intelligent Manufacturing Discipline Cluster Construction Fund (grant number: F2204).

References

1. Botero, A., Hyysalo, S.: Ageing together: steps towards evolutionary co-design in everyday practices. CoDesign **9**, 37–54 (2013). https://doi.org/10.1080/15710882.2012.760608
2. Boffi, M., Pola, L., Fumagalli, N., Fermani, E., Senes, G., Inghilleri, P.: Nature experiences of older people for active ageing: an interdisciplinary approach to the co-design of community gardens. Front. Psychol. **12**, 702525 (2021). https://doi.org/10.3389/fpsyg.2021.702525
3. Lo, B., Quill, T., Tulsky, J.: Discussing palliative care with patients. Ann. Int. Med. **130**, 744–749 (1999). https://doi.org/10.7326/0003-4819-130-9-199905040-00015
4. World Health Organization: Palliative care. Cuidados paliativos (2007)
5. Morrison, R.S., Meier, D.E.: Palliative care. N. Engl. J. Med. **350**, 2582–2590 (2004). https://doi.org/10.1056/NEJMcp035232
6. Ministry of Health of the People's Republic of China: Notice on the Issuance of the List of Medical Institutions' Diagnostic and Treatment Subjects (Weiheifa [1994] No. 27). https://www.waizi.org.cn/law/13556.html. Accessed 08 Feb 2023
7. National Health and Wellness Commission of the People's Republic of China: Notice of the Ministry of Health on the Issuance of Three Documents on the Principles for the Establishment of Urban Community Health Service Institutions. http://www.nhc.gov.cn/wjw/gfxwj/201304/499177a487ac4cbaac1a28dbf80123cb.shtml. Accessed 09 Feb 2023
8. General Office of the National Health and Health Commission: Notice of the General Office of the National Health and Health Commission on the Second Batch of Hospice Pilot Work (National Health Office of the Elderly Letter [2019] No. 483). http://www.nhc.gov.cn/lljks/s7785/201912/efe3ed3d9dce4f519bc7bba7997b59d8.shtml. Accessed 09 Feb 2023
9. Borgstrom, E., Barclay, S.: Experience-based design, co-design and experience-based co-design in palliative and end-of-life care. BMJ Support Palliat. Care. **9**, 60–66 (2019). https://doi.org/10.1136/bmjspcare-2016-001117
10. Blackwell, R.W., Lowton, K.N., Robert, G., Grudzen, C., Grocott, P.: Using experience-based co-design with older patients, their families and staff to improve palliative care experiences in the emergency department: a reflective critique on the process and outcomes. Int. J. Nurs. Stud. **68**, 83–94 (2017). https://doi.org/10.1016/j.ijnurstu.2017.01.002
11. French, T., Raman, S.: engaging people with lived experience in co-design of future palliative care services. Int. J. Public Adm. **44**, 778–789 (2021). https://doi.org/10.1080/01900692.2021.1920612
12. Macgregor, A., et al.: Palliative and end-of-life care in care homes: protocol for codesigning and implementing an appropriate scalable model of Needs Rounds in the UK. BMJ Open **11**, e049486 (2021). https://doi.org/10.1136/bmjopen-2021-049486
13. Jones, P.H.: Design for Care: Innovating Healthcare Experience. Rosenfeld Media, Brooklyn (2013)

14. Sanders, E.B.-N., Stappers, P.J.: Co-creation and the new landscapes of design. CoDesign **4**, 5–18 (2008). https://doi.org/10.1080/15710880701875068
15. Sanders, M.S., McCormick, E.J.: Human Factors in Engineering and Design. McGraw-Hill, New York (1993)
16. Kazadi, K., Lievens, A., Mahr, D.: Stakeholder co-creation during the innovation process: Identifying capabilities for knowledge creation among multiple stakeholders. J. Bus. Res. **69**, 525–540 (2016). https://doi.org/10.1016/j.jbusres.2015.05.009
17. Kildea, J., et al.: Design and development of a person-centered patient portal using participatory stakeholder co-design. J Med Internet Res. **21**, e11371 (2019). https://doi.org/10.2196/11371
18. Marent, B., Henwood, F., Darking, M.: EmERGE Consortium: development of an mhealth platform for HIV care: gathering user perspectives through co-design workshops and interviews. JMIR Mhealth Uhealth. **6**, e184 (2018). https://doi.org/10.2196/mhealth.9856
19. Sanders, E.B.-N., Stappers, P.J.: Probes, toolkits and prototypes: three approaches to making in codesigning. CoDesign **10**, 5–14 (2014). https://doi.org/10.1080/15710882.2014.888183
20. Steen, M.: Co-design as a process of joint inquiry and imagination. Des. Issues **29**, 16–28 (2013). https://doi.org/10.1162/DESI_a_00207
21. Steen, M., Manschot, M., De Koning, N.: Benefits of co-design in service design projects. Int. J. Des. **5**, 53–60 (2011)
22. Kleinsmann, M., Valkenburg, R.: Barriers and enablers for creating shared understanding in co-design projects. Des. Stud. **29**, 369–386 (2008). https://doi.org/10.1016/j.destud.2008.03.003
23. Liu, L., Jiang, Y., Dong, H., Lee, T.C., Liu, Q.Y.: The co-creation process of a platform for healthcare engineering design and innovation (HEDI). In: Langdon, P., Lazar, J., Heylighen, A., Dong, H. (eds.) CWUAAT 2020, pp. 47–55. Springer, Cham (2020). https://doi.org/10.1007/978-3-030-43865-4_5
24. Yue, J.: A study of medical co-creation media support based on service system design (2021)
25. Jiang, Y., Chen, J., Xu, Y., Xiao, S., Liu, L.: Eagle model: a future medical product innovative design model driven by human-technology symbiosis and co-design. In: Proceedings of 6th International Conference on Intelligent Human Systems Integration (IHSI 2023). AHFE Open Access, Venice, Italy (2023)
26. Yue, J., She, T., Li, F., Liu, M.: A mediated support service system model for the effectiveness of medical co-creation communication. In: Human Factors - Management - Design - Proceedings of the 20th Management Ergonomics and 1st Design Ergonomics Conference of the Chinese Society of Human Ergonomics. In: Human Factors - Management - Design - Proceedings of the 20th Management Ergonomics and Design Ergonomics Conference of the Chinese Society for Human Ergonomics. pp. 632–647
27. Zhang, H., Han, B.T., Tang, Z.: Constructing a nationwide interoperable health information system in China: the case study of Sichuan Province. Health Policy Technol. **6**, 142–151 (2017). https://doi.org/10.1016/j.hlpt.2017.01.002
28. Peng, F., Kurnia, S.: Understanding hospital information systems adoption in China. In: PACIS 2010 Proceedings. (2010)
29. Peres, S.C., Pham, T., Phillips, R.: Validation of the system usability scale (SUS). Proc. Human Fact. Ergon. Soc. Ann. Meet. **57**, 192–196 (2013). https://doi.org/10.1177/1541931213571043
30. Lewis, J.R.: Usability: lessons learned … and yet to be learned. Int. J. Hum.-Comput. Interact. **30**, 663–684 (2014). https://doi.org/10.1080/10447318.2014.930311
31. Bangor, A., Kortum, P.T., Miller, J.T.: An empirical evaluation of the system usability scale. Int. J. Hum.-Comput. Interact. **24**, 574–594 (2008). https://doi.org/10.1080/10447310802205776

32. Anam, H., Sadiq, M., Jamil, H.: Development of system usability scale (SUS) for the Urdu language. Int. J. Comput. Sci. Inf. Secur. **18**, 73–78 (2020)
33. Brooke, J.: SUS: A "Quick and Dirty" usability scale. In: Usability Evaluation in Industry. CRC Press (1996)
34. Sauro, J.: A Practical Guide to the System Usability Scale: Background, Benchmarks & Best Practices. Measuring Usability LLC (2011)
35. Adams, D.A., Nelson, R.R., Todd, P.A.: Perceived usefulness, ease of use, and usage of information technology: a replication. MIS Q. **16**, 227 (1992). https://doi.org/10.2307/249577
36. Branscomb, L.M., Thomas, J.C.: Ease of use: a system design challenge. IBM Syst. J. **23**, 224–235 (1984). https://doi.org/10.1147/sj.233.0224
37. Davis, F.D.: Perceived usefulness, perceived ease of use, and user acceptance of information technology. MIS Q. **13**, 319 (1989). https://doi.org/10.2307/249008
38. Peng, X., Zhang, H., Chen, Y.: Study on the promotion of ice and snow tourism industry on the economic development of Heilongjiang. J. Econ. Res. Introduct., 152–153 (2018)
39. Peng, X.: Research on the design of virtual reality system for ice and snow art based on somatosensory interaction. https://kns.cnki.net/kcms/detail/detail.aspx?dbcode=CMFD&dbname=CMFD201901&filename=1018892558.nh&uniplatform=NZKPT&v=1d6lCPsPLtvWLhJ67Ou5qiC9X6OW32tL4rotd_0qO8kvZrN_CXyGHhJ4OWlf1SNJ (2018)

Motivation Enhancement Design for Individual Exercise Habits Based on Multimodal Physiological Signals

Xiangyu Liu[1], Di Zhang[2(✉)], Jiayuan Lu[1], Bin Shi[1], Lv Ding[1], Yingjie Huang[1],
Ke Miao[1], and Hao Tang[1]

[1] College of Communication and Art Design, The University of Shanghai for Science and
Technology, Shanghai, China
[2] Xinhua Hospital, Affiliated with Shanghai Jiaotong University School of Medicine, Shanghai,
China
zhang-di@sjtu.edu.cn

Abstract. Regular exercise habit is beneficial for health maintenance and motor enhancement. People realize the importance of regular exercise, but few develop regular exercise habits. Regular exercise habit is hard to cultivate since it affected by various factors, including subjective feeling, exercise expectation, kinetic evaluation, and the same. Such factors could enforce continuous motivations via appreciable positive feedback. However, in practical applications, all the elements are discrete and temporal, which is hard to integrate into a design for motivation enhancement and habit form. Plenty of beginners may affect their future expectations due to a single poor exercise performance and abandon their regular exercise. Continuous positive feedback can help the beginner to establish the causality between single training and future expectations and alleviate anxiety since single poor performance. Wearable technology brings promising prospects for long-term exercise monitoring and provides an interdisciplinary platform for academic attempts. Prior studies have demonstrated wearable efficiency for sports and physical monitoring. Our study presents a motivation enhancement design for individual exercise habits based on multimodal physiological signals to track discrete exercise performance and predict future exercise performance. We applied surface Electromyography (sEMG) to represent the intensity of neuromuscular activation and as the prediction weight. Resting Heart Rate (RHR) to indicate physical fatigue, Sleep Duration (SD) to characterize the rest quality, Sports time (ST), and Heart Rate Difference (HRD) to show the performance of physical improvement. Such factors are integrated into prediction, and the infographic demonstrates forecasts. All participants reported positive psychological feedback to facilitate exercise motivation.

Keywords: Motivation Enhancement · Exercise Habits Development · Multimodal integration

V. G. Duffy (Ed.): HCII 2023, LNCS 14029, pp. 77–87, 2023.
https://doi.org/10.1007/978-3-031-35748-0_6

1   Introduction

Regular physical exercise is essential to improve physical health and motor performance. Developing exercise habits can benefit people in various aspects, such as Diabetes prevention [1], musculoskeletal maintenance [2], weight control [3], cancer prevention [4], and cardiovascular protection [2]. In addition, keeping regular strength training or aerobic exercise in midlife could help maintain independence and postpone disability in old age [5]. However, there are many obstacles to developing an individual exercise habit. Lack of motivation is a common obstacle to developing exercise habits [2, 6–8].

Motivation is at the core of various sports participation. It includes Intrinsic motivation, Extrinsic motivation, and Amotivation. Intrinsic motivation can motivate amateurs or athletes to attempt new things, accomplish tasks, and engage in a sport for pleasure and satisfaction. Extrinsic motivation could be prompted by external contingencies and implies a self-determination continuum, including External regulation, Introjection, and Identification. Amotivation is a negative psychological status, neither Intrinsic nor Extrinsic motivation in exercise training [7]. The concept of amotivation is analogous to learned helplessness and avolition. A person who is amotivated cannot perceive connections between exercise training and the training outcomes [9].

Motivation is associated with self-determination and self-efficacy, which can help people enhance their psychological function and develop individual exercise habits. Previous studies [9–11] have demonstrated motivation enhancement associated with increasing positive consequences and could transfer amotivation to intrinsic motivation. Furthermore, recent studies have proven that motivation enhancement is associated with better persistence [12], positive emotions [11], tremendous enthusiasm, and more satisfaction [13]. However, traditional motivation enhancement or stimulation relies on extrinsic motivation, such as coach inspiration or team encouragement. The influences of motivation caused by intrinsic motivation or amotivation are discussed rarely due to inaccurate measurements and inenarrable feelings.

Interdisciplinary development, such as biomedical engineering and computer science, shifted the perspective from external to internal stimulation. Physiological indexes have been applied to evaluate sports performance in practical scenarios. However, interdisciplinary cooperation increased the precision of performance monitoring, and the existing evaluation still lacks predictability by estimating past athletic performance. Lack of predictability decreased the exercise expectation, affecting sports motivation negatively.

The exercise motivation reinforcement relies on continuous positive feedback [7]. The positive feedback should include influences from past performance impact on the current kinematic status and future performance predictions and losses from irregular exercise habits. For this purpose, this study presents a motivation enhancement design for individual exercise habits based on multimodal physiological signals.

In our study, we present a linear prediction model that integrates five physiological signals to track current performance and predict future performance, including Surface Electromyography (sEMG), Resting Heart Rate (RHR), Sleep Duration (SD), Sports time (ST), Heart Rate Difference (HRD): the difference of Rest Heart Rate and Heart Rate Max. The prediction could provide positive consequences timely for amateurs.

Considering the data size and computational efficiency, we used machine learning to predict users' performance rather than deep learning.

2 Method

2.1 Participants and Experimental Setup

We invited four participants without kinematic or cardiovascular disorders to join our study. All participants signed the consent before the physiological recording. RHR, SD, ST, and HRM were recorded by bracelet (GARMIN Forerunner 245) for tracking and predicting exercise performance. GARMIN software "CONNECT" recorded the physical data. The sEMG was recorded by OT Sessantaquattro to represent the target neuromuscular activation and muscle recruitment.

The participants were required to wear the bracelet for at least one week, including sleeping and awakening timing, and finish a resistance exercise with OT devices. The 8 × 8 high density of electrodes was used to record the sEMG during the resistance exercise.

2.2 Data Analysis and Processing

Considering the impact of different data types, we use a five-scale score to rate the four physical performances and score standards listed in Table 1.

Table 1. Table of scores for exercise performance

Rest Heart Rate (RHR)	Sleep Duration SD)	Sport time (ST)	Heart Rate Difference (HRD)	Score
60–70 bpm	7 h	200–300 min	120–140	5
70–80 bpm	6 h	100–200 min	100–120	4
80–90 bpm	5 h	60–100 min	80–100	3
90–100 bpm	4 h	30–60 min	60–80	2
> 100 bpm	< 4 h	< 30 min	< 60	1

The baseline of RHR has adapted the average heart rate at awakening in participants' days due to participants' specificity. The SD standard uses seven hours as the threshold; more than seven hours will result in a higher score. The SD and ST were recorded by GARMIN Forerunner 245. The HRD standard is the difference between Heart Rate and Rest. The Heart Rate Max formula used $(209 - 0.7 \times age)$ demonstrated by Hirofumi et al. [14].

We extracted Root Mean Square (RMS) from sEMG to represent the single neuro-muscular activation and recruitment of strength. The resistance task was divided equally into two parts in the time domain to compare the RMS difference. The higher difference could represent a higher muscular activation level. Since athletic training has a cumulative positive effect on the whole body, we use sEMG as the weight coefficient of liner prediction.

2.3 Motivation Enhancement and Evaluation

The Exercise Causality Orientations Scale (ECOS) was initially used for extracting the design principles [15]. We summarized the causality with regular exercise habits and motivation enhancement in the questionnaire (ECOS) and placed the design principles from the questionnaire and semi-structured interview.

Then, we used an adjusted 7-point questionnaire integrated with The Perceived Environmental Supportiveness Scale (PESS) [16] and The Behavioral Regulation in Exercise Questionnaire (BREQ-3) [17] to evaluate the enhancement of our design, including 15 items for intrinsic motivation enhancement.

The options list in ECOS, PESS, and BREQ-3 set 1–5 scores which demonstrated "*1: Not true for me*" to "*5: Very true for me*". We also set the neutral option "*3: Sometimes true for me*" and willingness protection options *DK (Don't Know)* and *RF (Refusal choice)*.

Our questionnaire includes the following subscales:

- ECOS - Regular exercise habits (Sample item: "Sample item: "Evaluate your performance and provide yourself with positive feedback.")
- ECOS - Motivation enhancement (Sample item: "As a way to measure your progress and to feel proud of your achievements.")
- PESS - Motivation enhancement (Sample item: "Help me to feel confident about exercising.")
- BREQ - Integrated regulation (Sample item: "I exercise because it is consistent with my life goals")
- BREQ - Intrinsic regulation (Sample item: "I exercise because it's fun")

2.4 The Linear Prediction Models

In this work, we present two linear prediction models to evaluate a single exercise and the prediction of the long-term body on purpose for enhancing exercise enhancement. Daily physical data will predict the single exercise performance, and single exercise performance will be the basis for future body performance prediction. Considering the positive neuromuscular effect mentioned above, we used sEMG as the weight coefficient in the single exercise performance. GARMIN Forerunner 245 and Connect software record RHR, ST, and SD. In addition, HRD was calculated by the formula demonstrated by Hirofumi et al. [14]. All recordings were scored according to Table 2.

The single exercise performance evaluation is as follows:

$$X_i = x_{sEMG} \frac{1}{4} (x_{RHR} + x_{HRM} + x_{SD} + x_{ST}) + b \tag{1}$$

where X_i is the prediction of single exercise performance with multimodal physiological signals, x_{sEMG} is the weight for the prediction model, since its positive effect for the body, $x_{CapitalLetter}$ are the abbreviation of each physiological signals' score, and b is the error for modifying the model.

The cumulative exercise performance prediction is as follows:

$$\hat{x}_n = \sum_{i=1}^{n} a_i X_i \tag{2}$$

where $\hat{x}_n$ is performance prediction in time sequence, a_i is the coefficient for single exercise evaluation related by the exercise frequency, and X_i is single performance.

We set three a_i weights to represent "Regular Exercise," "Occasional Exercise," and "No Exercise." The a_i of Regular exercise increases since "1" to predict future physical performance. For Occasional Exercise, the a_i was less than "1", and the X_i was less than three points for more than three weeks; the a_i was adjusted to a negative number. After three weeks, if the X_i was lower than "2.5" points, the a_i will be adjusted to an integer multiple of "-1", and the physical performance will drop below the baseline. Smooth curves connected all score points.

The error of prediction is:

$$e_n = x_n - \hat{x}_n \tag{3}$$

where e_n is the prediction error, x_n is the actual performance, and $\hat{x}_n$ is the predicted performance: the e_n is an index of model precision for optimizing the prediction model.

3 Results

GARMIN CONNECT recorded the phycological data, including heart rate, exercise performance, and sleeping quality (Fig. 1). The participants reported that quantitative visualization consistently positively impacts the development of regular exercise habits.

We recorded the participants' exercises for one week and predicted their performance after 12 weeks (Fig. 2). The prediction curves show performance differences among Regular exercise (Green), Occasional exercise (Blue), and No exercise (Red). The curves imply that if amateur forms regular exercise habit, they could perform better in the future.

Each recorded exercise performance is a path integral to the curve, and the curve visualizes the prediction of exercise performance. Our study presented three consequences curves graphically (Fig. 2). The curve integrated all physiological signals to represent the impact of each training for future performance could be visually shown.

After the questionnaire and interviews, all participants reported positive feedback in three aspects: Perceptible positive feedback, Positive future expectations, and Intrinsic motivation enhancement.

Perceptible positive feedback includes single exercise recording/feedback and positive evaluation. Positive future expectation contains the causality between a single exercise and long-term physical performance. Intrinsic motivation enhancement is composed of consistent pleasures/willingness and exercise satisfaction.

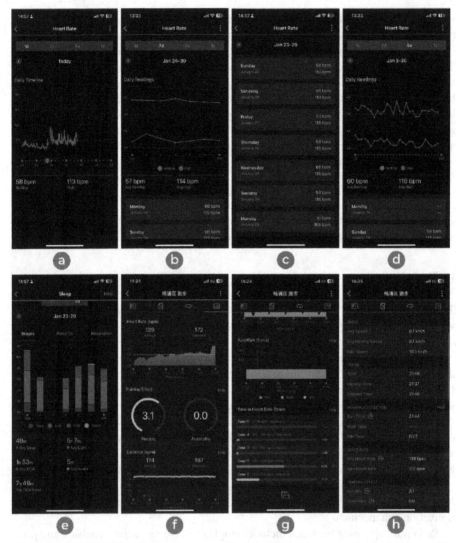

Fig. 1. GARMIN CONNECT interface screenshot (a: daily heart rate recording; b-c: weekly heart rate recording; d: monthly heart rate recording; e: weekly sleeping recording; f-h: aerobic exercise recording and physical details)

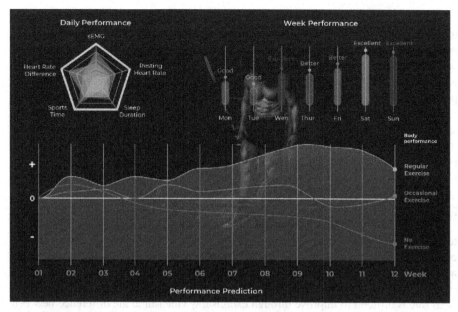

Fig. 2. The visual interface of motivation enhancement design (one participant)

4 Discussion

4.1 Perceptible Positive Feedback and Future Expectations

Our studies presented an exercise motivation enhancement design based on multimodal physiological signals by establishing causality between single/daily performance and future physical expectations to inspire intrinsic motivation for forming regular exercise habits. Previous attempts at motivation enhancement, such as external regulation, amotivation alleviation, and exercise intensity management, have become an emerging topic in areas [18]. The general purpose of exercise motivation enhancement is to form regular exercise habits, which can consistently improve physical performance for musculoskeletal maintenance, cancer prevention, and cardiovascular protection. The most commonly discussed areas of motivation enhancement include athletic psychology, exercise intensity regulation, and quantitative performance monitoring [19].

Although these prior studies have demonstrated specific feasibility and prospects in kinetic motivation improvement [20, 21], only some focus on the causality between intrinsic motivation enhancement and exercise willingness. The tension of the causality comes from the intricate connection between single exercise performance and future physical performance, which is hard to encourage beginners to form their exercise habits when they feel poor performance in a single exercise. Previous studies have demonstrated that exercise motivation was significantly connected with continuous positive feedback during or after the training, which shifted the promising motivation prospects from external regulation to intrinsic motivation enhancement, especially for the resident of urbanism habituated with individual exercise training.

With joint interdisciplinary cooperation and wearable multimodal physiological monitoring, quantitative exercise performance evaluation has impacted exercise training methodologies [22]. Wearable technologies and biomedical engineering bring new prospects in each training via multimodal signal recording and processing [23]. The joint advancement in product and interaction impacted the single exercise monitoring preciously. Although the data precision has been improved with design development, the causality with exercise performance and motivation enhancement has yet to be demonstrated. This work presents a prediction model based on single-exercise performance via multimodal physiological signals to link it with future performance. This link implies positive expectations for beginners to alleviate their anxiety due to single-poor performance and encourages them to exercise regularly. Our work combines multimodal physiological signals to predict future physical performance by evaluating a single/daily performance.

Our study combines five kinetic features, including sEMG, RHR, HRD, ST, and SD, to predict future performance. We used sEMG as the weight on the prediction model, considering the muscular positive effect on the entire body. The sEMG demonstrates neuromuscular activation intensity. The RHR, SD, and HRD represent comprehensive sport intensity, ensuring rest efficiency and avoiding cumulative fatigue. Since maximum heart rate is difficult to improve through exercise, we measured the difference between Maximum Heart Rate and Resting Heart Rate as an index for physical function. Furthermore, we used ST as an index of single exercise performance to precisely monitor exercise status.

4.2   Intrinsic Motivation Enhancement

Our findings demonstrated three aspects of motivation enhancement: (1) positive visual feedback includes single exercise recording/feedback and positive evaluation; (2) Positive future expectation contains the causality between single performance and long-term physical performance, which mainly focuses on establishing the connection in both physiological signals and sports expectation; and (3) intrinsic motivation enhancement is composed of consistent pleasures/willingness and exercise satisfaction, which mainly focus on kinetic psychology regulation and self-efficiency. All participants reported positive feedback, and future expectations could enhance their intrinsic motivation for exercise training. To the best we know, training beginners need help forming regular exercise habits since long-term benefits are hard to feel in a single activity [24]. In our work, we established a linear prediction model to link the single performance with long-term regular exercise benefits, which could help beginners to enhance their exercise motivation.

This study provided direct evidence for exercise motivation enhancement, which supported the hypothesis that intrinsic exercise motivation is driven by continuous positive feedback [7]. Exercise scientists have sought to identify the factors relevant to forming physical exercise habits [25–27]. Unfortunately, the research in areas has been primarily descriptive and has yet to guide hypotheses or practical interventions [28]. Our findings extended a more generalized prospect between self-efficacy perceptions and outcome expectations. For addictive exercise habits forming, outcome expectations are essential motivators bringing continuous positive stimulations. In addition, regular exercise also contributes to an expectancy of the desired outcome, including weight control, muscle maintenance, and training adherence. Furthermore, our findings also support that quantitative monitoring via wearable design and positive outcome expectations encourage those consistent with regular exercise programs [29].

4.3 Future Work

The presented work has demonstrated promising prospects of establishing causality between exercise motivation enhancement and exercise expectation. However, several issues need to be addressed in the future:

Validate the proposed model on a more significant number of participants: Although our findings demonstrated a specific efficiency in exercise motivation enhancement, validation on more extensive data is still essential.

Investigate various characteristics for exercise performance evaluation and sports habit forming: We applied sEMG, RHR, HRD, ST, and SD to enhance sport motivation and alleviate user anxiety from single poor exercise performance. Various physiological signals could be used to facilitate sports motivation enhancement. As an initial design, we presented a prediction model for enhancing users' desires and exercise expectations. In practical situations, users may face more complex exercise situations, such that different signal modes may involve in complex exercise scenarios.

Investigate the prediction robustness when monitoring in long-term exercise. This may extend the range of model applications. Although interdisciplinary integration and multimodal wearable technologies applied in the study may develop promising prospects in motivation enhancement, the attempt may affect the efficiency of wearable comfort and monitoring accuracy.

5   Conclusion

In this work, we presented an exercise motivation enhancement design via wearable multimodal physiological signals, which mainly focus on establishing continuous positive exercise expectations. The work consists of two parts, single/daily physical performance monitoring, and future performance prediction. The participants reported that the prediction design significantly enhanced their exercise motivation and kinetic desire. This design could motivate the users to exercise regularly, implying that each exercise will positively impact future performance, providing positive feedback continuously while alleviating the anxiety caused by a single poor performance. Through linear prediction base multimodal exercise factors, the design achieves positive feedback from the users at the regular exercise habit form and exercise motivation enhancement, indicating the high practical potential of the proposed method.

Acknowledgment. This work is sponsored by the Shanghai Sailing Program (22YF1430800).

References

1. Mayer-Davis, E.J., et al.: Intensity and amount of physical activity in relation to insulin sensitivity: The insulin resistance atherosclerosis study. JAMA **279**, 669–674 (1998)
2. Abramson, S., Stein, J., Schaufele, M., Frates, E., Rogan, S.: Personal exercise habits and counseling practices of primary care physicians: A national survey. Clin. J. Sport Med. **10**, 40–48 (2000). https://doi.org/10.1097/00042752-200001000-00008
3. Whelton, P.K., et al.: Sodium reduction and weight loss in the treatment of hypertension in older persons: a randomized controlled trial of nonpharmacologic interventions in the elderly (TONE). JAMA **279**, 839–846 (1998)
4. Lee, I.-M., Paffenbarger, R.S., Jr.: Physical activity and its relation to cancer risk: A prospective study of college alumni. Med. Sci. Sports Exerc. **26**, 831–837 (1994)
5. Shephard, R.J.: Exercise and aging: extending independence in older adults. Geriatrics **48** (1993)
6. Sylvester, B.D., Curran, T., Standage, M., Sabiston, C.M., Beauchamp, M.R.: Predicting exercise motivation and exercise behavior: A moderated mediation model testing the interaction between perceived exercise variety and basic psychological needs satisfaction. Psychol. Sport Exerc. **36**, 50–56 (2018). https://doi.org/10.1016/j.psychsport.2018.01.004
7. Pelletier, L.G., Tuson, K.M., Fortier, M.S., Vallerand, R.J., Briére, N.M., Blais, M.R.: Toward a new measure of intrinsic motivation, extrinsic motivation, and amotivation in sports: The sport motivation scale (SMS). J. Sport Exerc. Psychol. **17**, 35–53 (1995). https://doi.org/10.1123/jsep.17.1.35
8. Clancy, R.B., Herring, M.P., MacIntyre, T.E., Campbell, M.J.: A review of competitive sport motivation research. Psychol. Sport Exerc. **27**, 232–242 (2016). https://doi.org/10.1016/j.psychsport.2016.09.003
9. Vallerand, R.J., Pelletier, L.G., Blais, M.R., Brière, N.M., Senécal, C., Vallières, É.F.: On the assessment of intrinsic, extrinsic, and amotivation in education: Evidence on the concurrent and construct validity of the Academic Motivation Scale. Educ. Psychol. Measur. **53**, 159–172 (1993)
10. Vallerand, R.J., Deci, E.L., Ryan, R.M.: 12 intrinsic motivation in sport. Exerc. Sport Sci. Rev. **15**, 389–426 (1987)
11. Vallerand, R.J., Briere, N.M.: On the discriminant validity of the IM to know, to achieve, and to experience sensations in the sport domain. Unpublished manuscript, Research Laboratory on Social Behavior, Universite du Quebec a Montreal (1990)
12. Pelletier, L.G., Briere, N.M., Blais, M.R., Vallerand, R.J.: Persisting vs dropping out: A test of Deci and Ryan's theory. Can. Psychol. **29**, 600 (1988)
13. Brière, N.M., Vallerand, R.J., Blais, M.R., Pelletier, L.G.: Development and validation of a measure of intrinsic, extrinsic and amotivation in the sport context: the Échelle de Motivation dans les Sports (ÉMS). Int. J. Sport Psychol. **26**, 465–489 (1995)
14. Tanaka, H., Monahan, K.D., Seals, D.R.: Age-predicted maximal heart rate revisited. J. Am. Coll. Cardiol. **37**, 153–156 (2001). https://doi.org/10.1016/S0735-1097(00)01054-8
15. Rose, E.A., Parfitt, G., Williams, S.: Exercise causality orientations, behavioural regulation for exercise and stage of change for exercise: Exploring their relationships. Psychol. Sport Exerc. **6**, 399–414 (2005). https://doi.org/10.1016/j.psychsport.2004.07.002
16. Teixeira, D.S., et al.: Perceived environmental supportiveness scale: Portuguese translation, validation and adaptation to the physical education domain. Motriz: Rev. Educ. Fis. **25**, e101908 (2019). https://doi.org/10.1590/s1980-6574201900020003
17. Wilson, P.M., Rodgers, W.M., Fraser, S.N.: Examining the psychometric properties of the behavioral regulation in exercise questionnaire. Meas. Phys. Educ. Exerc. Sci. **6**, 1–21 (2002)

18. Calvo, T.G., Cervelló, E., Jiménez, R., Iglesias, D., Murcia, J.A.M.: Using self-determination theory to explain sport persistence and dropout in adolescent athletes. Span. j. psychol. **13**, 677–684 (2010). https://doi.org/10.1017/S1138741600002341
19. Chatzisarantis, N.L.D., Hagger, M.S., Biddle, S.J.H., Smith, B., Wang, J.C.K.: A meta-analysis of perceived locus of causality in exercise, sport, and physical education contexts. J. Sport Exerc. Psychol. **25**, 284–306 (2003). https://doi.org/10.1123/jsep.25.3.284
20. Cece, V., Lienhart, N., Nicaise, V., Guillet-Descas, E., Martinent, G.: Longitudinal sport motivation among young athletes in intensive training settings: Using methodological advances to explore temporal structure of youth behavioral regulation in sport questionnaire scores. J. Sport Exerc. Psychol. **41**, 24–35 (2019). https://doi.org/10.1123/jsep.2017-0194
21. Deci, E.L., Ryan, R.M.: Intrinsic Motivation and Self-Determination in Human Behavior. Springer, Boston (1985). https://doi.org/10.1007/978-1-4899-2271-7
22. Camomilla, V., Bergamini, E., Fantozzi, S., Vannozzi, G.: Trends supporting the in-field use of wearable inertial sensors for sport performance evaluation: A systematic review. Sensors **18**, 873 (2018). https://doi.org/10.3390/s18030873
23. Pernek, I., Kurillo, G., Stiglic, G., Bajcsy, R.: Recognizing the intensity of strength training exercises with wearable sensors. J. Biomed. Inform. **58**, 145–155 (2015). https://doi.org/10.1016/j.jbi.2015.09.020
24. Clavel San Emeterio, I., García-Unanue, J., Iglesias-Soler, E., Luis Felipe, J., Gallardo, L.: Prediction of abandonment in Spanish fitness centres. Eur. J. Sport Sci. **19**, 217–224 (2019). https://doi.org/10.1080/17461391.2018.1510036
25. Brand, R., Cheval, B.: Theories to explain exercise motivation and physical inactivity: Ways of expanding our current theoretical perspective. Front. Psychol. **10**, 1147 (2019). https://doi.org/10.3389/fpsyg.2019.01147
26. Fatt, S.J., Fardouly, J., Rapee, R.M.: #malefitspo: Links between viewing fitspiration posts, muscular-ideal internalisation, appearance comparisons, body satisfaction, and exercise motivation in men. New Media Soc. **21**, 1311–1325 (2019). https://doi.org/10.1177/1461444818821064
27. Neace, S.M., Hicks, A.M., DeCaro, M.S., Salmon, P.G.: Trait mindfulness and intrinsic exercise motivation uniquely contribute to exercise self-efficacy. J. Am. Coll. Health **70**, 13–17 (2022). https://doi.org/10.1080/07448481.2020.1748041
28. Dzewaltowski, D.A.: Toward a model of exercise motivation. J. Sport Exerc. Psychol. **11**, 251–269 (1989). https://doi.org/10.1123/jsep.11.3.251
29. Medrano-Ureña, M. del R., Ortega-Ruiz, R., Benítez-Sillero, J. de D.: Physical fitness, exercise self-efficacy, and quality of life in adulthood: A systematic review. IJERPH. **17**, 6343 (2020). https://doi.org/10.3390/ijerph17176343

Designing Relational AI-Powered Digital Health Coaching for Chronic Disease Prevention and Management

Yunmin Oh📷, Kika Arias📷, Lisa Auster-Gussman📷, and Sarah Graham(✉)📷

Lark Health, 2570 El Camino Real, Mountain View, CA, USA
sarah.graham@lark.com

Abstract. The healthcare industry is rapidly adopting digital coaching for chronic disease prevention and management. Human-computer interactions are affected by the way a digital coach communicates, including the tone of voice, choice of words, and type of feedback provided. A single interaction with a digital coach can be the determining factor in whether a user chooses to interact with the coach again. There is currently a dearth of research on the necessary characteristics of successful interactions between digital health coaches and users during long-term health coaching relationships. This research provides a conceptual framework of the coaching relationship between coaches and coachees for long-term chronic disease prevention and management that establishes a basis for the design and development of relational digital health coaching. We conducted qualitative interviews with expert healthcare providers to better understand key strategies and methods used by human coaches to 1) Guide coachees toward successful outcomes and 2) Build trust and rapport with coachees. We describe five coaching stages resulting from these interviews as well as key elements of coaching within each stage and the necessary personality of a digital health coach to accomplish the goals of each coaching stage. This work may inform the design of other digital coaches in the healthcare space.

Keywords: Automated agents · healthcare · lifestyle behavior change

1 Introduction

Digital apps have become more prolific in recent years, and the healthcare industry is one rapidly expanding use case [1]. As care has become less accessible for some due to pricing, supply, demand, or location [2], innovators have leveraged technology to improve access to healthcare programs [3]. Many healthcare providers have turned to telephonic, video, and text-based interactions with patients, which address some accessibility issues but are still limited in scale because they require human-to-human interactions.

More recently, the digital health coach, a completely virtual coach powered by artificial intelligence (AI) has emerged in the healthcare space [4]. For example, the World Health Organization recently launched a text messaging-based AI digital healthcare worker named Florence that provides information to users about physical and mental

© The Author(s), under exclusive license to Springer Nature Switzerland AG 2023
V. G. Duffy (Ed.): HCII 2023, LNCS 14029, pp. 88–103, 2023.
https://doi.org/10.1007/978-3-031-35748-0_7

health [5]. Digital health coaches have the advantage of offering active and ongoing support for chronic health conditions that require daily attention. The coach can provide customized health recommendations, track progress, and provide motivation, education, and resources to help users achieve their health goals [6]. However, as digital coaches become more prolific, it is important to examine the frameworks used to design these coaches, not in terms of the technology, but in terms of the coaching styles and strategies that developers imbue in digital coaches.

The developers of the original human-computer interfaces designed them to support one-off interactions rather than long-term coaching [7]. Therefore, the design of simple chatbots has historically focused on optimizing brief, simple interactions, like those for ecommerce, rather than addressing complex problems and relationship building over time. In contrast, a digital health coach must be able to work collaboratively with a user toward achieving health goals while considering user needs and preferences [8]. To do this, digital health coaches can be designed to interact with users in a manner that emulates how a human coach would interact with their coachees. Emulating human-to-human interactions can help establish trust, create a more engaging and personalized user experience, and improve the likelihood that users stick with a program over time [9, 10].

Trust is an essential element in any coach-coachee relationship, as are communication, empathy and compassion, shared decision-making, and patient centeredness [11, 12]. Human-computer interactions can be affected by the way a digital coach communicates, such as tone of voice, choice of words, and type of feedback provided. Some digital health coaches may be designed to be motivational and encouraging, while others may be more informative and educational. The effectiveness of these different styles of digital coaching remains unclear. Most research in this area has focused on user willingness or receptiveness to using digital health coaches [13]; there is currently a dearth of research on the necessary characteristics of successful interactions between digital health coaches and users.

We developed a conceptual framework of the health coach-coachee relationship in long-term chronic disease prevention and management to inform the design of digital health coaches in these domains. We specifically focused on aspects of the coach-coachee relationship that can be measured and manipulated in the programming environment in which digital coaches are developed. Our aims were to identify 1) Key stages of the coach-coachee relationship over time, 2) Key elements of coaching in each stage, and 3) Coaching strategies for long-term trust building that transcend coaching stages.

2 Related Work

2.1 Effective Health Coach-Coachee Dyads

Lattie et al., 2019 [14] provided recommendations for text-based mental health coaching focusing on the coach (characteristics, techniques), the workflow, the timing, and the content of messages. Highlights from these recommendations included the use of motivational interviewing techniques, brevity of messages, setting expectations around response latency, topic prioritization, and protocol flexibility. Some of these recommendations are relevant to inform the design of digital health coaches, such as the use of motivational interviewing techniques, brevity of messages, and topic prioritization, while others like protocol flexibility are less relevant because a digital coach cannot embellish upon a conversation or go "off-script" in the same manner as a human coach.

Thom et al., 2016 [15] conducted focus groups and individual interviews with patients, health coaches, and clinicians and identified seven themes for how health coaches help coachees to make decisions to improve their health: shared characteristics, availability, trusting relationship, education, personal support, decision support, and bridging between the coachee and primary care clinician. They further identified four themes of key coaching activities (education, personal support, practical support, and acting as a bridge between patients and clinicians). The authors intended these themes to be used for training and supporting human health coaches. However, they are also applicable to digital health, as the digital coach can be designed to support most of these themes and activities except for the human element of shared characteristics.

Gupta et al., 2020 [16] collected human-to-human text-based coaching conversations between a single certified health coach and 28 coachees to inform the design of a virtual health coach. They focused on the use of SMART (specificity, measurability, attainability, realism, and timing) goal attributes in the dialogues and the different stages and phases of the conversation flow. Two stages related to SMART goals emerged: Goal setting and goal implementation. Within each stage there were five phases with some overlap; for goal setting these were identification, refining, anticipating barriers, solving barriers, and negotiation. For goal implementation these were refining, anticipating barriers, solving barriers, negotiation, and follow-up. The researchers further developed a tagging system to identify the key components of a SMART goal within the coach-coachee dialogue. This SMART tagging system achieved an F1 score of 0.81 and performed similarly in a test dataset indicating that the SMART tag annotations were transferable to dialogues between different coach-coachee dyads.

Denneson et al., 2019 [17] demonstrated that self-determination theory provides a sound theoretical basis for health coaching. They analyzed the experiences of coachees rather than health coaches and discovered that coachees felt a sense of autonomy when coaches supported them in goal selection and recognized their ownership over their goals. Coachees felt competent when they were confident in their ability to tackle challenges, and they experienced a sense of relatedness when they had a consistently strong rapport with the coach. Thus, the authors proposed that patient autonomy, competence, and relatedness are important elements of health coaching from the patient's perspective.

2.2   Effective Human-Computer Interactions

Key elements that can be controlled during the design of conversational agents include what is discussed during coaching sessions and how it is discussed. Beinema et al., 2023 [18] created a blueprint topic model containing 30 topics and 115 actions validated by 11 experts that could be used to guide conversations between virtual agents and users. These authors proposed that tailoring a coaching conversation happens at five levels: Domain, conversation topic, action, dialogue act, and utterance. They determined that tailoring at each of these levels is important for increasing user adherence and engagement as opposed to a one-size fits all approach.

Gross et al., 2021 [19] investigated the coaching interaction style preferences of patients with chronic obstructive pulmonary disease and found that patient age and personal disease experience informed which interaction style they preferred. Patients with more severe disease preferred the paternalistic style (i.e., authority knows best), while younger patients and those with a less recent diagnosis preferred a deliberative interaction style (i.e., open to discussion). These findings highlight that users have different interaction style preferences and that enabling the user to choose the style of coaching they prefer may optimize outcomes.

Mitchell et al., 2021 [20] compared participants' coaching experiences with a conversational agent versus a human coach both delivered via text messaging. They found that participants in both groups reported generally positive experiences and that each type of coaching had its own advantages. Human coaches were able to embellish conversations and go "off-script" to inquire about other areas of participants' lives, which helped to develop rapport. In comparison, the agent was more consistent in providing participants with options rather than jumping to offer recommendations, which promoted participant autonomy.

Nißen et al., 2022 [21] examined how the social role of a chatbot affected a user's experience and the development of an affective bond with the chatbot. The social roles included those common in a healthcare setting: Institution, expert, peer, and dialogical self. They found that preferences for social roles depended on a user's age, with older users preferring the socially closer peer and dialogical-self roles and younger users the more distant roles. They further observed that users who were able to freely choose the chatbot's social role reported better experiences and bonds.

3   Research Objective

Although the number of health apps utilizing digital coaches has increased rapidly over the past few years [4], frameworks guiding the development and customization of digital health coach features remain sparse [22] and based on traditional theories of health behavior change [23], which focus primarily on the coachee rather than the coach-coachee relationship. We suggest that to develop the most effective digital health coach, designers must not only understand the key features and dynamics of the human coach-coachee relationship but also how these elements evolve over time.

Although human coach-coachee interactions provide a foundation for work in the human-computer interaction space, we believe human-computer interaction frameworks should be distinct in that they should emphasize aspects of the coach that are easily measured and manipulated in the digital space. The impact of text-based messaging should be at the forefront of framework development and suggestions for implementation. By focusing on these constructs, we aimed to develop a conceptual framework of digital health coaching that avoids the pitfalls of focusing on coaching styles and strategies that are too specific, unactionable, or ill-suited to a fully digital, text-based environment.

4 Methods

4.1 Approach

We conducted an exploratory qualitative analysis on a library of existing recordings and notes from 30-min moderated interviews with 11 different healthcare professionals including physicians, nurses, nutritionists, physical therapists, fitness coaches, and health educators who interact with patients or clients diagnosed with diabetes and/or prediabetes. We refer to these interviewees collectively as "human health coaches" from here on out. The original purpose of the interviews was to inform improvements to an existing marketplace digital health coach called Lark [24]. User researchers on the digital health coach design team recruited the interviewees using a moderated 1:1 interviewing platform called dscout. Interviewees responded to questions about their demographics and experience working with patients or clients.

4.2 Interviews

During 30-min, moderated 1:1 interviews, user researchers asked the interviewees questions around two main themes related to the key strategies or methods they use to 1) Guide coachees toward successful outcomes and 2) Build trust and rapport with coachees. Table 1 provides the full list of interview questions the user researchers asked the interviewees.

Table 1. Interview Questions

Question Type	Question Content
Warm-up question	1. Please introduce yourself and what you do? 2. Please elaborate on what you work with your coachees on? 3. What care do coachees usually ask for?
Human coach-coachee interactions	1. Please give some examples of how you talk to your coachees? a. How do you provide educational information to coachees? b. How do you communicate the coachee's current condition? c. How do you advise or encourage your coachees? 2. What are the best ways to interact with coachees that you've found that work? 3. What do you consider successful engagement with coachees? 4. What do coachees respond best to? 5. What challenges do you find in providing care to coachees? 6. What have you tried to overcome these challenges? 7. If you could describe your relationship with a coachee in one word, what would it be and why?
Human coach's Experience	1. What makes you feel the most discouraged or upset when providing care to coachees? Can you share a specific example or story about this? 2. What makes you feel the most rewarded about providing care to coachees? 3. If you could share one memorable anecdote or story about your experiences with coachees that you were proud of, what would it be?

4.3 Analyses

We transcribed all video-recorded interviews using the user research platform dscout, which supports auto-transcription and live notation. Using the resulting interview notes and transcripts, we conducted two rounds of affinity diagramming [25], a widely utilized qualitative analysis method in which researchers collaboratively sort a large volume of mixed information by clustering the information in an organized manner. This approach helps to synthesize information and insights during ideation in design thinking. Beginning with a single phrase or idea, and subsequently for each additional piece of data, the researchers chose whether it was similar or different from the previous piece of data based on the research topic. They collaboratively placed similar pieces of data into clusters and discussed any controversial parts of clusters or pieces of data in each cluster. Consensus was reached once all collaborators agreed on the defined clusters.

During the first round of affinity diagramming, we aimed to identify the stages of coaching. We organized the interview notes by the sequential order of coaching stages that the human coaches followed. We named each stage according to the coaching priorities aligned with that stage. For example, the first stage, Understanding the Coachee, involved coaches getting to know the coachee, their personal characteristics, and their motivation(s) for participating in health coaching.

During the second round of affinity diagramming, we aimed to identify key elements of the coaching stages that emerged from round one. We referred to a popular conversation design framework that described five elements of chatbot personalities (key behaviors, interaction goals, character traits, tone, and power dynamic) that can be considered during the development of a digital coach [26]. These elements occurred in each of the five coaching stages that we observed but varied across each stage as shown in the results.

Finally, we used thematic analysis [27] to examine any themes or overarching coaching strategies necessary for building long-term, trusting coach-coachee relationships regardless of the coaching stage. For example, digital coaches should be relational to be effective partners and companions for users. The overarching themes identified from the thematic analysis suggest how a digital coach may incorporate human qualities or characteristics that help to accomplish this goal. The researchers individually read the interview transcripts and coded for overarching themes. Two authors double-coded each of the transcripts and eight codes emerged. The authors grouped the codes into three overarching themes (i.e., Self-disclosure, Leveling, and Good Memory) that transcended the coaching stages.

5 Results

5.1 Participants

The 11 healthcare professionals from the library of interviews had a range of occupations and experience levels within the healthcare industry. There were nutritionists, physicians, fitness coaches, physical therapists, nurses, and health educators (Table 2). There was a wide range of years of experience: Three interviewees had fewer than five years of experience, two had five to nine years of experience, and six had over 10 years of experience. The demographic makeup of the interviewees was 73% female and 41 years old (range 28 to 60 years).

Table 2. Interviewee Demographics

Occupation	Sex	Experience (years)
Nutritionist	Female	5 to 9 years
Nutritionist	Female	5 to 9 years
Nutritionist	Female	5 to 9 years
Nutritionist	Female	10+ years
Fitness Coach	Female	10+ years
Fitness Coach	Female	10+ years
Physical Therapist	Female	10+ years
Nurse	Male	Less than 5 years
Physician	Male	Less than 5 years
Physician	Male	10+ years
Health Educator	Female	Less than 5 years

5.2   Conceptual Framework of Coaching Stages

The first round of affinity diagramming revealed five distinct temporal stages of coaching that repeat in a cycle: Understanding the Coachee, Educating the Coachee, Goal Setting, Tracking Progress, and Reassessing (Fig. 1).

Each coaching stage builds on information gained from prior stages and iterations. Examples of a digital health coach working with a user in each coaching stage are shown in Fig. 2. Based on the conceptual framework derived from human coach-coachee relationships, during stage 1, Understanding the Coachee, the digital coach should collect information and assess demographic context, unique situations, user knowledge, physical condition, and emotional challenges. During stage 2, Educating the Coachee, the digital coach should provide education while ensuring that users understand the information provided. The digital coach also provides educational resources as needed and addresses any user concerns. During stage 3, Goal Setting, the digital coach needs to understand and acknowledge a user's goal(s) and reasons for their goal(s). During stage 4, Tracking Progress, the digital coach helps to maintain continuity of care outside of synchronous interactions by providing resources, giving reminders, and continuing to keep users accountable to their goals. The coach should also record any progress captured in check-ins that happen during the goal-completion period. Finally, during stage 5, Reassessing, the digital coach should evaluate a user's progress toward their goal(s) and explain the evaluation to the user. If progress toward goal attainment is insufficient, or there are negative side effects to a user's physical or emotional health, the digital coach can offer alternatives. This final Reassessing stage also requires the digital coach

	STAGE 1	STAGE 2	STAGE 3	STAGE 4	STAGE 5
	Understanding the Coachee	Educating the Coachee	Goal Setting	Tracking Progress	Reassessing
Key Behaviors	Personalize Understand Be brief Empathize Listen Be sincere	Be knowledgeable Be clear Be accessible Teach Be accommodating Engage Be confident	Be goal-oriented Be practical Adapt Be patient Be creative Be respectful Encourage	Observe Be proactive Prompt Be available Encourage Support Be resourceful Communicate Provide feedback	Reflect Adapt Direct Seek information Be insightful Be positive Provide feedback
Interaction Goals	Trustworthy Accessible	Personalized Approachable	Personalized Accessible	Consistent Encouraging	Flexible Accurate
Character Traits	Open Compassionate	Honest Confident	Guiding Collaborative	Accessible Reliable	Encouraging Hopeful
Tones	Friendly Respectful	Informative Playful	Motivating	Caring Witty	Empathetic Informative

Fig. 1. Conceptual framework of relational AI coaching for long-term chronic disease management. Five stages of coaching along the top row, critical elements of coaching along the far-left column, and descriptive words within each cell from the interview transcripts and notes that embody the necessary personality of the coach within each stage.

to recall information gained in prior coaching stages to advance the care of, and working relationship with, a user.

From the second round of affinity diagramming, we found that each stage of the coaching framework varied in the nature of the coaching elements. For example, stage 1, Understanding the Coachee, has a unique set of key behaviors, interaction goals, character traits, tone, and power dynamics that make a coach most effective during this stage. The digital coach should exhibit key behaviors to personalize the coaching experience, listen to and understand a user, be brief with words (i.e., listen more than talk), empathize, and be sincere. The digital coach should interact with a user in a manner that is trustworthy and accessible. Character traits of stage 1 include the coach being open and compassionate. The coaching tone needs to be friendly and respectful. Finally, the power dynamic is closer to a peer-to-peer relationship (Fig. 3). We assigned unique coaching elements to each subsequent stage of coaching in the same manner.

5.3 Key Elements of Each Coaching Stage

Key behaviors describe the ways that a digital health coach should behave in each coaching stage (Fig. 1). These behaviors act as a guide to inform how a digital coach can be successful in accomplishing the focus of each coaching stage. An effective coach strives to empower the coachee and must strike a balance between how much they tell the coachee to do versus actions directed at promoting coachee autonomy. Thus, key behaviors inform how a digital coach can remain user-focused in each coaching stage.

Interaction goals are factors that are most important to the success of the overall interaction and dictate how a digital health coach should interact with users in each

Fig. 2. Examples of the Lark digital health coach working with users in each coaching stage. Top left panel: Stage 1, Understanding the Coachee; Top middle panel: Stage 2, Educating the Coachee; Top right panel: Stage 3, Goal Setting; Bottom left panel: Stage 4, Tracking Progress; Bottom right panel: Stage 5, Reassessing.

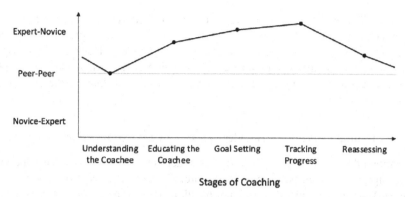

Fig. 3. Depiction of the power dynamic in each coaching stage of the conceptual framework.

coaching stage. The suggested interaction goals for a digital health coach are shown in Fig. 1. Interactions refer to the communication and relationship between a coach and coachee. This typically involves the coach providing guidance, support, and feedback to the coachee as they work toward specific goals. The coach-coachee relationship is built on trust, open communication, and a shared commitment to growth and development. The aim is for the coachee to gain new insights, develop new skills and strategies, and ultimately make meaningful progress toward their goals.

Character traits are the enduring qualities or attributes that define and describe the recommended personality of a digital health coach. The suggested character traits of a digital coach for each coaching stage are shown in Fig. 1. They describe the ways a digital coach should behave in the different coaching stages. A coach's character traits can significantly impact their coaching relationships either positively or negatively. For example, empathetic coaches who understand each coachee's experiences tend to build strong, trusting relationships with their coachees. Coaches with a patient and understanding demeanor are better equipped to help their coachees through challenging or frustrating situations. Certain character traits are leveraged more than others depending on the stage of coaching.

Tone conveys the attitude of a digital health coach as they engage in an interaction with a user. The suggested tones of a digital coach in each coaching stage are shown in Fig. 1. The tone used by a coach can significantly impact the coaching relationship and the success of the coaching experience. For example, a supportive and encouraging tone can help build a coachee's confidence and motivate them to achieve their goals, while a negative or dismissive tone can create feelings of frustration, insecurity, and mistrust in the coachee, hindering the effectiveness of the coaching relationship. Tone can be adjusted within each coaching stage to ensure that it is appropriate for the current focus of the coaching.

Power dynamics describe the level of influence or control that one entity has over another in an interaction. We describe the power dynamic using a spectrum from novice to expert, with the midpoint being peer-to-peer. With the application of health coaching in mind, a digital health coach's influence is never novice-to-peer in any of the five coaching stages. Figure 2 shows how the power dynamics progress throughout the stages of coaching. The first stage of coaching is best approached as peer-to-peer. Throughout the following stages of Educating, Goal Setting, and Tracking Progress, the influence becomes increasingly more expert-to-novice since a digital health coach should display a level of clinical expertise and guidance. This dynamic shifts back toward peer-to-peer during Reassessing to facilitate open dialogue with a user regarding their feelings about their progress.

5.4 Overarching Coaching Strategies for Human-Like Interactions

We identified three key strategies that human coaches use to build trust and long-term relationships with coachees: (1) Self-disclosure, (2) Leveling, and (3) Good memory (Table 3). We suggest ways that a digital health coach can adopt these key strategies with users.

Table 3. Summary of Coaching Strategies from the Thematic Analysis

Theme	Description	Code
Self-Disclosure	Exchange personal experience	Coach sharing Coachee sharing
Leveling	Meet coachees where they are at; "level" the playing field	Coach leveling Positive example Negative example Acknowledging effort
Good Memory	Recall coachee information and experiences	Recalling Looping back

Self-disclosure is one way that coaches can develop rapport with coachees. It involves sharing personal thoughts, information, feelings, goals, and experiences to build trust and strengthen relationships [28]. Coaches who share their own life stories and ask coachees about their personal experiences or history are more likely to build trusting relationships with coachees. However, self-disclosure must be appropriate and context-specific [28]. The infusion of self-disclosure in a human-computer interaction may require a digital health coach that has a name, uses "I" statements, and has a backstory (i.e., history or prior experiences). An example of an existing agent with this functionality is the Woebot digital health coach that tells users stories about its past experiences, likes, and dislikes [29]. In addition, a digital health coach can provide opportunities for users to share their own stories by asking questions about their prior experiences, which may help to establish rapport [30]. This can be achieved by including small talk, or light and casual conversations, during digital coach-user interactions.

Leveling involves an attitude of being non-judgmental, compassionate, and empathetic that human coaches assume to place themselves on a level playing field with coachees rather than in a hierarchical relationship. To achieve leveling, human coaches attentively listen to their coachees and try not to dismiss their concerns, myths, or misconceptions. The expert interviewees in this study pointed out that addressing coachee concerns early in the coaching experience is much more effective than ignoring or suppressing them.

We further found that human coaches often acknowledge a coachee's effort by putting themselves in the coachee's shoes. One physician mentioned that he commends his patients for cutting back on carbohydrates by saying, *"I know how hard it is to cut white rice and you're doing better than I would."* By offering this self-disclosure, he "levels" himself with his patient by highlighting that he is just another human being who is not better at eating healthily just because he is a physician. These types of interactions help coachees to feel seen, heard, understood, and feel better connected to coaches.

Another useful coaching approach for leveling is to share living proof or success stories of others with coachees. The expert interviewees in this study indicated that connecting coachees with peers experiencing similar health conditions motivates them by demonstrating desirable, tangible outcomes (i.e., providing reward-based motivation) and encourages them to become agents of change for others. In addition to success stories, some human coaches also provide examples of coachees who did not adhere to coaching recommendations. These coaches believe that fear-based motivation can also positively influence coachees' behavior (e.g., linking unhealthy food choices with developing diabetes). Regardless of the strategy, leveling provides diverse interaction styles that a digital health coach can adopt with coachees.

Good memory is a coach's ability to recall coachee information and experiences so that they can refer back to this information and demonstrate a deep understanding of coachees. Some studies show that physicians struggle to recall their interactions with patients, and as a result, patients feel unheard, which negatively affects their relationships with physicians [31]. The expert interviewees in this study asserted that recalling coachees' personal information and goals and integrating this information into follow-up conversations are both essential to building a long-term, trusting relationship. To construct a digital health coach with exceptional long-term memory, we recommended that the design team create a robust data model that collects and stores user data and responses during conversations. Designers or product owners should also establish a strong partnership with the data to inform design decisions that facilitate equipping a digital health coach with a good memory.

6   Discussion

Based on expert healthcare providers' coaching strategies and interaction styles, we developed a conceptual framework for digital health coaching that can be used as a guide for building and designing relational digital health coaches in the domain of long-term chronic disease prevention and management. We propose that this framework can be used to craft the right coaching style and strategies used by a digital health coach, which informs the design of a coach in the way it relates to a user, the information it gathers, power dynamics, and the evolution of the digital coach-user relationship over time.

Designing an effective digital health coach is a multi-step process including understanding the problem, defining user needs, creating a user-centered design, prototyping and testing the solution, and refining the design based on user feedback. The work in the present study supported the refining phase of an existing commercial digital health coach called Lark but may be used to inform the design of other digital coaches in the healthcare space.

Past researchers have suggested that humans subconsciously deduce personality traits not only when interacting with other humans but also when interacting with technology such as digital health coaches [26]. Therefore, a misaligned, generic, or undefined digital health coach personality can have a detrimental effect on the user experience. A single interaction with a digital coach can be the determining factor in whether a user chooses to interact with the digital coach again. Researchers have noted that when an autonomous agent's personality is consistent and approachable it signals that users are interacting with a trustworthy conversation partner [26]. A trustworthy conversation partner is especially important in long-term health coaching relationships. The conceptual coaching framework provided in this paper can help designers of digital health coaches ensure that these coaches are equipped with the right key behaviors, interaction styles, character traits, tone, and power dynamics to form effective, long-term coaching relationships with users.

Past research has suggested that one of the main disadvantages of digital health coaching is that successful coaching is about much more than goal achievement; it includes the ability to motivate clients and adapt to their dynamically changing needs [32]. We contend that if a digital health coach is designed with the human elements captured by this study, a digital coach can successfully emulate aspects of the human coach-coachee relationship required to personalize the coaching relationship and adapt to each unique user's needs.

6.1 Limitations

We only assessed the coach-coachee relationship from the coach's perspective and not the coachee's. We did not assess the effectiveness of a digital health coach following the implementation of this conceptual coaching framework. An important next step in this line of work is to validate the five coaching stages identified in this study as well as the key behaviors of coaches, interactions styles, character traits, tone, and power dynamics with users in terms of their experiences and outcomes following coaching.

Although we derived the stages and coaching strategies discovered in this study from an assessment of the human coach-coachee relationship, an AI-powered digital health coach does not act as a replacement for human health coaches and medical providers. Certain coaching stages may be more challenging to translate to a digital coaching intervention since they benefit from the transmission and interpretation of information that is unique to human-human interactions such as behavioral cues and emotional intelligence [33]. Although it is possible to develop a digital health coach that guides coachees through all five stages of coaching, it may be difficult to develop a high-fidelity digital coach that meets all a coachee's needs. There are certain aspects of each coaching stage that are well suited to the strengths of digital coaching such as data collection, tracking and interpretation, sharing resources and information, and providing reminders. Designing and developing technology that leverages these strengths can help create a continuous and personalized coaching experience.

7 Conclusions

This research provides a conceptual framework of the coaching relationship between coaches and coachees in long-term chronic disease prevention and management that establishes a basis for the design and development of relational, AI-powered, digital health coaching. We acknowledge that there is a need to further validate this framework with coachees as well as many opportunities for future research that tests the efficacy of digital health coaches that possess the characteristics proposed in this study. We hope that this conceptual framework provides opportunities for both researchers and design practitioners to develop trustworthy, effective, and humane digital health coaches that can facilitate better chronic disease prevention and management.

Acknowledgments. This work was funded by Lark Technologies. We thank our participants and UX researchers for their valuable contributions.

References

1. Iribarren, S.J., Akande, T.O., Kamp, K.J., Barry, D., Kader, Y.G., Suelzer, E.: Effectiveness of mobile apps to promote health and manage disease: Systematic review and meta-analysis of randomized controlled trials. JMIR Mhealth Uhealth 9(1), e21563 (2021)
2. Hart, L.G., Salsberg, E., Phillips, D.M., Lishner, D.M.: Rural health care providers in the United States. J. Rural Health 18(5), 211–231 (2002). https://doi.org/10.1111/j.1748-0361.2002.tb00932.x
3. Khairat, S., et al.: Advancing health equity and access using telemedicine: A geospatial assessment. J. Am. Med. Inform. Assoc. 26(8–9), 796–805 (2019)
4. Tudor Car, L., et al.: Conversational agents in health care: Scoping review and conceptual analysis. J. Med. Internet Res. 22(8), e17158 (2020). https://doi.org/10.2196/17158
5. WHO and partners launch world's most extensive freely accessible AI health worker (2022). https://www.who.int/news/item/04-10-2022-who-and-partners-launch-world-s-most-extensive-freely-accessible-ai-health-worker. Accessed 20 Oct 2022
6. El Kamali, M., et al.: Virtual coaches for older adults' wellbeing: A systematic review. IEEE Access. 21(8), 101884–101902 (2020)
7. Hussain, S., Ameri Sianaki, O., Ababneh, N.: A survey on conversational agents/chatbots classification and design techniques. In: Barolli, L., Takizawa, M., Xhafa, F., Enokido, T. (eds.) WAINA 2019. AISC, vol. 927, pp. 946–956. Springer, Cham (2019). https://doi.org/10.1007/978-3-030-15035-8_93
8. Bickmore, T., Trinh, H., Asadi, R., Olafsson, S.: Safety first: Conversational agents for health care. In: Studies in Conversational UX Design, pp. 33–57 (2018)
9. Chew, H.S.: The use of artificial intelligence–based conversational agents (chatbots) for weight loss: Scoping review and practical recommendations. JMIR Med. Inform. 10(4), e32578 (2022)
10. Paul, S.C., Bartmann, N., Clark, J.L.: Customizability in conversational agents and their impact on health engagement. Hum. Behav. Emerg. Technol. 3(5), 1141–1152 (2021)
11. Perlman, A.I., Abu Dabrh, A.M.: Health and wellness coaching in serving the needs of today's patients: a primer for healthcare professionals. Glob. Adv. Health Med. 9, 2164956120959274 (2020)
12. Singh, H.K., Kennedy, G.A., Stupans, I.: Competencies and training of health professionals engaged in health coaching: A systematic review. Chronic. Illn. 18(1), 58–85 (2022)

13. Nadarzynski, T., Miles, O., Cowie, A., Ridge, D.: Acceptability of artificial intelligence (AI)-led chatbot services in healthcare: A mixed-methods study. Digit. Health. **5**, 2055207619871808 (2019)
14. Lattie, E.G., Graham, A.K., Hadjistavropoulos, H.D., Dear, B.F., Titov, N., Mohr, D.C.: Guidance on defining the scope and development of text-based coaching protocols for digital mental health interventions. Digit. Health **5**, 2055207619896145 (2019)
15. Thom, D.H., et al.: A qualitative study of how health coaches support patients in making health-related decisions and behavioral changes. Ann. Family Med. **14**(6), 509–516 (2016)
16. Gupta, I., et al.: Human-human health coaching via text messages: Corpus, annotation, and analysis. In: Proceedings of the 21th Annual Meeting of the Special Interest Group on Discourse and Dialogue 2020, pp. 246–256 (2020)
17. Denneson, L.M., Ono, S.S., Trevino, A.Y., Kenyon, E., Dobscha, S.K.: The applicability of self-determination theory to health coaching: a qualitative analysis of patient experiences. Coaching: Int. J. Theory Res. Pract. **13**(2), 163–75 (2020)
18. Beinema, T., Op den Akker, H., Hermens, H.J., van Velsen, L.: What to discuss?—A blueprint topic model for health coaching dialogues with conversational agents. Int. J. Hum. Comput. Interact. **39**(1), 164–182 (2023)
19. Gross, C., et al.: Personalization of conversational agent-patient interaction styles for chronic disease management: Two consecutive cross-sectional questionnaire studies. J. Med. Internet Res. **23**(5), e26643 (2021)
20. Mitchell, E.G., et al.: Automated vs. human health coaching: Exploring participant and practitioner experiences. Proc. ACM Hum.-Comput. Interact. **5**(CSCW1), 1–37 (2021)
21. Nißen, M., et al.: The effects of health care chatbot personas with different social roles on the client-chatbot bond and usage intentions: Development of a design codebook and web-based study. J. Med. Internet Res. **24**(4), e32630 (2022)
22. Zhang, J., Oh, Y.J., Lange, P., Yu, Z., Fukuoka, Y.: Artificial intelligence chatbot behavior change model for designing artificial intelligence chatbots to promote physical activity and a healthy diet: Viewpoint. J. Med. Internet Res. **22**(9), e22845 (2020). https://doi.org/10.2196/22845
23. Kocaballi, A.B., et al.: The personalization of conversational agents in health care: Systematic review. J. Med. Internet Res. **21**(11), e15360 (2019). https://doi.org/10.2196/15360
24. Graham, S.A., Pitter, V., Hori, J.H., Stein, N., Branch, O.H.: Weight loss in a digital app-based diabetes prevention program powered by artificial intelligence. Digit. Health. **8** (2022). https://doi.org/10.1177/20552076221130619
25. Thornton, A.: User testing: How to use an affinity diagram to organize UX research. https://www.usertesting.com/blog/affinity-mapping#:~:text=What%20is%20an%20affinity%20diagram,analyzing%20qualitative%20data%20or%20observations. Accessed 25 Jan 2023
26. Deibel, D., Evanhoe, R., Vellos, K.: Conversations with Things: UX Design for Chat and Voice, pp. 40–68. Rosenfeld Media (2021)
27. Vaismoradi, M., Turunen, H., Bondas, T.: Content analysis and thematic analysis: Implications for conducting a qualitative descriptive study. Nurs. Health Sci. **15**(3), 398–405 (2013)
28. Jona, C.M.H., Sheen, J.A., Anderson, K., O'Shea, M.: Self-disclosure in a self-practice/self-reflection CBT group in professional psychology training. Train. Educ. Profess. Psychol. (2022)
29. Darcy, A., et al.: Anatomy of a Woebot®(WB001): agent guided CBT for women with postpartum depression. Exp. Rev. Med. Devices **19**(4), 287–301 (2022)
30. Lee, Y.C., Yamashita, N., Huang, Y., Fu, W.: "I Hear You, I Feel You": Encouraging deep self-disclosure through a chatbot. In: Proceedings of the 2020 CHI Conference on Human Factors in Computing Systems, pp. 1–12 (2020)

31. Taber, J.M., Leyva, B., Persoskie, A.: Why do people avoid medical care? A qualitative study using national data. J. Gen. Intern. Med. **30**, 290–297 (2015)

32. Rutjes, H., Willemsen, M.C., IJsselsteijn, W.A.: Beyond behavior: The coach's perspective on technology in health coaching. In: Proceedings of the 2019 CHI Conference on Human Factors in Computing Systems, pp. 1–14 (2019)

33. Denecke, K., Abd-Alrazaq, A., Househ, M.: Artificial intelligence for chatbots in mental health: Opportunities and challenges. In: Househ, M., Borycki, E., Kushniruk, A. (eds.) Multiple perspectives on artificial intelligence in healthcare. LNB, pp. 115–128. Springer, Cham (2021). https://doi.org/10.1007/978-3-030-67303-1_10

A Hybrid Multi-criteria Framework for Evaluating the Performance of Clinical Labs During the Covid-19 Pandemic

Miguel Ortiz-Barrios[1]([✉]) [iD], Andrea Espeleta-Aris[1] [iD], Genett Jiménez-Delgado[2] [iD],
Helder Jose Celani-De Souza[3] [iD], Jonas Santana-de Oliveira[4] [iD],
Alexandros Konios[5] [iD], Leonardo Campis-Freyle[6], and Eduardo Navarro-Jimenez[7] [iD]

[1] Department of Productivity and Innovation, Universidad de la Costa CUC,
080002 Barranquilla, Colombia
{mortiz1,aesplet}@cuc.edu.co
[2] Department of Industrial Engineering, Institución Universitaria de Barranquilla IUB,
080002 Barranquilla, Colombia
gjimenez@itsa.edu.co
[3] UNESP - Sao Paulo State University, Sao Paulo 12242250, Brazil
hjcelani@lidproj.com.br
[4] Sabin Medicina Diagnostica, Brasilia 70715-900, Brazil
jonas@sabin.com.br
[5] Department of Computer Science, Nottingham Trent University, Nottigham 4081112, UK
Alexandros.konios@ntu.ac.uk
[6] Department of Research and Innovation, Soltraf Ingeniería S.A.S., 080001 Barranquilla,
Colombia
[7] Department of Health Sciences, Universidad Simon Bolivar, 080001 Barranquilla, Colombia
eduardo.navarro@unisimon.edu.co

Abstract. Clinical laboratories were affected by the recent Covid-19 pandemic, evidencing the low preparedness of some clinical labs when responding to seasonal diseases, epidemics/pandemics, and other disastrous events. However, various operational shortcomings become glaring in the labs also propelled by the virus's ever-changing dynamics and rapid evolution. Therefore, this paper presents a novel hybrid intuitionistic Multi-criteria Decision-Making (MCDM) approach to evaluate the performance of clinical labs during the Covid-19 pandemic. First, we used Intuitionistic Fuzzy Analytic Hierarchy Process (IF-AHP) to estimate the relative weights of criteria and sub-criteria considering hesitancy and uncertainty properties. Second, we employed Intuitionistic Fuzzy Decision Making Trial and Evaluation Laboratory (IF-DEMATEL) to evaluate the interrelationships among performance criteria as often found in the healthcare context. Ultimately, the Combined Compromise Solution (CoCoSo) technique was applied to estimate the Performance Index (PI) of each clinical laboratory and pinpoint the main weaknesses hindering the effective response in presence of the Covid-19 and other disastrous events. This approach was validated in 9 clinical labs located in a Colombian region. The results evidenced that Operating capacity (global weight = 0.1985) and Occupational health and safety (global weight = 0.1924) are the most important aspects for increasing the overall response of the labs against new Covid-19 waves and future outbreaks. Besides, operating capacity (D + R = 37.486)

V. G. Duffy (Ed.): HCII 2023, LNCS 14029, pp. 104–122, 2023.
https://doi.org/10.1007/978-3-031-35748-0_8

and Equipment (D + R = 38.024) were concluded to be the main performance drivers. Also some clinical labs uncovered major shortcomings that may restrict their functioning in a future contingency.

Keywords: Multi-criteria Decision-Making (MCDM) · Intuitionistic Fuzzy Analytic Hierarchy Process (IF-AHP) · Intuitionistic Fuzzy Decision Making Trial and Evaluation Laboratory (IF-DEMATEL) · Combined Compromise Solution (CoCoSo) · Performance evaluation · Healthcare · Clinical Laboratories · Disaster management · Covid-19

1 Introduction

Despite the evolution of Clinical Labs, the Covid-19 pandemic has impacted a lot in the current automated scenario. Firstly, due to the sudden demand for tests 'volume increase, and secondly, the urgent need for specific workflow and procedures for quality compliance and accurate positive Covid-19 results. In the meantime, the occupational health and safety procedures for lab employees and patients have been modified to effectively address this outbreak.

During this turbulence, clinical laboratories all over the world have faced numerous challenges to offering agility in patient screening, improvements in the pre-analytical routines, and analytical and post-analytical workflow redesigns. Part of the test methods can be treated by automated tracks; others depend on stand-alone analyzers; and others are completely manual or semi-automatic. The managerial experience has been suggesting five public policy areas to be focused on: stopping the infection spread, budget management, ensuring service provision, and recovery to the level that is considered the new normal. As far as laboratories are concerned, the COVID-19 pandemic has clearly shown the goals of the four major stakeholders [1] (Table 1).

Table 1. Stakeholders' goals regarding clinical lab services

Stakeholder	Goal
Patient	Receive timely quality service
Laboratory Staff	Have all the necessary conditions for safe and quality work involving less stress and a higher level of motivation
Laboratory Management	Operate according to predefined procedures, without the need for ad hoc decisions, and be under less pressure while achieving better outcomes for their institutions
Distributors	Purchase equipment and consumables on time and distribute them to their customers without any difficulties

Depending on the clinical laboratory size, the impacts have been changing in intensity and unfortunately have forced small labs to shut down and others to review the strategy very fast.

In terms of Covid-19 diagnosis methods, Real-time PCR, Isothermal amplification, and serological testing have been more commonly used by clinical labs for Covid-19 diagnosis [2]. Serological testing for antibodies against SARS-CoV-2 is considered a complementary diagnosis in conjunction with the identification of convalescent plasma and epidemiologic studies. Some additional biochemical tests, including monitoring the change in blood cells, blood gas, coagulation, liver function, cardiac markers, and inflammatory responses such as cytokine levels in plasma, are also relevant to enhance the clinical laboratories' efforts [3]. This is another relevant influence factor that the fight against the pandemic will be able to reveal the strengths and weaknesses of laboratories.

Clinical Laboratories should establish standard operating procedures for risk management, in keeping with the policies for operating in extraordinary situations. This would also ensure that the supply chain is not threatened [1]. Despite many recommendations proposed in the literature to reach the state of the art in Clinical Laboratory management, one point is missing or rare to find and become the main objective of this paper: to present a novel hybrid intuitionistic Multi-criteria Decision-Making (MCDM) approach to evaluate the performance of clinical labs during the Covid-19 pandemic. Multi-Criteria Decision Making (MCDM) or Multi-Criteria Decision Analysis (MCDA), is one of the most accurate methods of decision-making, and it can be known as a revolution in this field [4, 5]. The Intuitionistic Fuzzy Analytic Hierarchy Process (IF-AHP) was primarily used to estimate the relative weights of criteria and sub-criteria considering hesitancy and uncertainty properties. IF-AHP resulted in the groundwork for designing short-term improvement plans in the clinical lab sub-sector. Just after, we employed Intuitionistic Fuzzy Decision-Making Trial and Evaluation (IF-DEMATEL) to identify the main performance drivers of clinical labs. Thereby, decision-makers linked to the Ministries of Health and local governments can establish long-term interventions focused on the most influencing decision elements. Ultimately, the Combined Compromise Solution (CoCoSo) technique was applied to estimate the Performance Index (PI) of each clinical laboratory and pinpoint the main weaknesses hindering the effective response of these institutions in presence of the Covid-19 and other disastrous events. This technique is robust and well-structured to have a practical problem-solving process in place and get the most accurate response for decision-making contemplating project environment, conflicts, problem-solving methods, and stakeholders' behavior [6].

The clinical laboratory operational capacity has been severely impacted by the fast test volume ramp-up. On the other hand, the waiting rooms preceding the outpatient specimen collection stations were overcrowded, increasing the probability of lab-acquired infections. On a different tack, stock-outs were reported in several sensitive materials required for specimen processing which also contributed to inefficiencies in the overall response of these institutions during this outbreak. All these difficulties were considered barriers restricting the effective clinical and diagnostic processes in hospital wards. These considerations evidence the low preparedness of some clinical labs when responding to seasonal diseases, epidemics/pandemics, and other disastrous events. It is then pivotal to measure the overall performance of these units against the Covid-19 outbreak and detect existing gaps restricting their response in presence of future outbreaks. Various operational shortcomings become glaring in the labs also propelled by the virus's ever-changing dynamics and rapid evolution [7].

In Equator, for instance, the national average time for case completion was 3 days; 12.1% of samples took $\geq$ 10 days to complete; the national average daily backlog was 29.1 tests per 100,000 people. Only 8 out of 24 provinces had authorized COVID-19 processing laboratories but not all processed samples and the percentage of pending results on April 30 was 67.1% [8]. In the UK, over 12 months of operation, the Defence Clinical Lab (DCL) was open for 289 days and tested over 72 000 samples. Six hundred military SARS-CoV-2-positive results were reported with a median E-gene quantitation cycle (Cq) value of 30.44. The lowest Cq value for a positive result observed was 11.20. Only 64 samples (0.09%) were voided due to assay inhibition after processing started [9]. In summary, everywhere we can observe challenges and enormous efforts to overpass the pandemic's impacts.

Occupational health and biosafety are other big issues to be addressed during and after the Covid-19 pandemic. SARS-CoV-2 has overwhelmed the public health system globally, challenged scientific knowledge, and upended our daily lives, requiring the effort and coordination of multiple government agencies, the medical and healthcare communities, and cross-functional scientific disciplines to develop testing platforms to better assist public health and clinical laboratories. Furthermore, this pandemic has presented several challenges specific to public health and clinical laboratories, including sustained high demands for specimen collection, testing, and rapid diagnostic turnaround times; shortages in testing reagents, personal protective equipment, and other resources; and extended work shifts. To make matters worse, some clinical laboratories have also seen a decline in their normal testing activity and have had to contend with lost revenue and financial challenges as well. It is often challenging to determine the appropriate safety measures to implement in a laboratory when working with a new infectious agent such as SARS-CoV-2. Considering the diversity of clinical laboratories management systems and strategies, they must determine the number of people that a laboratory can safely accommodate while maintaining social distancing, assessing cleaning procedures, and reviewing emergency operational plans, especially those focused on how to protect staff at higher risk for severe illness from COVID-19. It is strongly recommended for all clinical labs address this gap by implementing a consistent approach to training on risk assessments and appropriately managing risks to keep laboratories and their staff safe [10].

This paper is structured as follows. Section 2 presents the related work while Sect. 3 outlines the proposed methodology. Section 4 covers the results and discussion whereas Sect. 5 shows the conclusions and future work.

2 Literature Review

2.1 Introduction

The COVID-19 pandemic has posed unprecedented challenges for healthcare systems worldwide, overwhelming healthcare infrastructure, and leading to massive disruptions in healthcare services. The role of clinical laboratories in the COVID-19 pandemic has been vital in identifying, diagnosing, and managing infected patients. From the initial stages of the outbreak, clinical laboratories have been at the forefront of developing and implementing various diagnostic tools to identify the virus, determine its spread, and inform public health policies [11]. Clinical laboratories have also been instrumental in conducting clinical trials and research on potential treatments and vaccines for COVID-19 as they provided crucial data on the efficacy and safety of various treatments [12]. Consequently, clinical labs have been faced with significant burdens as they played a crucial role in combating the disease.

2.2   Challenges Faced by Clinical Labs During the Pandemic

One of the major challenges faced by healthcare systems was the shortage of medical supplies, including Personal Protective Equipment (PPE), ventilators, and testing kits. The scarcity of these critical resources led to delays in testing and treatment and increased the risk of infection for healthcare workers [13]. Additionally, healthcare systems faced challenges with resource allocation, particularly in areas where there was a surge in demand for healthcare services. Hospitals and clinics faced difficulties managing the influx of patients, leading to overcrowding, inadequate staffing, and long wait times [14].

Apart from hospitals and clinics, clinical labs were also significantly impacted during the pandemic. As a result of the increasing demand for COVID-19 testing, labs faced challenges with testing capacity, supply chain disruptions, and staff shortages [15]. In many countries, labs had to rapidly scale up their testing capacity to meet the demand, leading to delays in turnaround times and potential errors in testing [16]. There were also issues with the quality and reliability of testing kits, with reports of false positives and false negatives [17]. Furthermore, clinical labs were faced with a lack of standardization in testing protocols, which led to inconsistencies in testing results and difficulties in comparing data across different labs [18]. Therefore, labs had to adapt to new testing technologies and protocols leading to the necessity for retraining and certifying their staff [19].

Another major challenge faced by clinical labs during the pandemic has been turnaround times for PCR requests, which can have a significant impact on patient outcomes and public health.

In [20], the preparedness of clinical laboratories was investigated with respect to the increased demand for COVID-19 testing and it was found that while many labs had implemented measures to increase testing capacity, the time taken to process PCR requests was still a major challenge. This work emphasized the need for better coordination and communication between healthcare providers and clinical labs to ensure timely and accurate test results.

Overcrowding of waiting rooms at outpatient specimen collection stations was another issue that was noticed throughout the COVID-19 outbreak. This not only increased the risk of transmission of COVID-19 but also raised concerns about lab-acquired infections among healthcare workers. Ramaiah et al., in [21], noticed that some specimen collection centres had implemented measures such as online appointments and drive-through testing to reduce overcrowding and minimize the risk of transmission.

The shortage of supplies and reagents required for specimen processing was also a major challenge faced by clinical labs during the outbreak. Several studies have high-lighted the need for improved supply chain management and stockpiling of essential materials to ensure uninterrupted testing. For instance, Lin et al. revealed that shortages of swabs and transport media had a significant impact on the testing capacity of clinical labs [22].

It is worth noting that additionally to the aforementioned issues, several other factors have also impacted the response, efficiency, and performance of clinical labs and hospitals. These include the availability of trained staff, the use of different testing platforms with varying sensitivity and specificity, and the need for accurate and timely reporting of results to public health authorities.

2.3 Evaluating Preparedness and Performance of Clinical Labs Using Multi-criteria Decision-Making (MCDM) Techniques

There is limited literature on evaluating the performance and efficiency of clinical labs during epidemics/pandemics and other disastrous events. However, the existing studies have shown that some clinical labs are not well prepared to respond to seasonal diseases, epidemics/pandemics, and other disastrous events. With the ongoing Covid-19 outbreak, it is essential to measure the overall performance of clinical labs and identify gaps that may limit their response to future outbreaks.

Since clinical labs play an essential role in healthcare by providing diagnostic and monitoring services, their performance and efficiency can have a significant impact on patient care and outcomes. Therefore, decision-making approaches and techniques are used to evaluate their performance and efficiency. In the following paragraphs, some of the decision-making approaches and techniques used to evaluate the performance and efficiency of clinical labs are presented, with a particular focus on Multi-criteria decision-making (MCDM) techniques.

Singh et al. used a decision-making approach to evaluate the performance of clinical labs in India during the Covid-19 outbreak [23]. This study used the Analytic Hierarchy Process (AHP) to prioritize the criteria for evaluating the performance of the labs. The criteria included testing capacity, turnaround time, and quality of testing. The findings of their work highlight that the overall performance of the labs was satisfactory, but there were significant variations in testing capacity, turnaround time, and quality of testing among different labs [23].

Another decision-making approach was used in [24] to evaluate the efficiency of clinical labs in Pakistan during the Covid-19 outbreak. The study used the Data Envelopment Analysis (DEA) method to measure the efficiency of the labs. The study found that most labs were efficient, but there were some labs with low-efficiency scores, indicating the need for improvement.

One of the commonly used techniques for evaluating clinical lab performance is benchmarking, which involves comparing a lab's performance against established standards or best practices. For example, the College of American Pathologists (CAP) has established accreditation standards and checklists for clinical labs that cover a range of areas, including quality control, laboratory management, and patient safety. These standards provide a framework for evaluating the performance and efficiency of clinical labs [25].

Another technique used to evaluate the performance of clinical labs is Key Performance Indicators (KPIs). In [26], the authors discuss the importance of laboratory performance indicators to evaluate and improve the quality of laboratory testing. They also define Key Performance Indicators (KPIs) as measurable values that indicate how well a laboratory is performing in specific areas, and they provide examples of KPIs commonly used to evaluate the performance of clinical labs, such as turnaround time, error rates, and test volume. The authors suggest that KPIs can provide a quantitative measure of a lab's performance and can be used to identify areas for improvement.

In [27], it is presented a study in which multi-criteria decision-making (MCDM) techniques were used to evaluate the performance of medical laboratory centres in Iran. The authors explain that MCDM techniques involve evaluating multiple criteria or factors simultaneously and making a decision based on a combination of these factors. They note that MCDM techniques can provide a more comprehensive evaluation of clinical lab performance, considering multiple factors that may influence performance. The authors also describe the criteria used in their study to evaluate lab performance, which included factors such as test quality, equipment maintenance, and customer satisfaction. Their work managed to identify areas for improvement in the laboratory centres evaluated.

Another MCDM technique that has been applied to the evaluation of clinical lab performance is the Analytic Hierarchy Process (AHP). The authors, in [28], describe the criteria and sub-criteria used in their study to evaluate lab performance, which included factors such as quality of service, customer satisfaction, and reliability of test results. The findings of their work focused on identifying the strengths and weaknesses of the laboratories evaluated and suggesting improvements. Similarly, Liao et al., in [29], applied the Analytic Hierarchy Process (AHP) method to evaluate the performance of clinical laboratories in Taiwan during the Covid-19 pandemic. The authors identified the main weaknesses of the laboratories as being related to issues such as testing capacity, equipment availability, and turnaround time. This study demonstrated the potential of MCDM methods in evaluating laboratory performance and informing decision-making in the context of the Covid-19 pandemic.

In [30], the authors introduce an approach in which the Technique for Order of Preference by Similarity to Ideal Solution (TOPSIS) was used to evaluate the performance of clinical laboratories in Turkey. Initially, the authors explain that TOPSIS is a method for ranking alternatives based on their similarity to an ideal solution and their distance to the worst solution. In the context of clinical lab evaluation, the ideal solution may be a lab that performs perfectly in all criteria, while the worst solution may be a lab that performs poorly in all criteria. The authors also define the criteria used in their study to evaluate lab performance, which included factors such as turnaround time, quality of service, and cost-effectiveness. The results of the study were used to rank the performance of the clinical labs examined and to propose solutions that would help with the improvement of their performance. Another research work also applied the Technique for Order of Preference by Similarity to Ideal Solution (TOPSIS) method to evaluate the performance of clinical laboratories in Iran during the Covid-19 pandemic [31]. The authors found that the main weaknesses of the laboratories were related to issues such as turnaround time, quality control, and communication with healthcare providers.

Moreover, the Grey Relational Analysis (GRA) method is utilised in [32] to evaluate the performance of clinical laboratories in Pakistan during the Covid-19 pandemic. This work identified the main weaknesses of the laboratories as being related to issues such as testing capacity, quality control, and supply chain management. It is worth mentioning that this study demonstrated the applicability of MCDM methods to different contexts and the potential to improve laboratory performance in similar scenarios.

The Combined Compromise Solution (CoCoSo) technique is another Multi-Criteria Decision-Making method that aims to achieve the best compromise solution by balancing the different criteria involved in the decision-making process. This technique has been applied in various fields, including healthcare, to evaluate the performance of clinical laboratories and identify areas for improvement.

In the context of the COVID-19 pandemic, the CoCoSo technique has been used to assess the preparedness and response of clinical laboratories to the pandemic. A study by Delen et al. applied the CoCoSo technique to evaluate the performance of clinical laboratories in Turkey during the COVID-19 pandemic [33]. The authors identified the main weaknesses of the laboratories, including limited testing capacity, inadequate supply chain management, and lack of standardization in testing protocols.

Similarly, the application of the CoCoSo technique is used in [34] to evaluate the performance of clinical laboratories in China. This study identified the main weaknesses of the laboratories, such as a lack of communication and coordination among different institutions, limited access to testing resources, and inadequate training of staff. Other studies have also used the CoCoSo technique to evaluate the performance of clinical laboratories in other contexts.

All these considerations evidence the low preparedness of some clinical labs when responding to seasonal diseases, epidemics/pandemics, and other disastrous events. It is then pivotal to measure the overall performance of these units against the Covid-19 outbreak and detect existing gaps restricting their response in presence of future outbreaks. Therefore, this paper presents a novel hybrid intuitionistic Multi-criteria Decision-Making (MCDM) approach to evaluate the performance of clinical labs during the Covid-19 pandemic. First, we used Intuitionistic Fuzzy Analytic Hierarchy Process (IF-AHP) to estimate the relative weights of criteria and sub-criteria considering hesitancy and uncertainty properties. IF-AHP results serve as a groundwork for designing short-term improvement plans in the clinical lab sub-sector. Second, we employed Intuitionistic Fuzzy Decision-Making Trial and Evaluation Laboratory (IF-DEMATEL) to evaluate the interrelationships among performance criteria as often found in the healthcare context. Thereby, decision-makers linked to the Ministries of Health and local governments can establish long-term interventions focused on the most influencing decision elements. Ultimately, the Combined Compromise Solution (CoCoSo) technique was applied to estimate the Performance Index (PI) of each clinical laboratory and pinpoint the main weaknesses hindering the effective response of these institutions in presence of the Covid-19 and other disastrous events. This approach was validated in 9 clinical labs located in a Colombian region. A hybrid intuitionistic MCDM model containing 7 criteria and 24 sub-criteria was derived based on the pertinent scientific literature, the expert's opinion, and the applicable healthcare regulations. To the best of our knowledge, this is one the first studies in the literature demonstrating the use of hybrid intuitionistic fuzzy MCDM methods in the performance improvement of clinical labs during the Covid-19 period and its extension to similar scenarios.

3   Proposed Methodology

The novel hybrid intuitionistic Multi-criteria Decision-Making (MCDM) approach is proposed to evaluate the performance of clinical labs during the Covid-19 pandemic with three main objectives: 1) diagnose the general performance of clinical laboratories during the Covid-19 pandemic 19, 2) identify the main weaknesses that affect the effective response of these institutions to pandemic events and, 3) establish intervention plans focused on improving the performance of clinical laboratories to quickly adapt to complex and dynamic situations such as epidemics, pandemics, natural or public calamities, among others. The proposed model integrates the IF-AHP, IF-DEMATEL, and CoCoSo techniques and is composed of five phases (refer to Fig. 1). A brief explanation of the methodology is provided below.

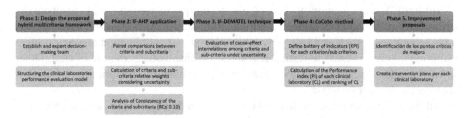

Fig. 1. Methodological framework for evaluating the Performance of Clinical Labs during the Covid-19 Pandemic

- **Phase 1. Design the proposed hybrid multicriteria framework:** A decision-making team is selected based on their experience in clinical laboratory management. The experts were invited to be part of the decision-making process to provide information on which criteria may influence the performance in clinical laboratories during the pandemic of Covid-19 and in applying the IF-AHP and IF-DEMATEL methods. Then, the performance evaluation model was structured by defining criteria and sub-criteria to establish a decision hierarchy considering the expertise of the decision-makers, the literature review, and good practices in clinical laboratory management. Subsequently, the surveys of the IF-FAHP and IF-DEMATEL methods were designed and applied.
- **Phase 2. IF-FAHP application:** In this phase, the IF-AHP method was applied to determine the relative weights of the criteria and subcriteria under conditions of vagueness and uncertainty in paired comparisons of the experts. With the results obtained from IF-AHP, the most relevant factors and subfactors were identified in the performance evaluation of clinical laboratories that will support the proposals for improvement in these institutions in the face of volatile and complex events such as pandemics. The mathematical formulation of the IF-AHP method is developed by Attanassov [35], Xu [36], and Ar et al. [37], among others.
- **Phase 3. IF-DEMATEL technique:** Subsequently, IF-DEMATEL is used to determine the significant interdependence between criteria and sub-criteria, considering the expected uncertainty of experts when evaluating the influence of the model factors [38, 39]. IF-DEMATEL identifies cause (dispatchers) and effect (receivers) factors.

Additionally, IF-DEMATEL provides information to decision-makers on the strength of the interrelationships for the medium and long-term design of interventions.

– **Phase 4. CoCoSo method**: In this stage, CoCoSo is applied to calculate the Performance Index (PI) of each clinical laboratory, taking into account some evaluation indicators aligned with the criteria of the model. Subsequently, the participating clinical laboratories were classified from the highest to the mentor IP value to distinguish those institutions with high performance and the clinical laboratories with lower performance that merit interventions for improvement. The mathematical model is developed by Yazdani et al. [40] and Stević et al. [41].

– **Phase 5. Improvement proposals:** In this last phase, based on the performance indicators (PI) and the ranking of clinical laboratories, the sub-criteria that most influence a poor response by these institutions to the Covid-19 pandemic were identified. Finally, intervention plans focused on improving the performance of clinical laboratories were established to respond promptly to new pandemics and catastrophes.

4 Results and Discussion

An intuitionistic hybrid model of MCDM containing 7 criteria and 24 sub-criteria was derived based on relevant scientific literature, expert opinion, and applicable health regulations. According to Table 2 and Fig. 2, *Operational capacity* (GW = 0.1985) and *Occupational Health and Safety* (GW = 0.1924) are the most important criteria when designing short-term improvement plans upgrading the overall performance of clinical labs during a pandemic event. On the one hand, insufficient operational capacity may result in delayed diagnosis and treatment which derives in more severe complications and increased mortality rates within emergency, hospitalization, and intensive care departments [42]. On a different tack, hospital-acquired infections in technical staff may downgrade the response of clinical labs against testing requirements during peak periods. Not less important is the low difference between the first-ranked (Operational Capacity) and the fourth-listed (Equipment) criteria in terms of relative importance (0.0508). Likewise, it is necessary to identify the most important sub-criteria. In this case, adherence to the PPE (GW = 0.1175) and delivery time for PCR results (GW = 0.0489) were found to be the most contributing to the clinical lab performance during the pandemic. To face this, remote-sensing technologies can be used to monitor whether the medical staff is wearing PPE at a particular time and location. For the latter, Grau et al. [43] establish that the LDH/leukocyte ratio could help prioritize rRT-PCR associated with infected patients. In the meantime, the queuing theory [44] and other analytical support methods [45] may be explored to estimate the necessary amount of doctors and nurses required to optimize the response against the increased demand. Thereby, it is possible to accelerate patient flow within the healthcare settings and consequently diminish overcrowding. It is also good to highlight that all matrixes in IFAHP were found to be consistent (Consistency ratio <10%) which reinforces the conclusions depicted above [46, 47].

On a different note, the interrelations among criteria/sub-criteria were mapped through the IF-DEMATEL approach (Table 3) [48]. Table 3 specifies the dispatchers and receivers. In this case, *Operating capacity (M2)* and *Equipment (M4)* were concluded to be dispatchers and can be therefore considered as the main intervention points within long-term plans upgrading the overall performance of clinical labs. Figure 3a,

Table 2. Global and local weights of decision elements – IFAHP method

CRITERION/SUBCRITERION	GW	LW
OCCUPATIONAL HEALTH AND SAFETY (M1)	0.1924	
Adherence to PPE (SM1)	0.1175	0.6107
Percentage of personnel infected by COVID-19(SM2)	0.0749	0.3892
OPERATING CAPACITY (M2)	0.1985	
PCR results delivery time (SM3)	0.0489	0.2463
Turnaround time for antigen results (SM4)	0.0458	0.2307
Average waiting time for sample collection (SM5)	0.0360	0.1814
Number of samples processed per day (SM6)	0.0323	0.1627
Maximum number of samples to be processed per day (SM7)	0.0353	0.1778
QUALITY (M3)	0.1726	
Diagnostic errors (SM8)	0.0430	0.2491
Customer satisfaction level (SM9)	0.0394	0.2283
Sample identification errors (SM10)	0.0319	0.1848
High quality accreditation (SM11)	0.0271	0.1570
Quality control on positive samples (SM12)	0.0188	0.1089
Quality control of negative samples (SM13)	0.0121	0.0701
EQUIPMENT (M4)	0.1477	
Availability of DX equipment (SM14)	0.0517	0.3500
Relevance of DX equipment (SM15)	0.0362	0.2451
DX equipment status (SM16)	0.0343	0.2322
Automation in the sample extraction process (SM17)	0.0254	0.1720
HUMAN RESOURCES (M5)	0.1075	
Availability of molecular biologists (SM18)	0.0686	0.6381
Staff experience in molecular biology (SM19)	0.0388	0.3609
PROTOCOLS AND PROCEDURES (M6)	0.0988	
Presence of protocols for sample handling COVID-19 (SM20)	0.0626	0.6336
Adherence to sample handling protocols COVID-19 (SM21)	0.0361	0.3654
MATERIALS (M7)	0.0820	
Availability of reagents for COVID-19 test processing (PCR) (SM22)	0.0311	0.3793
Availability of reagents for COVID-19 test processing (antigen)(SM23)	0.0300	0.3659
Pipette availability (SM24)	0.0209	0.2549

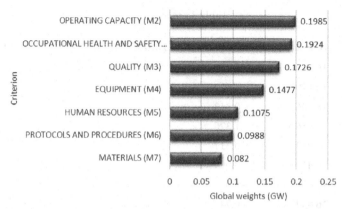

Fig. 2. Rank of criteria contributing to the performance of clinical labs during the Covid-19 pandemic

b outline the impact-digraph maps. The blue arrows indicate one-directional influences while the pink ones denote bi-directional interrelations. For instance, from Fig. 3b, it is evident that SM2 (Percentage of personnel infected by COVID-19) significantly influences sub-criterion SM1 (Adherence to PPE). Accordingly, improvements in the operational capacity through simulation models are highly advised to detect bottlenecks restricting the operational response of clinical labs [49, 50]. In fact, Grau et al. [43] state that the combined use of powerful analytical parameters could facilitate the medical management of patients, optimizing the human and material resources of clinical labs in presence of shortages derived from supply chain disruptions. In a similar vein, Muñoz et al. [51] argue that the implementation of digitalization practices and automation in clinical lab processes have a significant impact in reducing response times which may be useful to ramp up the disaster preparedness of the entire healthcare system.

Table 3. D + R and D-R values for decision criteria

	D + R	D − R	DISPATCHER	RECEIVER
M1	36.834	−0.022		*
SM1	75.55	−1.00		*
SM2	75.55	1.00	*	
M2	37.486	0.988	*	
SM3	13.197	−0.695		*
SM4	14.906	-0.922		*
SM5	14.325	0.768	*	
SM6	14.230	0.792	*	
M3	39.284	−0.306		*
SM8	17.016	0.493	*	
SM9	18.605	0.775	*	

(continued)

Table 3. (*continued*)

	D + R	D − R	DISPATCHER	RECEIVER
SM10	16.832	1.292	*	
SM11	18.170	−1.027		*
SM12	18.146	−0.213		*
SM13	17.656	−1.320		*
M4	38.024	0.317	*	
SM14	17.415	0.939	*	
SM15	17.006	−0.026		*
SM16	16.442	−0.747		*
SM17	16.552	−0.165		*
M5	38.091	−0.571		*
SM18	91.8	1	*	
SM19	91.8	−1		*
M6	39.698	−0.156		*
SM20	91.8000	1.0000	*	
SM21	91.8000	−1.0000		*
M7	37.417	−0.250		*
SM22	14.2964	0.7486	*	
SM23	14.0311	1.1177	*	
SM24	13.3747	−1.8663		*

CoCoSo allows us to establish a performance index revealing how well the clinical labs can respond to a pandemic event. Table 4 indicates the initial matrix containing the metrics values per each participant lab (n = 9) and decision element. Table 5 ranks the clinical labs considering the performance index Mi. According to the results, the laboratories with the worst functioning are L3 (Mi = 1.3269) and L4 (Mi = 1.5836) evidencing the need for immediate intervention to improve their processes. On a different note, it is observed that L2 and L6 (Mi = 2.3217 and Mi = 2.2401) are the most prepared when occurring these events. In consequence, the proposed model is therefore demonstrated to be an effective, efficient, and reliable alternative for creating focused solutions in the short and long term.

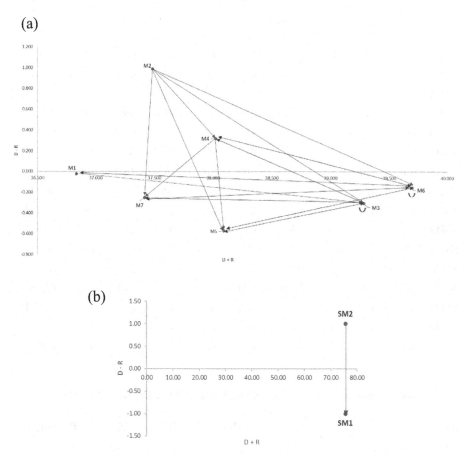

Fig. 3. Impact digraph maps for a) criteria and b) Occupational health and safety sub-criteria

Table 4. Initial CoCoSo decision matrix

	L1	L2	L3	L4	L5	L6	L7	L8	L9	GW
SM1	100%	100%	80%	100%	100%	100%	100%	100%	100%	0.1175
SM2	0%	2%	60%	60%	45%	10%	55%	30%	35%	0.0749
SM3	24	24	3	3	3	46	48	48	72	0.0489
SM4	3	2	3	1	48	15	24	22	12	0.0458
SM5	20	0	30	1	24	1	30	45	30	0.036
SM6	70	400	20	4	1000	106	250	350	180	0.0323
SM7	960	1000	150	20	400	464	300	500	250	0.0353
SM8	0%	0%	1%	5%	0%	0%	0%	1%	1%	0.043
SM9	98%	100%	100%	90%	100%	100%	95%	90%	85%	0.0394

(continued)

Table 4. (*continued*)

	L1	L2	L3	L4	L5	L6	L7	L8	L9	GW
SM10	0%	0%	1%	5%	0%	0%	0%	0%	0%	0.0319
SM11	2	2	2	1	2	2	1	1	1	0.0271
SM12	10%	97%	10%	20%	400%	55%	98%	98%	96%	0.0188
SM13	89	99	10	80	100	45	98	98	99%	0.0121
SM14	0	0	1	10	0	0	0	0	0	0.0517
SM15	9%	100%	80%	90%	50%	100%	100%	100%	100%	0.0362
SM16	90%	100%	100%	100%	100%	100%	100%	100%	100%	0.0343
SM17	2	2	1	1	2	2	1	2	1	0.0254
SM18	1	0	10	2	0	0	0	0	2%	0.0686
SM19	10	5	1	4	10	3	3	3	1	0.0388
SM20	2	2	2	2	2	2	2	2	2	0.0626
SM21	100%	100%	80%	90%	100%	100%	100%	100%	100%	0.0361
SM22	4	4	3	3	4	4	4	4	4	0.0311
SM23	4	4	4	4	4	4	4	4	4	0.03
SM24	0	0	2	0	0	0	0	0	0	0.0209

Table 5. Ranking of clinical laboratories based on the performance index (Mi)

AW	Si	Pi	Mia	Mib	Mic	Mi	Ranking
L1	0.8314	20.8597	0.1152	3.1130	0.8741	2.0468	4
L2	0.9246	23.8906	0.1318	3.5124	1.0000	2.3217	1
L3	0.5211	13.7440	0.0758	2.0000	0.5749	1.3269	9
L4	0.5980	16.7028	0.0919	2.3628	0.6972	1.5836	8
L5	0.8360	22.8130	0.1256	3.2640	0.9530	2.1787	3
L6	0.8388	23.7166	0.1305	3.3351	0.9895	2.2401	2
L7	0.6916	21.5229	0.1180	2.8930	0.8952	1.9757	5
L8	0.6924	20.6869	0.1136	2.8338	0.8615	1.9218	6
L9	0.6156	17.7379	0.0975	2.4718	0.7396	1.6658	7

5   Conclusions and Future Work

Clinical laboratories are recommended to use Multi-criteria Decision-Making (MCDM) tools including Intuitionistic Fuzzy Analytic Hierarchy Process (IF-AHP), Intuitionistic Fuzzy Decision Making Trial and Evaluation Laboratory (IF-DEMATEL), and Combined Compromise Solution (CoCoSo) to enhance their sustainability and operational excellence in periods of crisis. Besides, it helps to detect which aspects to focus on to improve by elucidating the most important and dispatching criteria which become pillars for the development of short- and long-term interventions.

It is suggested to implement improvement actions regarding operational capacity ($GW = 0.1985$) and Occupational Health and Safety ($GW = 0.1924$) through simulation methods and process digitalization. A closer look should be also taken at the equipment underpinning the clinical lab processes given its influencing nature in the overall response against the pandemic. Similarly, it is advised to train staff in the effective use of personal protective equipment and biosafety protocols propelling a safe work environment.

In future work, an extended version of the CoCoSo method is intended by using interval-type indicators. Secondly, it is suggested to implement the approach used in this article in other scenarios to set comparative studies identifying similarities and patterns. Finally, it is expected to include environmental-type criteria within the decision-making model to provide governments with a broader view of clinical lab performance from a circular economy perspective.

Acknowledgements. The authors would like to express their gratitude to Maria Fernanda Guzman Acosta and Jesús Soto Llanos for their valuable support during this research.

References

1. Stanković, S., Ašanin, M.: Clinical laboratories in the era of the COVID-19 pandemic: An analysis of experiences in Serbia. Serbian Med. J. **3**(3) (2021)
2. Tomo, S., Karli, S., Dharmalingam, K., Yadav, D., Sharma, P.: The clinical laboratory: A key player in diagnosis and management of COVID-19. Electron. J. Int. Feder. Clin. Chem. Lab. Med. **31**(4), 326–346 (2020)
3. Fang, B., Meng, Q.H.: The laboratory's role in combating COVID-19. Crit. Rev. Clin. Lab. Sci. **57**(6), 400–414 (2020). https://doi.org/10.1080/10408363.2020.1776675
4. Taherdoost, H., Madanchian, M.: Multi-Criteria decision making (MCDM) methods and concepts. Encyclopedia **3**, 77–87 (2023). https://doi.org/10.3390/encyclopedia3010006
5. Ortiz Barrios, M., Felizzola Jiménez, H., Nieto Isaza, S.: Comparative analysis between ANP and ANP- DEMATEL for six sigma project selection process in a healthcare provider. In: Pecchia, L., Chen, L.L., Nugent, C., Bravo, J. (eds.) IWAAL 2014. LNCS, vol. 8868, pp. 413–416. Springer, Cham (2014). https://doi.org/10.1007/978-3-319-13105-4_62
6. Yazdani, M., Zarate, P., Zavadskas, E.K., Turskis, Z.: A combined compromise solution (CoCoSo) method for multi-criteria decision-making problems. Manag. Decis. (2018). https://doi.org/10.1108/MD-05-2017-0458 Permanent link to this document: https://doi.org/10.1108/MD-05-2017-0458
7. Nuñez-Argote, L., Baker, D.P., Jones, A.P.: Initial clinical laboratory response to COVID-19: A survey of medical laboratory professionals. Lab Med. **52**(4), E115–E124 (2021). https://doi.org/10.1093/labmed/lmab021
8. Torres, I., Sippy, R., Sacoto, F.: Assessing Critical Gaps in COVID-19 Testing Capacity: The Case of Delayed Results in Ecuador. BMC Public Health (2021)
9. Weller, S.A., et al.: Development and operation of the defence COVID-19 lab as a SARS-CoV-2 diagnostic screening capability for UK military personnel (2022)
10. Salermon, R.M.: Biosafety challenges for clinical labs during the COVID-19 pandemic. Clinical Laboratory News (2020)

11. Lippi, G., Plebani, M.: The critical role of laboratory medicine during coronavirus disease 2019 (COVID-19) and other viral outbreaks. Clin. Chem. Lab. Med. **58**(7), 1063–1069 (2020)
12. Sanyaolu, A., et al.: Comorbidity and its Impact on Patients with COVID-19. SN Comprehens. Clin. Med. **2**(8), 1069–1076 (2020). https://doi.org/10.1007/s42399-020-00363-4
13. Rimmer, A.: Covid-19: The challenges of shielding the vulnerable and the NHS workforce. BMJ **369**, m1567 (2020)
14. Van den Berg, P., Yates, T.A., Haslam, N., et al.: The burden of COVID-19 in Eng-land's intensive care units: A report from the ICNARC Case Mix Programme. medRxiv (2020)
15. Singh, A., Shaikh, N., Singh, R., Singh, A.: COVID-19: Challenges and strategic initiatives in diagnostics in Indian clinical laboratory. Indian J. Pathol. Microbiol. **63**(Supplement), S138–S142 (2020)
16. Hanel, R., Getz, W.M.: COVID-19 and the workload of clinical laboratories: recommendations for the management of in vitro diagnostic services. medRxiv (2020)
17. Fang, Y., et al.: Sensitivity of chest CT for COVID-19: Comparison to RT-PCR. Radiology **296**(2), E115–E117 (2020)
18. Nardiello, S., et al.: Laboratory diagnosis of SARS-CoV-2 infection: A review of the available methods. Acta Biomed. **91**(3), e2020024 (2020)
19. Neidich, S.D., et al.: Increased risk of hospitalization in pa-tients with SARS-CoV-2 variant of concern B.1.1.7: A retrospective cohort study. E-Clin. Med. **37**, 100964 (2021)
20. Hogan, C.A., Sahoo, M.K., Pinsky, B.A.: Sample pooling as a strategy to detect community transmission of SARS-CoV-2. JAMA **323**(19), 1967–1969 (2021)
21. Ramaiah, A., Arora, N., Roux, L.: Drive-through testing: A unique, safe, and efficient way to test patients for COVID-19. Mayo Clin. Proc. **95**(7), 1420–1421 (2020)
22. Lin, Y.T., et al.: Laboratory outbreak of SARS-CoV-2 infection within a university hospital. J. Formos. Med. Assoc. **119**(7), 1239–1246 (2020)
23. Singh, A.K., Singh, A., Shaikh, A., Singh, R., Misra, A., Chakraborty, R.: Assessing the preparedness of COVID-19 testing laboratories in India: A nation-wide study. Med. J. Armed Forces India **76**(3), 296–302 (2020)
24. Cheema, S., Mahmood, A.: Efficiency assessment of clinical laboratories during COVID-19 pandemic: Data envelopment analysis approach. Clin. Epidemiol. Global Health **8**(4), 1065–1069 (2020)
25. Berwick, D.M., Hackbarth, A.D.: Eliminating waste in US health care. JAMA **307**(14), 1513–1516 (2012)
26. Salvagno, G.L., Lippi, G., Guidi, G.C.: Laboratory performance indicators and quality of testing. J. Lab. Precis. Med. **1**(1), 8–14 (2012)
27. Houshyar, A., Ayatollahi, H., Maleki, M.R.: Using multi-criteria decision-making (MCDM) techniques to evaluate the performance of medical laboratory centers in Iran. Med. J. Islam Repub. Iran **29**, 184 (2015)
28. Azadeh, A., Ghaderi, S.F., Saberi, M.: Performance evaluation of medical laboratories using analytic hierarchy process (AHP) technique. Iranian J. Publ. Health **40**(3), 48–55 (2011)
29. Liao, H.L., Yen, J.T., Ko, W.C., Huang, Y.T.: Evaluation of clinical laboratory performance during the COVID-19 pandemic using the analytic hierarchy process. BMC Med. Inform. Decis. Mak. **21**(1), 1–10 (2021)
30. Ozcanhan, M.H., Bilen, S.G.: Evaluation of clinical laboratory performances with TOPSIS method. J. Med. Syst. **43**(8), 1–8 (2019)
31. Khalilpourazary, S., Faraji, O., Eslamian, M.: Evaluation of clinical laboratories performance during the COVID-19 pandemic using TOPSIS. J. Med. Syst. **45**(4), 1–10 (2021)
32. Afsar, A., Memon, N.A., Memon, Z.A.: Performance evaluation of clinical laboratories during COVID-19 pandemic: A grey relational analysis approach. Pak. J. Med. Sci. **37**(4), 999–1004 (2021)

33. Delen, D., Demirkol, S., Gökmen, N.: Multi-criteria decision making approaches to evaluate COVID-19 testing centers. Health Care Manag. Sci. **24**(2), 238–248 (2021)
34. Wang, Z., Li, Y., Jiang, L., Li, X., Chen, S., Liu, B.: Performance (2020)
35. Atanassov, K.T.: Intuitionistic Fuzzy Sets, pp. 1–137 (1999)
36. Xu, Z.: Intuitionistic Preference Modeling and Interactive Decision Making, vol. 280. Springer, Heidelberg (2014)
37. Ar, I.M., Erol, I., Peker, I., Ozdemir, A.I., Medeni, T.D., Medeni, I.T.: Evaluating the feasibility of blockchain in logistics operations: A decision framework. Expert Syst. Appl. **158**, 113543 (2020). https://doi.org/10.1016/j.eswa.2020.113543
38. Ortíz-Barrios, M.A., Garcia-Constantino, M., Nugent, C., Alfaro-Sarmiento, I.: A novel integration of IF-DEMATEL and TOPSIS for the classifier selection problem in assistive technology adoption for people with dementia. Int. J. Environ. Res. Public Health **19**(3), 1133 (2022). https://doi.org/10.3390/ijerph19031133
39. Orji, I.J., Ojadi, F., Okwara, U.K.: Assessing the pre-conditions for the pedagogical use of digital tools in the Nigerian higher education sector. Int. J. Manag. Educ. **20**(2), 100626 (2022). https://doi.org/10.1016/j.ijme.2022.100626
40. Yazdani, M., Zarate, P., Kazimieras Zavadskas, E., Turskis, Z.: A combined compromise solution (CoCoSo) method for multi-criteria decision-making problems. Manag. Decis. **57**(9), 2501–2519 (2019). https://doi.org/10.1108/MD-05-2017-0458
41. Stević, Ž, Pamučar, D., Puška, A., Chatterjee, P.: Sustainable supplier selection in healthcare industries using a new MCDM method: Measurement of alternatives and ranking according to compromise solution (MARCOS). Comput. Ind. Eng. **140**, 106231 (2020). https://doi.org/10.1016/j.cie.2019.106231
42. Ortíz-Barrios, M.A., Alfaro-Saíz, J.-J.: Methodological approaches to support process improvement in emergency departments: A systematic review. Int. J. Environ. Res. Public Health **17**(8), 2664 (2020). https://doi.org/10.3390/ijerph17082664
43. Grau, C.M., et al.: Use of predictive tools in the management of COVID-19 patients: A key role of clinical laboratories. [Uso de herramientas predictivas en el manejo de pacientes COVID-19: El papel fundamental de los laboratorios clinicos] Adv. Lab. Med. **2**(2), 245–252 (2021). https://doi.org/10.1515/almed-2021-0019
44. Vega de la Cruz, L.O., Campaña, M.P., Pérez Vallejo, L.M., Tapia Claro, I.I.: Management of waiting lines through queuing theory in pharmaceutical facilities. [Gestión de las líneas de esperas a través de teoría de colas en entidades farma-céuticas] Rev. Cubana Farmacia **52**(2) (2019). www.scopus.com
45. Rivero, M.H.: An open-source application built with R programming language for clinical laboratories to innovate process of excellence and overcome the uncertain outlook during the global healthcare crisis. Paper presented at the Proceedings - 2020 International Conference on Computational Science and Computational Intelligence, CSCI 2020, pp. 870–871 (2020). https://doi.org/10.1109/CSCI51800.2020.00163. www.scopus.com
46. Lombardi Netto, A., Salomon, V.A.P., Ortiz Barrios, M.A.: Multi-criteria analysis of green bonds: Hybrid multi-method applications. Sustainability **13**(19), 10512 (2021). https://doi.org/10.3390/su131910512
47. Ortiz-Barrios, M., et al.: A multiple criteria decision-making approach for increasing the preparedness level of sales departments against COVID-19 and future pandemics: A real-world case. Int. J. Disaster Risk Reduct. **62**, 102411 (2021). https://doi.org/10.1016/j.ijdrr.2021.102411
48. Ortiz-Barrios, M., Nugent, C., Cleland, I., Donnelly, M., Verikas, A.: Selecting the most suitable classification algorithm for supporting assistive technology adoption for people with dementia: A multicriteria framework. J. Multi-Criteria Decis. Anal. **27**(1–2), 20–38 (2020). https://doi.org/10.1002/mcda.1678

49. Nuñez-Perez, N., Ortíz-Barrios, M., McClean, S., Salas-Navarro, K., Jimenez-Delgado, G., Castillo-Zea, A.: Discrete-Event Simulation to Reduce Waiting Time in Accident and Emergency Departments: A Case Study in a District General Clinic, pp. 352–363 (2017)
50. Ortiz-Barrios, M., Lopez-Meza, P., McClean, S., Polifroni-Avendaño, G.: Discrete-Event Simulation for Performance Evaluation and Improvement of Gynecology Outpatient Departments: A Case Study in the Public Sector, pp. 101–112 (2019)
51. Muñoz, W.A., Fuentes, D.B., Farfán Urzúa, M.J.: Role of public laboratories in the sars-cov-2 diagnosis in the covid-19 pandemic: Experience, challenges and opportunities. March 2021. [Rol de los laboratorios públicos en el di-agnóstico SARS-CoV-2 en la pandemia de COVID-19: Experiencia, desafíos y opor-tunidades Marzo 2021] Revista Chilena De Infectologia, **38**(2), 135–143 (2021). https://doi.org/10.4067/S0716-10182021000200135

The Role of Social Networks When Using Digital Health Interventions for Multimorbidity

Sara Polak[1]([⊠]) [iD], Cora van Leeuwen[1] [iD], Myriam Sillevis Smitt[1] [iD], Julie Doyle[2] [iD], Suzanne Cullen-Smith[2] [iD], and An Jacobs[1] [iD]

[1] imec-SMIT, Vrije Universiteit Brussel, Brussels, Belgium
sara.polak@imec.be
[2] NetwellCASALA, Dundalk Institute of Technology, Co. Louth, Ireland

Abstract. The use of a digital health intervention can be a valuable addition to the self-management journey of a person living with multiple chronic conditions (multimorbidity). However, digital technology is but one aspect of self-management. Different social actors, including formal and informal carers also contribute to various self-management efforts. This study investigated the role of social networks in the use of the digital health intervention ProACT, which was designed to support the self-management abilities of older people with multimorbidity (PwMs). Self-reports of social connection, using the Lubben Social Network Scale, and semi-structured interviews after up to one year of ProACT use were analyzed. Family, friends, healthcare professionals, and triage nurses were all found to be relevant actors in the social networks of PwMs. Several psychosocial mechanisms were identified through which different social relationships influenced PwMs' adoption and use of ProACT, including social support, social influence, social engagement, and person-to-person contact. Future digital health interventions should consider these mechanisms for effective implementation of such technology among PwMs.

Keywords: Digital Health · Self-Monitoring · Multimorbidity · Older Adults · Clinical Triage · Integrated Care · Interface for Disabled and Senior People

1 Introduction

Self-monitoring can provide more insights into someone's health compared to occasional clinical data collection [1]. This is achieved by collecting measures of everyday health and behavior. Insights derived from self-monitoring are especially important for people living with multiple chronic diseases (multimorbidity) to self-manage their complex health conditions [2]. The use of self-monitoring technology can help patients become more actively engaged with their health [3], resulting in more empowerment and autonomy of the patient making them a partner rather than simply a recipient of care [4–6]. Nevertheless, effectively managing multimorbidity remains subject to the combination of informal, professional, and self-care [7–9], which means that different social actors are involved in the disease management process.

The relevance of the relationship between social networks and self-management with a digital health intervention has been established, but there is a limited understanding

V. G. Duffy (Ed.): HCII 2023, LNCS 14029, pp. 123–137, 2023.
https://doi.org/10.1007/978-3-031-35748-0_9

of the mechanisms of this relationship [10, 11]. General theories exist on how social networks impact health or health behavior [12, 13], yet findings specific to the application of these theories, when using digital interventions for self-management, are limited. Furthermore, previous studies focus mostly on specific diseases as opposed to multimorbidity, while the burden of managing health and the impact of condition(s) on well-being adds up when dealing with multiple conditions simultaneously [14, 15]. As global rates of multimorbidity rise in tandem with ageing populations [16], it is necessary to examine the influence of social networks in these specific circumstances. To this end, we investigated the following research question: *What are the characteristics of a social network in relation to the use of a digital health intervention for self-management by people with multimorbidity?*

2 Background

Digital health interventions, including self-monitoring technology, have proven to be effective in improving health for certain diseases, such as hypertension, heart failure, or diabetes, by engaging the patient in their disease management [17–19] and have shown promising results in reducing health service utilization and being cost-reductive [20, 21]. Research on the interaction between self-monitoring technology and people living with chronic conditions mostly focused on understanding how the technology can enhance their quality of life. Yet, use of self-monitoring technology is not limited to the person living with chronic conditions, but also often involves caregivers and peers [22–24].

The combination of different social relationships surrounding an individual are usually referred to as a social network [12, 25]. Social networks can have various roles or functions, of which social support is a well-known example, usually provided in the form of supportive behaviors such as providing advice or practical help [25]. The role of social networks in self-care of older adults [9, 26] and self-management for chronic diseases [27] cannot be understated. It is known that social networks, including caregivers, family members, and friends are important for the self-care of older adults with multimorbidity [28, 29]. In a Canadian population of older adults above 65 years with chronic disease, social support was associated with positive mental health [30]. Similarly, lack of social support has been associated with an increase in morbidity and a decrease in general health and well-being, meaning that social connections are seen as an essential part of active and healthy ageing [9, 30–32].

Traditionally, family played a central role in supporting older adults as informal (unpaid) carers [26], often playing a role in healthcare decision making and condition management in the home. The influence of family and friends on self-management of older adults with chronic diseases has been found to be largely positive [27, 33]. As people age the likelihood of living with multiple chronic health conditions increases while social networks rarely grow, indeed social contacts are more likely to decline. Socio-demographic changes, such as smaller family units, migration of adult children for work (particularly from rural to urban locations) and single generation households, have placed pressure on familial social support networks. Consequently, the importance of a range of medical professionals as part of the social network of ageing adults has increased [34, 35]. Granovetter [36] has described the role of weak ties, represented by healthcare professionals in the social network of persons with multimorbidity (PwMs), providing relevant support without the influence of other social constraints such as dependence, intimacy or reciprocity expectations [35, 37].

Significant work has been done to investigate how these different social relationships impact health [38]. To this end, Berkman et al. [12] developed a conceptual model to explain the larger context of how social networks influence health behavior, showing that this is not simply a matter of social support (see Fig. 1). Other psychosocial mechanisms can be enabled by a social network, including: social influence, social engagement, person-to-person contact, and access to resources and material goods [12]. Members of a social network can have a general motivational function, due to their social influence, which allows them to help PwMs take up and continue self-management behaviors [39]. Social engagement, in the form of talking about (shared) situations regarding health, such as with peers, illustrates another way in which a social network can help with health-management [27]. Not all mechanisms in a social network apply in the same way in all health contexts. For example, person-to-person contact for PwMs self-managing their own health and wellbeing at home may be about the regular contact with their different healthcare providers, whereas in the original model this mechanism referred to contacts enabling transmission of diseases. Furthermore, some social mechanisms might have a negative instead of a positive impact. For example, even with access to multiple forms of health care, navigating between different care pathways can easily become burdensome rather than supportive for PwMs [40].

The mechanisms described above can impact health through different pathways. Some mechanisms, like social support, might directly impact health-related behavior. For example, when a spouse takes responsibility for cooking meals, their choice of ingredients will likely impact a PwM's adherence to their diet. On the other hand, emotional social support could affect a PwM psychologically by increasing their self-efficacy. Finally, social engagement in the form of a daily walk with friends might affect a PwMs general physiological health [12]. In this study, we investigate the working of these psychosocial mechanisms, and their pathways to health, in the context of the ProACT proof-of-concept trial, that evaluated a digital health intervention for multimorbidity self-management by older adults.

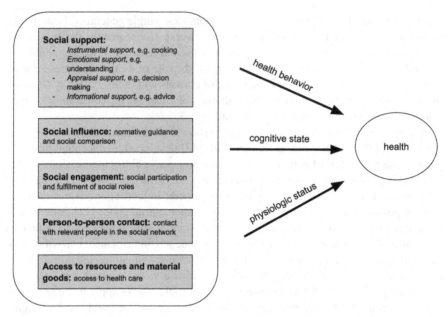

Fig. 1. The social and behavioral pathways to health model, adapted from Berkman et al. [12]

3 Method

3.1 The ProACT Platform

The perception and use of a digital self-management platform for PwMs was evaluated during the ProACT project, a H2020-funded proof-of-concept trial, conducted with 60 individuals of 65 years and older in Belgium (see Dinsmore et al. [41]). Participants had at least two conditions from the following disease categories: chronic obstructive pulmonary disease (COPD), congestive heart failure (CHF), chronic heart disease (CHD) and diabetes. They were provided with a tablet and Bluetooth devices which could be used to monitor health parameters such as weight, blood pressure, heart rate, blood glucose and blood oxygen through the ProACT platform [3] for a period of up to one year. The self-monitoring devices included a weight scale, smartwatch (measuring steps and sleep), blood pressure monitor, pulse oximeter and glucometer. All incoming data from the self-monitoring devices was telemonitored by a team of triage nurses who called participants in the event vital signs thresholds were exceeded [34]. For any technical assistance, a helpdesk was available which was monitored by members of the research team. The ProACT proof-of-concept trial received ethical approval of the Medical Ethics Committee of UZ Brussel.

3.2 Data Collection: Mixed Method Approach

Fiori et al. [42] suggest that social networks and the multidimensional support that they provide need to be examined holistically to provide a good understanding of their function. A mixed method approach was undertaken to provide a comprehensive view of the topic. Several data collection instruments were administered in the ProACT proof-of-concept trial, at four different timepoints (see Dinsmore et al. [41]). This study focuses on data collected at the end of the study. The Lubben Social Network Scale (LSNS) [43, 44] was administered to chart the networks of participants. Additionally, specific questions were asked during in-depth semi-structured interviews to further explore the influence of PwMs' social networks on their multimorbidity self-management using ProACT.

Of participants who completed the trial (n = 44), forty-two completed interviews about their experiences of self-monitoring with ProACT. Of those participants, 40 also completed the LSNS. All interviews were conducted in Dutch. Following verbatim transcription of the interviews, the data were coded in MAXQDA 2022 using the thematic analysis method outlined by Braun & Clarke [45]. Translation to English was completed by SP and CvL. Demographic data for the 42 participants included in this study can be found in Table 1.

Table 1. Demographic data of participants

Age mean, *SD* (range)	74.4, *5.4* (66–89)
Gender N (%)	
Male	33 (79)
Female	9 (21)
Highest education level N (%)	
None/primary	1 (2)
Lower high school	8 (19)
Higher high school	9 (21)
Higher education	12 (29)
University	12 (29)
Living situation N (%)	
Living alone	11 (26)
Living with others	31 (74)
Conditions N (%)	
CHD	41 (98)
CHF	16 (38)
COPD	14 (33)
Diabetes	24 (57)

4 Results

The average age of participants included in this study was 74.4 years (range 66–89 years) and participants were predominantly male (see Table 1 for more details). Using the 18-item Lubben Social Network Scale (LSNS), participants indicated their social connection with relatives, neighbors, and friends. This resulted in a total score between 0–90, as well as sub scores (between 0–30) for each of the social groups. According to Lubben et al. [46] total scores below 36 - and sub scores below 12 - could be an indication of people at risk of social isolation or overreliance on a single relationship. Though some individuals (n = 11) did fall into this at-risk category, on average, this does not apply to our sample as the mean total score reported was 42.8 (SD = 14.9). Means of 18.4 (SD = 5.7), 12.6 (SD = 6.4), and 11.8 (SD = 6.5) were reported for the subscales pertaining to relatives, neighbors, and friends, respectively. All but three participants scored above the cut-off point of 12 on the subscale of relatives, including those who had a low total score (i.e., <36). Neighbors were the second-most frequently involved group in the social network of our participants, with friends identified at a similar level of social connection as neighbors.

Semi-structured interviews provided more complete insights into the social networks of PwMs. Relationships outside of those reported in the LSNS were explored as well as the mechanisms and related types of impact that different relationships had on participants' self-management journeys with the ProACT platform. The themes and sub-themes identified from the interview data are presented according to the relevant psychosocial mechanisms from the model of Berkman et al. [12] (see Table 2).

4.1 Social Support

Different forms of social support exist, including instrumental (e.g., getting groceries), informational (e.g., providing advice), emotional (e.g., showing understanding), and appraisal (e.g., providing feedback) support. Instrumental support was the most visible type of social support provided to participants. When using the ProACT technology, participants sometimes required technical assistance. This type of support was provided by different people in the social network, including family members, healthcare professionals, and the helpdesk. Family members or formal carers helped participants to understand and use the platform: *"In the beginning, some things would block, so I couldn't return to the home page anymore. Eventually, I asked my 12-year old grandson and he has helped me with that"* (P63, male, 77 years, CHD + Diabetes). Other instances of instrumental social support included when friends and family joined self-management activities, such as going for a walk or a cycling trip, which motivated PwMs to continue their self-management efforts: *"since I'm alone, I needed to learn to go for a walk because that's not easy. That improved as I was with my brother or friends… then we would go for a walk"* (P98, female, 74 years, CHD + COPD). These examples show how people from the social network enabled PwMs to keep up their self-management activities while using the ProACT technology.

General Practitioners (GPs) or healthcare specialists were usually associated with more informational types of support, such as helping with the interpretation of health data: *"You can mention that to your doctor and say 'look, I see that I only sleep 2 h*

Table 2. Overview of psychosocial mechanisms and related themes

Psychosocial mechanism	Theme	Sub-theme
Social support	Instrumental support	Providing technical assistance
		Joining self-management activities
	Informational support	Interpretation of health data
	Emotional support	Providing reassurance
Social influence	Motivation	Initial technology adoption
		Maintaining self-management efforts
	Caregiver authority	
Social engagement	Retaining existing roles	Balancing social life
		Maintaining independence
	Restricted engagement	
Person-to-person contact	Regular contact with caregiver(s)	Data-supported contact
	Contact between appointments	Contact with triage
		Sharing data

per night in fact' [...] *and then they can say 'yes, it can be caused by your heart'* [...] *and they might be able to help you with that"* (P86, male, 71 years, CHD + CHF + Diabetes). Furthermore, PwMs depended on GPs or specialists to answer questions about their health: *"When I have a question, ok, I want to know how it works. And I go to the GP and there, and he, I have a GP thank god who makes time for me, if needed. And I won't abuse that, but when I have a question, I ask him and I get an answer. And they are always good answers, now he always has his books and a good explanation"* (P88, male, 72 years, CHD + Diabetes). Due to their professional background as a nurse, triage personnel - and sometimes friends or family members - were also trusted as a source of advice by PwMs when self-managing: *"they* [triage] *called and they said, this is the problem, or that is the problem, and we could communicate together what we could do or what would be best"* (P79, male, 70 years, CHD + Diabetes). For others, this process was less collaborative as they trusted their partner or their doctor to make the right decision for them: *"Yes because she* [wife] *always does* [...] *and this or that I cannot eat, then she doesn't prepare that"* (P89, male, 70 years, CHD + CHF + COPD).

Additionally, triage nurses and healthcare professionals played an important emotional role in reassuring participants: *"I was really content that they* [triage] *called me. I said to myself 'huh, they really do care'"* (P95, female, 85 years, CHD + CHF + COPD). Healthcare professionals supported PwMs by taking health measures with their own devices, which provided reassurance that the new self-monitoring technology could be trusted: *"the glucose measures, I check with my GP, with his devices. We find the same numbers at the same moment. That is important"* (P104, male, 69 years, CHF + Diabetes). For some participants, this reassuring role was fulfilled by the self-monitoring technology in between regular appointments: *"All the things you can measure, and then you can follow them. And then you can see that it all stays the same. Oh my blood pressure is still the same, that's still okay. […] then you feel more reassured with that* [the technology] *than without, because you don't see a doctor. You will have to wait"* (P64, male, 80 years, CHD + Diabetes). There were also a few instances where PwMs reported a lack of social support, not only due to healthcare professionals being unavailable to provide help when the PwM deemed they needed such support, but also by dismissive attitudes of healthcare providers. Not only was reassurance diminished in these instances, but PwMs also reported increased worry, as a result of the dismissal of concerns about health data: *"*[I] *discussed all the tables with doctor* [name] *and he says 'but that's nothing, that's just your arrhythmia'. So no action is taken. But then, sometimes you worry about it"* (P85, male, 82 years, CHD + CHF + Diabetes).

4.2 Social Influence

Different attitudes from the social network influenced the motivation of PwMs to use the self-monitoring technology, including the decision to start using ProACT. In many cases, it was adult children who encouraged PwMs to start using the platform: *"Well I thought, I'll never be able to do that. […] no, I didn't really see it but it is* [daughter] *who told me 'just try it'"* (P66, female, 70 years, CHD + Diabetes). Sometimes a little pressure from the social network was needed to take action and increase PwMs' self-management efforts. For example, use of the self-monitoring technology was sometimes nudged by a spouse: *"Yes, always the same routine […] Of course by my wife who faithfully presented the device every morning"* (P101, male, 72 years, CHD + CHF). However, from time to time, this type of nudging was experienced more negatively: *"My relationship has been affected by my wife who is ready in the morning to tell me 'don't dare to add 100 grammes'"* (P81, male, 69 years, CHD + CHF). Other times, the availability of someone to discuss experiences with provided the necessary motivation for PwMs to take actions in their digital self-management journey. For example, for one PwM discussing experiences with their sister-in-law resulted in the conclusion that they should keep working on self-management to maintain good health: *"That is what I recently said to my sister-in-law. Actually, your health, it's a constant work of yourself every day. It's not a given. You have to work for it"* (P115, female, 73 years, CHD + CHF). For PwMs feeling burdened by the need for help with different conditions, the triage nurses provided a positive social influence, as they motivated PwMs to contact their healthcare provider when needed: *"I found it very positive that they* [triage] *don't oblige you to do something. […] Then, at certain moments, I told myself, ok, I should do something about it […] That's the reason I went to get a second opinion with a cardiologist"* (P101, male, 72 years, CHD + CHF).

Many healthcare professionals, such as GPs, specialists and triage nurses provided support, e.g., by helping to interpret data from self-monitoring devices. This type of support was enabled by the authority PwMs assigned to this cohort of support actors in their social network. This was shown for general self-management topics: *"As the doctor always says, 'a little less salt', so I started to do that: eat less salt"* (P99, male,

74 years, CHD + Diabetes), but healthcare professionals also influenced the adoption of the technology. Since people turned to GPs and healthcare specialists for advice regarding health, the attitude of health professionals towards self-monitoring technology was taken seriously by PwMs, who were in turn (de)motivated to use technology on a regular basis: *"Daily measuring of your blood pressure is in fact not a good idea. From where do I get that idea? That idea comes from some cardiologists. It also comes from my GP"* (P102, male, 70 years, CHD + CHF).

4.3 Social Engagement

Many of the PwMs also had a social role as a spouse, (grand)parent or friend, outside their role as a person self-managing multimorbidity. For example, *"With New Year's I have promised my friend something. Every last Friday of the month, we drink a bottle of cava together [...] Normally I never drink it, it's not for me. But I have made a promise"* (P84, male, 81 years, CHD + Diabetes). Throughout the study, they maintained these roles, even though this would sometimes make it more difficult to stick to their self-management activities, as the partner of PwM79 (male, 70 years, CHD + Diabetes) explained *"Last week, we had the baptism of our grandchild, so he [PwM] has gained so much [weight] again"*. The involvement of triage nurses in the study created a new role in the social network of many PwMs, which some of them had to get used to. Even though the idea of the triage nurses monitoring and following up on readings appealed to some, other PwMs believed it was their own responsibility to check and act on their health data *"There are things that you identify yourself, uh, and you need to act on that by yourself [...] and you need to take appropriate measures by yourself"* (P68, male, 89 years, CHD + CHF).

Social engagement was a mechanism at play mostly with friends and family, where social roles and personal attachment showed more frequently than with other actors in the social networks, such as healthcare professionals. A downside of this familial engagement was displayed by overprotective children or spouses: *"But uh they are worried, you know the smallest thing I do, when I, dad you cannot do that, dad you cannot have that, dad. I say yes, but then dad has to stay in his seat and he can do nothing anymore"* (P111, male, 76 years, CHD + COPD + Diabetes). For some PwMs this led to reduced sharing of their self-management activities to avoid unnecessary worry: *"I don't think that my family members... my daughter... When there is something going on, when I tell them 'look, I started walking and doing..' Is there any concern? Yes, father, watch out, don't do too much that fatigues you"* (P84, male, 81 years, CHD + Diabetes).

4.4 Person-to-Person Contact

Many PwMs had regular personal contact with their healthcare providers to follow up on their symptoms, medication, and general health status: *"The doctor comes by every month, so you get a follow-up each month"* (P97, male, 74 years, CHD + CHF + Diabetes). Data sharing was an important element of staying in touch with carers, both for professionals and family members. In several cases, PwMs provided healthcare providers or family members with access to the ProACT platform to keep track of their health status and provide more appropriate follow-up at future appointments. Some

PwMs took the iPad with them to health consultations: *"Because they* [GP] *look at it as well. When I have that... for example on Friday she comes by. Then I can directly say: that is the average of this month"* (P78, male, 78 years, CHD + COPD). In this way, a synergy was created between the regular disease management by doctors and the self-management of PwMs. However, not everyone in the social network of PwMs could engage with the ProACT technology, leaving the nature of their direct contact and self-management support relationship with the PwM unchanged despite the PwM's use of the ProACT technology. *"But not the eldest* [daughter]. *Not that she was very interested, but yeah, she has so much, she has her family, she has her job* [...] *thus she is busy with that instead of me* [...] *she would want to do that, but she really doesn't have time for that"* (P103, female, 80 years, CHD + CHF + Diabetes).

For some, the triage nurses became the lever between the self-monitoring technology and their formal care, especially when the contact with the PwM's own healthcare providers was not very regular. PwMs identified triage monitoring and follow-up as a valuable resource while recognizing the necessary fluctuations in the frequency of direct engagement with the triage nurses: *"But it* [triage follow-up] *is an added value, when there are fluctuations. When differences occur, it is certainly an added value. Of course when nothing happens in 9 months... assuming my blood pressure would have remained constant, then I would have never received a call, which makes sense"* (P102, male, 70 years, CHD + CHF). Such comments by PwMs demonstrate the acceptance of a new support role within their social network, complementing other pre-existing roles providing self-management support with varied frequency and levels of involvement.

5 Discussion

Social relationships can impact health and affect management of multimorbidity in different ways [12, 27]. However, the nature of such relationships may change when digital interventions for self-management of chronic health conditions are introduced, partly in response to stretched healthcare resources worldwide. Digital health interventions are rapidly being added to the equation of social relationships and disease management. Traditionally, the focus has been on social support to assist people in their health management [25], which was indeed the most common way in which people from a social network influenced the use of self-monitoring technology for PwMs. In line with the LSNS scores reported for relatives, participants in this study reported significant social connection with family members. The tangible nature of their social support was easy to recognize for a PwM as supportive, during their introduction to the digital health intervention, such as when a family member provided help by solving technical problems.

Being able to use a digital health intervention is not enough for its adoption. PwMs need to trust the system and its output [47]. This is where healthcare providers played an important role. Doctors were often shown the data from the self-management devices, asked to help interpret readings and, at times, provided a second opinion. In the study by Gallant et al. [27] PwMs preferred advice from someone who had experienced a similar situation themselves. In our study, on the other hand, the authority of the person providing advice seemed to be more important. PwMs would not act on advice that they did not trust, or that was coming from a person or source that they did not trust with their health.

Once self-monitoring technology is in use by PwMs, there remains a continuous need for social resources. The combination of different conditions can lead to interaction of symptoms and medications [48], raising new questions for which PwMs seek advice. Normally, they would contact their GP or specialist in these situations, but the introduction of a triage service proved to be a valuable addition to the self-monitoring [34]. The triage nurses were available on a daily basis for advice and suggestions in the case of irregular health data, bridging the gap between the digital health intervention and the existing care pathways to healthcare professionals. Triage helped to reassure PwMs in the first instance, by explaining what was going on with their health data, providing psychological support found to reduce treatment burden by Gu et al. [14], and motivating PwMs to follow up on health readings of concern with their GP or specialist. Use of self-monitoring technology, combined with the social support offered by clinical triage monitoring, provided PwMs with needed support from a distance, while creating a sense of agency and control as personal self-management strategies evolved from the learning and engagement with both the technology and engagement with social network actors.

Some social mechanisms, such as person-to-person contact, might not necessarily change when a digital intervention is introduced, however, the nature and impact of these mechanisms can change. For example, person-to-person contact in regular doctor appointments was an important existing social mechanism that was enhanced by the introduction of self-monitoring technology. The ProACT platform provided a detailed overview of health status since the PwM's last appointment. As noted by Doyle et al. [3] this allowed for a more collaborative discussion of the care path, based on longitudinal data instead of decision-making based on single measurements during a given appointment. Nevertheless, some PwMs saw the process of recognizing that something was wrong with their health and taking action on it as their own responsibility and therefore did not recognize the triage team or other social actors as providing added value to their use of the digital health intervention ProACT. However, the extent to which social support actors' influence on PwM perceptions of self-management self-efficacy and autonomy is valued by PwMs requires further examination. This will be further explored in the SEURO H2020 project[1], which aims to evaluate the effectiveness and implementation of the ProACT platform with PwMs and their care networks in four countries.

Next to the use of the technology itself, additional behaviors are necessary for self-management, such as engaging in appropriate physical activity and healthy eating. Lower LSNS scores were reported for friends, yet, friends and family both had a clear role to play in providing support by joining in these types of self-management behaviors, which offered motivation for the PwM to maintain self-management efforts. Given the diversity of older adults, research is required with larger samples and with PwMs who have diverse types or sizes of social networks, to investigate if the role of social support is consistent in these variable contexts. For many PwMs, the use of technology in addition to their existing self-management behaviors was a new experience. Nonetheless, this experience was not always shared with their social network. For example, as also found by Gallant

---

[1] https://seuro2020.eu/

et al. [27], adult children were usually not actively updated on the results of using the digital health intervention, as PwMs felt that they should not be burdened with this information at the risk of causing worry about the PwM's health status.

Partners who lived in the same house as the PwM were often already involved in their self-management and continued to be so when the ProACT technology was introduced, even though this was not always appreciated by the PwM. Sharing of their experiences or worries was usually directed to friends, or sometimes to the triage nurses. McKinlay et al. [35] would suggest that the success of these non-familial support actors, in this role, may be explained by their provision of useful support as a weak tie, i.e., without being constrained by a close relationship such as a spouse. It has long been held that family ties cannot simply be replaced by new types of social relationships, such as those with triage nurses [49]. Indeed, family plays an important role in health promotion [50] and, as this study has shown, can be a critical support for those with multimorbidity seeking to use digital tools to enhance condition self-management. Nonetheless, for those who do not have a close social support network actively involved with disease management, support actors with weak ties may be easier to engage with as needed - as the triage nurses were available throughout work days in this study. Further exploration is required to establish how such support actors can enhance engagement with and effective use of digital health interventions to help PwMs maintain the range of behaviors necessary to self-manage multiple chronic health conditions effectively.

6 Conclusion

Different mechanisms within a social network can influence the use and effect of a digital health intervention for multimorbidity. Social influence plays an important role in the adoption of self-monitoring technology, whereas social support and social engagement are more salient as social mechanisms impacting health behavior while using a digital health intervention. Nonetheless, the impact of different social actors and social mechanisms might vary between users based on their needs and personal preferences, such as the desire to be independent or the need for external motivation by an authority figure. Furthermore, as social networks change, future digital health interventions should consider the potential role of new social actors, such as triage nurses, as complementary assets for effective use of the intervention.

Acknowledgements. The ProACT project received funding from the European Union's Horizon 2020 research and innovation programme under Grant Agreement no. 689996. The SEURO project received funding from the European Union's Horizon 2020 research and innovation programme under Grant Agreement no. 945449. We would like to thank all participants of this research for their valuable time.

References

1. Hallberg, I., Ranerup, A., Kjellgren, K.: Supporting the self-management of hypertension: Patients' experiences of using a mobile phone-based system. J. Hum. Hypertens. **30**, 141–146 (2016). https://doi.org/10.1038/jhh.2015.37

2. Nolte, E., McKee, M.: Caring for people with chronic conditions: An Introduction. In: Caring for people with chronic conditions: A health system perspective, pp. 1–14. Open University Press (2008)

3. Doyle, J., et al.: A digital platform to support self-management of multiple chronic conditions (ProACT): Findings in relation to engagement during a one-year proof-of-concept trial. J. Med. Internet Res. **23**(12), e22672 (2021). https://doi.org/10.2196/22672

4. Alkawaldeh, M.Y., Jacelon, C.S., Choi, J.: Older adults' experiences with a tablet-based self-management intervention for diabetes mellitus type II: A qualitative study. Geriatr. Nurs. **41**(3), 305–312 (2020). https://doi.org/10.1016/j.gerinurse.2019.11.010

5. Miyamoto, S., et al.: Empowering diabetes self-management through technology and nurse health coaching. Diabetes Educator **45**(6), 586–595 (2019). https://doi.org/10.1177/014572 1719879421

6. Park, S.K., Bang, C.H., Lee, S.H.: Evaluating the effect of a smartphone app-based self-management program for people with COPD: A randomized controlled trial. Appl. Nurs. Res. **52**, 151231 (2020). https://doi.org/10.1016/j.apnr.2020.151231

7. Gallant, M.P.: The influence of social support on chronic illness self-management: A review and directions for research. Health Educ. Behav. **30**(2), 170–195 (2003). https://doi.org/10.1177/1090198102251030

8. Heumann, M., Röhnsch, G., Hämel, K.: Primary healthcare nurses' involvement in patient and community participation in the context of chronic diseases: An integrative review. J. Adv. Nurs. **78**(1), 26–47 (2021). https://doi.org/10.1111/jan.14955

9. World Health Organization. Active ageing: a policy framework. https://apps.who.int/iris/handle/10665/67215. Accessed 06 Feb 2023

10. Koetsenruijter, J., et al.: Social support systems as determinants of self-management and quality of life of people with diabetes across Europe: Study protocol for an observational study. Health Quality Life Outcomes **12**(29) (2014). https://doi.org/10.1186/1477-7525-12-29

11. Vassilev, I., et al.: Social networks, social capital and chronic illness self-management: A realist review. Chronic Illn. **7**, 60–86 (2010). https://doi.org/10.1177/1742395310383338

12. Berkman, L.F., Glass, T., Brissette, I., Seeman, T.E.: From social integration to health: Durkheim in the new millennium. Soc. Sci. **51**(6), 843–857 (2000). https://doi.org/10.1016/S0277-9536(00)00065-4

13. Valente, T.W.: Social Networks and Health Behavior. In: Health Behavior: Theory, Research, and Practice, pp. 205–222 (2015)

14. Gu, J., Yang, C., Zhang, K., Zhang, Q.: Mediating role of psychological capital in the relationship between social support and treatment burden among older patients with chronic obstructive pulmonary disease. Geriatr. Nurs. **42**(5), 1172–1177 (2021). https://doi.org/10.1016/j.gerinurse.2021.07.006

15. Tran, V.-T., Barnes, C., Montori, V.M., Falissard, B., Ravaud, P.: Taxonomy of the burden of treatment: a multi-country web-based qualitative study of patients with chronic conditions. BMC Medicine **13**(115) (2015). https://doi.org/10.1186/s12916-015-0356-x

16. The Academy of Medical Sciences. Multimorbidity: a priority for global health research. https://acmedsci.ac.uk/file-download/82222577. Accessed 08 Feb 2023

17. Kirakalaprathapan, A., Oremus, M.: Efficacy of telehealth in integrated chronic disease management for older, multimorbid adults with heart failure: A systematic review. Int. J. Med. Inf. **162**, 104756 (2022). https://doi.org/10.1016/j.ijmedinf.2022.104756

18. McManus, R.J., et al.: Telemonitoring and self-management in the control of hypertension (TASMINH2): A randomised controlled trial. The Lancet **376**(9736), 163–172 (2010). https://doi.org/10.1016/S0140-6736(10)60964-6

19. Visser, L., Shahid, S., Al Mahmud, A.: Point-of-care testing for diabetes patients: investigating diabetes management by older adults. In: CHI '14 Extended Abstracts on Human Factors

in Computing Systems, pp. 1645–1650. Association for Computing Machinery, New York (2014). https://doi.org/10.1145/2559206.2581193

20. Panagioti, M., et al.: Self-management support interventions to reduce health care utilisation without compromising outcomes: A systematic review and meta-analysis. BMC Health Serv. Res. **14**, 356 (2014). https://doi.org/10.1186/1472-6963-14-356

21. Perl, S., et al.: Socio-economic effects and cost saving potential of remote patient monitoring (SAVE-HM trial). Int. J. Cardiol. **169**(6), 402–407 (2013). https://doi.org/10.1016/j.ijcard.2013.10.019

22. Danesi, G., Pralong, M., Panese, F., Burnand, B., Grossen, M.: Techno-social reconfigurations in diabetes (self-) care. Soc. Stud. Sci. **50**(2), 198–220 (2020). https://doi.org/10.1177/0306312720903493

23. Nunes, F., Verdezoto, N., Fitzpatrick, G., Kyng, M., Grönvall, E., Storni, C.: Self-care technologies in HCI: Trends, tensions, and opportunities. ACM Trans. Comput.-Hum. Interact. **22**(6), 33:1–33:45 (2015). https://doi.org/10.1145/2803173

24. Taylor, A., Godden, D., Aitken, A., Colligan, J., Wilson, R.: Delivering group-based services to the home via the Internet: Maximising clinical and social benefits. In: 2011 5th International Conference on Pervasive Computing Technologies for Healthcare (PervasiveHealth) and Workshops, pp. 384–388 (2011). https://doi.org/10.4108/icst.pervasivehealth.2011.246004

25. Heaney, C.A., Israel, B.A.: Social networks and social support. In: Health Behavior and Health Education, pp. 189–210. John Wiley & Sons (2008)

26. Hwu, Y.-J., Yu, C.-C.: Exploring health behavior determinants for people with chronic illness using the constructs of planned behavior theory. J. Nurs. Res. **14**(4), 261–270 (2006). https://doi.org/10.1097/01.JNR.0000387585.27587.4e

27. Gallant, M.P., Spitze, G.D., Prohaska, T.R.: Help or hindrance? How family and friends influence chronic illness self-management among older adults. Res. Aging **29**(5), 375–409 (2007). https://doi.org/10.1177/0164027507303169

28. Alqahtani, J., Alqahtani, I.: Self-care in the older adult population with chronic disease: Concept analysis. Heliyon **8**(7), e09991 (2022). https://doi.org/10.1016/j.heliyon.2022.e09991

29. Lawless, M.T., Tieu, M., Feo, R., Kitson, A.L.: Theories of self-care and self-management of long-term conditions by community-dwelling older adults: A systematic review and meta-ethnography. Soc. Sci. Med. **287**, 114393 (2021). https://doi.org/10.1016/j.socscimed.2021.114393

30. Yang, G., D'Arcy, C.: Physical activity and social support mediate the relationship between chronic diseases and positive mental health in a national sample of community-dwelling Canadians 65+: A structural equation analysis. J. Affect. Disord. **298**, 142–150 (2022). https://doi.org/10.1016/j.jad.2021.10.055

31. Chu, W.-M., et al.: Effect of different types of social support on physical frailty development among community-dwelling older adults in Japan: Evidence from a 10-year population-based cohort study. Arch. Gerontol. Geriatr. **108**, 104928 (2023). https://doi.org/10.1016/j.archger.2023.104928

32. Zhu, Y., et al.: Relationships among social support, self-efficacy, and patient activation in community-dwelling older adults living with coronary heart disease: A cross-sectional study. Geriatr. Nurs. **48**, 139–144 (2022). https://doi.org/10.1016/j.gerinurse.2022.09.008

33. Li, T., Zhang, Y.: Social network types and the health of older adults: Exploring reciprocal associations. Soc. Sci. Med. **130**, 59–68 (2015). https://doi.org/10.1016/j.socscimed.2015.02.007

34. Doyle, J., et al.: The role of phone-based triage nurses in supporting older adults with multimorbidity to digitally self-manage – Findings from the ProACT proof-of-concept study. Digit. Health **8**, 20552076221131140 (2022). https://doi.org/10.1177/20552076221131140

35. McKinlay, E., et al.: Social networks of patients with multimorbidity: A qualitative study of patients' and supporters' views. J. Prim. Health Care **9**(2), 153–161 (2017). https://doi.org/10.1071/HC16062

36. Granovetter, M.S.: The strength of weak ties. Am. J. Sociol. **78**(6), 1360–1380 (1973). https://doi.org/10.1086/225469

37. Rogers, A., Brooks, H., Vassilev, I., Kennedy, A., Blickem, C., Reeves, D.: Why less may be more: A mixed methods study of the work and relatedness of 'weak ties' in supporting long-term condition self-management. Implement. Sci. **9**, 19 (2014). https://doi.org/10.1186/1748-5908-9-19

38. Tsai, A.C., Papachristos, A.V.: From social networks to health: Durkheim after the turn of the millennium. Soc. Sci. Med. **125**, 1–7 (2015). https://doi.org/10.1016/j.socscimed.2014.10.045

39. Vassilev, I., Rogers, A., Kennedy, A., Koetsenruijter, J.: The influence of social networks on self-management support: A metasynthesis. BMC Publ. Health **14**, 719 (2014). https://doi.org/10.1186/1471-2458-14-719

40. Friis, K., Lasgaard, M., Pedersen, M.H., Duncan, P., Maindal, H.T.: Health literacy, multimorbidity, and patient-perceived treatment burden in individuals with cardiovascular disease. A Danish population-based study. Patient Educ. Counsel. **102**(10), 1932–1938 (2019). https://doi.org/10.1016/j.pec.2019.05.013

41. Dinsmore, J., et al.: A digital health platform for integrated and proactive patient-centered multimorbidity self-management and care (ProACT): Protocol for an action research proof-of-concept trial. JMIR Res. Protocols **10**(12), e22125 (2021). https://doi.org/10.2196/22125

42. Fiori, K.L., Smith, J., Antonucci, T.C.: Social network types among older adults: A multi-dimensional approach. J. Gerontol. B Psychol. Sci. Soc. Sci. **62**(6), 322–330 (2007). https://doi.org/10.1093/geronb/62.6.P322

43. Lubben, J.E.: Assessing social networks among elderly populations. Fam. Commun. Health **11**(3), 42–52 (1988)

44. Versions of the LSNS. https://www.bc.edu/content/bc-web/schools/ssw/sites/lubben/description/versions-of-the-lsns.html. Accessed 25 Jan 2023

45. Braun, V., Clarke, V.: Using thematic analysis in psychology. Qual. Res. Psychol. **3**(2), 77–101 (2006). https://doi.org/10.1191/1478088706qp063oa

46. Lubben, J., et al.: Performance of an abbreviated version of the Lubben social network scale among three European community-dwelling older adult populations. Gerontologist **46**(4), 503–513 (2006). https://doi.org/10.1093/geront/46.4.503

47. Weck, M., Afanassieva, M.: Toward the adoption of digital assistive technology: Factors affecting older people's initial trust formation. Telecommun. Policy 102483 (2022). https://doi.org/10.1016/j.telpol.2022.102483

48. Tripp-Reimer, T., et al.: An integrated model of multimorbidity and symptom science. Nurs. Outlook **68**(4), 430–439 (2020). https://doi.org/10.1016/j.outlook.2020.03.003

49. Ell, K.: Social networks, social support and coping with serious illness: The family connection. Soc. Sci. Med. **42**(2), 173–183 (1996). https://doi.org/10.1016/0277-9536(95)00100-X

50. Wu, F., Sheng, Y.: Social support network, social support, self-efficacy, health-promoting behavior and healthy aging among older adults: A pathway analysis. Arch. Gerontol. Geriatr. **85**, 103934 (2019). https://doi.org/10.1016/j.archger.2019.103934

Applying the Trajectories Conceptual Framework: A Case Study of an IoT Health Data Monitoring Application

Elizabeth Reisher⬛, Soundarya Jonnalagadda⬛, and Ann Fruhling(✉)⬛

University of Nebraska at Omaha, Omaha, NE 68182, USA
{erussman,sjonnalagadda,afruhling}@unomaha.edu

Abstract. We present a case study on the design and development of an IoT application, called Real-time Emergency Communication System for HAZMAT Incidents (REaCH). The REaCH application utilizes the latest IoT technologies to capture and monitor individual health data (heart rate, ECG, heat index) and provides an interactive dashboard to assist incident commanders to evaluate if a firefighter needs to be removed from the scene due to a potential threat to their health and well-being. In our study we examined the design and development of a dashboard utilizing the Trajectories Conceptual Framework (TCF) and Action Research (AR). The aim of this paper is to analyze if TCF can guide the development of a dashboard from research to industry. Our study consists of four cycles that span from the requirement gathering phase to delivering a minimal viable product. We conclude that the integration of TCF and AR provides a solid approach to evaluate the design and develop a real-time health monitoring IoT dashboard. We also propose the addition of a Developer Trajectory to address the technical aspects and help guide both the front-end and back-end developers through the various stages of the applications development using IoT technology.

Keywords: TCF · IoT · HCI · trajectories framework · dashboard design · Action Research

1 Introduction

"Human–Computer Interaction (HCI) is the study of the way in which computer technology influences human work and activities. HCI has an associated design discipline, sometimes called Interaction Design or User-Centered Design, focused on how to design computer technology so that it is as easy and pleasant to use as possible. A key aspect of the design discipline is the notion of "usability," which is often defined in terms of efficiency, effectiveness and satisfaction" [1]. Though Human Computer Interaction (HCI) is a well-established field of study where computer and information technologies are combined with social and behavioral sciences, there remains opportunities to improve the translation of HCI theories/frameworks and help operationalize best practices identified from applied research to industry practitioners and organizations' system design and evaluation strategies. The aim of this case study is to examine if the Trajectories Conceptual Framework (TCF) can be applied to help guide the development of a dashboard from a research laboratory setting to industry deployment.

We present a case study on the design and development of an IoT application, called the Real-time Emergency Communication System for HAZMAT Incidents (REaCH). The REaCH application utilizes the latest IoT technologies to capture and monitor individual health data (heart rate, ECG, heat index) and provides an interactive dashboard to assist incident commanders to evaluate if a firefighter needs to be removed from the scene due to a potential threat to their health and well-being. In our study we examine how we translated the design of a dashboard presenting the integration of multiple IoT sensor types and data from a pilot prototype to a field application, and the technical aspects associated with a minimally viable product (MVP). Our study presents how Benford's Trajectories Conceptual Framework (TCF) can guide the development of a dashboard from research stages to industry.

As part of this case study, we structured the paper as follows: Sect. 2 discusses the opportunities IoT offers in health data monitoring of first responders' health concerns, the gap between HCI research and practice, the TCF framework and the REaCH application under study. Section 3 presents our research method. Section 4 presents the results and observations from our laboratory tests, followed by a Sect. 5 discussion and Sect. 6 conclusion.

2   Background

We begin by providing a discussion on IoT, as we utilized IoT technologies for the development of the REaCH application.

2.1   Internet of Things (IoT)

Remote monitoring using IoT sensors has increased in popularity. Developing and using a dashboard to aggregate and display sensor data is common [2]. In industry, dashboards are often used to monitor employee safety, patient monitoring, product shipments, and asset tracking to name a few [2]. Today, interactive dashboards are even more dynamic, robust and complex due to emerging technologies and new areas where they can be utilized. One domain that has especially embraced dashboards is emergency management services. However, there are some unique challenges in emergency situations. Developing a dashboard to monitor first responder health data while the individual is actively engaged in an emergency requires the dashboard design to have real-time data and be more responsive than standard dashboard designs in the past.

IoT is defined as "An open and comprehensive network of intelligent objects that have the capacity to auto-organize, share information, data and resources, reacting and acting in face of situations and changes in the environment" [3]. IoT allows for human-to-human, human-to-things, and things-to-things communication and connection [3]. This type of communication and connection allows for many devices and sensors to be used in a way that enhances the life of the user. IoT strives to connect smart devices to provide services for users [3]. When developing a real-time interactive dashboard to monitor the health data of first responders, several Internet of Things (IoT) technologies could be utilized.

IoT computing consists of three components: (1) Hardware, e.g. sensors, actuators, and other embedded communication hardware, (2) Middleware, such as computing tools for data analytics with cloud and on-demand storage, and (3) Presentation, visualization and interpretation tools that are easy to understand and can be designed and modified for the individual applications [3]. Each component provides structure for all instances of IoT computing and allows for unifying protocols when IoT computing is done.

Challenges of implementing IoT applications include heterogeneity, interoperability, and scalability [4]. IoT dashboards must be configured to connect many different types of heterogeneous devices. In order to successfully implement IoT, a unifying architecture is needed in order to solve the challenge of heterogeneity [4]. In order to address the challenge of interoperability, a unifying protocol structure is required to ensure that the devices can successfully integrate and communicate with each other and ensure that data is secured during data transmission [4]. Scalability is a challenge that needs to be addressed because there often are many devices that need to be connected. When routing protocols and data storage are being designed, scalability needs to be addressed so that when the dashboard moves to the production where the demand for additional devices to be connected, it does not become overwhelmed and can seamlessly scale [4]. IoT technology is a useful platform to develop a real-time interactive dashboard that integrates and displays the health and environmental data captured from various smart devices and sensors.

Health monitoring is an important application of IoT as it provides a mechanism to monitor the health and safety of individuals remotely and can provide a more complete health scenario due to continuous monitoring [5]. Integrating wearable IoT devices and sensors allows for better remote monitoring as they can help provide areas where a healthcare intervention is necessary. HCI is necessary for health monitoring using IoT technologies as HCI provides a mechanism for disseminating the collected data [5]. Having good HCI design is needed for the IoT technologies to be used in the most ideal manner for monitoring. When designing a system, the UI design must be capable of meeting the various tasks at hand for the system [5]. These tasks can include various user roles, such as individual monitoring individuals, real-time data transmission, data availability, and a functioning system.

The collection of data pertaining to various IoT devices requires the use of sensors [6]. However, the emergence of the Internet of Things (IoT) poses new difficulties despite the alleged advantages we are getting from these sensors. Some of these have to do with managing IoT applications so that users can easily search, locate, and use their sensor data. Others have to do with creating the proper infrastructure to gather and store the enormous volume of heterogeneous sensor data [7]. The designers of sensor dashboards are under enormous pressure these days because of all these emerging technologies to organize the information more intelligently. Consolidating all the data from various technologies, displaying it on the dashboard in the most useful way, syncing the data from various technologies, and lastly reducing the cognitive load of dashboard users are the interface designer's most demanding challenges. Increased information also becomes the main cause of interface complexity that interface designer needs to consider while designing sensor dashboard [8].

2.2 First Responders

During a hazardous material (HAZMAT) incident, first responders such as firefighters are the first to reach the incident site. In doing so they put their lives at risk. For example, a fire inspector died after responding to an incident. The fire inspector had undergone strenuous and stressful work at a structure fire hours before he died at home [9]. His death was cardiac related. Circumstances like this one suggest a need for first responder health and environmental monitoring during HAZMAT incidents to ensure their safety and wellbeing. If the fire inspector had been monitored while responding to the incident, commanders may have noticed his health being compromised and removed him from the scene to be further evaluated, thus potentially saving his life.

In the United States, around 45% of on-duty deaths of firefighters are caused by cardiovascular events [10]. First responders are often asked to perform physically and physiologically demanding tasks over a long period of time. If not allowed adequate rest and recovery, first responders may develop fatigue and exhaustion due to physical stressors [11]. These stressors may cause the first responder to develop health problems, such as cardiovascular and pulmonary issues, and heat exhaustion. First responders need a monitoring system to alert incident commanders during a HAZMAT incident that the first responder's health could be compromised based on certain thresholds for heat index and heart rate.

2.3 Gap Between HCI Research and Practice

There is much value in what academic researchers discover through HCI research. However, research has shown that these findings are not always translated to industry practices [12]. The research-practice gap has previously been acknowledged as a HCI challenge as it minimizes the impact that academic research has on industry [12]. HCI design practitioners have identified barriers to implementing research findings into industry. These barriers include lack of access to peer-reviewed research, difficulties reading and comprehending academic research papers, and inability to translate findings into their design space [12]. Noting these barriers, it is important for academic researchers to provide new designs and methods that are HCI theory-based but are able to translate into design practice.

2.4 Trajectories Conceptual Framework

The Trajectories Conceptual Framework (TCF) stemmed from the work presented in various works by Steve Benford [13, 14] and is intended to help bridge the gap between HCI research results to industry best practices, especially for game design. Benford's [13] TCF framework uses trajectories to explain his framework. The trajectories are used to express the mapping between "story time" and "clock time". "Story time" is described as the "temporal structure of the underlying fiction" and "clock time" is defined as the time elapsed [14]. In this work, Benford introduces the 3 concepts of TCF: canonical (scripted), participant (actual), and historic (recounted) trajectories [15, 16]. In research, TCF can be used as a concept to explain how knowledge informs design, identify requirements for future technologies, and enable interactive user experiences [14]. TCF provides concepts that can describe various interactions in time (trajectories) for the purpose of helping to translate HCI theory to practice by identifying gaps between HCI research and industry UX practitioners' methods [15].

Canonical trajectories are the intended sequence of events or designer's plan for the experience [13]. These trajectories provide a space for the plot of the experience or event, allowing for structure in the event. In research, canonical trajectories are the researchers' vision for the application [16]. TCF was intended for use in game design and the canonical trajectory would be the plot of the game. In research applications, identifying canonical trajectories can provide a mechanism to express the main idea or reason behind doing the research.

Participant trajectories represent the experience of each individual participating in the experience or event [13]. From a gaming perspective, these trajectories can capture what occurs at each plot event of the canonical trajectory. In research, the participant trajectories represent the actual user experience [16]. Recording the experience of the user is key to completely grasp the key items that occurred at each plot point or step in the process.

Historic trajectories are the views of the experience after the experience has occurred [13]. Recounting historic trajectories allows for review of past events to potentially identify areas of strength or improvement. In research, historic trajectories are used to reflect on past experiences or iterations [16]. Reflecting on past experiences helps identify areas of growth or improvement for future experiments or tests.

2.5 Real-Time Emergency Communication System for HAZMAT Incidents (REaCH)

The goal of the REaCH application is to provide a real-time interactive dashboard application that captures and displays first responders' health data and environmental exposure data. The data displayed is utilized by incident commanders during a HAZMAT incident. Monitoring the health of first responders is essential as this work can be life threatening, real-time data collection allows for the health data of the first responders to be monitored, potentially eliminating episodes to occur on the scene if their health becomes compromised. The full discussion of the REaCH project can be found on the UNL MATC website [17].

The REaCH system utilizes the latest IoT technology that integrates multiple smart sensors which capture environmental and human health data. Unfortunately, there is no "all-in-one" sensor that can monitor all information types desired. Using IoT technology allows heterogenous devices and sensors to be integrated within the REaCH dashboard. Currently the REaCH application integrated the Kestrel DROP wireless sensor to collect environmental data to monitor the Ambient Heat Index and Polar H10 to collect heart rate from the sensors placed inside the First Responder's PPE suit.

The REaCH dashboard communication architecture is shown in Fig. 1. The sensors use Bluetooth to talk to the communication hub, which consists of a Raspberry Pi.

The Raspberry Pi collects data from the sensors and processes the data into the proper format for posting to the database, using the Django REST Framework. The application layer employs Django for the REaCH backend processing and Angular for the frontend applications. The application dashboard's user interface allows users to interact with the data. The application connects to a weather application programming interface (API) that displays real-time local weather and time information on the application dashboard.

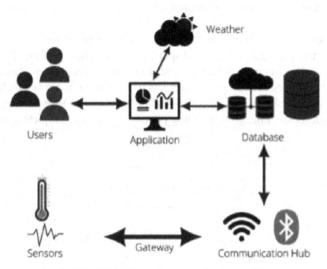

Fig. 1. REaCH dashboard communication architecture

3   Methods

In this section we present our research methodology to conduct cyclical integration testing of the REaCH application. We selected Action Research as our research approach and TCF as our theoretical foundation.

3.1   Action Research

Our research study employed the Action Research (AR) approach for our integration testing. AR aims to solve immediate problems (e.g., technical, performance, connectivity, data transmission, etc.) that arise during the iterative development and testing process [18]. AR allows for a continual research cycle that solves problems by interpreting what was observed and acting immediately on what was observed. AR allows for the research participants to be included in the research as the role of collaborator [18].

An ideal research social setting where AR can be used as a method is where the researcher can be actively involved, knowledge obtained can be applied immediately, and the research is a process that is able to link theory and practice (generally cyclical) [18]. AR often provides relevance to information systems research by including all participants. AR allows for problems to surface naturally during the experience and its collaborative nature empowers members of the research team to provide input on what issue or problem needs to be addressed [18].

Ortrun Zuber-Skerritt (Fig. 2) model consists of four stages, which can be repeated multiple times in a cyclic form [19]. The first stage, plan, concerns preparing the intervention and research location. Act concerns undergoing the intervention. Observe involves the data collection during the intervention that allows for evaluation. Reflect analyzes the data collected and discusses conclusions that may lead to a plan activity for a new cycle.

AR often can answer "how" and "why" research questions. This research is aimed toward improving our data collection, display, and functionality of our REaCH dashboard. Additionally, AR provides us a cyclical method for continuous learning in our project. As researchers, we can solve problems as they arise in our research and make improvements on our REaCH project with each iteration of changes. Using AR as our research design for each integration testing provides us with a complete framework for evaluation.

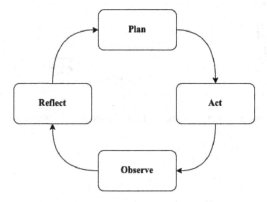

Fig. 2. Action Research Framework [19]

3.2 Operationalizing TCF Through AR

In Fig. 3, we propose how TCF can be operationalized through AR. During each AR cycle the three trajectories can help inform the direction of the next cycle.

Combining AR iterations with trajectories provides a clearer manner in the value each trajectory brings to the process (plan), how the trajectories are delivered (act), and how the Historic trajectory is being delivered (reflect) [16]. The canonical trajectories translate to the plan of the experience. Canonical trajectories are what the designer or developer intended to occur, which is the plan of the experience. The participant trajectories provide a space for the delivery of the experience to occur (act and observe), which then allows for a space to reflect and recount (historical trajectories) [16].

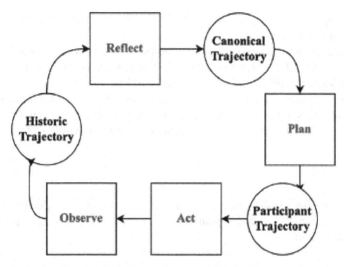

Fig. 3. Integration of Action Research and Trajectories Conceptual Framework

4 Case Study

In this study, REaCH development cycles were used to evaluate the integration of AR and TCF methods. As part of this study we conducted 4 cycles that allow for transla-tion from stakeholder meetings to an industry ready application. The 4 cycles are (1) initial meetings with stakeholders to capture requirements [20], (2) development of a high-fidelity wireframe, (3) development of a MVP single sensor dashboard, and (4) development of a multiple sensor integrated dashboard application for field testing.

The plan for Cycle 1 was to have a stakeholder focus group with various project stakeholders to brainstorm and identify initial system requirements. The session was held at the stakeholders; location e.g. Fire House during the normal work shift. This gave the research team an opportunity to view the existing equipment, tour the various vehicles, and establish rapport. The focus group produced a list of concerns that HAZ-MAT responders have when responding to an event [20]. This led to defining the initial requirements for the REaCH dashboard.

Cycle 2 took the output generated from Cycle 1 into consideration when developing the initial wireframe. The plan for this cycle was to have a high-fidelity wireframe evaluation. Developers followed an agile approach creating the wireframes and presented them routinely to stakeholders for feedback. Based on the feedback on the wireframe user interface, a first iteration of the MVP was developed and ready for validation testing.

Cycle 3 was a single sensor type integration and validation test with the newly developed dashboard. The plan was to test the minimum viable product developed. This test consisted of two simulated first responders each wearing one Kestrel Drop each (ambient heat index sensor). The goals of this test were to have successful integration of a single heat index sensor into the REaCH dashboard to connect Kestrel Drop via Bluetooth to data acquisition platform, to have the dashboard retrieve and show sensor data in a timely manner and demonstrate proof of concept to a stakeholder from a large metropolitan fire department.

Cycle 4 was a multiple sensor type integration test. The plan was to conduct expanded functionality testing of the REaCH system. The test consisted of integrating two Kestrel Drop heat index sensor devices and two POLAR H10 heart rate sensor devices. The goals of this test were to have multiple sensors and devices interacting with the REaCH system, ensure reliable and valid data transmission, validating thresholds and alert functionality, and moving proof of concept to a more production-oriented environment.

5 Results

In this section we discuss the observations and reflections for each cycle. The reflections of each cycle served as inputs for planning the next canonical trajectory phase of our dashboard development.

5.1 Cycle 1 – Stakeholder Focus Group

During the stakeholder focus group meeting, the concerns that first responders have during a hazardous materials event were identified. These concerns included short-term and long-term health effects from the exposure to hazardous materials during an incident. The stakeholders involved discussed the possibility of having their health monitored during the incident to help mitigate some health effects [20]. Heart rate and blood pressure were key vitals suggested for monitoring, as well as environmental effects such as oxygen level or the ambient heat index. Stakeholders were especially concerned about the carcinogens they may be taking home to their families. The also expressed the need for one application to display all the status of the equipment they used e.g. oxygen tank, walkie talkie battery, etc. Reflecting on Cycle 1, it was decided to move forward on creating a system that monitors health and environmental data on first responders during a HAZMAT incident.

5.2 Cycle 2 – High Fidelity Wireframe

Using the feedback from Cycle 1, a high fidelity wireframe (Fig. 4) was created. The wireframe provided a blueprint for the MVP. The developed wireframe provides a user interface display for monitoring individuals and crews on the scene, and device information and assignments. The users of the dashboard could view weather data and filter through crews and individuals at a scene. The wireframe simulated the functionality where the user could interact with the application and assign devices and sensors to a first responder and view the data in real-time to the dashboard for monitoring.

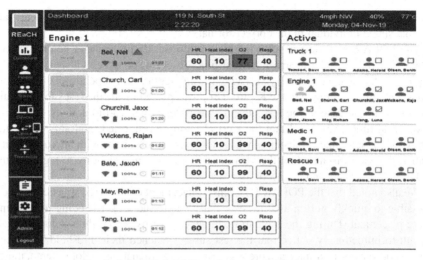

Fig. 4. Initial high-fidelity wireframe of REaCH system

5.3 Cycle 3 – Minimum Viable Product Validation

Minimum value product (MVP) evaluation is a crucial step in any software development project, as this step involves collecting feedback on the initial working prototype of the application. The MVP was developed based on the wireframe from Cycle 2 and we conducted a single sensor-type integration test using the developed REaCH system.

During this test, we observed successful integration of multiple Kestrel Drop device heat index sensors by confirming accurate and real-time data collection, confirming no issues with heterogeneity or scalability. However, one of the Kestrel Drop devices froze during the test and quit capturing data, uncovering an issue with interoperability. We also observed that the network needed to be set up locally and that the Raspberry Pi communication hub needed to be always carried by the simulated first responder, which could be challenging when we would like move to field testing phase.

We noted that it is important to assess each device independently before doing integration testing to validate and verify that the device's hardware and software is reliable and performs as expected/documented and meets the users' needs and expectations. We also realized that we need to have a detailed checklist on the steps to start up the dashboard and connect all the layers and devices/sensors. Developers learned that as the system scales and more devices and sensors are added, manual connection and setup procedures for each device become time consuming and error prone. We identified several automation enhancements to streamline the setup for the next testing iteration. After discussing Cycle 3 enhancements were made for Cycle 4 testing,

5.4 Cycle 4 – Expanded Functionality Testing

In Cycle 4, we expanded the dashboard functionality to have multiple sensors integrated. We then conducted a multiple sensor-type integration test building upon the feedback from Cycle 3. During this test, we observed successful data collection from multiple sensor devices to the dashboard, accurately attributing both heat index and heart rate data to a single individual in the correct format.

The POLAR H10 device fully integrated into the dashboard and heart rate data displayed on the dashboard correctly in real-time, observing no issues with heterogeneity. The sensor data was validated by verifying the ambient room temperature, ensuring an increase in temperature when the Kestrel Drop was placed inside the test subject's suit, and noting an increase in the test subject's heart rate when cardio activity was done. However, at times, we noted that the Kestrel Drop disconnected randomly, while the POLAR H10 maintained connection without issue, noting an issue with interoperability. Further, the team discussed on the idea of adding a system capability to highlight the availability of sensors and connectivity issues.

We also noted that the POLAR H10 sensor placement on the chest was not the most accessible to quickly put on and off, especially due to the sensor needing to be damp before placement. During the evaluation, the excessive use of brighter colors made it difficult to immediately notice that the test subject reached their threshold. The team reflected on various user interface presentation features such as the color scheme, image location changes, appropriate threshold flashing colors, and enhancing the filtering of first responders to be displayed e.g., active only or all available to further enhance the user experience. Regarding scalability, the system was not overwhelmed with three devices connected at once. To further prepare for scalability of additional sensors and more first responders wearing devices in the field test, the team discussed additional technical solutions to automate the device connectivity setup process and brainstormed new features that will allow the end user to activate the automated setup procedures, including smart device connection.

6   Discussion

During the requirement gathering, analysis and design, construction, and testing of the REaCH application the team was also able to capture feedback from all participants during each cycle, ensuring that all roles were incorporated into discussions. The natural recounting during each cycle's reflection allowed us to solidify the next canonical trajectory for the next cycle based on feedback on what needs to occur to make the REaCH dashboard design meet the end users' needs and ready for the next iteration of development. However, as discussed further in this section, we noted that our developers were not able to naturally provide technical input into the cycle or discussions due to their roles and the model focusing on more of the front-end design aspects of the REaCH dashboard and less on the technical implementation aspects. We propose that a new Developer trajectory be added to the TCF framework to provide a voice from the developers' perspectives.

6.1   Reflection on Each Trajectory

Reflecting on each of the three trajectories is a key component of the TCF. Reflections help drive the next steps to transition the research to practice. As described earlier, Canonical trajectories are the intended sequence of events or designer's plan for the experience [13]. Intended sequence of events was crucial for the REaCH dashboard to work as planned. For example, a sensor had to be assigned to an individual before an individual could be monitored. The individual had to be "active" in the event for the data from the sensor to be meaningful. The canonical trajectory aligned well with functionality of the REaCH system and how the sequence of events were critical to be able to monitor an individual.

Participant trajectories represent the experience of each individual participating in the experience or event [13]. This trajectory was key to the REaCH validation testing when participants were wearing the sensors. It was important to consider their experience wearing the hardware e.g., was it comfortable? Could it be easily worn? Did it get in the way of the main task at hand? Another key participant experience was the "acting" incident commander and their experience monitoring the participant's data. We were interested in if the data visualization was presented in the best format, was it readable, was it timely, easy to find, etc.

In general, it is important to continuously examine if the current IoT technologies used are the best for the task at hand. During this evaluation we noted that the POLAR H10 device was able to successfully complete the task of obtaining heart rate data. However, the POLAR H10 device might not be ideal in the field or during a real incident. The POLAR H10 device requires the device to be placed on the sternum, underneath all layers of clothing and the strap to be wet. A more useable device in the field could be one that is placed on the wrist as a wrist device does not require it to be placed underneath the clothes or need to have moisture before using. However, heart rate data collected closer to the core is more accurate than on other areas of the body. It should also be noted that the POLAR H10 device does provide important sensors to collect all the heart rate data and is described as the "gold standard in wireless heart rate monitoring". It can collect heart rate data based on ECG readings, allowing the REaCH application to measure bpm, ECG, and heart rate variability [21]. These are important design and implementation considerations as the application is transitioned from research to industry.

Historic trajectories are the views of the experience after the experience has occurred [13]. Recounting historic trajectories allows for review of past events to potentially identify areas of strength or improvement. The historic trajectory played a role in evaluating the adaptation or changes made from the previous cycle. This trajectory helped identify new functionality and areas that the current technology needed improvement. For example, the signal strength on how far the participant could be from the hub, battery life of the sensor, and response time in updating data, updating the dashboard, and sending an alert were all discussed as part of the Historical trajectories.

The team also reflected on specific IoT areas such as heterogeneity, interoperability, and scalability. The team noticed no apparent heterogeneity issues when testing, however, the sensors require different software frameworks to connect. The Kestrel Drop uses an open-source framework called Wizkers (http://www.wizkers.io/) and the POLAR H10 uses one developed from the manufacturer. Interoperability became an issue when the Kestrel Drops froze and disconnected. Scalability is a challenge that we will need to address as we move to field testing and issues will arise during a field test. Since these technical aspects did not fully align with the three trajectories, the researchers realized the possible need for an additional Trajectory which will be discussed next.

6.2 Enhancement of the Trajectories Conceptual Framework

We present a case study where various trajectories were considered as the application evolved. In several cases the TCF aligned well with each cycle and proved to be a solid approach for guiding the developing and testing cycles of the REaCH system; however, there were still some gaps in the translation from one cycle to the next cycle. To address some of the gaps, we propose adding a "Developer" Trajectory to address the technical aspects to help guide both the front-end and back-end developers' perspectives through the various cycles of the applications development. Further, the Developer Trajectory may include a visionary perspective on how the technology will scale when placed into practice. Especially during cycles 3 and 4, we noted that there was no explicit trajectory from the developer's point of view. Developing a real-time interactive dashboard requires a heavy lift on the developers and we think that TCF could be better enhanced by adding a trajectory that is the lens of the developer to address the technical aspects. During the reflection portions of the cycles, we noted that the developers could contribute to the conversation but their goals for the test were different than the rest of the team. Most of the team focused on the functionality of the dashboard and how it looked, while the developers wanted to ensure that the website is user-centric, has a scalable design, and accessible to all users. Finding the right balance between aesthetics and functionality, device connectivity and compatibility, data storage (backups) and maintaining optimal web performance were some of the technical challenges that can be addressed with a Developer trajectory. We propose a Developer trajectory that allows for the developers to have their own plan and discussion on the technical side of the dashboard and what they can improve to make the dashboard more functional and industry ready. A Developer trajectory would close gaps between participant perspectives and the technical functionality of the REaCH system.

A Developer trajectory would potentially be defined as the goal of the development team when testing a system functionality. In the new proposed model (Fig. 5), the Developer trajectory would sit in between act and observe. The Canonical trajectory sets the foundation for the cycle and acts as how the cycle plays out. The Developer trajectory sits between act and observe since system functionality tests that the developer's would like to have should occur during the act phase and be included in the overall observation of the cycle. Utilizing a Developer trajectory and having it implemented after the act phase could ensure that the developers have a space for discussion and reflection in later stages in the cycle while still allowing the plan of the cycle to occur. For example, in Cycle 4 we wanted to test the REaCH system functionality with two sensors. While implementing another sensor into the REaCH system was a heavy lift on the developers, monitoring the dashboard response and sensor use was also an important aspect of that cycle. Potentially allowing for the developers to have a trajectory near the beginning of the cycle could provide a space for their goals and tests to occur without taking away from the overarching plan of the cycle.

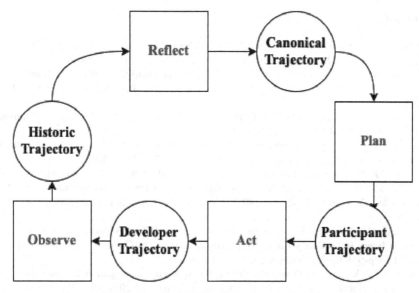

Fig. 5. Proposed TCF and AR Integrated Model

7 Conclusion

This case study presents an innovative approach for examining the usefulness of the TCF and proposes integrating TCF and Action Research. Further the authors propose extending the TCF to include a Developer Trajectory.

The main contribution from our case study are as follows 1) TCF can be used to guide the development of an IoT dashboard from research to industry 2) TCF can be operationalize through Action Research, and 3) the importance and need to consider developer's perspective in the testing phase when developing an IoT dashboard and therefore a new Developer trajectory is proposed. The authors recognize this is just one instantiation of integrating TCF and AR and thus opens the door for further examination and analysis.

Acknowledgments. This research was funded by the US Department of Transportation award number 69A355174107. This content is solely the opinions of the authors and does not necessarily represent the official views of the US Department of Transportation. We would like to express our gratitude to Dr. Aaron Yoder, University of Nebraska Medical Center; Dr. Sharon Medcalf, University of Nebraska Medical Center; Dr. Chandran Achutan, University of Nebraska Medical Center; Dr. Dario Ghersi, University of Nebraska at Omaha; and graduate students: Justin Fay, Troy Suwondo, Krishna Kumari, Dawei Li, and Ru Ng for their support of this project.

References

1. Dix, A.: Human-computer interaction. In: Liu, L., Özsu, M.T. (eds.) Encyclopedia of Database Systems. Springer, Boston (2009). https://doi.org/10.1007/978-0-387-39940-9_192
2. Vanden Hautte, S., et al.: A dynamic dashboarding application for fleet monitoring using semantic web of things technologies. Sensors **20**(4), 4 (2020). https://doi.org/10.3390/s20 041152
3. Group, S.M.A., et al.: Internet of Things (IoT): A literature review. J. Comput. Commun. **3**(5), 164 (2015). 10.4Ffig6/jcc.2015.35021
4. Sobin, C.C.: A survey on architecture, protocols and challenges in IoT. Wirel. Pers. Commun. **112**(3), 1383–1429 (2020). https://doi.org/10.1007/s11277-020-07108-5
5. Alrizq, M., Solangi, S., Alghamdi, A., Nizamani, M., Memon, M.A., Hamdi, M.: An architecture supporting intelligent mobile healthcare using human- computer interaction HCI principles. Comput. Syst. Sci. Eng. **40**, 557–569 (2021). https://doi.org/10.32604/csse.2022. 018800
6. Alqarni, H., Alnahari, W., Quasim, M.T.: Internet of Things (IoT) Security Requirements: Issues Related to Sensors. 2021 National Computing Colleges Conference (NCCC) (2021).https://doi.org/10.1109/nccc49330.2021.9428857
7. Sowe, S.K., Kimata, T., Dong, M., Zettsu, K.: Managing heterogeneous sensor data on a big data platform: IoT services for data-intensive science. In: 2014 IEEE 38th International Computer Software and Applications Conference Workshops (2014). https://doi.org/10.1109/ compsacw.2014.52
8. Kumar, N., Prajapati, S.: Challenges for interface designers in designing sensor dashboards in the context of Industry 4.0. Zenodo (2019). https://zenodo.org/record/3455623. Accessed 17 Jan 2023
9. At-home death of Lincoln fire inspector considered to be in line of duty, officials say | Crime and Courts | journalstar.com. (n.d.). https://journalstar.com/news/local/crime-and-courts/ at-home-death-of-lincoln-fire-inspector-considered-to-be-in-line-of-duty-officials/article_6 1047be7-760e-5b67-8e97-d4288ef8b4cf.html. Accessed 13 Dec 2022
10. Why do firefighters have an increased risk of heart attacks? (2017). https://www.medicalne wstoday.com/articles/316707
11. Corrigan, S.L., Roberts, S., Warmington, S., Drain, J., Main, L.C.: Monitoring stress and allostatic load in first responders and tactical operators using heart rate variability: A systematic review. BMC Publ. Health **21**(1), 1701 (2021)
12. Colusso, L., Bennett, C.L., Hsieh, G., Munson, S.A. (2017). Translation Resources: Reducing the Gap between Academic Research and HCI Practice. ACM Conferences. https://doi.org/ 10.1145/3064663.3064667. Accessed 19 Jan 2023
13. Benford, S., Giannachi, G.: Temporal trajectories in shared interactive narratives. In: Proceedings of the SIGCHI Conference on Human Factors in Computing Systems (CHI '08), pp. 73–82. Association for Computing Machinery, New York (2008). https://doi.org/10.1145/ 1357054.1357067
14. Benford, S., Giannachi, G., Koleva, B., Rodden, T.: From interaction to trajectories: designing coherent journeys through user experiences. In: Proceedings of the SIGCHI Conference on Human Factors in Computing Systems (CHI '09), pp. 709–718. Association for Computing Machinery, New York (2009). https://doi.org/10.1145/1518701.1518812
15. Velt, R., Benford, S., Reeves, S.: Translations and boundaries in the gap between HCI theory and design practice. ACM Trans. Comput.-Hum. Interact. **27**(4), 29:1–29:28 (2020). https:// doi.org/10.1145/3386247
16. Velt, R.: Putting trajectories to work: Translating a HCI framework into design practice [Thesis (University of Nottingham only)]. University of Nottingham (2018). http://eprints. nottingham.ac.uk/48412/

17. University of Nebraska–Lincoln. (n.d.). https://www1.unl.edu/search/#dept_results. Accessed 31 May 2022

18. Baskerville, R.: Investigating information systems with action research. Commun. Assoc. Inf. Syst. (1999). https://doi.org/10.17705/1CAIS.00219

19. Zuber-Skerritt, O.: Action Research for Change and Development. Gower Publishing, Aldershot (1991)

20. Medcalf, S., Hale, M.L., Achutan, C., Yoder, A.M., Fruhling, A., Shearer, S.W.: Requirements gathering through focus groups for a real time emergency communication system for HAZMAT incidents (REACH). J. Publ. Health Issu. Pract. **5**(2) (2021). https://doi.org/10.33790/jphip1100188

21. Polar H10. Polar H10 | Polar USA. (n.d.). https://www.polar.com/us-en/sensors/h10-heart-rate-sensor/. Accessed 1 June 2022

Multidimensional Data Integration and Analysis for Youth Health Care During the Covid-19 Pandemic

Jianlun Wu[1] , Yaping Ye[2] , Yuxi Li[3] , Ruichen Cong[3] , Yishan Bian[4] ,
Yuerong Chen[5] , Kiichi Tago[6] , Shoji Nishimura[7] , Atsushi Ogihara[7] ,
and Qun Jin[7(✉)]

[1] School of Public Health, Zhejiang Chinese Medical University, Hangzhou, China
[2] School of Humanities and Management, Zhejiang Chinese Medical University, Hangzhou, China
[3] Graduate School of Human Sciences, Waseda University, Tokorozawa, Japan
[4] The First Clinical Medical College, Zhejiang Chinese Medical University, Hangzhou, China
[5] The Third Clinical Medical College, Zhejiang Chinese Medical University, Hangzhou, China
[6] Department of Information and Network Science, Chiba Institute of Technology, Narashino, Japan
[7] Faculty of Human Sciences, Waseda University, Tokorozawa, Japan
jin@waseda.jp

Abstract. The COVID-19 pandemic has been making big impact on mental and physical health of youth. Recent research shows that the COVID-19 pandemic has exacerbated existing mental health problems due to the unique combination of public health crises and social isolation. The objective of this study is to integrate and analyze various health data sources to improve health care for youth during the COVID-19 pandemic. The focus of the research is to merge self-assessment data from individuals, data obtained from wearable devices, and health data based on Traditional Chinese Medicine (TCM), utilizing machine learning techniques to gain a comprehensive perspective of youth health. The experiment results showed that the correlation between the TCM-based Health Score (TCMHS) in the TCM dimension and the Wearable Device Stress-based Health Score (WDSHS) in wearable devices was stronger than the correlation between the Self-assessed Subjective Health Score (SSHS) and the WDSHS. On the other hand, activity calorie consumption was the most important feature to both the SSHS and WDSHS while resting heart rate affected the TCMHS most.

Keywords: Traditional Chinese medicine · Wearable Devices · LightGBM · Multidimensional health data analysis · COVID-19

1 Introduction

Youth health is a critical issue that needs to be addressed due to its impact on the overall well-being of adolescents and young adults. The holistic concept of youth health encompasses not only physical health but also mental, emotional, and social well-being.

V. G. Duffy (Ed.): HCII 2023, LNCS 14029, pp. 154–168, 2023.
https://doi.org/10.1007/978-3-031-35748-0_11

A positive state of physical, mental, and social functioning is necessary to enable young people to lead fulfilling lives and reach their full potential. In today's world, depression, anxiety, and stress (DAS) are the most common mental illnesses among youth [1], especially during the COVID-19 pandemic. Young people faced numerous challenges, such as remote online learning, social isolation, and economic uncertainty due to the COVID-19 pandemic, which affects their health and well-being [2]. To keep healthy in such a special period, youth are also paying more attention to their own health. Hence, it is important to ensure that young people have access to comprehensive and effective health care services.

Nowadays, wearable devices and health sensors are widely used to obtain the real-time health data [3, 4]. With the combination of sensors and wearable devices, we can easily identify the changes in regular activities of human body data. This application of digital health can be used for the early detection of symptoms and adverse changes in a patient's health status—which helps with timely medical interventions [5]. At the same time, machine learning algorithms can be applied to this data to provide personalized health recommendations based on individual characteristics and health conditions [6]. This has opened up new avenues for improving health care.

Additionally, Traditional Chinese Medicine (TCM) has been an integral part of health care for thousands of years, particularly in China and east Asia [7]. It focuses on the importance of balancing the physical, emotional, and spiritual aspects of health and considers the human body as an integrated system. TCM practitioners use four diagnostic methods, which are commonly called inspection (observation), auscultation and olfaction (listening and smelling), interrogation (questioning), and palpation (pulse examination), to gather information about a person's overall health and make a judgment about their health status [8]. The methods of TCM diagnosis are time-tested and effective and could also be used to collect one's health data.

This study aims to integrate and analyze multidimensional health data for youth health care during the COVID-19 pandemic. The research focuses on combining individual self-assessment data, data from wearable devices, and TCM health data, with machine learning to provide a comprehensive view of youth health.

Individual self-assessment of health data is highly subjective and may not accurately reflect an individual's actual health status. In contrast, data obtained from wearable devices can be relatively objective, but may lack a professional medical background. To address this issue, we incorporate the TCM approach of "four diagnostic methods" as a reference. By combining these three perspectives, a more comprehensive understanding of an individual's health can be achieved. The goal is to explore the relevant factors of the youth's health and build three regression models based on LightGBM (Light Gradient Boosting Machine) to use people's daily health features to better understand their health status.

Youth health requires comprehensive and effective health care services. By integrating multidimensional health data with modern data analysis techniques, a comprehensive view of youth health can be obtained, and personalized health care recommendations can be provided. This research contributes to advancing health care and improving youth health, particularly during the COVID-19 pandemic.

The rest of this paper is organized as follows. In Sect. 2, related work on wearable devices, the combination of TCM health assessment and wearable devices, and health data-related analysis using LightGBM are overviewed. In Sect. 3, we present the framework for multidimensional health data analysis in our study and describe the experiment procedures and analysis methods. In Sect. 4, experiment results are given and discussed. Finally, this study is summarized, the limitations are discussed, and potential avenues for future research are highlighted in Sect. 5.

2 Related Work

In this section, we succinctly present an overview of existing research works related to wearable devices, the combination of TCM health assessment and wearable devices, and health data related analysis using LightGBM.

2.1 Wearable Devices

In recent years, the widespread application of wearable devices in the field of health care and risk prevention has driven an ongoing surge of research related to wearable technology.

Especially during the COVID-19 pandemic, an increasing number of people are wearing wearable devices to monitor their health. Channa et al. [9] have shown that the COVID-19 pandemic has accelerated the growth of the wearables market, with increasing demand for devices that are multifunctional and easily customizable for specific applications. However, there are still challenges to be addressed in terms of design trade-offs, sensor improvements, power management, size reduction, computational algorithms, and security measures to fully realize the clinical potential of these wearables. On the other hand, Yen designed a three-parallel randomized controlled trial (RCT) to explore the effects of smart wearable devices on health-promoting lifestyles and quality of life [10]. The results showed that the smartwatch had significant effects on self-actualization, exercise, and stress management compared to the smartphone application, and the smart bracelet had a significant impact on self-actualization. The randomized controlled trial convinced us that smart wearable devices have potential benefits for promoting a healthy lifestyle and improving quality of life, which provided a foundation for our study.

2.2 The Combination of TCM Health Assessment and Wearable Devices

The integration of Traditional Chinese Medicine (TCM) diagnosis with modern technology has become a significant area of focus due to the advancements in information technology [11]. Zhou et al. [12] showed that the use of information and communications technology (ICT) devices allows for understanding the health status of the elderly and making behavior predictions, as well as using pulse manifestation data as a tool for health management and assisting in simple diagnoses. Dhinaharan et al. [13] pointed out that the implementation of advanced technology has resulted in the creation of the Typical Case Management System (TCMS), which provides support for TCM diagnosis and treatment. TCMS gathers a limited amount of personal information and carries out a comparative analysis of TCM knowledge maps to assess a person's health status, to ensure appropriate medical care.

2.3   LightGBM in Health Field

LightGBM was proposed by Ke et al. in 2017 [14], which contains two novel techniques: Gradient-based One-Side Sampling and Exclusive Feature Bundling to deal with a large number of data instances and a large number of features, respectively. Wang et al. [15] compared the performance of ML methods, including RF, XGBoost, and LightGBM, for miRNA identification in breast cancer patients. The evaluation was based on accuracy and logistic loss and LightGBM performed better, in which hsa-mir-139 was found to be a crucial target for breast cancer classification. The study showed that LightGBM is useful identifying and classifying miRNA targets in breast cancer. Rufo et al. [16] applied LightGBM to develop an accurate model for the diagnosis of diabetes. The results have shown that the LightGBM model outperformed other methods, such as KNN, SVM, NB, Bagging, RF, and XGBoost with an accuracy of 98.1%, an AUC of 98.1%, a sensitivity of 99.9%, and a specificity of 96.3% on the ZMHDD dataset.

3   Multidimensional Data Analysis Methods

In this section, we first present the framework of our study and the detailed procedures for multidimensional data analysis. Then, we introduce the methods for data analysis and modeling, which are correlation analysis and the LightGBM regression model.

3.1   Framework for Multidimensional Data Analysis

Figure 1 shows the framework for multidimensional data analysis in this study, which involves Data Collection, Data Integration and Cleaning, Statistical Analysis and Test, and Modeling with LightGBM Regression. The details are described as follows.

Data Collection.   The data is collected from multiple sources, such as the health indicators and activity records monitored and recorded by wearable devices, daily health self-assessment questionnaires reported by the subjects, and the TCM diagnosis and health assessment data.

Data Integration and Cleaning.   The data from multiple sources are integrated and cleaned. An integrated dataset is produced, for which independent variables are selected, and dependent variables are defined. In this study, three health scores as dependent variables are defined, namely Wearable Device Stress-based Health Score (WDSHS), Self-assessed Subjective Health Score (SSHS), and TCM-based Health Score (TCMHS), representing the three data sources.

Statistical Analysis and Test.   Firstly, correlations between variables in each dimension are analyzed and evaluated to understand the relationship between wearable devices, self-assessed health, and TCM-based health. Then, a statistical test is conducted to investigate the significance.

Modeling with LightGBM Regression.   Modeling with LightGBM regression is applied to compare the effects of these three targeted models to WDSHS, SSHS and TCMHS and determine the feature importance, respectively.

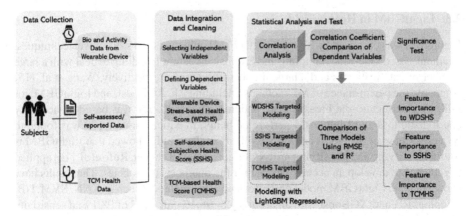

Fig. 1. The Framework for Multidimensional Data Analysis

3.2 Correlation Analysis and Statistical Test

The collected data is used to analyze the relationship between the daily health features recorded by the wearable devices, the subjective self-health report, and the TCM-based health assessment. We employ the correlation coefficient to examine the correlation between WDSHS, SSHS and TCMHS. The correlation coefficient is a statistical measure that is used to describe the relationship between two variables. It is a number that evaluates the strength of the linear relationship between these variables. By performing a correlation coefficient analysis on a dataset, it is possible to determine the presence of relationships between variables and predict if a change in one variable will lead to another change. Additionally, the strength of the relationship between two variables can be evaluated and if there is a non-linear relationship, it can also be detected.

There are three commonly used methods for calculating the correlation coefficient, including the Pearson Correlation Coefficient (PCC), the Spearman's rank correlation coefficient and Kendall rank correlation coefficient. The PCC requires that the variables follow a normal distribution, but the other two methods do not.

In this study, we further use a statistical test to investigate whether the obtained correlation coefficients have statistical significance. It assesses the statistical significance of the correlation coefficient by comparing it to a critical value (such as a normal distribution) and calculating the p-value. The p-value is then used to determine if the correlation coefficient is statistically significant.

3.3 Regression and Feature Importance Analysis Using LightGBM

In this study, LightGBM is adopted to model and analyze the importance of multiple dimensions in the dataset. LightGBM is a gradient boosting framework that uses tree-based learning. The key to the success of a tree model is to find the best split. While all other boosting methods solve it by growing the tree horizontally, LightGBM enables the tree to grow vertically, which treats leaves of the same layer differently, and thus avoiding unnecessary or low split gain. For example, the XGboost and LightGBM use the same loss reduction function to drop leaves that are not behaving well, while LightGBM restricts it as one-side sampling [17].

One reason that LightGBM can fulfill our need for this study is that the distribution of our selected features varies a lot. For example, the step number can be more than ten thousand while the resting heart rate is generally under one hundred. LightGBM can solve this problem without the need to bear normalization loss [18]. A more important reason we use LightGBM is that not only is it a tree based boosting model which can give us feature importance, but also it can provide us with more accurate regression score predictions [14]. Additionally, compared to other boosting tree models, training a LightGBM model apparently requires less memory and is much faster, and the result tends to be better.

As mentioned above in Sect. 3.1, we define three health scores, namely WDSHS, SSHS and TCMHS, to evaluate the health status of our experiment subjects. In this study, both our defined independent variables (i.e., WDSHS, SSHS and TCMHS) and selected dependent variables (concerned wearable device health features) are numeric. As a regression model can only have one dependent variable, three regression models are built corresponding to those three independent variables, respectively.

We build three targeted models to WDSHS, SSHS and TCMHS, and use RMSE (Root Mean Squared Error) and R^2 (Coefficient of Determination), expressed in Eqs. (1) and (2), to evaluate the effects of these models and determine the feature importance.

$$RMSE = \sqrt{\frac{1}{n} \sum_{i=1}^{n} (y_i - \widehat{y_i})^2} \tag{1}$$

$$R^2 = 1 - \frac{\sum_i (\widehat{y_i} - y_i)^2}{\sum_i (\overline{y_i} - y_i)^2} \tag{2}$$

4 Experiment Result and Discussion

4.1 Experiment Overview

In this study, we recruited 22 university students as the subjects, including 11 males and 11 females. This study was conducted under the approval of the Ethics Review Committee on Research with Human Subjects of Waseda University, Japan (No. 2018-092), and all subjects for this experiment signed the informed consent.

In our experiment, subjects are requested to wear the wearable device (Huawei Band 7) to monitor and record the daily health indicators and activity data from December 5, 2022 to January 26, 2023. In addition, SSHS on a scale of one to five is recorded by subjects every day and reported weekly during the period of the experiment every day. Furthermore, TCM-based health data was collected once a week using TCM diagnostic methods, including inspection, listening, palpation, and auscultation, and a health score with the range of one to ten is given according to TCM health data of the past week.

At the end of the experiment, 20 full datasets were submitted from subjects. Then, we removed the four datasets with too many missing values. Finally, 16 datasets were used for analysis, which represented the health data of 16 subjects (7 males and 9 females at the ages of the twenties) in 53 days, a total of 848 records.

4.2 Data Preprocessing

To integrate these 16 datasets into one dataset for analysis in this study, we selected 15 independent variables from the health feature data recorded in the wearable device, which is shown in Table 1.

Table 1. Variables for Feature Data from Wearable Devices

Group	Variable Name	Description
Bio Indicators	RestingHeartRate	Resting Heart Rate
	MinBloodOxygen	Minimum Blood Oxygen
	MaxBloodOxygen	Maximum Blood Oxygen
Sleep Indicators	SleepScore	Sleep Score
	DeepSleepContinuity	Deep Sleep Continuity
	WakeUpCounts	Wake Up Counts
	BreathingQuality	Breathing Quality
	TotalSleepDuration	Total Sleep Duration
	TotalDeepSleepDuration	Total Deep Sleep Duration
	TotalLightSleepDuration	Total Light Sleep Duration
	TotalREMSleepDuration	Total Rapid Eye Movement Sleep Duration
Activity Indicators	ActivityCalConsumption	Activity Calories Consumption
	StepNumber	Step Number
	StepDistance	Step Distance
	MHIntensityExcerciseTime	Moderate to High Intensity Exercise Time

The three defined dependent variables, WDSHS, SSHS and TCMHS, are obtained as follows. Firstly, WDSHS is calculated from the stress score given by the wearable device, expressed in Eq. (3).

$$WDSHS = 5 - \frac{StressScore}{20} \qquad (3)$$

where *StressScore* is ranged from 0 to 100, and the score is higher, the stress is greater. We convert it to a scale of one to five. Next, SSHS is the score which is directly assessed and reported by the subjects themselves in a scale of one to five. Thirdly, TCMHS is converted from the original TCM-based assessment score (*TCMAssessmentScore*) with a range of one to ten by Eq. (4), resulting in a value of one to five.

$$TCMHS = \frac{TCMAssessmentScore}{2} \qquad (4)$$

For the missing values in data, including the stress score, from wearable devices, we fill them with the mean of each variable for each subject. Since the values of SSHS and TCMHS are given weekly, we simply transfer them into daily values for the past week.

4.3   Correlation Analysis Results

After preprocessing the data, we found that most of the variables in the dataset do not follow a normal distribution. Therefore, we could only take Spearman's rank correlation coefficient and Kendall's rank correlation coefficient into consideration. However, there were too many common rankings in the data sampled if using the Spearman method. Finally, Kendall's rank correlation coefficient was chosen for the evaluation.

The following steps were taken to provide a measure of the strength and direction of the relationship between two variables and the evidence of the statistical significance of the relationship:

1. Calculation of the Kendall Correlation Coefficient (tau): The Kendall Correlation Coefficient (tau) was calculated as a measure of the strength and direction of the relationship between two variables.
2. Hypothesis Testing: Using statistical methods to perform a hypothesis test to determine the statistical significance of the correlation coefficient by comparing the calculated tau statistic to a critical value from the normal distribution and calculating the p-value.
3. Interpretation of the p-value: The p-value was used to determine the statistical significance of the correlation coefficient, with a p-value less than 0.05 indicating that the correlation is statistically significant and suggesting that the relationship between two variables is not due to chance.

As mentioned above, the purpose of correlation analysis is to evaluate the correlation between variables in each dimension, and to understand the relationship between TCM-based health, self-assessed health, and health score by wearable devices. Due to the non-normal distribution of variables in the dataset and the inability of the Pearson test to handle multi-variable rankings, we used Kendall rank correlation analysis as a statistical method to evaluate the correlation coefficients between the variables in the dataset.

We used the R software to evaluate the Kendall Correlation Coefficient (tau). Figure 2 shows the heatmap of correlations among variables. Finally, we determined the correlation between each variable based on the p-value obtained from the hypothesis test for statistical significance.

In the wearable devices dimension, the indicators monitored by wearable devices are divided into five subdimensions of exercise, sleep, breathing, heart rate, and stress scores. To avoid potential collinearity problems, the relationship between variables in these five subdimensions is no longer analyzed. The results showed that in the TCM dimension, the correlation between two variables is extremely weak. The highest Kendall Correlation Coefficient (tau) between the variables TCMHS and WDSHS was 0.34, with a p-value < 0.001. Therefore, we consider TCMHS and WDSHS to have weak correlation in the TCM dimension. In the self-assessed health dimension, the number of variables with weak correlations is less than that in the TCM dimension, but the average correlation coefficient between variables is slightly higher compared to the TCM dimension. Among the variables that belong to the self-assessed health dimension, the highest correlation was between Resting Heart Rate and SSHS, with a correlation score of -0.218, a p-value < 0.001, and a significance level of 0.05. Therefore, we consider that Resting Heart Rate and SSHS have a weak negative correlation in the self-assessed health dimension. In

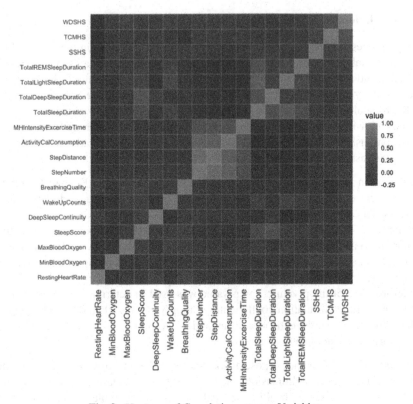

Fig. 2. Heatmap of Correlations among Variables

the wearable devices dimension, the correlation between variables is roughly equal to that in the TCM dimension. Besides the variables TCMHS and WDSHS, the strongest correlation was found between Resting Heart Rate and WDSHS, with a correlation score of -0.26, a p-value of <0.001, and a significance level of 0.05, indicating a weak negative correlation.

According to the analysis results, it was easy to see that the variables TCMHS, SSHS, RestingHeartRate, and variable WDSHS have the strongest correlation among them. Considering that RestingHeartRate and WDSHS belong to the wearable device dimension, the WDSHS with the highest correlation score is selected as the representative variable for wearable devices for further analysis.

Figure 3 shows that the correlation coefficients between the three representative variables of the three dimensions are generally lower than 0.4, but the p-values are all less than 0.001. Therefore, there was a correlation between these three variables. Among the three variables, the strongest correlation was found between TCMHS and WDSHS, followed by the correlation between SSHS and WDSHS, and finally, the correlation between SSHS and TCMHS.

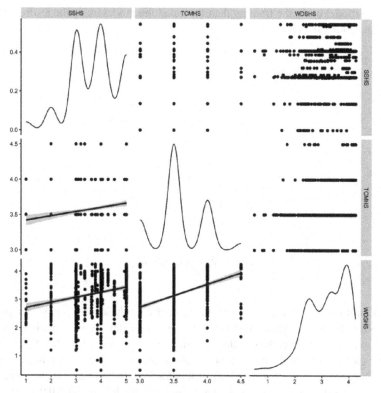

Fig. 3. Correlation Matrix Plot between WDSHS, SSHS and TCMHS

4.4 LightGBM Regression Analysis Results

Modeling Procedure. Our built models were run based on Python's Jupyter Notebook, which provided a runtime environment consisting of Python 3.9, NumPy 1.19.5, scikit-learn 1.0.2, and the package of LightGBM. Firstly, we built three models with 3 Ys respectively standing for three independent variables, i.e., WDSHS, SSHS and TCMHS. Secondly, we split the training and testing dataset 80 to 20 percent randomly. Thirdly, we tried and modified the model parameters to achieve the best fit. After several attempts, the parameters shown in Fig. 4 were determined.

As shown in the Fig. 4, 'task': 'train' means that our task was to train the model. Gradient boosting decision tree ('gbdt') was used. Since we took a regression model, the objective is regression. The parameter 'metric': {'rmse'} means that we only save the result if the RMSE is smaller. We did not change the default setting of 'learning_rate' as 0.1'. The most important one is 'num_leaves', which stands for how many leaves are on one tree. It directly affects the shape of a tree, which in turn greatly affects the results. After seven trials, we found the RMSE is the least when this parameter is equal to 23. And 'num_iteration' is set to 1000, which stands for that we were iterating 1000 times. The other parameters are default settings, and we did not change them. Finally, we trained the model using the training dataset, tested the model using the testing dataset, and calculated the feature importance.

```
params = {
           'task' : 'train',
           'boosting_type' : 'gbdt',
           'objective' : 'regression',
           'metric' : {'rmse'},
           'learning_rate' : 0.1,
           'num_leaves' : 23,
           'min_data_in_leaf' : 1,
           'num_iteration' : 1000,
           'verbose' : 0
}
```

Fig. 4. Parameter Setting

Model Evaluation. Table 2 shows the contrast between these three regression models. In the table, the RMSE value represents the degree of deviation of predicted values and true values. Therefore, the smaller the value, the better the model fits. On the other hand, R^2 can be commonly understood as using the mean as the error benchmark to see whether the forecast error is greater or less than the mean, and it is the greater the value, the better the model fits. As shown in the table, for RMSE, TCMHS < WDSHS < SSHS, which means that the model best predicted the TCM Health Score, while the model is not good at predicting the trend of the variation of SSHS. This may be because the SSHS indicator is too subjective, and the health score obtained by pulse diagnosis of TCM may have more regular patterns. This also implies that when it comes to the judgment of health status, TCM diagnosis is more reliable than the other two methods. It is interesting that the table shows that for R^2, WDSHS > TCMHS > ISHS. This means the WDSHS model best fits, since the stress score itself is calculated by a certain pattern of these health feature data. However, a significant contrast can also be found that is similar to the findings of RMSE described above, which shows the model predicting TCM-based health scores behaves better.

Table 2. Results for LightGBM Regression Model Comparison

Targeted Model	RMSE	R^2
WDSHS	0.56	0.35
SSHS	0.86	0.15
TCMHS	0.31	0.32

Feature Importance. The results are shown in Figs. 5, 6 and 7. Figure 5 shows the feature importance when predicting WDSHS. It is not difficult to find that the ActivityCalConsumption of the activity group, the TotalSleepDuration of the sleep group and the RestingHeartRate of the bio group are the top three. However, it can also be found that wearable devices attach great importance to sleep, counting for three of the top five. From Fig. 5, we can see that there is a strong correlation between the calculation of wearable device stress value and overall sleep.

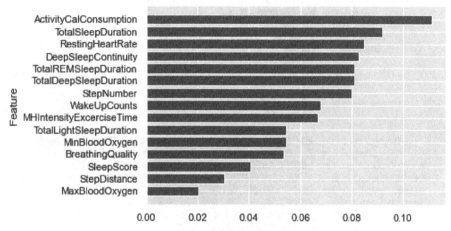

Fig. 5. Feature Importance to WDSHS

From Fig. 6, we can see that the factors that most affect self-assessment is the daily activity calorie consumption, the same as for WDSHS. This feature is the only one in the activity group that ranks in the top five of SSHS, which could be regarded as the direct correlation between activity calories and fatigue. In the second and the fifth places are the RestingHeartRate and MinBloodOxygen, both from the bio group, which are indicators of direct discomfort caused by abnormalities. It is natural to affect people's self-health cognition to such a large extent. Finally, the third and fourth places belong to the sleep group. These two indicators determine how a person rests, which largely affects people's self-assessment in subjective feelings.

Figure 7 shows the importance of these health features to the diagnosis of TCM. Of the top five most important features, the top one is the resting heart rate of the bio group, and the second and third places are all daily activities. It is worth mentioning that two activity features come up in the top three. And two features of the sleep group are in fourth and fifth places. We can conclude that these indicators are more objective than subjective self-assessments, which proves the pattern and regularity of TCM's diagnosis for health scores.

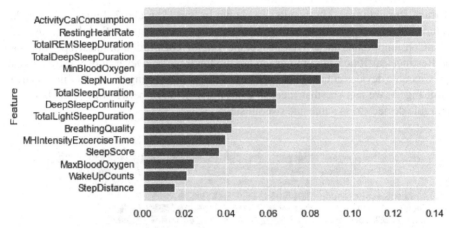

Fig. 6. Feature Importance to SSHS

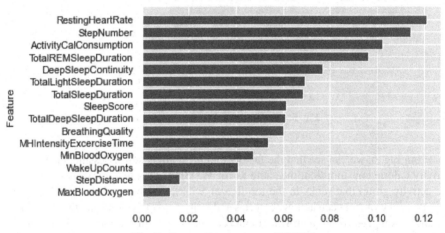

Fig. 7. Feature Importance to TCMHS

5 Conclusion

The findings of this study provide insights into the relationship between the three dimensions of health assessment. By understanding the correlation between the various variables, future studies can focus on developing more comprehensive and accurate methods for data analysis and health assessment. It is also worth mentioning that the results of the feature importance analysis highlight the significance of daily activities in determining one's health status. This indicates the importance of maintaining a healthy lifestyle, not just in terms of physical activity, but also in terms of diet and calorie consumption. Overall, this study provides valuable insights into the relationship between TCM pulse diagnosis, wearable devices, and self-assessed health scores. The results demonstrate the importance of taking a holistic approach to health assessment and the significance of daily activities in determining one's health status.

This study has two limitations. First, due to the impact of the pandemic and time constraints, the sample size utilized in this experiment is relatively limited. Consequently, the model developed from these data may exhibit an insufficient degree of stability. Second, during the experiment, a multitude of variables pertaining to the physiological health of adolescents was scrutinized. However, the consideration given to their psychological health was inadequate. Despite incorporating stress as a factor in our observations, we contend that there remains a necessity for additional research in the realm of mental health among adolescents.

In future research, we aim to focus on variable selection and examine the accuracy of the model while reducing the number of variables in the model to find the features with high importance, and weight them to obtain a personalized health score, which is expected to provide an improved understanding of individual health compared to the existing health score. Additionally, we will explore the relevance of TCM in providing theoretical support for the results of this study, and define a new composite health measure taking into account of multidimensional evidence based on wearable devices, individual self-subjective assessments and medical diagnoses to provide a comprehensive understanding of individual health.

Acknowledgement. The work was supported in part by 2022–2024 Masaru Ibuka Foundation Research Project on Oriental Medicine, 2020–2025 JSPS A3 Foresight Program (Grant No. JPJSA3F20200001), and 2022 JST SPRING (Grant No. JPMJSP2128).

References

1. Hicks, T., Heastie, S.: High school to college transition: a profile of the stressors, physical and psychological health issues that affect the first-year on-campus college student. J. Cult. Divers. **15**(3), 143–147 (2008)
2. Courtney, D., Watson, P., Battaglia, M., Mulsant, B.H., Szatmari, P.: COVID-19 impacts on child and youth anxiety and depression: challenges and opportunities. Can. J. Psychiatry **65**(10), 688–691 (2020)
3. Tago, K., Takagi, K., Jin, Q.: Detection of health abnormality considering latent factors inducing a disease. IEEE Access **8**, 139433–139443 (2020)
4. Tago, K., Nishimura, S., Ogihara, A., Jin, Q.: Improving diagnosis estimation by considering the periodic span of the life cycle based on personal health data. Big Data Res. **23** (2020)
5. Vijayalakshmi, K., Uma, S., Bhuvanya, R., Suresh, A.: A demand for wearable devices in health care. Int. J. Eng. Technol. (UAE) **7**, 1–4 (2018)
6. Ghazal, T.M., et al.: IoT for smart cities: machine learning approaches in smart healthcare—a review. Future Internet **13**, 218 (2021)
7. Wang, W., Zhou, H., Yang, Y.F., Sang, B.S., Liu, L.: Current policies and measures on the development of traditional Chinese medicine in China. Pharmacol. Res. **163**, 105187 (2020)
8. Zhao, C., Li, G.Z., Wang, C., Niu, J.: Advances in patient classification for traditional Chinese medicine: a machine learning perspective. Evid.-Based Complement. Altern. Med. eCAM (2015)
9. Channa, A., Popescu, N., Skibinska, J., Burget, R.: The rise of wearable devices during the COVID-19 pandemic: a systematic review. Sensors (Basel) **21**(17), 5787 (2021)
10. Yen, H.-Y.: Smart wearable devices as a psychological intervention for healthy lifestyle and quality of life: a randomized controlled trial. Qual. Life Res. **30**(3), 791–802 (2020). https://doi.org/10.1007/s11136-020-02680-6

11. Cao, R., Cao, C., Xie, Q., Jia, Z.: Practical research of conceptual system framework based on TCM basic theory. In: Proceedings of 2012 IEEE 14th International Conference on e-Health Networking, Applications and Services (Healthcom), pp. 357–360, Beijing, China (2012)
12. Zhou, S., Ogihara, A., Nishimura, S., Jin, Q.: Analysis of health changes and the association of health indicators in the elderly using TCM pulse diagnosis assisted with ICT devices: a time series study. Eur. J. Integr. Med. **27**, 105–113 (2019)
13. Nagamalai, D., Renault, E., Dhanuskodi, M.: Advances in Parallel, Distributed Computing. Communications in Computer and Information Science, vol. 203 (2011)
14. Ke, G., et al.: LightGBM: a highly efficient gradient boosting decision tree. In: Proceedings of 31st Conference on Neural Information Processing Systems (NIPS 2017), Long Beach, CA, USA (2017)
15. Wang, D., Zhang, Y., Zhao, Y.: LightGBM: an effective miRNA classification method in breast cancer patients. In: Proceedings of 2017 International Conference on Computational Biology and Bioinformatics (ICCBB 2017), pp. 7–11, Newark, NJ, USA (2017)
16. Rufo, D., Debelee, T., Ibenthal, A., Negera, W.: Diagnosis of diabetes mellitus using gradient boosting machine (LightGBM). Diagnostics **11**, 1714 (2021)
17. Chen, T., Carlos G.: XGBoost: a scalable tree boosting system. In: Proceedings of 22nd ACM SIGKDD International Conference on Knowledge Discovery and Data Mining (KDD 2016), pp. 785–794, New York, NY, USA (2016)
18. Sekine, Y., Kasuya, S., Tago, K.: Influence analysis of the screen time on daily exercise based on the personal activity factor model. In: Proceedings of 2022 IEEE 10th Region 10 Humanitarian Technology Conference (R10-HTC), Hyderabad, India (2022)

Design for Shoulder and Neck Pain Based on Yoga Asanas Practice

Yeqi Wu[1], Ziyan Dong[1], Xinran Liu[1], Xiang Wu[1], Tianfeng Xu[1], Xiangyu Liu[2(✉)], and Li Xu[1(✉)]

[1] School of Art Design and Media, East China University of Science and Technology, Shanghai, China
xuli@ecust.edu.cn
[2] College of Communication and Art Design, University of Shanghai for Science and Technology, Shanghai, China
liuxiangyu@usst.edu.cn

Abstract. With shoulder and neck pain prevalent worldwide and getting younger, yoga as physical therapy can effectively relieve shoulder and neck pain. However, in daily yoga training, the inability to achieve standard movements affects the exercise effect and causes bodily injury. The paper proposes the necessity and significance of monitoring the yoga exercise in place, frequency, intensity time, etc. Through experiments, we provide data reference for the later product design, define the product's demand point and propose the wearable device's creation. It can guide the user to perform the correct yoga exercise to relieve shoulder and neck pain and has particular social significance.

Keywords: Shoulder and neck pain · Yoga · Product Design

1 Introduction

1.1 Background

Shoulder and Neck Pain. Shoulder and neck pain is caused by repetitive strain on the musculoskeletal system. It is considered a musculoskeletal disorder (MSD) in severe cases and one of the top five chronic illnesses in developing countries. It is found all over the world [1]. The prevalence in the adult population is 30–50%, peaking at roughly 45 years of age [1]. More than one-third of patients endure recurrence after recovery, with women being more likely than men to develop shoulder and neck discomfort [2]. According to studies, shoulder and neck pain affects breathing, prevents blood from flowing easily to the brain, squeezes the nerves around the neck, and causes lesions in body regions. In addition to raising medical expenditures and lowing the quality of life, it diminishes job productivity, increases the risk of future long-term sick leave, impairs one's career, and places a substantial socioeconomic burden on patients and society.

Our constant use of cell phones and computers at work and daily life puts our shoulders and necks in a fixed position for extended periods. This incorrect posture strains the muscles and raises their level of tension, unintentionally causing shoulder and neck pain. In addition, younger people have increasingly begun to experience shoulder and neck pain in recent years due to the rapid development of technology and the economy, in recent years. According to a study looking into factors associated with neck and shoulder pain in young adults, increased screen-based activities (prolonged computer and cell phone use) without physical exercise led to a higher prevalence of neck pain in adults [3]. Therefore, it is reasonable to anticipate that the sickness will affect many individuals in the coming decades [1], which will substantially impact them. Therefore, it is crucial to treat and alleviate shoulder and neck pain quickly.

Yoga. According to a study, physical therapies, including Tui Na (a type of Chinese manual medicine), massage, acupuncture, tai chi, yoga, Pilates, etc., are helpful alleviated neck discomfort in addition to surgical treatment. Yoga can effectively relieve shoulder and neck muscular fatigue as a kind of strength and flexibility training and rectify postural errors and muscle imbalances. It can also promote joint mobility and muscle strength. Holger Cramer et al. [4] conducted a comprehensive literature review on the benefits of yoga on chronic neck pain and its related disability, quality of life, and mood, indicating that yoga may be a promising therapeutic option. Abhinav Mohan [5] discovered that yoga therapies lowered pain intensity in adults with CNNP (chronic non-specific neck pain) and increased cervical spine range of motion and quality of life with yoga interventions. Yoga and general exercise were each evaluated in-dependently for their impact on neck discomfort by Holger Cramer et al. [6]. Patients in the yoga group experienced neck pain that was much less severe than that of the exercise group after the 9-week investigation, indicating that yoga is more beneficial than general exercise in treating chronic non-specific neck pain. Jaclyn N Chopp-Hurley et al. [7] used electromyography to recode muscle activity in the trapezius and serratus anterior throughout 15 yoga positions. They discovered that muscle activity changed depending on the carriage stance. Yoga does not require a lot of fitness equipment and only takes up a little space; it is also simple to practice and understand. Moreover, Jari Ylinen [8] discovered that pain alleviation could be first dictated with low-cost stretching activities as an acceptable intervention therapy. As a result, yoga is more suited as an intervention therapy for those who suffer from shoulder and neck pain.

1.2 Status

The standard yoga positions are difficult for beginners to learn by watching videos alone, which can have two impacts. Firstly ineffective, producing little overall progress. Second, despite the public's perception that yoga is a gentle and risk-free kind of exercise, yoga contains the same risks of injury as any other form of physical activity [9]. According to research, performing yoga exercises on one's own by someone unfamiliar with conventional poses can result in many problems, including overstretching and repetitive muscle strain [10]. A study by Melody Lee [11] indicated that those with low bone mass or osteoporosis could potentially sustain compression fractures or deformities in excessive spinal flexion and extension postures.

1.3 Purpose and Significance

This paper demonstrated the effects of various yoga asanas (Bull Face Pose, Camel Pose, and Cobra Pose) on shoulder and neck muscles to evaluate whether it is essential to track the location, frequency, and intensity of yoga exercises. We will use the experiment to gather data for future product design, identify the market for the product, and propose developing a wearable gadget to instruct users on how to practice yoga correctly, prevent accidents linked to yoga, and assist people with shoulder and neck problems.

2 Methods

2.1 Overview of Testing Protocol

16 Participants were randomly assigned to the control group (n = 4), the bull-faced group (n = 4), the camel group (n = 4), and the cobra group (n = 4) for a 2-week intervention. This study had two assessments: one before the practice and one after. Before and after the test, the visual analog scale values for neck pain and neck muscle endurance were recorded. Afterward, each participant received instruction in yoga asana exercises, and the examiner recorded the values of EMG activity. The test lasted two weeks (3 days of training per week). Each yoga practice session had a time constraint of 30 s and lasted between 5 and 15 min. The data were then condensed and statistically examined. Each participant provided written informed consent.

2.2 Participants

Sixteen volunteers (eight females and eight males) between the ages of 21 and 30 were invited to participate in this study. The average age of the sample was 25.6 years (minimum 22 years and maximum 27 years). They were requested to complete an online survey before the test to provide information about each subject. None suffered a spinal cord injury or a congenital or acquired neuromuscular illness. Before the experiment, each participant was fully informed of all the specifics, including that:

- Neck pain intensity assessment.
- Neck muscle endurance tests.
- EMG electrode placement, MVC testing, and selected yoga pose.
- Potential dermatological risk of allergy during the test. Temporary soreness of the shoulder and neck muscles at the end of the investigation.

2.3 Procedures

Neck Pain Intensity Assessment. The Visual Analogue Scale (VAS) is often utilized in pain evaluation approaches. Participants do not need to fill out a lengthy form during testing; instead, they look at the VAS scale and say a number between 0 and 10. The numbers "0" and "10" represent "no pain" and "maximum pain," respectively [12]. Neck pain, muscle tightness in the back of the shoulder, and pain from palpable muscle pressure are the three essential criteria for identifying shoulder and neck muscle pain [13].

The test was carried out as follows. The examiner standardized the participants' sitting positions so that there were fewer disparities between them and no compensatory trunk movements could occur. All participants sat in the same chair with their feet on the floor and their hands placed under their hips [14, 15]. To promote soft tissue compliance in the neck, each participant had a neck warm-up as directed by the examiner [14]. Before collecting data, the examiner would show the actions to the participants (flexion, extension, rotation, and lateral bending) [16] (see Fig. 1). Participants were required to attain an extended possible range of motion in the cervical spine while providing VAS values. To achieve the average values, all participants completed three tests before (Pre-VAS) and After (Post-VAS) the yoga exercise. The test was repeated two weeks later.

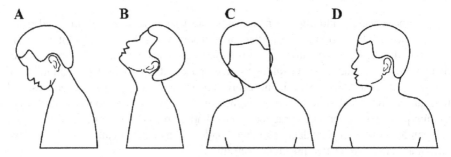

Fig. 1. Cervical spine movements: (A) flexion, (B) extension, (C) lateral bending, (D) rotation.

Neck Muscle Endurance Tests. The neck flexor and extensor endurance tests are valid and dependable in testing static neck muscular endurance.

Muscular Endurance of the Neck Flexors. The following is how the test was carried out. The participant was lying on a flat surface. All participants were instructed to place their palm on a table precisely behind the participant's head, resulting in a slightly flexed upper neck posture (see Fig. 2). The participant was asked to gently bend the upper neck, which involves lifting the head and holding isometric forcing until it is about 2.5 cm from the examiner's hand. The test was stopped if the participant couldn't keep their head in position and was terminated after more than 60 s [17, 18], and the length was measured in seconds [19]. The maximum hold time was recorded when the test was conducted twice, with a three-minute break in between. The cervical extensor endurance test was performed after 20 min of rest following the completion of the cervical flexor endurance test.

Muscular Endurance of the Neck Extensors. The procedure for the test was as follows. The participant was required to maintain a horizontal cervical spine and retract their chin while lying on a flat platform with their arms by their sides and their head protruding beyond the border of the surface. An examiner from the staff wrapped a goniometer around the participant's head and fastened an elastic magic band to it above the head. The strap was then used to suspend a weight, which lifted the weight off the ground (see Fig. 3). When the examiner removed the support from the participant's head, the

Fig. 2. Position of the subject during the neck flexor endurance test.

test began. The test was terminated if the neck position deviated more than 5° from horizontal (as assessed by a goniometer). After more than 180 s of testing, it was stopped [17, 18]. The longest hold time was reported when the test was conducted twice with a three-minute break in between.

The above tests must be performed again in two weeks.

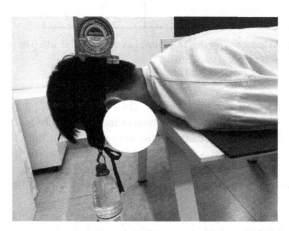

Fig. 3. Position of the subject during the neck extensor endurance test.

Surface Electromyography

Selection of Muscles for Seems Analysis. The following right arm muscles were chosen for shoulder and neck pain investigation: Trapezius, Scalenes, and Levator Scap, since they are the primary muscles involved in the mobility and control of the shoulder and neck.

Preparation of Skin and Placement of Electrodes. The skin was cleaned with a scrub and 70% alcohol to minimize resistance before applying the electrodes. If necessary, the skin was further shaved. Then high-density surface electromyography electrodes (HD-sEMG) were placed on the participant's muscles. The electrodes for the trapezius and scapular lift muscles were identified with the center of the electrode located two-thirds of the distance from the seventh cervical spine at the vertebra (C7) to the lateral edge of the acromion; the electrodes for the rhomboid muscle were placed lateral and superior to the neck and clavicular junction (see Fig. 4). Finally, the medical tape was used to secure the electrodes. A 5-second resting recording was conducted after the electrode implantation [20] to eliminate the underlying noise from the recording. The participant contracted the muscle and checked the electrode's placement by observing the EMG signal on an oscilloscope.

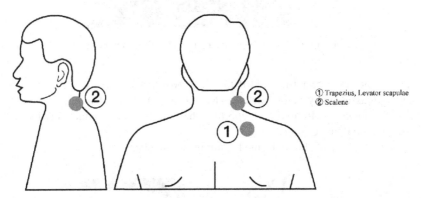

Fig. 4. Placement of electrodes for the Trapezius, Levator scapulae site. The same electrode was used on the Levator scapulae and trapezius.

Maximum Voluntary Contractions (MVCs). The Maximum Voluntary Isometric Contractions (MVCs) test is a standardized method of measuring muscle strength in patients with neuromuscular diseases. It can evaluate how strong their muscles are and assess how successful treatment approaches are (yoga). The power of the participant's right shoulder was selected for this test to collect EMG data. The test position matched the manual muscle testing position depicted in texts that physical therapists frequently refer to.

The examiner was to apply as much manual resistance as possible gradually. Participants were instructed to exert their entire potential force for one second, hold it for five seconds, and then relax for the remaining time. During the test, examiners verbally encouraged participants and loudly counted the seconds to enhance muscle activation. The examiner thoroughly observed participants to ensure they did not try compensatory exercises. If the test was inaccurate, it was stopped and redone [21]. For Trapezius and Levator scapulae, the participant sat in a chair with knees and hips bent at 90°, placed the dominant arm at 90° abducted on the frontal plane, hands facing down, and neck extended and rotated to the non-dominant side (examiner was positioned behind the individual and provided elbow resistance.) (shown in Fig. 5); For Scalenes, the participant was supine, hands were placed at their sides, and the neck was extended and rotated to the non-dominant side (examiner was positioned next to the individual and provided head resistance.) (shown in Fig. 6). Each muscle received MVC test twice, with a 30-second break in between each test.

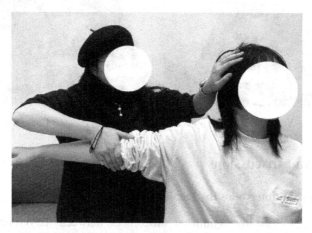

Fig. 5. Trapezius and Levator scapulae MVC test position.

Fig. 6. Scalenes MVC test position

Yoga Poses. The examiner gives verbal and written directions and reference photographs for each posture. On their yoga mats, participants practiced the Bull Face Pose, Cobra Pose, and Camel Pose (see Fig. 7). Participants were needed to hold each standard stance for 15 s to complete the trial. The yoga intervention lasted two weeks, with three training days per week, and electromyographic data were gathered at the first and last practice sessions.

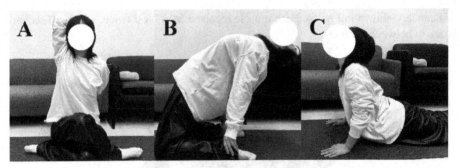

Fig. 7. Yoga Pose: (A) Bull Face Pose, (B) Cobra Pose, (C) Camel Pose.

3 Results and Discussions

3.1 Basic Information About the Participants

There were no statistically significant differences between the groups regarding participants' age, BMI, gender, or disease duration. It is shown in Table 1.

Table 1. Personal information of subjects participating in the experiment

Subjects	Gender	Age(year)	Height(cm)	Weight(kg)	BMI
1	F	23	161	56	21.6
2	F	23	162	46	17.5
3	F	24	164	48	17.8
4	F	23	161	52	20.1
5	M	26	175	68	22.2
6	F	25	160	70	27.34
7	F	23	168	58	20.5
8	F	23	158	47	18.8
9	M	21	173	63	21.0
10	M	22	183	62	18.5
11	M	23	170	60	20.7
12	F	21	152	55	23.8
13	M	24	170	55	19.0
14	M	25	173	65	21.7
15	M	26	172	68	23.0
16	M	26	172	86	29.1

3.2 Neck Pain Intensity and Neck Muscle Endurance

Visual Analogue Scale (VAS): Table 2 displays the pain intensity differences between the experimental and control groups and the statistical analysis of the groups. This is similar to another study. Anders et al. [22] also used an analog scale to quantify the pain level in the patient's muscles. When the pain intensity of the experimental and control groups was compared after two weeks of yoga intervention, there was a significant difference between the two groups. The pain was significantly reduced in the experimental group compared to the control group. Several other studies comparing the results of various workout regimens on the shoulder and neck muscles were discovered while exploring the literature. According to a survey by Lars L. Andersen [23], the VAS values likewise showed a decline and significant pain alleviation after ten weeks of targeted training for the shoulder and arm muscles. The effect persisted even after the exercises stopped. Since muscle activation helps to relieve muscle pain and stiffness, this study implies that practicing yoga is a task that involves muscle activation. Various stances showed different improvements. Additionally, because VAS values are primarily subjective, future research must explore more impartial and trustworthy ways to measure the intensity of muscular pain.

Table 2. The Visual Analogue Scale (VAS) results between the treatment and control groups.

	Subjects	Mean	SD	P
Treatment Group	1	2.61 ± 1.14	0.22 ± 0.17	0.003**
	2	2.11 ± 0.96	0.67 ± 0.70	0.001**
	3	3.22 ± 1.44	1.44 ± 0.98	0.003**
	4	4.06 ± 1.47	1.83 ± 0.62	0.007**
	5	2.39 ± 0.33	1.22 ± 0.40	0.006**
	6	2.22 ± 1.93	1.44 ± 2.01	0.034*
	7	3.00 ± 1.79	2.17 ± 1.24	0.022*
	8	1.33 ± 0.94	0.39 ± 0.49	0.034*
	9	0.94 ± 0.83	0.33 ± 0.30	0.048*
	10	2.22 ± 1.05	1.17 ± 0.86	0.008**
	11	2.61 ± 0.77	1.61 ± 0.65	0.000**
	12	1.28 ± 0.80	0.89 ± 0.72	0.013*
Control Group	13	1.61 ± 1.02	1.56 ± 0.83	0.741
	14	1.78 ± 1.17	1.50 ± 0.78	0.383
	15	1.56 ± 0.96	1.39 ± 0.77	0.203
	16	1.28 ± 1.02	1.33 ± 0.60	0.889

Abbreviations: * $p < 0.05$ ** $p < 0.01$

Neck Endurance Test: According to the neck endurance test results, all experimental groups had significantly longer neck flexor and extensor endurance times than the control group following two weeks of yoga intervention, as indicated in Table 3. A neck muscle endurance test was also used to assess muscle status in a study by Stephen J. [19], and he concluded that it was trustworthy. Yoga stretches the muscles, which can improve the deep neck flexors' static endurance. This is consistent with D. Falla's study [24], which involved testing and massaging several shoulder and neck muscular groups. Falla concluded that by stretching the muscles, their activation level at rest or low fatigue might decrease, increasing neck endurance. So, from this result, practicing yoga can raise the neck muscles' static endurance, effectively alleviating neck pain and enhancing neck function. The level of effort of the participants influences the static neck endurance test. Therefore, future research could eliminate testing errors by objectifying pain indices data using more measurement techniques.

Table 3. Mean holding time for an endurance test.

	PRE	POST
Neck flexor test	23.3	28.9
Range	8–56	10–76
Neck extensor test	104.4	121.7
Range	33–170	38–178

3.3 EMG

The Root means square of EMG activation expressed as %MVIC for each muscle analyzed in the three yoga poses is presented. The most significant Trapezius and Levator scapulae activation occurred in the Bull Face pose, followed by the type Camel Pose. Bull Face Pose and then Cobra Pose most significant greatest scalenus activation occurred in Camel Pose, followed by Bull Face Pose.

As previously hypothesized, it was able to observe that yoga exercises all activated the shoulder and neck muscles to varying degrees. For muscle activity comparison, 0–20% MVIC was considered as low muscle activity, 21–40% MVIC as moderate muscle activity, 41–60% MVIC as high muscle activity, and >60% MVIC as very high muscle activity [25]. Exercises that produce moderate EMG activity (21–40% MVIC) have been created to create stimuli that increase muscular endurance, while those submitted make high and very high EMG activity (41–60% MVIC and above 61% MVIC, respectively, make appropriate stimuli to induce strength increases [26]. Secondly, the degree of activation of muscle activity varied among the different yoga asanas in this sample. Therefore, yoga may be a beneficial exercise practice that activates the muscles at the shoulder and neck, helping to develop muscle strength and reduce shoulder and neck muscle pain caused by work. Limitations of the study also need to be considered. First, the yoga exercises were provided to the participants only with verbal and pictorial postural correction cues, which may have led to the participants' lack of standard postures. In addition, the current study only considered unilateral muscle activity in healthy participants.

This study found that these three yoga poses can stretch the shoulder and neck muscles and improve the exercise of neck and shoulder girdle strength, thus increasing the static endurance of deep neck flexors, promoting muscle movement, and relieving muscle pain. In other words, it will have a positive impact effect after the correctness of yoga poses is guaranteed. And but in daily yoga training, it is difficult to make the muscles get enough stimulation because of the inability to reach the average, thus affecting the effect of the exercise. In the usual practice, it isn't easy to ensure the impact of the exerted rain. I designed a wearable product to guide the user to perform the correct yoga practice and relieve shoulder and neck pain.

4   Product Design

4.1   Definition

This design is a clinically validated wearable device that can track muscle in real time. It is worn by the user during exercise and monitors the power level in real-time. It is synchronized via Bluetooth to a smartphone companion app for saving and Analysis. It uses color charts to display exercise intensity and optimize training results, allowing people with shoulder and neck pain to perform a good yoga practice, effectively relieving shoulder and neck pain.

4.2   Design

This wearable device's surface is made of lightweight, stain-resistant plastic. The interior is lined with soft fabric that fits closely against the skin, and the middle is filled with foam for fastening and cushioning. There are four monitoring zones, each employing specialized electrodes to track muscle activity continuously. Adjustable silicone straps are used to hold the gadget to the body securely. Silicone is a soft material that won't irritate the skin and has the added benefit of being durable and non-deforming (shown in Fig. 8 and Fig. 9).

The user puts it on, as shown in Fig. 10. When the user begins their yoga practice, the device will remind them by sound and light, with three levels in the cueing program. The tone will progressively get louder, and the light bands on either side will gradually shift from white to green as the muscles gently contract, encouraging the user to fully extend the muscles. The device will also keep track of the user's yoga practice time and alert the user when their allotted time is up. The user is prompted to pay attention and correct their posture when the light changes from green to red and the tone becomes extremely urgent during the monitoring of the muscle state over the head (shown in Fig. 11). These will be returned and recorded by the associated mobile app.

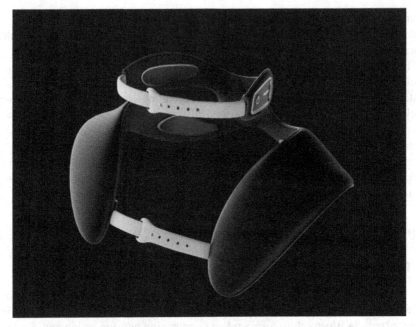

Fig. 8. Visual representation of the product design.

Fig. 9. Details of the product design.

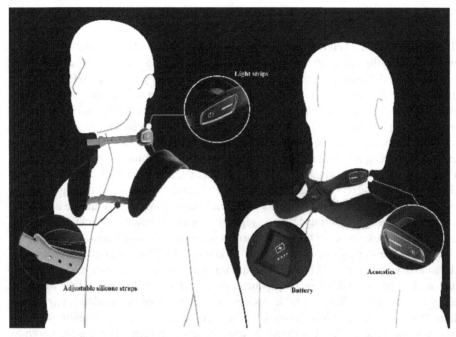

Fig. 10. The product's application.

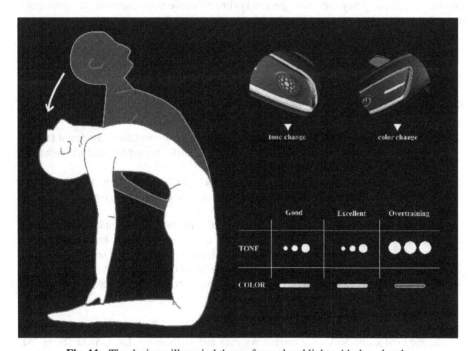

Fig. 11. The device will remind them of sound and light with three levels.

182   Y. Wu et al.

5 Conclusion

The prevalence of shoulder and neck discomfort significantly impacts society and medicine globally. Long durations of studying or working on a computer or phone can result in shoulder and neck pain, and in recent years, younger people have been experiencing the condition more frequently. Yoga can help reduce neck and shoulder pain. However, because it cannot perform regular movements during daily yoga training, ensuring that the muscles are sufficiently stimulated is challenging, reducing the exercise's effectiveness. Three famous yoga poses were chosen, and 16 volunteers were enlisted to participate in an analog scale for neck pain, neck muscle endurance test, and EMG numerical measurements. It was concluded that, after two weeks of intervention, the experimental group showed a decrease in the values of the visual analog scale for neck pain, an increase in neck muscle endurance, and an increase in muscle activation compared to the control group. Yoga engages the neck and shoulder muscles, so positive outcomes are possible once the proper form is maintained during training.

This article suggests that it is essential to keep track of the position, frequency, and duration of yoga exercises. Through the experiment, it offers data for later product design, and at the end, it establishes the product's demand point and suggests that wearable gadgets be produced. This wearable device can track the state of muscle activity in real time. Wearers of this product can track their level of muscle activation in real-time while working out, synchronize it with the smartphone app that supports it via Bluetooth to save and analyze the data, display exercise intensity using color charts, and maximize the training effect. They can more precisely direct people with shoulder and neck pain to perform a better yoga practice, effectively relieving their pain.

Acknowledgment. This work is sponsored by the Shanghai Sailing Program (22YF1430800).

References

1. Hoy, D., et al.: The global burden of neck pain: estimates from the Global Burden of Disease 2010 study. Ann. Rheum. Dis. **73**(2014), 1309–1315 (2010). https://doi.org/10.1136/annrhe umdis-2013-204431
2. Shin, D.W., et al.: Global, regional, and national neck pain burden in the general population, 1990–2019: an analysis of the global burden of disease study 2019. Front. Neurol. **13**, 955367 (2022). https://doi.org/10.3389/fneur.2022.955367
3. Büyükturan, B., Şaş, S., Kararti, C., Büyükturan, Ö.: The effects of combined sternocleido-mastoid muscle stretching and massage on pain, disability, endurance, kinesiophobia, and range of motion in individuals with chronic neck pain: a randomized, single-blind study. Musculoskeletal Sci. Pract. **55**, 102417 (2021). https://doi.org/10.1016/j.msksp.2021.102417
4. Cramer, H., Klose, P., Brinkhaus, B., Michalsen, A., Dobos, G.: Effects of yoga on chronic neck pain: a systematic review and meta-analysis. Clin. Rehabil. **31**, 1457–1465 (2017). https://doi.org/10.1177/0269215517698735
5. Mohan, A., Tijmes, S., Mehta, A., Cohen, J.G.: Therapeutic yoga for the management of chronic nonspecific neck pain: current evidence and mechanisms. Int. J. Yoga Therap. **32**, Article 5 (2022). https://doi.org/10.17761/2022-D-21-00007

6. Cramer, H., et al.: Randomized-controlled trial comparing yoga and home-based exercise for chronic neck pain. Clin. J. Pain **29**, 216–223 (2013). https://doi.org/10.1097/AJP.0b013e318 251026c

7. Chopp-Hurley, J.N., Prophet, C., Thistle, B., Pollice, J., Maly, M.R.: Scapular muscle activity during static yoga postures. J. Orthop. Sports Phys. Ther. **48**, 504–509 (2018). https://doi.org/ 10.2519/jospt.2018.7311

8. Ylinen, J., Wirén, K., Häkkinen, A.: Stretching exercises vs manual therapy in treatment of chronic neck pain: a randomized, controlled cross-over trial. Acta Derm. Venereol. **39**, 126–132 (2007). https://doi.org/10.2340/16501977-0015

9. Awan, R., Laskowski, E.R.: Yoga: safe for all? Mayo Clinic Proc. S0025619619300746 (2019). https://doi.org/10.1016/j.mayocp.2019.01.015

10. Swain, T.A., McGwin, G.: Yoga-related injuries in the United States From 2001 to 2014. Orthop. J. Sports Med. **4**, 232596711667170 (2016). https://doi.org/10.1177/232596711667 1703

11. Lee, M., Huntoon, E.A., Sinaki, M.: Soft tissue and bony injuries attributed to the practice of yoga: a biomechanical analysis and implications for management. Mayo Clin. Proc. **94**, 424–431 (2019). https://doi.org/10.1016/j.mayocp.2018.09.024

12. Hudswell, S., von Mengersen, M., Lucas, N.: The cranio-cervical flexion test using pressure biofeedback: a useful measure of cervical dysfunction in the clinical setting? Int. J. Osteopath. Med. **8**, 98–105 (2005). https://doi.org/10.1016/j.ijosm.2005.07.003

13. Bech, K.T., Larsen, C.M., Sjøgaard, G., Holtermann, A., Taylor, J.L., Søgaard, K.: Voluntary activation of the trapezius muscle in cases with neck/shoulder pain compared to healthy controls. J. Electromyogr. Kinesiol. **36**, 56–64 (2017). https://doi.org/10.1016/j.jelekin.2017. 07.006

14. Youdas, J.W., Carey, J.R., Garrett, T.R.: Reliability of measurements of cervical spine range of motion—comparison of three methods. Phys. Ther. **71**, 98–104 (1991). https://doi.org/10. 1093/ptj/71.2.98

15. Park, K.-N., Kwon, O.-Y., Ha, S.-M., Kim, S.-J., Choi, H.-J., Weon, J.-H.: Comparison of electromyographic activity and range of neck motion in violin students with and without neck pain during playing. Med. Probl. Perform. Artists. **27**, 188–192 (2012). https://doi.org/ 10.21091/mppa.2012.4035

16. Criswell, E., Cram, J.R. (eds.): Cram's Introduction to Surface Electromyography, 2nd edn. Jones and Bartlett, Sudbury (2011)

17. Ljungquist, T., Harms-Ringdahl, K., Nygren, Å., Jensen, I.: Intra- and inter-rater reliability of an 11-test package for assessing dysfunction due to back or neck pain. Physiother. Res. Int. **4**, 214–232 (1999). https://doi.org/10.1002/pri.167

18. Paksaichol, A., Lawsirirat, C., Janwantanakul, P.: Contribution of biopsychosocial risk factors to nonspecific neck pain in office workers: a path analysis model. J. Occup. Health. **57**, 100–109 (2015). https://doi.org/10.1539/joh.14-0124-OA

19. Edmondston, S.J., Wallumrød, M.E., MacLéid, F., Kvamme, L.S., Joebges, S., Brabham, G.C.: Reliability of isometric muscle endurance tests in subjects with postural neck pain. J. Manipulative Physiol. Ther. **31**, 348–354 (2008). https://doi.org/10.1016/j.jmpt.2008.04.010

20. Cid, M.M., Januario, L.B., Zanca, G.G., Mattiello, S.M., Oliveira, A.B.: Normalization of the trapezius sEMG signal - a reliability study on women with and without neck-shoulder pain. Braz. J. Phys. Ther. **22**, 110–119 (2018). https://doi.org/10.1016/j.bjpt.2017.09.007

21. Kelly, B.T., Kadrmas, W.R., Kirkendall, D.T., Speer, K.P.: Optimal normalization tests for shoulder muscle activation: an electromyographic study. J. Orthop. Res. **14**, 647–653 (1996). https://doi.org/10.1002/jor.1100140421

22. Andersen, L.L., Nielsen, P.K., Søgaard, K., Andersen, C.H., Skotte, J., Sjøgaard, G.: Torque–EMG–velocity relationship in female workers with chronic neck muscle pain. J. Biomech. **41**, 2029–2035 (2008). https://doi.org/10.1016/j.jbiomech.2008.03.016

23. Andersen, L.L., Kjær, M., Søgaard, K., Hansen, L., Kryger, A.I., Sjøgaard, G.: Effect of two contrasting types of physical exercise on chronic neck muscle pain. Arthritis Care Res. **59**, 84–91 (2008). https://doi.org/10.1002/art.23256

24. Falla, D., Jull, G., Hodges, P., Vicenzino, B.: An endurance-strength training regime is effective in reducing myoelectric manifestations of cervical flexor muscle fatigue in females with chronic neck pain. Clin. Neurophysiol. **117**, 828–837 (2006). https://doi.org/10.1016/j.clinph.2005.12.025

25. Uhl, T.L., Muir, T.A., Lawson, L.: Electromyographical assessment of passive active assistive, and active shoulder rehabilitation exercises. PM&R **2**, 132–141 (2010). https://doi.org/10.1016/j.pmrj.2010.01.002

26. Beazley, D., Patel, S., Davis, B., Vinson, S., Bolgla, L.: Trunk and hip muscle activation during yoga poses: implications for physical therapy practice. Complement. Ther. Clin. Pract. **29**, 130–135 (2017). https://doi.org/10.1016/j.ctcp.2017.09.009

Proposal for Family Health Management Service Based on Personal Medical and Lifelog Data, and Genetic Information

Jae Sun Yi[✉] ⓘ and Mingyeong Kim ⓘ

Handong Global University, Pohang, Korea
`creative1@handong.edu`

Abstract. Unlike most OECD countries, people in Korea not only easily visit hospitals and medical institutions to receive procedures and prescriptions at low cost but also have easy access to their own health data. However, they have difficulty interpreting their health data, so it was limited to checking the current status rather than applying to preventive management. In addition, the collected health data does not directly lead to health management, due to Koreans' particular consumption pattern. They value the recommendation of acquaintances and brand awareness more than their actual health condition and the suggestion from medical personnels. Moreover, women in their 30s to 50s are the most health-conscious group in Korea and they tend to manage their parents' and children's health.

Therefore, this study utilized the DTC genetic test service to help Koreans find a health management suitable for their inborn constitution, collected and accumulated scattered health data to track current health conditions and risks, and compared and analyzed changes in health data. Lastly, we proposed a mobile-based healthcare service platform that can connect and manage the health data of three generation family. Based on usability tests, the platform has been improved so that users can better visually recognize and manage data that is difficult to understand without medical experts. Through this study, individuals will be able to comprehensively understand their constitution, current health status, future health risks, and obtain appropriate family health management methods for healthier lives.

Keywords: Service Design · Health Management

1 Introduction

Recently, the healthcare market has continued to expand worldwide. Also, interest in health care is increasing in Korea. According to a 2020 survey, 93.1% of Koreans said they were interested in health, three out of four Koreans (75.2%) said they were making efforts towards managing their health [1]. Furthermore, managing health has gained much attention in recent years, leading Korea as one of the fastest-growing medical expense countries compared to its GDP among the OECD members [2]. The widening gap between life expectancy and healthy life expectancy [3], the increase in habit-related

V. G. Duffy (Ed.): HCII 2023, LNCS 14029, pp. 185–196, 2023.
https://doi.org/10.1007/978-3-031-35748-0_13

chronic diseases and in the proportion of the elderly population as well as an increase in health-related social costs have led to a rise in the awareness of knowing how to live a long life rather than knowing how long to live [4, 5]. In turn, this seems to contribute the public's high interest in health.

Amid high interest in health care, Koreans are in an environment where it is easy to manage their health through hospitals. According to a 2021 survey [6], about 71.6% of Koreans receive outpatient treatment without an appointment. On the day of treatment, the average waiting time after reception is approximately 14.6 min, indicating that compared to other countries, Koreans can visit hospitals whenever they want to. Furthermore, the burden of medical expenses is low since Koreans are covered by the National Health Insurance [7]. Studies show that per capita medical expenses are the lowest among 22 OECD high-income countries [8], indicating that Koreans are accessible to health services both physically and cost-effectively. Therefore, the number of outpatient treatments per person in Korea is 14.7 per year, the highest among OECD countries [9]. For example, in 2019, more than 40% of the total Korean population received endoscopy [10], which is about 1/100 of the cost compared to US hospitals and 1/14 that of UK public hospitals [11]. Also, 36% of the examinees received it for medical examinations and not for treatment [10]. This indicates that Korea is an environment where it is easy to obtain medical data through medical institutions even if it is not an emergency.

In addition to visiting a doctor for health examination, Koreans are provided with a health examination service for the entire nation to regularly obtain precise health status data. Additionally, Korea, which has the world's second-largest ICT Development Index in 2017 [12] due to low infrastructure costs and various competitive structures which result from high population density [13], is creating IT-based healthcare services through good ICT infrastructure. Moreover, with the implementation of the MyData policy in early 2021, individuals can manage medical information that was previously submitted to a medical institution or a platform in one place [14]. This creates an environment where people can manage their health through data. Health data collected through various channels can be useful for health care, but despite the growing proportion of data inside and outside medical institutions, data is only interpreted at the time of acquisition and is not aggregated [15], making it more difficult to apply to individual health care. In an environment where a lot of health information can be collected and managed, this study aims to identify the current status and characteristics of Korean health care and suggests health care measures that reflect their needs and complementary points to allow individuals to use various medical and health data obtained from each platform and service.

2   Healthcare System Utilization Status

Koreans have good access to various health-related services and tend to actively use them, and the national health examination service, which is provided every two years to the entire population, has been increasing over the past 10 years except during the pandemic. Experts recommend that people in their 20s and 30s should compare the results of the examination items to correct their lifestyle and emphasize the need to check all the changes from previous tests after their 40s [16]. Nevertheless, according to statistics related to medical checkups, a majority of service users were receiving results through mail receipt, but 42.8% of recipients said they do not keep the results of the last examination [17]. Moreover, about 71% of them answered they did not understand the results [18], indicating that the examination data is not being accumulated but is being lost, and that it is difficult to interpret even if they check the results. Through this, even though regular data collection infrastructure is established, it can be seen that Koreans are not using health care through national health examinations in an appropriate way, but only checking their current health status.

Other methods Koreans are using to obtain health data include mobile applications related to lifelog collected through various devices such as smart scales and wearable devices. According to a 2018 survey, smartphone ownership rate in Korea is top of the world [19]. 95% of Koreans own smartphones and COVID-19 has led the nation to use digital services more actively than before [19]. Particularly in the healthcare area, people record their health status and management status through various devices such as mobile application (58.6%), smartphone-linked device (33.3%), and smartwatch (27.1%) [20]. Due to the development of measurement technology, data such as oxygen saturation, electrocardiogram, blood pressure, body fat, and muscle mass can be collected in real time. Efficient management of the collected data is considered important [21], but data collected from various lifelog systems are diverse and complex, and collected data are uneven depending on the collection device and company [22]. Thus, there is a limit to users' overall recognition and application of health information to health care.

In order to make good use of health data, it is necessary to accumulate and interpret difficult and complex health data, not just to collect them, but to derive health care directions. Therefore, if lifelog data, which adds continuity of personal health records to regular health examination results, and constitution data can be integrated and managed, individuals will be able to manage their health more effectively. However, it is not easy for individuals to identify changes in health status by comprehensively accumulating data distributed across platforms, such as health examination results belonging to medical institutions and lifelog data belonging to each company platform. It is also difficult to interpret accumulated data, so there are many obstacles when managing health based on data, which needs to be improved.

3   User Analysis

3.1   Health Management Based on Consumption Patterns

According to a survey conducted in 2023, Koreans perform activities for health care such as disease management (65%), diet management and health functional food intake (64%), and exercise (48%) [23]. The trend of use in the disease management industry shows that more and more people have been spending more money on disease management over the past three years [23], and the amount of medical/assistance appliance use has also tended to surge over the past three years, indicating that health-related consumption is increasing. According to the 2022 Health Care Trend Survey, information on healthy diets is more likely to refer to the Internet (42.2%) and acquaintances (42.1%) than recommended by doctors and pharmacists (18.4%) [24]. In addition, according to a survey of about 1,000 Koreans, Koreans buy health functional foods based on reviews

(25.4%), acquaintances (19.6%), recognition (18.5%) and brands (16.8%) more than professional recommendations (13.5%), indicating that they consume based on trends rather than professional medical information [20]. In Korea, there is also a trend in diet and exercise methods, so health care methods that become a hot topic through SNS or various media, such as low-carbon diet and intermittent fasting, become the trend. The reason for this phenomenon is because Koreans are willing to follow the trend so that they may not fall behind from their group since they have experienced a short period of economic growth during their growth period. Accordingly, they have a trend-sensitive consumption pattern, which is no exception when deciding to purchase health-related services or products.

However, considering that everyone has a different constitution, health care methods based on trends, recommendations and reviews of others are unlikely to be effective and may have adverse or side-effects on the individual [25–27]. Additionally, each person has different deficiencies according to various characteristics such as environment, lifestyle, occupation, and genetic factors. Health status is also very different among the same age [28]. So even if people consume for health care, they need to know what the most necessary factors are and manage their health accurately. When people take care of their health in a way that is not suitable for them, they may not get the intended results. The higher the experience of trying in the past, the higher the expectation of failure. So if people experience a persistent sense of failure, it can lead to resignation of health management and failure in health behavior [29]. So for sustainable health care, people need to manage health according to their inborn constitution.

3.2 Characteristics of Potential Main Users

In Korea, consumers who spend the most on health care are in their 30s to 50s [30], and major buyers of health functional foods are also in the same age group [24], indicating that they are the group that is most interested in health care among all generations in Korea. Because they value parental love and filial piety under the influence of Confucianism, they tend to perform family health care together. In the case of parents, they tend to act as parents to their children even when their children become adults, helping their adult children's health care and also actively participating in older parents' health care. According to the 2022 Health Care Trend Report, in the case of people in their 20s and 60s, the proportion of family members and others purchasing their health functional foods is 33.6% and 40.1% respectively, more than twice as high compared to other age people [24]. This supports that in the case of children's generation and parents' generation, health is managed by the family, especially by the middle generation. People are directly or indirectly affected by health behavior in the family system [31], and studies on middle-aged health behavior show that men's health behavior varies depending on the presence of their spouses [32]. Women's behavior changes depending on the presence of their children, regardless of whether they have a spouse or not [32], indicating that married women in their 30s to 50s who have children are actively managing their family's health.

According to a 2021 survey of married parents with children, immunity was a priority health concern for their children under teens to 30s, growth and nutrition for underage children, and eye health for children in their 20s [30]. When they take care of their children's health, the answer to "consume health functional foods" was higher than diet control, exercise, and rest [24]. They encourage their adult children to consume health functional foods related to immunity due to COVID-19 [24], showing that parents actively care their children's health through consumption. These middle-aged generations also feel responsible for supporting their parents' generation by the value of filial piety. They provide economic and non-economic support [33], including parental health care. According to a 2018 survey, 47% of old parents' medical expenses are supported by their children [34], indicating that the middle generation is deeply involved in parental health care.

On the other hand, the middle generation, a health manager, performs consumption-oriented health care when managing the health of the family, and manages overall health care such as immunity and growth rather than data-based. However, since health care methods may not work for each family member due to different characteristics such as age, gender, and lifestyle [28], it is necessary to know what each individual needs most and which behaviors are needed based on the family's health data to manage their health accurately according to their family history, and their own constitution.

4   Service Direction

Based on the previous survey, in order to enable Koreans to manage health based on their own data, this study proposes services including 1) health care direction based on their natural constitution, 2) comprehensive interpretation by accumulating collected data, and 3) way to manage the health of each family members.

4.1   Health Management Method Based on Inborn Constitution

An example of knowing an individual's inborn constitution is Direct to Customer-Genetic Testing (DTC-GT), which identifies user-specific genetic characteristics without using expensive and complex genetic testing through medical institutions. Examples of DTC-GT services include services that analyze genetic diseases and present health care methods suitable for personal genetic information, and services that recommend products fit for individuals. According to a 2021 survey, 4.9% of Koreans have already experienced the test, which is not a small number in terms of the current status of the Korean industry [35]. At the same time, government and industry interest in the DTC-GT market is also increasing, so various regulations are also being eased, and the accessibility and utilization of DTC genetic tests by Korean consumers are expected to increase significantly. According to the survey, more than half of 70% of those who intend to purchase DTC genetic tests were found to be "performing preventive health care" and "finding non-medical genetic characteristics", and the lower the age group, the more it was found to prefer "non-genetic characteristics identification" and "preventive health care" to "disease treatment" [36], indicating that young people with better health conditions are conducting DTC genetic tests for preventive health care purposes compared to the elderly at high risk.

In other words, people who have no problem with their current health condition but are interested in their future health are already performing DTC-GT, so DTC genetic tests can be useful for recognizing individual's unique health characteristics and preventive health care. As another example of getting inborn constitution data, Korean medicine has a concept of providing different health care methods considering four constitution differences [37], but it must be diagnosed by a Korean medicine doctor in person. According to a related study, the degree of consistency between experts in diagnosis of constitution varies from 33.5% to more than 90% [38]. Thus, if incorrectly diagnosed, there is a limit to health care that may not suit them. Thus, in order to identify accurate and unchanged constitution data, we apply DTC genetic testing to the service. It is suitable for use in this service because users can collect samples and receive results directly through kits at home without visiting medical institutions, so users can meet their needs to preventative health without being constrained by time and space.

4.2 Method of Providing Comprehensive Interpretation by Accumulating Collected Data

Currently, Koreans only use regularly collected health examination data and lifelog to diagnose the condition at the moment of collection. So a method is needed that makes the accumulation to monitor the changes of data possible on one platform while making it easy for users to recognize it. Accordingly, it is necessary to include health examination data and lifelog in the service and provide them in an easy-to-interpret manner so that accumulations and changes can be easily identified. In addition, if genetic data obtained through DTC genetic testing is included, preventive health care through genetic data and current status through health examination results and lifelog can be checked at the same time, which can have a positive impact on health care.

However, genetic data results and current diagnostic data may be difficult to interpret simultaneously, such as when a user has a gene involved in obesity but the user's current weight or body fat rate is in the normal range. For another example, genetic results show cardiovascular items in the "cardiovascular" category, but health examination results show cardiovascular-impacting items such as blood pressure, triglycerides, and cholesterol as individual items without categories, making it difficult to think in conjunction with cardiovascular. Therefore, if the two types of data, genetic results and current status data, are combined and provided inside the service, users will be able to intuitively recognize their health status and management direction and manage health. Instead of listing and presenting categories derived from genetic testing and medical examination data respectively, each result item is grouped with indicators of common or similar properties so that genetic data and current data can be compared and viewed within the same article with new classification criteria, users will be able to easily recognize what they lack genetically or in their current behavior, improve the current status, or preventively manage their health. Based on the characteristics that Koreans are sensitive to trends, we newly classified items as eight categories of cardiovascular, bone, eyes, kidney, immunity, hair loss, skin, and diet that Korean are most interested in.

4.3 Ways to Manage the Health of Family Members

Families share not only genetic factors but also living environments and lifestyles. So similar diseases can be shared which is useful to prepare for common risk factors if families manage their health together. Seven of the top 10 diseases in which Koreans die the most are chronic diseases and chronic diseases are usually caused by lifestyle or genetic factors in the family so intensive management is needed. According to a study, chronic diseases increase rapidly after one's 40s and the majority of people under their 20s have a family history of chronic diseases [39]. So family-based health care based on data is needed to effectively prevent more fatal health hazards to individuals across generations. Additionally, cancer, heart disease, and cerebrovascular disease, which account for a high proportion of Korean deaths, are all related to family history due to large proportions of genetic factors and family-sharing lifestyles, and high blood pressure, a representative disease of family history, increases the probability of development by 50% and diabetes increases by 30–40% when people have a family history [40]. Nevertheless, according to a previous study, people with a family history of stomach cancer show inappropriate eating habits such as excessive sodium intake (95%), lack of vitamin C intake (30%), and lack of dietary fiber intake (85%), showing that even those with family history do not take preventive measures such as fixing their lifestyle [41]. Therefore, when performing health care on a family basis, recognizing risk factors from family history and one's data and managing lifestyle is essential. Thus, it is important to share family history when managing family members, and to suggest the direction of lifestyle management that needs to be managed in relation to the genetic factors that cause these diseases.

Through the DTC-GT, parents will be able to identify their children's constitution and find information about their child's effective nutrition, growth-related bones, or athletic ability. However, in Korea, regulations on DTC genetic testing for minors are still being discussed [42]. So based on the parents' genetic expression rate data of 'bone', 'athletic ability', and 'nutrient concentration' through DTC-GT, children can also be more properly managed by narrowing the scope of health functional foods or food intake. In addition, improving lifestyle habits such as maintaining muscle mass or improving eating habits is more effective in managing the health of the elderly than trendy health functional foods or excessive health examinations through hospitals. The middle generation can help their parents perform DTC-GT at home without having to move a long distance or spend a lot of time in a large hospital for their parents' checkups. Through parents' "athletic ability" items, the middle generation can encourage their parents by suggesting the most effective exercise method, and the "nutrient concentration" items in the test results can help them manage their health in a more personalized way, such as diet or nutrient intake. If the manager identifies vulnerable diseases of family members or ill-matched health care methods through genetic risk and family history management and suggests health care directions tailored to the vulnerability, effective health care can be achieved through data tailored to each member.

5   Service Suggestion

Based on previous research, to enable users to perform health care based on various health data including genetic data, DTC genetic testing process must be performed and the results should be checked. Additionally, the national health examination results and lifelog collected from various smart healthcare devices should be regularly and continuously updated to the service, and the whole data should be reflected in comprehensive health results. Moreover, in order to collect family health data and present customized health care methods for each member, it should be easy to collect and update family health data, and a large amount of information accumulated for each family member should be managed. To this end, it will be efficient to perform the service on the platform that users use the most to utilize health care information. Consequently, this study chose the mobile platform that Koreans are currently most actively using for health status records [20].

5.1 Information Architecture and Wireframe

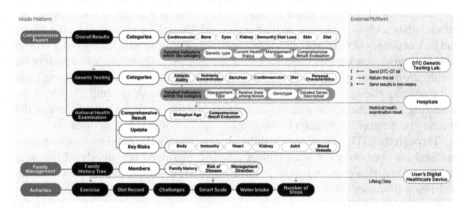

Fig. 1. Information Architecture

Based on the defined problems and solutions, we produced a service information architecture (IA) and a service wireframe (Fig. 1). When the user applies for DTC genetic testing through the service, an external DTC genetic testing institution will deliver the sample kit. After the user returns the kit, the result will be presented through the mobile platform two weeks later. Then, the comprehensive report, which combines user genetic data and medical examination data received from medical institutions, provides information on the genetic type, current health status, and management types by category, and each examination data also can be checked. A lifestyle management function is placed on the main screen so that users can manage their lifestyle according to their usual health goals, and a family management function presents the family tree that indicates the family history and each member's health status and data to manage family health easily. Then, the study created a corresponding prototype wireframe to conduct usability testing.

5.2 Service Development Through Usability Testing

In order to find usability problems and derive improvements by analyzing users' prototype usage methods, service usability tests were conducted on 11 married women in their 30s to 50s three times using wireframe. The test was conducted by placing an experimental smartphone with the wireframe prototype installed so that the user can operate it and recording the operating scene and the smartphone screen at the same time and analyzing it later. The user performed the assigned tasks through oral and screen guidance. Through the first test, the name of a function that the user did not understand was changed, and it was reflected in the service knowing that it was taken more seriously when health status was indicated by age than good/bad indicators. Through the second usability test, access to functions that users are not well aware of was improved, and the service tutorial was strengthened by identifying the need for a detailed explanation of genetic testing cost. Through the last test insight, the flow that was not smooth in performing the service, such as the screen that was converted after receiving the genetic testing result, was modified. Through post-interviews after the test, various types of indicators such as genetic information, medical examination result, comprehensive reports, and lifelog, which are the core of this study, were modified to make it easy for users to recognize.

5.3   Final Content and Design

The final service application design reflecting the usability testing is shown in the figure below (Fig. 2). (1) (2) First of all, the lifelog is accumulated by linking with the basic health application in the device and digital healthcare devices (smart scale, smart band, etc.). (3) In the case of health examination data, it is possible to easily link the results of health examination only with the name and social security number, thereby lowering the hurdle for data accumulation. (4) Health data of the simple enumeration method, which were previously difficult to interpret, are classified by major categories, and data that indicate danger are exposed first to make people easier to recognize. In addition, the comprehensive results are expressed by age, a familiar data notation, to help intuitive understanding by comparing the biometric age with the current age, and to provide a management direction that can compensate for the current health condition by placing a simple comprehensive evaluation. (5) When applying for DTC genetic testing in the application, after completing the payment process, the user will go through a two-week process from receiving the DTC-GT kit to completing sample analysis, allowing them to check their data test status in the app. Upon completion of the analysis, push notification of the results arrival app is sent so that it can be checked immediately. (6) Within the result sheet, detailed gene items can be checked by category. Categories that require management are exposed first to make people recognize the need for care. (7) Detailed indicators within the category show the user's state, overall description, relative state among Korean, and detailed genes description involved in the results to increase user confidence. (8) Users who upload health examination data and undergo DTC genetic testing can check a comprehensive report that integrates the results. Each data is divided into eight categories that Koreans are most interested in, and genetic data is expressed as bad, caution, and fine levels, and current data collected by medical checkups are expressed in age, allowing users to check their conditions at a glance. (9) For each category, a pop-up window consisting of two tabs appears. Through the first tab, users can check management types, simple comprehensive reviews, the number of risk genes they have, and check how old their bodies are to help them understand their status. The second tab exposes detailed indicator-specific results within the category so that users can know what data they have, making them aware of what they need to be managed with special care. (10) On the Family Management tab, each member can be added to the family history tree. Medical history can be listed and their health data can be uploaded and updated. Through DTC-GT, serious family genetic disease and disorder is shown visually and be able to predict children's future genetic illness and natural constitution.

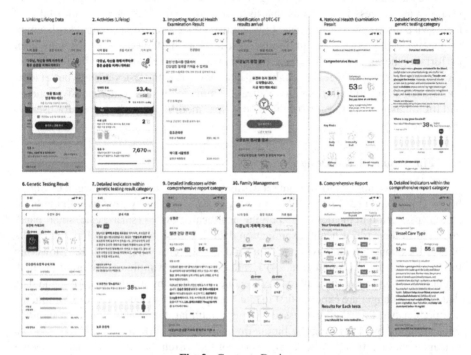

Fig. 2. Contents Design

The service offers health care directions to the user in the form of lifelog goals such as the number of steps goals and weight goals on the Activities tab according to the input information, so that family health care and personal health care can be properly managed.

6 Conclusion

To help Koreans manage their health properly, this study identified how Koreans are currently using the Korean healthcare system, and what characteristics Koreans have. As a result, it was found that Koreans are actively obtaining health data through medical infrastructure, but the results are vast and difficult to interpret, making it difficult to apply them in health care. We also found that they are managing their health based on trends even though they are likely to be ineffective, and that women in their 30s and 50s, who are most health-conscious, want to care the health of their parents and children together. Accordingly, this study proposed a mobile service platform including the following functions. 1) To enable individuals to manage their health based on their unique constitution, it allows DTC-GT to be performed on the service, and they can check the results. 2) By synthesizing national health examination data, lifelog, and genetic data, users can easily compare and analyze the data, and apply it to health care. 3) In order to manage the health of the family together, by adding health data for each member, health care directions are presented for each member. Through this service platform, individuals will be able to comprehensively recognize their innate constitution, current health status, and future risks, reflect them in health care, and secure appropriate family health care methods, so that they can lead a healthy life.

References

1. Trendmonitor. https://www.trendmonitor.co.kr/tmweb/trend/allTrend/detail.do?bIdx=1919&code=0501&trendType=CKOREA. Accessed 9 Feb 2023
2. Ministry of Health and Welfare, Korea Institute for Health and Social Affairs: OECD Health Statistics 2021. Ministry of Health and Welfare, South Korea (2021)
3. Newsmp. http://www.newsmp.com/news/articleView.html?idxno=208269. Accessed 9 Feb 2023
4. Samsung Securities. https://www.samsungpop.com/mobile/invest/poptv.do?cmd=fileDown&FileNm=uma_200724.html. Accessed 9 Feb 2023
5. Lee, E., Kim, W.: Establishment of community public smart healthcare model for disease Prevention and Health Life Extension. Issue Anal. **331**, 1–20 (2018)
6. Shin, J., et al.: Survey on the Experience with Healthcare Service in 2021, Ministry of Health and Welfare, Korea Institute for Health and Social Affairs (2021)
7. National Health Insurance Service. https://www.nhis.or.kr/nhis/policy/wbhada01700m01.do. Accessed 9 Feb 2023
8. Chow R.D., Bradley E.H., Gross C.P.: Comparison of cancer-related spending and mortality rates in the US vs 21 high-income countries. JAMA Health Forum **3**(5), 5 (2022)
9. Ministry of Health and Welfare, Korea Institute for Health and Social Affairs: OECD Health Statistics 2022. Ministry of Health and Welfare, South Korea (2022)
10. Health Chosun. https://m.health.chosun.com/svc/news_view.html?contid=2021070701677. Accessed 9 Feb 2023
11. Cheung, D.: The comparison of the costs for endoscopy-related procedures among different countries; Korean Health Insurance payment is reasonable? Korean Soc. Gastrointest. Endoscopy Seminar **55**, 166–169 (2016)
12. ICT Development Index 2017. https://www.itu.int/net4/ITU-D/idi/2017/#undefined. Accessed 9 Feb 2023
13. IDG Connect. https://www.idgconnect.com/article/3580022/five-reasons-south-korea-has-the-fastest-internet.html. Accessed 9 Feb 2023
14. Lee, G.: Current status of MyData policy and tasks in health and welfare. Health Welfare Policy Forum 52–68 (2021)
15. Doctorstimes. http://www.doctorstimes.com/news/articleView.html?idxno=213791. Accessed 9 Feb 2023
16. Health Chosun. https://health.chosun.com/site/data/html_dir/2016/11/30/2016113001291.html. Accessed 9 Feb 2023
17. Medipharmhealth. http://medipharmhealth.co.kr/news/article.html?no=77389. Accessed 9 Feb 2023
18. Datasom. http://www.datasom.co.kr/news/articleView.html?idxno=104973. Accessed 9 Feb 2023

19. Taylor, K., Silver, L: Smartphone Ownership is Growing Rapidly Around the World, But Not Always Equally. Pew Research Center, 1–46 (2019)
20. Opensurvey, Healthcare Trend Report 2021. Opensurvey, pp. 1–36 (2021)
21. Yi, M., Whangbo, T.: A selective lifelog management scheme for personalized healthcare services. J. Korean Inst. Next Gener. Comput. **10**(6), 14–21 (2014)
22. Park, J.: Actuality and prospects of digital health care. KHIDI J. Perspect. **1**(2), 52–59 (2021)
23. Card, S.: The importance of healthy daily life - health care, how are you doing? Samsung Datatalk **10**, 1–10 (2023)
24. Opensurvey, Healthcare Trend Report 2022. Opensurvey, pp. 1–46 (2022)
25. Health Chosun. https://m.health.chosun.com/svc/news_view.html?contid=2021030802292. Accessed 9 Feb 2023
26. The JoongAng. https://www.joongang.co.kr/article/8549039#home. Accessed 9 Feb 2023
27. Health Chosun. https://health.chosun.com/site/data/html_dir/2018/09/14/2018091400039.html. Accessed 9 Feb 2023
28. Lee, B., Sohn, Y., Lee, S., Yoon, M., Kim, M., Kim, C.: An efficacy of social cognitive theory to predict health behavior a meta-analysis on the health belief model studies in Korea. J. Public Relat. **18**(2), 163–206 (2014)
29. Kim, Y., Zang, H., Choi, J.: Goal determination in diet trying. J. Bus. Convergence **6**(4), 39–43 (2021)
30. Korea Health Supplements Association: Health Supplement Market Status and Consumer Research 2021. Korea Health Supplements Association (2021)
31. Umberson, D.: Family status and health behaviors: social control as a dimension of social integration. J. Health Soc. Behav. **28**, 306–319 (1987)
32. Lee, E., Jun, H.: Gender differences in the relationships between family structure and health-related behaviors in midlife. Family Cult. **27**(2), 157–179 (2015)
33. Oh, H., Hwang, W.: 2019 Korean Workingmom Report. KB Financial Laboratory, pp. 1–61 (2019)
34. Yonhap News. https://www.yna.co.kr/view/AKR20180820052700002. Accessed 9 Feb 2023
35. Medigate News. https://medigatenews.com/news/1839154928. Accessed 9 Feb 2023
36. Park, I., Jun, I.: A study on factors influencing consumer purchase intentions and purposes in direct-to-consumer genetic test. J. Digital Convergence **17**(7), 167–177 (2019)
37. Lee, J., Lee, S., Chung, Y., Lee, Y., Moon, Y.: Design and implementation of the database system for personalized food and diet recommendation based on 8-oriental body constitution and physical information. Proc. Korean Soc. Comput. Inf. Conf. **28**(1), 187–188 (2020)
38. Han, E., Kwon, Y.: Inter-expert agreement and diagnostic accuracy of Sasang Constitution medicine. J. Physiol. Pathol. Korean Med. **32**(4), 185–196 (2018)
39. Lee, N., Kim, M., Choi, H., Lee, J., Jung, D.: A Study on the prevalence and risk of family history for chronic diseases: findings from the Korea National Health and Nutrition examination survey 2019. J. Convergence Inf. Technol. **11**(8), 160–167 (2021)
40. Lee, J.: Family tree diseases: family history diseases. Med. Rep. **38**(8), 38–39 (2014)
41. Kim, S., Lee, B., Oh, S., Lee, D., Kim, S., Ko, Y.: The influence of family history of Ischemic heart disease on healthy behaviors. Korean J. Family Pract. **12**(1), 16–21 (2022)
42. Medicaltimes. https://www.medicaltimes.com/Users/News/NewsView.html?ID=1142851. Accessed 9 Feb 2023

An Interactive Design Solution for Sleep Persuasion Based on Health Risk Visualization

Kaiqiao Zheng, Jing Luo$^{(\boxtimes)}$, and Yuqing Yan

College of Art and Design, Division of Arts, Shenzhen University, Shenzhen, Guangdong, China
luojng@szu.edu.cn

Abstract. With the increasing development of the Internet and mobile phone technology, bedtime procrastination caused by mobile phone addiction is infringing on people's health and causing distress to them. In order to make users deeply aware of the health risks caused by bedtime procrastination, this project proposes an interactive persuasion scheme based on health risk visualization. First, we design a preliminary solution based on risk perception and information visualization. Secondly, we find user needs through user research. And then we combined the user needs to optimize the scheme and developed an interaction design scheme for sleep persuasion based on health risk visualization. Finally, the feasibility of the scheme was verified through qualitative experiments and positive feedback from users was obtained. At the same time, the design pattern can also be used to help people correct other vices, such as being sedentary, not exercising, not drinking water, and supervise the development of healthy behaviors.

Keywords: bedtime procrastination · mobile phone addiction · visualization · risk perception · sleep persuasion

1 Introduction

Sleep is the most essential physiological need of humans. Adequate sleep allows the brain, heart, stomach and other organs to relax and rest. On the contrary, prolonged sleep deprivation will lead to memory loss, endocrine disorders, and increased risk of cardiovascular diseases and cancer [1–3], which have serious negative effects on people's physiological health and psychological health. According to the 2022 China Sleep Index Report, sleep deprivation is widespread among the Chinese urban population, and there are many reasons for sleep deprivation, besides physiological, work and other irresistible factors, the main reason is poor lifestyle habits, such as using cell phones before bedtime. With the continuous development of the Internet and mobile phone technology, increasing numbers of people have adopted the habit of using mobile phones before going to bed, especially the younger generation. The survey results show that only 2.76% of college students said they do not use their mobile phones before going to bed, in contrast to 61.53% of college students who use their mobile phones before going to bed every day [4]. Surveys from abroad have also shown that more than 90% of young people use their mobile phones to access the Internet before bedtime. It has

V. G. Duffy (Ed.): HCII 2023, LNCS 14029, pp. 197–210, 2023.
https://doi.org/10.1007/978-3-031-35748-0_14

been shown that the habit of using cell phones before bedtime affects people's mood and biorhythms, and the Blue-ray from the mobile phone screen inhibits the normal secretion of melatonin from the pineal gland, which has an adverse effect on sleep quality [5, 6].

Excessive mobile phone addiction disrupts the original daily rhythm of people's lives and it is one of the main reasons for bedtime procrastination. This behavior of delaying the time to fall asleep without external factors preventing them and indulging in other non-essential activities at the time when they should be sleeping is a manifestation of bedtime procrastination [7]. Even though they are sleepy, they still get deeply immersed in the world of the Internet and cannot extricate themselves from it, and the pleasure from the Internet information always makes them want to delay sleeping for a little further. Given that smartphones have become widely available, it is feasible to achieve sleep persuasion by mobile phones which help people correct the bad behavior habit of bedtime procrastination to get better sleep.

As sleep procrastination has become a norm, there is a rising number of scholars researching the topic of bedtime procrastination. However, research has mainly gathered to reveal the nature and causes of bedtime procrastination, and to make sleep recommendations based on this, while there are fewer experiments on actual intervention studies. It has been suggested that good sleep hygiene habits can help reduce the tendency for bedtime procrastination [8, 9], such as creating a quiet sleep environment, not eating or drinking before bedtime, and reducing coffee intake. It has also been noted that negative emotions such as anxiety and depression can contribute to sleep procrastination [10]. Meditating positively can help people fall asleep by slowing down their brain activity so that negative emotions fade away [11]. In addition, it was suggested that people's lack of education about sleep health is also an important cause of bedtime procrastination. A comparative study on bedtime procrastination intervention was conducted by Baodan Zhang et al. The study showed that people's bedtime procrastination significantly decreased after they were aware of the hazards of late sleep through health education [12]. Out of self-protective instinct, when people are fully aware of the dangers associated with staying up late, they will choose to stop doing so to avoid negative effects. This shows that negative information can increase people's risk perception, which in turn has a positive effect on sleep persuasion.

As people become more aware of healthy sleep, the demand for sleep-aid products is also on the rise. In recent years, a large number of products about sleep management have appeared in the market, with 228 sleep management apps in the apple store alone in this category. Their functions are mainly focused on helping users to fall asleep quickly, monitoring their sleep, and waking up regularly [13, 14]. Despite their rich features, they lack targeted interventions for bedtime procrastination. Unlike insomnia, most sleep procrastinators do not have sleep disorders, and they are often willing to sacrifice sleep time for immediate pleasure, but regret it when they feel groggy the next day, or even fluke that occasional indulgence does not have substantial and irreversible negative effects on their health.

In order to remind users of the health effects of staying up late at night and persuade them to stop sleep procrastination, this study proposes the concept of health risk visualization. Information visualization can transform complex and abstract information into concise and clear graphical information, helping users to organize information and discover the structural relationships embedded between them [15]. It has been stated that risk perception has a significant positive effect on protective behavior [16]. Visualization can effectively reduce the cost of communication between humans and computers. This means that by visualizing health risk information, users can visualize the changes in the corresponding risk of disease caused by their staying up late on the interactive interface. The display of the probability of illness will help people to break the positive self-bias. Overall, the design aims to visually present the possible negative effects of staying up late to users through the medium of mobile phones, and to persuade people to avoid the health risks associated with bedtime procrastination.

2 User Research

In this stage, questionnaire research and user interviews were used to conduct the research. First, we collected data through questionnaires to analyze the behavioral habits, psychological characteristics and the use of sleep management products of bedtime procrastinators. Based on the questionnaire results and health risk visualization, a preliminary design was created. Second, further user interviews were conducted to learn more about the reasons for the formation of sleep procrastination habits and to verify the feasibility of the preliminary design idea.

2.1 Questionnaire

Participants. The questionnaire was distributed through online social media platforms and was completed with 287 participants. The data of participants who themselves suffered from sleep disorders or worked at night were excluded. After screening, 236 (109 males, 127 females) valid questionnaires were obtained. 88.56% of the participants are in the age group of 18–30 years old, and most of them are college students (n = 118: 50%) or full-time employed youth (n = 107: 45.34%).

Research Approach. The questionnaire includes four sections: (a) personal basal information. (b) Participants' sleep habits. Participants were required to fill in their ideal sleep time versus their actual sleep time, and the main reasons that prevented them from going to bed on time. If the option of "playing on the mobile phone" was selected, they were asked to answer the average duration and frequency of playing it before bedtime and other relevant specifics. (c) Participants' perceptions of sleep procrastination. Participants were asked to make a general assessment of their own sleep procrastination and then complete the Chinese version of the Sleep Procrastination Scale (SDSS-C) to verify the accuracy of the previous assessment. Then, participants were also asked to select the three most worrisome items among the numerous hazards of sleep procrastination. (d) Participants' use of sleep applications. Participants were asked to answer whether they had used any sleep applications. Then, they were asked to choose how often they used them and answer any problems they had experienced while using them. If they had never used the related application before, they were asked to answer the reason for not using it.

Result. The results of the questionnaire study showed that 76.27% of the participants expressed that they were aware of the harm of sleep delay and were worried about the health risks associated with sleep deprivation happening to them. Probably the majority of the participants in the study were young people, who are more concerned about their external image. Among the risks of sleep deprivation, they were most concerned about hair loss (64.83%), sudden death (61.44%), and skin deterioration (60.59%). Regarding the use of sleep apps, a total of 74 participants expressed that they had used sleep applications, but 82.44% of users said they used such applications very infrequently. The complex and uninteresting interactive interface and the lack of obvious persuasive effect are the main reasons that prevent them from persisting in using them. Regarding the currently available sleep product suggestions, words such as more concise, easy to use, and forced to turn off the phone were mentioned by users several times (Fig. 1).

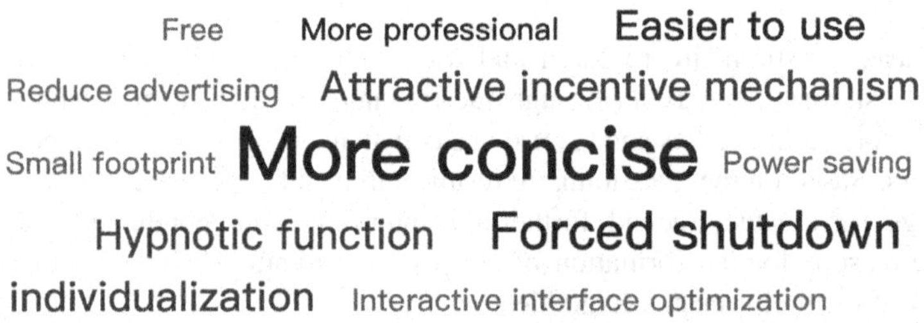

Free   More professional   Easier to use

Reduce advertising   Attractive incentive mechanism

Small footprint   More concise   Power saving

Hypnotic function   Forced shutdown

individualization   Interactive interface optimization

Fig. 1. User demand keywords

2.2 Preliminary Conception

Based on the theories related to health risk visualization and the results of questionnaire research, we propose a preliminary design idea. First, the probability of illness is displayed to break people's positive self-bias. And use the red warning to strengthen users' concerns about their health condition. Secondly, we learned in the questionnaire collection stage that people are more concerned about the deterioration of their skin due to staying up late. As staying up late can impair liver function and cause toxins to deposit in the skin, which leads to skin diseases. To better resonate with users in the follow-up user interviews, the liver pattern was used in the initial program. A healthy liver will gradually become ugly and terrible with the delay in sleeping to warn people to sleep on time (Fig. 2).

2.3 Interview

Participants. During the questionnaire study, we screened 100 participants who had more pronounced bedtime procrastination behavior and had the habit of using mobile phones at bedtime (bedtime procrastination scale score ≥ 3.5). We randomly interviewed 10 of these participants, 5 males, and 5 females, with a mean age of 24.8 years (SD = 2.79; age range: 21–31) (Table 1).

Research Approach. Based on the questionnaire research, we used interviews to gain insight into participants' psychological activities during bedtime procrastination and to

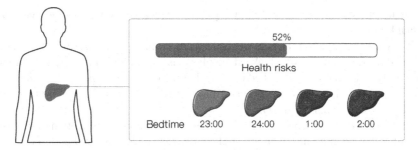

Fig. 2. Preliminary design scheme (Color figure online)

Table 1. Respondent characteristics

Participant ID	Gender	Age	Job	Bedtime Procrastination Scale Score	Average mobile phone time	Use of sleep apps
P1	Male	22	Student	5	≥2 h	Yes
P2	Male	31	Full-time	4.2	1.5–2 h	No
P3	Male	28	Full-time	3.78	≥2 h	No
P4	Male	23	Student	3.78	≥2 h	No
P5	Male	24	Full-time	3.78	≥2h	Yes
P6	Female	21	Student	4.33	1.2–2 h	Yes
P7	Female	24	Full-time	3.78	0.5–1 h	Yes
P8	Female	26	Full-time	4	≥2 h	No
P9	Female	24	Student	3.89	1–1.5 h	Yes
P10	Female	25	Full-time	3.67	0.5–1 h	No

verify the feasibility of the initial design idea. The interview process lasted about 20 min for each group, and the whole process was recorded with the participants' consent. Finally, the interviews were transcribed, organized, and summarized to provide more ideas for the design of the program. The interviews consisted of the following four parts: (a) Reasons for using phone before bedtime and common phone apps used before bedtime. (b) Whether attempts were tried to remedy sleep procrastination habits. (c) Details of the use of sleep apps and the feeling of using them, or detailed reasons for not using them. (d) Opinions and suggestions on the preliminary conceptualization of the health risk visualization sleep persuasion interaction design.

Result. All 10 participants reported that their habit of checking their phones before bedtime had lasted for more than 2 years and was accompanied with increasingly longer usage times. Checking the phone during free time had formed a conditioned reflex in them, otherwise they would be anxious. Brushing short videos, binge-watching, playing games and other forms of entertainment make them enjoyable and ignore the hazards of staying up late. However, the following day, the lack of sleep often interferes with normal life,

When asked if they had corrected their sleep procrastination habits, seven participants indicated that they had tried to make sleep plans, use smart health bracelets, or turn off lights early to get themselves to bed on time, but the results were poor. The other three participants thought they were in good health and that sleep delay had not brought them any obvious substantial harm so far.

Of the 10 respondents, 5 of them had used sleep management applications. All 5 users stated that they would only open the application occasionally when they remembered. Although they had set sleep alarms, they often ignored the application's reminders, which often only reminding at the set time. If users choose to continue playing with their phones, the app will not have any reminders. In addition to the usage problems mentioned in the questionnaire, one of the users also questioned the professionalism of the application. When he used a smart health bracelet and a sleep app to record sleep quality at the same time, the final monitoring data presented by the two was different (P7). Another user said that the system's reward and punishment mechanism was not attractive to him, which means that it doesn't matter if he doesn't follow the sleep schedule (P1). Another four participants also indicated that this was one of the main reasons why they were not interested in using such applications.

When discussing the preliminary design options during the interviews (Fig. 2), both 10 participants agreed that the visualization increased their perception of health risks and had a positive effect on persuading them to sleep on time. Specifically, the participant identified that the progressive ugliness of the liver pattern over time caused feelings of fear, which prompted him to desire to take action to stop it to happen (P4). The red progress bar prevented them from ignoring the health risks associated with sleep procrastination (P2). Meanwhile, participants who had experience with the same type of app were concerned about being able to stick with the app. This is because they rarely actively opened such apps when playing with their phones before bed, or even forgot that they had downloaded such an app.

3   Design Process

3.1   Design Requirement

Problem Feedback. Based on the questionnaire research and in-depth interviews, we can analyze and summarize 3 problems existing when users use sleep persuasion products:

(a) The interactive interface is complex and has more content. The lack of a clear classification of common and non-common functions for users leads to confusion and may even dissuade some users in the process of use.

(b) The product cannot attract users to stick to it. The formation of good sleep habits requires a long period of persistence. Persuasion as the core function of this type of application is often ignored by users and fails to guide them to fall asleep on time. When users realize that their sleep procrastination fails to change, they may choose to give up using it.

(c) Users are eager to get more feedback in the process of using this kind of application. Some of the existing feedback models and reward and punishment mechanisms are difficult to resonate with them and relatively unconvincing. As users do not get the feedback and emotional value they desired, their trust in the application will decrease.

Design Philosophy. In response to the above feedback, we wanted to find a simple interaction solution that would entice users to stick with it for a long time and persuade them to stop procrastinating on sleep. Firstly, the design solution should follow the principle of minimalist design and focus on the key function of health risk visualization. Secondly, as a persuasion tool, it needs to break through the traditional persuasion interaction and make users notice the existence of the persuasion message. Anthropomorphism as one of the visualization methods is more helpful for health knowledge dissemination than the traditional way [17]. Finally, the effectiveness of persuasion is based on the trust of the user. The difficulty of designing persuasion tools is to consistently achieve the trust of users. In the field of psychological suggestion, the principle of similarity has a strong persuasive effect [18]. Therefore, in the interaction scheme, we will use the user's base situation as the starting data to establish a link between the product and the user. The effect of persuasive tools may diminish with time, nevertheless, emotional resonance helps to maintain the user's trust in the persuasive tool [19].

3.2   Content Frame

The sleep persuasion process can be divided into three stages: information entry, prompting, and sleep feedback (Fig. 3). With the above analysis, we combine user behavior and user psychology to add details to the persuasion process to improve the persuasion effect (Fig. 4).

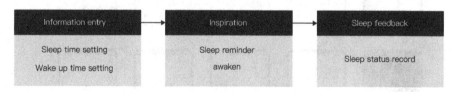

Fig. 3. Sleep persuasion frame

204   K. Zheng et al.

Fig. 4. Upgraded sleep persuasion frame

3.3 High-Fidelity Prototype

The high-fidelity prototype diagram was categorized according to the three stages mentioned above (Fig. 5). In the information entry phase, users need to complete the Sleep

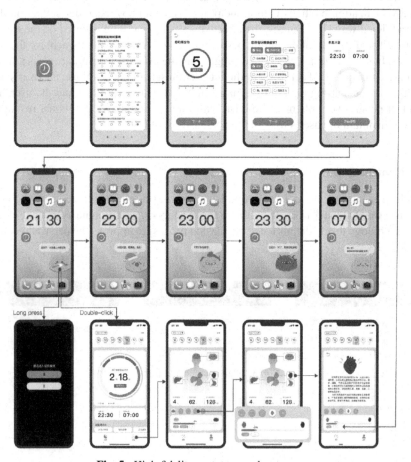

Fig. 5. High-fidelity prototype and use process

Procrastination Scale test so that they have a clearer awareness of their bedtime procrastination. Secondly, users are supposed to select the diseases that they are rather worried about caused by bedtime procrastination, so that the application can push customized and targeted healthy sleep suggestions to assist users in better avoiding health risks. Finally, users need to set a sleep schedule, that is, the time to go to bed and the time to wake up.

Different from the traditional top banner message reminder, this design solution anthropomorphizes the images of human organs and adopts the interaction form similar to desktop pets to attract users' attention (Fig. 6). Based on the initial idea, we added rich expressions and actions to the organ images to enhance the interest of the interaction process. To allow users to accurately understand the intention expressed by the anthropomorphic image, the text dialog box is retained and suggestions are conveyed to users in a friendly tone. The anthropomorphic image presents different states to the user according to the time change (Fig. 7). Specifically, it presents the state of brushing teeth half an hour before the set bedtime, and the state of yawning at bedtime. When the user starts to delay bedtime, it reminds the user of the increased risk of certain diseases if they do not sleep on time, based on the information collected during the information entry phase. In order to make users interact with the application and enhance user stickiness, we set up tips to help them fall asleep on time, such as completing work tasks on time and reducing the intake of coffee or tea during the day, in addition to bedtime. The anthropomorphic image is hovered at the top of the phone interface, and users can stop themselves from playing with the phone by long-pressing to open the lock function. When the anthropomorphic image hinders the normal use of the phone, the user can hide it by swiping. And it will pop up again automatically when the status is refreshed.

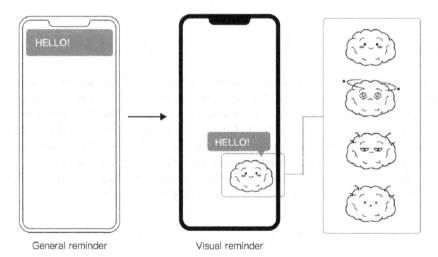

General reminder   Visual reminder

Fig. 6. Improvement of interaction mode

In the app, users can modify the basic information previously entered, and view records of sleep delays and health risk levels. Delayed sleep times are marked in red.

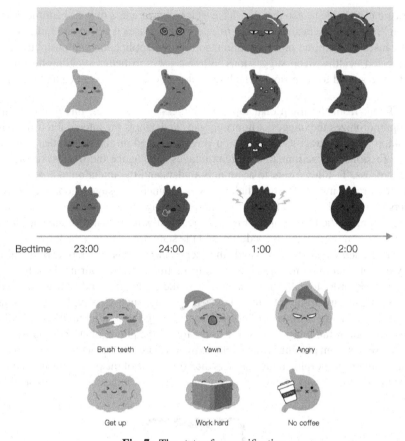

Fig. 7. The state of personification

The sleep time is synchronized with the time when the phone is turned off, as no other technology is currently available. The more time the user has procrastinated, the higher the health risk. The information visualization allows users to visualize the damage to their organs and the increase in the probability of related diseases caused by bedtime delay. The specific disease risk of each organ can be toggled at the bottom to view. By clicking on the organ icon, a health knowledge card pops up with an explanation of how bedtime procrastination causes the onset of disease and suggestions for remedial measures. When the user follows the plan, the health risk will decrease.

4 User Study

In this phase, it was aimed to verify the feasibility of the interaction design solution and to collect user feedback.

Participants. Twenty participants (8 males, 12 females) with an average age of 25.9 years (SD = 3.80; age range: 21–33) were recruited through online social networking platforms in this phase of the study. All of them had significant bedtime procrastination behavior (bedtime procrastination scale score greater than or equal to 3.5), had the habit of using cell phones before bedtime, and were in good physical condition without sleep disorders.

Experimental Design. Participants were randomly divided into two groups. Group A was the control group, who used a sleep persuasion application based on health persuasion. Group B was the experimental group, who used a sleep persuasion application that visualized health risks. Before the start of the experiment, users were asked to fill out a questionnaire. It consisted of the following 3 parts: (a) health risk perception was measured by 8 sentences (e.g., "Procrastination before bedtime increases my risk of cardiovascular disease"). (b) Attitude toward bedtime procrastination. It was measured by 5 sentences, including 2 reverse questions. (c) Intention to correct bedtime procrastination was measured by 6 sentences (e.g., "I want to reduce the number of occurrences of sleep procrastination"). After completion, the corresponding interaction design prototype was presented to each of the two groups of participants, and participants were asked to freely manipulate the interaction prototype while substituting it into the actual usage scenario. At the end of the experiment, participants were asked to fill out the questionnaire again. Finally, they were given a usability questionnaire to complete. The questionnaires adopted the form of Richter's five-point scale.

Result. The experimental results showed that the users' health risk perceptions improved after receiving sleep health education. The visualization application had a significant role in enhancing users' health risk perceptions (Fig. 8). With the health risk visualization persuasion, users' negative attitudes toward bedtime procrastination significantly increased (Fig. 9) and were more concerned about the negative health effects of bedtime procrastination than before the persuasion. In addition, the experimental results also reflected significant differences in users' willingness to correct bedtime procrastination (Fig. 10). Individuals in the visual persuasion condition were more willing than those in the non-visual persuasion condition.

The International Organization for Standardization (ISO) classifies computer usability into 3 metrics, including effectiveness, efficiency, and user satisfaction. Participants in both groups evaluated the sleep persuasion prototype used (Fig. 11). In the effectiveness dimension, the persuasion success rate was significantly higher in group B. In the efficiency dimension, the risk visualization significantly increased the frequency of interaction between the user and the application to shorten the time to complete the persuasion task. In the user satisfaction dimension, user satisfaction was higher in group B. The satisfaction rate of the key function "sleep persuasion" was significantly higher than that of group A.

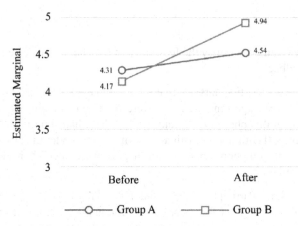

Fig. 8. Impact of visualization on health risk perception

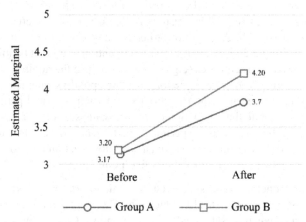

Fig. 9. Impact of visualization on bedtime procrastination attitudes

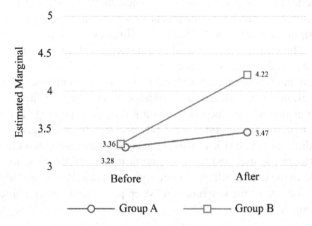

Fig. 10. Impact of risk perception on intention to correct sleep procrastination

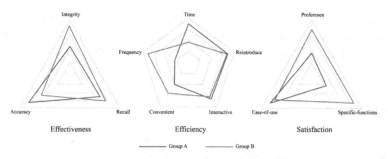

Fig. 11. Usability test of interaction scheme

5 Discussion

Adequate sleep is an important part of maintaining a person's normal activities. And with the development of society and technology, people's lifestyles have changed. Besides the causes of work and illness, the problem of sleep deprivation triggered by bedtime procrastination also needs attention. Firstly, we found in the previous study that the increase in health risk perception helps people to make protective behaviors. Moreover, information visualization helps to improve risk perception. Therefore, we take health risk visualization as an approach point for the design of the sleep persuasion inter-action program. In addition, we combined questionnaire research and semi-structured interviews to further understand users' bedtime behavioral habits, emotions, and usage needs. The preliminary design scheme based on theoretical research received positive feedback from the participants to initially determine the feasibility of the design idea. Based on the user research results, we optimized and designed the interaction design scheme in depth. Finally, we verified the positive effect of health risk visualization in sleep persuasion through comparative experiments. And it was approved by users in the usability testing session.

At the same time, there are some limitations in this study. Firstly, the formation of bedtime procrastination is complicated and cannot be accurately controlled only by the use of mobile applications. Its professionalism needs to be improved. Secondly, correcting bedtime procrastination requires long-term intervention, and this study only verified the effectiveness of the sleep persuasion tool in the short term, and additional experiments are needed for long-term effectiveness.

6 Conclusion and Future Work

In this paper, we propose a sleep persuasion interaction design scheme based on health risk visualization, aiming to improve users' risk perception level and persuade them to sleep on time through information visualization. Combining persuasion theory, risk perception theory, visualization theory and user research, we developed a high-fidelity prototype and tested its usability. The results show that health risk visualization has a significant positive impact on sleep procrastination persuasion. This interaction design solution is presented as a mobile application, which has the advantages of lower cost and easier scalability. The design pattern can also be used to persuade people to correct other vices, such as being sedentary, not exercising, and not drinking water, and to urge people to develop good health behaviors. It provides a new solution for healthy product design.

References

1. Buxton, O.M., Marcelli, E.: Short and long sleep are positively associated with obesity, diabetes, hypertension, and cardiovascular disease among adults in the United States. Soc. Sci. Med. **71**(5), 1027–1036 (2010)
2. Luyster, F.S., Strollo, P.J., Zee, P.C., Walsh, J.K.: Sleep: a health imperative. Sleep **35**(6), 727–734 (2012)
3. Irwin, M.R.: Why sleep is important for health: a psychoneuroimmunology perspective. Annu. Rev. Psychol. **66**, 143 (2015)
4. Wang, X.J., Zhang, Y., Liu, Y.Y.: Chinese Sleep Research Report. Social Science Literature Press (2022)
5. Chung, S.J., An, H., Suh, S.: What do people do before going to bed? A study of bedtime procrastination using time use surveys. Sleep **43**(4), zsz267 (2020)
6. Hodge, B.A., et al.: Dietary restriction and the transcription factor clock delay eye aging to extend lifespan in Drosophila Melanogaster. Nat. Commun. **13**(1), 3156 (2022)
7. Kroese, F.M., De Ridder, D.T., Evers, C., Adriaanse, M.A.: Bedtime procrastination: introducing a new area of procrastination. Front. Psychol. **611** (2014)
8. Kadzikowska-Wrzosek, R.: Insufficient sleep among adolescents: the role of bedtime procrastination, chronotype and autonomous vs. controlled motivational regulations. Curr. Psychol. **39**, 1031–1040 (2020)
9. Jankowski, K.S., Randler, C., Itzek-Greulich, H., et al.: Morningness-eveningness correlates with sleep time, quality, and hygiene in secondary school students: a multilevel analysis. Sleep Med. **30**(C), 151–159 (2017)
10. Sirois, F.M., Nauts, S., Molnar, D.S.: Self-compassion and bedtime procrastination: an emotion regulation perspective. Mindfulness **10**, 434–445 (2019)
11. Rusch, H.L., et al.: The effect of mindfulness meditation on sleep quality: a systematic review and meta-analysis of randomized controlled trials. Ann. N. Y. Acad. Sci. **1445**(1), 5–16 (2019)
12. Zhang, B.D., et al.: Effect of health education on the late sleep phenomenon among medical students. Health Research (2016)
13. Behar, J., Roebuck, A., Domingos, J.S., Gederi, E., Clifford, G.D.: A review of current sleep screening applications for smartphones. Physiol. Meas. **34**(7), R29 (2013)
14. Choi, Y.K., et al.: Smartphone applications to support sleep self-management: review and evaluation. J. Clin. Sleep Med. **14**(10), 1783–1790 (2018)
15. Ware, C.: Information Visualization: Perception for Design. Morgan Kaufmann (2019)
16. Pligt, J.: Risk perception and self-protective behaviour. Eur. Psychol. **1**(1), 34–43 (1996)
17. Wang, L., Touré-Tillery, M., McGill, A.L.: The effect of disease anthropomorphism on compliance with health recommendations. J. Acad. Mark. Sci. 1–20 (2022)
18. Fogg, B.J.: Persuasive technology: using computers to change what we think and do. Ubiquity **2002**(December), 2 (2002)
19. Ahmad, W.N.W., Ali, N.M.: A study on persuasive technologies: the relationship between user emotions, trust and persuasion (2018)

Comparison of Physiological Responses to Stroop Word Color Test and IAPS Stimulation

Sayyedjavad Ziaratnia[(✉)], Peeraya Sripian, Tipporn Laohakangvalvit, and Midori Sugaya

College of Engineering, Shibaura Institute of Technology, 3-7-5, Toyosu, Koto-ku 135-8548, Tokyo, Japan
{am20008,peeraya,tipporn,doly}@shibaura-it.ac.jp

Abstract. The impact of stress on physical and mental health is widely acknowledged, with an estimated 90% of all primary care physician visits being attributed to stress-related problems. Despite this, there is a need for further research on stress-inducing experiments. This study aims to fill this gap (need) by examining the feasibility of stress-inducing experiments such as the Stroop word color test and IAPS images and evaluating the resulting stress levels through physiological data. This study evaluated the distribution of stress indicators, including pNN20, pNN50, and LF/HF, across different tasks using the Friedman test and time series analysis. The aim was to compare the stress-inducing potential of the Stroop Word Color Test and the International Affective Picture System (IAPS) task. Results from the time series graph suggest that participants perceived the Stroop Word Color Test as less stress-inducing compared to the IAPS task.

Keywords: Stress Analysis · Stress Inducing Experiments · Stroop Word Color Test · International Affective Picture System (IAPS)

1 Introduction

Stress has been linked to a wide variety of physical and mental health problems. It is estimated that up to 90% of all visits to primary care physicians are for stress-related problems [1]. Studies have shown that stress can contribute to the top six causes of: cancer, coronary heart disease, accidental injuries, respiratory disorders, cirrhosis of the liver, and suicide [1]. Also, it is a major factor in a number of other conditions, including ulcers, insomnia, anxiety, and depression. In a study it was found that those who reported high levels of stress were more likely to be obese, have high blood pressure, and be less physically active than those who reported low levels of stress [2]. Stress has also been shown to have a negative impact on cognitive function. In another study, it was found that those who reported high levels of stress were more likely to have poorer memory and attention skills than those who reported low levels of stress [3]. There are several theories as to the reason that stress is so harmful to our health. One theory is that stress causes our bodies to release a hormone called cortisol. Cortisol is a stress hormone that has negative effects on our bodies, including increasing our blood pressure, suppressing

V. G. Duffy (Ed.): HCII 2023, LNCS 14029, pp. 211–222, 2023.
https://doi.org/10.1007/978-3-031-35748-0_15

our immune system, and increasing our appetite [4]. Another theory is that stress creates a state of chronic inflammation in our bodies. Although inflammation is a natural process that helps our bodies heal from injuries, chronic inflammation can lead to a number of health problems, including heart disease, cancer, and Alzheimer's disease [5].

To reduce stress levels, some of the most effective stress-reduction techniques are exercise, meditation, and relaxation. Exercise is a great way to reduce stress because it helps to release endorphins, which are hormones that have a positive effect on our mood [6]. Meditation is another effective stress-reduction technique. Meditation helps to focus our attention on the present moment and can help to clear our mind of negative thoughts [7]. Relaxation techniques, such as yoga and deep breathing, can also help to reduce stress by promoting a state of relaxation [8].

To better understand and quantify the effects of stress, it is necessary to perform experiments that induce stress in a controlled environment. This type of experimentation allows researchers to measure and observe the physiological and psychological responses to stress, and to create a model that accurately estimate stress levels. One of the key challenges in creating such a model is the development of a comprehensive database of stress responses. This database is crucial for determining the effectiveness of the stress induction procedures and for validating the stress estimation model. To create this database, it is necessary to conduct a large number of experiments, each involving a different group of participants and a range of stress induction methods. The data collected from these experiments will be used to train and validate the stress estimation model. It is important to note that the development of a stress estimation model will have significant practical applications in the fields of medicine, psychology, and health promotion. By providing a tool for estimating stress levels, researchers and clinicians will be able to identify individuals at risk of developing stress-related health problems and to intervene early to prevent or mitigate these problems. Additionally, the development of a stress estimation model will facilitate the study of stress and its effects and may lead to the development of new and effective stress management strategies.

In this work, we will perform a preliminary experiment to compare the effect Stroop Word Color test and IAPS images on the physiological signals.

2 Background

2.1 Stress Estimation Methods

Stress is a psychological and physiological phenomenon experienced by individuals in response to demanding or challenging situations. Measuring stress levels is important to understand the impact of stress and develop effective interventions. There are several methods for measuring stress levels, including self-report questionnaires and physiological measures.

Self-report questionnaires are a commonly used method for measuring stress levels. One of the most widely used self-report questionnaires is the State-Trait Anxiety Inventory (STAI) [9], which measures an individual's level of anxiety. The STAI consists of two separate scales: the state anxiety scale, which measures anxiety in response to a specific situation, and the trait anxiety scale, which measures a person's general level of anxiety. Self-report questionnaires have the advantage of being easy to administer, but they may be subject to biases such as social desirability, which can affect the accuracy of the results.

Physiological measures are objective measures that assess physiological responses associated with stress, such as heart rate, blood pressure, and cortisol levels. One commonly used psychophysiological measure is heart rate variability (HRV) analysis, which involves the measurement of the variations in time between heartbeats. Two measures of HRV that are often used are the low-frequency (LF) and high-frequency (HF) components, which provide information about different aspects of HRV. Additionally, pNN50 and pNN20 are measures of HRV that indicate the proportion of normal-to-normal R-R intervals that differ by more than 50ms (pNN50) or 20ms (pNN20). Higher values of pNN50 and pNN20 are associated with increased sympathetic nervous system activation [10] and higher levels of stress.

pNNx. pNNx is a measure of HRV that is widely used in research to study the effects of stress on the autonomic nervous system. The pNNx is defined as the percentage of successive normal-to-normal (NN) intervals that differ by more than x milliseconds [11].

$$pNNx = \sum_{n=1}^{t}(if\,(a_n - a_{n-1>x}); z = z + 1) \div t \qquad (1)$$

Studies have shown that pNNx is negatively correlated with stress [12], meaning that as stress levels increase, HRV decreases and the pNN50 decreases. This decrease in HRV is thought to reflect the effects of stress on the autonomic nervous system, which regulates physiological functions such as heart rate, blood pressure, and respiration.

LF/HF. LF/HF is a ratio of low-frequency (LF) to high-frequency (HF) power in the frequency domain analysis of HRV. The LF and HF components of HRV are used to represent different aspects of the autonomic nervous system's regulation of heart rate.

The LF component is thought to reflect the combined effects of both sympathetic and parasympathetic nervous system activity, while the HF component is thought to reflect primarily parasympathetic nervous system activity. The LF/HF ratio is therefore used as an index of sympathovagal balance, with higher values indicating a greater relative contribution of sympathetic nervous system activity [13].

Research has shown that the LF/HF ratio is positively correlated with stress, meaning that as stress levels increase, the relative contribution of sympathetic nervous system activity increases, and the LF/HF ratio increases [14].

2.2 Stress Induction for Experiment

The induction of stress in research studies is a crucial tool for investigating the effects of stress on various physiological and psychological outcomes. There are several methods used to induce stress, including physical, psychological, and social stressors.

Physical stressors are methods that induce stress through physical means. Examples include the cold pressor test, in which participants immerse their hand in cold water, and the handgrip test, where participants squeeze a handgrip for a set time. These methods have been used to study the effects of stress on cardiovascular and autonomic nervous system function.

Psychological stressors are methods that induce stress through mental or cognitive means. Examples include the Stroop word-color test, in which participants are asked to name the color of incongruent words and colors, and mental arithmetic, in which participants are asked to perform mathematical calculations under time pressure. These methods have been used to study the effects of stress on cognitive function and executive control.

Social stressors are methods that induce stress through social evaluation or exclusion. Examples include public speaking, in which participants are asked to give a speech in front of an audience, and social exclusion, in which participants are excluded from social interaction. These methods were used to study stress on social behavior and interpersonal relationships.

The induction of stress in research studies is a crucial tool for investigating the effects of stress on various physiological and psychological outcomes. The choice of method will depend on the specific research question and the desired level of stress induction. Physical, psychological, and social stressors are some of the commonly used methods for stress induction in research studies.

Stroop Word Color Test. The Stroop Word Color Test, also known as the Stroop task, is a well-established tool for measuring cognitive processing speed and control in psychology [15]. The task involves presenting participants with a list of color names (e.g., "red," "blue," "green") that are printed in a different ink color than the word itself. Participants are asked to name the ink color as quickly and accurately as possible while ignoring the word's meaning. This creates a conflict between the automatic tendency to read the word and the requirement to attend to the ink color, leading to slower and less accurate performance compared to when the word and ink color match.

Recent studies have shown that the Stroop task can also be used to induce stress, as the cognitive demands of the task have been found to activate the physiological stress response. The physiological response to the Stroop task has been shown to include increased heart rate and blood pressure, which are all markers of the body's stress response [16]. This makes the Stroop task a useful tool for studying the impact of stress on cognitive performance and the underlying physiological mechanisms.

IAPS Images. IAPS stands for the International Affective Picture System. It is a standardized set of images rated for emotional valence (positive, neutral, or negative) and arousal levels (low, medium, or high) [17]. The IAPS images are widely used in research to study the effects of emotions on various physiological and psychological outcomes.

Researchers can use the IAPS images to induce various levels of emotional stress in participants by presenting them with images that have been rated as high in arousal or negative valence. For example, images that depict scenes of violence or injury are often used to induce elevated levels of stress. The IAPS images can also be used to study the effects of positive emotions, such as happiness or contentment, by presenting participants with images that have been rated as high in positive valence.

The use of IAPS images allows researchers to standardize and control the level of emotional stress induced in participants, providing a useful tool for investigating the effects of emotions on various outcomes.

According to an investigation, pictures with a mean valence of 2.62 ± 0.3 and a mean arousal score of 5.79 ± 0.4 were found to elicit stress [18]. Consequently, for the purpose of inducing stress in participants, images were chosen from the same domain as identified by this study.

3 Research Objective

The main objective of this study is to compare the stress-inducing effects of two commonly used experiments, the Stroop Word Color test, and IAPS images, to determine the validity of these experiments as tools for inducing stress. This study aims to provide a comprehensive examination of the stress-inducing capacity of these two experiments and to ensure that the experiment blocks used meet the necessary requirements for inducing stress in participants. This study's findings will contribute to a better understanding of the methods used to induce stress in research settings and will provide valuable information for future studies exploring the impact of stress on various outcomes.

4 Experiment

4.1 Participants

A total of 9 participants were recruited for the study from the Shibaura Institute of Technology community, including both students and faculty members. The sample consisted of 7 male and 2 female participants, with an age range of 18 to 32 years.

4.2 Measurements

In this study, two types of measurements were utilized to gather data. A PulseSensor was used to measure the photoplethysmography (PPG) signal, which provides information about the blood flow and pulse rate. A Logitech C920n RGB camera was also used for subject monitoring purposes, allowing for real-time observation of the participant's behavior and physiological responses during the experiment. These measurements were chosen as they are non-invasive and widely used in physiological research, providing reliable and accurate data to support the study's objectives.

4.3 Experiment Procedure

The experiment consisted of 6 blocks, as depicted in Fig. 1. In the first block, participants were asked to complete a questionnaire. The second block was a 5-min period of rest, during which participants were instructed to close their eyes, stay relaxed, and refrain from moving. The third block was the Stroop Word Color Test, which lasted approximately 5–8 min. After completing the Stroop Word Color test, participants took another period of rest. In the fifth block, participants were shown stressful images as part of the International Affective Picture System (IAPS) task. Finally, the last block was another period of rest. These blocks were designed to examine the effect of stress on cognitive and physiological responses.

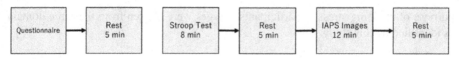

Fig. 1. Experiment Procedure

5   Result and Discussion

5.1   Data Pre-processing

The experiment data pre-processing involves a series of steps to mitigate the impact of noise on the results of the photoplethysmography (PPG) analysis. The pre-processing pipeline consists of four key stages:

1. Interpolation: This stage involves filling in any missing data points in the PPG signal to ensure a continuous and complete signal for further analysis. Additionally, some peaks in the signal may have a flat area, which can affect the analysis results. To avoid this, the interpolation step specifically targets these peaks by interpolating them to preserve the overall shape of the signal.
2. Low-pass filter: A low-pass filter with a cutoff frequency of 2 Hz is applied to the interpolated signal to remove high-frequency noise that may affect the results.
3. High-pass filter: A high-pass filter with a cutoff frequency of 50 Hz is then applied to remove low-frequency noise that may obscure the PPG signal.
4. Butterworth filter: A Butterworth filter is applied to further improve the signal quality by suppressing both low and high-frequency noise.

The implementation of these pre-processing steps is critical to obtaining accurate results in the PPG analysis, as they help to minimize the impact of noise and ensure that the signal remains intact and interpretable.

5.2   Data Analysis

The aim of this analysis was to evaluate the efficacy of the Stroop Word Color test and the IAPS images in inducing stress. To accomplish this objective, three indexes were utilized as indicators of stress, including the LF/HF ratio, pNN50, and pNN20.

Overall Comparison. In order to evaluate the overall distribution of three HRV indexes, namely pNN20, pNN50, and LF-HF, across five different tasks, including Rest 1, Stroop World Color test, Rest 2, IAPS images, and Rest 3, we compute the average value of the HRV indexes during each of the five tasks and show the box plots in Figs. 2, 3 and 4. Then Friedman test was employed for further statistical analysis. The Friedman test is a non-parametric statistical test used to assess the differences between groups on a dependent variable measured on an ordinal scale, and is commonly used when data violate the assumptions of normality, homogeneity of variance, and independence required by parametric tests. By conducting this analysis, we aimed to determine whether the distributions of the indexes differed significantly across the different tasks.

The results showed that the Friedman statistic was not significant for pNN20 ($\chi 2$ (4) = 3.700, p = 0.448) and pNN50 ($\chi 2$ (4) = 7.500, p = 0.112). This implies that the scores for pNN20 and pNN50 did not differ significantly among the conditions, and thus, these variables may not be sensitive enough to detect differences in autonomic function among different tasks. However, the Friedman statistic was significant for LF/HF ($\chi 2$ (4) = 10.700, p = 0.030). Further analysis revealed that the significant difference was between the Stroop Word Color test and Rest 3, which is not the appropriate pair for comparison. Therefore, the results suggest that there is no significant difference for LF/HF among all tasks.

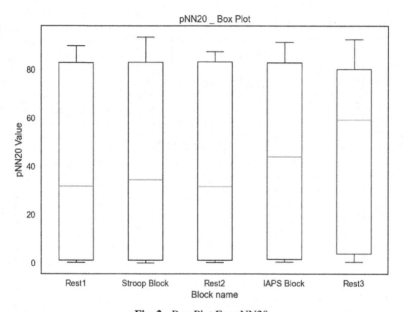

Fig. 2. Box Plot For pNN20

Time Series Analysis. Furthermore, to assess the trends more in detail, time-series plots were generated for each of the indexes as shown in Fig. 7, the trend of the LF/HF ratio was observed to decrease during the Stroop Word Color test but increase during the IAPS block. Conversely, as illustrated in Figs. 5 and 6 the trends of pNN50 and pNN20 were increasing for the Stroop test and the IAPS task. Results suggest that the Stroop Word Color test may not have been as effective in inducing stress compared to the IAPS task. The decrease in the LF/HF ratio during the Stroop test may indicate a shift toward parasympathetic activity, while the increase in pNN50 and pNN20 for both tasks suggest an increase in autonomic nerve activity, which is indicative of stress.

In conclusion, the results of this analysis provide evidence that the IAPS task was more effective in inducing stress compared to the Stroop Word Color test. Further research is needed to fully understand the reasons for these findings and to explore other potential stress-inducing tasks.

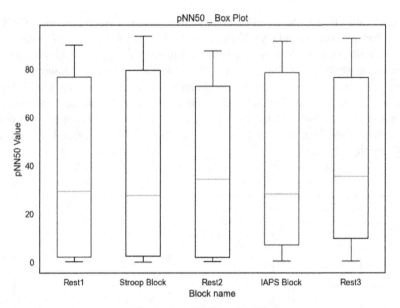

Fig. 3. Box Plot For pNN50

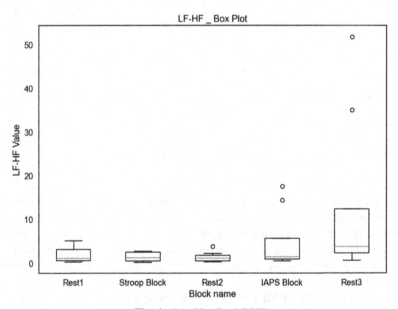

Fig. 4. Box Plot For LF/HF

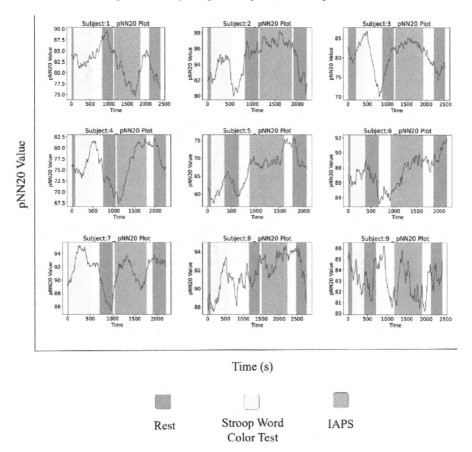

Time (s)

Rest   Stroop Word   IAPS
                Color Test

Fig. 5. Subjective Time Series For pNN20

5.3 Discussion

The study aimed to evaluate the differences in the distribution of HRV indexes: pNN20, pNN50, and LF/HF, across different tasks using the Friedman test. The results indicate that pNN20 and pNN50 may not have a significant difference across the tasks. On the other hand, the LF/HF ratio only showed a significant difference between the Stroop Word Color test and Rest 3. Further analysis using time series plots revealed that the IAPS task was more effective in inducing stress compared to the Stroop Word Color test. The decrease in the LF/HF ratio during the Stroop test may indicate a shift toward parasympathetic activity, while the increase in pNN50 and pNN20 for both tasks suggest an increase in autonomic nerve activity, which is indicative of stress.

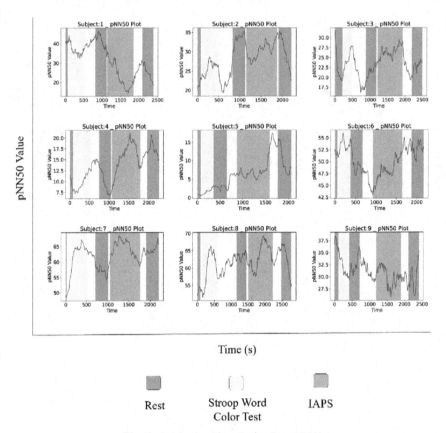

Fig. 6. Subjective Time Series For pNN50

Additionally, In the present study, participants were asked about their subjective experience of stress while performing both the Stroop word color test and the IAPS. Consistent with previous research, all participants reported feeling stressed when viewing the IAPS images. However, younger participants reported enjoying the Stroop Word Color test and did not report experiencing stress while completing the task. These findings suggest that the relationship between age and stress-inducing cognitive tasks may be more nuanced than previously thought, and that additional research is needed to fully understand the mechanisms underlying these effects.

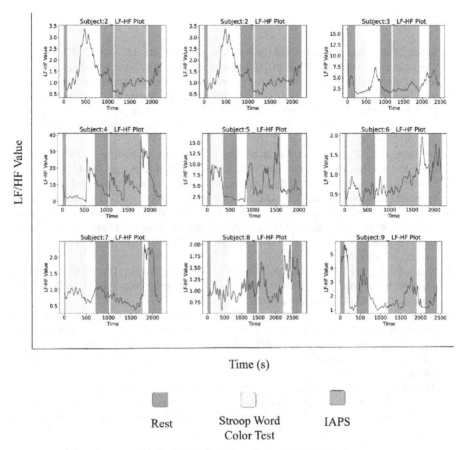

LF/HF Value

Time (s)

Rest   Stroop Word   IAPS
                Color Test

Fig. 7. Subjective Time Series For LF/HF

6   Conclusion

The results of the time series graph suggest that the Stroop Word Color Test was perceived as less stress-inducing compared to the International Affective Picture System (IAPS) task. This hypothesis was generated based on the patterns observed in the time series graph, which showed that the physiological responses of the participants were lower during the Stroop test compared to the IAPS task. Further research is needed to confirm these findings and to explore the underlying mechanisms that may contribute to the perceived stress levels during these tasks. Nevertheless, this study provides valuable insights into the comparison of two commonly used stress-inducing experiments and highlights the importance of considering the subjective experiences of participants when designing stress induction protocols.

Acknowledgements. This study is partly supported by JSPS KAKENHI Grant Number JP19K20302. We thank all the participants for their cooperation in the experiment.

References

1. Salleh, M.R.: Life event, stress and illness. Malays. J. Med. Sci. **15**, 9–18 (2008)
2. Gasperin, D., Netuveli, G., Soares Dias-da-Costa, J., Pascoal Pattussi, M.: Effect of psychological stress on blood pressure increase: a meta-analysis of cohort studies Efeito do estresse psicológico no aumento da pressão arterial: uma metanálise de estudos de coorte (2009)
3. Lupien, S.J., McEwen, B.S., Gunnar, M.R., Heim, C.: Effects of stress throughout the lifespan on the brain, behaviour and cognition. Nat. Rev. Neurosci. **10**, 434–445 (2009). https://doi.org/10.1038/nrn2639
4. McEwen, B.S.: Physiology and neurobiology of stress and adaptation: central role of the brain. Physiol Rev. **87**, 873–904 (2007). https://doi.org/10.1152/physrev.00041.2006
5. Moieni, M., Eisenberger, N.I.: Effects of inflammation on social processes and implications for health. Ann. N. Y. Acad. Sci. **1428**, 5–13 (2018). https://doi.org/10.1111/nyas.13864
6. Hildebrandt, T., Shope, S., Varangis, E., Klein, D., Pfaff, D.W., Yehuda, R.: Exercise reinforcement, stress, and β-endorphins: an initial examination of exercise in anabolic–androgenic steroid dependence. Drug Alcohol Depend. **139**, 86–92 (2014). https://doi.org/10.1016/j.drugalcdep.2014.03.008
7. Evans, S., Ferrando, S., Findler, M., Stowell, C., Smart, C., Haglin, D.: Mindfulness-based cognitive therapy for generalized anxiety disorder. J. Anxiety Disord. **22**, 716–721 (2008). https://doi.org/10.1016/j.janxdis.2007.07.005
8. Toussaint, L., et al.: Effectiveness of progressive muscle relaxation, deep breathing, and guided imagery in promoting psychological and physiological states of relaxation. Evid.-Based Complement. Altern. Med. **2021**, 1–8 (2021). https://doi.org/10.1155/2021/5924040
9. Spielberger, C.D., Goruch, R., Lushene, R., Vagg, P., Jacobs, G.: Manual for the state-trait inventory STAI (form Y). Mind Garden, Palo Alto, CA, USA (1983)
10. Ahmed, T., Qassem, M., Kyriacou, P.A.: Physiological monitoring of stress and major depression: A review of the current monitoring techniques and considerations for the future. Biomed. Signal Process Control. **75**, 103591 (2022). https://doi.org/10.1016/j.bspc.2022.103591
11. Mietus, J.E., Peng, C.-K., Henry, I., Goldsmith, R.L., Goldberger, A.L.: The pNNx files: re-examining a widely used heart rate variability measure. Heart **88**, 378 (2002). https://doi.org/10.1136/heart.88.4.378
12. Trimmel, M.: Relationship of Heart Rate Variability (HRV) parameters including pNNxx with the subjective experience of stress, depression, well-being, and every-day trait moods (TRIM-T): a pilot study. Ergon. Open J. **8**, 32–37 (2015). https://doi.org/10.2174/1875934301508010032
13. Kim, H.-G., Cheon, E.-J., Bai, D.-S., Lee, Y.H., Koo, B.-H.: Stress and heart rate variability: a meta-analysis and review of the literature. Psychiatry Investig. **15**, 235–245 (2018). https://doi.org/10.30773/pi.2017.08.17
14. Sloan, R.P., et al.: Effect of mental stress throughout the day on cardiac autonomic control. Biol. Psychol. **37**, 89–99 (1994). https://doi.org/10.1016/0301-0511(94)90024-8
15. Jensen, A.R., Rohwer, W.D.: The stroop color-word test: a review. Acta Psychol. (AMST) **25**, 36–93 (1966). https://doi.org/10.1016/0001-6918(66)90004-7
16. Pehlivanoğlu, B., Durmazlar, N., Balkancı, D.: Computer adapted stroop colour-word conflict test as a laboratory stress model. Erciyes Med. J. **27**, 58–63 (2005)
17. Lang, P.J., Bradley, M.M., Cuthbert, B.N.: International affective picture system (IAPS): Technical manual and affective ratings. NIMH Center Study Emotion Attention **1**, 3 (1997)
18. Mochizuki-Kawai, H., Matsuda, I., Mochizuki, S.: Viewing a flower image provides automatic recovery effects after psychological stress. J. Environ. Psychol. **70**, 101445 (2020). https://doi.org/10.1016/j.jenvp.2020.101445

IoT and AI in Medicine and Healthcare

Artificial Intelligence for Clinical Intensive Care in the Hospital: Opportunities and Challenges

Kirsten Brukamp[(✉)]

Research Group Health – Technology – Ethics, Protestant University Ludwigsburg,
Paulusweg 6, 71638 Ludwigsburg, Germany
k.brukamp@eh-ludwigsburg.de

Abstract. Innovative technologies promise to substantially transform clinical health care. In particular, applications of artificial intelligence are currently emerging as part of medical devices. Clinical intensive care in the hospital has traditionally been a setting in which health care professionals are extensively supported by technical products. Post-operative care after cardiac surgery constitutes a highly relevant realm for evaluating novel approaches with medical devices. Technological innovations may include probability estimates for diagnosis and prognosis by an artificial intelligence analysis of data combinations from different sources, voice and gesture control, remote assessment of skin perfusion, as well as optimized representation and visualization of clinical data. A requirements analysis, using empirical methods of social science research, was conducted in order to include stakeholders' perspectives. Thereby, a participatory design was realized in the research and development processes. Ethical, legal, and social implications (ELSI) were specifically addressed to identify potentials for improving both acceptance and acceptability during future steps.

Keywords: Innovative technologies · Artificial intelligence · Health care · Intensive care · Hospital · Empirical methods of social science research · Requirements analysis · Ethical, legal, and social implications (ELSI)

1 Introduction

1.1 Technological Innovations for Clinical Intensive Care in the Hospital

Artificial intelligence (AI) applications are currently transforming health care fundamentally. Examples concern a wide range of disciplines, such as surgery and psychiatry, radiology and pharmacology [1]. Automated analysis is increasingly offered for images, which may be generated by both expensive medical devices in hospitals and by users via their own mobile devices. Thereby, opportunities arise for hospital management as well as individual patient empowerment. While the routes to technological progress explore the potential of various strategies, questions surface regarding the conditions for an acceptable use from a societal standpoint.

The research and development project "AI-based post-operative care for patients after cardiac surgery" (i.e. "KI-gesteuerte postoperative Versorgung herzchirurgischer

V. G. Duffy (Ed.): HCII 2023, LNCS 14029, pp. 225–235, 2023.
https://doi.org/10.1007/978-3-031-35748-0_16

Patienten" KIPos in German) focuses on AI applications in clinical intensive care after surgery. The intensive care units are based in a large university hospital in Germany. Additional partners include research groups on vision and imaging, on gesture recognition, on remote blood flow detection, as well as a company that concentrates on artificial intelligence for personalized medicine. The project receives funding from the Federal Ministry of Education and Research in Germany (i.e. "Bundesministerium für Bildung und Forschung" BMBF in German).

The technical approaches are planned to specifically improve patient care at the bedside and its immediate environment. Visual representations of patient data from the records are optimized and displayed on large screens, and physicians and nurses use gesture recognition to steer through the available data. In particular, radiological images are analyzed for daily changes during the patient's stay. Vital signs are deduced from the remote detection of blood flow in the skin. On an overarching patient management level, AI predictions are calculated regarding the patients' readiness to be safely transferred out of the intensive care environment, depending on the available data from previous practice.

Specific approaches and devices are selected for the purpose of enhancing intensive care in the Department of Cardiothoracic Surgery at the University Hospital Düsseldorf in Germany. The innovations include an artificial intelligence analysis of a data combination from different sources for diagnostic and prognostic probability estimates, voice and gesture control, remote assessment of perfusion, as well as optimized representation and visualization of clinical data. Prior to implementation, a requirements analysis was conducted with physicians, nurses, and former patients, and the results were evaluated towards specific aims for the implementation process.

The objective of this study is to examine the technological developments for clinical health care from a societal perspective. The focus is on user orientation and user experience as topics of human-technology interaction (HTI) in the framework of ethical, legal, and social implications (ELSI).

1.2   Brief Overview Regarding the Current Practice in Health Care

Potential applications of machine learning in cardiovascular health care, according to the literature, include automated imaging interpretation, natural language processing, and predictive analytics [2]. Image interpretation extends to electrocardiography, echocardiography, chest x-rays, computed tomographic angiography, and invasive coronary angiography [2]. Language analysis is based on clinical notes and electronic health records in general [2]. Predictions concern mortality, complications after procedures, as well as early and late outcomes after therapy [2].

A review identified five areas for applications of machine learning in thoracic surgery: aiding diagnosis and preoperative management, augmenting intraoperative surgical performance, surgical observation and evaluation/skill assessment, post-surgical prognosis/post-procedure prognostication, and accelerating translational research [3]. A scoping review of artificial intelligence in thoracic surgery lists the following five areas for applications: machine learning for diagnostic augmentation, preoperative predictions, postoperative complication prediction, prediction using molecular markers, and postoperative survival prediction [4]. A narrative review of artificial intelligence in thoracic surgery named the following applications: thoracic lesion management, preoperative evaluation and risk assessment, surgical performance and planning, pathology, and prognosis [5]. An additional article calls attention to the following areas for artificial intelligence in cardiothoracic surgery: diagnostic augmentation, human-machine teaming and computer vision, preoperative performance and safety in cardiothoracic surgery, intraoperative performance and safety in cardiac/cardiothoracic surgery, and post-operative management [6].

The database Medical Information Mart for Intensive Care (MIMIC-III) was used to predict long-term mortality after cardiac surgery [7]. 18.15% of the patients died within four years, and age, congestive heart failure, and urine output were among the key predictors [7].

Touchless user interfaces appear to be very convenient for computer systems in hospitals. A systematic literature search yielded more than forty suitable articles since 2010 [8]. Motivational factors for these types of innovations included hygiene and frequent hand use [8]. The most frequent task was image navigation, and the environment that was considered most often was the operating room [8]. Many studies had small sample sizes and focused on gesture-recognition accuracy as well as feasibility [8].

1.3 Details of Technological Innovations

Technological innovations in the research and development project KIPos include applications of artificial intelligence, voice and gesture control, remote assessment of blood perfusion in the skin [9–11], as well as optimized representation and comprehensive visualization of clinical data [12].

The perfusion of visible human tissues may be inferred from video recordings with optical, contactless, remote photoplethysmography (rPPG) signals [10]. The latter technique is also utilized to measure oxygen saturation by pulse oximetry. Heart beats result in pulses that lead to repeat changes in skin color, which cannot normally be detected by the human eye. After local definitions for regions of interest, the heart rate and the perfusion are deduced [10]. This technique can be applied to face and neck, and it detects facial coverings, such as masks [11].

A novel dashboard approach presents both classic patient data and AI assessments. A concise data depiction is especially meaningful in critical post-operative care situations with increased mortality and morbidity. The interactive dashboard was developed with a user-centered focus, which took into account a survey with twenty-five cardiac surgeons and interviews with physicians from different wards [12]. The users may choose their own preferences for the depictions, thereby individualizing the details [12].

Figure 1 shows a concept image [13], which illustrates several innovations that the project KIPos introduces into clinical intensive care, namely gesture control and improved visualization. Figure 2 shows a passive leg raise test [14], which illustrates one use case in the project KIPos. Clinical health care professionals raise a patient's leg in order to predict fluid responsiveness, i.e. the response to rapid fluid loading, from hemodynamic parameters, such as heart rate and blood pressure.

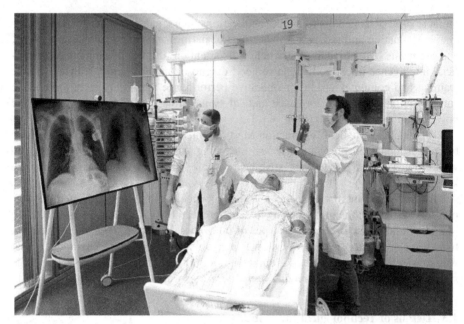

Fig. 1. Concept image. The figure [13] illustrates several innovations for clinical intensive care in the research and development project KIPos: gesture control and improved visualization.

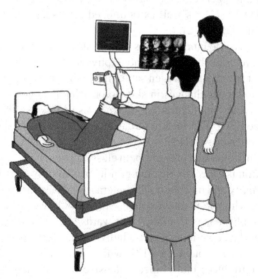

Fig. 2. Leg raise test. The figure [14] illustrates a use case in the research and development project KIPos: the clinical passive leg raise test for fluid responsiveness.

2 Methods

Methods include empirical social science research, integration of expert knowledge, project workshops, and literature reviews. Qualitative methods from empirical research were employed, as part of a requirements analysis, to gain insights into the needs and desires of important target groups for artificial intelligence on intensive care units. Interviews were conducted with physicians, nurses, and former patients. Interview guidelines were developed based on project plans and literature reviews. The transcripts were analyzed according to qualitative content analysis [15]. In addition, project members from technical and social disciplines engaged in participant observation to gain a better understanding of the clinical care processes. The results were discussed in project workshops, from which conclusions were deduced for future directions and implementation of specific technological approaches. The workshops focused on general requirements as well as ethical, legal, and social implications (ELSI). Specialists provided expertise regarding medical device law, emerging artificial intelligence law, and data protection.

3 Results

3.1 Requirements Analysis

The requirements analysis, which primarily relies on the content analysis of interviews with physicians, nurses, and patients, yields highly relevant results for the development of the project. User orientation and user experience are understood as important components in the consideration of ethical, legal, and social implications (ELSI). Numerous recommendations were inferred for the use settings and the designs of the technological products.

For instance, warning signals during or before emergency situations may be deduced from vital signs, laboratory values, and various examination procedures. Health care professionals could be automatically notified of alarming developments. The expanded detection of early warning signs may improve prognosis and survival in post-operative intensive care.

Applications could include pain management. Subjective pain fluctuations may be signaled by objective and measurable changes in vital signs, vegetative responses, and movements. An automated assessment could benefit patients because a reliable prediction might lead to preventive administration of pain medication.

Possibilities were pondered to modify alarms. Noise reduction in intensive care units has been a notorious, long-standing topic in the face of increasingly technology-filled work environments. Nevertheless, the life-threatening conditions in intensive care preclude far-reaching changes in current practice.

Documentation of clinical progress is an important, but also time-consuming task in the hospital. Technical support could assist in calculating statistical measures and autonomously presenting them to decision-makers, e.g. as means and changes over time. This information could be combined with reminders for personnel. Diagnostic and therapeutic procedures might be scheduled more conveniently, if all hospital information systems were technically synchronized, aside from any potential enhancement by artificial intelligence.

Long-term, the clinical software systems may be meaningfully completed by the integration of guidelines according to evidence-based practice in health care. This approach could take place on different levels, which may correspond to the coming technical advancements: In a first step, the AI-supported system suggests appropriate guidelines, which relate to the clinical questions at hand. In a second step, the system analyzes the details of guidelines for passages that fit clinically, across different guidelines. In a third step, the system recommends newer clinical studies, which became available after guideline publication, for a comprehensive, current contextualization of guidelines.

AI applications would ideally not only help professionals to make decisions, but also support patient education. Both search queries from patients and their conditions themselves could lead to suitable offers of educational material via media, at a level that is appropriate for the patients' current cognitive abilities. Due to the fragile patient conditions in intensive care, this opportunity could instead be offered to relatives and friends at this critical time, according to the patients' own wishes.

Overall, stakeholders sought an improved analysis and an increased linkage of data. Health care procedures generate much information, but the data may not always be analyzed to the full extent that is currently possible by technological means. Results from different procedures should be more intensely linked in the future in order to gain novel insights into pathophysiology, treatment interactions, and prognosis.

3.2 Ethical Implications

The four principles of biomedical ethics [16] provide a framework for the ethical analysis of topics in applied ethics. These principles include respect for autonomy, beneficence, non-maleficence, and justice. They have been complemented by additional dimensions in applied ethics for technology, such as privacy, safety, security, participation, and self-image [17]. Ethical questions for the research and development project KIPos in particular concern respect for autonomy, privacy, safety, explainability, and avoidance of harm in the format of bias for or against patient groups, such as women.

The principle of respect for autonomy gives rise to the concept of informed consent, which relies on the interaction and communication between patients and physicians. Patients have to receive all information for treatments in advance, and they need to give informed consent for all interventions. The standards for information about research interventions in health care are frequently supposed to be higher than for medically necessary procedures.

Health care professionals may experience conflicts of interest between their roles as clinicians and as researchers. As clinicians, they are inclined to provide the best possible care to their patients. Nevertheless, as researchers, they may offer interventions that have yet to be proven safe and effective. Such conflicts are addressed in the field of human research ethics.

According to the requirements analysis, technical assistance can support patient education. Nevertheless, it is an ethical question when and how patient education should take place. Most jurisdictions guarantee patients access to their own clinical files. A competent patient with emotional stability can act according to this right at any time. In contrast, patients in intensive care and after surgery frequently exhibit limitations and fluctuations of their cognitive abilities as well as emotional instability. Therefore, a cautious use of educational materials, tailored towards the individual patient situation, can be advised for a successful recovery process, especially while the patients are in critical care after surgery. Thereby, the principle of respect for autonomy is balanced with the principle of beneficence.

Applications utilizing artificial intelligence may realize improvements in health care for many patients, in line with the principle of beneficence. Nevertheless, challenges of non-maleficence also need to be taken into account. Risks exist due to automated data assessments when seemingly neutral automation algorithms analyze skewed data collections or incorporate categories of bias from society, for example regarding age, gender, or ethnic origin. At this time, human expertise is frequently considered necessary in decision-making processes that involve artificial intelligence.

Both the dimension of beneficence and the dimension of non-maleficence lead to the practice of evidence-based intensive care. Experts negotiate guidelines, recommendations, and standards. For this purpose, novel studies deliver scientific results for progress in health care. Insofar, research is needed, even though it cannot fully exclude risks during the clinical collection of new data.

The principle of justice calls for widespread clinical access, surpassing boundaries of education or finances. Clear patient benefits should also be broadly discernable. During the research and development process, the dimension of justice encourages participation from all user groups.

Privacy is an ethical topic that is related to several of the principles above, in particular to individual patient wishes, according to the principle of respect for autonomy. Extensive data collection and analysis could further infringe on individual privacy in an already precarious setting. Nevertheless, the patients' situations are already so threatening in intensive care that the principle of beneficence typically takes precedence, such that the promises to save patients' lives are pursued despite potential risks.

3.3 Social Implications

Social implications occasionally demonstrate a close overlap with ethical implications. They concern communication and interaction, in small groups or in society as a whole.

User orientation and user experience are topics of human-technology interaction (HTI). From a user perspective, technical devices and interfaces should possess opportunities to be individualized or personalized. This way, technology becomes more convenient and understandable. Still, a common ground needs to be laid in critical areas of collaboration at work. For example, colors such as red, yellow, and green carry established meanings with them. Diverging individual definitions would most probably lead to confusion in a shared working environment.

Projects that seek to transform health care in a fundamental way may change established practices. Thereby, they require human adaptation. Hospital organization slowly change over time and necessitate additional skills, which personnel should be enabled and empowered to acquire.

When AI explainability is limited, health care providers need information, guidance, and support from technical developers in order to act as mediators between patients and technological products. Health care professionals cannot be expected to develop a complete second expertise in computer science, digital medicine, artificial intelligence, and engineering. Nevertheless, the professionals directly interact with patients, and the latter expect them to provide explanations for the technical background. Health care experts can be expected to undergo continuing education in order to update their knowledge about technical advancements.

3.4 Legal Implications

The legal requirements for AI-based medical devices are strong and will become even more important. The Medical Device Regulation (MDR) of the European Union [18] was introduced as the legal framework for medical devices in 2017. The oversight for manufacturers is fairly strict. On this basis, limitations abound for academic researchers and developers to transfer their innovations into marketable products. Consequently, the vision of a fully AI-equipped intensive care unit, or general hospital ward, will probably not materialize in a widespread manner soon. Rather, the hospitals probably need to wait for commercial certification of individual products, which gradually become available for practical use over a prolonged period of time. Technological innovations carry risks that require legal provisions regarding liability.

The proposed Artificial Intelligence Act (AI Act) of the European Commission [19] is likely to enhance this effect. According to the planned AI Act, designated notified bodies assess the artificial intelligence components of medical devices.

The General Data Protection Regulation (GDPR) in the European Union [20] provides the general framework for the utilization of technology in health care, together with patients' rights. Results from artificial intelligence may continuously improve, when more and more data are provided for learning. Collection and use of comprehensive clinical data need to be justified and made transparent to patients and health care institutions alike.

4 Discussion

Innovative technologies for health care possess the potential to significantly transform intensive care even further. For post-operative care after cardiac surgery, the requirements analysis in the research and development project KIPos demonstrates highly relevant contributions from stakeholders, such as physicians, nurses, and patients. The recommendations, concerns, and comments are expected to lead to increases for acceptance and acceptability of the final applications and products in the intended setting. Thereby, the participation of target groups constitutes a meaningful approach to co-creation in the project, and this concept was realized in an exemplary fashion.

The study could be broadened by including a higher number of study subjects as well as the inclusion of additional, potential target groups, such as physical therapists, pharmacists, and supportive hospital staff. Nevertheless, the study completely fulfills its role as an initial requirements analysis, and additional requirements will be assessed during the progress of the project. The assessment of the requirements by the expert panel was limited by the need for timely decisions to select certain technological approaches, but to leave out others, due to the restricted time frame for implementation during the three allotted years for the entire project. Next steps include technological development, iterative testing phases, adjustments of the requirements as well as the monitoring of their effects, and plans for the study design of an empirical evaluation during the demonstration model phase with quantitative and qualitative research methods.

According to the concept of research integration, ethical, legal, and social implications (ELSI) are included and examined in the study. The integration of ethical issues into health technology assessment, for example, has been suggested for more than a decade [21]. The consideration of dedicated ELSI categories [16, 17] in the requirements analysis constitutes a definite strength in the project KIPos overall, as well as particularly in the early stages, because a perspective of integration may promote acceptance and acceptability of the envisioned technologies on the individual, organizational, and societal levels later on. Important obstacles were identified, as well as legal frameworks to be followed.

The potential for transfer of the project results to adjacent and more remote areas of care is immense. The technological innovations themselves as well as the concepts for their clinical applications may be transferred to intensive care in general, post-operative care in general, cardiac surgery and cardiac care, general in-hospital care, and integration of in-hospital and ambulatory care.

The research and the development steps towards technologies are highly relevant for future health care, and empirical data is fundamental in order to consider the recommendations from the target groups. This way, technology use may be optimized for human-centered interaction, which is expected to raise health care quality for patients and work satisfaction in health care providers.

5   Conclusion

Innovations in technologies, particularly artificial intelligence, for use in health care promise substantial advancements in life expectancy and quality of life in the near future. Cardiovascular medicine and intensive care, as a care area that has traditionally strongly relied on technology use, are of utmost public health importance. Therefore, technological innovations in cardiac critical care are both rooted in continuity and slated for expansion.

In summary, a requirements analysis demonstrates that novel technological applications, including in artificial intelligence, offer meaningful opportunities to improve clinical intensive care. At the same time, challenges need to be addressed regarding ethical, legal, and social implications (ELSI) in order to realize health innovations in an acceptable way.

Acknowledgments. The project "Artificial-intelligence-based post-operative care: testing and evaluation" (i.e. "Künstliche-Intelligenz-basierte postoperative Versorgung: Testung und Evaluation" KIPos-TE in German), as a part of the joint project "AI-based post-operative care for patients after cardiac surgery" (i.e. "KI-gesteuerte postoperative Versorgung herzchirurgischer Patienten" KIPos in German), is funded by the Federal Ministry of Education and Research in Germany (i.e. "Bundesministerium für Bildung und Forschung" BMBF in German) under grant funding number 16SV8603. The interview study was positively evaluated by the responsible research ethics committee at the regional medical association State Chamber of Physicians. The interviews were conducted by Shirin Gatter, research fellow in the Research Group Health – Technology – Ethics.

The KIPos-TE researchers should like to thank the study participants and all members of the KIPos project consortium, in particular at the Digital Health Lab, Department of Cardiothoracic Surgery, University Hospital Düsseldorf, Düsseldorf, Germany, and the Fraunhofer Heinrich Hertz Institute, Berlin, Germany.

References

1. Brukamp, K.: Human-machine interaction in medicine. [In German: Mensch-Maschine-Interaktion in der Medizin.] In: Chibanguza, K., Kuß, C., Steege, H. (eds.) Artificial Intelligence. Law and Practice of Automatized and Autonomous Systems. [In German: Künstliche Intelligenz. Recht und Praxis automatisierter und autonomer Systeme.] Nomos, Baden-Baden (2022)
2. Kilic, A.: Artificial intelligence and machine learning in cardiovascular health care. Ann. Thorac. Surg. **109**(5), 1323–1329 (2020). https://doi.org/10.1016/j.athoracsur.2019.09.042. Accessed 10 Feb 2023
3. Ostberg, N.P., Zafar, M.A., Elefteriades, J.A.: Machine learning: principles and applications for thoracic surgery. Eur. J. Cardiothorac. Surg. **60**(2), 213–221 (2021). https://doi.org/10.1093/ejcts/ezab095,lastaccessed23/02/10
4. Seastedt, K.P., et al.: A scoping review of artificial intelligence applications in thoracic surgery. Eur. J. Cardiothorac. Surg. **61**(2), 239–248 (2022). https://doi.org/10.1093/ejcts/ezab422. Accessed 10 Feb 2023
5. Bellini, B., Valente, M., Del Rio, P., Bignami, E.: Artificial intelligence in thoracic surgery: a narrative review. J. Thorac. Dis. **13**(12), 6963–6975 (2021). https://doi.org/10.21037/jtd-21-761. Accessed 10 Feb 2023
6. Mumtaz, H., et al.: The future of cardiothoracic surgery in artificial intelligence. Ann. Med. Surg. (Lond.) **80**, 104251 (2022). https://doi.org/10.1016/j.amsu.2022.104251. Accessed 10 Feb 2023
7. Yu, Y., et al.: Machine learning methods for predicting long-term mortality in patients after cardiac surgery. Front. Cardiovasc. Med. **9**, 831390 (2022). https://doi.org/10.3389/fcvm.2022.831390. Accessed 10 Feb 2023
8. Cronin, S., Doherty, G.: Touchless computer interfaces in hospitals: a review. Health Informatics J. **25**(4), 1325–1342 (2019). https://doi.org/10.1177/1460458217748342. Accessed 10 Feb 2023
9. Kossack, B., Wisotzky, E., Hänsch, R., Hilsmann, A., Eisert, P.: Local blood flow analysis and visualization from RGB-video sequences. Curr. Dir. Biomed. Eng. **5**(1), 373–376 (2019). https://doi.org/10.1515/cdbme-2019-0094. Accessed 10 Feb 2023
10. Kossack, B., Wisotzky, E., Hilsmann, A., Eisert, P.: Automatic region-based heart rate measurement using remote photoplethysmography. In: IEEE/CVF International Conference on Computer Vision (ICCV) Workshops, pp. 2755–2759 (2021)
11. Kossack, B., Wisotzky, E., Hilsmann, A., Eisert, P.: Local remote photoplethysmography signal analysis for application in presentation attack detection. In: Schulz, H.-J., Teschner, M., Wimmer, M. (eds.) Vision, Modeling, and Visualization. Eurographics Association Proceedings, pp. 135–142 (2019). https://doi.org/10.2312/vmv.20191327. Accessed 10 Feb 2023
12. Kalkhoff, S., Korlakov, S., Lichtenberg, A., Aubin, H., Schmid, F.: Comprehensive visualization of AI decisions for early complication detection of cardiac surgery patients. Thorac. Cardiovasc. Surg. **70**(S 01), S1–S61 (2022). https://doi.org/10.1055/s-0042-1742835. Accessed 10 Feb 2023

13. KIPos consortium: KIPos project information: concept image. Bundesministerium für Bildung und Forschung, Bonn (2021). https://www.interaktive-technologien.de/projekte/kipos. Accessed 10 Feb 2023

14. KIPos consortium: KIPos results: leg raise test image. Fraunhofer-Institut für Nachrichtentechnik, Berlin (2022). https://projekt-kipos.de/ergebnisse. Accessed 10 Feb 2023

15. Mayring, P.: Qualitative content analysis: theoretical foundation, basic procedures and software solution. SSOAR Open Access Repository, Klagenfurt (2014). https://www.ssoar.info/ssoar/bitstream/handle/document/39517/ssoar-2014-mayring-Qualitative_content_analysis_theoretical_foundation.pdf. Accessed 10 Feb 2023

16. Beauchamp, T.L., Childress, J.F.: Principles of Biomedical Ethics. Oxford University Press, Oxford (1979)

17. Weber, K.: MEESTAR^2 – an extended model for the ethical evaluation of socio-technical arrangements. [In German: MEESTAR^2 – Ein erweitertes Modell zur ethischen Evaluierung soziotechnischer Arrangements.] In: Weidner, R. (ed.) Technical Support Systems that Humans Really Want. [In German: Technische Unterstützungssysteme, die die Menschen wirklich wollen.] Helmut Schmidt University Hamburg [in German: Helmut-Schmidt-Universität Hamburg], Hamburg (2016)

18. Medical Device Regulation 2017: Regulation (EU) 2017/745 of the European Parliament and of the Council of 5 April 2017 on medical devices, amending Directive 2001/83/EC, Regulation (EC) No 178/2002 and Regulation (EC) No 1223/2009 and repealing Council Directives 90/385/EEC and 93/42/EEC. Official J. Eur. Union L 117 (2017). https://eur-lex.europa.eu/legal-content/EN/TXT/PDF/?uri=CELEX:32017R0745&qid=1675874782576&from=EN. Accessed 10 Feb 2023

19. Artificial Intelligence Act Proposal 2021: European Commission: Proposal for a Regulation of the European Parliament and of the Council Laying Down Harmonised Rules on Artificial Intelligence (Artificial Intelligence Act) and Amending Certain Union Legislative Acts {SEC(2021) 167 final} - {SWD(2021) 84 final} - {SWD(2021) 85 final}. COM(2021) 206 final; 2021/0106 (COD) (2021). https://eur-lex.europa.eu/resource.html?uri=cellar:e0649735-a372-11eb-9585-01aa75ed71a1.0001.02/DOC_1&format=PDF. Accessed 10 Feb 2023

20. General Data Protection Regulation 2016: Regulation (EU) 2016/679 of the European Parliament and of the Council of 27 April 2016 on the protection of natural persons with regard to the processing of personal data and on the free movement of such data, and repealing Directive 95/46/EC. Official J. Eur. Union L 119 (2016). https://eur-lex.europa.eu/legal-content/EN/TXT/PDF/?uri=CELEX:32016R0679. Accessed 10 Feb 2023

21. Burls, A., et al.: Tackling ethical issues in health technology assessment: a proposed framework. Int. J. Technol. Assess. Health Care 27(3), 230–237 (2011). https://doi.org/10.1017/S0266462311000250. Accessed 10 Feb 2023

Proposal of a Prototype Wireless Network Based on IoT that Allows the Monitoring of Vital Signs of Patients

Leonel Hernandez[1]([✉]), Aji Prasetya[2], Jainer Enrique Molina-Romero[3], Leonardo Campis[4], Jose Ruiz Ariza[5], Hugo Hernández Palma[6], and Emilse María Vásquez Avendaño[3]

[1] Faculty of Engineering, Institución Universitaria de Barranquilla IUB, Barranquilla, Colombia
lhernandezc@unibarranquilla.edu.co
[2] Faculty of Engineering, Universitas Negeri Malang, Malang, Indonesia
aji.prasetya.ft@um.ac.id
[3] Faculty of Health Sciences, Universidad Libre, Barranquilla, Colombia
{jainer.molina,vasqueza}@unilibre.edu.co
[4] SOLTRAF Ingeniería SAS, Barranquilla, Colombia
[5] Department of Computer Science and Electronics, Universidad de la Costa CUC, Barranquilla, Colombia
jruiz18@cuc.edu.co
[6] Faculty of Engineering, Corporación Universitaria Latinoamericana CUL, Barranquilla, Colombia
hhernandez@ul.edu.co

Abstract. This study proposed developing a wireless network that monitors patients' vital signs using the Top-Down methodology. The project begins by giving a general overview of a current problem and showing a solution from the telecommunications environment. Ultimately, it should provide a practical and efficient solution through an IoT architecture. We seek to establish how a network of this type can improve response times and, consequently, the internal processes of the organization so that doctors who would be one of the end-users benefits can have an improvement in the process of monitoring vital signs of patients under their care since they will have the facility to validate this information from anywhere in the clinic. The network will allow the convergence of the data collected by the various clinical monitoring equipment. This would enable storing the data of each patient, and this could help the medical staff make decisions more agilely and receive timely alerts when the patient's vital signs are altered. The information of all monitored patients would help managers make decisions regarding the improvement or adjustment of internal processes, patient treatments, and others. The data would be centralized to generate different statistics, allowing a clear picture of the capacity status and future or possible saturation in care. Finally, a functional prototype of a wireless network based on IoT will be delivered, allowing the implementation of new network trends such as SDWN.

Keywords: Internet of Things (IoT) · Monitoring · Packet Tracer · Wireless Networks · Patients

V. G. Duffy (Ed.): HCII 2023, LNCS 14029, pp. 236–249, 2023.
https://doi.org/10.1007/978-3-031-35748-0_17

1 Introduction

The health system presents various problems that have led to this sector's crisis. The problem can be visibly evidenced in emergency rooms and physical spaces for hospitalizations, given that the constant flow of patients demands that internal processes be increasingly efficient. For these health services to fulfill their purpose of optimal and professional care that can contribute to improving the patient's health and, in most cases, saving their life, in 2020, according to the Ministry of Health, patients that required hospitalization were 87,459 nationwide [1], which shows that the flow of patients is high, making it necessary to have a technological infrastructure with which an optimal service can be provided. To strengthen this infrastructure, new alternatives are required that support medical processes and tasks in such a way as to minimize the number of adverse situations of these health services and guarantee reliable and permanent access of doctors to information of each patient to improve the recovery process of each user of the health system.

In Colombia, we are experiencing a critical moment for the health system that shows how important it is to have clear and timely information to make decisions that can save lives. The non-availability of the data means that it is unavailable to interested users when required, either in the database or in the information repositories provided for that purpose. This failure in the process means that one of the information security principles, which is available, is being breached. Wireless networks are the best connectivity option since you do not have to be at a fixed point within the clinic to access some information. Still, it is possible to access different applications from mobile devices from any location, such as cell phones, tablets, and laptops.

IoT plays a fundamental role in health, which has made it possible to optimize access to information and equipment that benefit the patient [2]. Information on health issues is too essential since if it is not received on time and correctly, a person's life or integrity can be at risk [3]. Data poorly studied or provided out of time can compromise a patient's life. The proposed system seeks to offer an agile tool so that the information obtained from it in real-time is used to make precise decisions at the time required. The design consists of traditional wireless equipment, on which they connect IoT sensors and actuators, which allow high availability and connectivity for the equipment of the various medical spaces.

In this project, the TOP-DOWN methodology was used, which proposes an incremental development of the system requirements throughout the network, identifying clear and concise activities in its iterations to implement a technological infrastructure prototype in a network simulator that serves as a strategy to improve the processes of a solution that provides care to users who require this type of service. When implementing the prototype, a performance analysis of the network was made, obtaining good response times that fit the requirement of the health center under study. The rest of the paper is organized as follows: the general concepts of wireless networks and IoT are exposed, presenting the appropriate literature review. Subsequently, the methodology used for the development of the study is exposed. Then the results of the simulated prototype are revealed, presenting the design, list of equipment, basic configurations, and response times to culminate with the general conclusions and future work.

2   Literature Review

In the existing literature, works like the prototype proposed by the project have been found. The first corresponds to a comparative analysis entitled "System for Monitoring the Heart Rhythm." It had the objective of Designing a filter for the electrocardiogram signal to obtain the heart rate. Unfortunately, many people worldwide suffer from cardiovascular diseases and would benefit from continuous monitoring of their cardiac constants. This project allowed us to know how to work on the reading or cardiac signal of the person in which it is reflected in the mobile device and thus be able to determine and analyze through a specialized medical staff to say that the patient is well or your heart rhythm is wrong [3].

In the methodology explained by [4], a descriptive research study was presented by the method proposed in the SCG. The series of instantaneous heart rates obtained from the ECG is used as a reference. The algorithm used in the ECG is summarized in 2 steps: a preprocessor and a decision rule. The preprocessor removes baseband line drift and enhances the QRS complex. [5] made a descriptive research study using an experimental method based on the network tests, seeing its efficiency and reliability and making changes to provide optimal results. In addition to tests on vital signs with the prototype compared to conventional methods, to analyze and validate results, which can only be evaluated through observation, comparison, and monitoring. [6] describes the results obtained through an IoT-based ECG system to diagnose specific cardiac pathologies. [7] carry out a complete analysis of the impact of IoT-ML solutions for healthcare applications, in which the importance of agility in decision-making for health protection is highlighted.

[8] explain the strong interaction between solutions called the Internet of Medical Things (IoMT) and a wireless network category called WBAN (Wireless Body Area Network), noting that both go hand in hand for the design and implementation of patient monitoring systems, consultations by health specialists and stakeholders.

Security is a core factor in wireless networks and IoT devices that connect to these infrastructures. [9] mentions IoHT as a variant of IoT focused on health care. Security guidelines must be established to prevent data interception or connectivity damage, such as jamming attacks. In this sense, similar investigation advances were carried out by [10], in which encryption methods are explained to protect the IoHT network devices, the WBAN infrastructure, and the data of patients with COVID-19, specifically via the SIMON lightweight block cipher.

IoT is closely related to wireless network infrastructures to strengthen health care, facilitate connectivity and communication between patients and health professionals, and promote secure access to relevant data from medical records. IoT has a robust application in healthcare through various architectures such as Bluetooth, ZigBee, and LoWPAN [11–14]. IoT can also be applied in other fields, such as installing sensors for monitoring environmental conditions in data centers, research developed by [15], or tracking people to prevent kidnapping, such as the work produced by [16]. [17] configured a prototype for intelligent buildings, using packet tracer to establish a redundant IoT topology through HSRP protocol.

Packet Tracer is a widely used simulator for network education owned by Cisco Systems, with which all kinds of network topologies are designed. In his comparative study of simulators for teaching wireless networks, [18] positions Packet Tracer in good shape and places it as an excellent alternative for designing and prototyping wireless networks. Packet tracer has been used to simulate several WLAN implementations, as [19–22] did in their respective investigations, and as an educational tool for networking learning [23, 24].

3   Methodology

To achieve the proposed objectives, it was intended to adjust the Top-down network design methodology, focused on customer requirements [25, 26]. The authors developed the project in four phases. The first phase corresponds to the requirements analysis, where researchers analyze the customer's needs. In stage 2, researchers proposed the network's logical design, the general diagram of the system's operation, and the WLAN design, following the stipulations of the Top-down network design methodology. In phase 3, the authors selected the equipment, tools, and other elements necessary for the prototype's correct operation. Finally, stage 4 develops tests, optimization, and network design documentation. Researchers conducted various tests to verify the network's performance [27]. The system was also optimized, taking as input the partial and global tests carried out on the prototype to adjust the aspects presented [28]. Figure 1 shows the stages of the project.

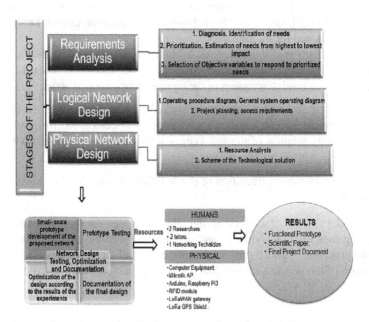

Fig. 1. Stages of the project

4 Results and Discussion

This project seeks to respond to connectivity and efficient access to information required by the different users interested in the clinic. The proposed prototype will be implemented based on an IoT solution. By having a connectivity solution design, nursing and medical staff care will be provided with a quality service to carry out their research activities and clinical data in real-time. With the diagnosis of the current state of the WLAN network, it is intended to survey network infrastructure plans to identify the areas of wireless coverage and improve the service provided. In the same way, medical and assistance personnel will be able to count on a mobile (wireless) internet access service that will give them more independence and mobility within the infrastructure and that will respond to their requirements and demands for the development of their activities, which require constant access to the Internet, as well as monitoring of patients. Administrative staff will be allowed to work in various spaces that are not limited by the direct connection of their equipment (desktop computers) to the LAN network. Instead, they will be allowed a link that provides them with mobility if required.

4.1 Network Simulation

For the development of the prototype, the Packet Tracer simulator version 8.1.1 was used, in which a wide variety of functions related to networks can be carried out, such as designing and building a network from scratch, working on pre-built projects, testing new designs, and network topologies, test network changes before applying them to the network, examine the flow of data through a network, run simulations of the Internet of Things similar to [29], or prepare for networking certification exams. Figure 2 shows the topology designed for the prototype.

For the construction of the prototype, the IoT devices provided by the Packet Tracer tool were used. These devices are doors with card reader access, RFID cards, and RFID readers. Below is a brief description of the equipment mentioned above:

- RFID card: It is about preventing unauthorized persons from accessing the facilities and speeding up the entry and exit of workers and customers. [twenty]. Figure 3 shows the configuration of the IoT Gate 4 with the activation of the wireless port [30]:

Figure 4 shows the configuration of the IoT Gate 4 with the Wireless0, the SSID, and its password:

- RFID reader: they oversee feeding the labels and tags through the antennas while capturing their data, decoding it, and transmitting it to the corresponding software for interpretation. Figure 5 shows the configuration of the RACK RFID card with the activation of the wireless port so that it can be managed from the IoT management console:

- IoT Server: consists of an object that has been provided with an Internet connection and specific software intelligence, on which physical parameters can be measured or act remotely, and that therefore allows an ecosystem of services to be generated

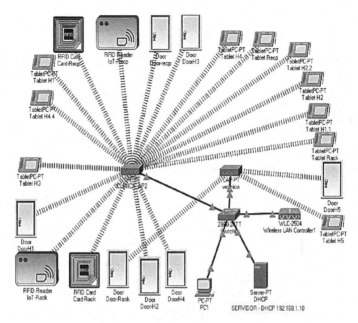

Fig. 2. Physical Design of the Network

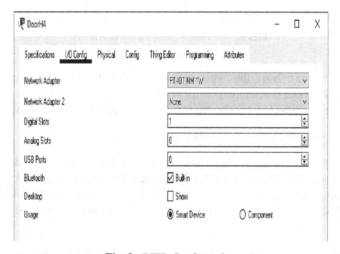

Fig. 3. RFID Configuration

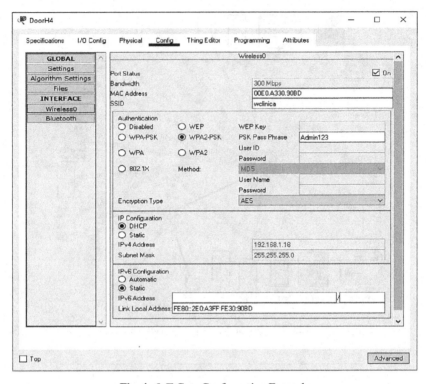

Fig. 4. IoT Gate Configuration Example

around it. Figure 6 shows the configuration of the DHCP services in the central server and the IoT service is activated, the user and the assigned key will allow access to the administration console from the browser of any computer connected to the network:

Figure 7 shows the IoT service configuration in the server:

- WLC (Wireless LAN Controller): In a Wireless LAN (WLAN) network, we can use WLC to centralize the control of the APs (Access Points or Access Points) instead of delegating management to each one of them. Figure 8 shows the list of IoT devices that interact in the topology displayed from the browser of one of the connected devices:

Figure 9 below shows the physical connections in the communications rack and the different network devices, such as the server, switch, and WLC in the rack:

For the operation of network connectivity, the following tests are carried out by sending packets from different IoT devices, which will be reflected in Fig. 10, highlighting the correct operation of the topology:

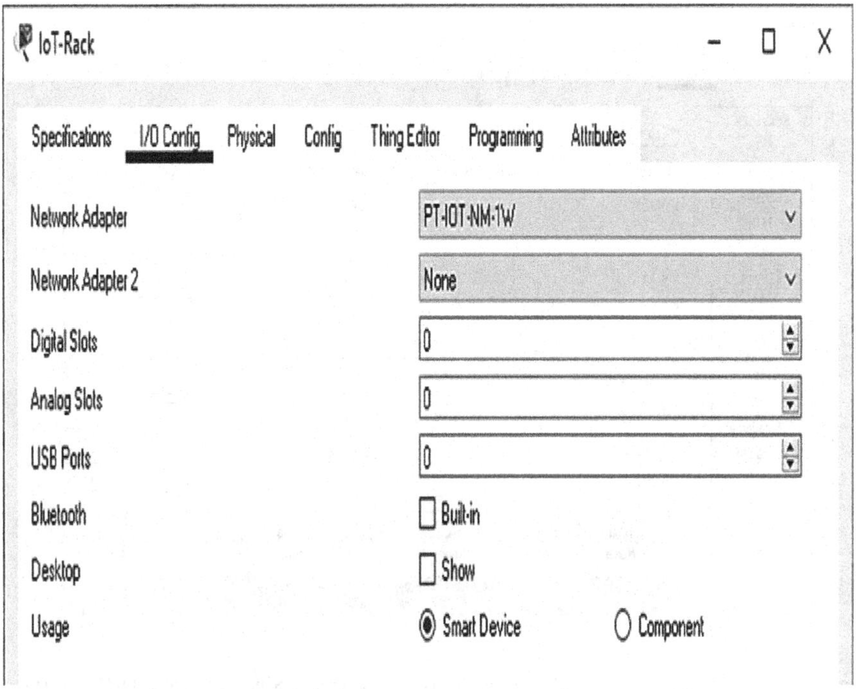

Fig. 5. RACK RFID Configuration with Wireless Port Activation

Successful: This means that the packet sent arrived correctly at its destination. Example: it was sent from the DHCP Server to the WLC. It came perfectly, it was also dispatched from an H3 Tablet and arrived correctly, and a packet was also sent from a Port, and all the packages that were sent also arrived at their destination.

4.2 Network Performance Indicators

The following tests are made for response times by pinging the DHCP server from any host in the topology. The response times in which the packets were sent and received were always favorable, with positive responses of (0) zero lost data packets shown in Table 1 (partial results) with some IoT devices.

In implementing this class, it is relevant to calculate, in addition to the response times, the delay, and the Jitter, which are indicators that validate the network's excellent performance. Jitter is the first consequence of a signal delay. Delay specifies how long a data bit travels through the network from a source node to an end node. At the same time, Jitter is defined as the temporal variability during the sending of digital signals, a slight deviation from the accuracy of the signal. Of clock, Jitter is often thought of as an unwanted noise signal. In general, Jitter is called an unwanted and abrupt change in the property of a signal. This can affect both the amplitude and the frequency and phase situation.

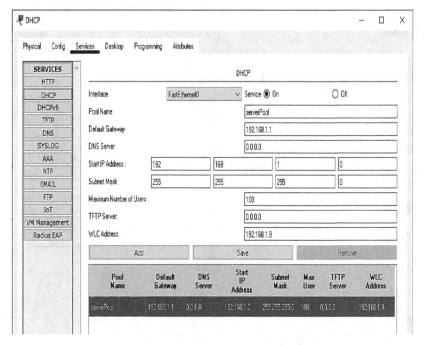

Fig. 6. Server Configuration by DHCP in Cisco Packet Tracer Simulator from DHCP Services

Even though the prototype is built in a simulated environment, the response times, delay, and jitter values are highly satisfactory, which allows for estimating an adequate performance of the infrastructure at the time of implementation. Equation 1 was used for delay calculation:

$$d_{end-end} = N\left(d_{proc} + d_{trans} + d_{prop}\right) \tag{1}$$

where N is the number of nodes, dproc is the delay produced by the traffic analysis of the network equipment, dtrans is the transmission delay, and dprop is the propagation delay. Equation 2 was used for jitter calculation:

$$J_{per} = T_{per(1)} - T_0 \tag{2}$$

where $T_{per(1)}$ is the oscillation period of the first oscillation after the initiating event and T_0 the ideal oscillation period. Table 2 shows the delay and jitter values for traffic between Tablet H1 and Tablet H4:

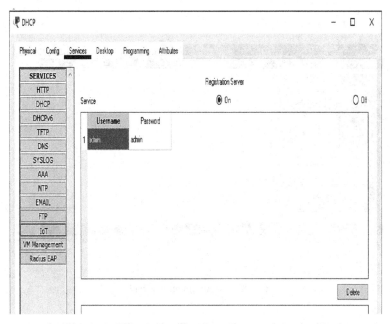

Fig. 7. Configuring the IoT Service on the Cisco Packet Tracer Simulator Server

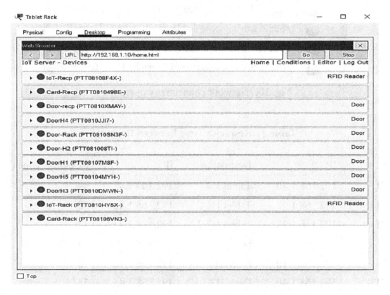

Fig. 8. Devices connected to the server

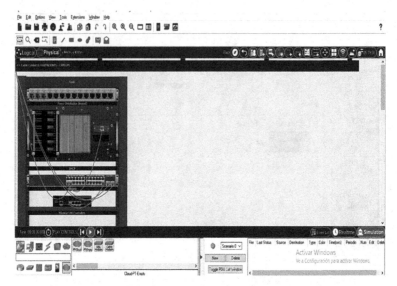

Fig. 9. Communications Rack

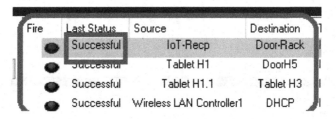

Fig. 10. Network connectivity operation

Table 1. Response Time Between Devices

Source	IP	Destination	IP	Response Time (ms)
Tablet H1	192.168.1.46	Tablet H4	192.168.1.42	49
Tablet H4	192.168.1.42	Tablet H1	192.168.1.46	38
Tablet H4.4	192.168.1.28	Tablet H2.2	192.168.1.43	42
Tablet Recp	192.168.1.37	Server	192.168.1.10	14
Server	192.168.1.10	DoorH1	192.168.1.12	18
Tablet H3	192.168.1.40	Door-H2	192.168.1.45	55
PC1	192.168.1.13	Card-Recp	192.168.1.38	15

Table 2. Delay and Jitter Values

Time Response	Delay	Jitter
49	−0,029	0,009
20	−0,02	0,032
30	−0,03	0,056
10	0,005	−0,015
15	−0,01	0,01
12	0,014	−0,035
26	−0,021	-0,01

5   Conclusions and Future Works

This project allowed the design of a wireless network prototype that allows and helps to improve the patient monitoring process, using Packet Tracer as a simulator. An IoT-based design was carried out. The tests that allowed evaluating the device response times could be carried out, concluding that this type of network can be adapted to a clinic infrastructure efficiently.

All those devices connected to a wireless network can be linked to the network, making IoT devices interact with patient monitoring equipment. The project highlights that since access to the network or the server can be given from any location in the clinic, being within WiFi coverage, patient information can be accessed. In addition, IoT devices can improve access to patient monitoring rooms. The prototype allows the use of devices such as doors, cards, and RFID readers, which show the environment of a clinic with the implementation of the Internet of things. The tablets were used as a monitor in each room for practical use, and the connection with the server was established. This allowed tests to be carried out with packet shipments from each physical location of the hospitalization rooms to the server.

Finally, after the packet sending tests, it was possible to evaluate the response times and the percentage of packet loss, obtaining the following results: a minimum time of 14 ms and a maximum of 55 ms, with a rate of 0% packet loss, low delay levels and therefore Jitter. With this, it can be concluded that the network design provides adequate results, offering optimal response times that contribute to the improvement of the internal processes of the clinic. In future work, the prototype implementation can be mentioned and carried out in the short term, as security configuration and tests, which were not considered at this stage of the project. Additionally, a different network paradigm can be considered, such as SDWN. Better results of performance indicators (such as delay and Jitter) have been verified compared to the traditional WLAN [31].

References

1. Fernandez, J., Molina, A., Camargo, L.: Catálogo de indicadores básicos de salud 2020 (2021). https://www.minsalud.gov.co/sites/rid/paginas/freesearchresultsf.aspx?k=Indicadoresbásicosdesalud2020. Accessed 0 Mar 2021

2. Sharma, N.K., Gautam, D.K., Sahu, L.K., Khan, M.R.: First wave of covid-19 in India using IoT for identification of virus. Mater. Today Proc. (2021). https://doi.org/10.1016/J.MATPR.2021.05.492

3. Cotorruelo, A.: Sistema para monitorización del ritmo cardíaco mediante Smartphone, Universidad de Sevilla (2017)

4. Alarcó Pérez, J., Parada Medina, R., Monzo Sánchez, C.: Diseño de una Smart UCI para la monitorización de pacientes, Universitat Oberta de Catalunya (2019)

5. Gutierrez, J.P.: Implementación de un Prototipo de una Red Inalámbrica de Sensores Biomédicos, para la Adquisición y Almacenamiento de Datos, Usando Cloud Computing, para Pacientes en Casa, Universidad Nacional de San Agustín de Arequipa (2019)

6. Morello, R., Ruffa, F., Jablonski, I., Fabbiano, L., De Capua, C.: An IoT-based ECG system to diagnose cardiac pathologies for healthcare applications in smart cities. Measurement **190**, 1–14 (2022)

7. Sabrin Sworna, N., Muzahidul Islam, A.K., Shatabda, S., Islam, S.: Towards development of IoT-ML driven healthcare systems: a survey. J. Netw. Comput. Appl. **196** (2021). https://doi.org/10.1016/j.jnca.2021.103244

8. Aski, V.J., Kumar, S., Verma, S., Rawat, D.B.: Advances on networked eHealth information access and sharing: status, challenges, and prospects. Comput. Netw. **204** (2022). https://doi.org/10.1016/j.comnet.2021.108687

9. Sharma, K.: Internet of healthcare things security vulnerabilities and jamming attack analysis. Exp. Syst. **39**(3) (2022). https://doi.org/10.1111/exsy.12853

10. Mohsin, F., Elmedany, W.: A secure internet of healthcare things for tackling COVID-19. In: 2021 International Conference on Innovation and Intelligence for Informatics, Computing, and Technologies, 3ICT 2021, pp. 98–104 (2021). https://doi.org/10.1109/3ICT53449.2021.9581819

11. Ahmadi, H., Arji, G., Shahmoradi, L., Safdari, R., Nilashi, M., Alizadeh, M.: The application of internet of things in healthcare: a systematic literature review and classification. Univ. Access Inf. Soc. **18**(4), 837–869 (2018). https://doi.org/10.1007/s10209-018-0618-4

12. Dhanvijay, M.M., Patil, S.C.: Internet of Things: a survey of enabling technologies in healthcare and its applications. Comput. Netw. **153**, 113–131 (2019). https://doi.org/10.1016/j.comnet.2019.03.006

13. Hernandez, L., Marquez, L., Correa, S., Simanca, T.: Design and prototyping of a scalable IoT solution based on LoRaWAN to improve the service of school routes in the south west location of Barranquilla. In: 2020 6th International Conference on Science in Information Technology: Embracing Industry 4.0: Towards Innovation in Disaster Management, ICSITech 2020 (2020). https://doi.org/10.1109/ICSITech49800.2020.9392062

14. AbdulGhaffar, A., Mostafa, S.M., Alsaleh, A., Sheltami, T., Shakshuki, E.M.: Internet of Things based multiple disease monitoring and health improvement system. J. Ambient. Intell. Humaniz. Comput. **11**(3), 1021–1029 (2019). https://doi.org/10.1007/s12652-019-01204-6

15. Hernandez, L., Calderon, Y., Martinez, H., Pranolo, A., Riyanto, I.: Design of a system for detection of environmental variables applied in data centers. In: Proceeding - 2017 3rd International Conference on Science in Information Technology: Theory and Application of IT for Education, Industry, and Society in Big Data Era, ICSITech 2017 (2017). https://doi.org/10.1109/ICSITech.2017.8257144

16. Hernandez, L., Prasetya, A., Dwiyanto, F.: Design of a network prototype based on LoRaWAN for the implementation of a mobile anti-kidnapping monitoring platform. In: 2021 7th International Conference on Electrical, Electronics and Information Engineering (ICEEIE) (2021). https://doi.org/10.1109/ICEEIE52663.2021.9616785

17. Reddy, G.P., Kumar, Y.V.P.: Retrofitted IoT based communication network with hot standby router protocol and advanced features for smart buildings. Int. J. Renew. Energy Res. **11**(3), 1354–1369 (2020)

18. Richards, T., Gamess, E., Thornton, D.: A survey of wireless network simulation and/or emulation software for use in higher education. In: Proceedings 2021 ACMSE Conference - ACMSE 2021 Annual ACM Southeast Conference, pp. 63–70 (2021). https://doi.org/10.1145/3409334.3452066

19. Prajwal, K., Amistaree, P., Vamshi, G.R., Kirthika, D.V.: Wireless communication network-based smart grid system. In: 1st International Conference on Pervasive Computing and Social Networking, pp. 673–694 (2021). https://doi.org/10.1007/978-981-16-5640-8_51

20. Ashok, G.L., Saleem, A.P., Sai, N.M., Nagasaikumar, J., Vamshi, A.: Implementation of smart home by using packet tracer. Int. J. Sci. Technol. Res. **9**(2), 678–685 (2020)

21. Elhaloui, L., Elfilali, S., Tabaa, M., Benlahmer, E.H.: Toward a monitoring system based on IoT devices for smart buildings. In: Saeed, F., Al-Hadhrami, T., Mohammed, F., Mohammed, E. (eds.) Advances on Smart and Soft Computing. AISC, vol. 1188, pp. 285–293. Springer, Singapore (2021). https://doi.org/10.1007/978-981-15-6048-4_25

22. Sony, K., Durga Indira, N., Vinay Kumar, S., Bhanu Prakash, V., Jaya Chandra Sekhar, D.: Electronic devices monitoring based wireless gateway network using cisco packet tracer. Int. J. Adv. Trends Comput. Sci. Eng. **8**(6), 2935–2963 (2019). https://doi.org/10.30534/ijatcse/2019/41862019

23. Al-Hamadani, M.N., Sattam, I.A., Daoud, R.W., Shehab, S.N., Kamel, H.A.: Design and implement a self-managed computer network for electronic exams and sharing. Indones. J. Electr. Eng. Comput. Sci. **19**(1), 466–475 (2020). https://doi.org/10.11591/ijeecs.v19.i1.pp4 66-475

24. Muniasamy, V., Eljailani, I.M., Anadhavalli, M.: Student's performance assessment and learning skill towards Wireless Network Simulation tool - Cisco Packet Tracer. Int. J. Emerg. Technol. Learn. **14**(7), 196–208 (2019). https://doi.org/10.3991/ijet.v14i07.10351

25. Oppenheimer, P.: Top-down Network Design, 3rd edn. Cisco Press, Indianapolis (2011)

26. Kurose, J.F., et al.: Computer Networking A Top-Down Approach Seventh Edition, 7th ed. (2017)

27. Hernandez, L., Jimenez, G., Pranolo, A., Rios, C.U.: Comparative performance analysis between software-defined networks and conventional IP networks. In: Proceedings 5th International Conference on Science in Information Technology, ICSITech 2019 (2019)

28. Hernandez, L., et al.: Optimization of a WiFi wireless network that maximizes the level of satisfaction of users and allows the use of new technological trends in higher education institutions. In: Streitz, N., Konomi, S. (eds.) HCII 2019. LNCS, vol. 11587, pp. 144–160. Springer, Cham (2019). https://doi.org/10.1007/978-3-030-21935-2_12

29. Kumar, V., Sakya, G., Shankar, C.: WSN and IoT based smart city model using the MQTT protocol. J. Discret. Math. Sci. Cryptogr. **22**(8), 1423–1434 (2019). https://doi.org/10.1080/09720529.2019.1692449

30. Hwang, Y.M., Kim, M.G., Rho, J.J.: Understanding the Internet of Things (IoT) diffusion: focusing on value configuration of RFID and sensors in business cases (2008–2012). Inf. Dev. **32**(4), 969–985 (2016). https://doi.org/10.1177/0266666915578201

31. Hernández, L., Rios, C.E.U., Pranolo, A.: Design a model-based on nonlinear multiple regression to predict the level of user satisfaction when optimizing a traditional WLAN using SDWN. Int. J. Adv. Sci. Eng. Inf. Technol. **11**(4), 1487–1493 (2021). https://doi.org/10.18517/ijaseit.11.4.14463

Mel Frequency Cepstral Coefficients and Support Vector Machines for Cough Detection

Mpho Mashika⬭ and Dustin van der Haar[(✉)]⬭

Academy of Computer Science and Software Engineering,
University of Johannesburg, Auckland Park, Johannesburg, Gauteng, South Africa
dvanderhaar@uj.ac.za

Abstract. Asthma, pneumonia, chronic obstructive pulmonary disease (COPD), and most recently, the covid-19 illness all include cough as one of its most noticeable symptoms. This paper proposes a method that uses audio signals to detect cough events. To train the models, we used data obtained from the ESC-50 dataset. We built models based on different features selected from Mel Frequency Cepstral Coefficients (MFCC), Zero Crossing Rate (ZCR), and Energy. The classification algorithms are K-NN, Support Vector Machine (SVM), and Multilayer Perceptron (MLP). The best model used the MFFC features and the SVM classification algorithm. The best model realised an accuracy of 92.20%, a precision of 92.86%, a recall of 91.55%, and an F1-score of 92.20%.

Keywords: Cough Detection · mel-frequency cepstral coefficient · support vector machine

1 Introduction

A cough is a voluntary or involuntary act that clears the throat of foreign particles. A cough is one of the easiest-to-recognize signs of several respiratory illnesses, including laryngitis, asthma, pneumonia, bronchitis, and chronic obstructive pulmonary disease.

Three steps make up a cough: inhalation, increased pressure in the throat and lungs caused by the vocal cords closing, and finally, an explosive release of air caused by the vocal cords opening, which produces the cough's distinctive sound [1]. A cough is divided into two main categories, acute and chronic. In the case of acute cough, the most common cause is an infection in the upper respiratory tract that affects the throat, known as URTI (upper respiratory tract infection). A chronic cough may be caused by smoking, post-nasal drip, gastroesophageal reflux disease, and asthma [2]. Treatments for cough include postnasal drip, antibiotics, and acid reflux.

Laconte et al. found a correlation between cough frequency and the perceived quality of life [18]. Counting cough frequency manually is an error-prone task,

V. G. Duffy (Ed.): HCII 2023, LNCS 14029, pp. 250–259, 2023.
https://doi.org/10.1007/978-3-031-35748-0_18

which brings about the need for automated cough detectors. Since individuals with various diseases exhibit distinct coughing patterns, automated cough detectors can help doctors establish diagnosis [3].

Coughing frequently results in the emission of some sound; a cough detector is implemented in this study using audio signals from these emissions. Computing MFCC as a feature set allows for processing audio signals from microphone-acquired cough sounds; these features feed an SVM classifier with minimum sequential optimisation. Our findings demonstrate the potential of MFCC features for remote cough detection. This study shows that an effective remote cough detection system can be built with few features or complex machine learning approaches.

Following this introduction, this paper is divided into the following sections: Section 2 discusses related research, Sect. 3 describes the experimental setup and dataset we used to train our model, Sect. 4 goes into depth about the methodology we followed in this study, Sect. 5 provides a summary of the findings with performance matrices, and Sect. 6 makes conclusions.

2 Similar Work

Various work has been done on cough detection in the recent past. Amoh and Odame considered two approaches to using deep neural networks for cough detection: a convolutional neural network and a recurrent neural network [4]. Between the two, the convolutional network did better with a specificity of 92.70%, whereas the recurrent network achieved a sensitivity of 87.70%. Monge-Alvarez et al. proposed an automated cough detection model using local Hu-moments as a robust feature set; the audio signals were acquired using a smartphone [5]. Using k-NN as a classifier, the model achieved a sensitivity of up to 88.51% and specificity of up to 99.77% in various noisy environments.

Teyhouee and Osgood looked at the possibility of categorising various coughing conditions using Hidden Markov Models (HMM) [6]. They utilised the models to separate coughing episodes from background noise and successfully classified cough episodes with an area under the curve of 92%. Chen and Zhai proposed a model for cough detection where they used 20 features selected from MFCCs by the Uniform Variable Elimination (UVE) algorithm and classified them using the SVM classifier [7]. The dataset used to train the model combined data from the ESC-50 dataset and self-recorded cough recordings. The model archived an accuracy of 94.90%, a recall of 97.10%, a precision of 93.1%, and a recall of 95%. Miranda et al. Did a comparative study on different deep architectures for cough detection [18]. They evaluated deep neural networks (DNN), convolution neural networks (CNN) and long-short-term models (LSTM), using STFT, FMB and MFCC as features to classify cough from non-cough events.

3 Experimental Setup

The dataset consists of audio samples labelled cough and non-cough, collected from the Environmental Sound Classifier (ESC-50) dataset [17].

The ESC-50 dataset comprises standardised brief environmental recordings (5-s clips, 44.1 kHz, single channel). The non-cough samples are drawn from the ESC-50 dataset's labelled ambient recordings, which include animal noises, natural sounds, human sounds, interior sounds, and other noises. We obtained 670 samples from the dataset, 335 cough and 335 non-cough samples. We used 80% of the data to train our model and 20% to test the model. In total, the training data had 266 cough samples and 266 non-cough samples. We used Weka [13] to implement the SVM and MLP classifiers, and we implemented the KNN classifier manually.

4   Methods

4.1   Pre-processing

We broke down the pre-processing into three processes, as shown in Fig. 1. In the first process, pre-emphasis, we emphasised the higher frequencies to increase the signal energy at higher frequencies. The next process is framing, in which we segment the audio samples in segments of 25 ms with a 50% overlap between segments. Signal windowing is a method of temporally weighting signals that produce limited support (nonzero section) by multiplying the signal by a function that places more emphasis on desirable portions of the signal and often attenuates it outside of this range, usually to zero [14] and the windowing function we used for this study is the Hamming windowing function.

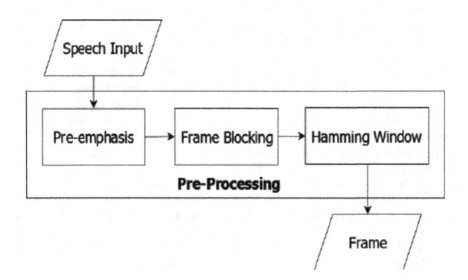

Fig. 1. Audio signal pre-processing.

4.2   Feature Selection

Mel-Frequency Cepstral Coefficients. We adopted Mel Frequency Cepstral
Coefficients (MFCC) as features because they are the most popular features in
this field; they are based on the human hearing mechanism and have a high
degree of accuracy [15] (Fig. 2).

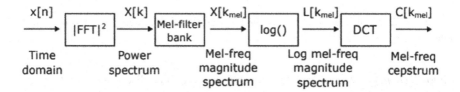

Fig. 2. MFCCs for a single analysis window is calculated using this method.

Calculating the short-time Fourier transform's magnitude is the first stage
in this procedure.

$$X(k,m) = |\sum_{n=0}^{N-1} w(n)x(n+mH)e^{-j2\pi k/n}| \quad (1)$$

where x represents the input signal, N represents the frame size, k represents the
discrete-frequency index, m represents the hop number for the analysis window,
and H represents the hop size. For the widow function w, a Hamming window
is utilised. $X(k,m)$ is evaluated for $k = 0, ..., N/2$ and the magnitudes of these
components are preserved. We utilised 1024 frame size and 512 hop size.

Next, convert the linear frequency scale of the STFT to the mel-frequency
scale by employing a mel-filter bank. The Mel-filter bank consists of several
triangular filters that overlay one another whose centre frequencies are evenly
distributed along the lower and higher frequency value on the mel-frequency
scale. The filter bank is built using (2)

$$H_p(k) = \begin{cases} 0, k < f(p-1) \\ \frac{k-f(p-1)}{f(p)-f(p-1)}, f(p-1) \le k \le f(p) \\ \frac{f(p+1)-k}{f(p+1)-f(p)}, f(p) \le k \le f(p+1) \\ 0, k > f(p+1) \end{cases} \quad (2)$$

Here the triangle filter with the pth centre frequency is called H_p. An example
of a triangular filter bank produced by (2) is seen in Fig. 3.

Following that, the log of the filter bank energies $L(p,m)$ is determined by
the use of the filter bank on the power spectrogram for all P filters.

$$L(p,m) = log[\sum_{k=0}^{N/2} \hat{X}(k,m)H_p]0 \le p \le P-1 \quad (3)$$

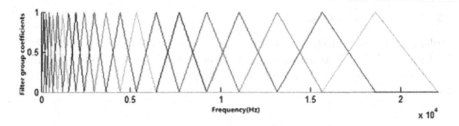

Fig. 3. An array of triangle filters is used to determine the energy of each band in the mel-scale

where $\hat{X}(k,m) = X(k,m)^2$ is the power spectrum. The discrete cosine transform (DCT) is applied column-wise to $L(p,m)$ as the last step in computing the MFCCs.

$$C(c,m) = \sum_{p=0}^{P-1} \frac{\pi}{P}(p + \frac{1}{2}) \tag{4}$$

where C is the discrete frequency index c's mel-frequency cepstrum. We extracted 13 coefficient as it has been discovered that they produce better results [12].

Short-Term Energy. Short-term energy is a time-domain feature of speech signals that is frequently used to discriminate between voiced and unvoiced speech segments. Assuming that $w(n)$ frames are used to process the windowing function and the speech waveform time domain signal, $y_i(n)$ is the ith frame of the speech signal, and it meets the requirements of formula (5):

$$y_i(n) = w(n)(i-1)d + n) \tag{5}$$

$$1 \leq n \leq L, 1 \leq i \leq f_n \tag{6}$$

where fn is the total number of frames, L is the frame length, d is the frame shift length, and $w(n)$ is the hamming windowing function.

(7) can be used to express the short-term energy of the i-th frame's voice signal.

$$E(i) = \sum_{n=0}^{L-1} y_i^2(n), 1 \leq i \leq f_n \tag{7}$$

Zero-Crossing Rate (ZCR). A zero crossing rate occurs when successive samples of a discrete-time signal change sign. The ZRC counts the number of times a signal's amplitude changes sign within a specific signal and is a reliable predictor of the signal's frequency content. A signal's low-frequency content suggests that the ZCR will also be low, while a signal's high-frequency content suggests that the ZRC will likewise be high [16] and (8) can be used to compute the ZRC on a short-term basis.

$$ZCR(m) = \sum_{n=1}^{N-1} |sgn[x(n+mH)] - sgn[x(n+mH-1)]| \qquad (8)$$

where,

$$sgn[x(n)] = \left\{ \begin{array}{l} 1, \quad x(n) \geq 0 \\ -1, x(n) < 0 \end{array} \right\} \qquad (9)$$

4.3   Cough and Non-cough Classification

K-Nearest Neighbor (kNN). K-NN is a non-parametric supervised learning method; it classifies an unknown item based on the plurality of the votes of the k closest neighbours of the unknown item; if k = 1, then the unknown item will be classified as belonging to the same class as its closest neighbour. The neighbourhood can be calculated using different formulae. We calculated the separation between our data points using the Euclidean (x, y) formula for our implementation, and we found empirically that k = 1 produces the best results.

Support Vector Machine (SVM). Support vector machines are examples of supervised learning models that examine data for regression and classification purposes. Created by AT&T employees Vladimir Vapnik and others [8], SVM is one of the most reliable prediction techniques [9]. Finding the most significant margin between two or more classes is the goal of SVM, as it seeks to maximise the difference between two or more classes. It will occasionally use a kernel function to convert the input set into a higher dimension to discover the ideal margin. The Gaussian kernel, polynomial, and linear kernels are the most frequently used kernel functions.

Finding the best SVM margin during training is a quadratic problem that may be solved by minimum sequential optimization (SMO) [10]. In this study, we implemented SVM SMO using the Gaussian kernel.

Multilayer Perceptron (MLP). A multilayer perceptron is a feed-forward artificial neural network having at least three layers of nodes: an input layer for gathering input signals, an output layer for making a judgment on the input signals, and a hidden layer between these two layers [11].

We use MFFC features to train the neural network. 13 input neurons, a hidden layer containing three neurons, and two output neurons are present. We have employed the sigmoid activation function and backpropagation technique to train our model.

Table 1. Results of our classifier models.

Classifier	Feature	Accuracy	Precision	Recall	F1-score
KNN	ZCR	59,97%	58,97%	64,79%	61,74%
	Short-Term Energy	59,86%	59,00%	62,23%	60,61%
	MFCC	79,58%	79,17%	80,28%	79,72%
SVM	Short-Term Energy	64.79%	49,30%	71,43%	58,33%
	MFCC	92,20%	92,86%	91,55%	92,20%
MLP	MFCC	85,50%	83.43%	74,79%	78,87%

5   Classification Results

We created a total of 6 experiments and evaluated their performance against the test portion of the dataset. These classification results are summarised in Table 1. According to the summary in the above table, we can see that MFCC features classified with the SVM algorithm archived the best results, with accuracy, precision, recall and F1-score of 92.20%, 92.86%, 91.55%, 92.20% respectively. These findings suggest that using MFCC coefficients and the SVM SMO classifier, our model can accurately detect cough with a 92.20 % accuracy rate. When the results of the k-NN classifier with different features are compared, it is evident that the MFCC features outperform both ZCR and Short-Term Energy.

In Table 2, we compare our model against existing work. We can see that in terms of accuracy, it comes in third place, first place being the work of [4], which includes post-processing. When compared with [3] deep learning approaches of convolutional and recurrent networks, our model performed the best.

5.1   Discussion

Our model highlighted how we might use MFFC features to build a cough detection system. Our model has low complexity and is straightforward enough to be used extensively. Our model can be beneficial for identifying patients based on long-term cough observation, counting cough occurrences, and monitoring cough in real-time.

The following parameters limit our recognition model in terms of performance:

- The calibre of the training and test samples: Our training dataset is not large enough. To enhance our cough detection model, we will use a larger dataset in the future.
- Our model uses a limited number of speech signal characteristics extracted throughout the feature extraction phase: Spectral features like spectral centroid and flatness can be studied in the future.

Table 2. Comparison of our model performance with existing work

Reference	Methods	Accuracy	Dataset
Our model	13 MFFCs and SVM	92,20%	ESC-50 dataset(266 coughs and 266 non-cough samples). 80% data for training the mode and 20% for testing
(Amos & Odame) [4]	Convolutional network and recurrent network	89.70% and 84,90% respectively	Collected recordings from 14 healthy individuals, each individual produced 40 cough recordings. For non-cough sounds, each read 20 phonetically balanced prompts
(Monge-Alvarez) [5]	k-NN & Hu-moments	95.28% after post-processing	Recorded raw signals of cough events, non-cough events and background noises
(Teyhouee & Osgood) [6]	HMM	82.00%	Authors collected cough sounds from individuals at the University of Saskatchewan
(Chen & Zhai) [7]	20 MFCC features by UVE	94.9%	Authors combine data from the ESC-50 dataset and self recorded sounds from patients with respiratory diseases

6   Conclusion

In this study, we propose a suitability analysis of different spectral features and three classifiers for automated cough detection. The study resulted in the development of a system using MFCC as a feature set, with the best SVM classifier, with accuracy and precision values of up to 92,20% and 92.86%, respectively. This cough detection model can be used in detecting cough patterns of patients, as different illnesses have different cough patterns [2]. Our findings indicate that it is possible to develop a technology that is both convenient and least disturbing for patients and practitioners may trust.

Our next goal is to optimise the model by optimising the database, using more audio features and implementing a post-processing stage to reject false positives and false negatives.

References

1. European Respiratory Society (ERS): The economic burden of lung disease. In: European Lung White Book. Lausanne, Switzerland: ERS, ch. 2, pp. 16–27 (2005)
2. Hoyos-Barceló, C., Monge-Álvarez, J., Zeeshan, S.M., Alcaraz-Calero, J.-M., Casaseca-de-la-Higuera, P.: Efficient k-NN implementation for real-time detection of cough events in smartphones. IEEE J. Biomed. Health Inform. **22**(5), 1662–1671 (2018). https://doi.org/10.1109/JBHI.2017.2768162
3. Ranjani, S., Santhiya, V., Jayapreetha, A.: A real-time cough monitor for classification of various pulmonary diseases. In: Proceedings 3rd International Conference on Emerging Applications of Information Technology, Kolkata, India, 29 November 2012, pp. 102–105 (2012)
4. Amoh, J., Odame, K.: Deep neural networks for identifying cough sounds. IEEE Trans. Biomed. Circuits Syst. **10**(5), 1003–1011 (2016). https://doi.org/10.1109/TBCAS.2016.2598794
5. Monge-Alvarez, J., Hoyos-Barcelo, C., Lesso, P., Casaseca-de-la-Higuera, P.: Robust detection of audio-cough events using local Hu moments. IEEE J. Biomed. Health Inform. **23**(1), 184–196 (2019)
6. Teyhouee, A., Osgood, N.D.: Cough detection using hidden Markov models. In: Thomson, R., Bisgin, H., Dancy, C., Hyder, A. (eds.) SBP-BRiMS 2019. LNCS, vol. 11549, pp. 266–276. Springer, Cham (2019). https://doi.org/10.1007/978-3-030-21741-9_27
7. Chen, X., Hu, M., Zhai, G.: Cough detection using selected informative features from audio signals. In: 2021 14th International Congress on Image and Signal Processing, BioMedical Engineering and Informatics (CISP-BMEI) (2021)
8. Cortes, C., Vapnik, V.: Support-vector networks. Mach. Learn. **20**(3), 273–297 (1995)
9. Mansour, A., Lachiri, Z.: SVM based emotional speaker recognition using MFCC-SDC features. Int. J. Adv. Comput. Sci. Appl. **8**(4), 12 (2017)
10. Huang, X., Shi, L., Suykens, J.: Sequential minimal optimization for SVM with pinball loss. Neurocomputing **149**, 1596–1603 (2015)
11. Dutta, J., Chanda, D.: Music emotion recognition in assamese songs using MFCC features and MLP classifier. In: 2021 International Conference on Intelligent Technologies (CONIT) (2021)
12. Mokgonyane, T.B., Sefara, T.J., Modipa, T.I., Mogale, M.M., Manamela, M.J., Manamela, P.J.: Automatic speaker recognition system based on machine learning algorithms. In: 2019 Southern African Universities Power Engineering Conference/Robotics and Mechatronics/Pattern Recognition Association of South Africa (SAUPEC/RobMech/PRASA), pp. 141–146 (2019). https://doi.org/10.1109/RoboMech.2019.8704837
13. Hall, M., Frank, E., Holmes, G., Pfahringer, B., Reutemann, P., Witten, I.H.: The we-ka data mining software: an update. ACM SIGKDD Explor. Newsl. **11**(1), 10–18 (2009)

14. Karjalainen M., Paatero T.: Frequency-dependent signal windowing. In: Proceedings of the 2001 IEEE Workshop on the Applications of Signal Processing to Audio and Acoustics (Cat. No.01TH8575), pp. 35–38 (2001). https://doi.org/10.1109/ASPAA.2001.969536

15. Chen, Y., Xie, Y., Song, L., Chen, F., Tang, T.: A survey of accelerator architectures for deep neural networks. Engineering **6**(3), 264–274 (2020)

16. Bachu, R., Kopparthi, S., Adapa, B., Barkana, B.: Separation of voiced and unvoiced using zero crossing rate and energy of the speech signal. In: American Society for Engineering Education (ASEE) Zone Conference Proceedings, pp. 1–7 (2008)

17. Piczak, K.: ESC: dataset for environmental sound classification. In: Proceedings of the 23rd ACM International Conference on Multimedia, pp. 1015–1018 (2015)

18. Miranda, I.D., Diacon, A.H., Niesler, T.R.: A comparative study of features for acoustic cough detection using deep architectures. In: 2019 41st Annual International Conference of the IEEE Engineering in Medicine and Biology Society (EMBC) (2019). https://doi.org/10.1109/embc.2019.8856412

Multi-stakeholder Approach for Designing an AI Model to Predict Treatment Adherence

Beatriz Merino-Barbancho[1], Peña Arroyo[1], Miguel Rujas[1], Ana Cipric[2],
Nicholas Ciccone[2], Francisco Lupiáñez-Villanueva[3], Ana Roca-Umbert Würth[3],
Frans Folkvord[3,4], María Fernanda Cabrera[1], María Teresa Arredondo[1],
and Giuseppe Fico[1(✉)]

[1] Life Supporting Technologies Research Group, Universidad Politécnica de Madrid, Avda
Complutense 30, 28040 Madrid, Spain
gfico@lst.tfo.upm.es
[2] SaMD Innovation, Novo Nordisk A/S, Vandtårnsvej 108-110, 2860 Søborg, Denmark
[3] PredictBy, Barcelona, Spain
[4] Tilburg Center for Cognition and Communication (TiCC), Department of Communication and
Cognition, Tilburg University, Tilburg, The Netherlands

Abstract. Artificial intelligence (AI) can transform healthcare by improving
treatment outcomes and reducing associated costs. AI is increasingly being
adopted in healthcare. In this regard, one area where AI can have a significant
impact is in improving adherence to treatment, which is critical to achieving
desired health outcomes. It is well known that poor adherence can lead to treatment
failure, disease progression and increased healthcare costs. However, the factors
that influence adherence to treatment remain unclear. In this context, this study
sought to implement an open innovation methodology based on co-creation to
understand the requirements for the development of an AI model to aid in the prediction of treatment adherence. Semi-structured interviews were conducted with
eleven stakeholders from four groups: patients, healthcare professionals, data scientists and pharmacists. The needs and requirements received were categorized
into four key aspects that were translated into requirements and needs: understanding the nature of the drivers, scope and impact of the problem; identifying
data sources; understanding relevant data points; and addressing potential ethical
issues.

Keywords: AI · adherence · cocreation · stakeholders · innovation

1 Introduction

Artificial intelligence (AI) is already established in our daily tasks and is poised to
become a permanent phenomenon. In the healthcare sector, in particular, it has the
potential to transform healthcare by improving treatment outcomes and patient care as
well as reducing associated costs and burden for healthcare professionals [1]. Specifically, the design and implementation of artificial intelligence models can analyze large
amounts of patient data and identify patterns that can help inform the customisation of

V. G. Duffy (Ed.): HCII 2023, LNCS 14029, pp. 260–271, 2023.
https://doi.org/10.1007/978-3-031-35748-0_19

treatment plans and provide patients with personalised interventions. In addition, healthcare professionals can intervene early and take proactive measures to improve outcomes and consequently the quality of life of patients. In this regard, one of the areas where AI models have a major impact is in the consideration of adherence to treatment as non-adherence is estimated to cost the healthcare system billions of dollars each year.

Adherence to treatment is critical for achieving the desired health outcomes and is one of the most essential factors in the success of any medical intervention. Non-adherence is responsible for a staggering number of premature deaths in the US (125,000 each year) and the EU (200,000 each year), causing personal suffering and imposing significant financial burden on healthcare systems. Approximately 25% of patients are non-adherent to preventive and disease management activities, such as medication intake, appointment scheduling, screening, exercise, and dietary changes [2, 3]. It also contributes to unnecessary healthcare costs and a significant burden on healthcare systems. Ensuring adherence to treatment is particularly important for chronic diseases such as diabetes, hypertension, and cancer, where adherence can significantly impact disease management and patient outcomes.

Despite the critical impact of non-adherence, there is a lack of uniformity in the terminology used to describe deviations from prescribed therapies and a lack of comprehensive theoretical and empirical understanding of the underlying factors driving adherence [4]. Improving adherence to treatment and understanding the factors that influence adherence remains a highly critical goal in the healthcare setting. To this end, the development of accurate artificial intelligence models to understand these factors and predict adherence to treatment greatly assists key stakeholders in tailoring interventions to improve patient outcomes. To achieve this, the European BEAMER project [5] is currently working on the creation of a data-driven AI-based disease diagnosis model that can improve healthcare outcomes and cost-effectiveness through population segmentation and treatment adherence prediction. However, given the involvement of multiple stakeholders in the decision-making process to design the model and the impact it has on them, it is essential to understand their different requirements and needs in order to build a meaningful model for all of them [6]. In this light, the conventional innovation paradigm of bringing research directly to the market is undergoing a transformation that is leading to the emergence of open innovation as a novel form of collaboration and knowledge sharing between different stakeholders, including the public and private sectors, healthcare professionals and researchers, as well as patients and citizens. This approach leads to more efficient and effective research and development processes, resulting in the creation of innovative solutions better adapted to the needs of end-users, leading to better health outcomes, increased patient satisfaction and improved access to healthcare [7].

The objective of this article is to describe how a systematic open innovation methodology has contributed to the extraction of functional, non-functional, business and legal requirements for the design and development of an AI-based treatment adherence model, as well as the understanding of what those requirements are, and the barriers and challenges presented by each of the stakeholders for the utilization of this model.

2 Materials and Methods

2.1 BEAMER Project

The BEAMER Project [5] funded through the Innovative Medicines Initiative (IMI2) and now under the Innovative Health Initiative (IHI), is a European research project (Grant agreement number: 101034369). The primary goal of the project is to develop a disease-agnostic behavioral and adherence model that enhances the quality, outcomes, and cost-effectiveness of healthcare, by improving patients' quality of life, promoting healthcare accessibility, and ensuring sustainability. The model is designed to personalize patient care based on Real World Data obtained from patients' behaviors and health system information, revolutionizing the way healthcare professionals interact with patients to optimize their understanding of their condition and adherence levels during their patient journey. To optimize the disease-agnostic adherence model, BEAMER will be tested through real-life proof of concept in 18 different pilots across six European countries, including over 18,000 patients (3,000 patients in each thematic area).

2.2 Multi-stakeholder Engagement

During the development of a multi-stakeholder AI model, such as the one undertaken by the BEAMER project, it is essential to build an end-to-end strategy that lays the foundation for a co-creation environment. This enables the involvement of several stakeholders, each with their unique perspectives and insights, in the development process, allowing for the achievement of functional requirements that facilitate the conceptualisation of the Model.

To implement this kind of multi-stakeholder engagement methodology, the process was structured into four sequential steps. These steps (see Fig. 1) aimed at identifying the key stakeholders, building customized interviews to capture relevant information and requirements for the AI model, engaging stakeholders in video call interviews and transcribing and analysing the interview data to extract the different requirements.

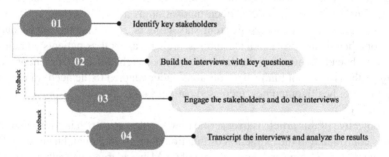

Fig. 1. Methodology overview

1. **Identify key stakeholders.** The process of identifying the key stakeholders for the BEAMER AI model required a thorough analysis of the different stakeholders in terms

of the information they could provide on the needs and preferences to be considered for the BEAMER model, in accordance with the project's criteria. This approach not only enables the identification of the key stakeholders, but also determines the nature and scope of their potential contributions.

2. **Build the interviews (key questions).** Customized interviews were created for each of the identified key stakeholders as they can contribute in different aspects of Model development, such as requirements gathering, risk identification, barriers to adoption, model validation and potential use cases. While each interview was tailored to the specific stakeholder group, all questionnaires followed a common structure to obtain an overview of each stakeholder's input. This structure comprised three main sections as reflected in Table 1. Literature [8] defines semi-structured interviews as guided conversations where the interviewer has a clear understanding of the information they seek to obtain, yet the conversation is allowed to diverge and may substantially change. These interviews typically utilize topic guides that contain core questions used consistently across interviews, while allowing for variations in the sequencing of questions and the depth of information probed by the interviewer. The primary data collection method for this study was chosen to be semi-structured interviews, as the authors had prior knowledge of the sample and sought to elicit participants' opinions, beliefs, and thoughts related to the research topic.

Table 1. Interview sections

Section	Objective
General Introductory Questions	Gather information about the interviewee's position or role, their experience with AI systems and their perspective on the potential of the model
Expectations of the Model	Compile the intended use of the model, the essential features it should have and the highest outcome they envision from it
Risk/Limitations of the Model	Compile risks and limitations that their stakeholder type might face in relation to similar systems

3. **Engage and do the interviews with stakeholders.** The engagement with the key stakeholders was performed using video call interviews, each lasting approximately 60 min, to ensure that all stakeholders had a comprehensive understanding of the BEAMER model. The interviews adhered to a structured format consisting of three segments. The first segment involved a 10-min presentation and introduction to the Model to ensure that all stakeholders, including external parties, had a clear understanding of the Model's objectives. The second segment comprised 30 min of questioning related to the three pre-defined blocks of questions described earlier. The third section, reserved for 20 min, was for further discussion, allowing to obtain additional insights or feedback from the stakeholders. This approach facilitated the gathering of valuable input from the stakeholders in a timely and efficient manner.

4. **Transcribe the interviews and analyze the results.** After each interview, the data was transcribed using a speech-to-text system called "Whisper" [9]. The transcribed data was then structured and analyzed to identify the requirements and expectations of the BEAMER model. This process ensured a consistent and efficient approach to data management, resulting in a well-organized foundation for extracting key insights and requirements from the stakeholder perspectives. A visual representation of the base outline is presented in Fig. 2.

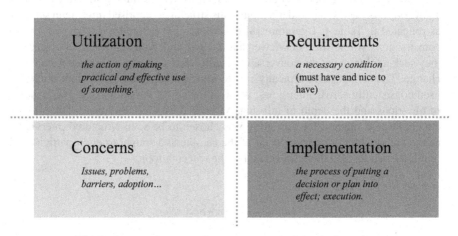

Fig. 2. Systematic approach to extract results from the interviews

2.3 Requirements Extraction

The design of an effective model requires a thorough consideration of various types of requirements, including functional, non-functional, business, and legal requirements. Functional requirements define the specific capabilities and essential functions that the model needs to fulfill, while non-functional requirements outline the quality attributes such as reliability, performance, maintainability, scalability, and usability. Business requirements describe the project's goals and objectives, and legal requirements refer to the regulation, laws, and ethical considerations that must be complied with.

The BEAMER model's success relies on a systematic approach that considers all these requirements to ensure that the final product is functional, efficient, and compliant with relevant regulations. Table 2 summarizes the exact definition of each of these requirements which has been used as the basis for the extraction of them.

To extract the requirements, the VOLERE methodology [10] was used, which allowed for a structured and systematic approach to ensure that all relevant requirements were studied in the design and development process of the BEAMER model. The use of this methodology made it easier to extract requirements that were understandable to all stakeholders and helped to develop a model that satisfied all their expectations

Table 2. Requirements definition

Type of requirement	Description
Functional Requirements (F)	Functional requirements define "how" the system/ person/ process needs to behave in order to achieve the goal
Non-functional Requirements (NF)	Non-functional Requirements define system attributes such as reliability, performance, maintainability, scalability and usability
Business Requirements (B)	Business requirements define "what" needs to be done (goal) and "why" it is important
Legal Requirements (L)	Legal requirements define the rules and standards that have to be legally complied with (i.e., GDPR)

[11]. Interviews were conducted with different stakeholders to document their vision, objectives, limitations, expectations, and requirements related to the BEAMER model.

The interviews were recorded and transcribed manually and through the use of Whisper [9], an automatic speech recognition system. Once all transcripts were completed, the requirements were extracted by different members of the consortium, who documented the type, description, rationale, priority, priority description, feasibility issues, and type of stakeholder in an Excel file.

Finally, the requirements were divided based on their typology to identify the aspects that needed to be considered in the design of the BEAMER model (see Fig. 3). This approach ensured that the BEAMER model was developed with a co-creational multi-stakeholder approach, which considered the expectations and requirements of all stakeholders to create a robust and sustainable solution for predicting treatment adherence.

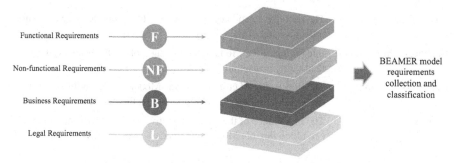

Fig. 3. Requirements flow

2.4 User Stories Definition

To identify potential use cases, UML diagrams [12] were also used to model and visualize the system architecture of the BEAMER system. This standardized visual modeling language helped to provide a clear understanding of the system's components, their relationships, and the flow of data within the system.

UML diagrams played a critical role in the design and development of the BEAMER system, allowing for effective communication and collaboration among stakeholders and providing a clear understanding of the system's structure and behavior. Overall, their use helped to improve the efficiency and accuracy of the development process, leading to a more effective and functional software system.

3 Results

3.1 Multi-stakeholder Engagement

Following the execution of the multi-stakeholder engagement strategy, a total of 11 individual interviews were conducted with key stakeholders, each lasting around 60 min and involving open discussions and question-and-answer sessions. The interviewees consisted of a diverse range of stakeholders, including 6 pharmaceutical companies, 1 patient association, 3 health professionals from different areas of expertise, and 1 data scientist.

Furthermore, the multi-stakeholder engagement process yielded a fundamental outline of the vision that each stakeholder contributed, serving as the foundation for the extraction of the diverse requirements of the BEAMER model. This base outline is summarised in the Table 3.

Table 3. Base outline for the different stakeholders

Stakeholder	Base outline
Data Scientist	The need for a validated methodology based on literature to ensure reliability and explainability of the Model development process
Healthcare Professional	Integration of the Model into existing tools of the health system facilitating its usability
Patient Association	The importance of customizing the Model to meet individual patient needs and assist them in comprehending their condition
Pharma	The importance of the usability in diverse clinical settings and the need for a flexible Model able to adapt to population changes

3.2 Requirements' Collection

The requirements gathering phase involved stakeholders from different areas of expertise, including healthcare professionals, patients, pharmaceutical companies and data scientists. A total of 89 requirements were identified and classified based on their type, priority level and the stakeholder who identified them. Table 4 shows the distribution of requirements based on their type and priority level.

Table 4. Distribution of requirements based on their type and priority level.

Type of requirement	High priority (p = 4)	High/Medium priority (p = 3)	Medium/low priority (p = 2)	Low priority (p = 1)	Total
Functional Requirements (F)	14	11	10	5	**40**
Non-functional Requirements (NF)	16	8	3	2	**29**
Business Requirements (B)	5	8	2	2	**17**
Legal Requirements (L)	4	0	0	0	**3**

As a result, it emerges from the requirements extracted that a thorough understanding of the behavioural and structural elements underlying the patient's behaviour is required. However, it is important to note that the behavioural dimensions are only part of the explanation, and that a more complete model must take into account the structural elements that influence the patient's behaviour. The structural part of the model is being considered on an empirical basis, and this is crucial for the success of the predictive model. In terms of data input requirements, the algorithm should be able to calculate the outcome from a minimum patient input (taking into account legal requirements such as the protection of patient data) and be complemented by data from other sources, such as medical records, registers and textual sources. Patient-reported behavioural data should be collected using validated instruments to ensure the quality of the information obtained. Similarly, the quality of the data used must be assured to allow generalisability of the model. Broadly speaking, two categories of data can be considered, coming from the different data sources mentioned above: structural factors and behavioural factors. On top of that, efforts were made to identify data sources that stakeholders can contribute to train the IA model. Relevant data points were understood, including patient demographics, medical history, medication use, lifestyle, social determinants of health and other factors that affect treatment adherence, these being structural data but also what types of behavioural data are relevant to the model. It was discussed which technical endpoints should be taken into account such as accuracy, ease of use and acceptability of the AI model in order to refine the model by evaluating its performance in real-life settings, identifying strengths and weaknesses of the model along with suggestions for improvements.

Finally, the main results expected from the use of the BEAMER tool are twofold. Firstly, the BEAMER tool is expected to be able to segment the population based on behavioural data and finetuning with structural data as well as a prediction of the user's adherence level. The utilisation of the results will also be two-fold. Firstly, the patient-oriented solution will aim to raise awareness of personal non-adherence. Secondly, the pharmacy- and hospital-oriented solution will aim to provide information on the segmented distribution of the target population or the individual patient. The following table (see Table 5) lists the most important requirements to be incorporated in the development of the final model.

Table 5. Requirements extraction for BEAMER model

Functionality	Definition
Actionability	Professional will be responsible for making decisions regarding treatment recommendations based on the output of the BEAMER model, such as modifying a treatment, rather than the patients themselves
Data Protection	Ensuring the accurate and transparent handling of patients' information is an utmost priority, as it cultivates trust among both patients and end-users
Explicability	The underlying model of the BEAMER tool will operate transparently and be explainable to end-user, thus providing trustworthy by relying on the extracted outputs
Generalizability	The BEAMER model will be able to generalize, giving valid and functional outputs that avoid any kind of bias
Integration	Guidelines will be provided that enable the integration of the BEAMER model with various specific systems as required by users for future applications. It can also function as a stand-alone solution
Prediction	Based on the different inputs, the BEAMER model will provide a prediction of the level of adherence to treatment personalized for each patient
Segmentation	As one of the outputs of the model, segmentation will provide the characterization of the different patient groups, representing an added value for all end users
Usability	The BEAMER tool will strive to provide ease to use for all the end-users, thereby reducing the burden associated with adopting new technologies

The insights received has been categorised into eight essential aspects that were translated into requirements and needs. The nature, scope and impact of the problem, i.e. the development of the IA model for predicting adherence to treatment was understood by considering the possible barriers to adoption, implementation, utilisation and challenges in the short term. Efforts were made to identify data sources that stakeholders can contribute to train the IA model. Relevant data points were understood, including patient demographics, medical history, medication use, lifestyle, social determinants of health and other factors that affect treatment adherence, these being structural data but also what types of behavioural data are relevant to the model. It was discussed which technical endpoints should be taken into account such as accuracy, ease of use and acceptability of the AI model in order to refine the model by evaluating its performance in real-life settings, identifying strengths and weaknesses of the model along with suggestions for improvements. Finally, potential ethical issues were addressed and suggested ways to mitigate them, such as ensuring patient privacy, avoiding bias and ensuring that the model is transparent and understandable to patients and healthcare professionals.

3.3 User Stories Defined from the Extracted Requirements

To explore the potential preliminary use cases for the BEAMER system, stakeholder profiles were created, outlining the respective roles and relevant functionalities related to the BEAMER system. Using these stakeholder profiles as a reference, a range of use cases were identified, representing the most common route of using the model for each actor. The following two subsections describe the high-level related to the healthcare professionals and pharmaceutical profiles, representing a description of action for each of these users.

Healthcare Professional Profile

Jaime is a healthcare professional, aged 35 years, who is engaged in his daily work routine. As a primary care physician, he logs into his regular platform and reviews the consultations that he has for the day. Upon viewing the screen, Jaime can easily see the list of patients, along with a color-coded column indicating the level of adherence predicted in each patient by the model. This feature is particularly helpful for Jaime to identify patients who are at a higher risk of non-adherence.

Furthermore, when Jaime selects a patient, the system provides him with a set of characteristics that explain the reasons for the adherence level categorization. The information is presented in both written and visual formats, making it easier for Jaime to explain to the patient and improve their understanding of the situation. If there are any inconsistencies in the results or predictions, Jaime can notify the system and make necessary modifications.

Pharmaceutical profile

Pauline, aged 43 years, is a professional who works in a pharmaceutical company and is responsible for developing a new product. She decides to leverage the BEAMER Model that has already been developed to reduce production costs. As the model is adaptable, Pauline can modify it to align with the objectives of her study.

Before commencing the development of the product, Pauline needs to conduct an analysis taking into consideration the target population of her study and their characteristics. To do this, she will rely on the information from the different clusters and phenotypes characterized by the BEAMER Model, which is validated both theoretically and empirically. This approach will enable Pauline to gain a better understanding of her target audience and ensure that the new product is designed to meet their specific needs and preferences.

4 Conclusions

This study implemented an open innovation approach based on co-creation and semi-structured interviews to involve stakeholders in the process of designing an AI model for predicting adherence to treatment. The methodology allowed stakeholders, including patients, healthcare professionals, data scientists and pharmacists, to provide insights and suggestions on requirements and needs related to the problem, data sources, relevant data points, technical endpoints and potential ethical issues. This approach supported to guarantee that the resulting IA model met the needs of all stakeholders and was robust in such a way that all perspectives are thoughtfully factored into the design of the model. From the 11 semi-structured interviews, 89 requirements were extracted and summarised into eight essential blocks, which were translated into requirements and needs. This will serve as a fundamental input for the design and further development of the BEAMER model since in order to design an effective AI model for predicting treatment adherence, it is essential to understand the nature, scope and impact of the problem, identify potential barriers to adoption, implementation and utilisation, and address short-term challenges.

Acknowledgment. This project has received funding from the Innovative Medicines Initiative 2 Joint Undertaking (JU) under grant agreement No 101034369. The JU receives support from the European Union's Horizon 2020 research and innovation programme and EFPIA and LINK2TRIALS BV.

References

1. Yu, K.-H., Beam, A.L., Kohane, I.S.: Artificial intelligence in healthcare. Nat. Biomed. Eng. **2**(10) (2018). Art. no. 10. https://doi.org/10.1038/s41551-018-0305-z
2. van Boven, J.F., et al.: European network to advance best practices and technology on medication adherence: mission statement. Front. Pharmacol. **12** (2021). Accessed 6 Mar 2023. https://www.frontiersin.org/articles/10.3389/fphar.2021.748702
3. Parsey, L.: €125 billion lost each year across Europe due to non-adherence to medication. ILCUK, 7 April 2022. https://ilcuk.org.uk/125-billion-lost-each-year-due-to-non-adherence/. Accessed 6 Mar 2023
4. Mathes, T., Jaschinski, T., Pieper, D.: Adherence influencing factors – a systematic review of systematic reviews. Arch. Public Health **72**(1), 37 (2014). https://doi.org/10.1186/2049-3258-72-37
5. _Beamer Home: BEAMER. https://beamerproject.eu/. Accessed 6 Mar 2023
6. Horkoff, J.: Non-functional requirements for machine learning: challenges and new directions. In: 2019 IEEE 27th International Requirements Engineering Conference (RE), pp. 386–391, September 2019. https://doi.org/10.1109/RE.2019.00050
7. Elmquist, M., Fredberg, T., Ollila, S.: Exploring the field of open innovation. Eur. J. Innov. Manag. **12**(3), 326–345 (2009). https://doi.org/10.1108/14601060910974219
8. Miles, J., Gilbert, P. (eds.): A Handbook of Research Methods for Clinical and Health Psychology, pp. xi, 315. Oxford University Press, New York (2005). https://doi.org/10.1093/med:psych/9780198527565.001.0001
9. Radford, A., Kim, J.W., Xu, T., Brockman, G., McLeavey, C., Sutskever, I.: Robust speech recognition via large-scale weak supervisión. arXiv, 6 December 2022. https://doi.org/10.48550/arXiv.2212.04356
10. Volere Requirements: Volere Requirements. https://www.volere.org/. Accessed 23 Feb 23
11. Volere – the Evolution of Successful Requirements Techniques: IRM Connects, by IRM UK | IT Blog, 27 July 2016. https://www.irmconnects.com/volere-evolution-successful-requirements-techniques/. Accessed 23 Feb 2023

12. 'Unified Modeling Language (UML) description: UML diagram examples, tutorials and reference for all types of UML diagrams - use case diagrams, class, package, component, composite structure diagrams, deployments, activities, interactions, profiles, etc.' https://www.uml-dia grams.org/. Accessed 23 Feb 2023
13. Eckhardt, J., Kaletka, C., Krüger, D., Maldonado-Mariscal, K., Schulz, A.C.: Ecosystems of co-creation. Front. Sociol. **6** (2021). Accessed 2 Feb 2023. https://www.frontiersin.org/art icles/10.3389/fsoc.2021.642289

Using Lean Six Sigma and Discrete-Event Simulation to Reduce Patient Waiting Time Before Sample Collection: A Clinical Lab Case Study

Miguel Ortiz-Barrios[1]([⊠]) [iD], Matías García-Constantino[2] [iD], Zahiry Castro-Camargo[1],
Cindy Charris-Maldonado[1], Sulay Escorcia-Charris[1], Gisell Sierra-Urbina[1],
Estefany Molinares-Ramirez[1], Alina Torres-Mercado[1], Armando Pérez-Aguilar[3,4],
and Pedro López-Meza[5]

[1] Department of Productivity and Innovation, Universidad de la Costa CUC, 080002
Barranquilla, Colombia
{mortiz1,zcastro4,ccharris5,sescorci7,gsierra10,emolinar,
atorres68}@cuc.edu.co
[2] School of Computing, Computer Science Research Institute, Ulster University, Belfast BT37
0QB, UK
m.garcia-constantino@ulster.ac.uk
[3] Academic Division of Computer, Juarez Autonomous University of Tabasco, Cunduacan,
Tabasco, Mexico
211H18001@alumno.ujat.mx, armando.pa@laventa.tecnm.mx
[4] Academic Division of Computer Systems Engineering, Instituto Tecnológico Superior de Villa
la Venta, La Venta, Huimanguillo, Tabasco, México
[5] Facultad de Ciencias Económicas, Administrativas y Contables, Corporación Universitaria
Reformada, Barranquilla, Colombia
p.lopez@unireformada.edu.co

Abstract. Prolonged waiting time has been identified as a common shortcoming in different clinical labs and has been associated with delayed diagnosis, untimely treatment, cost overruns, a major risk of more severe health complications, and higher mortality rates. The problem is even more sharpened if the target population is composed of pregnant women who may experience dizziness, headache, vomiting, or fainting in case of extended delays before sample collection. Therefore, this paper proposes a combination between Lean Six Sigma (LSS) and Discrete-Event Simulation (DES) to minimize the waiting time before blood collection in clinical laboratories. We first described the process and its interactions with other departments using a SIPOC diagram. Second, we evaluated the measurement system reliability and performed a non-normal capability analysis to verify the current process performance. Afterward, we analyzed the main causes of the waiting time problem by employing the fishbone diagram, Value Stream Mapping (VSM), Correlogram, and DES. Following this, various improvement strategies were pretested using a DES model. Once these interventions were applied in the wild, a before-and-after analysis was undertaken to evidence how much the waiting time before sampling had lowered. Finally, X-R process control charts were elaborated to monitor this variable and underpin continuous improvement. A real

© The Author(s), under exclusive license to Springer Nature Switzerland AG 2023
V. G. Duffy (Ed.): HCII 2023, LNCS 14029, pp. 272–283, 2023.
https://doi.org/10.1007/978-3-031-35748-0_20

case study in a private clinical laboratory is presented to validate this approach. As a result, the mean waiting time before sample collection passed from 61 to 21.5 min per patient while the parts per million (ppm) decreased from 873920 to 145714.

Keywords: Lean Six Sigma (LSS) · Discrete-Event Simulation (DES) · Healthcare · Clinical Laboratories

1 Introduction

According to the World Health Organisation (WHO), in the first two decades of the 21st century life expectancy has increased by more than 6 years, that is from 66.8 years in 2000 to 73.4 years in 2019 [1]. In addition to the global increase in life expectancy, the population has also increased, which has impacted the health systems with larger numbers of patients that require urgent or routine medical consultation. The COVID-19 pandemic had an even greater impact with limited or scarce access to health services, for which patients have to wait for a longer time compared to pre-pandemic services. Prolonged waiting time has been identified as a common shortcoming in different healthcare settings. It has been associated with delayed diagnosis, untimely treatment, cost overruns, a major risk of more severe health complications, and higher mortality rates. Clinical labs are not the exception to this rule, and in many cases, it is critical to have clinical lab results on time so that health professionals can continue with the treatment of a condition on a patient, for example in deciding to perform surgery to extract malignant tissues from a patient or in deciding the best treatment to follow. Although patients with chronic diseases might be some of the patients that need to have clinical lab results frequently and timely, there are other types of patients, like pregnant women, which require similar access at least during a defined period.

Several works have focused on reducing the turnaround time using advanced process improvement methods [2–4]. However, the evidence base is very limited regarding the application of these approaches to reduce the waiting time before sample collection, hence the relevance of the present study. The importance of waiting time as a metric is critical because it involves patient dissatisfaction, higher complaint rates, and the need of satisfying government specifications. Moreover, a more efficient workflow when providing health services to patients could be achieved and the costs derived from waiting time could be reduced. Note that one of the cases in which the problem is even more sharpened is when the target population is composed of pregnant women who arrive at clinical labs for urinalysis, general blood tests, and glucose curves prescribed by their gynecologists during prenatal care. As these tests require patients to fast, extended delays before sample collection may increase the likelihood of experiencing dizziness, headache, vomiting, or fainting which may trigger canceled appointments, waste of time, and low customer satisfaction. In extreme scenarios, the health of both the pregnant woman and the baby could be negatively affected.

This paper proposes a combination between the Lean Six Sigma (LSS) and Discrete-Event Simulation (DES) methods to minimize the waiting time before blood collection in clinical laboratories. The remainder of the paper is organized as follows: Section 2 presents the related work in simulation applied to waiting times, in particular with the Lean Six Sigma (LSS) and the Discrete-Event Simulation (DES) methods. Section 3 describes the proposed approach. Section 4 presents the experiments that were carried out and the results obtained. Finally, Sect. 5 presents the conclusions.

2 Literature Review

For clinical laboratories, as well as for many other companies, quality entails the deployment of improvement opportunities meeting the needs and expectations of all relevant stakeholders [5]. Thereby, it is possible to improve the key management indicators of the organization and, therefore, the efficiency of its processes [6].

Many organizations have used methodologies such as Lean Six Sigma (LSS) for supporting process improvement and productivity [3]. This methodology helps to reduce the variation of the defects identified in the processes [5], lessen non-quality costs, and meet stakeholder needs [7]. For example, the implementation of this approach has had a significant impact on clinical laboratories in terms of the number of processed samples per day which was found to increase by 20% approximately [8].

LSS applications have been proven to be effective when tackling different operational challenges in clinical labs. According to the reported evidence, 93% of errors in these healthcare settings occur in the pre- and post-analysis phases with a margin of 46%–68.2% [8, 9]. Other aspects of relevant interest are the waiting times before sampling and result reporting which have been significantly associated with diagnosis and treatment processes in more complex healthcare services [3, 6, 10]. The benefits of deploying LSS are also evident in the review performed by Thakur et al. [11], Ialongo & Bernardini [12], and Antony et al. [13].

On the other hand, Thakur et al. [14] implemented LSS to shorten excessive quality control material use and the associated total annual expenditure in The Eastern Health Clinical Biochemistry Laboratories. In another application, Stoiljkovic et al. [15] employed LSS to reduce process time and resource investment in sample analysis of a microbiology laboratory.

A gap detected in the literature is that only 20% of interventions using LSS in healthcare services show post-intervention data which is not sufficient to demonstrate the sustainability of LSS projects in a real clinical scenario [16]. Besides, the evidence base does not present LSS interventions in clinical labs during the recent Covid-19 pandemic which would be beneficial when elucidating how these units can cope with complex and uncertain scenarios with this approach. Also, the LSS has not been merged with other advanced Operational Research methods in the clinical lab context which may be explored to upgrade the overall quality of their services. Finally, waiting time before sample collection has been poorly addressed in the literature, more especially when considering the characteristics of highly vulnerable populations including pregnant women. In view of the above, this paper bridges these gaps by presenting a novel application that combines LSS and DES to provide clinical lab managers with methodological support helping to reduce the likelihood of dizziness, headache, vomiting, or fainting by minimizing the waiting time before sample collection experienced by pregnant women.

3   Proposed Methodology

The purpose of this methodological approach is to reduce waiting times before sample collection in clinical laboratories. The proposed methodology consists of 5 phases following the DMAIC cycle [17] and Discrete-Event Simulation (DES) [18] (Fig. 1):

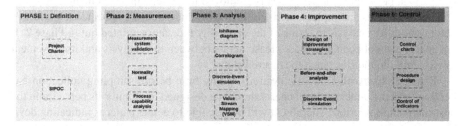

Fig. 1. Proposed methodology for lessening waiting times before sample collection in clinical laboratories.

Phase 1: Definition. In this phase, the project guidelines are established according to the needs and expectations of the laboratory. To this aim, a project charter containing the objectives, scope, problem definition, LSS team, business goals, performance metrics, and project schedule. Also, the activities and interactions of clinical labs with other services/departments are outlined using the Supplier-Input-Process-Output-Customers (SIPOC) diagram [19, 20].

Phase 2: Measurement. The measurement system first needs to be validated before collecting the waiting time data. A paired T-test is useful to deal with this activity as it can establish whether this system can generate high-quality data supporting the statistical analysis required in the LSS-DES approach. Once this has been verified, the waiting time data are gathered to underpin the normal/non-normal capability analysis. In this step, several indicators including Cpk, Ppk, Ppu, short-term/long-term sigma level, and Parts Per Million (PPM) are calculated to define the current process performance. The Minitab 20® software has been defined to cope with all these tasks.

Phase 3: Analysis. This phase describes all the methods that need to be employed to pinpoint the causes separating the clinical lab from the desired performance in terms of waiting time before sample collection. The following tools are used for the analysis: Ishikawa diagram, Value Stream Mapping (VSM), Correlogram, and DES. The use of the Ishikawa Diagram is justified by the need of establishing the possible causes augmenting the waiting time experienced by the patients. On the other hand, a VSM is utilized to detail the laboratory process and identify the non-value activities. Using the Smartdraw® software is then possible to additionally evaluate how these activities have impacted the target metric [21]. In parallel, a correlogram is built to identify which other process variables are highly correlated to the waiting time problem and can be therefore considered an intervention point during the improvement phase. This technique helps to describe the degree to which one variable is linearly related to another. Finally, DES is employed to elucidate how interactions with other departments and services affect the target indicator which entails a holistic view of the process while facilitating engagement with decision-makers in the practical context. The Arena® software is employed to model and simulate the lab computationally.

Phase 4: Improvement. In this stage, various improvements are designed together with the decision-makers associated with the laboratory to diminish the waiting time experienced by the patients before sample collection. Each strategy is pretested with the aid of the DES model to determine if it effectively diminishes the waiting time. A comparison between means/medians is employed to validate this statement. After this, effective strategies are implemented. Following this, new data are collected to perform a before-and-after analysis in terms of the capability indicators pointed out in Phase 2. If the goals have not been achieved, please iterate between the analysis and improvement phases until the metrics reach the desired status.

Phase 5: Control. Once the desired waiting time before sampling collection has been enhanced, suitable control charts should be designed to monitor its behavior in the post-intervention period. Thereby, it will be possible to detect patterns indicating deviations from the expected performance. Likewise, it is necessary to include the process modifications derived from Phase 4 in the related clinical lab procedures so that the current and new organization members can implement them in the daily routine. Complementary to these activities, it is essential to control the indicators governing each project objective using appropriate graphs and descriptive statistics.

4 Results and Discussion

The proposed methodology was implemented in a private clinical laboratory mostly attending pregnant women from vulnerable regions in a low-and-middle-income country. The following sub-sections outline the results achieved during the LSS project and what practical implications were derived in support of the decision-making processes pillaring the clinical lab sustainability.

4.1 Definition

In the clinical laboratory, most patients are pregnant women, so it is essential that the average waiting time before sample collection mustn't exceed 20 min. Thereby, it will be possible to diminish the likelihood of experiencing dizziness, headache, vomiting, or fainting while staying in the lab. However, this metric was found to be 60.6 min on average with a standard deviation of 35.96 min from the shift assignment to the sample collection. Consequently, written complaints have been received from the insurance companies which may put contracts on hold if no intervention is made. Besides, there is an increase in non-quality costs due to the reprocessing caused by the long waiting time. A summary of the intervention can be found in Fig. 2. The project was scheduled to be completed within 6 months and requires the involvement of 29 professionals from different knowledge areas.

Figure 3 depicts the SIPOC diagram elaborated for describing the process interactions with other healthcare services and departments. Thereby, we can design improvement strategies enhancing communication flows among units with a special focus on minimizing the waiting before sample collection.

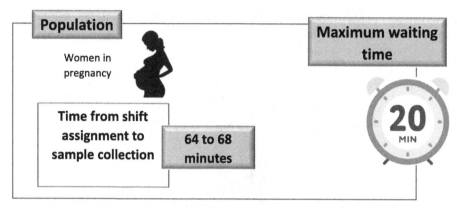

Fig. 2. Problem statement for the LSS project in the showcased clinical lab

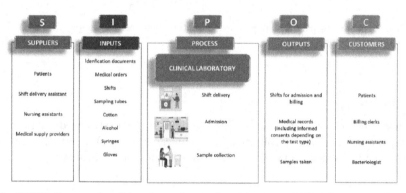

Fig. 3. SIPOC diagram describing the patient pathway between shift assignment and sample collection.

4.2 Measure

With a p-value of 0.515 (T = −0.66), the card-based measurement system was concluded to generate precise waiting time data. A paired t-test was utilized to compare how similar the data produced by the current system were compared to the ones reported by a temporal measurement scheme created for the validation activity. Once the data quality was verified, a capability analysis was performed to determine the current response of the clinical lab in terms of waiting time before sampling collection. As the variable was found to be non-normal, the data were transformed using the Johnson approach. As a result, the process capability assessment was undertaken now based on a normal assumption. The results are shown in Fig. 4.

In summary, Fig. 4 evidences that most waiting times are higher than the specification limit (dashed red line). This is coherent with the capability indicators derived from this analysis: Cpk (−0.54), Ppk (−0.38), Ppu (−0.38), short-term sigma level (0.35), and long-term sigma level (−1.15). All these metrics indicate that the process is currently catastrophic and needs profound and serious interventions to achieve the desired performance. In fact, 873,920 out of 1,000,000 patients attending this lab, will have to wait for more than 20 min before sample collection.

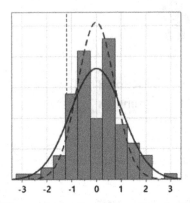

Fig. 4. The process capability graph for the waiting time before sample collection in the showcased clinical lab

4.3 Analysis

A fishbone diagram was used to discriminate the potential causes producing extended waiting times before sample collection in the clinical lab (Fig. 5). This tool serves as an initial mapping supporting the investigation of the real problem drivers.

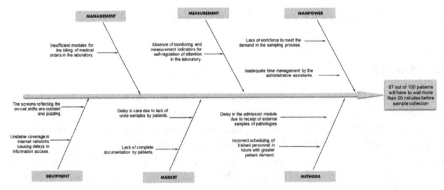

Fig. 5. The fishbone diagram reflecting the causes behind the extended waiting time before sample collection.

The next step is to implement a VSM to detect the non-value-added activities and measure how they impact the target metric (Fig. 6). It is evident that there are significant waits: shift delivery-admission (WT: SD-A) and admission-sample collection (WT: A-SC). It can be also concluded that 87.8% of the time spent by pregnant women in the lab corresponds to waiting periods.

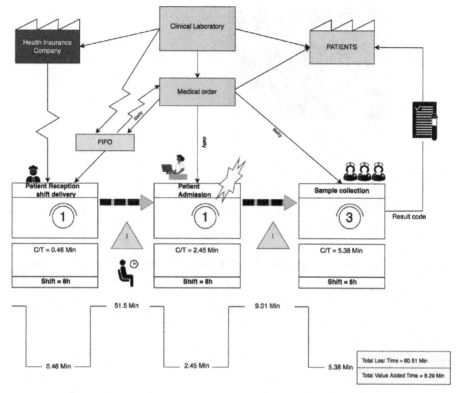

Fig. 6. The VSM describing the pathway from the shift delivery to sample collection.

A correlogram (Fig. 7) was additionally deployed to establish how different times between activities may influence the target metric. It is significant to note the high positive correlation (0.97) between WT: SD-A and WT: SD-SC which confirms the findings derived from the VSM method. Ultimately, a DES model was designed with the help of Arena® software to represent the patient flow and interactions with other services and departments.

4.4 Improvement

Two major improvement strategies were pretested and implemented in the wild: i) the adoption of tablets accelerating calls to patients and minimizing the time invested in signing the informed consents required before the sample collection, and ii) the inclusion of one more admission agent during the peak hours.

The validation process of each scenario was supported by the DES model (Fig. 8). A comparison between medians (p-value < 0.05) proved that the waiting before sample collection passed from 60.6 min to 21.5 min (percentage reduction: 68.34%).

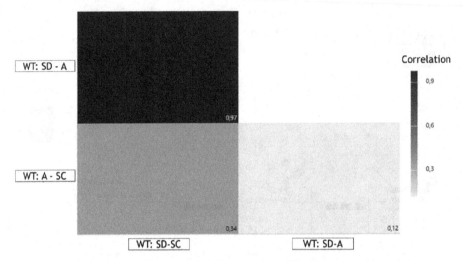

Fig. 7. The correlogram analyzing interrelations between different intra-process waiting times.

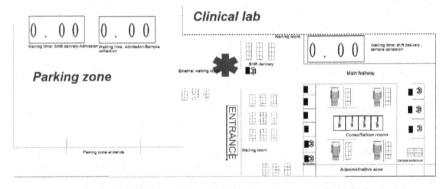

Fig. 8. The DES model representing the showcased clinical lab.

4.5 Control

To maintain the improvements achieved in the "Improve" phase, it was necessary to develop three action lines: i) design individual I-MR control charts to monitor the average and variations in the waiting time before sample collection (Fig. 9), ii) officially modify the admission and sample collection procedures in the clinical lab, and iii) monitor an indicator measuring the satisfaction level of pregnant women regarding the timeliness of the admission and sample collection processes.

In this case, the I-MR control chart can outline several variation problems including points out of the limits and increasing trends which can be timely intervened and therefore avoid a negative effect on the process sigma level. Likewise, the implemented improvement strategies were inserted into the Quality Management System of the lab thereby indicating that the associated new/current staff must follow them in the daily operability. Ultimately, a line chart was suggested to verify how the satisfaction level of

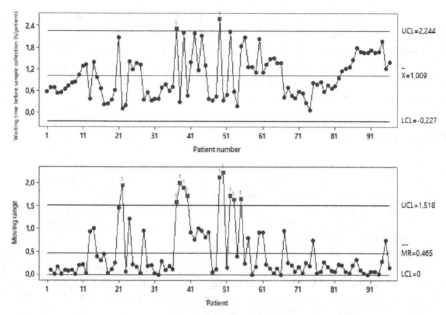

Fig. 9. I-MR control chart for monitoring the behavior of waiting times before sample collection

pregnant women has evolved after intervention and consequently devise improvement plans if new process deviations are detected regarding the process timeliness.

5   Conclusions and Future Work

The use of Lean Six Sigma and Discrete-Event Simulation can be an effective approach to reducing patient waiting times before sample collection in clinical laboratories. The case study highlights the successful implementation of this approach, resulting in significant improvements in patient satisfaction and staff productivity.

The project team identified the root causes of the problem, including inefficient sample collection processes, lack of standardized procedures, and inadequate staffing levels. They used Lean Six Sigma tools such as SIPOC, Value Stream Mapping, and Correlogram to identify and eliminate non-value-added activities. Discrete-Event Simulation was used to simulate various scenarios and evaluate the impact of different changes on patient waiting times. This allowed the team to optimize the process and identify the most effective solutions.

The resulting metrics indicate that the process is currently catastrophic and needs profound and serious interventions to achieve the desired performance. The implementation of standardized procedures and the use of simulation technologies also resulted in increased staff productivity and improved patient satisfaction. In fact, the waiting before sample collection passed from 60.6 min to 21.5 min. Overall, this case study demonstrates the potential benefits of using Lean Six Sigma and Discrete-Event Simulation in healthcare settings including upgraded process efficiency and better patient outcomes.

For future work, it is recommended to extend this application to other healthcare processes where LSS and DES can be employed to optimize patient flow in emergency departments, improve surgical scheduling, and reduce medication errors. Also, the proposed approach can be integrated with data science techniques such as Artificial Intelligence to make the methodological groundwork more robust and useful for supporting the healthcare decision-making process.

References

1. World Health Organization (WHO): Global Health Estimates: Life expectancy and healthy life expectancy. https://www.who.int/data/gho/data/themes/mortality-and-global-health-estimates/ghe-life-expectancy-and-healthy-life-expectancy
2. Gupta, S., Kapil, S., Sharma, M.: Improvement of laboratory turnaround time using lean methodology. Int. J. Health Care Qual. Assur. **31**(4), 295–308 (2018). https://doi.org/10.1108/IJHCQA-08-2016-0116
3. Inal, T.C., et al.: Lean six sigma methodologies improve clinical laboratory efficiency and reduce turnaround times. J. Clin. Lab. Anal. **32**(1) (2018). https://doi.org/10.1002/jcla.22180
4. White, B.A., Baron, J.M., Dighe, A.S., Camargo, C.A., Jr., Brown, D.F.M.: Applying lean methodologies reduces ED laboratory turnaround times. Am. J. Emerg. Med. **33**(11), 1572–1576 (2015). https://doi.org/10.1016/j.ajem.2015.06.013
5. Ibrahim, I., Sultan, M., Yassine, O.G., Zaki, A., Elamir, H., Guirguis, W.: Using lean six sigma to improve timeliness of clinical laboratory test results in a university hospital in Egypt. Int. J. Lean Six Sigma **13**(5), 1159–1183 (2022). https://doi.org/10.1108/IJLSS-08-2021-0138
6. Nevalainen, D., Berte, L., Kraft, C., Leigh, E., Picaso, L., Morgan, T.: Evaluating laboratory performance on quality indicators with the six sigma scale. Arch. Pathol. Lab. Med. **124**(4), 516–519 (2000)
7. Gras, J.M., Philippe, M.: Application of the six sigma concept in clinical laboratories: a review. Clin. Chem. Lab. Med. **45**(6), 789–796 (2007). https://doi.org/10.1515/CCLM.2007.135
8. Badrick, T., Ge, Y., Gou, G., Wong, W.: What factors are associated with improvements in productivity in clinical laboratories in the Asia pacific region? Clin. Biochem. **99**, 103–110 (2022). https://doi.org/10.1016/j.clinbiochem.2021.10.008
9. Zhou, B., Wu, Y., He, H., Li, C., Tan, L., Cao, Y.: Practical application of six sigma management in analytical biochemistry processes in clinical settings. J. Clin. Lab. Anal. **34**(1) (2020). https://doi.org/10.1002/jcla.23126
10. Lima-Oliveira, G., Volanski, W., Lippi, G., Picheth, G., Guidi, G.C.: Pre-analytical phase management: a review of the procedures from patient preparation to laboratory analysis. Scand. J. Clin. Lab. Invest. **77**(3), 153–163 (2017). https://doi.org/10.1080/00365513.2017.1295317
11. Thakur, V., Akerele, O.A., Randell, E.: Lean and six sigma as continuous quality improvement frameworks in the clinical diagnostic laboratory. Crit. Rev. Clin. Lab. Sci. **60**(1), 63–81 (2023). https://doi.org/10.1080/10408363.2022.2106544
12. Ialongo, C., Bernardini, S.: Long story short: an introduction to the short-term and longterm six sigma quality and its importance in laboratory medicine for the management of extra-analytical processes. Clin. Chem. Lab. Med. **56**(11), 1838–1845 (2018). https://doi.org/10.1515/cclm-2018-0310
13. Antony, J., Palsuk, P., Gupta, S., Mishra, D., Barach, P.: Six sigma in healthcare: a systematic review of the literature. Int. J. Qual. Reliab. Manag. **35**(5), 1075–1092 (2018). https://doi.org/10.1108/IJQRM-02-2017-0027

14. Samanta, A.K., Varaprasad, G., Gurumurthy, A.: Implementing lean six sigma in health care: a review of case studies. Int. J. Lean Six Sigma **14**(1), 158–189 (2023). https://doi.org/10.1108/IJLSS-08-2021-0133

15. Stoiljković, V., Trajković, J., Stoiljković, B.: Lean six sigma sample analysis process in a microbiology laboratory. J. Med. Biochem. **30**(4), 346–353 (2011). https://doi.org/10.2478/v10011-011-0018-2

16. Thakur, V., et al.: Use of a lean six sigma approach to investigate excessive quality control (QC) material use and resulting costs. Clin. Biochem. **112**, 53–60 (2023). https://doi.org/10.1016/j.clinbiochem.2022.12.001

17. Ortiz Barrios, M.A., Felizzola Jiménez, H.: Use of six sigma methodology to reduce appointment lead-time in obstetrics outpatient department. J. Med. Syst. **40**(10), 1–15 (2016). https://doi.org/10.1007/s10916-016-0577-3

18. Ortiz-Barrios, M., Alfaro-Saiz, J.: An integrated approach for designing in-time and economically sustainable emergency care networks: a case study in the public sector. PLoS ONE **15** (2020). https://doi.org/10.1371/journal.pone.0234984

19. Chaurasia, B., Garg, D., Agarwal, A.: Lean six sigma approach: a strategy to enhance performance of first through time and scrap reduction in an automotive industry. Int. J. Bus. Excell. **17**(1), 42–57 (2019). https://doi.org/10.1504/IJBEX.2019.096903

20. Ortiz Barrios, M., Felizzola Jiménez, H.: Reduction of average lead time in outpatient service of obstetrics through six sigma methodology. In: Bravo, J., Hervás, R., Villarreal, V. (eds.) AmIHEALTH 2015. LNCS, vol. 9456, pp. 293–302. Springer, Cham (2015). https://doi.org/10.1007/978-3-319-26508-7_29

21. Ortíz-Barrios, M.A., Escorcia-Caballero, J.P., Sánchez-Sánchez, F., De Felice, F., Petrillo, A.: Efficiency analysis of integrated public hospital networks in outpatient internal medicine. J. Med. Syst. **41**(10), 1–18 (2017). https://doi.org/10.1007/s10916-017-0812-6

A Hybrid Fuzzy MCDM Approach to Identify the Intervention Priority Level of Covid-19 Patients in the Emergency Department: A Case Study

Armando Perez-Aguilar[1,3]($\boxtimes$), Miguel Ortiz-Barrios[2], Pablo Pancardo[1], and Fernando Orrante-Weber-Burque[4]

[1] Academic Division of Information Science and Technology, Juarez Autonomous University of Tabasco, Cunduacan, Tabasco, Mexico
211H18001@alumno.ujat.mx, armando.pa@laventa.tecnm.mx,
pablo.pancardo@ujat.mx

[2] Department of Productivity and Innovation, Universidad de la Costa CUC, Barranquilla, Colombia
mortiz1@cuc.edu.co

[3] Academic Division of Computer Systems Engineering, Technological National of Mexico/Higher Technological Institute of Villa La Venta, Huimanguillo, Tabasco, Mexico

[4] Secretaría de Salud, Hospital Comunitario la Venta, La Venta, Huimanguillo, Tabasco, México

Abstract. Several efforts have been made by hospital administrators to provide high-quality care for Covid-19-infected patients admitted to the Emergency Department (ED). Estimating the intervention priority level of Covid-19 patients is pivotal to underpin this process. However, diagnoses vary from one doctor to another considering various factors including experience, intuition, and education level. This problem is even more sharpened especially in absence of patient background and medical records. In addition, there is a large volume of infected persons requiring emergency care and a wide range of health and socio-personal particularities that need to be considered when deciding if these patients will be only treated at the ED, hospitalized, or returned home. Therefore, this study proposes a new integrated Multi-Criteria Decision-Making (MCDM) approach to identify the intervention priority level of Covid-19 infected patients. First, the Trapezoidal Neutrosophic Fuzzy Analytic Hierarchy Process (TNF-AHP) method was implemented to calculate the criteria and sub-criteria weights considering uncertainty and knowledge level. Second, the Intuitionistic Fuzzy Compromise Combined Solution (IF-CoCoSo) was applied to estimate the intervention priority level of Covid-19 patients and define actions to improve their health condition. The proposed approach was validated in a Mexican public hospital. As a result, an MCDM model comprising 5 criteria and 27 sub-criteria was designed to support this decision. Specifically, "Socio-personal characteristics" (overall weight = 0.195), "Hypogeusia" (overall weight = 0.0812), and "Chronic lung disease" (overall weight = 0.089) were found to be the most important decision elements in defining the intervention priority level of Covid-19 patients.

© The Author(s), under exclusive license to Springer Nature Switzerland AG 2023
V. G. Duffy (Ed.): HCII 2023, LNCS 14029, pp. 284–297, 2023.
https://doi.org/10.1007/978-3-031-35748-0_21

Keywords: Trapezoidal Neutrosophic Fuzzy Analytic Hierarchy Process (TNF-AHP) · Intuitionistic Fuzzy Combined Compromise Solution (IF-CoCoSo) · Multiple Criteria Decision-Making (MCDM) · Covid-19 · Emergency Department (ED)

1 Background

Decision-making is a practice that is carried out in everyday life constantly. Some decisions can be made without the help of any tool. However, there are decisions involving several options and a large and complex amount of information with multiple criteria. In many cases, these criteria are ambiguous or diffuse, making it difficult to reach direct decisions. This activity becomes more complex when decision-making concerns the health or life of a person while entailing large amounts of information that must be analyzed in a short time. Multiple Criteria Decision-Making (MCDM) methods have been developed to deal with this context [1–3] and several applications have evidenced their effectiveness in the practical healthcare scenario [4, 5].

The current Covid-19 pandemic has stressed the healthcare system and continuously demands robust decision-making processes assisting medical staff in its in-time diagnosis and treatment. Particularly, researchers are concerned about the early prediction of mortality risk in patients infected with Covid-19 as mentioned by Hu et al. [6] and Ortíz-Barrios et al. [7]. These models work with machine learning but their sample size is relatively small so the interpretation of their findings may be limited. On the other hand, although some criteria (e.g. age, diabetes mellitus, and race) identified in hospitalized Covid-19 infected patients have been incorporated into these applications [8], they do not represent the existing relationship between these criteria and uncertainty often found in new decision-making contexts. MCDM methods can be useful in these circumstances, especially when the criteria have imprecise characteristics and are more complex to manage. By combining MCDM with fuzzy Trapezoidal Neutrosophic Fuzzy (TNF) sets, the results are more efficient and realistic [9]. This evidences an evolution of the MCDM methods to cope with new and more multifaceted scenarios [10] as the one exposed during the pandemic.

The decision-making context here described arises from the need to allocate scarce resources and timely intervene in Covid-19 patients with a high risk of mortality or permanent sequelae. Some studies have been performed for risk prioritization in Covid-19 patients using multi-criteria decision-making methods. For instance, Albahri et al. [11] used a patient dataset containing laboratory criteria to address this activity. Özkan et al. [12] prioritized Covid-19 patients admitted to public hospitals for intensive care unit admission using multi-criteria decision-making methods. However, they did not consider ambiguous or fuzzy information. On a different tack, it can be observed that the criteria that have been deemed in this context are conflicting and must be therefore prioritized by a suitable weighting method.

The proposed approach was validated in a Mexican hospital serving a population of approximately 30,000 patients. The manuscript is structured as follows. First, Sect. 2 presents the methodology. Section 3 outlines the results and discusses the main findings. Ultimately, Sect. 4 depicts the conclusions and future work.

2 Methodology

An integrated methodology comprising five phases (Fig. 1) is proposed to determine the intervention level for Covid-19 patients attending the emergency medical unit:

Phase 1 – Creation of a Decision-Making Group: A group of experts with experience in the care of Covid-19 patients is selected to support the design of the prioritization model, as well as to underpin the calculation of criteria/sub-criteria weights and analyze the cause-effect interrelationships between these decision elements.

Phase 2 - Design of the Prioritization Model (Objective, Criteria, Sub-criteria, and Alternatives): The model is constructed taking into account the criteria and sub-criteria derived from the experts' opinions, the Health Ministry regulations, and the related scientific literature.

Phase 3 - Weighting: The TNF-AHP method is applied to calculate the relative importance of criteria and sub-criteria considering the uncertainty, vagueness, and knowledge level of the experts.

Phase 4 – Calculation of Intervention Priority Level (IPL): In this phase, the IPL is calculated for the alternatives (patients) using IF-CoCoSo. Depending on the IPL, the patient is then decided to discharge at home or stay at the hospital.

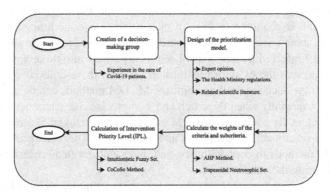

Fig. 1. Proposed methodology for prioritizing the intervention level of Covid-19 patients admitted to the emergency department.

Following this, we provide a detailed description of the mathematical procedures supporting TNF-AHP and IF-CoCoSo applications used in this study.

2.1 Trapezoidal Neutrosophic Fuzzy Analytic Hierarchy Process (TNF-AHP)

Combining the Trapezoidal Neutrosophic Fuzzy (TNF) sets with the Analytic Hierarchy Process (AHP) was decided to estimate the criteria and sub-criteria weights while considering the knowledge of truth, indeterminacy, and falsity of human thought when comparing two decision elements pairwisely [9]. The general procedure of the TNF-AHP algorithm is explained below:

Step 1: Contrast the criteria/sub-criteria using linguistic terms.

$$A^k = \begin{bmatrix} c_{11}^k & c_{12}^k & \cdots & c_{1n}^k \\ c_{21}^k & c_{22}^k & \cdots & c_{2n}^k \\ \cdots\cdots\cdots\cdots\cdots \\ c_{n1}^k & c_{n2}^k & \cdots & c_{nn}^k \end{bmatrix} \tag{1}$$

Step 2: In case of group decision-making, the comparisons (c_{ij}^k) are averaged as stated in Eq. 2.

$$c_{ij} = \frac{\sum_{k=1}^{k} c_{ij}^k}{K} \tag{2}$$

Step 3: The pairwise comparison matrix is updated with the c_{ij} values as shown in Eq. 3.

$$A = \begin{bmatrix} c_{11} & c_{12} & \cdots & c_{1n} \\ c_{21} & c_{22} & \cdots & c_{2n} \\ \cdots\cdots\cdots\cdots\cdots \\ c_{n1} & c_{n2} & \cdots & c_{nn} \end{bmatrix} \tag{3}$$

Step 4: The geometric mean of fuzzy comparison values associated with each criterion/sub-criterion is calculated as presented in Eq. 4. Here, si denotes a trapezoidal neutrosophic fuzzy number.

$$S_i = \left[\prod_{j=1}^{n} c_{ij} \right]^{\frac{1}{n}}, i = 1, 2 \ldots\ldots.n \tag{4}$$

Step 5: The fuzzy weight of each decision element is achieved by following Eq. 5.

$$\begin{aligned} w_i &= s_i \otimes (s_1 \otimes s_2 \otimes s_3 \otimes \ldots . \otimes s_n)^{-1} \\ &= \langle lwi, mwi, uwi, vwi), T_\beta, I_\beta, F_\beta \rangle \end{aligned} \tag{5}$$

Step 6: The ranking method is used to convert wi, a trapezoidal neutrosophic number, into a crisp value [13]. Equation 6 is then applied considering that the problem is of maximization nature.

$$R(wi) = \left(\frac{lwi + 2(mwi + uwi)}{2} \right) + (T_\beta - I_\beta - F_\beta) \tag{6}$$

Step 7: Ultimately, $R(wi)$ is derived by implementing Eq. 7.

$$w_i = \frac{R(wi)}{\sum_{i=1}^{n} R(wi)} \tag{7}$$

2.2   Intuitionistic Fuzzy Combined Compromise Solution (IF-CoCoSo)

In this section, we aim to describe the IF-CoCoSo approach. This is an extension of the CoCoSo method described in Yazdani et al. [14] and Ortíz-Barrios et al. [10]. The inclusion of intuitionistic fuzzy sets helps to deal with imprecise knowledge and lack of data often found in complex decision-making environments [15]. The IF-CoCoSo procedure is as follows:

Step 1: Build the Linguistic Decision Matrix (LDM).

The experts arrange the LDM to assess his/her decision on patient Hi regarding a criterion Pj. Then, we derive the performance assessment matrix $Y_k = \left[y_{ij}^r\right]_{mxn}$ considering the group of criteria (Eq. 8)

$$
Y_k = (y_{ij}^r)_{mxn} = \begin{array}{c} H_1 \\ \vdots \\ H_m \end{array} \begin{array}{c} P_1 \quad \cdots \quad P_{n.} \\ \left[\begin{array}{ccc} (\mu_{11r}, \nu_{11r}) & \cdots & (\mu_{1nr}\nu_{1nr}) \\ \vdots & \ddots & \vdots \\ (\mu_{m1r}, \nu_{m1r}) & \cdots & (\mu_{mnr}\nu_{mnr}) \end{array} \right] \end{array}, \forall r. \tag{8}
$$

Step 2: Estimate the importance of decision-makers.

The importance ratings of decision-makers are defined as $\xi_r = (\mu_r, \nu_r), r = 1, 2, \cdots, \ell$. The crisp weights of experts are derived applying Eq. 9.

$$
\varpi_r = \frac{\mu_r(2 - \mu_r - \nu_r)}{\sum_{r=1}^{\ell}[\mu_r(2 - \mu_r - \nu_r)]}, r = 1, 2, \ldots, \ell. \tag{9}
$$

Step 3: Build the Aggregated Intuitionistic Fuzzy Decision Matrix (A-IF-DM) by applying the IFWA operator. Let $D = \left[y_{ij}\right]_{mxn}$ be the A-IF-DM, where $y_{ij} = (\mu_{ij}, \nu_{ij}), i = 1, 2, \ldots, m, j = 1, 2, \ldots, n$ (Eq. 10)

$$
y_{ij} = \left\langle 1 - \prod_{r-1}^{\ell}\left(1 - \mu_{ijr}\right)^{\varpi_r}, \prod_{r-1}^{\ell}\left(1 - \nu_{ijr}\right)^{\varpi_r}, \right\rangle. \tag{10}
$$

Step 4: Construct the Normalized Aggregated Intuitionistic Fuzzy Decision Matrix (NA-IF-DM).

The NA-IF-DM $M = \left[\varsigma_{ij}\right]_{mxn}$ is computed by implementing Eq. 11.

$$
\varsigma_{ij} = \begin{cases} y_{ij} = (\mu_{ij}, \nu_{ij}), \text{ for benefit criterion,} \\ (y_{ij})^c = (\nu_{ij}, \mu_{ij}), \text{ for cost criterion.} \end{cases} \tag{11}
$$

Step 5: Estimate the Weighted Sum Method (WSM) and Weighted Product Method (WPM) scores.

The WSM $\left(\wp_i^{(1)}\right)$ score for each patient is computed by applying the Intuitionistic Fuzzy Weighted Average (IFWA) operator (Eq. 12). Here φ_j represents the weight of decision element j.

$$
\wp_i^{(1)} = \bigoplus_{j=1}^{n} \varphi_j \varsigma_{ij}. \tag{12}
$$

The EWPM $\left(\wp_i^{(2)}\right)$ score for each patient is computed using the Intuitionistic Fuzzy Weighted Geometric (IFWG) operator (Eq. 13).

$$\wp_i^{(2)} = \overset{n}{\underset{j=1}{\oplus}} \; \varphi_j \varsigma_{ij}. \tag{13}$$

Step 6: Determine the Balanced Compromise Score (BCS) of each Covid-19 patient. $\mathcal{Q}_i^{(1)}$, $\mathcal{Q}_i^{(2)}$, and $\mathcal{Q}_i^{(3)}$ are utilized to rank the patients (Eq. 14, 15, and 16).

$$\mathcal{Q}_i^{(1)} = \frac{S^*\left(\wp_i^{(1)}\right) + S^*\left(\wp_i^{(2)}\right)}{\sum_{i=1}^{m}\left(S^*\left(\wp_i^{(1)}\right) + S^*\left(\wp_i^{(2)}\right)\right)}, \tag{14}$$

$$\mathcal{Q}_i^{(2)} = \frac{S^*\left(\wp_i^{(1)}\right)}{\min_i S^*\left(\wp_i^{(1)}\right)} + \frac{S^*\left(\wp_i^{(2)}\right)}{\min_i S^*\left(\wp_i^{(2)}\right)}, \tag{15}$$

$$\mathcal{Q}_i^{(3)} = \frac{\vartheta S^*\left(\wp_i^{(1)}\right) + (1-\vartheta)S^*\left(\wp_i^{(2)}\right)}{\vartheta \min_i S^*\left(\wp_i^{(1)}\right) + (1-\vartheta)\min_i S^*\left(\wp_i^{(2)}\right)}, \tag{16}$$

where ϑ is a coefficient with $\vartheta \in [0,1]$. As this is the first study dealing with this decision-making context, we take $\vartheta = 0.5$.

Step 8: Calculate the overall compromise solution of Covid-19 patients ($\mathcal{Q}_i$) by utilizing Eq. 17.

$$\mathcal{Q}_i = \left(\mathcal{Q}_i^{(1)}\mathcal{Q}_i^{(2)}\mathcal{Q}_i^{(3)}\right)^{\frac{1}{3}} + \frac{1}{3}\left(\mathcal{Q}_i^{(1)}\mathcal{Q}_i^{(2)}\mathcal{Q}_i^{(3)}\right). \tag{17}$$

Finally, prioritize the patients by arranging the $\mathcal{Q}_i$ values in descending order.

3 Results and Discussion

3.1 Creation of a Decision-Making Group

10 experts were selected to form the decision-making group as depicted in Table 1. A preliminary interview was conducted to verify the accomplishment of some inclusion criteria including length of experience, time caring for Covid-19 patients in the Emergency Department (ED), and educational background.

3.2 Design of the Prioritization Model

The working group proposed the inclusion of several decision elements to be deemed when defining the intervention priority of Covid-19 patients admitted to the ED. This information was complemented with the criteria/sub-criteria considered in similar studies, and the specifications of the Health Ministry regulations regarding the Covid-19 pandemic. The result is a model comprising 5 criteria and 27 sub-criteria which helps doctors to prioritize Covid-19 patients and define the most appropriate intervention route (Fig. 2).

Table 1. Profile of experts participating in the decision-making group

Experts	Educational background	Length of experience (years)	Time caring for Covid-19 patients (years)
Expert 1	Bachelor in Medical Surgeon	18	2
	Master of Science in Public Health		
	Master in Education and Teaching		
	PhD. in Public Health and Health Management		
Expert 2	Bachelor in Medical Surgeon	18	2
	Master of Science in Public Health with an emphasis on Epidemiology		
	PhD. in Public Health and Health Management		
Expert 3	Bachelor in Medical Surgeon	16	1.8
	Specialty in Medical Emergencies		
Expert 4	Bachelor in Medical Surgeon	14	1.8
Expert 5	Bachelor in Medical Surgeon	11	1
	Master in Public Health Sciences		
Expert 6	Bachelor in Medical surgeon	19	2
Expert 7	Bachelor in Medical surgeon	15	1.9
Expert 8	Bachelor in Medical surgeon	22	1.6
	Master in Public Health Sciences		
Expert 9	Bachelor in Medical surgeon	6	1.8

(*continued*)

Table 1. (*continued*)

Experts	Educational background	Length of experience (years)	Time caring for Covid-19 patients (years)
Expert 10	Bachelor in Medical surgeon	4	1.8

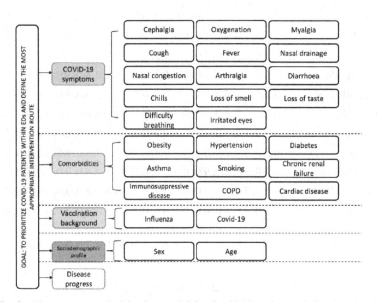

Fig. 2. The proposed prioritization model for Covid-19 patients admitted to the ED

3.3 Weights of Criteria and Sub-criteria

The decision-makers performed pairwise comparisons between criteria/sub-criteria based on the TNF-AHP procedure (see sub-Sect. 2.1). These judgments were collected through a survey where the experts could establish the importance ratings in a linguistic manner. The responses were then translated to the corresponding TNF number and averaged to derive the aggregated pairwise comparison matrix (Eq. 1, 2, and 3). An example of this step is provided in Table 2. After this, the fuzzy weights of criteria and sub-criteria are derived after implementing Eq. 4 and 5 (Table 3). The ranking method is then employed to defuzzify these priorities (Eq. 6). These values are later normalized applying Eq. 7 to generate the overall and local weights of the decision elements incorporated into the model (Table 4).

According to the results, it has become glaring that *Cephalgia* - SC1 and *Oxygenation* - SC2 (NGW = 0.08) are the most relevant sub-criteria when defining the intervention priority of Covid-19 patients in the ED. These symptoms have been identified to be significantly associated with poor health outcomes if not intervened timely [16, 17] It is also seen that *Disease Progress* – C5 (NGW = 0.055) and *Covid-19* - SC25 (NGW = 0.055) highly contribute to the decision of what healthcare pathway should be followed

Table 2. Aggregated pairwise comparisons in TNF numbers - Covid-19 symptoms sub-criteria Vs Cephalgia and Oxygenation

Sub-criteria/Covid-19 symptoms	Cephalgia (SC1)	Oxygenation (SC2)
Cephalgia (SC1)	⟨(1.0, 1.0, 1.0, 1.0) 1.0, 0.0, 0.0⟩	⟨(0.2, 0.2, 0.2, 0.3) 0.8, 0.5, 0.2⟩
Oxygenation (SC2)	⟨(3.0, 4.0, 5.0, 6.0) 0.8, 0.5, 0.2⟩	⟨(1.0, 1.0, 1.0, 1.0) 1.0, 0.0, 0.0⟩
Myalgia (SC3)	⟨(4.0, 4.5, 5.0, 6.0) 0.9, 0.3, 0.2⟩	⟨(7.0, 8.0, 8.0, 9.0) 0.9, 0.5, 0.1⟩
Cough (SC4)	⟨(2.5, 3.0, 3.5, 4.0) 0.9, 0.2, 0.2⟩	⟨(6.0, 6.0, 6.0, 7.0) 0.9, 0.3, 0.1⟩
Fever (SC5)	⟨(3.0, 3.5, 4.0, 5.0) 0.9, 0.3, 0.2⟩	⟨(6.0, 7.0, 7.0, 7.0) 0.9, 0.4, 0.1⟩
Nasal drainage (SC6)	⟨(5.0, 5.0, 6.1, 7.0) 0.9, 0.4, 0.2⟩	⟨(7.0, 8.0, 9.0, 9.0) 0.9, 0.5, 0.2⟩
Nasal congestion (SC7)	⟨(3.5, 0.3, 4.5, 5.0) 0.9, 0.2, 0.1⟩	⟨(8.0, 8.0, 9.0, 9.0) 0.8, 0.4, 0.2⟩
Arthalgia (SC8)	⟨(2.3, 3.0, 3.0, 3.5) 0.9, 0.2, 0.1⟩	⟨(7.0, 8.0, 8.0, 9.0) 0.9, 0.5, 0.2⟩
Diarrhoea (SC9)	⟨(3.5, 4.0, 5.0, 6.0) 0.8, 0.4, 0.2⟩	⟨(7.0, 8.0, 8.0, 9.0) 0.9, 0.3, 0.1⟩
Chills (SC10)	⟨(5.0, 6.0, 7.0, 8.0) 0.9, 0.4, 0.2⟩	⟨(7.5, 8.0, 8.5, 9.0) 0.9, 0.5, 0.2⟩
Loss of smell (SC11)	⟨(7.0, 7.0, 8.0, 9.0) 0.9, 0.5, 0.1⟩	⟨(8.0, 8.0, 9.0, 9.0) 0.8, 0.4, 0.2⟩
Loss of taste (SC12)	⟨(6.0, 7.0, 7.0, 8.0) 0.9, 0.4, 0.1⟩	⟨(8.0, 8.0, 9.0, 9.0) 0.8, 0.4, 0.2⟩
Difficulty breathing (SC13)	⟨(3.0, 4.0, 5.0, 6.0) 0.8, 0.4, 0.2⟩	⟨(3.0, 3.0, 3.0, 3.5) 1.0, 0.1, 0.1⟩
Irritated eyes (SC14)	⟨(3.5, 4.0, 5.0, 6.0) 0.9, 0.4, 0.2⟩	⟨(6.0, 7.0, 7.0, 7.0) 0.9, 0.4, 0.1⟩

Table 3. Criteria and sub-criteria weights in TNF numbers

Sub-criteria/Covid-19 symptoms	Weights in TNF numbers
Cephalgia (SC1)	⟨(0.187, 0.164, 0.197, 0.204) 0.079, 0.094, 0.100⟩
Oxygenation (SC2)	⟨(0.240, 0.235, 0.216, 0.205) 0.079, 0.095, 0.104⟩
Myalgia (SC3)	⟨(0.118, 0.126, 0.124, 0.124) 0.079, 0.094, 0.105⟩
Cough (SC4)	⟨(0.103, 0.106, 0.102, 0.101) 0.079, 0.093, 0.103⟩
Fever (SC5)	⟨(0.092, 0.094, 0.089, 0.088) 0.079, 0.094, 0.104⟩
Nasal drainage (SC6)	⟨(0.047, 0.051, 0.052, 0.053) 0.079, 0.094, 0.105⟩
Nasal congestion (SC7)	⟨(0.045, 0.048, 0.047, 0.048) 0.079, 0.094, 0.105⟩
Arthalgia (SC8)	⟨(0.046, 0.048, 0.048, 0.048) 0.079, 0.094, 0.104⟩
Diarrhoea (SC9)	⟨(0.044, 0.045, 0.044, 0.045) 0.079, 0.093, 0.105⟩
Chills (SC10)	⟨(0.025, 0.026, 0.026, 0.026) 0.058, 0.032, 0.013⟩
Loss of smell (SC11)	⟨(0.015, 0.015, 0.015, 0.015) 0.059, 0.031, 0.011⟩
Loss of taste (SC12)	⟨(0.014, 0.015, 0.014, 0.014) 0.059, 0.031, 0.011⟩
Difficulty breathing (SC13)	⟨(0.015, 0.017, 0.017, 0.019) 0.057, 0.031, 0.017⟩
Irritated eyes (SC14)	⟨(0.010, 0.010, 0.010, 0.010) 0.058, 0.029, 0.013⟩

Table 4. Defuzzified and normalized global weights of criteria and sub-criteria

Criterion/sub-criterion	Defuzzified weight	Normalized Global Weight (NGW)
Cephalgia (SC1)	0.160	0.080
Oxygenation (SC2)	0.160	0.080
Myalgia (SC3)	0.100	0.050
Cough (SC4)	0.074	0.037
Fever (SC5)	0.090	0.045
Nasal drainage (SC6)	0.040	0.020
Nasal congestion (SC7)	0.044	0.022
Arthalgia (SC8)	0.026	0.013
Diarrhoea (SC9)	0.038	0.019
Chills (SC10)	0.076	0.038
Loss of smell (SC11)	0.048	0.024
Loss of taste (SC12)	0.048	0.024
Difficulty breathing (SC13)	0.101	0.051
Irritated eyes (SC14)	0.046	0.023
Obesity (SC15)	0.050	0.025
Hypertension (SC16)	0.100	0.050
Diabetes (SC17)	0.058	0.029
Asthma (SC18)	0.039	0.019
Smoking (SC19)	0.038	0.019
Chronic renal failure (SC20)	0.034	0.017
Immunosuppressive disease (SC21)	0.029	0.014
COPD (SC22)	0.096	0.048
Cardiac disease (SC23)	0.044	0.022
Influenza (SC24)	0.100	0.050
Covid-19 (SC25)	0.110	0.055
Age (SC26)	0.050	0.025
Sex (SC27)	0.096	0.048
Disease progress (C5)	0.110	0.055

by a Covid-19 patient. In particular, the Covid-19 evolution has been detected as a predictor for future Intensive Care admission [18, 19]. The rapid progression of this disease will make it necessary to transfer the patient to more complex services for avoiding the appearance of long-term sequelae and shortening the mortality risk. On the other hand, different vaccines have been proven to be successful in preventing severe health deterioration in Covid-19 patients which consequently influences the medical decision-making process supporting diagnosis and treatment [20, 21]. Although these aspects are the most significant in the prioritization process, it is evident that there are low differences with most of the remaining sub-criteria which denotes the need for diagnosing these patients based on an ample criterion set. In general, the most relevant criterion is *Covid-19 symptoms* - C1 (NGW = 0.526) which represents more than half of the intervention decision. Finally, it should be noted that no inconsistency problems were found in the aggregated pairwise comparison matrixes which underpin the reliability of the findings here described.

3.4   Calculation of Intervention Priority Level (IPL)

At this stage, the IF-CoCoSo method was applied to calculate the Intervention Priority Level (IPL) of each Covid-19 patient arriving at the ED. First, we calculated the relative importance of each decision-maker considering the linguistic variables (LV) and the intuitionistic fuzzy numbers used by Alrasheedi et al. [22] (Eq. 8–9). Table 5 shows the experts' weights.

Table 5. The relative priorities of experts in IF and crisp numbers

Expert	LV	IFNs	Non-normalized weights	Normalized weights
1	EE	(0.9, 0.05, 0.05)	0.398	0.1197
2	EE	(0.9, 0.05, 0.05)	0.398	0.1197
3	ME	(0.7, 0.2, 0.1)	0.324	0.0975
4	ME	(0.7, 0.2, 0.1)	0.324	0.0975
5	ME	(0.7, 0.2, 0.1)	0.324	0.0975
6	M	(0.6, 0.3, 0.1)	0.278	0.0836
7	M	(0.6, 0.3, 0.1)	0.278	0.0836
8	ME	(0.7, 0.2, 0.1)	0.324	0.0975
9	EE	(0.9, 0.05, 0.05)	0.398	0.1197
10	M	(0.6, 0.3, 0.1)	0.278	0.0836

* EE: Exceeds expectations; ME: Meet expectations; M: Moderate

Equation 10–13 were later applied to support the BCS calculations. Following this, Eq. 14–16 were implemented to compute the $Q_i^{(1)}$, $Q_i^{(2)}$, and $Q_i^{(3)}$ scores (Table 6) of each triaged Covid-19 patient. Ultimately, Q_i (Intervention Priority Level – IPL) was estimated for each patient (n = 17) arriving at the showcased Mexican hospital during a peak day (Table 6). In this case, the lower IPL the higher risk of developing more severe complications if no intervention is made. The outcomes revealed that patient H_{10} was found to be the one with the smallest IPL (0.891) while H_4 was concluded to have the highest IPL (1.717). Patients with IPL < 1.000 (H_{10}) are considered with very high risk and must be cared for in the hospital urgently, even transferred to more complex services. On the other hand, patients with IPL higher than 1.450 (H_1, H_5, H_7, H_{12}, H_{13},

H_{15}, H_{16}, and H_{17}) are concluded to have a low risk of serious health complications and can be therefore discharged at home.

Table 6. Intervention Priority Level (IPL) for the cohort of Covid-19 patients in the showcased Mexican Hospital

Covid-19 patient	$\wp_i^{(1)}$	$\wp_i^{(2)}$	$Q_i^{(1)}$	$Q_i^{(2)}$	$Q_i^{(3)}$	$Q_i(\vartheta)$	Ranking Order
H_1	0.934	0.044	0.063	3.332	0.960	1.502	12
H_2	0.699	0.042	0.047	2.855	0.727	1.234	3
H_3	0.937	0.031	0.062	2.820	0.950	1.319	5
H_4	0.900	0.062	0.062	3.974	0.944	1.717	17
H_5	0.920	0.047	0.062	3.428	0.949	1.530	14
H_6	0.937	0.034	0.062	2.932	0.953	1.359	7
H_7	0.924	0.042	0.062	3.250	0.949	1.468	9
H_8	0.642	0.036	0.043	2.512	0.665	1.092	2
H_9	0.926	0.033	0.061	2.898	0.942	1.342	6
H_{10}	0.584	0.025	0.039	2.000	0.598	0.891	1
H_{11}	0.942	0.030	0.062	2.813	0.954	1.318	4
H_{12}	0.925	0.042	0.062	3.261	0.950	1.472	10
H_{13}	0.926	0.043	0.062	3.266	0.951	1.474	11
H_{14}	0.932	0.038	0.062	3.083	0.952	1.411	8
H_{15}	0.914	0.053	0.062	3.661	0.949	1.611	15
H_{16}	0.925	0.045	0.062	3.360	0.952	1.508	13
H_{17}	0.957	0.056	0.065	3.837	0.994	1.694	16

4   Conclusions and Future Work

A hybrid MCDM approach integrated by TNF-AHP and IF-CoCoSo methods was proposed to provide triage physicians with a decision support system that rapidly prioritizes the use of scarce medical resources during peak demand while defining appropriate intervention pathways for Covid-19 patients based on their IPL. Thereby, it is possible to diminish the risk of mortality and the development of long-term sequelae compromising the life quality of these patients while alleviating the burden experienced by their families.

The result of this application is a prioritization model containing 5 criteria and 27 sub-criteria. In this case, the most important factor when defining the intervention priority of Covid-19 patients is *Covid-19 symptoms* - C1 (NGW $= 0.526$). Besides, the IF-CoCoSo application uncovered that approximately 50% of the patients have a low risk of severe health complications and can be thus discharged at home safely.

Further comparative studies may be considered as future work. Considering interval data on quantitative variables and alternative methods such as IF-BWM and IF-COPRAS may be fruitful research pathways to make this proposal more solid and robust. The use of fuzzy sets types 1 and 2 can be also implemented to explore how variations in uncertainty management may affect the IPL of Covid-19 patients and the consequent diagnosis/treatment decisions.

References

1. Peng, X., Yuan, H., Yang, Y.: Pythagorean fuzzy information measures and their applications. Int. J. Intell. Syst. **32**(10), 991–1029 (2017). https://doi.org/10.1002/int.21880
2. Ortiz Barrios, M., Felizzola Jimenez, H., Nieto Isaza, S.: Comparative analysis between ANP and ANP-DEMATEL for six sigma project selection process in a healthcare provider (2014)
3. Pedrycz, W., Ekel, P., Parreiras, R.: Fuzzy multicriteria decision-making: Models, methods and applications. In: Fuzzy Multicriteria Decision-Making: Models, Methods and Applications, pp. 1–338 (2010). https://doi.org/10.1002/9780470974032
4. Glaize, A., Duenas, A., Di Martinelly, C., Fagnot, I.: Healthcare decision-making applications using multicriteria decision analysis: a scoping review. J. Multi-Criteria Decis. Anal. **26**(1–2), 62–83 (2019). https://doi.org/10.1002/mcda.1659
5. Ortíz-Barrios, M.A., Alfaro-Saíz, J.-J.: Methodological approaches to support process improvement in emergency departments: a systematic review. Int. J. Environ. Res. Public Health **17**(8), 2664 (2020). https://doi.org/10.3390/ijerph17082664
6. Hu, C., et al.: Early prediction of mortality risk among patients with severe COVID-19, using machine learning. Int. J. Epidemiol. **49**(6), 1918–1929 (2020). https://doi.org/10.1093/ije/dyaa171
7. Ortíz-Barrios, M., Arias-Fonseca, S., Ishizaka, A., Barbati, M., Avendaño-Collante, B., Jiménez-Navarro, E.: Artificial intelligence and discrete-event simulation for capacity management of intensive care units during the covid-19 pandemic: a case study. J. Bus. Res. (2023). https://doi.org/10.1016/j.jbusres.2023.113806
8. Killerby, M.E., et al.: Characteristics associated with hospitalization among patients with covid-19 - metropolitan atlanta, georgia, march-april 2020. Morb. Mortal. Wkly Rep. **69**(25), 790–794 (2020). https://doi.org/10.15585/MMWR.MM6925E1
9. Singh, A., Das, A., Bera, U.K., Lee, G.M.: Prediction of transportation costs using trapezoidal neutrosophic fuzzy analytic hierarchy process and artificial neural networks. IEEE Access **9**, 103497–103512 (2021). https://doi.org/10.1109/ACCESS.2021.3098657
10. Ortiz-Barrios, M., Silvera-Natera, E., Petrillo, A., Gul, M., Yucesan, M.: A multicriteria approach to integrating occupational safety & health performance and industry systems productivity in the context of aging workforce: a case study. Saf. Sci. **152**, 105764 (2022). https://doi.org/10.1016/j.ssci.2022.105764
11. Albahri, A.S., Hamid, R.A., Albahri, O.S., Zaidan, A.A.: Detection-based prioritisation: framework of multi-laboratory characteristics for asymptomatic COVID-19 carriers based on integrated Entropy–TOPSIS methods. Artif. Intell. Med. **111**, 101983 (2021). https://doi.org/10.1016/j.artmed.2020.101983
12. Özkan, B., Özceylan, E., Kabak, M., Dikmen, A.U.: Evaluation of criteria and COVID-19 patients for intensive care unit admission in the era of pandemic: a multi-criteria decision making approach. Comput. Methods Programs Biomed. **209**, 106348 (2021). https://doi.org/10.1016/j.cmpb.2021.106348
13. Darehmiraki, M.: A solution for the neutrosophic linear programming problem with a new ranking function. In: Optimization Theory Based on Neutrosophic and Plithogenic Sets, pp. 235–259 (2020). https://doi.org/10.1016/B978-0-12-819670-0.00011-1

14. Yazdani, M., Zarate, P., Kazimieras Zavadskas, E., Turskis, Z.: A combined compromise solution (CoCoSo) method for multi-criteria decision-making problems. Manag. Decis. **57**(9), 2501–2519 (2019). https://doi.org/10.1108/MD-05-2017-0458

15. Ortiz-Barrios, M., Gul, M., Yucesan, M., Alfaro-Sarmiento, I., Navarro-Jiménez, E., Jiménez-Delgado, G.: A fuzzy hybrid decision-making framework for increasing the hospital disaster preparedness: the colombian case. Int. J. Disast. Risk Reduct. **72**, 102831 (2022). https://doi.org/10.1016/j.ijdrr.2022.102831

16. García-Azorín, D., et al.: Frequency and phenotype of headache in covid-19: a study of 2194 patients. Sci. Rep. **11**(1), 1–10 (2021). https://doi.org/10.1038/s41598-021-94220-6

17. Akhavan, A.R., et al.: Risk stratification of covid-19 patients using ambulatory oxygen saturation in the emergency department. West. J. Emerg. Med. **21**(6), 5 (2020). https://doi.org/10.5811/WESTJEM.2020.8.48701

18. Jain, V., Yuan, J.-M.: Predictive symptoms and comorbidities for severe COVID-19 and intensive care unit admission: a systematic review and meta-analysis. Int. J. Public Health **65**(5), 533–546 (2020). https://doi.org/10.1007/s00038-020-01390-7

19. Galloway, J.B., et al.: A clinical risk score to identify patients with COVID-19 at high risk of critical care admission or death: an observational cohort study. J. Infect. **81**(2), 282–288 (2020). https://doi.org/10.1016/j.jinf.2020.05.064

20. Zheng, C., Shao, W., Chen, X., Zhang, B., Wang, G., Zhang, W.: Real-world effectiveness of COVID-19 vaccines: a literature review and meta-analysis. Int. J. Infect. Dis. **114**, 252–260 (2022). https://doi.org/10.1016/j.ijid.2021.11.009

21. Shao, W., et al.: Effectiveness of COVID-19 vaccines against SARS-CoV-2 variants of concern in real-world: a literature review and meta-analysis. Emerg. Microbes Infect. **11**(1), 2383–2392 (2022). https://doi.org/10.1080/22221751.2022.2122582

22. Alrasheedi, M., Mardani, A., Mishra, A.R., Streimikiene, D., Liao, H., Al-nefaie, A.H.: Evaluating the green growth indicators to achieve sustainable development: a novel extended interval-valued intuitionistic fuzzy-combined compromise solution approach. Sustain. Dev. **29**(1), 120–142 (2021). https://doi.org/10.1002/sd.2136

Generation of Consistent Slip, Trip and Fall Kinematic Data via Instability Detection and Recovery Performance Analysis for Use in Machine Learning Algorithms for (Near) Fall Detection

Moritz Schneider[1]([✉]) [iD], Anika Weber[3,4], Mirko Kaufmann[2,3], Annette Kluge[2], Ulrich Hartmann[3], Kiros Karamanidis[4], and Rolf Ellegast[1]

[1] Institute for Occupational Safety and Health of the German Social Accident Insurance, St. Augustin, Germany
Moritz.Schneider@dguv.de
[2] Business and Organizational Psychology, Faculty of Psychology, Ruhr-University Bochum, Bochum, Germany
[3] RheinAhrCampus, Koblenz University of Applied Sciences, Remagen, Germany
[4] Sport and Exercise Science Research Centre, School of Applied Sciences, London South Bank University, London, UK

Abstract. Slip, trip and fall (STF) accidents are a major problem for companies in many industries and cause massive work absences. According to the German employers' liability insurance associations, this type of accident has been leading the list of reportable occupational accidents in the traffic, transport and logistics sector for years. A total of 172,045 STF accidents occurred during the reporting period of the German Social Accident Insurance (DGUV Report 2021) seven of which were fatal, and 2,694 new accident pensions. This paper focuses on the standardized acquisition of kinematic data of STF events and its use to assess dynamic stability control during locomotion for machine learning. Accurate detection of near falls via machine learning could help to identify subjects at high risk of falling and ensure that fall prevention interventions are provided to targeted individuals.

Keywords: slip · trip · fall · kinematic data · near fall · machine learning

1 Introduction

Every 5th occupational accident is caused by slipping, tripping and falling (STF) [1]. STF accidents are a significant problem for companies in a wide range of industries and result in expressive work absences [2, 3]. According to the German employers' liability insurance associations, this type of accident has been leading the list of reportable occupational accidents in the traffic, transport and logistics sector for years [4, 5]. A trip occurs when the swing phase of the foot is unexpectedly interrupted because it does not sufficiently negotiate the ground or obstacles. A slip occurs when the friction between

V. G. Duffy (Ed.): HCII 2023, LNCS 14029, pp. 298–305, 2023.
https://doi.org/10.1007/978-3-031-35748-0_22

the shoe sole and the ground is not adequate to counteract the forces occurring between the foot and the ground while stepping. A fall is defined as the unintentional contact of the body with the ground, which can happen for a variety of reasons, including twisting an ankle, miss stepping, tripping or slipping. In 2021, 172,045 STF accidents overall were reported from the DGUV (seven of which were fatal) resulting in 2,694 accident pensions [6]. 33%, of STF accidents occur in the commercial sector (e.g. in production, in workshops, at loading and unloading points); 17% in the public environment in generally accessible public places and in outdoor areas (e.g. path, parking lot, waiting room, see [6]). Slip hazards are caused by reduced surface friction, e.g., due to oil, wetness, polished surfaces, but also by weather conditions, e.g., rain, ice and snow. Uneven surfaces (steps, slopes/waviness, openings/depressions) stepped elevated edges or step edge profiles can, for example, pose a trip, twist or misstep hazard [3]. Certain occupational groups in the commercial sector, such as employees in the steel industry, associated plant fire departments, as well as firefighters in general [7], and people working in the public sector, such as mail and parcel delivery workers [8], are particularly at risk of slipping and tripping.

1.1 State of the Art STF Prevention

To prevent slip accidents, the state of the art offers a wide range of protective measures according to the hierarchy of controls through the STOP model [9–11]:

1. S: Substitution (e.g., replacement of slippery floor with anti-slip one)
2. T: Technical protective measures (such as floor covering, elimination of slip-promoting substances)
3. O: Organizational protective measures (such as the organization of working hours, planning of maintenance and repair measures)
4. P: Personal protective measures (such as footwear, experience, reaction, physical aspects and gait)

The protective measures with the most far-reaching effect are to be preferred [9]. The addressee for the STOP design sequence is the entrepreneur/employer and it specifies his methodology in dealing with STF hazards. In order to reduce the number of STF accidents, DGUV rules are made available to companies and organizations to provide assistance in the implementation of the obligations arising from state occupational health and safety regulations or accident prevention regulations. DGUV Information 208–046, for example, provides information on the responsibility of companies to provide and wear suitable personal protective equipment such as footwear, weather protective clothing and safety equipment. Many technical, organizational and personal factors are involved in the occurrence of STF accidents [12, 13]. With the implementation of the STOP model, workplaces are made safer with regard to STF accidents.

However, hazards for newspaper, mail and parcel delivery staff arise from road traffic, adverse weather conditions such as rain or snow, and factors beyond the company's control (local conditions of delivery routes, roads, sidewalks, driveways, stairways and stairwells in buildings). An evaluation of STF accidents among postal delivery workers [14] showed that in most cases they were due to snow and ice (70%). Half of all falls occurred during the months of November through February, and three-fourths of the falls occurred between 7 a.m. and 9 a.m. In 50% of the accidents, a combination of slippery conditions, use of shoes with poor tread, and time-saving behaviours, such as the unsafe practice of preparing the mail for the next delivery while walking, was identified [14, 15]. The research suggests that unsafe work practices, such as reading addresses while walking and taking shortcuts, increase the risk of falls [8].

In such cases, the following measures to prevent STF accidents are described in DGUV Information 208–035 (2020) [16]:

- Training in the conscious perception of STF hazards, e.g., tripping obstacles
- Education on suitable footwear for delivery, e.g., shoe sole material
- Advice on safe walking, e.g., no sorting while walking

In particular, this research project aims to address those hazardous locations where substitutional and technical measures to protect against STF accidents have been exhausted due to the location of the accident sites (in private and publicly accessible properties such as homes, or in the case of extensive outdoor facilities in the open air) by using a hazard awareness training and a perturbation-based training to improve reactive fall skills.

1.2 State of the Art Near Fall Classification

A "near fall" is a situation where a person trips, slips, or missteps, but is able to catch themselves and not touch the ground with any part of their body other than their feet. It is thought to be a complicated and heterogeneous event that can be influenced by a variety of factors, including physical, cognitive, and environmental factors. Current methods for detecting (near) falls are mainly based on thresholds (e.g., single- or multi-phase) or follow the machine learning (ML) approach. To classify the accuracy of fall detection algorithms a variety of metrics are used including sensitivity (the ability to correctly identify falls), specificity (the ability to correctly identify non-fall events), positive predictive value (the proportion of identified falls that are actually falls), negative predictive value (the proportion of identified non-fall events that are actually non-fall events) and the area under the receiver operating characteristic (ROC) curve.

Comparison of TH with ML shows higher sensitivities in ML (TH: 72.9% to 99.7% vs. ML: 84.6% to 99.8%), higher area under the ROC curve (TH: 0.83 to 0.96 vs. ML: 0.93 to 0.99) and lower false positive 3 (TH: 5% to 10.9 vs. ML: 0.6% to 5.1%) [17–20]. Based on previous studies it can be said that near falls and Activities of Daily Living (ADLs) lead to high false positive rates in TH-based methods for fall detection [17]. In addition, thresholds are commonly calibrated using simulated fall signals and are therefore often inappropriate for real fall signals because the fall phases of simulated falls are different from those of real falls [19]. Fall detection rates determined by ML are influenced by the different sensors used, sampling rates of the sensors, type of movements, as well as different characteristics of the subjects [18]. Despite the good recognition rates, however, this shows that the algorithms cannot simply be transferred to other configurations. Falls are generally a rare event, which has a strong impact on the parameter of specificity in particular. Real falls recorded in previous studies come from very specific subject collectives (e.g., Parkinson's disease patients), which makes it difficult to generalize the results to other groups of people. Accordingly, TH methods are easy to implement and require little computational effort. However, they are difficult to generalize across different individuals/activities and also show poor results when applied to real falls. ML methods, on the other hand, require more computational effort and are inherently highly dependent on their training data, but provide better results when applied to real falls. With a better sensitivity and a lower false positive rate, it appears that machine learning algorithms often beat threshold-based algorithms in terms of accuracy and dependability. In order to validate and expand on these findings in different circumstances, more study would be required. According to a review article [20] only two studies examined more than one type of near falls and distinguished between near-falls and falls [21, 22].

Inspired by these findings and ongoing research, a ML approach for detection of real (near) falls will be developed and tested. This algorithm should be able to distinguish between trips, slips, and missteps, and to differentiate near falls from falls.

2 Materials and Methods

The consistent slip, trip and fall kinematic data for use in machine learning algorithms for (near) fall detection are generated within a DGUV-funded project ENTRAPon. The project aims to develop additional training elements for the prevention of STF accidents. The projects primary objective is to supplement existing training tools (e.g. warehouse simulator) by setting up and evaluating a perturbation-based training.

2.1 Participants

In this project in total 140 employees, 70 from steel industry and 70 postal delivery, are to be recruited in advance for voluntary participation in the study ENTRAPon. The study is looking for both male and female participants who wish to take part in the study voluntarily. Only healthy workers, who are able to perform the given tasks without restrictions, can take part in the study. Workers who are unable to perform the tasks due to physical or neurological impairments, caused for example by injuries or previous illnesses of the musculoskeletal system, will be excluded from participation.

2.2 Experimental Setup

An STF-parkours (Fig. 1) is used in this study, consisting of a 15 m walkway in which a total of 18 STF elements are integrated equally divided into the following categories: unexpected trip- and slip-like perturbations, and changes in surface compliance. The black stepping tiles are placed 70 cm apart.

Slips were induced by a movable tile on two hidden rails with linear bearings that could slide forward up to 14 cm upon foot contact. Trips were induced using a 19 cm height tripping board that flips up from the walkway at mid-swing using a hidden contact sensor. Missteps were triggered by a foam block (11 cm high) that compresses to about 5 cm when stepped on. The perturbation elements can be activated at different points on the parkour by means of modular elements and are integrated into the floor in such a way that the participants are not aware of which disturbance occurs at which point. The participants faced away from the walkway before each trial so that the positioning

Fig. 1. Set-up of a slip, trip and fall (STF)-parkour including an overhead safety system (ceiling) at one cooperation partner's premises.

of the hazards could not be seen. Thus, they have to reactively adjust their gait to each perturbation. Participants wore a safety harness that was attached to on overhead safety rail. Furthermore they were equipped with shin guards.

During training and transfer testing the participants are fully instrumented with ambulatory inertial measurement units (IMUs) that are widely used in human motion analysis and determination of gait stability [20, 23, 24]. Therefore, they wear a whole body measuring suit (Xsens Link, Enschede, Netherlands) consisting of 17 IMU sensors.

2.3 Experimental Protocol

First, the anthropometric data of the participants were measured according to the instructions of Xsens. They were then fitted with a fall arrest harness and the Xsens system. Then, with the safety harness latched to the fall arrest system, participants were positioned at the beginning of the parkour and instructed to walk back and forth at their normal walking speed to familiarize themselves with the distance between the black tiles (at least 3 trials). After familiarization, participants continued to walk repeatedly on the parkour, but were additionally informed that from now on a perturbation in walking might occur. However, they were not given any further information about the perturbation, such as at which repetition a perturbation will occur, where a perturbation may occur, and what type of perturbation will occur. In addition, participants were instructed to wait at the start and end points until they received the command to turn around and start walking. Participants completed the parkour assessment first at their normal walking speed and then at a fast-walking speed. At each of the walking speeds, they were exposed ones to each of the three hazards (slipping, tripping, and compliant surface). After the gait perturbation, they walked without perturbation for at least one trial.

2.4 Definition of Near Falls in the Context of Workers

Near-falls are often defined and identified based on observations and arbitrary interpretations of circumstances, so there is no precise mathematical description of them. In laboratory environments it is possible to monitor and evaluate a number of variables, including distance travelled while slipping, severity of loss of balance, and forces during the fall recovery process. In the current literature, there are no specific parameters or thresholds that can be used to uniquely identify a near fall in STF accidents. The definition and identification of near falls is generally based on subjective assessments of the situation, and the specific parameters and thresholds used may vary depending on the context and the goals of the analysis. This work uses a data-driven approach to the design of wearable sensors and other monitoring tools that may be used to evaluate balance and mobility in real-time. These tools assess numerous elements of movement and balance using a range of sensors, including accelerometers, gyroscopes, and magnetometers. An accelerometer, for instance, may be used to monitor acceleration and deceleration, which can reveal information about the movement's speed and direction. The measurement of angular velocity and direction by a gyroscope, on the other hand, may be used to detect changes in balance.

In our assessment there are 3 categories of data: no fall (normal walking, standing, …), near fall (with subsequent fall (pre-impact phase) and without subsequent fall) and fall. For further evaluations of falls and near falls the cause has to be further analysed.

In a first step, sample data sets are considered in which subjects "lightly" and "heavily" near fall by "stumbling", "slipping" and "missstepping". For this purpose, multivariate time series of sensor data and the corresponding video sequences are synchronised and the biomechanical gait stability assessment parameters are calculated. Parameters like margin of stability, spatio-temporal components, step duration and length, time to touchdown from perturbation (recovery performance) and velocity of centre of mass at touchdown are considered in the classification. When these data are available in a synchronised form, the next step is to investigate which evaluation channels and their combinations allow a particularly good prediction for which type of STF and at what intensity, in order to develop an algorithm for marking of near falls due to the different types of STF.

The developed near-fall algorithm will then be tested on new data sets to determine the extent to which it can detect near-falls and their graduation "lightly" and "heavily", so that all measurement data of the ENTRAPon parkour can be labelled with it. In the last step, the quality of the algorithm would then be tested by manual expert evaluation, if necessary. The high-quality classified database then serves as the starting point for training artificial intelligence.

3 Conclusion

The standardized STF events provided by the parcours will be used to categorize near falls and provide a database of kinematic human data for use in machine learning methods. Near falls will be defined according to existing research and literature findings based on comprehensible parameters. In addition, graduations are made for the pre-impact phase and (near) falls according to anatomical orientations/directions and causes of falls (STF). There are also graduations for the pre-impact phase and (near) falls according to anatomical orientations/fall directions and causes of falls.

The determination of near falls will be made after a thorough evaluation of all pertinent facts, taking into consideration the unique context and analytical aims. Identifying near falls does not have a one-size-fits-all approach, and the particular criteria and thresholds that we are employed may need to be customized to the unique circumstances of each instance. If it can be shown in the initial investigations of the generated data that (near) fall accidents can be detected with sufficient accuracy by machine learning on a feature-rich database ("whole body measurement suit"), it can be sensibly reduced (fewer information channels). This reduces the number of sensors required and thus increases wearing comfort. In this context, the limitations with which (near) fall accidents can be detected should be investigated. This is to be done with the aim of developing a broadly suitable prevention warning system for use in professional practice, in order to effectively reduce STF accidents in operational practice in the long term.

The ability to detect near falls will allow for more accurate profiles of critical situations, more precise risk assessments, and possibly even prediction of personal fall risk to prevent falls early. The final goal is to develop a prevention warning system suitable for broad use in occupational practice, in order to effectively reduce trip, slip and fall accidents in occupational practice in the long term.

References

1. DGUV. Statistik Arbeitsunfallgeschehen 2019 (2020). https://www.dguv.de/de/zahlen-fak ten/index.jsp.
2. Hsiao, H.: Fall prevention research and practice: a total worker safety approach. Ind. Health **52**, 381–392 (2014)
3. BAuA, Sturz, Ausrutschen, Stolpern, Umknicken (2021).https://www.baua.de/DE/Themen/ Arbeitsgestaltung-im-Betrieb/Gefaehrdungsbeurteilung/Expertenwissen/Mechanische-Gef aehrdungen/Sturz-Ausrutschen-Stolpern-Umknicken/Sturz-Ausrutschen-Stolpern-Umknic ken_node.html
4. BGHM. Vorsicht, Rutschgefahr! Stolpern, Ausrutschen, Stürzen - Die häufigsten Unfallursachen bei der Arbeit (2021). https://www.bghm.de/bghm/presseservice/text-portal-fuer-int erne-kommunikation/vorsicht-rutschgefahr

5. Verkehr, B.: Stolpern, Rutschen, Stürzen (2021). https://www.bg-verkehr.de/arbeitssiche rheit-gesundheit/branchen/gueterkraftverkehr/animationsfilme/stolpern-rutschen-stuerzen
6. DGUV. Statistik Arbeitsunfallgeschehen 2021 (2021). https://www.dguv.de/de/zahlen-fak ten/index.jsp.
7. Mohr, J.O.: Fit gegen das Stolpern – Projektstudie der HFUK Nord. 6. DGUV-Fachgespräch Ergonomie, pp. 125–127 (2017)
8. Bentley, T.A.: Slip, trip and fall accidents occurring during the delivery of mail. Ergonomics **41**, 1859–1872 (1998)
9. Wetzel, C.: Entwicklung einer Rutschhemmungsmatrix zur Auswahl von Bodenbelägen und Schuhen zur Reduzierung von Ausgleitunfällen. Bergische Universität Wuppertal (2013)
10. Lehto, M.R., Cook, B.T.: Occupational health and safety management. In: Handbook of Human Factors and Ergonomics, pp. 701–733 (2012)
11. E. O. F. D. 89/391/EEC. The introduction of measures to encourage improvements in the safety and health of workers at work. Official Journal of the European Union L 183, 29/06/1989, pp. 1–8 (2008)
12. Paridon, H.: Entstehung von Stolper-, Rutsch- und Sturzunfälle. BGAG-Report 1/05 (2005)
13. Chang, W.-R., Leclercq, S., Lockhart, T.E., Haslam, R.: State of science: occupational slips, trips and falls on the same level. In: Ergonomics, pp. 861–883 (2016)
14. Haslam, R.A., Bentley, T.A.: Follow-up investigations of slip, trip and fall accidents among postal delivery workers. In: Safety Science, pp. 33–47 (1999)
15. Bentley, T.A., Halsam, R.A.: Identification of risk factors and countermeasures for slip, trip and fall accidents during the delivery of mail. In: Applied Ergonomics, pp. 127–134 (2001)
16. DGUV. DGUV Information 208–035 - Zustellen von Sendungen (2020)
17. Aziz, O., Musngi, M., Park, E.J., Mori, G., Robinovitch, S.N.: A comparison of accuracy of fall detection algorithms (threshold-based vs. machine learning) using waist-mounted tri-axial accelerometer signals from a comprehensive set of falls and non-fall trials. Med. Biol. Eng. Compu. **55**(1), 45–55 (2016). https://doi.org/10.1007/s11517-016-1504-y
18. Casilari, E., Lora-Rivera, R., García-Lagos, F.: A study on the application of convolutional neural networks to fall detection evaluated with multiple public datasets. Sensors **20**(5), 2020 (2020)
19. Bagalà, F., et al.: Evaluation of Accelerometer-Based Fall Detection Algorithms on Real-World Falls. PLoS ONE **7**(5) (2012)
20. I. Pang, Y. Okubo, D. Sturnieks, S. R. Lord und M. A. Brodie, „Detection of Near Falls Using Wearable Devices," *Journal of Geriatric Physical Therapy,* pp. 48–56, 2019
21. Lee, J.K., Robinovitch, S.N., Park, E.J.: Inertial sensing-based pre-impact de-tection of falls involving near-fall scenarios. IEEE Trans. Neural Syst. Rehabil. Eng. **23**(2), 258–266 (2015)
22. Albert, M.V., Kording, K., Herrmann, M., Jayaraman, A.: Fall classification by machine learning using mobile phones. PloS One **7**(5) (2012)
23. Kangas, M., Konttila, A., Lindgren, P., Winblad, I., Jämsä, T.: Comparison of low-complexity fall detection algorithms for body attached accelerometers. Gait Posture, 285–291 (2008)
24. Nyan, M.N., Tay, F.E.H., Murugasu, E.: A wearable system for pre-impact fall detection. J. Biomech., 3475–3481 (2008)

Safe Environments to Understand Medical AI - Designing a Diabetes Simulation Interface for Users of Automated Insulin Delivery

Tim Schrills[1]([✉]) [ID], Marthe Gruner[1] [ID], Heiko Peuscher[2] [ID],
and Thomas Franke[1] [ID]

[1] University of Lübeck, Ratzeburger Allee 160, 23560 Lübeck, Germany
{schrills,gruner,franke}@imis.uni-luebeck.de
[2] Technische Hochschule Ulm, Prittwitzstraße 10, 89075 Ulm, Germany
Heiko.Peuscher@thu.de

Abstract. Modern therapy for type 1 diabetes requires patients to interact with intelligent systems designed for automated insulin delivery (AID). Despite substantial medical advantages, patients often experience low trust in and predictability of AID systems. To mitigate adverse effects on human-AI cooperation, AID simulations may be used in training of patients. The goal of the present research is to identify requirements for human-centered AID simulation. To this end, we conducted an interview study ($N = 12$) in which stakeholders were queried on their expectations regarding AID systems, mainly addressing interactivity and explanation of simulation parameters. In addition, a prototypical simulation was used in a within-subject online experiment with $N = 32$ participants to evaluate effects on perceived trustworthiness and traceability. While the latter improved significantly, no difference in perceived trustworthiness was found. Our results indicate that interactive simulations can contribute to improving human cooperation with AID systems in a safe environment.

Keywords: Human-Automation Interaction · Diabetes Therapy · Explainability

1 Introduction

To support the therapy of type 1 diabetes mellitus (T1DM), intelligent systems are used to automate the control of glucose levels. To do so, they integrate machine learning as part of a user-specific adaptation process [1]. Several studies report positive effects on therapy quality (see [2] and [3]). However, high numbers of discontinuation of automated therapy (see [4]) can be observed. Given the lack of human-centered design of such highly automated systems [5], current research focuses on methods to improve therapy adherence as well as user experience. Boughton [6], e.g., describes an onboarding process, where users learn how to correctly interact with an AID system before actually connecting it to their

V. G. Duffy (Ed.): HCII 2023, LNCS 14029, pp. 306–328, 2023.
https://doi.org/10.1007/978-3-031-35748-0_23

bodies. Already at this early stage, misconceptions leading to disappointment and abandonment could be prevented. To exploit this potential, research from engineering psychology, especially in human-automation interaction, can be a promising approach.

Patients and highly automated systems for diabetes therapy, often referred to as AID systems (*Automated Insulin Delivery*, [7]), share the same goal: they aim to stabilize glucose levels by delivering the correct amount of insulin needed (usually through an insulin pump). Yet in contrast to patients, AID systems are currently not able to infer all information needed to perform (the necessary) calculations (e.g., food intake or physical activity, [2]). Therefore, it is particularly important that patients understand exactly what information the system needs from them and when, and what information the system can infer and process independently. Thus, the performance of many AID systems regularly relies on information inputs by the user [7,8], that is, cooperation between patients and AID systems. Accordingly, requirements defined for cooperation between humans and AI (c.f [9]) must be met to avoid critical effects regarding the quality of therapy. Patients must be able to predict how their interaction with the system influences the system's information processing. However, to establish mutual predictability, intelligent systems often need to be redesigned [10], which remains a challenge, although it is important to achieve reliable medical devices, like AID systems (see [11]). Potential solutions involve intense training for patients, including ways to improve AID system's traceability and patients' ability to predict how their cooperation affects the quality of their therapy [12].

Even though first empirical studies suggest that people with T1DM can benefit significantly from AID systems [3,13,14], several recent studies [4,15,16] explicate the need for human-centered development of AID systems, especially to manage patients' expectations. To address the effects known from human-automation interaction and respect the high risk associated with unpredictable AID systems in actual use, it is important to create a safe environment for patients as well as professionals to experience AID information processing. Within such an environment, patients can be supported to correct their mental model of the system (c.f. [17]), especially in situations where an AID system's performance is unsatisfactory or even dangerous.

One key effect in the field of human-automation-interaction is the *first failure effect*, where a significant reduction of users' trust in a system results from an unexpected failure after an (initial) period without failures [18]. This effect could be mitigated by demonstrating constraints of system capabilities in an early stage of interaction, thus allowing users to form more precise expectations about the system's behavior [19]. However, in the medical domain, especially when therapy parameters such as medicine dosages are automatically adapted, an early real-world experience of system failure is not desirable for patients or professionals. First-failure effects can also be experienced in a simulated environment [20]. Yet, while several open-source frameworks for diabetes simulation exist (see [21] or [22]), those systems are not yet developed to be used by patients and medical professionals. To the best of our knowledge, a precise description of the requirements for a patient-centered AID simulation as well as design criteria for the interaction with it is missing so far.

Accordingly, the goal of the present research is to analyze requirements for a human-centered simulation of AID systems that allows users to experience the limitations of AID systems, thus mitigating, e.g., first-failure effects. The leading research questions are

RQ1 *How does the interface of a simulation of an AID system have to be designed in order to improve the user experience before the use of the actual system?*

RQ2 *To what extent can simulation improve the perceived traceability and trustworthiness of a machine-learning-based AID system?*

To this end, we 1) identified relevant stakeholders, 2) conducted $N = 12$ interviews to extract system requirements, and 3) defined desired properties of an AID simulation for training purposes. In addition, we designed a simulation experiment ($N = 32$) where we tested an initial implementation of the elicited features and measured participants' performance as well as their experienced trustworthiness and traceability.

2 Background

2.1 Intelligent Systems for Automated Insulin Delivery (AID)

In recent developments in diabetes therapy, intelligent systems are increasingly used to automatically calculate the amount of insulin required. To this end, they mainly rely on glucose levels and further variables influencing insulin sensitivity (e.g., time of day or currently acting insulin). AID systems usually consist of several components. For example, the DBLG1 system consists of a sensor for continuous glucose monitoring [23], an insulin pump, and a handheld that contains the calculation and control algorithm [24]. It is not completely automated, because patients are still required to communicate information, e.g., on food intake [25], which is why it is also referred to as a hybrid closed-loop system. The prefix hybrid indicates a lower level of automation [26].

Empirical studies indicate that AID systems - with varying levels of automation, can improve diabetes therapy and quality of life in patients with diabetes [27,28]. While the degree of improvement depends on a wide range of medical factors (e.g., the therapy quality prior to AID therapy, [2,4]), a majority of patients report improved psychological ratings, e.g., on stress or disease-related workload [28,29]. In a meta-study, Farrington et al. [16] found a variety of benefits of closed-loop systems for users. These ranged from improved glycemic control, reduced fear of hypoglycemia, reassurance of family or partners, reduced stress, improved sleep habits, increased self-confidence, and greater ability to take action in daily life. These effects are found to be independent of specific manufacturers or systems [30].

However, [31] demonstrated in a study that around 33% of participants discontinued the use of an AID system one year after the end of the study.

They identified difficulties with the calibration of the sensors and alarms (when glucose levels exceed certain limits) but also problems intensely studied in human-computer interaction: users developed wrong expectations concerning the system's way to process information [32], potentially due to different approaches in glucose control between patients and AID systems. For example, AID systems can react every five minutes to a change in the glucose level (c.f. [33]), while manual treatment usually has less frequent control. As a consequence, e.g., AID systems may initially calculate lower amounts of insulin to correct high glucose levels than users. Also, for users who continued to use the system, the usage time of the automatic mode decreased over time [31]. This raises the question of what challenges patients with diabetes face in adopting and using closed-loop systems and whether initial challenges of human-automation interaction (c.f. first failure effect) might contribute to that development.

2.2   User Experience of Information Processing in AID Systems

Transparently demonstrating limitations of automated systems such as an AID system, potentially increases users' perceived trustworthiness [34], e.g., by enabling users to classify incorrect outputs of the algorithm. In AID systems, for example, users could observe that the algorithm does not adequately integrate the effects of alcohol consumption. Thus, by explicitly demonstrating which information an AID system can process, users are supported in developing a correct mental model and valid expectations regarding system performance. In addition, the way in which AID systems calculate often remains opaque to users, as in a wide range of AI-based systems [35]. Previous studies demonstrated that explanations of software systems increase the acceptance of, e.g., movie recommendations [36]. Schrills & Franke [12] found that users request multiple information about an AID system's insulin calculation, although it is not clear whether all information is used when evaluating the system. All in all, it can be assumed that the user experience of AID systems can be improved through the human-centered displaying of information.

The effects of explanations on users' perceived traceability can vary between context and prior knowledge of users (c.f. [37]). While Cai et al. [38] found an improvement in users' perceived traceability, Springer & Whittaker [39] demonstrated users' confusion after interacting with explanations. For example, Bansal et al. [40] showed that explanations in a machine-learning context increase the chance that an incorrect output result of a model will be wrongly accepted by the user. Pelaje et al. [41] demonstrated that providing explanations can have unintended consequences, such as information overload and a more convincing (c.f. [40]) but not necessarily accurate mental model of the system. For example, users may perceive the system as more trustworthy after receiving an explanation, even if it is not as reliable as they believe. This also applies in the medical domain: in a study by Bussone et al. [42] users who trusted the algorithm tended to be disproportionately dependent on the system, while users who reported lower levels of trust also decided against the system's suggestions when they were correct.

With regard to closed-loop systems, research demonstrates that increased levels of trust of patients with diabetes in a closed-loop system lead to a reduced burden of treatment, relieves them of decision-making effort, and increases the quality of life [43]. Yet, overtrust or complacency (c.f. [44]) in medical systems such as AID systems can lead to severe medical consequences. Accordingly, when systems are modified to support patients' understanding of, e.g., insulin calculation, empirical evaluation of effects on perceived trustworthiness and traceability, is crucial to avoid complacency. Schrills & Franke [12] also demonstrated that explanations' effects on user experience potentially need longer periods (see [45]) and depend on the interactions with the system (see [46]). Using a simulation could enable interactions that are otherwise limited, such as checking one's own predictions about system behavior or testing out the effects of different points in time to communicate information. Following Chromik et al. [46], this could lead to a change in the perceived traceability of the system.

2.3   Simulation of Type 1 Diabetes and AID Systems

Given severe consequences in case of errors, simulations became an essential part of the training of medical professionals and those to be. Ethical and medical constraints require trialing of complex systems prior to clinical adoption [47]. Many complex medical devices, though, are now commonly used in domestic settings by laypersons, as in the case of self-directed management of diabetes. In this respect, simulation can be equally valuable as a training method. AID simulations offer this possibility, as they consist of a physiological model (e.g., [48,49]) and an algorithm to simulate the behavior of an AID system. So far, these simulations have been used primarily for training machine learning and evaluating control algorithms or their performance. Sufficiently user-centered, however, they also present training opportunities for AID system users in appropriate cooperation with the systems. Possible examples of such simulations include *AAU-T2D* [50], *CarbMetSim* [51], *cgmsim* [52], *LT1* [21], or *simglucose* [22]. Constraints such as inadequate graphical user interfaces and the need for programming skills limit the extent to which simulations can be employed in settings involving patients or healthcare providers who lack in-depth technical knowledge.

2.4   Supporting Traceability and Trust Through Interactive Simulation

Users' experience of a system's trustworthiness and traceability is influenced by the type of interaction they were able to perform with the system. For example, answering questions about an AI's information processing may result in a change of perceived traceability, while observing an AI system has lesser effects [12, 46]. The advantages of explanations to support trust dynamics in human-AI cooperation are debated based on a variety of results [53–55].

Currently, many explanation methods applied to support human-AI cooperation are static, e.g., when users are presented with highlighted features of images. Here, users can request in-depth information for cases that arise in the use of the system. However, it is not possible to set specific scenarios yourself, for example, adopting the physiological parameters an AID system has to consider (see [21]). In contrast, interactive explanations enable users to actively explore and familiarize themselves with, e.g., a machine learning model (see [56]). While an interactive approach has been used in several studies (e.g., [57]), free exploration can be challenging, especially in complex systems. In an interactive AID simulation such as LT1 [21], users are potentially able to adapt a variety of parameters, they potentially never encountered before. The design of the instructions of an AID simulation is thus central before deploying it as a safe way of training and preparation for actual use without overwhelming users.

Diabetes affects a range of stakeholders: in addition to the patients themselves, depending on the healthcare system, a variety of healthcare professionals are involved, such as diabetes counselors, diabetology specialists, or even school nurses, for example. In addition, family members, especially parents in the case of children with diabetes, are often involved in the management of the disease (potentially leading to stress for parents, see [58]). This variety means that technologies in the diabetes context need to cater to different user requirements. In particular, the use of AID systems increases the initial training workload of diabetes advisors [59], for example, for whom a high level of guidance is required when introducing patients to such systems. The increasing integration of technology in diabetes therapy also poses a great challenge to, for example, school nurses or parents [60], who need to be aware of and understand differences between, e.g., AID systems from different manufacturers. Consequently, an AID simulation must not only take into account the requirements of individual patients but also offer interfaces for other stakeholders who want to use the simulation for training patients or for their own continuing education.

3   Study 1: Interviews with Health Care Providers and Patients

To design a user-centered AID simulation for different stakeholders (patients, physicians, and diabetes counselors), an interview study was first conducted. The goal was to analyze the requirements for the system as well as a target group-specific list of necessary functions.

3.1   Participants

Participants were recruited from internet forums focused on type 1 diabetes and received no separate compensation for their participation. A total of $N = 12$ individuals participated in the interviews. The participants included three physicians, three counselors, and six patients, two of whom were already using an AID system at the time of the interview. Participants were between 21 and 56 years of age and had between 4 and 23 years of prior experience with T1DM, which for patients refers to the duration of the disease and for healthcare professionals refers to the duration of their professional experience.

3.2 Material and Procedure

The interviews in this study were semi-standardized. To this end, questions were defined before the study was conducted. These differed between patients with diabetes and healthcare professionals. First, a brief description of what an AID system is and how they generally work was provided. The first part of the interview for patients included general questions about their experience with diabetes and experience with different treatment formats. The second part asked about expectations and attitudes toward AID systems. In the final third part, explicit questions were asked about patients' requirements and functionalities concerning to an AID simulation. For the health care providers, the interview was also conducted in three parts after an analogous introduction: in the first part, the experiences in the treatment with AID systems, in the second part, typical problems of patients with AID systems and in the third part, how an AID simulation could be used in the training of patients.

After written informed consent was obtained, each interview was conducted individually and lasted between 60 and 90 min. All interviews were conducted digitally. The interviews were recorded and transcribed for subsequent analysis.

3.3 Thematic Analysis

Based on the transcribed interview data, a thematic analysis [61] was conducted. Here, an inductive and latent approach was followed, that is, we aimed to identify underlying concepts of functionalities for AID simulations without a prior definition of a theoretical framework. Accordingly, a constructivist perspective was adopted for coding and theme creation, meaning that the statements made by the participants were used to reconstruct the settings, classifying, for example, their experience and the therapeutic context. Data from healthcare providers and patients were analyzed together.

In the first step, codes for the interviews were created by two persons working independently and in two successive steps. These codes were used in a workshop with four experts to identify topics and thus summarized them into requirements. Subsequently, the recorded requirements were reviewed with an expert from the health care providers, who had also originally participated in the interviews.

3.4 Results of Study 1

From this analysis, five different simulation functions were derived that should be made available within a simulation: 1) The interactive individualization of parameters processed by the simulation allowing to examine personal questions or hypotheses of the users, 2) a dynamic and real-time modification of the simulation based on the changed parameters supporting exploration of the simulation, 3) pre-defined standard situations that are easy to access and provide a parameter configuration that can, e.g., illustrate the limits of the AID algorithm, 4) detailed information on the parameters covered by the simulation, since these are model-dependent and may not be known depending on the individual therapy and experience with diabetes. Finally, users requested 5) to get insight into the algorithm's calculation, demanding more detail in the simulation than in everyday usage. We also identified different goals users pursue when using the simulation, mainly the improvement of experienced traceability and safety.

Interactive Individualisation of Parameters. Users stated that a simulation can be interactively adjusted to them personally. Herein they referred both to the interactive adjustment of parameters for the metabolic model (e.g., different insulin sensitivity at certain times of the day) and to the simple modification of parameters of the simulated situation (e.g., the amount and type of food ingested). In addition, they expressed the desire for therapy goals (such as desired minimal or maximum glucose level) to be easily adjustable, which in turn should affect the functioning of the simulated AID systems.

Patient: I need to see how the system reacts to different amounts of carbohydrates at once, so yeah, I think I would like to change that and compare.

Real-time Modification of Parameters. Interview partners expressed the desirability of immediate adaptation of the simulation after changing the parameters. Especially among health care providers, this is mentioned as a prerequisite for the use of a simulation, e.g., in the context of training courses or individual training. Furthermore, the adjustment of the parameters should not only be done numerically but e.g., via sliders, to better represent different extents of food intake.

Healthcare Provider: If I click, I would like to see how that changes, how the AID system corrects differently than before. I don't want to have many printouts to compare them.

Pre-defined Scenarios. In the interviews, various situations were highlighted that the interviewees considered particularly interesting or important. This includes, for example, the situations *exam, alcohol intake,* or *long journey.* Patients refer to those situations as challenging for the control of glucose levels in everyday life, which is why their consideration in the simulation is of particular interest. An AID simulation should allow a quick selection of these situations (by automatically configuring appropriate parameters).

Healthcare Provider: Many patients ask about the night because they sleep, they can't do anything, and they trust the system. I would like to jump directly to that topic and show them, what will be happening.

Explanation of Integrated Parameters. Since some of the models used in AID systems employ proprietary parameters, participants expressed the necessity to have them adequately explained. For example, the dimension should be clearly marked for all parameters and it should be possible to switch, e.g., between mg/dl and mmol/l (two typical units for describing the glucose level). Furthermore, less familiar parameters, e.g., values for calculating physical activity, should be explained more precisely on request.

> Patient: I find some words very confusing, I don't know, I learned 'bolus' and that's it. When a system uses other words, I need to know, they mean 'bolus'.

Explanation of AID Calculation. Consistent with what [12] described, the requirement described in the interviews was that the exact calculation of the system is explained as part of the simulation. Patients with type 1 use calculations based on factors e.g. the number of carbohydrates ingested in other forms of therapy. Most of the patients interviewed stated that they wanted the system to display this calculation transparently and thus know the factors used. This was also identified by healthcare providers as an explanation often requested by patients.

> Patient: The system needs to show me the calculation, how much insulin is to correct my glucose level, how much is for food, and so on. I need to see, whether it got the correct equation.

3.5 Implementation of Requirements in Existing Simulations

To rank the requirements identified in study 1, we also reviewed existing simulators. Table 1 shows the extent to which the requirements are already implemented by users in existing simulation frameworks.

Users' Goals for AID Simulation. In addition to the identified functions necessary to answer the first research question, healthcare providers and patients indicated several goals to be achieved by the simulation. Highlighted are the 1) development of safe use of the AID system, 2) maintenance of a sense of control for patients, 3) the opportunity to have their own experience prior to actual use, 4) the opportunity (especially for low-tech users) to learn all functions of the system in a safe environment, and 5) the development of confidence in AID-based therapy.

4   Study 2: Experimental Evaluation of an Interactive Diabetes Simulation

For the second study, the requirements identified in the first study were implemented in a prototypical user-centered AID simulation. Allowing for an online

Table 1. Comparison of Existing Diabetes Simulations

	Interactive Individualisation of Parameters	Real-time Modification of Parameters	Pre-defined Scenarios
AAU-T2D	Code & MatLab App	Not implemented	Not implemented
CarbMetSim	Code	Not implemented	Example Pre-Sets
cgmsim	WebApp	WebApp	Not implemented
lt1	WebApp	WebApp	Not implemented
mgipsim	Graphical User Interface	Not implemented	Not implemented
simglucose	Commandline Interface	Not implemented	Random Generator

	Explanation of Integrated Parameters	Explanation of AID Calculation	
AAU-T2D	Code documentation	Code documentation	
CarbMetSim	Code documentation	Code documentation	
cgmsim	In GitHub	In GitHub	
lt1	WebApp	Not integrated	
mgipsim	Unknown	Unknown	
simglucose	Not integrated	Not integrated	

experiment to address the second research question, we investigated the extent to which an interactive simulation can influence perceived trustworthiness and traceability.

4.1 Participants

Participants for study 2 were recruited via university mail as well as diabetes-related online forums. Both participants with and without diabetes were allowed to participate in the experiment. To obtain a rough estimate of the participants' knowledge of diabetes, they answered several questions on theoretical concepts of diabetes treatment as part of the online experiment. Since all participants answered more than 60% correctly ($M = 76\%$, $SD = 13\%$), nobody was excluded.

In total, $N = 32$ persons participated in the experiment. The mean age of the participants was $M = 32$ years ($SD = 6.7$ years). The youngest participant was 19 years old, and the oldest participant was 61 years old. Of the 32 participants, 20 were patients with type 1 diabetes.

To better classify the sample concerning user diversity (i.e., diversity in human-technology interaction), the Affinity for Technology Interaction (ATI) scale [62] was assessed. The sample had an average value of $M = 4.22$ ($SD = 1.31$), thus being above the medium range (possible ATI score range $= 1$–6) and higher than reported for the general population (3.5 as described in [62]).

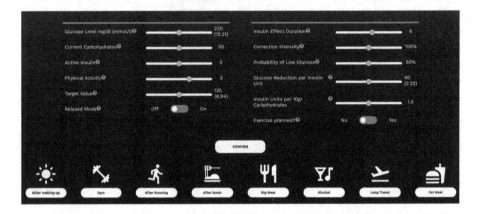

Fig. 1. Depiction of the prototypical Simulation Interface

4.2   Material

Diabetes Simulation. A dedicated diabetes simulation was set up to conduct the study. This consisted of a random forest model for insulin calculation, which was generated based on synthetic data. This could be operated by means of an online web interface. The synthetic data set of information relevant to AID systems was developed to be independent of individual medical data and the complications that come with it in terms of using personal health data. Each instance in the data set consisted of 12 different attributes and the insulin requirement. The individual data sets represent different individuals and therefore contain individualized factors as features, such as the amount of correction for high glucose levels. The different attributes were based on data that is already used in various clinically tested AID systems (c.f. [33]). After creation, the data set was reviewed by two independent professionals. Both independently rated the data set as plausible. In total, over 480 instances (i.e., data points) were created to train and test the model.

The front-end, developed as a web application, provided a prototypical insulin calculation through an interactive simulation (with basic functions of interaction such as changing input parameters). The application is client-server based and was designed as a Python application using the Django framework. A representation of the interface of the interactive simulation can be found in Fig. 1. In line with the results of study 1, Table 2 depicts which interface elements have been used to implement the diabetes simulation requirements described in study 1.

Table 2. Requirements and corresponding interface elements

Human-Centered Requirement	Interface Elements
Interactive Individualisation of Parameters	Integration of slider controllers with dimension description for the adjustment of parameters
Real-time Modification of Parameters	Immediate update of the result by pressing the *Confirm Calculation* button
Pre-defined Scenarios	Buttons with different scenarios marked as pictogram and text
Explanation of Integrated Parameters	Icons with question marks that can be hovered over to display more information
Explanation of AID Calculation	Not integrated

Questionnaires. *Affinity for Technology Interaction.* User diversity can significantly impact individual user experience and, for example, initial trust in a system [63]. To examine the role of user diversity in experienced interaction with an AID system, ATI was collected [62]. Based on the personality trait need for cognition [64], the construct describes the individual tendency to actively engage in intensive technology interaction. ATI was measured with a validated scale [62]. The ATI scale uses a 6-point Likert response scale from completely disagree = 1, largely disagree = 2, slightly disagree = 3, slightly agree = 4, largely agree = 5, to completely agree = 6. A higher score indicates a higher affinity for technology. The present sample was assessed as rather affine to interact with technology (see section Participants above).

Subjective Information Processing Awareness Scale. The SIPA scale measures the degree to which a user feels capable of perceiving, understanding, and predicting a system's information processing. The metric aims to assess the perceived traceability of automated information processing. SIPA can be evaluated by calculating three subfacets (transparency, understandability, and predictability) as well as an overall average. The SIPA scale uses a 6-point Likert response scale from completely disagree = 1, largely disagree = 2, slightly disagree = 3, slightly agree = 4, largely agree = 5, to completely agree = 6. Accordingly, higher SIPA values indicate that users experienced higher traceability in the system.

Facets of System Trustworthiness Scale. The FOST scale [65] was used to assess trust. With 5 items, this allows a more economical repeated-measures experiment compared to, for example, the widely used scale of [66]. As for trust, the mean value of the FOST items was calculated for each point of measurement. It uses the same 6-point Likert scale as the SIPA and ATI scales.

NASA Task Load Index. The NASA-TLX is a metric for subjectively perceived task load [67]. For this study, only two of the six dimensions were considered, mental demand and perceived frustration. As the remaining four dimensions did not fit the experimental task, they were omitted. For both items, the same 6-point Likert scale was used, and the mean score was calculated. Higher values indicate that participants experienced a higher workload regarding to the two assessed facets.

Mental Model Accuracy: To assess comprehension of the insulin calculation algorithm, participants were asked a series of What-If questions after each explanation (as shown in Figure X). This allowed the determination of the accuracy of participants' mental models. This question type was chosen because it is assumed that an interactive explanation mainly affects the users' ability to predict how the model reacts to changes in, e.g., the input information. For each question, participants were shown a parameter assignment of the simulation. Then they were asked to predict in which direction the calculated amount of insulin would change, i.e., whether it would increase, decrease, stay the same, or whether the algorithm would detect an insulin surplus. Participants could also indicate that they did not have an answer to the question. The percentage of correct answers was calculated and used as an indicator of the accuracy of the participants' mental model.

4.3   Procedure

The experiment followed a within-subject design, evaluating how two different explanation methods (static vs. interactive) affect the understanding of a prototypical AID simulation.

After a pre-experimental questionnaire assessing whether participants had type 1 diabetes or not, a series of multiple-choice questions were used to determine the theoretical understanding of type 1 diabetes and insulin therapy. The experiment was then divided into two experimental blocks. In the first section, participants were given a static explanation of the AID system. They were shown eight images, each depicting a parameter configuration and the prediction of the insulin calculation algorithm for this exact configuration. In the second section, participants were given access to the prototypical simulation via a web interface and could explore the algorithm. For both explanation methods, the participants were restricted to interact or observe for five minutes, respectively. There was no randomization of explanations order (static was always prior to interactive explanation). The fixed order was chosen because we assumed that the formation of an accurate mental model by the interactive condition would affect the results of the following section. Since we expected a less accurate mental model in the static condition, it was presented first. After each experimental block, participants' SIPA, NASA-TLX, FOST, and mental model accuracy were assessed.

4.4   Hypotheses and Statistical Analysis

Following hypotheses were tested within the study to examine whether interactive explanation improves both the user experience and the accuracy of the mental model in AID simulation:

H1 *Subjective Information Processing Awareness is higher after the interactive than after the static explanation.*

H2 *Perceived Trustworthiness is higher after the interactive than after the static explanation.*

H3 *Perceived Workload is lower in the interactive explanation than in the static explanation.*

H4 *Mental Model Accuracy is higher for the interactive explanation than for the static explanation.*

All hypotheses were tested using paired-sample t-tests with p-values corrected according to Bonferroni-Holm. Effect size is reported as Cohen's d and was analyzed according to [68] with respect to [69], which suggests a less strict interpretation of Cohen's d in psychological research.

The extent to which experienced traceability of the system and the accuracy of the mental model were related was examined exploratively. For this purpose, Pearson's r between the SIPA facets and the accuracy of the mental model was calculated for both conditions. They were compared using Fisher's z-test [70].

4.5   Results of Study 2

The descriptive data of all variables and the results of all t-tests can be found in Table 3. For SIPA transparency and SIPA understandability, there was no significant difference between static condition and interactive condition. However, SIPA predictability was rated significantly higher for the interactive condition than the static condition. While the effect size for SIPA transparency is negligible, effect sizes for understandability and predictability suggest a large effect on the interactive simulation. Hence, **H1** can neither be fully discarded nor supported based on the data.

Trust rating did not differ significantly between interactive and static conditions ($p = .315$), showing only a small effect size ($d = 0.09$). Accordingly, our results provide no support for **H2**. The subjectively estimated workload was higher for the static condition compared to the interactive condition ($p < .001$) and a very large effect ($d = 0.70$) was found. Accordingly, the results provide support for **H3**. Participants' mental model accuracy was significantly higher after the interactive than the static condition ($p < .001$). Again, a large effect size emerged ($d = 0.67$). Based on these results, **H4** can be supported.

The correlation of SIPA with mental model accuracy was calculated to understand the possible calibration of user experience and performance. Respective values can be found in Table 4. For the correlation between mental model accuracy and SIPA Transparency, Fisher's z-test revealed a significant difference

Table 3. Descriptive data and t-test results for connected samples for all variables, comparing static and interactive AID explanation

	Static	Interactive	t	df	p	d
SIPA Transparency	$M = 4.16$ $SD = 1.11$	$M = 4.14$ $SD = 1.40$	0.1	31	.525	0.01
SIPA Understandability	$M = 3.02$ $SD = 1.29$	$M = 3.47$ $SD = 1.16$	1.6	31	.059	0.28
SIPA Predictability	$M = 2.80$ $SD = 1.24$	$M = 3.23$ $SD = 1.07$	1.9	31	.032	0.34
FOST	$M = 3.63$ $SD = 1.20$	$M = 3.52$ $SD = 1.20$	0.5	31	.315	0.09
NASA-TLX	$M = 3.37$ $SD = 1.01$	$M = 2.55$ $SD = 1.25$	3.9	31	.001	0.70
Mental Model Accuracy	$M = 31\%$ $SD = 23\%$	$M = 49\%$ $SD = 27\%$	3.8	31	.001	0.67

between the static and interactive condition ($z(30) = 1.89, p = .029$). The correlation between SIPA Understandability and mental model accuracy did not differ significantly between the conditions ($z(30) = 1.01$, $p = .135$). Likewise, the correlation between SIPA Predictability and mental model accuracy did not differ significantly between the conditions ($z(30) = 0.56$, $p = .289$).

Table 4. Correlations between SIPA facets and mental model accuracy

		Mental Model Accuracy	
		Static	Interactive
SIPA Transparency	Pearson's r	.24	.63
	p	.095	<.001
SIPA Understandability	Pearson's r	.37	.59
	p	.019	<.001
SIPA Predictability	Pearson's r	.36	.48
	p	.023	.003

5 Discussion

5.1 Summary of Results

The objective of the study was to investigate the requirements for an AID simulation and to test a prototype implementation. In the interviews with two key stakeholder groups - patients and health care providers - several requirements could be identified: 1) the individual adaptation of simulation parameters to and by the users, 2) the real-time adaptation of the simulation after the change of parameters, 3) the use of preset scenarios to quickly look at certain parameter configurations, 4) the explanation of the displayed parameters as well as 5) the explanation of the concrete calculations of the AID system. All in all, it can be stated that the elicited requirements could enable users to construct individual and for them relevant situations in the simulation and to get a detailed representation of which decision the system makes. The simulation must therefore be suitable to allow patients and health care providers to adjust parameters (through explanation and suitable interface elements such as sliders) and to directly check the resulting changes. Overall, our research demonstrates that currently available open-source simulations do not yet meet all the requirements formulated by relevant stakeholders and human-centered development is still needed.

Based on the requirements found, a prototype simulation was developed and evaluated in an experiment. It was shown that the interactive elements of a simulation can improve the accuracy of the mental model and perceived predictability (as assessed by the SIPA scale facet). The present data did not support the hypothesis that subjective information processing awareness and confidence in general increase by using an interactive explanation. In an exploratory analysis, it was also found that the correlation between perceived transparency and the accuracy of the mental model increased after using the interactive explanation.

5.2   Implications

The results of the interview study show that the use of interactive simulations can be an important contribution to the human-centered design of AID systems. Compared to current systems, additional functions must be integrated: in particular, users must be able to test to what extent their individual predictions about the functioning of the AID system are accurate. Morrison & Rosenthal [71] describe that an improvement of the mental model can be stimulated by active exploration in safe environments or practice fields. When using an AID system, hypotheses emerge (in the mental model) about how a system responds to specific inputs. As long as these are incorrect, cooperation is compromised (see [72], e.g., because the sense of directability is no longer present). Since correcting incorrect hypotheses in ongoing use can be hazardous to health, it is necessary to do this in the context of simulations. That is, preventing user experiences such as the first failure effect (c.f. [18] could help to reduce the number of discontinued AID therapies [4].

Thereby, the results of the experimental evaluation also point to the fact that an interactive use of the simulation can lead to better results in the accuracy of the mental model. The higher correlation between the accuracy of the mental model and user experience after the interactive simulation also indicates that the emergence of warranted trust [73] is supported by active testing of one's own hypotheses compared to processes involving the illusion of explanatory depth [46] or XAI pitfalls [74].

While previous studies suggest that explanations increase the workload of users (e.g., [75]) and can thus lead to information overload [76], this is not the case in our experiment. The participants reported low values for effort after they were able to work with the interactive explanation. The reason for this could be related to the high cognitive demand for working memory during hypothesis testing [77]. While previous instances in an observation role must be remembered to test hypotheses (i.e., perform abductive reasoning), an interactive simulation allows users to reconfigure the parameters. However, saving the results of specific tests and having them presented while further exploring the AID system's functionality could improve mental model accuracy.

A central requirement of the users was the possibility to select pre-defined scenarios. This could compensate for the disadvantages of free exploration and limit the unsystematic use of the system. The customization of the pre-defined scenarios could preserve the advantages of individual exploration with higher guidance, e.g., for less experienced users.

Overall, the present research shows that the use of AID simulations can close an important gap in the preparation of AID-based therapies for patients with diabetes. To provide a human-centered simulation, the following design guidelines should be considered:

DG1 AID simulation should offer interactive adaption of parameters regarding the individual's physiology as well as the simulated situation.

DG2 AID simulations should offer real-time feedback on changes in parameters.

DG3 AID simulations should highlight users' information communication as part of the simulation to demonstrate how user behavior affects cooperation.

DG4 AID simulations should include scenarios that demonstrate challenging situations for glucose management, as well as the limits of the system.

DG5 AID simulations should encourage users to test and develop hypotheses regarding the AID system's information processing.

5.3   Limitations and Further Research

Although different stakeholders have been considered for the requirements elicitation, it needs to be examined whether other deployment scenarios of AID systems require further investigation. For example, AID systems are now also used with children under 2 years [78], which makes the role of parents, for example, more important. While many requirements elicited in this study can be transferred to these groups, it is unclear whether onboarding needs to address more fundamental aspects here. Furthermore, all participants in our interview study had previous experience with another form of diabetes therapy (e.g., pen). A comparison to persons who start directly with an AID therapy, for example, could change the requirements for onboarding, since the change of the mental model of the therapy could proceed differently than a completely new setup.

Moreover, the evaluation carried out was done only with a prototypical simulation, meaning that neither all guidelines presented were implemented nor was the physiological model sufficiently tested before. Thus, the update of the insulin calculation could only be triggered by pressing a button and not in real-time. This meant that this usage requirement could not be fully verified. In addition to the sample size, an even more target population-oriented sample should be used in future studies. The prior knowledge about diabetes was controlled by an initial test, but it is not clear to what extent the sample is representative e.g. for the assessment of trustworthiness since possible risks are only presented (and have not already been experienced). In the design of the evaluation, randomization was deliberately omitted - thus it cannot be ruled out that the effects found are based on the sequence or the longer interaction with the system (c.f. [12,45]). However, due to the overall shortness of the experiment, it seems more likely that the different conditions were responsible for the effects found.

In future studies, an established model or an open-source simulation should be used for the creation of stimuli or explanations. The model used in this study was prone to errors with unknown parameter configurations and was only comparable to a limited extent with systems that have or are seeking clinical approval.

In order to improve simulation-based and safe training of patients and health care providers, the cognitive processes during the use of an AID simulation should be considered in more detail. It is not yet clear how exactly hypotheses are formed by the users and which information they use to reject or accept thise hypotheses. It is also important to distinguish between different levels of experience with diabetes and with the use of simulations, as the response to explanations may differ between experts and novices [37].

6   Conclusion

User-centered design of medical simulations offers many opportunities to improve AI-assisted therapies. To do so, it is necessary to understand the requirements for stakeholder use and to empirically test which design approaches for these simulations lead to desirable outcomes. In this sense, the present work contributes to establishing guidelines for the design of human-centered AID simulations based on interviews with stakeholders. Furthermore, the evaluation shows the added value of interactive simulations for the improvement of the user experience and the accuracy of the mental model. Further research can build on these results and develop systems for training, education, and therapy using available open-source technology by applying the guidelines we discussed.

Acknowledgements. We would like to thank Jerom Schult, who was responsible for the design and implementation of the simulation interface as part of his master's thesis and essentially mutually supervised the implementation of the evaluation. This research has been supported by funding from the Federal Ministry of Education and Research of Germany in the framework of the project CoCoAI (Cooperative and Communicating AI, project number 01GP1908).

References

1. Lewis, D.: How it started, how it is going: the future of artificial pancreas systems (automated insulin delivery systems). J. Diab. Sci. Technol. **15**(6), 1258–1261 (2021)
2. Berget, C., et al.: Six months of hybrid closed loop in the real-world: an evaluation of children and young adults using the 670G system. Pediatr. Diab. **21**(2), 310–318 (2020)
3. Bisio, A., et al.: The impact of a recently approved automated insulin delivery system on glycemic, sleep, and psychosocial outcomes in older adults with type 1 diabetes: a pilot study. J. Diab. Sci. Technol. **16**(3), 663–669 (2022)
4. Messer, L.H., et al.: Real world hybrid closed-loop discontinuation: predictors and perceptions of youth discontinuing the 670G system in the first 6 months. Pediatr. Diab. **21**(2), 319–327 (2020)
5. Smith, M.B., et al.: Human factors associated with continuous glucose monitor use in patients with diabetes: a systematic review. Diab. Technol. Therapeut. **21**(10), 589–601 (2019)
6. Boughton, C.K., Hartnell, S., Allen, J.M., Fuchs, J., Hovorka, R.: Training and support for hybrid closed-loop therapy. J. Diab. Sci. Technol. **16**(1), 218–223 (2022)
7. Trevitt, S., Simpson, S., Wood, A.: Artificial pancreas device systems for the closed-loop control of type 1 diabetes: what systems are in development? J. Diab. Sci. Technol. **10**(3), 714–723 (2016)
8. Boughton, C.K.: Fully closed-loop insulin delivery—are we nearly there yet? Lancet Dig. Health **3**(11), e689–e690 (2021)
9. Klein, G., Woods, D., Bradshaw, J., Hoffman, R., Feltovich, P.: Ten challenges for making automation a "team player" in joint human-agent activity. IEEE Intell. Syst. **19**(06), 91–95 (2004)
10. Johnson, M., Vera, A.: No AI is an island: the case for teaming intelligence. AI Mag. **40**(1), 16–28 (2019)
11. Kerasidou, C.X., Kerasidou, A., Buscher, M., Wilkinson, S.: Before and beyond trust: reliance in medical AI. J. Med. Ethics (2021). medethics-2020-107095
12. Schrills, T.P.P., Franke, T.: How do users experience traceability of AI systems? examining subjective information processing awareness in automated insulin delivery (AID) systems (2022)
13. Knoll, C., et al.: Real-world evidence on clinical outcomes of people with type 1 diabetes using open-source and commercial automated insulin dosing systems: a systematic review. Diab. Med. (2021)
14. Abraham, M.B.: Effect of a hybrid closed-loop system on glycemic and psychosocial outcomes in children and adolescents with type 1 diabetes: a randomized clinical trial. JAMA Pediat. **175**(12), 1227 (2021)
15. Adams, R.N., et al.: Psychosocial and human factors during a trial of a hybrid closed loop system for type 1 diabetes management. Diab. Technol. Therapeut. **20**(10), 648–653 (2018)
16. Farrington, C.: Psychosocial impacts of hybrid closed-loop systems in the management of diabetes: a review. Diab. Med. **35**(4), 436–449 (2018)
17. Carroll, J.M., Olson, J.R.: Mental models in human-computer interaction. In: Handbook of Human-Computer Interaction, pp. 45–65 (1988)
18. Wickens, C.D., Xu, X.: Automation trust, reliability and attention HMI 02–03. Technical report, University oif Illinois (2002)

19. Bowden, V.K., Griffiths, N., Strickland, L., Loft, S.: Detecting a Single automation failure: the impact of expected (but not experienced) automation reliability. Human Fact. J. Human Fact. Ergon. Soc., 001872082110371 (2021)
20. Clegg, B.A., Vieane, A.Z., Wickens, C.D., Gutzwiller, R.S., Sebok, A.L.: The effects of automation-induced complacency on fault diagnosis and management performance in process control. Proc. Human Fact. Ergon. Soc. Annual Meet. **58**(1), 844–848 (2014)
21. Schmitzer, J., Strobel, C., Blechschmidt, R., Tappe, A., Peuscher, H.: Efficient closed loop simulation of do-it-yourself artificial pancreas systems. J. Diab. Sci. Technol. **16**(1), 61–69 (2022)
22. Xie, J.: Simglucose v0. 2.1 (2018). https://github.com/jxx123/simglucose. Accessed 20 Jan 2020
23. Bode, B.W.: Clinical utility of the continuous glucose monitoring system. Diab. Technol. Therapeut. **2**(1, Supplement 1), 35–41 (2000)
24. Amadou, C., et al.: Diabeloop DBLG1 closed-loop system enables patients with type 1 diabetes to significantly improve their glycemic control in real-life situations without serious adverse events: 6-month follow-up. Diab. Care **44**(3), 844–846 (2021)
25. Boughton, C., et al.: Assessing the effect of closed-loop insulin delivery from onset of type 1 diabetes in youth on residual beta-cell function compared to standard insulin therapy (CLOuD study): a randomised parallel study protocol. BMJ Open **10**(3), e033500 (2020)
26. Parasuraman, R., Sheridan, T., Wickens, C.: A model for types and levels of human interaction with automation. IEEE Trans. Syst. Man Cybern. - Part A: Syst. Humans **30**(3), 286–297 (2000)
27. Suttiratana, S.C., et al.: Qualitative study of user experiences with loop, an open-source automated insulin delivery system. Diab. Technol. Therapeut. **24**(6), 416–423 (2022)
28. Nefs, G.: The psychological implications of automated insulin delivery systems in type 1 diabetes care. Front. Clin. Diab. Healthcare **3**, 846162 (2022)
29. Grando, M.A., et al.: Patient perception and satisfaction with insulin pump system: pilot user experience survey. J. Diab. Sci. Technol. **13**(6), 1142–1148 (2019)
30. Bekiari, E., et al.: Artificial pancreas treatment for outpatients with type 1 diabetes: systematic review and meta-analysis. BMJ k1310 (2018)
31. Lal, R.A., Basina, M., Maahs, D.M., Hood, K., Buckingham, B., Wilson, D.M.: One year clinical experience of the first commercial hybrid closed-loop system. Diab. Care **42**(12), 2190–2196 (2019)
32. Bansal, G., Nushi, B., Kamar, E., Lasecki, W.S., Weld, D.S., Horvitz, E.: Beyond accuracy: the role of mental models in human-AI team performance. In: Proceedings of the AAAI Conference on Human Computation and Crowdsourcing, vol. 7, pp. 2–11 (2019)
33. Benhamou, P.Y., Huneker, E., Franc, S., Doron, M., Charpentier, G., Consortium, D.: Customization of home closed-loop insulin delivery in adult patients with type 1 diabetes, assisted with structured remote monitoring: the pilot WP7 Diabeloop study. Acta Diabetol. **55**, 549–556 (2018)
34. Dzindolet, M.T., Peterson, S.A., Pomranky, R.A., Pierce, L.G., Beck, H.P.: The role of trust in automation reliance. Int. J. Hum Comput Stud. **58**(6), 697–718 (2003)
35. Adadi, A., Berrada, M.: Peeking inside the black-box: a survey on explainable artificial intelligence (XAI). IEEE Access **6**, 52138–52160 (2018)

36. Herlocker, J.L., Konstan, J.A., Riedl, J.: Explaining collaborative filtering recommendations. In: Proceedings of the 2000 ACM Conference on Computer Supported Cooperative Work, Philadelphia, Pennsylvania, USA, pp. 241–250. ACM (2000)
37. Szymanski, M., Millecamp, M., Verbert, K.: Visual, textual or hybrid: The effect of user expertise on different explanations. In: 26th International Conference on Intelligent User Interfaces, College Station, TX, USA, pp. 109–119. ACM (2021)
38. Cai, C.J., Jongejan, J., Holbrook, J.: The effects of example-based explanations in a machine learning interface. In: Proceedings of the 24th International Conference on Intelligent User Interfaces, Marina del Ray, California, pp. 258–262. ACM (2019)
39. Springer, A., Whittaker, S.: Progressive disclosure: empirically motivated approaches to designing effective transparency. In: Proceedings of the 24th International Conference on Intelligent User Interfaces, Marina del Ray, California, pp. 107–120. ACM (2019)
40. Bansal, G., et al.: Does the whole exceed its parts? the effect of AI explanations on complementary team performance (2021)
41. Paleja, R., Ghuy, M., Ranawaka Arachchige, N., Jensen, R., Gombolay, M.: The utility of explainable AI in ad hoc human-machine teaming. Adv. Neural. Inf. Process. Syst. **34**, 610–623 (2021)
42. Bussone, A., Stumpf, S., O'Sullivan, D.: The role of explanations on trust and reliance in clinical decision support systems. In: 2015 International Conference on Healthcare Informatics, Dallas, TX, USA, pp. 160–169. IEEE (2015)
43. Tanenbaum, M.L., et al.: Trust in hybrid closed loop among people with diabetes: perspectives of experienced system users. J. Health Psychol. **25**(4), 429–438 (2020)
44. Parasuraman, R., Manzey, D.H.: Complacency and bias in human use of automation: an attentional integration. Human Fact. J. Human Fact. Ergon. Soc. **52**(3), 381–410 (2010)
45. Holliday, D., Wilson, S., Stumpf, S.: User trust in intelligent systems: a journey over time. In: Proceedings of the 21st International Conference on Intelligent User Interfaces, Sonoma, California, USA, pp. 164–168. ACM (2016)
46. Chromik, M., Eiband, M., Buchner, F., Krüger, A., Butz, A.: I think i get your point, AI! the illusion of explanatory depth in explainable AI. In: 26th International Conference on Intelligent User Interfaces, College Station, TX, USA, pp. 307–317. ACM (2021)
47. Herrera-Aliaga, E., Estrada, L.D.: Trends and innovations of simulation for twenty first century medical education. Front. Public Health **10**, 619769 (2022)
48. Dalla Man, C., Raimondo, D.M., Rizza, R.A., Cobelli, C.: GIM, simulation software of meal glucose—insulin model. J. Diab. Sci. Technol. **1**(3), 323–330 (2007)
49. Hovorka, R., et al.: Nonlinear model predictive control of glucose concentration in subjects with type 1 diabetes. Physiol. Meas. **25**(4), 905–920 (2004)
50. Ahdab, M.A., Leth, J., Knudsen, T., Vestergaard, P., Clausen, H.G.: Glucose-insulin mathematical model for the combined effect of medications and life style of Type 2 diabetic patients. Biochem. Eng. J. **176**, 108170 (2021)
51. Goyal, M.: CarbMetSim (2023)
52. Tuomaala, A.K., Sandini, L., Haro, S.: Kohti keinohaimaa. Suomen lääkärilehti (2018)
53. Dikmen, M., Burns, C.: The effects of domain knowledge on trust in explainable AI and task performance: a case of peer-to-peer lending. Int. J. Hum Comput Stud. **162**, 102792 (2022)
54. Wang, X., Yin, M.: Are explanations helpful? a comparative study of the effects of explanations in AI-assisted decision-making. In: 26th International Conference on Intelligent User Interfaces, College Station, TX, USA, pp. 318–328. ACM (2021)

55. Alufaisan, Y., Marusich, L.R., Bakdash, J.Z., Zhou, Y., Kantarcioglu, M.: Does explainable artificial intelligence improve human decision-making? In: Proceedings of the AAAI Conference on Artificial Intelligence, vol. 35, no. 8, pp. 6618–6626 (2021)
56. Collaris, D., van Wijk, J.J.: ExplainExplore: visual exploration of machine learning explanations. In: 2020 IEEE Pacific Visualization Symposium (PacificVis), Tianjin, China, pp. 26–35. IEEE (2020)
57. Eiband, M., Anlauff, C., Ordenewitz, T., Zürn, M., Hussmann, H.: Understanding algorithms through exploration: supporting knowledge acquisition in primary tasks. In: Proceedings of Mensch Und Computer 2019, Hamburg, Germany, pp. 127–136. ACM (2019)
58. Streisand, R., Swift, E., Wickmark, T., Chen, R., Holmes, C.S.: Pediatric parenting stress among parents of children with type 1 diabetes: the role of self-efficacy, responsibility, and fear. J. Pediatr. Psychol. **30**(6), 513–521 (2005)
59. Kimbell, B., et al.: on behalf of the CLOuD consortium: what training, support, and resourcing do health professionals need to support people using a closed-loop system? a qualitative interview study with health professionals involved in the closed loop from onset in type 1 diabetes (CLOuD) trial. Diab. Technol. Therapeut. **22**(6), 468–475 (2020)
60. March, C.A., Nanni, M., Kazmerski, T.M., Siminerio, L.M., Miller, E., Libman, I.M.: Modern diabetes devices in the school setting: perspectives from school nurses. Pediatr. Diab. **21**(5), 832–840 (2020)
61. Braun, V., Clarke, V.: Using thematic analysis in psychology. Qual. Res. Psychol. **3**(2), 77–101 (2006)
62. Franke, T., Attig, C., Wessel, D.: A personal resource for technology interaction: development and validation of the affinity for technology interaction (ATI) scale. Int. J. Human-Comput. Interact. **35**(6), 456–467 (2019)
63. Attig, C., Wessel, D., Franke, T.: Assessing personality differences in human-technology interaction: an overview of key self-report scales to predict successful interaction. In: Stephanidis, C. (ed.) HCI 2017. CCIS, vol. 713, pp. 19–29. Springer, Cham (2017). https://doi.org/10.1007/978-3-319-58750-9_3
64. Cacioppo, J.T., Petty, R.E.: The need for cognition. J. Pers. Soc. Psychol. **42**(1), 116–131 (1982)
65. Trommler, D., Attig, C., Franke, T.: Trust in activity tracker measurement and its link to user acceptance. In: Dachselt, R., Weber, G. (eds.) Mensch Und Computer 2018 - Tagungsband, Bonn, Gesellschaft für Informatik e.V. (2018)
66. Jian, J.Y., Bisantz, A.M., Drury, C.G.: Foundations for an empirically determined scale of trust in automated systems. Int. J. Cogn. Ergon. **4**(1), 53–71 (2000)
67. Hart, S.G., Staveland, L.E.: Development of NASA-TLX (task load index): results of empirical and theoretical research. In: Advances in Psychology, vol. 52, pp. 139–183. Elsevier (1988)
68. Cohen, J.: Statistical power analysis. Curr. Dir. Psychol. Sci. **1**(3), 98–101 (1992)
69. Funder, D.C., Ozer, D.J.: Evaluating effect size in psychological research: sense and nonsense. Adv. Methods Pract. Psychol. Sci. **2**(2), 156–168 (2019)
70. Meng, X.L., Rosenthal, R., Rubin, D.B.: Comparing correlated correlation coefficients. Psychol. Bull. **111**(1), 172 (1992)
71. Morrison, M., Rosenthal, A.: Exploring learning organizations: enacting mental models - the power of the rosenthal stage. J. Work. Learn. **9**(4), 124–129 (1997)
72. Chiou, E.K., Lee, J.D.: Trusting automation: designing for responsivity and resilience. Human Fact. J. Human Fact. Ergon. Soc. **65**(1), 137–165 (2023)

73. Jacovi, A., Marasović, A., Miller, T., Goldberg, Y.: Formalizing trust in artificial intelligence: prerequisites, causes and goals of human trust in AI. In: Proceedings of the 2021 ACM Conference on Fairness, Accountability, and Transparency. FAccT 2021, pp. 624–635. Association for Computing Machinery, New York (2021)
74. Ehsan, U., Riedl, M.O.: Explainability Pitfalls: Beyond Dark Patterns in Explainable AI (2021)
75. Sanneman, L., Shah, J.A.: An empirical study of reward explanations with human-robot interaction applications. IEEE Rob. Autom. Lett. **7**(4), 8956–8963 (2022)
76. Ghassemi, M., Oakden-Rayner, L., Beam, A.L.: The false hope of current approaches to explainable artificial intelligence in health care. Lancet Dig. Health **3**(11), e745–e750 (2021)
77. Klichowicz, A., Lippoldt, D.E., Rosner, A., Krems, J.F.: Information stored in memory affects abductive reasoning. Psychol. Res. **85**(8), 3119–3133 (2021)
78. Tseretopoulou, X., et al.: Safe and effective use of a hybrid closed-loop system from diagnosis in children under 18 months with type 1 diabetes. Pediatr. Diab. **23**(1), 90–97 (2022)

Advanced Artificial Intelligence Methods for Medical Applications

Thitirat Siriborvornratanakul[✉]

Graduate School of Applied Statistics,
National Institute of Development Administration (NIDA),
148 SeriThai Rd., Bangkapi, Bangkok 10240, Thailand
thitirat@as.nida.ac.th

Abstract. Although analyzing high-stakes medical images is challenging, it is what recent deep neural networks quite excel at. Noticing that there are still many concerns regarding the adoption of vision AI-based digital human models in actual medical practices, this paper goes through challenges that occur in each development stage of vision AI in medical applications. Focusing on modeling patients' internal organisms via medical imaging, we found that most existing vision-based AI systems share similar challenges, ranging from huge computational resources, laborious data annotation, domain shifting, and unexplainability. Data collection in this era of data privacy law is another challenge that is rarely discussed in previous works conducting technical implementations of deep neural networks. In the end, our conclusion is that leading researchers in deep neural networks tend to put more concern into introducing techniques that allow newer, bigger, and more precise networks to be easily trained and evaluated based on some quantitative evaluation metrics. Meanwhile, physicians and data protection laws seem to hold a different concern regarding qualitative issues about how to make these deep networks trustworthy, ethical, and able to explain their decisions as well as underneath logic in a meaningful manner.

Keywords: digital human model · artificial intelligence · computer vision · deep neural network · medical imaging

1 Introduction

Recently, the uprising trend of artificial intelligence (AI) has become obvious that its services and applications can be found in almost every sector. In the healthcare sector, there exists AI services and applications to assist not only medical diagnosis but also other healthcare-related tasks like infection risk prediction [26], healthcare cognitive assistants [25], automation of non-patient-care administrative workflow [14], automatic medical stock check [21], etc. According to the 2022 survey of AI in healthcare [22], it is interesting that the adoption of AI has recently shifted from AI researchers and data scientists to domain expert users in healthcare. Hence, in order for AI to successfully deploy to the healthcare sector, not only AI researchers and data scientists but also physicians must all be satisfied.

© The Author(s), under exclusive license to Springer Nature Switzerland AG 2023
V. G. Duffy (Ed.): HCII 2023, LNCS 14029, pp. 329–340, 2023.
https://doi.org/10.1007/978-3-031-35748-0_24

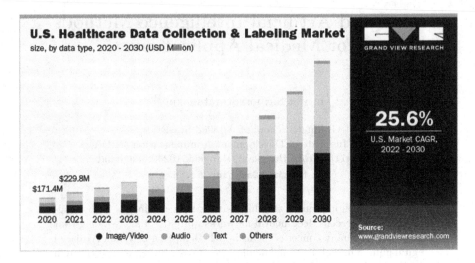

Fig. 1. The predicted growth of healthcare data collection and labeling market. Image courtesy of Grand View Research [9].

In the work of [9], the growth of AI adoption in the healthcare sector is shown via a report of the global healthcare data collection and labeling market; the market is expected to grow continuously at an annual rate of 26.9% from 2022 to 2030, as illustrated in Fig. 1. Among many data modalities in this report, image and video had the largest revenue share of over 40% in 2021. Focusing on vision-based unimodal AI or vision AI, research communities have made it clear lately that powerful vision AI models and algorithms can truly open up a new frontier, allowing various aspects of human's internal organism as well as other external behaviors to be digitally modeled, learned, and predicted. Nevertheless, the study of this paper will be limited to the use of vision AI to model patient's internal organisms as its applications directly contribute to the core value of the healthcare sector.

To foresee how far vision AI's services and applications can digitally model human organisms for the purpose of medical diagnosis, this paper conducts an in-depth investigation that closely aligns recent advances in vision AI with actual tasks performed by physicians. Fortunately, the workflow of recent data-driven AI (which is considered a branch of data science) shares many things in common with the workflow of medical image processing, as shown in Fig. 2. Although the two workflows look different at the first glance, many of their processes refer to the same tasks, particularly the part of data preparation (data management) and modeling (analytics). Therefore, it should be quite straightforward to map existing challenges/practices in recent data-driven AI to actual medical tasks.

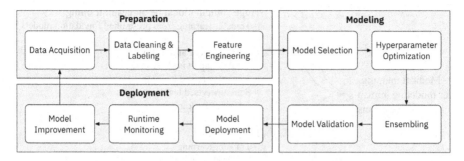

(a) A data science workflow [32].

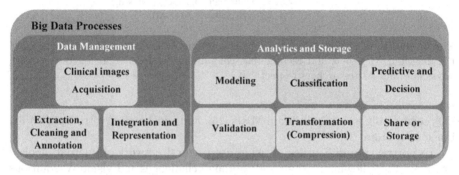

(b) A big data workflow for biomedical image processing [19].

Fig. 2. Comparing the two workflows of (a) general data science and (b) big data for medical image processing. Images courtesy of Wang el al. [32] and Kouanou et al. [19] respectively.

2   Background of Medical Imaging

For modeling human's internal organisms, medical imaging (a.k.a., radiology) is a very important practice that has assisted physicians in diagnosis and treatment for more than a century, starting from X-ray (since 1896), ultrasound (first used clinically in 1970s), magnetic resonance imaging (MRI) (evolved during 1970s), and computerized tomography (CT) scan (invented in the early 1970s) [3]. Medical imaging alone allows physicians to perform non-intrusive diagnostics, better assess the internal organism, track an ongoing illness, and aid surgical procedures. As medical imaging often infers scarce specialists for interpretation, an overwhelming amount of data, and time-consuming tasks, using AI in this practice has been actively observed for decades.

Nevertheless, it is the recent advances in vision AI that have made the integration of AI and medical imaging more prominent than ever, particularly the advances in deep neural networks for complicated visual analysis. For example, spotting diseases in X-ray images [2], locating kidney mass in a series of multi-axis CT image slices [18], screening for breast cancer in digital mammography

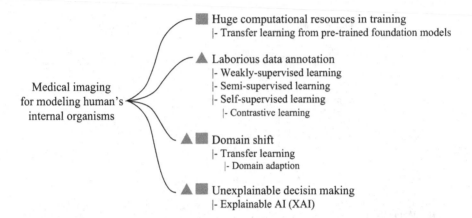

Fig. 3. Outline of challenges and vision AI solutions to be discussed in this study. In the diagram, triangular and rectangular icons indicate burdens/challenges regarding physicians and AI researchers respectively.

[20], segmenting anomaly in brain MRIs [13], and constructing a transparent 3D image of a brain [29].

To portray the difficulties of using deep neural networks in actual medical practices, the following sections walk through challenges and vision AI solutions of recently published works. Figure 3 outlines all challenges and solutions to be discussed in this study.

3   Modeling Patient's Internal Organism: Challenges

In the work of [18] published in 2022, kidney mass segmentation is done automatically for a series of multi-axis CT image slices using two Convolutional Neural Networks (CNNs) named 2.5D ResUNet and 2.5D DenseUNet. Although training deep neural networks in a fully-supervised manner sounds straightforward, this work emphasizes three non-trivial challenges of deep neural networks in medical imaging practices—huge computational resources, laborious data annotation, and domain shift.

First, the big-data and high-dimensional nature of medical images infers **huge computational resources** that limit researchers' choices in choosing network architectures as well as related hyperparameters, leading to non-optimal performances. When training a deep neural network, the current best practice in research communities is to batch many training samples together before passing the batches through the network; using an appropriate batch size is also said to be one of the key factors for obtaining optimal results in CNNs upon a medical image dataset, according to [17]. However, in this work of kidney mass segmentation [18], the size of CT data regarding a batch of patients is relatively large, limiting researchers from experimenting with large batch sizes due to insufficient computational resources. This large amount of memory required by batching patients' CT data during network training is also the reason that [18] uses the architecture of 2.5D UNet instead of exploiting the popular but more-memory-hungry architecture of 3D UNet.

The second challenge mentioned in [18], which is probably one of the most challenging problems in applying deep neural networks in real-world practices, is **laborious data annotation**. In [18], the process of ground-truth annotation for kidney mass segmentation cost an experienced urologist about 70–350 min of time just to precisely annotate 70 CT image slices belonging to one patient. Unfortunately, for classic fully-supervised learning, this precise per-pixel annotation cannot be compromised as it will directly affect the final performance of the trained networks.

Thirdly, [18] discusses the classic **domain-shift** challenge encountered by most machine learning-based algorithms including deep neural networks. Because of discrepancies between the training dataset (a public repository collected from American patients) and the test dataset (collected from Thai patients by the researchers), it is found that the performances of the trained models drop when being applied to the test dataset. This conveys that it may not be possible to share and use an already-trained deep neural network among hospitals. This is because data collected from different hospitals often have unique data characteristics or distributions that result from a combination of factors like different CT scanners, scanning parameters, patient demographic, and patient cohorts. Hence, unless the data from different hospitals are very similar to one another or researchers are able to train their networks on a huge training dataset that covers most data diversities, utilizing a deep neural network for medical images may require each hospital to do time-intensive tasks of collecting data, annotating data, and training their own version of the network, all by themselves.

Apart from the three challenges mentioned above, another challenge shared by most complicated deep neural networks is the infamous black-box problem, meaning that these deep AI networks are opaque and **unexplainable**. Despite the highly accurate predictions that these networks can produce, even researchers and developers who designed and trained the networks themselves cannot explain the reasons behind their networks' decisions. In the context of high-stakes applications like interpreting patients' medical image data, unexplainability is a major barrier that prevents deep neural networks from actual clinical deployment [12,15,16]. According to [31], the concern about how deep neural networks make their decisions is not only from physicians but also from European Union's regulations as General Data Protection Regulation (GDPR) states that it is the right of patients to "receive meaningful information about the logic involved" any automated decision making.

Compared to other data modalities, image-based deep neural networks have some visualization techniques that allow peeking inside the black box and making some sense of how the networks make decisions. For example, the work of [24] utilizes Gradient-weighted Class Activation Map (Grad-CAM) to display the regions of lungs infected by COVID-19 in both chest X-ray and CT-scan images, as shown in Fig. 4; using Grad-CAM allows them to interpret the detection

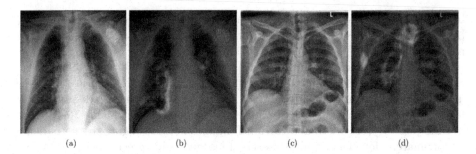

(a)   (b)   (c)   (d)

Fig. 4. Grad-CAM visualization on chest X-ray images. Image courtesy of Panwar et al. [24].

results and determine further actions. While Grad-CAM is able to highlight regions that contribute most to each class-specific decision, it provides neither meaningful explanation nor logic about how and why the network chooses to concentrate on some regions and neglect others. Besides, as Grad-CAM is a result of upsampling low-resolution 2D feature maps from the last convolutional layer, Grad-CAM image is coarse and can easily miss highlighting fine-grained detail.

Recently, Automated Machine Learning (AutoML) is another rising trend that focuses on automating and accelerating the development pipeline of machine learning and deep learning. The work of [1] uses an AutoML named AutoGluon to train 2D slices of CT images and aggregate the results to get the final prediction of 3D CT images. However, according to the work of [27], the latest AutoML tools still lack in terms of transparency and explainability, making them inappropriate for being used in high-stakes medical practices. In addition, using AutoML to randomly try infinite possibilities of deep neural networks demands even more training resources compared to traditional human-guided training.

4   Modeling Patient's Internal Organism: Solutions

To deal with the challenge of huge computational resources during deep network training, the use of **transfer learning** upon one or more well-trained **foundation models** is a standard solution for vision AI practitioners. According to the survey of [6] in the context of medical imaging, this strategy of transfer learning is applicable even when tasks, domains, or both regarding the foundation model and the downstream model, are different. An obvious example is the famous ImageNet dataset. Although natural images in ImageNet are significantly different from medical images, deep neural networks pre-trained on ImageNet are said to be the de-facto approach when transfer learning is used for medical images [23]. Nevertheless, despite significant computational resource reduction when training downstream models, the huge cost regarding pre-training those foundation models remains unchanged.

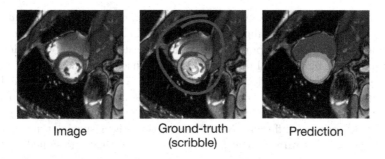

Image   Ground-truth   Prediction
                 (scribble)

Fig. 5. Weakly-supervised image segmentation with scribbles. Image courtesy of Valvano et al. [30].

To tackle the challenge of laborious data annotation, the work of [30] uses the concept of **weakly supervised learning** that allows medical-image annotators to roughly (weakly) annotate with scribbles (as shown in Fig. 5) instead of the usual fine-grained per-pixel annotation. This weakly supervised solution is developed by training a multi-scale Generative Adversarial Network (GAN) with a novel attention-gating mechanism. The researchers mention that the weakly supervised setup helps reduce annotation effort and in turn, increases the number of annotations to 15x more compared to the fully supervised setup. Experimental results on many medical and non-medical image segmentation datasets also show matching performances between this weakly-supervised approach and previous works of fully-supervised approaches.

Recently, another popular strategy to reduce annotation effort is to involve unlabeled data in deep networks' training; this is usually done by the concepts called semi-supervised learning and self-supervised learning. **Semi-supervised learning**, on one hand, is a practice that uses both labeled and unlabeled training data. According to the survey of [6], semi-supervised learning is a common scenario in medical imaging where annotators only label some images, leaving the other images unlabeled. The works of [11,33], for example, mix labeled and unlabeled data to train their deep neural networks on liver and chest CT scan images respectively.

Self-supervised learning, on the other hand, refers to a practice that unlabeled data get annotated by some internal mechanism of the network. Once the unlabeled data become the (self-)labeled data, the network can proceed using them as training data in a fully-supervised manner. For vision AI, popular self-supervised learning approaches usually involve contrastive learning [5] where general features of an unlabeled image dataset are learned by pre-training the network to spot similar and different training samples. Once the pre-training's finished, the pre-trained network can be further fine-tuned on a smaller dataset for several downstream tasks. For example, the work of [4] extends contrastive self-supervised learning to the segmentation of volumetric medical images on MRI datasets in the semi-supervised setting. Another self-supervised contrastive learning solution that can completely eliminate the need for image annotation is recently proposed in CheXzero [28]. In this work, chest X-ray images are classified by contrastively learning between the unlabeled X-ray images and their corresponding pathology reports written in natural language (text). However, using image-text multimodal data is beyond the discussion scope of our paper.

Transfer learning is sometimes mentioned as a solution for the challenge of domain shift as it helps fine-tune the network trained on a domain A for a task T_a to work well in a domain B for a task T_b, when either domain or task, or both can be different. Nevertheless, there is a special type of transfer learning called **domain adaptation** that is specifically designed to tackle the domain shift challenge, focusing on scenarios when both tasks and domain feature spaces are the same only marginal data distributions are different. The aim of domain adaptation is to minimize the distribution gap between source (training) data and target (test) data. According to the 2022 survey [10], there exist several methods proposed for domain adaptation in medical image analysis. However, volumetric representation (often 3D or 4D) of medical images increases the problem complexity compared to 2D images. Also, off-the-shelf pre-trained deep neural networks are mostly designed to work with 2D images, and transferring from these networks does not benefit much in performance for medical imaging analysis [10]. Last but not least, [10] mentioned that different medical scanning methods (e.g., CT, MRI, X-ray) introduce a new challenge of inter-modality heterogeneity—each scanning method produces unique visual characteristics that differ from the others, making knowledge transferring and domain adaptation even more difficult.

Explainable AI (XAI) refers to any method whose attempt is to render the decision making of AI more transparent, explainable, and interpretable. In the 2022 survey of [31], XAI in medical image analysis is categorized into four categories based on two criteria—model-based versus post hoc explanation, and model-specific versus model-agnostic explanation. Despite many attempts to build deep learning-based XAI, the survey suggests that introducing the concept of XAI to deep neural networks is still very difficult without sacrificing some model complexity and prediction accuracy; this is due to the huge number of parameters in deep neural networks. Hence, for most deep networks, a common XAI solution is the post hoc explanation when we analyze the already-trained model in order to learn insight into how it makes each decision. Examples of post hoc explanations include saliency map visualization, feature importance, learned feature inspection, and interaction among features. Unfortunately, these explanations are still not out-of-the-box explanations that physicians can use to explain to patients.

5   Discussion

In this section, we discuss our discovery regarding the adoption of vision AI in the practices of modeling human internal organisms via medical image analysis. First, it can be seen that most mature deep neural networks are based on supervised learning. This means that they basically require a huge amount of training data as well as high-quality annotation. Although collecting patient data is not easy due to recent laws in data privacy and protection, it is a lot more problematic and laborious for physicians to deliberately annotate these data while maintaining their daily duties of patient treatment. To tackle this concern of data-hungry and laborious annotation, researchers have recently turned their interest to cutting-edge techniques of weakly-supervised learning, semi-supervised learning, and self-supervised learning. Nevertheless, these cutting-edge training techniques do not help reduce the computational resources required during the network's training. The use of foundation models extensively pre-trained by world-leading researchers is by far an easy and practical solution to jump-start the training of our (smaller) custom networks.

Second, there is a significant trade-off between accuracy and explainability. This trade-off makes state-of-the-art deep neural networks very infamous for their black-box decision making which also violates some regulations regarding patients' rights. Besides, according to the work of [8] in 2022, AI still cannot meet ethical standards regarding the codes of conduct that govern human physicians. Hence, letting AI take sole responsibility for core medical diagnostics is still too risky, and professional physicians may feel awkward about using AI in their high-stakes professional practices. Third, learning-based AI like deep neural networks heavily depends on training data which is quite fragile to data changes. Therefore, a solid quality assurance procedure is needed to ensure long-term reliability regarding AI in medical diagnosis [7]. While research solutions in domain adaptation are being investigated, periodic system re-training is the main direction in current AI adoption.

As concluded in Fig. 3, all challenges discussed in this paper are burdens for either AI researchers or physicians, or sometimes both. While huge computation is a main burden for AI researchers and developers, data annotation is usually a direct burden for physicians that slows down or even stalls the whole development process. Another interesting issue is a challenge in training data collection due to increasingly intense data-related regulations lately and the emerging new-generation AI called Generative AI (e.g., ChatGPT, Midjourney). However, this issue requires aligning the rule of law, AI technicality, and medical practices altogether which is beyond the scope of our paper.

6 Conclusion

Recently, artificial intelligence (AI) has revolutionized and disrupted many professional sectors around the world, including the healthcare sector. Focusing on image-based patient organism modeling and the prominent trend of deep neural networks for visual analysis, it is found that previous works struggle with several challenges when trying to develop and utilize deep neural networks in medical practices. For deep neural network researchers and developers, challenges exist in every stage from the beginning stage of data collection to the ending stage of system deployment. These challenges result in significant delays in time, expensiveness in development bills, non-optimal performances, and/or performance degradation in production. Although researchers have continuously proposed solutions for these challenges, in our opinion, it is the challenge of unexplainable AI that remains a great concern for physicians and also a major barrier to AI adoption in the medical profession. Hence, to encourage more widespread and legitimate AI adoption in medical practices, future works should focus on not only how precisely a deep network can produce correct outputs but also how meaningfully and logically a deep network can describe its own outputs. Human-physician-in-the-loop is one possible direction to make the future development of vision AI closely align with both actual medical practices and the code of ethics of the medical profession.

References

1. Anwar, T.: COVID19 diagnosis using AutoML from 3D CT scans. In: IEEE/CVF International Conference on Computer Vision Workshops (ICCVW) (2021). https://doi.org/10.1109/ICCVW54120.2021.00061
2. Borkowski, A.A., Viswanadhan, N.A., Thomas, L.B., Guzman, R.D., Deland, L.A., Mastorides, S.M.: Using artificial intelligence for COVID-19 chest x-ray diagnosis. Federal Pract. **37**(9), 398–404 (2020). https://doi.org/10.12788/fp.0045
3. Bradley, W.G.: History of medical imaging. In: Proceedings of the American Philosophical Society, vol. 152, pp. 349–361 (2008). http://websites.umich.edu/ners580/ners-bioe_481/lectures/pdfs/2008-09-procAmerPhilSoc_Bradley-MedicalImagingHistory.pdf
4. Chaitanya, K., Erdil, E., Karani, N., Konukoglu, E.: Contrastive learning of global and local features for medical image segmentation with limited annotations. In: Conference on Neural Information Processing Systems (NeurIPS) (2020)
5. Chen, T., Kornblith, S., Norouzi, M., Hinton, G.: A simple framework for contrastive learning of visual representations. In: International Conference on Machine Learning (ICML), pp. 1597–1607 (2020)
6. Cheplygina, V., Bruijne, M., Pluim, J.: Not-so-supervised: a survey of semi-supervised, multi-instance, and transfer learning in medical image analysis. Med. Image Anal. **54**, 280–296 (2019). https://doi.org/10.1016/j.media.2019.03.009
7. Feng, J., et al.: Clinical artificial intelligence quality improvement: towards continual monitoring and updating of AI algorithms in healthcare. NPJ Dig. Med. **5**(66) (2022). https://doi.org/10.1038/s41746-022-00611-y
8. Gillies, A., Smith, P.: Can AI systems meet the ethical requirements of professional decision-making in health care? AI Ethics **2**, 41–47 (2022). https://doi.org/10.1007/s43681-021-00085-w
9. Grand View Research: Healthcare data collection and labeling market size, share and trends analysis report by data type (image/video, audio, text), by region (North America, Europe, APAC, LATAM, MEA), and segment forecasts (2022–2030). https://www.grandviewresearch.com/industry-analysis/healthcare-data-collection-labeling-market-report. Accessed 24 Jan 2023
10. Guan, H., Liu, M.: Domain adaptation for medical image analysis: a survey. IEEE Trans. Biomed. Eng. **69**(3), 1173–1185 (2022). https://doi.org/10.1109/TBME.2021.3117407
11. Han, K., et al.: An effective semi-supervised approach for liver CT image segmentation. IEEE J. Biomed. Health Inf. **26**(8), 3999–4007 (2022). https://doi.org/10.1109/JBHI.2022.3167384

12. He, J., Baxter, S.L., Xu, J., Xu, J., Zhou, X., Zhang, K.: The practical implementation of artificial intelligence technologies in medicine. Nat. Med. **25**, 30–36 (2019). https://doi.org/10.1038/s41591-018-0307-0
13. Hespen, K.M., Zwanenburg, J.J.M., Dankbaar, J.W., Geerlings, M.I., Hendrikse, J., Kuijf, H.J.: An anomaly detection approach to identify chronic brain infarcts on MRI. Sci. Rep. **11**(7714) (2021). https://doi.org/10.1038/s41598-021-87013-4
14. Hinson, J.S., et al.: Multisite implementation of a workflow-integrated machine learning system to optimize COVID-19 hospital admission decisions. NPJ Dig. Med. **5**(94) (2022). https://doi.org/10.1038/s41746-022-00646-1
15. Jia, X., Ren, L., Cai, J.: Clinical implementation of AI technologies will require interpretable AI models. Int. J. Med. Phys. Res. Pract. **47**(1), 1–4 (2020). https://doi.org/10.1002/mp.13891
16. Jin, W., Fatehi, M., Abhishek, K., Mallya, M., Toyota, B., Hamarneh, G.: Artificial intelligence in glioma imaging: challenges and advances. J. Neural Eng. **17**(2) (2020). https://doi.org/10.1088/1741-2552/ab8131
17. Kandel, I., Castelli, M.: The effect of batch size on the generalizability of the convolutional neural networks on a histopathology dataset. ICT Express **6**(4), 312–315 (2020). https://doi.org/10.1016/j.icte.2020.04.010
18. Kittipongdaja, P., Siriborvornratanakul, T.: Automatic kidney segmentation using 2.5D ResUNet and 2.5D DenseUNet for malignant potential analysis in complex renal cyst based on CT images. EURASIP J. Image Video Process. **2022**(1), 1–15 (2022). https://doi.org/10.1186/s13640-022-00581-x
19. Kouanou, A.T., Tchiotsop, D., Kengne, R., Zephirin, D.T., Armele, N.M.A., Tchinda, R.: An optimal big data workflow for biomedical image analysis. Inf. Med. Unlocked **11**(2018), 68–74 (2018). https://doi.org/10.1016/j.imu.2018.05.001
20. Leibig, C., Brehmer, M., Bunk, S., Byng, D., Pinker, K., Umutlu, L.: Combining the strengths of radiologists and AI for breast cancer screening: a retrospective analysis. Lancet Digit Health **4**(7) (2022). https://doi.org/10.1016/S2589-7500(22)00070-X
21. Lertsawatwicha, P., Phathong, P., Tantasanee, N., Sarawutthinun, K., Siriborvornratanakul, T.: A novel stock counting system for detecting lot numbers using Tesseract OCR. Int. J. Inf. Technol. (2022). https://doi.org/10.1007/s41870-022-01107-4
22. Lorica, B., Nathan, P.: 2022 AI in Healthcare Survey Report (2022). https://gradientflow.com/2022aihealthsurvey/. Accessed 14 Oct 2022
23. Matsoukas, C., Haslum, J.F., Sorkhei, M., Söderberg, M., Smith, K.: What makes transfer learning work for medical images: feature reuse & other factors. In: IEEE/CVF International Conference on Computer Vision and Pattern Recognition (CVPR) (2022). https://doi.org/10.1109/CVPR52688.2022.00901
24. Panwar, H., Gupta, P., Siddiqui, M.K., Morales-Menendez, R., Bhardwaj, P., Singh, V.: A deep learning and grad-CAM based color visualization approach for fast detection of COVID-19 cases using chest X-ray and CT-Scan images. Chaos Solit. Fract. **140** (2020). https://doi.org/10.1016/j.chaos.2020.110190
25. Preum, S.M., et al.: A review of cognitive assistants for healthcare: trends, prospects, and future directions. ACM Comput. Surv. **53**(6) (2021). https://doi.org/10.1145/3419368
26. Raza, M.M., Venkatesh, K.P., Kvedar, J.C.: Intelligent risk prediction in public health using wearable device data. NPJ Dig. Med. **5**(153) (2022). https://doi.org/10.1038/s41746-022-00701-x
27. Siriborvornratanakul, T.: Human behavior in image-based road health inspection systems despite the emerging AutoML. J. Big Data **9**(96) (2022). https://doi.org/10.1186/s40537-022-00646-8

28. Tiu, E., Talius, E., Patel, P., Langlotz, C.P., Ng, A.Y., Rajpurkar, P.: Expert-level detection of pathologies from unannotated chest X-ray images via self-supervised learning. Nat. Biomed. Eng. (2022). https://doi.org/10.1038/s41551-022-00936-9
29. Todorov, M.I.: Machine learning analysis of whole mouse brain vasculature. Nat. Methods **17**, 442–449 (2020). https://doi.org/10.1038/s41592-020-0792-1
30. Valvano, G., Leo, A., Tsaftaris, S.A.: Learning to segment from scribbles using multi-scale adversarial attention gates. IEEE Trans. Med. Imaging **40**(8), 1990–2001 (2021). https://doi.org/10.1109/TMI.2021.3069634
31. Velden, B., Kuijf, H.J., Gilhuijs, K.G., Viergever, M.A.: Explainable artificial intelligence (XAI) in deep learning-based medical image analysis. Med. Image Anal. **79** (2022). https://doi.org/10.1016/j.media.2022.102470
32. Wang, D., et al.: Human-AI collaboration in data science: exploring data scientists' perceptions of automated AI. In: Proceedings of the ACM on Human-Computer Interaction, vol. 3(CSCW), pp. 1–24 (2019). https://doi.org/10.1145/3359313
33. Zhang, Y., Su, L., Liu, Z., Tan, W., Jiang, Y., Cheng, C.: A semi-supervised learning approach for COVID-19 detection from chest CT scans. Neurocomputing **503**(7), 314–324 (2022). https://doi.org/10.1016/j.neucom.2022.06.076

Automated Nystagmus Parameter Determination: Differentiating Nystagmic from Voluntary Eye-Movements

Alexander Walther[1]([✉]), Julian Striegl[1,2], Claudia Loitsch[2],
Sebastian Pannasch[3], and Gerhard Weber[1]

[1] Chair of Human-Computer Interaction, TU Dresden, 01187 Dresden, Germany
`alexander.walther1@tu-dresden.de`
[2] ScaDS.AI Dresden/Leipzig, Center for Scalable Data Analytics and Artificial
Intelligence, 01187 Dresden, Germany
[3] Chair of Engineering Psychology and Applied Cognitive Research, TU Dresden,
01069 Dresden, Germany

Abstract. Nystagmus describes an involuntary oscillation of one or
both eyes. Depending on its origin, it decreases visual acuity and may
lead to vertigo, oscillopsia, physical strain, and social anxiety. Available
assistive technology only accounts for the limited sight, rather than compensating the nystagmus itself. When designing and using a system for
nystagmus compensation, it is necessary to create a user model that
covers the user's nystagmus as detailed as possible, due to the various
specific manifestations of the illness. Determining nystagmus parameters
involves a time-consuming manual inspection of eye movement recordings
and requires considerable expertise. So far, no algorithm for automatic
nystagmus parameter detection and categorization of eye movements has
been established. Therefore, the here presented paper strives to address
this gap by presenting a novel approach for automatic nystagmus parameter determination and real-time eye movement categorization. The algorithm for automatically determining nystagmus parameters is evaluated
through a pilot study with subjects from the target group, focusing on
the accuracy of parameter detection.

Keywords: User Modelling · Nystagmus Parameter Determination ·
Eye-Movement Classification

1 Introduction

Nystagmus is a rare condition [19, 23] that describes an involuntary oscillation
of one or both eyes [21]. It can be present at birth or develop during the first
few months of life (e.g. in the form of infantile/congenital nystagmus) or may

---

A. Walther and J. Striegl—The authors contributed equally to this research.

Supplementary Information The online version contains supplementary material
available at https://doi.org/10.1007/978-3-031-35748-0_25.

V. G. Duffy (Ed.): HCII 2023, LNCS 14029, pp. 341–354, 2023.
https://doi.org/10.1007/978-3-031-35748-0_25

be acquired later in life (acquired nystagmus) [21]. Literature provides a variety of manifestations, which are defined by the nystagmus origin and specific values of several parameters [1,8].

In addition to a decreased visual acuity [21], nystagmus may cause several other side effects. Individuals with acquired nystagmus often suffer from vertigo and the visual disorder oscillopsia [1,21]. Patients with infantile nystagmus also report vertigo [8,21], but it usually occurs only when they are stressed [9]. As a compensation strategy, many patients develop a forced head posture [8] to reduce the nystagmus intensity [21], which in turn can lead to physical strain, especially to the neck [18]. Furthermore, patients often feel socially unconfident due to their involuntary eye movements and the forced head posture [17]. With regard to accessibility issues when working with a computer, patients with nystagmus experience almost the same problems as people with low vision in general. Possible barriers include small font sizes, usage of serif or embellished fonts, low distinctiveness of single characters, capital writings, and low contrasts.[1] To overcome these issues, assistive software such as screen magnifiers, screen readers, speech recognition software and other accessibility functionalities are recommended[2] as well as certain wearables[3], handhelds[4] and stationary devices[5].

The aforementioned assistive technologies help people with nystagmus to overcome visual barriers in daily life. However, no assistive technology has yet been developed specifically for nystagmus, in particular, to compensate for involuntary eye movements. Since the exact characteristics of nystagmus vary greatly from person to person, novel assistive technologies, which aim to compensate for involuntary eye movements, must provide tailored and adaptive assistance according to individual characteristics of nystagmus. This requires a user model that describes the nystagmus in appropriate detail. Currently, a manual analysis of a patient's eye movement recordings is necessary to determine the concrete manifestation and thereby create such a user model. As this is a time-consuming procedure requiring considerable expertise, an automated approach would be beneficial but has yet to be established and evaluated. This paper provides a contribution in this direction.

This paper presents a novel approach for automatically determining the waveform, direction, amplitude, and frequency of nystagmus by analyzing eye movement recordings with a heuristic approach. The developed algorithm is evaluated in a pilot study whose results are discussed at the end of this paper.

---

[1] WCAG Impact Matrix; https://www.w3.org/WAI/GL/WCAG-impact-matrix; Access Date: 18.02.21.

[2] Nystagmus Network - Assistive Technology; https://nystagmusnetwork.org/support-with-education-contents/assistive-technology/; Access Date: 29.03.2022.

[3] EASTIN - eSight; http://www.eastin.eu/de-de/searches/products/detail/database-handicat/id-31479; Access Date: 29.03.2022.

[4] EASTIN - Mobilux; http://www.eastin.eu/de-de/searches/products/detail/databa se-hj\%C3\%A6lpemiddelbasen/id-68298; Access Date: 29.03.2022.

[5] EASTIN - ClearView; http://www.eastin.eu/de-de/searches/products/detail/datab ase-hj\%C3\%A6lpemiddelbasen/id-73472; Access Date: 29.03.2022.

Furthermore, a second algorithm is described, which aims to categorize eye movements in real time based on the identified parameters.

2   State of the Art

Current research in the field of nystagmus focuses mostly on medical procedures.[6] However, as such solutions require significant surgical or drug-based interventions, there is some research in the field of non-medical, computer-based nystagmus compensation.

Johannfunke [12] developed a concept and system for computer-based compensation of pathological horizontal nystagmus using eye tracker-based motion data. In their system, the horizontal position of visual stimuli was adjusted based on eye movement. For a conducted study, the used eye tracker was not calibrated for individual subjects, as the high frequency of the nystagmus of test subjects made a fixation of stimuli difficult and as the view direction was neglected in the scope of the study. Participants had to perform several tasks with either an actively adjusted image (experimental condition) or with an unadjusted image (control condition). Reaction times, duration of fixations, and number and length of saccades were measured during the experiment. The results showed that reaction times and the number of fixations decreased in subjects with a visual acuity of at least 0.1 in the experimental group, which was taken as an indication of a more stable image perception. Furthermore, 3 out of 16 subjects found the compensation to be comfortable. However, a deterioration of the measured values was observed for participants with a visual acuity of less than 0.1.

Pölzer and Miesenberger [20] investigated how latencies, which occur during the processing of the recorded eye movement, can be minimized by predicting the next gaze point based on the last three measured gaze points and eye movements. Recorded eye movements formed the data basis for the mathematical model that can predict – to some extent – the eye movements of a person with congenital horizontal pendular nystagmus. While especially at local extrema (e.g. transitions of the individual nystagmus phases) the prediction deviated significantly from the real value, the usefulness of the publication by Pölzer and Miesenberger lies in the presented approach to predict the eye movements of a person with nystagmus.

Teufel et al. [24] showed that the visual acuity of subjects with downbeat nystagmus syndrome (DBN) can be improved through computer-assisted adaptation of display contents. In their study, test subjects were asked to indicate the position of the opening of a Landolt ring [28] displayed on a monitor. If the answer was correct, the size of the Landolt ring was reduced. If the answer was repeatedly incorrect, the test was terminated and the size of the last detected Landolt ring was used to determine visual acuity. The experiment was performed under two conditions: first with a fixed and second with a dynamically adjusted position of the Landolt ring. In the latter, the ring was displaced according to

---

[6] IN-VISION   Organization;   https://in-vision.org.uk/research/;   Access   Date: 28.01.2021.

involuntary eye movement. In each trial, visual acuity was measured in three directions of gaze: straight ahead, 20° to the left, and 20° to the right. Results indicated that the dynamic movement of the centered Landolt ring (straight ahead condition) did not improve visual acuity compared to the static presentation. However, five out of ten subjects showed an improvement in visual acuity when looking sideways.

Smith et al. [22] developed prototypical eyeglasses, designed to stabilize the wearer's field of vision using optical methods. In a conducted experiment, acquired pendular nystagmus (APN) was induced in subjects by moving a screen with imprinted Landolt rings uniformly back and forth. Thereby, the experiment was conducted under simulated nystagmus condition, similar to the works of Iijima et al. [11] and Landry et al. [16]. Each subject completed three visual tests under different test conditions: (1) Nystagmus glasses off and screen unmoved (=normal vision test), (2) nystagmus glasses off, and (3) screen moved (untreated APN), and nystagmus glasses on and screen moved (treated APN). It was shown that in the second setting, no subject was able to detect the largest ring, while in the third condition results were obtained, which were comparable to those of the normal eye test. Although Smith et al. obtained very good results, their work is only related to a limited extent, since they use a physical-optical approach to compensate for involuntary eye movements. In the present work, however, a digital approach is investigated.

Juhola et al. [13] used angular velocity for the recognition of nystagmus beats in otoneurological patients with spontaneous nystagmus. Their method rejected outlier beat candidates and candidates corrupted by noise through multiple classification approaches. Parameters for the classification comprise slow phase amplitudes (of horizontal and vertical movement) and torsional components. The authors experimented with several classification algorithms, including forms of discriminant analysis, k-nearest neighbor, naive Bayes, multilayer perceptron networks, and support vector machines. Results on test data indicated that nearest neighbor searching with data standardization and without cleaning yields the highest accuracy for the classification. The authors suggest a combination of manual and automatic selection for the creation of training sets.

In summary, while the idea of retinal image stabilization for people with nystagmus has been examined before, no established approach exists by now to distinguish between intentional and nystagmic gaze automatically and the automatic determination of specific nystagmus parameters still remains an open research question. This paper aims to address this gap with two algorithms, described in the following Section.

3   Algorithm-Based User Modeling for People with Nystagmus

Based on the findings of related research and on a conducted context analysis - comprising a focus group with individuals affected by nystagmus - we developed two algorithms to, firstly, automatically determine nystagmus parameters and, secondly, categorize eye movements in real-time, based on those parameters.

3.1   Automated Nystagmus Parameter Determination

Nystagmus can take various forms and can have different origins [8,21]. Among others, the following parameters can be used to describe a specific manifestation of the illness [1]:

- waveform: The shape of the graph resulting from a one-dimensional eye recording. The wave may be sinusoidal (= pendular nystagmus) or jerk (= jerk nystagmus).
- direction: The direction of the nystagmus' fast phase.
- amplitude: The maximum degree the eye is deviated by the nystagmus.
- frequency: The number of nystagmic cycles per second.
- conjugacy: The degree of conjugacy between the nystagmic movement of both eyes.
- slow phase velocity: The eye movement's velocity during the slow phase of the nystagmus.

The hereafter presented algorithm aims to automatically detect the first four parameters (waveform, direction, amplitude, and frequency). Based on these detected parameters, eye movements can be further classified by our second algorithm, which is described in Sect. 3.2. Since the second algorithm solely relies on saccades detected in real-time, the conjugacy and slow-phase-velocity were omited during the automated parameter determination.

The algorithm's core concept lies in analyzing fast eye movements, also known as saccades. In healthy eye conditions, those occur when quickly shifting the focus from one object to another. In patients with nystagmus, the fast phase, in which the eye is being moved to its original gaze position, is often defined by a saccade [21]. The data set used by the algorithm shall therefore include the duration of the eye recording and a set of saccades, where each entry contains the time range the saccade occurred at as well as its amplitude and direction in degrees. The algorithm relies on eye movement data recorded by a spatially and temporally highly accurate eye tracker, while the subject is asked to focus on a single target. The latter requirement aims to reduce the number of voluntary gazes to zero in the best case. For simplicity, it is assumed that only one eye has been recorded. Therefore, the parameters will only be computed for that specific eye and the algorithm does not account for disconjugate eye movements - such as in see-saw-nystagmus [21]. The following paragraphs describe how each parameter may be determined by utilizing the given saccades. Since pendular nystagmus contains no saccades [21], the direction, amplitude and frequency can only be determined for patients with jerk nystagmus. The algorithm has been implemented in Python and run on a Fujitsu (Windows 10) with a 3.00 GHz Intel Core i5-9500 processor and 8.0 GB of RAM.

Preprocessing. Given the assumption, that the used eye tracker has a high temporal and spatial resolution, the data basis may contain voluntary saccades of a very small amplitude. This is due to the fact that people show a small amplitude tremor regardless of the health status of the eye [14]. Therefore, a filter removes all saccades with an amplitude of less than 1°. This threshold was determined by analyzing several publications for common nystagmus amplitudes (see Table 1). The lowest valued was used.

Table 1. Nystagmus amplitudes observed in literature.

Nystagmus	Amplitude [°]	Ref.
idiopathic infantile nystagmus	3.3–7.9	[4]
	2.8–5.5	[2]
PLAHF nystagmus	2	[27]
undefined	1–4	[6]
	small: <5 average: 5–15 large: >15	[15]
	small: <5 average: 5–10 large: >10	[7]
horizontal jerk nystagmus	3–4	[25]
manifest latent nystagmus	1.8–5	[2]

Waveform. As described in the literature, a cycle of pendular nystagmus does not contain saccades [21]. Therefore, it is assumed that the waveform can be determined by the number of registered saccades. To account for rare voluntary saccades, a threshold is again used. This threshold was set based on the hypothesis that the data set of a person with jerk nystagmus contains more than one saccade per two seconds. The value was obtained by analyzing several publications for common nystagmus frequencies (see Table 2). The lowest value was used. Hence, if an eye recording lasted one minute, the algorithm assumes a pendular nystagmus if less than 30 saccades were detected. Otherwise, jerk nystagmus is considered.

Direction. Assuming a conjugate movement of both eyes, the fast phase of nystagmus may either beat vertically (upbeat/ downbeat nystagmus) or horizontally in both directions [8,21]. When determining this direction using the given set of saccades, the algorithm counts the number of saccades for both directions and assumes the one with the most occurrences to be the representative one for the nystagmus. Special manifestations with alternating directions are not accounted for.

Amplitude. For determining the nystagmic amplitude, the median amplitude of all registered saccades is computed. The median is used to ignore outliers and get the amplitude most representative for the nystagmus.

Table 2. Nystagmus frequencies observed in literature.

Nystagmus	Frequency [Hz]	Ref.
acquired pendular nystagmus	3–4	[21]
horizontal pendular nystagmus	6.25	[29]
horizontal jerk nystagmus	2–4	[25]
spasmus nutans	3–11	[21]
	>10	[8]
idiopathic infantile nystagmus	3.89/4.08	[26]
	3.2	[10]
	2.93–4.0	[4]
	3.5–5	[2]
congenital nystagmus in relation to albinism	2.5	[10]
physiologic end point nystagmus	1–2.8	[3]
PLAHF nystagmus	5–10	[27]
manifest latent	2–3	[2]

Frequency. Given the duration of the eye recording, the frequency of the nystagmus may be computed by dividing the number of registered saccades by the duration in seconds.

3.2 Automated Eye-movement Categorization

In this section an algorithm for automatically categorizing eye movements is described. The data basis of the algorithm are the nystagmus parameters determined in Sect. 3.1 and real-time information on registered saccades. The algorithm shows an example of how nystagmus parameter determination can be automated.

By comparing the attributes of a registered saccade with the parameters detected by the algorithm described in the previous Section, recorded eye movements can be classified either as nystagmic (involuntary) or non-nystagmic (voluntary). The following heuristic is visualized in Fig. 1. Firstly, it is checked, if the previous algorithm detected a pendular nystagmus. If so, all incoming saccades are assumed to be voluntary (since pendular nystagmus does not contain any saccades). If a jerk nystagmus was detected, the incoming saccade's direction is checked to be similar to the one of the nystagmus. The directions are considered to be similar if they differ by ± 22.5° at most. If that is not the case, the saccade is considered to be voluntary. Otherwise, it will be checked if the saccade's amplitude is less than half or more than twice as big as the amplitude typical to the subject's nystagmus, the saccade is classified as voluntary. Otherwise, the saccade is seen as too similar to the ones caused by the nystagmus and is therefore assumed to be nystagmic.

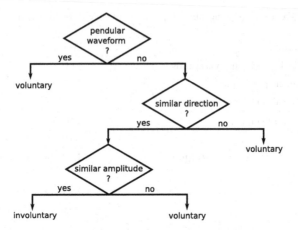

Fig. 1. Schema of the classification algorithm's heuristic. Directions are considered to be similar if they differ by $\pm 22.5°$ at most. Amplitudes are assumed to be similar if one of the currently observed saccades is at least half and at most twice as big as the one typical for the user's nystagmus.

4   Evaluation

To evaluate the accuracy of the automated nystagmus parameter detection, a pilot study was conducted. Consequently, the used methodology, participating group, and results will be described and discussed.

4.1   Methodology

Four patients (one male and three females) with congenital nystagmus were included in the participating group. None of them had previously been subjected to a detailed determination of the nystagmus parameters by a doctor. All participants had to sign a privacy policy and consent form to comply with data protection provisions. Furthermore, all participants had either reached the age of majority or were in the presence of a legal guardian to comply with ethical and legal requirements.

During the study, each participant was asked to sit upright in front of a monitor (Asus VG248QE[7], 120 Hz) at a distance of 55 cm, while placing their head on a chin-forehead-rest. An EyeLink 1000+[8] (1000 Hz) was used to record the movements of the right eye. EyeLink's default settings for saccade recognition were used. To guarantee equal lighting conditions during each trial and between participants, the roller blinds were closed and the ceiling lights were turned on.

---

[7] Product information Asus VG248QE; https://www.asus.com/de/Displays-Deskto ps/Monitors/All-series/VG248QE/; Access Date: 11.06.2021.

[8] EyeLink User Manual;
http://sr-research.jp/support/EyeLink%201000%20User%20Manual%201.5.0.pdf;
Access Date: 17.03.2021.

The nystagmus parameters were determined in two trials, five minutes apart. During the break, a questionnaire was filled out about the experiences users faced during the trial. The participants' task in each trial was to focus on a stimulus (5 mm red dotted circle on a white background) that was presented in changing positions (± seven degrees relative to the vertical head position, three times each) for three seconds each. The eye movements recorded 0.5 s after and before a change of the stimulus position were were algorithmically analyzed according to the heuristic described in Sect. 3.1. Overall the study took about fifteen minutes for each participant.

To evaluate the automatically determined parameters, recorded eye movement data of both trials were manually inspected by the facilitator using OMTools[9] for preprocessing and MATLAB (v. R2020b)[10] for visualization.

4.2 Results

The results of both the automatic and manual eye movement data analysis are compared in Table 3 and evaluated in the following sections. The result of the heuristic is considered as correct if it matches the result of the manual analysis performed by the facilitator.

Table 3. Comparison of nystagmus parameters determined automatically and manually (MI = Manual Inspection; J = jerk nystagmus; P = pendular nystagmus)

subject		1	2	3	4
waveform	Trial 1	J	J	J	P
	Trial 2	J	J	J	J
	MI	P	J	J	J
direction	Trial 1	right	right	right	–
	Trial 2	right	right	right	right
	MI	–	right	right	right(left)
amplitude [°]	Trial 1	1.91	3.59	3.73	–
	Trial 2	10.91	2.96	2.14	1.20
	MI	5	6	6.5	1
frequency [Hz]	Trial 1	2.40	3.47	3.67	–
	Trial 2	1.27	3.25	2.60	2.20
	MI	2.5	4	4	6

---

[9] Homepage OMTools; http://www.omlab.org/software/software.html; Access Date: 16.06.2021.
[10] Homepage MATLAB; https://www.mathworks.com/products/matlab.html; Access Date: 14.06.2021.

Waveform. The manual analysis of the eye recordings showed that three participants had jerk nystagmus, whereas one subject had pendular nystagmus. The algorithm determined the waveform correctly in five out of eight trials, which leads to an accuracy of 62.5%.

Direction. The manual analysis of subject 4 resulted in a nystagmus with alternating directions, where the majority of the saccades beat to the right side, which the algorithm detected correctly in one of the two trials. Regarding the determination of the nystagmus direction, the algorithm achieved an accuracy of 62.5%.

Amplitude. The automatically determined amplitudes exceed the ones of the manual analysis in one trial and fall below them in five trials. Allowing a tolerance of 20%, a correct amplitude was only found in the second trial of subject 4. This results in an accuracy of 12.5% for the automated amplitude determination.

Frequency. Allowing a tolerance of 20%, the algorithm determined the frequency correctly in four out of eight trials.

4.3   Discussion

The results indicate that the presented heuristic is suitable for determining the parameters of a patient's nystagmus to a certain extend, but still has potential for improvement. As described in Sect. 3.1, the algorithm solely relies on the saccades detected by the used eye tracker. A manual inspection of these saccades revealed some weak spots of this approach. Firstly, some of the registered saccades include parts of both the slow phase and the fast phase (see Fig. 2), which leads to a decreased amplitude. Furthermore, registered saccades do not represent the whole fast phase in some cases, as visualized in Fig. 2, which also results in a divergence between the automatically computed amplitudes and the manually analyzed ones. These incorrect amplitudes also affect the computed frequencies, since only saccades categorized as nystagmic are taken into account. If a saccade's amplitude is decreased below the median amplitude (due to the inclusion of parts of the slow and fast phase) and is therefore categorized as a voluntary one, it will not be used to compute the frequency, which is thereby decreased. Another reason for the incorrectly determined frequencies can be found in the threshold used to filter small voluntary saccades (see Sect. 3.1). Since the amplitude of subject 4 is around 1, most of the nystagmic saccades were categorized as voluntary ones, which decreased the frequency determined by the algorithm.

Limitations. The intention of the conducted study was to demonstrate the feasibility of the algorithm in a first pilot study. Therefore, several limitations should be mentioned. Firstly, the number of participants was too low to support a quantitative analysis of the implementation of the algorithm. In addition to this only patients with congenital nystagmus could be recruited for the study, which meant that the applicability of the algorithm in acquired nystagmus could not be tested. While evaluating the study results, the manual analysis of the recorded eye movements was performed by the facilitator and should in future studies be verified by an experienced ophthalmologist. The achieved accuracy of all four parameters is not sufficient to indicate a robust algorithm and may be improved by the proposals of Sect. 4.3, among others. Finally, the algorithm has been tested on one device only, whose installed hardware may have influenced the results. With regard to the repeatability of the pilot study, the setup lacks the information of the lab's exact illumination.

Proposals for Improvement. Regarding the revealed weak spots, the presented algorithm may be improved by using local extrema of the recorded eye movements rather than only the registered saccades. This way only the recordings of the fast phase would be taken into account, avoiding the saccades that also contain parts of the slow phase. Furthermore, all data of the fast phase could be included in the computation and not just the saccadic part. An alternative could be the application of certain algorithms from the field of waveform analysis. Additionally, the threshold for filtering saccades of small amplitude should be decreased to account for nystagmus with low amplitudes. Finally, the parameters for the saccade detection algorithm of the used eye tracker could be experimented with, to see if they impact the quality of detected saccades.

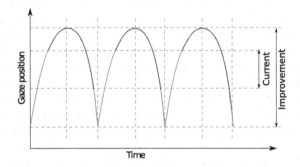

Fig. 2. Comparison of the current amplitude determination and the suggested improvement. Eye movement recordings (blue) and saccades detected by the eye tracker (red), which contain parts of the slow and fast phase. (Color figure online)

Future Work. As the research in non-medical nystagmus treatment is rather limited, the presented user modeling approach may be used in further research, e.g. to automatically adapt a user interface to a patient's specific nystagmus. Since most of the nystagmus side effects originate from continuous involuntary eye movements, we made the hypothesis that they may be reduced by shifting the patients surrounding simultaneously to the nystagmus. This way, a focused object is held in the viewer's fovea, which eventually extends the fixation period of the nystagmus. As described by Dell'Osso [5], this would increase the subject's visual acuity. We assume that this also leads to a reduced forced head posture since the nystagmus compensation would be performed by the image-shifting system and the head posture would no longer be needed. Finally, a non-present or reduced forced head posture may also have a positive impact on the patient's social confidence. Such a system may utilize both described algorithms to determine a viewer's specific nystagmus manifestation at first and then e.g. shift a monitor's content simultaneously to the nystagmus, using the eye movement categorization. Thus the algorithms presented in this paper represent a first step to a novel assistive technology; thereby impacting the field of HCI. Future work should strive to improve the here presented algorithms, specifically regarding their accuracy, to deploy them to compensate nystagmic eye movements digitally for affected individuals using computer systems. A follow-up study should further include a larger sample size to achieve more resilient results.

5   Conclusion

Nystagmus describes an involuntary oscillation of one or both eyes. Depending on the specific manifestation it decreases the visual acuity and may lead to vertigo, oscillopsia, physical strain, and social anxiety. Available assistive technologies help patients to overcome visual barriers, but none has yet been developed to compensate the involuntary eye movements in particular. When designing and using such a system, it is necessary to create a user model that covers the user's nystagmus as detailed as possible, due to the various specific manifestations existing. Determining nystagmus parameters involves a time-intensive manual analysis of eye movement recordings and requires considerable expertise. At this point no approach for automated nystagmus parameter determination exists so far and the presented algorithm represents a first step in this direction. This paper presents a novel approach of determining nystagmus parameters automatically. In addition, a heuristic for a second algorithm was presented, that aims to categorize eye movements in real time based on the determined nystagmus parameters. The automatic parameter determination has been evaluated in a pilot study, which included four participants. Overall, the evaluation resulted in an accuracy of 62.5% for the waveform and direction, 50% for the frequency, and 12.5% for the amplitude. The results show, that the algorithm is feasible for determining the parameters of a patient's nystagmus to a certain extent, but still has potential for improvement. Further developments need to improve the automated parameter determination and include an evaluation of the presented eye movement categorization. There are certain limitations with regard to the algorithms and the study presented here, but it should be understood as a first step towards a computer-based nystagmus compensation and may be the basis for a novel assistive technology in the future.

References

1. Abadi, R.V.: Mechanisms underlying nystagmus. J. Roy. Soc. Med. **95**(5), 231–234 (2002)
2. Abadi, R.V., Scallan, C.J., Clement, R.A.: The characteristics of dynamic overshoots in square-wave jerks, and in congenital and manifest latent nystagmus. Vision Res. **40**(20), 2813–2829 (2000)
3. Abel, L., Parker, L., Daroff, R., Dell'Osso, L.: End-point nystagmus. Invest. Ophthalmol. Visual Sci. **17**, 539–44 (1978)
4. Clement, R.A., Whittle, J.P., Muldoon, M.R., Abadi, R.V., Broomhead, D.S., Akman, O.: Characterisation of congenital nystagmus waveforms in terms of periodic orbits. Vision Res. **42**(17), 2123–2130 (2002)
5. Dell'osso, L.F., Steen, J.V.D., Steinman, R.M., Coleewijn, H.: Foveation dynamics in congenital nystagmus i: fixation. Documenta Ophthalmologica **79**(1), 1–23 (1992)
6. von dem Hagen, E.A., Houston, G.C., Hoffmann, M.B., Morland, A.B.: Pigmentation predicts the shift in the line of decussation in humans with albinism. Eur. J. Neurosci. **25**(2), 503–511 (2007)
7. Happe, W.: Augenheilkunde. Hippokrates Verl., Stuttgart, 2, überarb. und erw. aufl edn. (1999)
8. Hertle, R.W., et al.: A classification of eye movement abnormalities and strabismus (cemas). In: Report of a National Eye Institute Sponsored Workshop from the committee for the Classification of Eye Movement Abnormalities and Strabismus (CEMAS) Workshop, vol. 56, pp. l. National Eye Institute (NEI), Bethesda (2001)
9. Hertle, R.W., Dell'Osso, L.F.: Nystagmus In Infancy and Childhood: Current Concepts in Mechanisms, Diagnoses, and Management, illustrated edn. OUP USA, New York (2013)
10. Huurneman, B., Boonstra, F., Goossens, J.: Perceptual learning in children with infantile nystagmus: effects on 2d oculomotor behavior. Invest. Ophthalmol. Visual Sci. **57**, 4229–4238 (2016)
11. Iijima, A., Minamitani, H., Ishikawa, N.: Image analysis of quick phase eye movements in nystagmus with high-speed video system. Med. Biol. Eng. Comput. **39**, 2–7 (2001)
12. Johannfunke, M.: Blickkontingente Kompensation des pathologischen Nystagmus. Diploma thesis, Universität Bielefeld (2008)
13. Juhola, M., Aalto, H., Joutsijoki, H., Hirvonen, T.P.: The classification of valid and invalid beats of three-dimensional nystagmus eye movement signals using machine learning methods. Adv. Artif. Neural Syst. **2013**, 1–11 (2013)
14. Krauzlis, R.J.: Chapter 32 - eye movements. In: Squire, L.R., Berg, D., Bloom, F.E., du Lac, S., Ghosh, A., Spitzer, N.C. (eds.) Fundamental Neuroscience, 4th edn., pp. 697–714. Academic Press, San Diego (2013)
15. Käsmann-Kellner, B.: Nystagmus: Klinische charakteristika, therapeutische optionen. Spektrum der Augenheilkunde **31**(1), 27–48 (2017)
16. Landry, J., Lee, P., Madduri, M.: Nystagmus simulating and compensating for eye motion blur with eye tribe (2015). https://stanford.edu/class/ee367/Winter2015/report_landry_lee_madduri.pdf, not published as scientific paper
17. McLean, R.J., Windridge, K.C., Gottlob, I.: Living with nystagmus: a qualitative study. Brit. J. Ophthalmol. **96**(7), 981–986 (2012)
18. Morris, B., Smith, V., Elphick, J., Laws, D.E.: Compensatory head posture and neck problems: is there an association? a cohort study of nystagmus patients. Eye **23**(2), 279–283 (2008)

19. Orssaud, D.C.: Congenital nystagmus (2003). https://www.orpha.net/data/patho/GB/uk-nystagmus.pdf, not published as scientific paper
20. Polzer, S., Miesenberger, K.: Assisting people with nystagmus through image stabilization: using an arx model to overcome processing delays. In: 2017 39th Annual International Conference of the IEEE Engineering in Medicine and Biology Society (EMBC), vol. 2017, pp. 1222–1225 (07 2017)
21. Quiros, P.A., Yee, R.D.: Nystagmus, saccadic intrusions, and oscillations. In: Ophthalmology, chap. 9.18, 3rd edn, pp. 1040–1048. Elsevier, Mosby (2009)
22. Smith, R., Oomen, B., Stahl, J.: Image-shifting optics for a nystagmus treatment device. J. Rehabil. Res. Dev. **41**, 325–336 (2004)
23. Sarvananthan, N., et al.: The prevalence of nystagmus: the leicestershire nystagmus survey. Invest. Opthalmol. Visual Sci. **50**(11), 5201 (2009)
24. Teufel, J., et al.: Real-time computer-based visual feedback improves visual acuity in downbeat nystagmus - a pilot study. J. Neuroeng. Rehabil. **13**, 1743–0003 (2016)
25. Thomas, S., Proudlock, F.A., Sarvananthan, N., Constantinescu, C., Gottlob, I.: Nystagmus characteristics and MRI findings of patients with perinatal central nervous system injury. Invest. Ophthalmol. Visual Sci. **47**(13), 2510–2510 (2006)
26. Thomas, S., et al.: Phenotypical characteristics of idiopathic infantile nystagmus with and without mutations in frmd7. Brain J. Neurol. **131**, 1259–1267 (2008)
27. Wang, P., Ya, P., Li, D., Lv, S., Yang, D.: Nystagmus with pendular low amplitude, high frequency components (plahf) in association with retinal disease. Strabismus **28**(1), 3–6 (2020)
28. Wesemann, W., Heinrich, S., Jägle, H., Schiefer, U., Bach, M.: Neue din- und iso-normen zur sehschärfebestimmungnew din and iso norms for determination of visual acuity. Der Ophthalmologe **117** (2019)
29. Winkelman, B.H.J., et al.: Nystagmus in patients with congenital stationary night blindness (CSNB) originates from synchronously firing retinal ganglion cells. PLOS Biol. **17**(9), e3000174 (2019)

Modeling Complex Human Behavior
and Phenomena

Disaster Mitigation Education Through the Use of the InaRISK Personal Application in Indonesia

Afisa[1]([⊠]), Achmad Nurmandi[2], Misran[1], and Dimas Subekti[1]

[1] Department of Government Affairs and Administration, Universitas Muhammadiyah Yogyakarta, Yogyakarta, Indonesia
{afisa.psc22,misran.psc20,dimas.subekti.psc20}@mail.umy.ac.id
[2] Department of Government Affairs and Administration Jusuf Kalla School of Government, Universitas Muhammadiyah Yogyakarta, Yogyakarta, Indonesia
nurmandi_achmad@umy.ac.id

Abstract. This study aims to analyze the InaRisk Personal Application in improving disaster mitigation in Indonesia, including its obstacles. The researcher used a qualitative descriptive approach. The research data was taken from the National Disaster Management Agency (BNPB) website and online media and processed using the NVivo 12 Plus software. Researchers used three indicators of Disaster Communication: Information, Communication, and Coordination. The results showed that if the Information indicator data got a percentage of 42%, which means it is good, this is supported by various supporting features and the latest so that it is easily accessible at any time with a stable connection. Communication gets a percentage of 31%, so it is pretty active in providing a fast response to disaster detection around users and the best advice for disaster mitigation. Coordination gets a percentage of 26%, where BNPB continues to try to provide socialization to introduce the InaRISK Personal application by involving many stakeholders, including volunteers and the community, in developing services on this application. It's just that only a few people download and use the InaRISK Personal application, especially those who live in disaster-prone areas.

Keywords: Information Technology · Disaster Mitigation · InaRisk Personal App

1 Introduction

Disasters are always scary, and the impact is very wary of them. Indonesia is one of the countries that are prone to disasters [1]. This is because Indonesia is located between the confluence of three active plates: the Indo-Australian, Eurasian, and Pacific. [2]. Therefore, Indonesia is often referred to as an area in the Pacific Ring of Fire or a room with a high potential for natural disasters [3]. Okezone.com reports that the National Disaster Management Agency (BNPB) has recorded data on natural disasters in Indonesia from January 1 to June 26, 2022, where there were 1,902 incidents, of which 1,788 or

94% of them were wet hydrometeorological disasters the form of floods, landslides, and landslides extreme weather [4]. These disasters have caused many victims, including 98 people dying, 679 people being injured, 15 people missing, and 2,399,287 people suffering and having to evacuate [5].

Through the National Disaster Management Agency (BNPB), the Government launched an online-based disaster mitigation application called InaRisk Personal as a monitoring tool for reducing the disaster risk index, developed on November 10, 2016 [6]. The InaRISK Personal application is also used for socialization and education through a self-assessment method for the risk of COVID-19 transmission as a basis for decision-making considerations in formulating strategies, policies, and programs to tackle disaster risk nationally and regionally [7].

Previous research from Ferry Lismanto et al. (2022) found that the people of Pur-wodadi, North Bengkulu, know the risk of being exposed to Covid-19 based on their lifestyle and advice on preventing Covid-19 transmission and education about health protocols [8]. The research of Dewi 'Izzatus Tsamroh et al. (2021) obtained the results of an independent assessment of the risk of COVID-19 transmission through InaRISK Personal on students in English Village, including behavior patterns towards health pro-tocols [9]. Yusuf's research (2018) shows that using web-based information and com-munication technology or applications has become a trend in every region in Indonesia to facilitate and accelerate government services [10].

The difference between this study and previous research is that this study exam-ines disaster communication carried out by the Government to the community through the InaRISK Personal application in disasters that often occur in Indonesia, not only focusing on the Covid-19 pandemic. This paper is prepared to explain the effectiveness of using the InaRisk Application to increase understanding of disasters effectively and efficiently. This paper will answer two questions: RQ1: How is the development of using the InaRISK Personal application? RQ2: How is the Government's disaster mitigation communication in the InaRISK Personal application to create a disaster-resilient society?

2   Literature Review

2.1   Information Technology Management in Disaster Mitigation

Disaster mitigation aims to reduce the risks posed by disasters [11]. Mitigation includes all actions taken before, during, and after the occurrence of natural events to mitigate their effects, including avoiding hazards, providing warnings, and evacuation in the period before the danger [12]. Disaster events do not escape the study of public policy because they involve actions that must be taken or not be done (do or not to do) by the Government [13]. A general understanding of appropriate and effective mitigation or community preparedness in dealing with disasters can be seen in how they respond to disasters [14].

Disaster mitigation must be carried out in a planned and comprehensive manner through various efforts and approaches. First, a technical process, namely technically disaster mitigation, is carried out to reduce the impact of a disaster. Second, human policy aims to form people who understand and know the dangers of disasters. Third, the administrative approach, which is the approach usually taken by the government or organizational leaders, can be a managerial approach in disaster management, especially at the mitigation stage. Fourth, the cultural approach is an approach to increase awareness about disasters [15].

There are four critical things in disaster mitigation, namely; First, the availability of information and maps of disaster-prone areas for each type of Disaster. Second, socialization increases public understanding and awareness in dealing with disasters. Third, there is regulation and arrangement of disaster-prone regions to reduce the threat of catastrophe [16].

Effective disaster mitigation must have three main elements: First, a hazard assessment to identify the population and assets that are threatened, as well as the level of threat that will produce a Disaster Potential Map. Second, a warning based on disaster data occurs as an early warning and uses communication channels to give messages to the authorities and the public. Third, preparedness provides knowledge about areas likely to be affected by disasters and warning systems for evacuation [17].

Lack of information and public knowledge about disaster preparedness can cause panic, making it difficult to overcome and reduce disaster risk [18]. Advances in technology and the increasingly diverse presence of mobile devices have led to a new culture in society, so it is necessary to change educational media through mobile applications that can increase understanding of behavior in the community [19]. Expanding the knowledge and attitude of the community in disaster mitigation will prevent the occurrence of a more considerable disaster impact [20].

ICT can help deal with the consequences of natural disasters through two main channels: awareness-raising and public education and rapid response channels [21]. Information systems are needed to improve disaster mitigation behavior and prevent disaster risks based on android applications. Information and Communication Technologies (ICT) is a multimedia-based learning system (technology involving text, images, sound, and video) capable of making the presentation of a topic fascinating, and it has a significant and strategic role to be able to develop clear and powerful learning activities. A wide range [22]. Therefore, disaster mitigation and preparation of IT-based information (Information and Technology) on matters that support community preparedness for disasters are essential [23].

2.2 InaRiskPersonal Application

InaRISK Personal is an application that contains information on the level of danger in an area, including the threat of disasters, affected populations, and potential physical, economic, and environmental losses. It is equipped with recommendations for actions to anticipate them in a participatory manner [24]. InaRISK Personal is a development of the InaRISK portal, officially launched on November 10, 2016, by the Head of the National Disaster Management Agency (BNPB). The presence of the inaRISK Personal application on mobile phone users is expected to make the Indonesian nation resilient to disasters and meet the demands of technological advancement [25].

Several goals are expected from the InaRISK Personal application, including a tool for disseminating the results of disaster risk studies to the Government, Regional Government, and other stakeholders as a basis for planning disaster risk reduction programs. Assisting the Government, Regional Government, and other parties in formulating strategies for implementing programs, policies, and activities to reduce disaster risk at the national to regional levels. Assist the Government in monitoring the achievement of reducing the disaster risk index in Indonesia. As well as providing spatial data for other analytical purposes, such as GCDS (Global Center Disaster Statistics), MHEWS, revision of spatial planning, etc.

There are several features of the InaRISK Personal Application. First, the menu for the latest earthquake event information. Second, the Settings menu Column location search. Third, the button to determine the level of danger at the cursor location. Fourth, the threat layer display button. Fifth, InaRisk's other feature menu (especially Covid-19 risk assessment and preparedness for personnel, family, and village) [26]. Meanwhile, currently, there are 13 lists of types of disasters provided by the InaRISK Personal application, including floods, flash floods, extreme weather, extreme waves and abrasion, earthquakes, forest and land fires, droughts, volcanic eruptions, landslides, tsunamis, multi-hazards., and Covid-19.

3   Method

This study uses a qualitative descriptive research method to broadly describe the InaRISK Personal application in increasing disaster mitigation knowledge for its users. The analysis of this research uses the help of Q-DAS (Qualitative Data Analysis Software), namely Nvivo 12 plus software, to collect, manage, and analyze data effectively, efficiently, and with validity. Data sources for this research include the National Disaster Management Agency (BNPB)'s the official website, InaRISK's online news, and previous analyses related to InaRISK and Disaster Mitigation.

Table 1. Websites and Online Media

Website		Amount of Data
BNPB RI	https://bnpb.go.id/	10
InaRISK BNPB RI	https://inarisk.bnpb.go.id/	5
Online Media		
Kompas.com	https://www.kompas.com/	6
AntaraNews.com	https://www.antaranews.com/	6
CnnIndonesia.com	https://www.cnnindonesia.com/	6
Republika.com	https://www.republika.co.id/	6

The data was obtained using the Ncapture feature on Nvivo 12 plus with Web Chrome to capture web content in the form of website, social media, and other document content.

Visualization of the Nvivo 12 plus analysis in this study uses four features, namely, the Crosstab Query feature, to find automatic calculations between all data. Chart Analysis feature to study, process data in research, and analyze answers. The Word Cloud Analysis feature finds occurring words from data findings or views frequently spoken terms. Cluster Analysis feature to visualize and collect data/words with similarities and differences Table 1.

4 Result and Discussion

4.1 InaRISK Personal Application Information

Since the Covid-19 pandemic, the Government has started implementing electronic system-based public services [27]. The ease of using the InaRISK Personal application can be seen from the various information presented through four main features [28].

1. Information on Disaster Hazards and Mitigation
2. Users will be provided with information regarding the level of danger in the vicinity, along with suggestions for mitigation. There is also practical education on the dangers of disaster threats. Digital-based hazard maps can identify risk areas more accurately, informatively, and quickly, so they need to be introduced to Disaster Risk Reduction education [29].
3. Covid-19 Self Assessment.
4. Users will be asked to answer several questions as a self-assessment. Then, the application will display the results of the assessment as well as recommendations for the closest referral hospital to the user's location. The more appropriate and accurate the answers the user gives, the more accurate the results and recommendations. The COVID-19 pandemic paves the way for theoretically extending and integrating technology acceptance models, addressing public concerns based on feedback, and ultimately increasing the use of detection applications [30].
5. Report Prevention Activities
6. This feature serves as a Covid-19 prevention activity around the user. The results of the activity report will be placed spatially and forwarded to local authorities as material for consideration of programs and policies related to handling Covid-19. Information on disasters needs to be collected to analyze the impact of disasters and the priority of disaster risk mitigation based on the risk analysis results [31].
7. ACeBS Survey Feature (Quick Assessment of Simple Buildings)
8. This feature assesses earthquake-resistant house standards and education about earthquake-resistant building planning through a visual assessment survey containing questions about elements of earthquake-safe structural rules. Foundations/slops, columns, walls, roof beams/ring balks, details of reinforcement at the end nodes of beams and columns, connections, roof support structures or trusses, roof support structures in the form of camping/mountains, and roof coverings [32].

The data above shows that the information in the InaRISK Personal application is suitable for providing disaster education to the public. Based on the four data sources, it is proven that the total percentage of the information contained in InaRISK Personal is 42% or is in the first position Fig. 1. The supporting features influence this, the choice

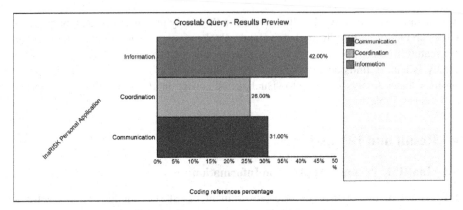

Fig. 1. Quality Information on InaRISK Personal App

of exciting words and the information conveyed quickly, clearly, and accurately on the condition that the user has filled out some of the questions available in the application to find out the vulnerability of disaster threats. The information must reflect the intent and purpose, not be late in conveying and be useful [33]. Information is an essential factor in assessing the success of an application because if the information provided matches what is needed, then people will not want to use the application [34].

4.2 InaRISK Personal Application Communication

The InaRISK Personal application is committed to providing excellent and real-time communication services to each user so that the community participates in disaster mitigation [35]. When users start accessing the InaRISK Personal application to find out about the Disaster they are worried about, the application will respond quickly. Still, the user's internet network condition must also be ensured to support. Using communication and crisis management through technology is becoming increasingly important to analyze and address the needs of diverse stakeholders for timely and reliable information [36] Fig. 2.

The following analysis uses the Word Cloud feature to find words that often appear and are discussed in the research topic. Word Cloud will clearly show the types of words that appear in online media and the BNPB website regarding the InaRISK Personal application. The following are the results of the 50 most dominating comments on this topic from several research sources, which can be seen in Fig. 3 below:

The data from the analysis of the Would Cloud feature above shows that the words that often appear are Disaster and Mitigation. The Law of the Republic of Indonesia Number 24 of 2007 concerning Disaster Management states that a disaster is an event or series of events that threatens and disrupts people's lives and livelihoods caused, both by natural factors and non-natural factors as well as human factors, resulting in human casualties, environmental damage, property loss, and psychological impact [37]. Disaster mitigation is essential as an immediate action to reduce disaster risk, especially concerning human victims [38]. The analysis results above show that the InaRISK Personal Application provides easy access for the application user community to gain knowledge

Fig. 2. Communication on InaRISK Personal App

and understanding related to disaster management according to the primary purpose of creating the InaRISK Personal application. Then the next word that often appears is the InaRISK Personal, Education, Information, and Risk application which is the topic of this research. The disaster mitigation recommendation mechanism already available in the InaRISK Personal application has been adapted to disaster conditions around the user, with additional mitigation knowledge displayed in simple and easy-to-understand language.

4.3 Coordination of InaRISK Personal Applications

The National Disaster Management Agency (BNPB), as the pioneer of the InaRISK Personal application, tries to introduce this application widely through several socialization activities at the community and volunteer levels. This is done because the users of this application are still relatively low, while the Coordination carried out by BNPB with several stakeholders has been going well. The InaRISK Personal application receives support from various parties, such as the Ministry of Energy and Mineral Resources, the Ministry of Public Works and Public Housing, BMKG, and other institutions, especially the provision of data. Cooperation is very much needed, especially at all societal levels, to realize a program to achieve the previously planned goals [39]. In-depth campaigns are needed through opportunities to collaborate with government agencies such as the Ministry of Education and the Disaster Management Agency to expand mobile applications so that parents, teachers, and children can use them [40].

The cluster analysis feature above shows the interrelationships between all indicators. The cluster analysis results help determine the coordination connectivity that is established for the success of the InaRISK Personal application. Based on the table above, it is the coefficient number between indicators, where the information coefficient has the most substantial relationship with the communication coefficient, as much as 0.863034. The coordination coefficient with the communication coefficient also includes a strong relationship of 0.840994. Meanwhile, the weakest coefficient relationship is information with Coordination, with a coefficient of 0.676237. This shows that the Coordination can still be developed because, currently, there are few users of the InaRISK Personal application. Follow-up actions are needed to realize disaster mitigation, such as socialization to all components of society, especially in areas with potential disasters. Community disaster education is essential in minimizing disaster risk, including Information systems, Warning systems, and Response mechanisms [41]. Preparedness is reflected in the characteristics of the actors (i.e., their experience, knowledge, and skills), the roles and responsibilities assigned to each other, and the existing structures and networks [42].

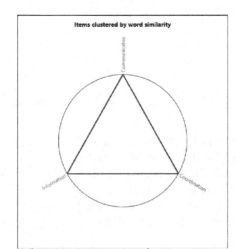

Code A	Code B	Pearson correlation coefficient
Information	Communication	0.863034
Coordination	Communication	0.840994
Information	Coordination	0.676237

Fig. 3. Connectivity Coordination with other indicators

5   Conclusions

Disaster mitigation programs are needed to monitor, plan, and improve disaster management systems, especially in the digital era. The InaRISK Personal application is expected to increase public awareness of surrounding disasters, especially during the Covid-19 pandemic. An application designed to be easy to use and up to date as a medium for disaster mitigation education. However, it is necessary to increase socialization in all components of society, especially in areas with potential disasters. The results showed that the disaster mitigation information contained in the InaRISK Personal application was good, with the highest score of 42%, then the communication carried out was also reasonably good, with a percentage of 31%. It is just that Coordination shows the lowest rate of 26%, so it must be improved, especially in terms of socialization. Innovations in disaster mitigation will continue to be carried out, especially adjusting the development of digital technology. The story of the InaRISK Personal application must continue to be encouraged to provide disaster education to the public more broadly, effectively, and efficiently. This study has limited research on social media in describing disaster communication contained in the InaRISK Personal application, so further research is expected to examine social media strategies in attracting interest in using these applications to increase additional literacy related to disaster mitigation applications.

References

1. Buchari, R.A.: Manajemen Mitigasi Bencana dengan Kelembagaan Masyarakat di Daerah Rawan Bencana Kabupaten Garut Indonesia. Sawala J. Pengabdi. Masy. Pembang. Sos. Desa dan Masy. **1**(1), 1, (2020). https://doi.org/10.24198/sawala.v1i1.25836
2. Karim, R., Conoras, W.A., Rasai, J.: Identifikasi Daerah Rawan Bencana Alam Gerakan Tanah Di Wilayah Maluku Utara. Dintek **12**(September), 58–67 (2019)
3. Masum, M., Ali Akbar, M.: The pacific ring of fire are working as a home country of geothermal resources in the world. IOP Conf. Ser. Earth Environ. Sci. **249**(1), 1 (2019). https://doi.org/10.1088/1755-1315/249/1/012020
4. cnbcindonesia.com, "Kepala BNPB: Hingga 26 Juni, 1.902 Bencana Alam Terjadi di RI." https://www.cnbcindonesia.com/news/20220627153814-4-350721/kepala-bnpb-hingga-26-juni-1902-bencana-alam-terjadi-di-ri
5. Mufarida, B.: BNPB Catat 1.902 Bencana Melanda Indonesia hingga Juni 2022. Okezone.com (2022). https://nasional.okezone.com/read/2022/06/27/337/2619000/bnpb-catat-1-902-bencana-melanda-indonesia-hingga-juni-2022
6. BNPB luncurkan inaRISK, Risiko Bencana Indonesia Teridentifikasi. https://bogorkab.go.id/post/detail/bnpb-luncurkan-inarisk-risiko-bencana-indonesia-teridentifikasi
7. Sufiyanto, S., Yuniarti, S., Andrijono, D.: Sosialisasi dan edukasi penilaian mandiri terhadap risiko penularan COVID-19 melalui InaRISK Personal. Abdimas: Jurnal Pengabdian Masyarakat Universitas Merdeka Malang **5**(3), 209–219 (2020). https://doi.org/10.26905/abdimas.v5i3.5004
8. Syaiful, F.L., Fitria, D.: Penerapan Inarisk Personal Bagi Masyarakat Purwodadi Di Kecamatan Argamakmur Kabupaten Bengkulu Utara Sebagai Upaya Mitigasi Bencana Dan Penularan Covid-19. **5**(2), 77–89 (2022). https://doi.org/10.25077/jhi.v5i2.605
9. Tsamroh, D.I., Devi Permata Wijaya, N., Zuhria Sugeha, A.: Penilaian Risiko Penularan Covid-19 pada Peserta Didik di Kampung Inggris Menggunakan Aplikasi InaRisk. Pros. Semin. Nas. Pengabdi. Masy. Univ. Ma Chung **1**, 231–239 (2021). https://doi.org/10.33479/senampengmas.2021.1.1.231-239
10. Yusuf, R.M.S., Jumhur, H.M.: Penerapan E-Government Dalam Membangun Smart City Pada Kota Bandung Tahun 2018 E- Government Implementation in Building Smart City in Bandung 2018. E-Proceeding Manag. **5**(3), pp. 3126–3130 (2018). https://journal.trunojoyo.ac.id/iniciolegis/article/download/8822/4912
11. Davis, A., Carter, F.: Disaster Mitigation. Idosr J. Sci. Technol. **5**(1), 18–22 (2020)
12. Wekke, I.S.: Mitigasi Bencana, I. Indramayu, Jawa Barat: Penerbit Adab, 2021
13. Faturahman, B.M.: Konseptualisasi Mitigasi Bencana Melalui Perspektif Kebijakan Publik. PUBLISIA J. Ilmu Adm. Publik **3**(2), 123–133 (2018)

14. Henstra, D., Minano, A., Thistlethwaite, J.: Communicating disaster risk? An evaluation of the availability and quality of flood maps. Nat. Hazards Earth Syst. Sci. **19**(1), 313–323 (2019). https://doi.org/10.5194/nhess-19-313-2019

15. Utami, S.P.: Kesiapsiagaan Warga Sekolah Dalam Menghadapi Bencana Gempa Bumi Di SMP-SMA Plus Amanah Muhammadiyah Kota Siliwangi. (2018)

16. Lestari, P.: Model Komunikasi Bencana Berbasis Masyarakat, 1st ed. Sleman, Yogyakarta: PT Kanisius (2018)

17. Bahan Pembelajaran Pencegahan dan Mitigasi. Kementerian Pertahanan RI Badan Pendidikan dan Pelatihan. (2016)

18. Idris, B.N.A., Yugiantari, G., Hadi, I.: Upaya Peningkatan Perilaku Mitigasi Bencana Berbasis Aplikasi Pencegahan Resiko Insiden Pandemi Covid-19 Pada Remaja Daerah Pesisir. J. Ilmu Keperawatan Jiwa **4**(1), 79–86 (2021)

19. Rudiastuti, A.W., Suryanegara, E., Prihanto, Y.: Application Design: Community Response to Disaster Information System Features, pp. 82–89 (2022). https://doi.org/10.5220/001079 4700003317

20. Putra, A.W.S., Podo, Y.: Faktor-faktor yang mempengaruhi tingkat pengetahuan masyarakat dalam mitigasi bencana alam tanah longsor. Urecol 6th, pp. 305–314 (2017)

21. Djoumessi, Y.F., de B. Mbongo, L.: An analysis of information communication technologies for natural disaster management in Africa. Int. J. Disaster Risk Reduct. **68**, (2022). https://doi.org/10.1016/j.ijdrr.2021.102722

22. Adisel, Prananosa, A.G.: Penggunaan Teknologi Informasi dan Komunikasi dalam Sistem Manajemen Pembelajaran pada Masa Pandemi Covid 19. ALIGNMENTJournal Adm. Educ. Manag. **3**(1), 1–10 (2020). https://doi.org/10.31539/alignment.v3i1.1291

23. Wijayanti, D.: Pelatihan pembuatan dokumen penanggulangan bencana berbasis IT di LPB MDMC PDM Bantul. Masy. Berdaya dan Inov. **3**(1), 1–4 (2022)

24. InaRISK Personal. https://inarisk.bnpb.go.id/about

25. Kurniawan, N., et al: The use of personal inarisk media in improving the concept of disaster information literacy in social studies learning. Ristic **1**(1), 1–11 (2020)

26. Kuliah Tamu 'Mengenal Aplikasi Kebencanaan INARISK' bersama Ridwan Yunus dari BNPB (2022). https://www.its.ac.id/tgeofisika/id/kuliah-tamu-mengenal-aplikasi-keb encanaan-inarisk-bersama-ridwan-yunus-dari-bnpb/

27. Katz, R.L., Callorda, F.M., Jung, J.: Can Digitization Mitigate COVID-19 Damages? Evidence from Developing Countries. SSRN Electron. J.1–25 (2020). https://doi.org/10.2139/ssrn.360 0829

28. "Panduan Singkat InaRISK Personal." https://inarisk.bnpb.go.id/panduan_singkat_ina.pdf

29. Jiali, S., Yamauchi, H., Oguchi, T., Ogura, T.: Application of Web Hazard Maps to High School Education for Disaster Risk Reduction. Int. J. Disaster Risk Reduct., **72**(1) (2022). https://doi.org/10.1016/j.ijdrr.2022.102866

30. Alsyouf, A., et al.: Exposure detection applications acceptance: the case of COVID-19. Int. J. Environ. Res. Public health **19**(12), (2022). https://doi.org/10.3390/ijerph19127307

31. Rahardjo, S.: Mengelola Cagar Budaya di Wilayah Rawan Bencana Apakah Indonesia Sudah Siap?. Pros. Balai Arkeol. Jawa Barat, pp. 283–303 (2021). https://doi.org/10.24164/prosid ing.v4i1.26

32. Hamzah, A., Amri, M.R., Rozita, E., Yunus, R.: Penilaian Bangunan Sederhana di Kawasan Rawan Gempabumi: Studi Kasus di Kota Bengkulu dan Kabupaten Bengkulu Tengah. J. Dialog Penanggulangan Bencana **11**(1), 13–21 (2020)

33. Yuni, F.: Analisis Pemanfaatan Berbagai Media Sosial sebagai Sarana Penyebaran Informasi bagi Masyarakat. Paradig. - J. Komput. dan Inform. **19**(2), 152 (2017)

34. Ragini, J.R., Anand, P.M.R., Bhaskar, V.: Big data analytics for disaster response and recovery through sentiment analysis. Int. J. Inf. Manage. **42**(May), 13–24 (2018). https://doi.org/10.1016/j.ijinfomgt.2018.05.004

35. Barata, G.K., Lestari, P., Hendariningrum, R.: Model Komunikasi Untuk Penanggulangan Bencana Gunung Merapi Melalui Aplikasi Plewengan. J. Commun. Spectr. **7**(2), 31–45 (2018). https://doi.org/10.36782/jcs.v7i2.1782

36. Stute, M., Maass, M., Schons, T., Kaufhold, M.A., Reuter, C., Hollick, M.: Empirical insights for designing information and communication technology for international disaster response. Int. J. Disaster Risk Reduct. **47**(July), 2020 (2019). https://doi.org/10.1016/j.ijdrr.2020.101598

37. *Undang-Undang Republik Indonesia Nomor 24 Tahun 2007 Tentang Penanggulangan Bencana*

38. Que, T., Wu, Y., Hu, S., Cai, J., Jiang, N., Xing, H.: Factors influencing public participation in community disaster mitigation activities: a comparison of model and nonmodel disaster mitigation communities. Int. J. Environ. Res. Public Health **19**(19), 12278 (2022). https://doi.org/10.3390/ijerph191912278

39. Nainggolan, D.P.: Strategi Penerapan E-Government di Kota Pekanbaru. JOM FISIP **5**(1), 1–13 (2018)

40. Thontowi, M.: Bumikita Mobile Application: The Starting Point of a Children-Centred Approach for Multi Hazard Early Warning System in Indonesia. In: Murayama, Y., Velev, D., Zlateva, P. (eds.) ITDRR 2020. IAICT, vol. 622, pp. 102–115. Springer, Cham (2021). https://doi.org/10.1007/978-3-030-81469-4_9

41. Fuady, M., Munadi, R., Fuady, M.A.K.: Disaster mitigation in Indonesia: between plans and reality. IOP Conf. Ser. Mater. Sci. Eng. **1087**(1), 012011 (2021). https://doi.org/10.1088/1757-899x/1087/1/012011

42. Nespeca, V., Comes, T., Meesters, K., Brazier, F.: Towards coordinated self-organization: An actor-centered framework for the design of disaster management information systems. Int. J. Disaster Risk Reduct. **51**, 101887 (2020). https://doi.org/10.1016/j.ijdrr.2020.101887

Using Agent-Based Modeling to Understand Complex Social Phenomena - A Curriculum Approach

André Calero Valdez[1]([✉]) [iD], Johannes Nakayama[2] [iD], Luisa Vervier[2] [iD],
Hendrik Nunner[1] [iD], and Martina Ziefle[2] [iD]

[1] Institute for Multimedia and Interactive Systems, University of Lübeck,
Ratzeburger Allee 160, 23562 Lübeck, Germany
{calerovaldez,nunner}@imis.uni-luebeck.de
[2] Human-Computer Interaction Center, RWTH Aachen University,
Campus Boulevard 57, 52076 Aachen, Germany
johannes.nakayama@rwth-aachen.de, {vervier,ziefle}@comm.rwth-aachen.de

Abstract. Agent-based modeling (ABM) is a powerful tool for studying complex systems that involve multiple agents interacting with each other and their environment. However, there is a lack of comprehensive and easily accessible resources for learning about ABM and its applications. To address this issue, collaboration on developing an open curriculum on ABM for university seminars is proposed. An open curriculum would allow for the sharing of expertise and knowledge across disciplines and institutions, be more accessible to a broader audience, and foster greater collaboration and cooperation among researchers and practitioners in the field of ABM. This would ultimately improve the accessibility and impact of ABM as a tool for understanding and predicting the behavior of complex systems. We propose a curriculum comprising six modules covering the introduction to ABM, building an ABM, analyzing and interpreting results, real-world applications, advanced topics, and future directions.

Keywords: Agent-based modeling

1 Introduction

In today's world, phenomena are becoming increasingly complex due to the interplay between people and technology, which can result in **emergent behavior and feedback loops**. Understanding and predicting these phenomena require the use of complexity-enabled methods, which combine empirical and theoretical elements. One such method that has gained popularity in recent years is agent-based modeling (ABM).

ABM is a computational method that **simulates the behavior of individual agents and their interactions within a complex system**. It allows researchers to model complex systems and analyze the emergent behavior that arises from the interactions of individual agents. ABM has been used to model a wide range of complex systems, including social, economic, and environmental systems.

Despite the growing popularity of ABM, it is still **not widely incorporated into university and school curricula**. This is because ABM requires knowledge from multiple disciplines, and interdisciplinary education is still lacking in many institutions. However, there have been some efforts to develop curricula that incorporate ABM into social science education.

For example, the Center for the Study of Complex Systems at the University of Michigan offers a graduate-level course in agent-based modeling for social science research. The course covers the basics of ABM, including agent behavior, agent interactions, and model validation, and **introduces students to the NetLogo programming language**, which is commonly used for ABM.

Similarly, the Santa Fe Institute offers a short course on agent-based modeling for the social sciences, which covers the fundamentals of ABM and its applications in various fields, including economics, sociology, and political science.

To demonstrate the effectiveness of ABM in understanding complex phenomena, researchers have used it to model a wide range of systems, including the spread of infectious diseases, the dynamics of financial markets, and the behavior of social networks.

For example, Epstein and Axtell in 1996 [10] used the emergence of residential segregation in a city **constructed from first principles**, demonstrating how individual preferences for neighborhood diversity can lead to the formation of segregated neighborhoods. Another study by Eubank et al. in 2004 [11] used ABM to **model the spread of infectious diseases**, showing how different control strategies can affect the spread of disease.

ABM is a powerful tool for modeling complex systems and understanding emergent behavior. While its interdisciplinary nature presents challenges for incorporating it into social science curricula, there have been efforts to develop ABM-focused courses and resources to support its adoption. To support these efforts, we propose an open curriculum for teaching ABM in the social sciences.

2   Related Work

This section briefly overviews agent-based modeling (ABM) as a tool and its historical development. Additionally, it discusses the essential aspects that must be considered while developing a curriculum for ABM. A proposed content outline is also presented, along with a discussion of the significance of collaboration in creating an Open Curriculum for ABM.

2.1   Agent-Based Modeling

An agent-based model comprises **three essential components** [10]. The central element of an agent-based model is the **agent** itself. An agent has internal states that change dynamically upon interaction with other agents or the environment. The second component is the **environment**, representing the space the agents populate. In Epstein and Axtell's words, the environment is "a medium separate from the agents, on which the agents operate and with which they interact" [10]. The last component is a **set of rules** that links the agents with their environment by defining how they change their internal states and environment in the simulation [9].

One of the **first agent-based models** that gained traction in the social sciences was put forward by Schelling in 1971 [15], who described a model intended to depict **racial segregation in urban areas**. In its most basic layout, the model consists of two types of agents (e.g., conceptualized as blue and orange agents) that live on a square lattice. Based on the fraction of similar agents in their Moore neighborhood [13], agents determine whether they are satisfied or unsatisfied with their current "home" in the network. The condition for **satisfaction is given by a global threshold**, which defines the fraction of agents in an agent's neighborhood, which must be similar. Unsatisfied agents relocate to a random empty square on the lattice. When this model is played out for a sufficient amount of simulation steps, **segregated neighborhoods of agents of the same color emerge**. The most striking property of Schelling's model was that this **segregation is even observable for high tolerance values** as defined by the satisfaction threshold.

Schelling's approach would later heavily influence a series of modeling attempts that can be summarized under the umbrella of **generative social science** as described by Epstein and Axtell [10], and Epstein [7]. The authors argue that specific macroscopic system-level patterns should be investigated from the bottom up. The distinguishing element of this approach is a shift in focus from the particular **individual strategy to the macroscopic pattern**. If a measure of fit between the simulated and the (empirically) observed pattern can be developed, the new paradigm is to generate candidate rules that give rise to emergent patterns. The fitness with regard to the observed patterns becomes the quality metric of the model [7]. To our knowledge, there is still no consensus about a formal metric of this kind. In many modeling attempts, **the fit of the simulated pattern with the observed phenomena was mainly determined qualitatively**, predominantly through visualization.

One early example that explicitly adhered to the paradigm put forward by Epstein and Axtell [10] was Axelrod's model of the **dissemination of culture** [1]. The model aimed to generate candidate explanations for a conundrum Axelrod puzzled over. If one assumes that **people that are close to each other converge in their views and opinions**, why does everyone not become the same eventually, and **how can global polarization still occur**?

In the model, agents are organized on a fully populated square lattice, meaning each agent is connected to its four neighbors (think north, east, south, and west). Each agent has a "culture", which is represented by a vector of fixed length whose elements are instances of an arbitrary categorical alphabet. The

cultural similarity between two agents is calculated as the fraction of cultural traits they share (i.e., dimensions of the vector that are identical).

In each step of the simulation, one agent is chosen at random. This agent then applies one simple rule to update its internal state represented by the culture vector. He calculates the similarity with one randomly chosen neighbor. Then he **changes one of his dissimilar cultural dimensions to that of the other agent with a probability equal to their similarity.** When these rules are played out sufficiently long in a simulation, **regions of cultural similarity that are entirely separate from each other emerge.**

The crucial detail that led to this global pattern was that Axelrod made the **local convergence of culture conditional on the ex-ante similarity** of the two agents. That is to say that locally proximal individuals do not unconditionally converge in their views and opinions but only do so if they already share certain traits.

On a related note, Epstein [8] studied the opposite phenomenon of why some behaviors are widely adopted by the majority of a population, i.e., **the emergence of social norms.** In this model, agents inhabit a one-dimensional lattice and possess the **two attributes of norm and radius.** The norm is a binary factor whose states are represented by the letters L and R (for driving on the left or the right side of the road, respectively, which Epstein uses as an example norm). The **radii are heterogeneous between agents**, and they determine the number of agents that an agent samples to both of their sides when updating their internal norm.

As in the model of the dissemination of culture, the state updates in this model happen asynchronously and randomly. In each simulation step, the agents are activated in random order and update their norm according to a set of simple rules. First, an activated agent checks the predominant norm in her neighborhood as defined by her internal radius attribute. Then, the agent checks **if the resulting norm would change if the radius were increased by one.** If this is the case, the agent increases her radius by one. If the norm does not change, the agent determines whether the norm would change if she decreased her radius by 1. If it does not, the agent decreases her radius by one. Otherwise, she leaves her radius at the original value.

Epstein describes this kind of normative perception with the **intuitive conceptualization of "lazy statisticians."** The agents will reduce the size of the samples they use to determine the predominant social norm if this does not change the result, and they only increase their sample sizes when the results do change. Put differently, they are "lazy" in the sense that they minimize their samples to determine the predominant norm.

Running a series of experiments with this model, Epstein was able to produce **patterns that exhibit local conformity and global diversity**, meaning that the model allows for both local convergence of behavior as well as regional emergence of different norms.

There are several available software options to implement agent-based models. The recent improvements and broader accessibility of computational resources have made the approach of ABMS significantly more viable. A **well-established and popular option is the NetLogo software** [17] introduced by Wilensky in 1999 that provides a simple programming language based on the educational language Logo along with an integrated visualization framework for agent-based models.

More recently, the programming language **Julia** [3] **has been considered to be a promising option for agent-based modeling**. Burbach et al. [4] compared both options and concluded that each of them has favorable properties. However, they prefer Julia as a more reliable option for more computationally and conceptually complex models. A framework for agent-based modeling in Julia is provided by a software package called Agents.jl [16] which implements a domain-specific language for ABMs and includes data collection and visualization capabilities.

3   Designing Curricula

Developing a curriculum is a complex and multifaceted process involving several different factors and considerations. In general, **a well-designed curriculum should be based on a clear understanding of the program's goals and objectives**, the students' needs and interests, and the latest research and best practices in the field, which in our case, will be agent-based modeling.

Recent literature on curriculum development emphasizes the importance of a **learner-centered approach,** which focuses on the needs and interests of the students and the development of their **critical thinking, problem-solving, and communication skills** [2]. This approach can involve a range of pedagogical strategies, such as active learning, collaborative learning, and problem-based learning, which can help to engage students and promote their learning and development.

In the specific case of a university seminar on agent-based modeling, the curriculum would need to cover the fundamental principles and concepts of this approach, as well as the latest developments and applications in the field. This could include topics such as the basics of agent-based modeling, the benefits and limitations of this approach, and how to implement and evaluate agent-based models.

Overall, developing a curriculum is a dynamic and ongoing process that requires careful planning, research, and collaboration. By taking into account the **latest research and best practices** and by involving experts and stakeholders in the process, it is possible to **develop a curriculum that is effective, engaging, and relevant for students** [12].

4   Curriculum Development

ABM is a computational approach for modeling and simulating the actions and interactions of autonomous agents within a system. It is **a powerful tool for**

understanding and predicting the behavior of complex systems, particularly those that involve multiple agents interacting with each other and their environment [6].

In the following we present an outline for an empirical-based curriculum on ABM for a university seminar using six modules:

1. Introduction to Agent-Based Modeling. The first module of a course on Agent-Based Modeling (ABM) should introduce students to the **key concepts and principles** of this tool for studying complex systems. In the first session, the course should start with an overview of ABM, including its definition and key characteristics. It should discuss why ABM is useful for studying complex systems, using examples such as social networks, traffic flow, and economic systems. A second session should focus on the basic **concepts and terminology** of ABM. Students will learn about agents, which are the individual entities that make up the system being modeled, and the rules and interactions that govern their behavior. They will also explore how agents can be programmed to interact with each other and the environment and how these **interactions can give rise to emergent behavior** at the system level.

2. Building an Agent-Based Model. In the second module, students should learn how to define **agents and their properties**, specify the rules and interactions among agents, and implement the model in a programming language. They will also learn how to validate and calibrate the model to ensure that it accurately represents the real-world system being studied.

3. Analyzing and Interpreting the Results. The third module should focus on analyzing and interpreting the results of the model. Students will learn how to visualize and analyze the output of the model, interpret the results in the context of the real-world system being modeled, and evaluate the robustness and sensitivity of the model.

4. Applications of Agent-Based Modeling. In the fourth module, students should explore **real-world applications** (e.g., disease dynamics [14]) of agent-based modeling and the role of ABM in **policy and decision-making**. They will also discuss the ethical implications of using ABM to model complex systems.

5. Advanced Topics in Agent-Based Modeling. The fifth module should cover advanced topics in agent-based modeling, such as incorporating **spatial and temporal dynamics**, modeling **networked systems** (see Fig. 1 or [5]), and incorporating **machine learning and data analytics** into ABM.

6. Conclusions and Future Directions. Finally, in the sixth module, students should summarize the key takeaways from the course and discuss emerging **trends and challenges** in ABM research and practice. By the end of the course, students will have the skills and knowledge to create and analyze agent-based models of complex systems and will be prepared to **apply these techniques in their own research** and professional practice.

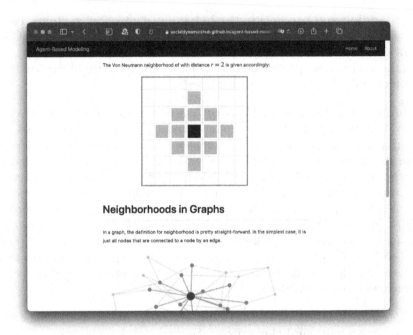

Fig. 1. Comparing different types of spaces in ABM

5   Call for Collaboration on the Open Curriculum

ABM involves the creation of computational models that simulate the actions and interactions of autonomous agents within a system and has been applied to a wide range of fields, including e.g., economics, biology, and sociology, among others. Despite its growing importance, however, there is a **lack of comprehensive and easily accessible resources for learning about ABM** and its applications. This is particularly true for university seminars, where students and researchers may not have access to specialized courses or textbooks on the subject. This is where collaboration on the development of an open curriculum on ABM for university seminars becomes crucial. Such a curriculum, created through the collective efforts of researchers and practitioners from diverse disciplines and backgrounds, would **provide a valuable resource for students and researchers** seeking to learn about ABM and its applications.

There are several potential benefits to this type of collaboration. First, an open curriculum would allow for the **sharing of expertise and knowledge across disciplines and institutions**. Researchers and practitioners from different fields could contribute their unique perspectives and experiences, resulting in a more comprehensive and diverse resource.

Second, an open curriculum would be more **easily accessible to a broader audience**, including students and researchers who may not have access to specialized courses or textbooks. This could help to expand the reach and impact of ABM as a tool for understanding and predicting the behavior of complex systems.

Finally, an open curriculum could **foster greater collaboration and coop-eration** among researchers and practitioners in the field of ABM. By working together to create a shared resource, researchers and practitioners could foster a sense of community and collaboration that would benefit the field as a whole.

In conclusion, collaboration on the development of an open curriculum on ABM for university seminars is an important step towards improving the accessibility and impact of ABM as a tool for understanding and predicting the behavior of complex systems. By bringing together researchers and practitioners from diverse disciplines and backgrounds, such a curriculum could serve as a valuable resource for students and researchers seeking to learn about ABM and its applications.

5.1 Social Dynamics Hub

We propose to organize such an open curriculum in a way that directly supports the decentralized creation of documents as used in the open-source community, i.e., GitHub. For this purpose, we have created a Github organization SocialDynamicsHub (https://github.com/socialdynamicshub) were individual repositories contain either content of modules or interactive notebooks for teaching ABM. One repository automatically renders to a website (see Fig. 2 and Fig. 3) that can serve as a starting point for interested researchers at https://socialdynamicshub.github.io/.

We would be happy to welcome collaborators on this platform.

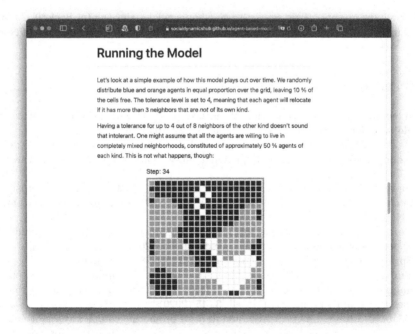

Fig. 2. Screenshot from the website tutorial on the Schelling Model

Fig. 3. Screenshot from the website tutorial on the Forest fire model

Acknowledgements. This research was supported by the Digital Society research program funded by the Ministry of Culture and Science of the German State of North Rhine-Westphalia.

References

1. Axelrod, R.: The dissemination of culture: a model with local convergence and global polarization. J. Conflict Resolut. **41**(2), 203–226 (1997)
2. Baldoni, M., Baroglio, C., Brunkhorst, I., Henze, N., Marengo, E., Patti, V.: Constraint modeling for curriculum planning and validation. Interact. Learn. Environ. **19**(1), 81–123 (2011)
3. Bezanson, J., Edelman, A., Karpinski, S., Shah, V.B.: Julia: a fresh approach to numerical computing. SIAM Rev. **59**(1), 65–98 (2017). https://doi.org/10.1137/141000671
4. Burbach, L., et al.: Netlogo vs. Julia: evaluating different options for the simulation of opinion dynamics. In: Duffy, V.G. (ed.) HCII 2020. LNCS, vol. 12199, pp. 3–19. Springer, Cham (2020). https://doi.org/10.1007/978-3-030-49907-5_1
5. Burbach, L., Halbach, P., Ziefle, M., Calero Valdez, A.: Opinion formation on the internet: the influence of personality, network structure, and content on sharing messages online. Front. Artif. Intell. **3**, 45 (2020)
6. Eilam, B., Reisfeld, D.: A curriculum unit for promoting complex system thinking: the case of combined system dynamics and agent based models for population growth. J. Adv. Educ. Res. **2**(2), 39–60 (2017)

7. Epstein, J.M.: Agent-based computational models and generative social science. Complexity **4**(5), 41–60 (1999)
8. Epstein, J.M.: Learning to be thoughtless: social norms and individual computation. Comput. Econ. **18**, 9–24 (2001)
9. Epstein, J.M.: Modeling civil violence: an agent-based computational approach. Proc. Nat. Acad. Sci. **99**(suppl_3), 7243–7250 (2002)
10. Epstein, J.M., Axtell, R.: Growing Artificial Societies: Social Science from the Bottom Up. MIT Press (1996)
11. Eubank, S.G., et al.: Modelling disease outbreaks in realistic urban social networks. Nature **429**(6988), 180–184 (2004)
12. Matkovic, P., Tumbas, P., Sakal, M., Pavlicevic, V.: University stakeholders in the analysis phase of curriculum development process model. In: Proceedings of International Conference of Education, Research and Innovation (ICERI) 2014 Conference, pp. 2340–1095. International Academy of Technology, Education and Development (IATED), Seville (2014)
13. Moore, E.F.: Machine models of self-reproduction. In: Proceedings of the Symposium on Principles of Self-Organization, pp. 17–33 (1962)
14. Retzlaff, C.O., et al.: Fear, behaviour, and the covid-19 pandemic: a city-scale agent-based model using socio-demographic and spatial map data. J. Artif. Soc. Soc. Simul. **25**(1) (2022)
15. Schelling, T.C.: Dynamic models of segregation. J. Math. Sociol. **1**(2), 143–186 (1971)
16. Vahdati, A.R.: Agents.jl: agent-based modeling framework in Julia. J. Open Source Softw. **4**(42), 1611 (2019)
17. Wilensky, U., Rand, W.: An Introduction to Agent-Based Modeling: Modeling Natural, Social, and Engineered Complex Systems with NetLogo. MIT Press (2015)

Policy-Based Reinforcement Learning for Assortative Matching in Human Behavior Modeling

Ou Deng$^{(\boxtimes)}$ and Qun Jin$^{(\boxtimes)}$

Graduate School of Human Sciences, Waseda University, Tokorozawa, Japan
dengou@toki.waseda.jp, jin@waseda.jp

Abstract. This paper explores human behavior in virtual networked communities, specifically individuals or groups' potential and expressive capacity to respond to internal and external stimuli, with assortative matching as a typical example. A modeling approach based on Multi-Agent Reinforcement Learning (MARL) is proposed, adding a multi-head attention function to the A3C algorithm to enhance learning effectiveness. This approach simulates human behavior in certain scenarios through various environmental parameter settings and agent action strategies. In our experiment, reinforcement learning is employed to serve specific agents that learn from environment status and competitor behaviors, optimizing strategies to achieve better results. The simulation includes individual and group levels, displaying possible paths to forming competitive advantages. This modeling approach provides a means for further analysis of the evolutionary dynamics of human behavior, communities, and organizations in various socioeconomic issues.

Keywords: Multiagent system · Reinforcement learning · Game theory · Human behavior modeling

1 Introduction

The exploration of human behavior patterns has mainly relied on quantitative and qualitative actual investigation and analysis and social experiments under certain conditions. These traditional methods cannot avoid many practical limitations, such as the budgetary cost of conducting social surveys and experiments, the difficulty of obtaining data resources, and even ethical and moral constraints. Due to these limitations and difficulties, multiagent system (MAS) simulation and artificial intelligence methods are utilized to assist traditional social investigation and analysis. Even for some social experiments that cannot carry out by ethical or moral restrictions, a well-designed simulation can provide a certain degree of reliable results or help to do counterfactuals in social experiments.

Considering the high complexity of human behavior patterns, we choose a simple but fundamental human behavior – assortative matching – for our social

© The Author(s), under exclusive license to Springer Nature Switzerland AG 2023
V. G. Duffy (Ed.): HCII 2023, LNCS 14029, pp. 378–391, 2023.
https://doi.org/10.1007/978-3-031-35748-0_28

experiments. The matching theory has essential applications in social and economic fields, e.g., labor market, industry planning, and international trade. This study was inspired by a coupling game conceived by Dan Ariely [1], who claimed and guessed that the result would be an *equal matching* when single men and women play such a coupling game under specific rules, without experimenting.

We design and implement simulation experiments with multi-agent systems and machine learning methods, which verify the common-sense-based *equal matching*. In the designed virtual environment, our policy-based reinforcement method improves strategies to enable some agents to obtain competitive advantages over others. The experiments examine the transformation conditions of these competitive advantages and the transformation process, which are essential to the evolving dynamic of social communities.

2 Related Works

Policy-based reinforcement learning is a subfield of reinforcement learning focused on developing algorithms for learning control policies to manage agents in complex environments. The application of policy-based reinforcement learning to assortative matching in human behavior modeling is a relatively new research area.

This area of research emerged in the 2010s,s, when computer scientists and computational social scientists explored the use of reinforcement learning techniques to model and predict relationship formation in large-scale social networks. Early work focused on developing algorithms that can influence relationship formation by incentivizing individuals to form relationships with others who are similar to themselves in specific characteristics.

The use of deep neural networks in reinforcement learning was introduced by Mnih et al. from Google DeepMind [2]. In 2015, the same research group introduced the Deep Q-Network (DQN) algorithm [3], which uses deep neural networks to approximate the action-value function. The algorithm demonstrated superhuman performance in many Atari games. In 2016, the Asynchronous Advantage Actor-Critic (A3C) algorithm [4] was introduced, which uses multiple parallel actors to interact with the environment and reduce the time needed for convergence.

Since then, the field has developed new policy-based reinforcement learning algorithms for assortative matching in online social networks, online dating platforms, and mobile communication networks. These algorithms have been applied to real-world data and provided new insights into the factors that shape relationships and social networks.

The Trust Region Policy Optimization (TRPO) algorithm was introduced by Schulman et al. of OpenAI [5], which uses a trust region constraint to ensure stable updates to the policy. The Proximal Policy Optimization (PPO) algorithm [6] was introduced in 2017, which combines ideas from policy gradient methods and trust region methods to provide a flexible and computationally efficient approach to policy optimization.

Recent research has explored the use of deep reinforcement learning techniques for policy-based assortative matching, which can improve the performance of algorithms and address challenges associated with traditional reinforcement learning algorithms.

However, limited research applied policy-based reinforcement learning to assortative matching in human behavior modeling, a multidisciplinary field combining economics, sociology, and computer science techniques to study the factors that shape relationships and social networks. Most researches in this field have been based on analytical and computational models rather than reinforcement learning approaches.

3   Methods

This study presents a novel reinforcement learning algorithm, the Multi-Head Attention Asynchronous Advantage Actor-Critic (MA-A3C) algorithm, shown in Fig. 1. This approach integrates the Multi-Head Attention mechanism with the classic Asynchronous Advantage Actor-Critic (A3C) algorithm and is specifically designed to address assortative matching problems in reinforcement learning. Given the inherent complexities of human behavior patterns, the proposed MA-A3C algorithm provides a more effective solution for modeling these patterns. Additionally, the algorithm demonstrates scalability and has the potential for more comprehensive applications in research domains involving human behavior modeling.

The A3C algorithm is a widely recognized multi-agent reinforcement learning (MARL) technique that incorporates the actor-critic framework and parallel computing. This multi-agent model is particularly well suited for simulating human behavior, as it employs multiple parallel processing units to learn a policy asynchronously, thus enabling more efficient state space exploration.

Adding the MA-A3C algorithm can improve its performance. This is because the Multi-Head Attention function enables the algorithm to attend to different state space elements more flexibly and in a more fine-grained way. Multi-Head Attention is a common technique in deep learning that allows for creation of multiple attention mechanisms that can be applied to different input elements.

In reinforcement learning, Multi-Head Attention can be used to enable the A3C algorithm to attend to different states based on their relative importance. This can help improve the efficiency of the learning process by enabling the algorithm to focus on the most important elements of the state while ignoring the less important ones.

3.1   Multi-Head Attention Function in A3C Algorithm (MA-A3C)

Let S be the state representation, W_i be the weight matrix for the ith head, and b_i be the bias vector for the ith head. The attention scores for the ith head can be calculated as the dot product of S and W_i with softmax normalization: $a_i = \text{softmax}(S \cdot W_i + b_i)$. Next, the attention scores are used to weight the features

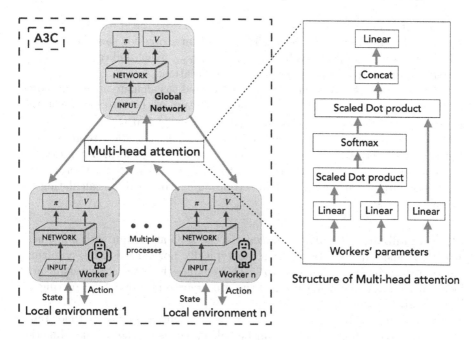

Fig. 1. Multi-Head Attention Asynchronous Advantage Actor-Critic (MA-A3C) network structure. The left section shows the general structure of MA-A3C. The right expand section shows the details of the multi-head attention mechanism.

of the state representation: $S_i = a_i \cdot S$. Finally, the weighted features from each head are concatenated to produce the final enhanced state representation: $S_{\text{final}} = [S_1, S_2, ..., S_H]$, where H is the number of heads. The enhanced state representation is then passed to the policy network to determine the action.

3.2 General Procedures of MA-A3C Algorithm

(1) Enhancing State Representation. The state of the environment can be represented as a vector of features. This representation can be enhanced using normalization, dimensionality reduction, and feature selection techniques. Let $x_t \in R^n$ be the state of the environment at time t, and let $x_t' \in R^m$ be the enhanced representation, where m is the number of features after enhancement. The enhancement process can be expressed as $x_t' = f(x_t)$, where $f(\cdot)$ implements normalization, dimensionality reduction, and feature selection techniques.

For instance, normalization can be performed using the mean and standard deviation of the features. Dimensionality reduction can be achieved using principal component analysis (PCA) or singular value decomposition (SVD) techniques. Feature selection can be performed by selecting the most important features based on some criteria.

(2) Calculating Attention Scores. To compute attention scores for each head, we can use various methods such as dot product attention, scaled dot product attention, or MLP attention. Let $x't \in R^m$ be the state representation and let h be the number of heads. The attention scores for each head can be calculated as a set of scalar values $a_{t,1}, a_{t,2}, ..., a_{t,m}$, which indicate the relative importance of each feature in the state representation.

The dot product attention method can be used to calculate attention scores, where $a_{t,j} = (x't,j)^T \cdot wj$, and $x'_{t,j}$ is the jth feature of the state representation x'_t, and w_j is the weight vector associated with the jth feature.

The attention scores are used to weight each head's state representation features. The weighted features can then be combined to form a context vector representing the state's multi-head attention representation. Alternatively, scaled dot product attention or MLP attention can be used for calculating the attention scores.

(3) Normalizing Attention Scores. In the A3C algorithm with multi-head attention function, attention scores are typically normalized using a softmax function to ensure that they sum to 1. This enables the attention mechanism to focus on the most significant parts of the state representation while ignoring the less important ones.

Let $a_t = [a_{t,1}, a_{t,2}, ..., a_{t,m}]$ be the vector of attention scores for time step t. The normalized attention scores can be calculated using the softmax function expressed in Eq. 1.

$$p_t = \text{softmax}(a_t) = \frac{\exp(a_t)}{\sum_{j=1}^{m} \exp(a_{t,j})} \tag{1}$$

The softmax function maps a vector of real numbers to a probability distribution, ensuring that the attention scores sum to 1, i.e., $\sum_{j=1}^{m} p_{t,j} = 1$.

Normalizing the attention scores allows the A3C algorithm to dynamically weight the features in the state representation based on their importance, resulting in a more effective representation of the state. The attention mechanism can focus on the most important parts of the state representation while ignoring the less important elements, which can improve the performance of the policy-based reinforcement learning algorithm.

(4) Weighting Features. The attention scores are used to weight the features of the state representation. The weighted features are combined using a linear transformation to produce a new, enhanced state representation.

Let $s_t = [s_{t,1}, s_{t,2}, ..., s_{t,n}]$ be the state representation at time step t, and $p_t = [p_{t,1}, p_{t,2}, ..., p_{t,m}]$ be the corresponding normalized attention scores. The weighted state representation can be calculated by Eq. 2.

$$z_t = \sum_{j=1}^{m} p_{t,j} \cdot s_{t,j} \tag{2}$$

This weighted state representation dynamically emphasizes the most important features of the state while ignoring the less important ones. The weighted state representation can then be fed into a neural network or machine learning model for further processing. This results in a more effective representation of the state that can be used for decision-making in the policy-based reinforcement learning algorithm.

(5) Passing Enhanced State to Policy Network. The process of calculating attention scores, normalizing the scores, weighting the features, and passing the enhanced state to the policy network is repeated for each head. This allows the policy network to attend to different parts of the state space using multiple fine-grained attention mechanisms.

Let θ be the parameters of the policy network and $f_\theta(z_t)$ be the function representing the policy network that maps the enhanced state representation z_t to a set of actions. The policy network can be formulated as Eq. 3.

$$a_t = f_\theta(z_t) \tag{3}$$

where $a_t = [a_{t,1}, a_{t,2}, ..., a_{t,k}]$ is the vector of actions output by the policy network for time step t.

The policy network can be trained to maximize a reward signal that reflects the elements' performance in the environment.

The enhanced state representation is fed into the policy network, which outputs a set of actions that can be taken by the elements in the environment. This results in a more effective representation of the state and improved decision-making in the policy-based reinforcement learning algorithm.

(6) Multi-head Attention. To enable the policy network to attend to different parts of the state space using multiple fine-grained attention mechanisms, we repeat the process of calculating attention scores, normalizing the scores, weighting the features, and passing the enhanced state to the policy network for each head.

Let H be the number of heads in the multi-head attention function, and $h \in 1, 2, ..., H$ be the index for each head. For each head h, we calculate the attention scores, $\alpha_{t,h} = [\alpha_{t,h,1}, \alpha_{t,h,2}, ..., \alpha_{t,h,n}]$, using a method such as dot product attention, scaled dot product attention, or multi-layer perceptron attention. We then normalize the attention scores using the softmax function to obtain the normalized attention scores by Eq. 4.

$$\beta_{t,h} = \text{softmax}(\alpha_{t,h}) \tag{4}$$

We then weight the features of the state representation, $s_t = [s_{t,1}, s_{t,2}, ..., s_{t,n}]$, using the normalized attention scores to obtain the weighted features by Eq. 5.

$$z_{t,h} = \sum_{i=1}^{n} \beta_{t,h,i} s_{t,i} \tag{5}$$

Finally, we obtain the enhanced state representation for each head by concatenating the weighted features for each head. That is, $z_t = [z_{t,1}, z_{t,2}, ..., z_{t,H}]$, and this enhanced state representation can then be passed to the policy network to produce a set of actions, $a_t = f_\theta(z_t)$.

This process of applying the multi-head attention function in the A3C algorithm is repeated for each head to allow the policy network to attend to different parts of the state space using multiple fine-grained attention mechanisms.

(7) Updating Policy Network. The policy network is updated using the gradient of the policy objective, which is calculated using the observed rewards and estimated state values. The policy objective is defined as the difference between the expected return and the estimated value of each state, and the gradient of this objective is used to update the policy network.

Let $J(\theta)$ be the policy objective, where θ is the set of parameters of the policy network; R_t is the reward observed at time step t; $V(s_t; \phi)$ is the estimated value of state s_t; γ is the discount factor; and ϕ are the parameters of the value function.

The expected return from state s_t is given by Eq. 6.

$$G_t = R_t + \gamma \cdot V(s_{t+1}; \phi) + \gamma^2 \cdot V(s_{t+2}; \phi) + ... \tag{6}$$

The policy objective is the negative logarithm of the policy, weighted by the advantage function, and is given by Eq. 7.

$$J(\theta) = -\frac{1}{T} \sum_{t=1}^{T} \log \pi_\theta(a_t|s_t) A_t \tag{7}$$

where $\pi_\theta(a_t|s_t)$ is the policy network, and $A_t = G_t - V(s_t; \phi)$ is the advantage function. The gradient of the policy objective concerning the parameters of the policy network is given by Eq. 8.

$$\nabla_\theta J(\theta) = -\frac{1}{T} \sum_{t=1}^{T} \nabla_\theta \log \pi_\theta(a_t|s_t) A_t \tag{8}$$

This gradient is used to update the parameters of the policy network using the Adam optimization algorithm, a variant of stochastic gradient descent. The value function is updated using the mean squared error between the observed returns and the estimated returns.

The policy network is updated iteratively until convergence, at which point the policy network has learned an optimal policy for mapping states to actions. The A3C algorithm has been shown to achieve state-of-the-art performance on a range of benchmark reinforcement learning problems.

4   Experiment and Discussion

4.1   Experimental Environment

Assortative matching games are fundamental games that combine both competition and cooperation. In this study, we develop a simulation model, shown in Fig. 2, using Netlogo (https://ccl.northwestern.edu/netlogo/) based on the "love coupling" idea introduced by Dan Ariely [1]. The model includes a set of basic strategies to simulate human behavior, with the simulation consisting of a population of male and female agents (default=25 each gender) divided into control and experimental groups. The control group only employs the basic strategies predefined in the model, while the experimental group can accept strategy optimization from the python-based MA-A3C reinforcement learning engine during the simulation, shown in Fig. 3.

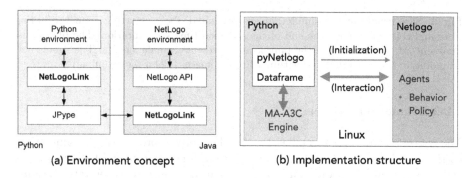

(a) Environment concept   (b) Implementation structure

Fig. 2. Environment construction. (a) Environment concept shows the Multi-agent Reinforcement Learning (MARL) environment concept using Netlogo and Python. (b) Implementation structure shows the MA-A3C engine embedded system implementation structure in this study.

4.2   Experiment Design

4.2.1 General Rules for Agents

Each agent has a unique numerical label (default value in the range [0,24]) and moves within a predefined activity space, searching for agents with higher numerical labels within their visual range. Agents can request pairing with others who accept or reject based on individual strategies. If pairing is successful, the reward value is equal to the sum of the numerical labels of both agents, which is shared equally by the successful agents. The aim of all agents is to obtain higher rewards.

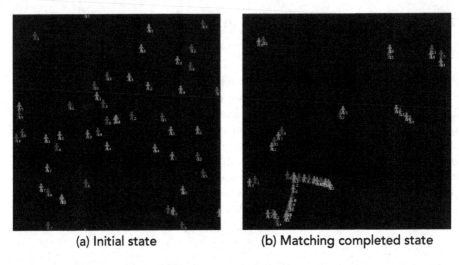

(a) Initial state   (b) Matching completed state

Fig. 3. Screenshots of the simulation are presented above, starting from the initial state and continuing until the end of the specified time step duration. The blue icons represent 'Male' agents, and the pink icons represent 'Female' agents. The agents act according to their own policies within a limited space. (Color figure online)

4.2.2 Evaluation Criteria

The control group serves as a baseline for the study, representing the simulation pairing results without external intervention. The experimental group evaluates whether the MA-A3C reinforcement learning can achieve better-matching results, including whether the agents in the experimental group can successfully match with opposite-sex partners with higher numerical labels compared to those in the control group with the same numerical label. The agents in the experimental group serve as MA-A3C reinforcement learning workers, with their policy network adopting few steps update method and their global network adopting a round-based update method. This study explores the effectiveness of reinforcement learning algorithms in improving assortative matching game outcomes and provides valuable insights into the potential applications of reinforcement learning in social simulation.

4.2.3 Initial Policies and Learnable Variables

For all agents, the following initial strategies are adopted.

Move Policy. The agent selects a target. The target is the opposite-sex agent with the highest numerical label that has not yet successfully paired within the agent's visual range and whose label is not the most recent one in the 'being declined list' (to avoid the excessive pursuit of the same potential partner). If there are no eligible targets, the agent moves randomly.

Offer Policy. The agent sends a pairing offer if the target is within a distance of three steps. At this point, both the sender and the recipient of the offer pause their movement. The recipient of the offer decides to accept or decline based on their decline and accept decision policy.

Decline Policy. For the first n offers received, the agent declines them unconditionally and records the sender's label in their own 'decline list'. The sender of the declined offer records the label of the target in their 'being declined list'. For offers received after the first n, if the sender's label is lower than the maximum value in the 'decline list', the offer is declined.

Accept Policy. For the first n offers received, the agent does not accept any of them. For offers received after the first n, if the sender's label is greater than or equal to the maximum value in the 'decline list', the offer is accepted, and the matching is completed.

Policy Optimization. Different experimental conditions were applied to the control and experimental groups during the game. The control group remained with the same initial policies and underwent no stochastic changes. In contrast, the experimental group underwent policy optimization, with their learnable variables, such as move direction, first decline n, decline list, and being declined list, updated accordingly.

4.3   Experiment Result

Simulation Result of Control Group (Baseline). Based on the evaluation criteria described in Sect. 4.2.2, the experiments simulated the results of all agents in the control group. The goal was to analyze how **equal matching** was affected by different conditions, especially the view range of the agents. As shown in Table 1, a larger view range led to more equal matching. In other words, if some agents in the experimental group were able to match with partners whose numerical labels had a higher-than-average gap, it indicated that the MA-A3C algorithm was effective.

MA-A3C Reinforcement Learning for Policy Optimization. The results of the baseline experiment showed that equal matching was relatively better with a view range of 25, making it appropriate to conduct a mixed experiment with a control and experimental group. We introduced an experimental group (optimized by the MA-A3C reinforcement learning) to examine how much assortative matching changed under this condition. We used the same 50×50 space and agent initialization, similar to the baseline experiment. The only difference was that we selected the smallest 10 labels (i.e., labels in $[0, 9]$) of male and female agents as the experimental group, which was tested within the same time step duration. After the matching was completed, compared to the baseline, the absolute difference of each pairing increased from 1.02 to 7.09, and the variance

Table 1. Baseline results of assortative matching on different view ranges

Abs. label diff.	View range	Trial #1	#2	#3	#4	#5	Ttrials Avg.
Avg. label diff.	5	8.80	8.40	7.56	7.44	6.36	7.71
Standard deviation		5.94	5.88	5.93	6.19	4.70	5.73
Avg. label diff.	15	7.28	3.84	2.96	2.76	5.36	4.44
Standard deviation		6.41	3.31	3.22	3.41	3.76	4.02
Avg. label diff.	25	0.96	0.88	0.64	0.84	1.76	1.02
Standard deviation		1.14	1.01	0.95	1.28	1.56	1.19

Note: Abs. label diff.: Absolute label difference of paired agents.

Avg. label diff.: Average of Abs. label diff.

from 1.19 to 5.80. This indicates that the experimental group agents with smaller label values increased their competitiveness after policy optimization and could match with partners with larger label values. Table 2 shows the detailed results of the experiment conducted five times.

4.4   Discussion

In our experiments, we found that view range had the most significant effect on the absolute deviation of matched pairs, as shown in Table.1. In a non-sparse space, a larger view range typically means more information can be obtained. This information represents potential competitive advantages for agent actions. Individuals with wider fields of view have more reference points for their behavior when they obtain more external information, enabling them to leverage their potential competitive advantages. This characteristic is also reflected in macrosocial and economic behavior, where increased information flow is conducive to better resource flow and matching.

Although the control group and experimental group had the same view range and were in the same environment, the agents in the experimental group had more competitive advantages through the MA-A3C optimization strategy. Specifically, the agents in the experimental group are the "workers" in the policy algorithm. The global network selectively learns their actions and policy experiences in the local environment. This selection is achieved through the multi-head attention mechanism. The experimental results show that not all agents in the experimental group performed well every time. Due to many objective random factors in the environment, a good action result is likely due to luck rather than strategy. Therefore, although the multi-head attention mechanism cannot completely filter and exclude this random luck, it can effectively give more attention to factors less affected by randomness during learning.

From the prior knowledge of the Secretary problem [13] in human behavior analysis, we know that the optimal cutoff tends to n/e as n increases, and the best applicant is selected with probability $1/e$. The MA-A3C engine can also obtain

Table 2. Simulation results of the control group and experimental group in five trials (view range = 25).

Rough steps	Trial #1 Female	Male	#2 Female	Male	#3 Female	Male	#4 Female	Male	#5 Female	Male
10	19	5	22	18	22	14	16	7	14	19
	24	22	13	12	23	13	18	19	19	17
	20	14	18	24	24	22	19	24	12	21
	16	23	10	21	15	16	14	21	23	4
100	21	24	20	20	21	3	15	23	16	12
	7	20	15	5	19	1	22	15	11	15
	17	21	23	6	17	2	13	18	12	1
	1	17	16	16	13	15	5	20	15	6
	2	16	11	11	18	24	20	11	18	18
200	5	15	19	17	16	12	23	17	22	9
	18	8	17	21	14	7	4	20	24	13
	15	7	24	6	11	17	24	1	17	14
	22	5	1	14	2	20	11	12	21	5
	23	2	21	10	1	11	3	16	8	24
300	13	11	8	15	20	10	21	5	20	3
	11	15	4	13	12	8	2	9	2	10
	0	2	7	8	4	21	12	10	10	8
	14	10	14	9	10	9	10	8	9	20
	8	3	9	7	9	19	8	4	7	7
400	10	9	12	5	6	5	7	3	5	11
	9	6	6	1	5	4	9	6	4	2
	4	1	3	4	8	23	17	7	0	16
	6	4	2	1	7	18	0	2	6	5
	12	0	5	2	3	6	6	3	3	0
500	3	3	0	0	0	0	1	0	1	2
C.Gr.Avg.Diff.	-2.63	-1.90	-1.80	-1.07	-2.73	-2.07	-1.90	-1.57	-3.00	-1.80
E.Gr.Avg.Diff.	2.10	4.70	1.00	3.30	4.10	3.10	1.90	3.30	2.60	4.60
Avg. label diff.	7.32		5.52		7.92		7.16		7.52	
STD deviation	5.84		5.32		6.13		5.69		6.02	

Note:　C.Gr.Avg.Diff.: Control group average difference of paired agents.
E.Gr.Avg.Diff.: Experimental group average difference of paired agents.
represents the outstanding agent in experimental group, which gains a higher label partner than group average.

similar experiences in repeated reinforcement learning, thereby improving the agent's initial setting of n.

From the records of the experimental group's target selection, we found that sometimes agents follow the same-sex agents with high label values instead of the high label values of the opposite-sex agents in the conventional strategy. Opposite-sex agents favor same-sex agents with high label values, and following them may have more opportunities to interact with high-label value opposite-sex agents. Similar wisdom can also be found in human behavior patterns. Education can be understood as students following teachers to a certain extent.

5   Conclusion

In most environments handled by reinforcement learning, such as Atari2600, the agent's and environment's relationship is independent. However, in human behavior modeling, the association is more complex and richer.

This paper chose a fundamental human behavior pattern in which the agent's actions entirely determine the environment. The results of this modeling imply similar phenomena of human behavior in the real world. For example, under the economic man hypothesis, follow-up and collaborative strategies are the dynamic basis for forming an entrepreneurship and management team. In this study, we propose the MA-A3C algorithm, which combines the A3C algorithm with the multi-head attention mechanism to optimize the policy of a small number of agents in the experimental group and break the balance of equal matching.

From the experiment, we realized that equal matching is likely a specific manifestation of the Nash equilibrium in human behavior patterns. However, the underlying game mechanism requires further in-depth study in future research. Learning to act in multi-agent systems has received attention primarily from game theory, focusing on algorithms that converge to the Nash equilibrium. Reinforcement learning, on the other hand, focuses on acting optimally in stochastic scenarios. The learning process of systems of intelligent interacting agents is highly complex due to the complexity of single-agent learning combined with their communications and networked information dynamics, which is a topic for future work.

References

1. Ariely, D.: The Upside of Irrationality: The Unexpected Benefits of Defying Logic at Work and at Home. Harper (2010)
2. Mnih, V., et al.: Playing Atari with Deep Reinforcement Learning. Proc, NIPS Deep Learning Workshop (2013)
3. Mnih, V., et al.: Human-level control through deep reinforcement learning. Nature **518**, 529–533 (2015)
4. Mnih, V., et al.: Asynchronous Methods for Deep Reinforcement Learning. In: Proc. International Conference on Learning Representations (ICLR) (2016)
5. Schulman, J., et al.: Proceedings of the 32nd International Conference on Machine Learning. PMLR **37**, 1889–1897 (2015)
6. Schulman, J., et al.: Proximal Policy Optimization Algorithms (2017)
7. Hoffman, M., et al.: Reinforcement Learning with Deep Energy-Based Policies. In: Proc. 34th International Conference on Machine Learning (ICML 2017)
8. Haarnoja, T., et al.: Soft Actor-Critic: Off-Policy Maximum Entropy Deep Reinforcement Learning with a Stochastic Actor. In: Proc. Conference on Neural Information Processing Systems (NeurIPS 2018)
9. Zhao, C., et al.: Attentional Communication Framework for Multi-Agent Reinforcement Learning in Partially Communicable Scenarios. Electronics (2022)
10. Buşoniu, L., et al.: A comprehensive survey of multi-agent reinforcement learning. IEEE Transactions on Systems, Man, and Cybernetics, Part C (Applications and Reviews), vol. 38, no. 2, pp. 156–172 (2008)

11. Madani, K., et al.: A game theory-reinforcement learning (GT-RL) method to develop optimal operation policies for multi-operator reservoir systems. J. Hydrol. **519**, Part A (2014)
12. Nowé, A. et al.: Game Theory and Multi-agent Reinforcement Learning. Wiering, M., van Otterlo, M. (eds) Reinforcement Learning. Adaptation, Learning, and Optimization, vol 12. Springer. (2012). https://doi.org/10.1007/978-3-642-27645-3_14
13. Ferguson, T.S.: Who solved the secretary problem? Statist. Sci. **4**, 282–296 (1988)

The Influence of Background Color and Font Size of Mobile Payment App Interface on Elderly User Experience

Hongyu Du[1], Weilin Liu[1(✉)], Peicheng Wang[1], Xiang Sun[1], and Wenping Zhang[2]

[1] School of Management Engineering, Qingdao University of Technology, Qingdao 266520,
People's Republic of China
lwl0446@163.com

[2] School of Business, Qingdao University of Technology, Qingdao 266520, People's Republic of China

Abstract. At present, the functions of mobile payment Apps are increasing, and the interface elements are more diversified, which is more suitable for young people. However, the elderly are different from young people. They have special group characteristics, especially visual aging. This paper will use eye-tracking technology to record the behavior performance and visual experience data of the elderly subjects when using different mobile payment Apps, obtain the subjective experience data of the elderly subjects by combining the questionnaire survey method, and then analyze the impact of color design and font size design of the Apps interface on the overall user experience of the elderly. The difference in Apps interface is reflected in background color and font size. The research results can provide an important reference for the interface design of mobile payment Apps for the elderly, help to improve the user experience level of App, enable the elderly to better use high-tech products, and also enrich the human-computer interaction interface design theories.

Keywords: Interface design · Elderly-oriented · Font Size · Color

1 Introduction

According to the results of the seventh National Population Census released by the National Bureau of Statistics of China on May 11, 2021, the population aged 60 and over is 264 million, accounting for 18.70%, and the population aged 65 and over is 190 million, accounting for 13.50% [1]. Compared with the sixth National Population Census in 2010, the proportion of the population aged 60 and over increased by 5.44 percentage points, and the proportion of the population aged 65 and above increased by 4.63 Percentage points. According to the United Nations classification standards on aging, when a country's population over 60 years old accounts for more than 10% of the total population or the proportion of the population over 65 years old exceeds 7%, it means that it has entered a mildly aging society; The proportion of people over 60 years old in the total population exceeds 20% or the proportion of people over 65 years old

V. G. Duffy (Ed.): HCII 2023, LNCS 14029, pp. 392–401, 2023.
https://doi.org/10.1007/978-3-031-35748-0_29

exceeds 14%, indicating that they have entered a moderately aging society. In today's increasingly large elderly population, how to make the elderly more convenient in all aspects of life is an unavoidable problem in Chinese society.

With the rapid development of information technology such as the Internet and big data, mobile payment application has covered people's clothing, food, housing, transportation and other aspects with the advantages of convenience, security and speed. It has become an important means of consumer payment. The elderly, as an important part of society, naturally account for a large proportion of Internet use. As of June 2022 (see Fig. 1), the proportion of Internet users aged 60 and above was 11.3% [2], compared with 2009 [3] (see Fig. 2), it has increased by about five times, and the elderly are gradually adapting to the Internet era. However, the continuous increase of App functions, the diversification of interface elements, and the complex interaction process have made many elderly users discouraged from mobile payment Apps. Fundamentally, one of the aspects is that some senior citizens do not agree that they have derailed from the times. More importantly, the eye function of the elderly is seriously degraded, not only the eyeball but also the muscles responsible for observing color near the eyes, which leads to the decline of the eyesight of the elderly and the weak perception of color, too small font size is not easy to see, for pale colors and slightly similar color differences are also difficult to distinguish. Because their vision is weakened, their sense of security in human-computer interaction (HCI) is greatly reduced. And older people generally like warm colors, they can find security in them, while younger people are different.

Therefore, this study will take elderly users as the target group, analyze the real experience of elderly users on mobile payment App interfaces with different background color and font size designs, reveal the impact of different background colors and font sizes on the user experience of the elderly, and provide design guidance for the interface design of mobile payment Apps from the perspective of the elderly.

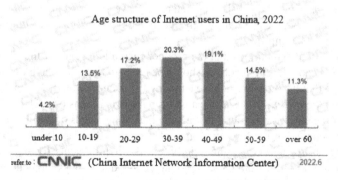

Fig. 1. Age structure of netizens in China, 2022

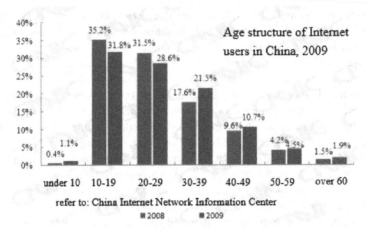

Fig. 2. Age structure of netizens in China, 2009

2   Related Research

Internationally, in the book "Emotional Design", Norman divides the goals of design and design into three levels: instinctive layer, behavior layer, and reflection layer, and explains these three layers of concepts [4]. Cooper's "The Inmates are Running the Asylum" lists many real and credible practical examples, which shows that there is currently a common problem of "difficult to use" in software products and software-based high-tech products. The authors argue that the "difficult to use" problem is caused by the high degree of "cognitive friction" in these products, and the root cause of this problem is the lack of an early "interaction design" stage in the current software development process for the benefit of users [5]. Hirokawa, Inoue, Iwaki, et al. build three hierarchical models and obtain four kinds of interfaces [6]. These interfaces have improved in integrating interface elements so that users can directly rely on memory operations, but the quantitative analysis needs to be improved.

In China, An also mentions that the product design language for the elderly should be concise and capable, and feedback should be given to the elderly in human-computer interaction so that the elderly can have empathy [7]. Dong, through in-depth interviews and grounded theoretical analysis, research from the two dimensions of care concept and the needs of the elderly, it is found that a large part of the needs of the elderly coincides with young people, but the level or degree of needs are different [8]. For example, air conditioning is also needed by the elderly, but the requirements for wind speed and temperature are different from those of young people due to physiological reasons. We cannot ignore the demands of older persons in this regard. According to the current aging design of related mobile payment Apps in China, it is found that some Apps have indeed launched an elderly mode. But many elderly mode switching entry is not displayed on the home page but is hidden in the "Settings" bar, and users need to look for it again to open the elder mod. In addition, the interface settings are only superficial, and some Apps' home page font is adjusted to be suitable for the elderly to read, but after clicking on the secondary page, the layout and font of the interface are the same as the normal version, which does not fundamentally solve the problem of the elderly using the App. Moreover, some Apps just have a simple enlargement of icons and fonts, which does not take the actual needs of the elderly into account at all. The difficulty of operation does not decrease but increases.

3 Method

3.1 Experimental Design

This study used a two-factor within-subjects design, two of which are background color and font size. There are two background colors: blue (RGB: 39, 140, 255) and green (RGB: 87, 171, 109), and two levels of font-size: 36pixels(px) (small font) and 44px (large font). The dependent variables are the task completion time, fixation count and fixation duration time. They are all obtained by the eye-tracking tester.

3.2 Experimental Materials

We divide the experimental interface into four types, green background color-large font, green background color-small font, blue background color-large font, and blue background color-small font. Figure 3 shows the self-designed interface legends of four mobile payment App that are saved in PNG format at a resolution of 428×926 px. In recent mobile Apps adapted for aging, the icons of the elderly mode are mostly designed as four rows and four columns. Therefore, we selected 16 icons commonly used by the elderly as experimental icons. These icons are selected from the mobile payment Apps commonly used in China: WeChat and Alipay. Under different experimental conditions, various icons are the actual shapes designed by the App icon designer, selected in iPhone 13 pro max. The background color of the four experimental materials were adjusted by image processing software. The icons are distributed randomly across the four interfaces to avoid errors due to different positions.

3.3 Experimental Equipment

The experiment was conducted in the eye-tracking laboratory of the Qingdao University of Technology. Figure 4 shows the SMI iView X™ RED eye tracker system used for the experiment, at 500 Hz, for collecting eye movement data. The system consists of a laptop (Dell M4800), a monitor (Dell P2213, screen size approx. 47.4 cm × 29.6 cm, 1680 × 1050 px definition), and an infrared tracking component. Software is installed on laptops, including Experiment Center 3.7, iView X RED, and Begaze 3.7. Experiment Center 3.7 is used to design and control the overall experiment. iView X RED collects eye-tracking data that can be analyzed offline by Begaze 3.7.

3.4 Participant

Due to the impact of COVID-19 in China, universities are in "semi-closed" states, so we look for participants on campus. We choose to go to the campus cafeteria to

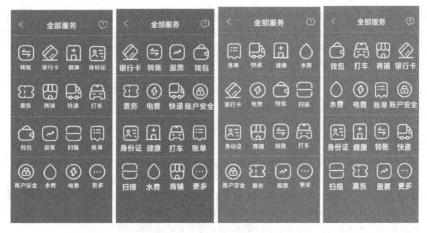

Fig. 3. Experimental materials

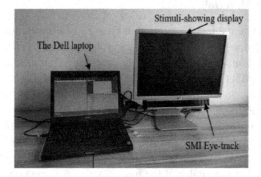

Fig. 4. Eye-tracking system for experimentation

randomly invite female workers to the laboratory alone in the afternoon when the canteen is not working. Male participants are randomly selected after the nucleic acid test in the morning, and we invite them to the laboratory alone. Finally, a total of 29 older adults (19 women and 10 men) working at Qingdao University of Technology participated. Their age ranged from 57 to 68 years old. All participants had experience using smartphones. And the corrected vision is normal.

3.5   Experimental Process

We save the designed interface in JPG format, upload it to the eye-tracking system, and ask the elderly to complete the experiment in the Human Factors & Ergonomics Lab. Before the experiment begins, we will reassure the elderly and ask them not to be nervous. When the experiment starts, we first explain the process and requirements of the experiment to the participants, and then they are asked to sit in front of the screen with the distance between participants and the monitor adjusted to about 70 cm. The eye-tracking system is then calibrated using the five-point method, and once the calibration accuracy of both eyes is less than 0.6, a preliminary experiment will be started. The preliminary experiment is to ask the elderly to look for target icons in an existing App interface. The purpose is to make the elderly understand what needs to be done next and determine whether they can continue to complete the experiment. Next, it will enter the interface to be tested, and let the elderly look for different target icons in the four interfaces in turn. The eye-tracking system will automatically record the completion time of the task. To avoid the influence of the target position on the result, all four different target icons are evenly distributed in the four corners of the interfaces. During the experiment, we will give verbal guidance to the elderly to help them complete the experiment correctly. At the end of the experiment, the four interfaces are presented one by one on the mobile phone, and the participants are asked to explain which background color and font size they preferred according to their own experience.

4   Data Analysis

The analysis of face-to-face interviews after the experiment found that 72.4% (21 people) of subjects prefer blue, and 20.7% (6 people) believe that large font sizes are advantageous or make it easier to find information. In order to make a more objective analysis of the results, statistical analysis of the experimental data will be conducted. All statistical analyses are performed by SPSS 26.0 with a 0.05 α level. During repeated measurement ANOVA, the Greenhouse-Geisser method is used to correct the degrees of freedom and P-values.

4.1   Task Completion Time Analysis

The statistical results of task completion time are shown in Table 1, and the two-factor repeated measurement ANOVA analysis of 2 (background color difference) $\times$ 2 (font size difference) shows that:

The interaction effect of background color and font size is insignificant ($F = 0.839$, $p = 0.368$, $\eta^2 = 0.029$), and the main effect of background color is not significant ($F = 0.034$, $p = 0.855$, $\eta^2 = 0.001$). In contrast, the main effect of font size is significant ($F = 8.299$, $p = 0.008$, $\eta^2 = 0.229$); the paired comparison results show that task completion time under large font size is significantly 1274 ms longer than that under the condition of the small font size.

Table 1. Statistical results of task completion time [ms]

	A1		A2	
	B1	B2	B1	B2
Mean	3137.755	5148.341	3792.283	4329.824
Std. Deviation	2989.419	6564.579	3100.812	3176.898

Note: A1 is green background color, A2 is blue background color, B1 is small font, and B2 is large font

4.2 Eyes Movement Behavior Analysis

The statistical results of fixation count and fixation duration time are shown in Table 2, and the two-factor repeated measurement ANOVA analysis of 2 (background color difference) × 2 (font size difference) shows that:

Table 2. Statistical results of fixation count and fixation duration time

		A1		A2	
		B1	B2	B1	B2
Fixation count [n]	Mean	8.276	16.690	11.552	13.517
	Std. Deviation	5.897	16.123	6.690	9.387
fixation duration time [ms]	Mean	2021.159	3828.166	2556.246	2964.631
	Std. Deviation	1352.946	4451.754	1913.583	2278.055

Note: A1 is green background color, A2 is blue background color, B1 is small font, and B2 is large font

Fixation Count Analysis
The interaction effect of background color and font size is not significant ($F = 3.013$, $p = 0.094$, $\eta^2 = 0.097$), and the main effect of background color is not significant ($F = 0.001$, $p = 0.973$, $\eta^2 < 0.001$). In contrast, the main effect of font size is significant ($F = 13.968$, $p = 0.001$, $\eta^2 = 0.333$); the paired comparison results show that fixation count time under large font size is significantly 5.2 more than that under the condition of the small font size.

Fixation Duration Time Analysis
The interaction effect of background color and font size is insignificant ($F = 1.802$, $p = 0.190$, $\eta^2 = 0.060$), and the main effect of background color is not significant ($F = 0.257$, $p = 0.616$, $\eta^2 = 0.009$). In contrast, the main effect of font size is significant ($F = 11.738$, $p = 0.002$, $\eta^2 = 0.295$); the paired comparison results show that fixation duration time under large font size is significantly 1108 ms longer than that under the condition of the small font size.

5 Discussion

This study analyzes the effects of font size and background color on the use of mobile payment Apps by the elderly. For the elderly, the interaction between appropriate fonts and background colors can enhance the readability of the text [9]. Therefore, this study aims to find the appropriate font with the appropriate background color, so as to provide elderly users with a better user experience and reduce the barriers to their use of mobile payment Apps.

From the above analysis, font size significantly affects the total time for the elderly to complete the task, and also significantly affects the fixation count and fixation duration time. Specifically, on the small-font interface, the elderly take less time to complete the task, have a smaller number of fixations, and have a shorter fixation during time. The shorter the task completion time, the more favorable the interface design, and the more convenient for the elderly to find. Fixation count and fixation duration time have been widely applied as effective indicators to measure the visual attention that users devote to specific objects [10]. The less fixation count and fixation duration time, the less visual attention is required, and the more advantageous the elderly search will be. Thus, a smaller 36px font size is superior to a larger 44px font. Generally, large font size is easier for the elderly to read than small font size. However, due to the limitation of the size of mobile phone screen, too large font size and spacing can also cause reading efficiency problems. Katzir, Hershko and Halamish tested 100 children in grades two and five and found that for 5th graders, reducing the font size resulted in higher comprehension scores [11]. Another study by Halamish also found that small fonts sometimes have memory advantages [12]. The smaller font size of 36px can significantly improve the reading experience of App interfaces for the elderly, which is consistent with the subjective feelings of the elderly. Therefore, in the elderly-oriented transformation of mobile payment Apps, the font size can be appropriately reduced to meet the readability of the UI design; that is, the smaller font size (36px) can be selected as the preferred font size for software fonts when designing an interface. However, the different degrees of visual degradation of the elderly will lead to their different needs for font size. Therefore, in the process of elderly-oriented transformation of mobile payment Apps, it is better to provide optional font size. From the face-to-face interview data after the eye-tracking experiment, we can also notice that there are still some of the older participants who respond faster to large font size (such as participant P01, participant P26).

Regarding the effect of background color on the use of Apps interface for the elderly, the main effect of background color in this study is not significant for the experimental performance, i.e., task completion time, fixation count and fixation duration time. Hsieh uses card classification and other methods to determine the importance of color to perception, the results show that color is closely related to visual appeal, and the study also confirms that correct color information is critical to the accuracy of naming and the speed of icon recognition [13]. In the study of Tanaka and Presnell, participants are asked to identify the color version of HCD (high color diagnostic) objects based on a color diagnostic hypothesis, and the results show that color plays a role in recognition of HCD objects [14]. In addition, different colors can affect people's endocrine system through vision, which leads to the increase or decrease of human hormones, so that people's mood changes. This means that different colors trigger different emotions in users. If the elderly are in a positive emotional state when using the mobile payment app, it can increase their trust in the app to some extent, so as to improve their user experience. But, in our study, the statistical analysis results show that the two different colors, namely green and blue, have no significant difference in the experimental data, only the face-to-face interview data shows that 72.4% (21 people) of the participants prefer blue. The main reason for the lack of significance may be that both green and blue background color can improve the user experience for the elderly, and the difference between them is only a little. Because color plays an important role in target recognition and emotion arousal, we can't ignore the impact of color on user experience when the background color is not green and blue at the same time. With the aging of the body, the elderly have serious weaknesses in vision, such as retinal thinning, reduced number of photoreceptors and retinal neurons, lens shrinkage and hardening, and other problems, so in the aspect of color aging suitable design, it is necessary to improve the brightness and contrast of color so as to improve the color perception and recognition by the elderly.

6 Conclusions

Based on the results of this study, for the elderly, the selection of appropriate font size and background color on the interface of mobile payment App can help improve the readability of text in the interactive interface, improve the convenience of using Apps, and help reduce their anxiety when using high-tech products. The main conclusions of this study are: (1) Compared with 44px font, 36px font can better meet the user experience of most elderly people when using mobile payment Apps. (2) Blue and green background color have no significant impact on the user experience of mobile payment Apps for the elderly, but blue may be slightly better.

The limitations of this study are mainly reflected in: (1) The sample size is not large enough. Because of covid-19, the state of college closure makes us look for older participants on campus. The invited elderly participants are all the logistics staff of the canteen and security department, which cannot cover all the elderly groups in China. They are mainly aged between 57 and 68. It is necessary to expand the survey scope of elderly users in the future. (2) Background color difference and font size difference are only divided into two cases. That is, there are only four experimental conditions. The influence of more background color and font size on the user experience of the elderly needs to be further explored.

References

1. Bulletin of the Seventh National Population Census of the National Bureau of Statistics of China (中国国家统计局第七次全国人口普查公报). http://www.stats.gov.cn/tjsj/tjgb/rkpcgb/qgrkpcgb/202106/t20210628_1818824.html
2. The 50th Statistical Report on Internet Development in China (第50次中国互联网络发展状况统计报告). http://www.cnnic.cn/n4/2022/0914/c88-10226.html
3. The 25th Statistical Report on Internet Development in China (第25次中国互联网络发展状况统计报告). http://www.cnnic.cn/n4/2022/0401/c88-808.html
4. Norman, D.A.: Emotional Design. Basic Books, the United States(2005)
5. Cooper, A.: The Inmates are Running the Asylum. Sams, the United States(2004)
6. Hirokawa, M., Inoue, K., Iwaki, T., Kashima, T.: Fundamental study on an intuitive interface design theory (直感的インタフェースデザインの設計論の基礎の考察). Trans. Japan Society Kansei Eng. **13**(5), 543–554 (2014). https://doi.org/10.5057/jjske.13.543
7. An, Q.: Research on design of household elderly escort robot based on demand level(基于需求层次的家用老年陪护机器人设计研究). Indust. Design, (**5**), 119–121(2022). http://dx.chinadoi.cn/https://doi.org/10.3969/j.issn.1672-7053.2022.05.052
8. Dong, C.Y.: Research on the Design of Electronic Products for the Elderly Based on the Concept of Care(基于关怀理念的老年人电子产品设计研究). Zhejiang Sci-Tech University, (2021). http://dx.chinadoi.cn/ https://doi.org/10.27786/d.cnki.gzjlg.2021.001060

9. Hou, G.H., Ning, W.N., Dong, H.: The Effect of Age and Font Size on Digital Reading Experience(字号、间距影响数字阅读体验的年龄差异研究). Library **0**(8):97–102(2018). http://dx.chinadoi.cn/ https://doi.org/10.3969/j.issn.1002-1558.2018.08.019

10. Liu, W., Liang, X., Liu, F.: The effect of webpage complexity and banner animation on banner effectiveness in a free browsing task. Int. J. Human-Comput. Interact. **35**(13), 1192–1202 (2019). https://doi.org/10.1080/10447318.2018.1516843

11. Katzir, T., Hershko, S., Halamish, V.: The effect of font size on reading comprehension on second and fifth grade children: Bigger is not always better. PloS One, **8**(9), e74061 (2013) https://doi.org/10.1371/journal.pone.0074061

12. Halamish, V.: Can very small font size enhance memory? Mem. Cognit. **46**(6), 979–993 (2018). https://doi.org/10.3758/s13421-018-0816-6

13. Hsieh, T.: Multiple roles of color information in the perception of icon-type images. Color. Res. Appl. **42**(6), 740–752 (2017). https://doi.org/10.1002/col.22140

14. Tanaka, J.W., Presnell, L.M.: Color diagnosticity in object recognition. Percept. Psychophys. **61**, 1140–1153 (1999). https://doi.org/10.3758/BF03207619

A Roadmap for Technological Innovation in Multimodal Communication Research

Alina Gregori[1]([⊠]) [iD], Federica Amici[2] [iD], Ingmar Brilmayer[3] [iD],
Aleksandra Ćwiek[4] [iD], Lennart Fritzsche[1], Susanne Fuchs[4] [iD],
Alexander Henlein[1] [iD], Oliver Herbort[5], Frank Kügler[1] [iD], Jens Lemanski[6,7] [iD],
Katja Liebal[2], Andy Lücking[1] [iD], Alexander Mehler[1] [iD], Kim Tien Nguyen[1],
Wim Pouw[8] [iD], Pilar Prieto[9,10], Patrick Louis Rohrer[10,11] [iD],
Paula G. Sánchez-Ramón[1,10] [iD], Martin Schulte-Rüther[12] [iD],
Petra B. Schumacher[3] [iD], Stefan R. Schweinberger[13] [iD], Volker Struckmeier[1],
Patrick C. Trettenbrein[14] [iD], and Celina I. von Eiff[13]

[1] Goethe University Frankfurt/M., Frankfurt am Main, Germany
gregori@lingua.uni-frankurt.de
[2] University of Leipzig, Leipzig, Germany
[3] University of Cologne, Cologne, Germany
[4] Leibniz Centre General Linguistics, Berlin, Germany
[5] Julius-Maximilians-University of Würzburg, Würzburg, Germany
[6] WWU Münster, Münster, Germany
[7] University of Hagen, Hagen, Germany
[8] Donders Institute for Brain, Cognition, and Behaviour, Radboud University Nijmegen, Nijmegen, The Netherlands
[9] ICREA (Institució de Recerca i Estudis Avançats), Barcelona, Spain
[10] Universitat Pompeu Fabra, Barcelona, Spain
[11] Nantes Université, Nantes, France
[12] University Medical Center Göttingen, Göttingen, Germany
[13] Friedrich Schiller University of Jena, Jena, Germany
[14] Max Planck Institute for Human Cognitive and Brain Sciences, Leipzig, Germany

Abstract. Multimodal communication research focuses on how different means of signalling coordinate to communicate effectively. This line of research is traditionally influenced by fields such as cognitive and neuroscience, human-computer interaction, and linguistics. With new technologies becoming available in fields such as natural language processing and computer vision, the field can increasingly avail itself of new ways of analyzing and understanding multimodal communication. As a result, there is a general hope that multimodal research may be at the "precipice of greatness" due to technological advances in computer science and

Supported by the DFG priority program *Visual Communication* (ViCom).
I. Brilmayer and P. L. Rohrer—External collaborator
A. Gregori, F. Amici, I. Brilmayer, A. Ćwiek, L. Fritzsche, S. Fuchs, A. Henlein, O. Herbort, F. Kügler, J. Lemanski, K. Liebal, A. Lücking, A. Mehler, K. T. Nguyen, W. Pouw, P. Prieto, P. L. Rohrer, P. G. Sánchez-Ramón, M. Schulte-Rüther, P. B. Schumacher, S. R. Schweinberger, V. Struckmeier, P. C. Trettenbrein, C. I. von Eiff—For the ViCom Consortium, alphabetical order except lead author.

V. G. Duffy (Ed.): HCII 2023, LNCS 14029, pp. 402–438, 2023.
https://doi.org/10.1007/978-3-031-35748-0_30

resulting extended empirical coverage. However, for this to come about there must be sufficient guidance on key (theoretical) needs of innovation in the field of multimodal communication. Absent such guidance, the research focus of computer scientists might increasingly diverge from crucial issues in multimodal communication. With this paper, we want to further promote interaction between these fields, which may enormously benefit both communities. The multimodal research community (represented here by a consortium of researchers from the Visual Communication [ViCom] Priority Programme) can engage in the innovation by clearly stating which technological tools are needed to make progress in the field of multimodal communication. In this article, we try to facilitate the establishment of a much needed common ground on feasible expectations (e.g., in terms of terminology and measures to be able to train machine learning algorithms) and to critically reflect possibly idle hopes for technical advances, informed by recent successes and challenges in computer science, social signal processing, and related domains.

Keywords: Multimodal communication · Natural language processing · Technical innovation

1   Introduction: Multimodal Communication

When people talk to each other, they naturally communicate with their whole bodies (e.g., [58]). That is, besides speech or sign they use facial expressions, move their hands and arms for gesturing, laugh, gaze, shrug, nod, sigh, among other things. All these signals cohere into social interactions (e.g, [119]) and are interpreted in relation to one another [76]. While some of these signals are perceived in the acoustic modality, others are perceived visually, tactilely or olfactorily. Thus, interactions are not only produced by the whole body, but also perceived by various sense modalities. Hence, communication is multimodal, captured in the eponymous term of *multimodal communication.*

We are researchers with different backgrounds working on multimodal communication, specifically on gestures, sign languages, didactic and clinical aspects of visual communication, animal communication, and human-computer interaction systems. Our work contributes to the Priority Programme *Visual Communication* (ViCom), supported by the German Research Foundation (DFG). ViCom aims at disclosing the specific characteristics of the visual modality as a communication channel and its interaction with other channels (especially the acoustic one) to develop models of human communication and their cognitive and evolutionary foundations. We share an interest in visual communication and are particularly interested in exploring to what extent vocal or signed linguistic communication is multimodal at its core and substantially shaped by (social) interaction [56,77]. We differ in the theoretical frameworks we employ [37], the populations and species we work with, and the methodologies we use. What ties us together is the idea that mutual progress can be made by employing principles of open science, sharing our expertise on different scientific strands, and paving the way for cooperative science to move beyond the border of a single discipline.

Many aspects of multimodal communication remain unknown, including the mechanisms by which multiple signals are quickly integrated in perception and coordinated in production [6,187]. The study of multiple signals is therefore required, and in need of technological advancement to be explored. The detailed investigation of different signals in isolation, as well as their cross-modal integration in different populations and species, requires tools and methods that differ from those developed for written (and usually digitized) text. Over the past years, tools and methods have been developed for simultaneously keeping track of signals on various channels, but not necessarily in a joint effort by computer science (expertise in data processing), linguistics (expertise in linguistic structure and its contributions to meaning, etc.), and other disciplines investigating principles of communicative behavior.

1.1 Goals of This Article

Not least due to advances in audiovisual technology (i.e., recording and storing ephemeral utterance events by means of camera and microphone for analysis), an empirically grounded theory of multimodal language use and interaction is developing [38] – "a scientific tool whose importance to our discipline equals that of the microscope to biology" [178, p. 275].

We believe that multimodal research is necessary to advance theoretical research on human and non-human animal communication. Here, we survey the state-of-the-art of existing research tools that can and have been applied in multimodal research on communication. We evaluate current approaches, point out short- and long-term aims, and identify the scientific innovations that such aims imply. We further provide suggestions for tools and applications, which we believe might help move the interdisciplinary research dialogue between cognitive and computer science forward. Finally, we highlight the availability of these tools, not only to increase their familiarity among linguists, but also to highlight how some tools are now primarily used by computer scientists due to high technical skills required to wield these tools.

1.2 Overarching Terms

"Multimodal communication" is a broad field of research that considers not merely acoustic signals (which may be grouped into meaningful units) as being able to move communication forward. While most of this paper will revolve around the acoustic and visual modes of communication, note that tactile cues (e.g., in languages of the deaf-blind) or olfactory signals (e.g., in animal communication) are used for communication as well. Typical examples of visual communication are sign languages, gesturing, facial expressions, eye gaze, and orofacial movements, but also diagrams, emojis, and written text, cf. Fig. 1. Multimodality can refer to the sensory channels (e.g., acoustic, visual) or different content types within a sensory channel (e.g., signs and facial expressions, eye gaze, text and emojis).

Some forms of multimodal communication comprise complex grammar and can express a potentially infinite range of different ideas (e.g., discourse in sign languages), others have lexicalized meanings (e.g., individual signs or symbolic and highly conventionalized gestures), or may refer to specific aspects of the current situation (e.g., deictic gestures indicating spatial relations). In addition, the different forms vary in complexity: For example, lexical items of a sign language are highly complex signals that consist of discrete parameters (i.e., hand shape, place of articulation, movement, and orientation), while symbolic gestures may be formed in a simpler manner. Moreover, some forms of visual communication such as sign languages are highly conventionalized (vertical axis of Fig. 1), while others, such as iconic gestures, may be created spontaneously. Within gesture studies, degrees of conventionalization of hand-and-arm movements are located on *Kendon's Continuum*, popularized by [113, p. 37]. Note that the level of conventionalization may differ within each form. For example, a simple drawing of an object, like a hammer, is first and foremost its representation in the iconic sense – it refers to a hammer through a sense of resemblance (but see [17,25,57] for critical discussions of reducing reference to resemblance). However, if a hammer is combined with a sickle in a specific manner, it may stand for a symbolic and conventional representation of Marxist-Leninist philosophy.

Lastly, forms vary in the specific effectors – the medium used for expression (e.g., hands, face, paper/screen, cf. colored in Fig. 1) they are typically tied to – or their dynamicity (deictic gestures often being relatively static, while beat gestures are dynamic). The use of visual cues in communication – which makes it multimodal – can also set an implicit "tone" to the communicative situation. This can be shown in the expression of emotional states or reversing the meaning of what is said. Note also that multimodal communication may happen without intention, or without consciously controlling effectors to communicate (e.g., in non-human animal research).

2   Development of Multimodal Research

2.1   Establishing Multimodal Research

While the idea of communication being multimodal is not new itself, multimodality has yet to be adequately incorporated and modelled in linguistic theories. In sharp contrast to the well-established interest in written and/or spoken language understood as a unimodal phenomenon, multimodal aspects of communication have received only some initial attention.

Multimodal communication research has emerged on the foundation of work from pioneering scholars from the late 20th century (e.g., [79,80,113]), who claimed that gesture had to be understood as an integral part of communication. Since then, visual cues have been gradually accepted as a central component of many communicative scenarios from a variety of perspectives. Crucially, this acceptance has been triggered by cutting-edge studies on both signed and spoken languages. This makes important contributions to the assumption that the study of visual aspects of communication should definitely be considered a worthwhile

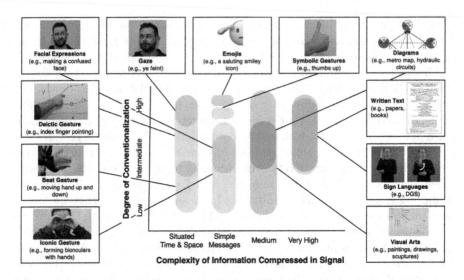

Fig. 1. Examples of a variety of different forms of visual communication (non-exhaustive). Different forms of visual communication are organized horizontally according to the complexity of the information that could potentially be conveyed and vertically according to their level of conventionalization. Colors indicate the effectors that are primarily involved (hands: blue, face: green, paper/screens: red). Images are re-used courtesy of Oliver Herbort. Still images of DGS signs are copyright [184] and re-used under Creative Commons Attribution 4.0 International License. (Color figure online)

(or even necessary) addition to theories. This relates not only to "communication" in the abstract sense but also more centrally to specifically linguistic theories (e.g., [143] for a review, [42,43] for gesture, [155] for signed languages, [65] for the gesture–sign interface, [105] for the gesture–grammar interface).

It is our belief that the incorporation of multimodal aspects of communication into linguistic theories may well come to resemble the inclusion of prosodic aspects into grammatical models of language. Prosody initially was not deemed important with regard to its effects on other linguistic subfields such as syntax, semantics, lexical analysis, or information structure, cf. [36,174]. This changed only when the established methods of the neighboring subfields started considering that prosody has a productive impact on the language system as a linguistic subfield in its own right (e.g., [69,179]). Important research by [60,92,146] demonstrated the phonological status of intonation across languages. Nowadays, prosody has been shown to not only constitute an essential module of grammar but also having an impact on language production and processing (see [153] for a review).

There is some level of agreement that multimodality can be an important factor for communication research as well. However, from a wider perspective, multimodal communication research has not yet agreed on standard definitions (e.g., for concepts, categories, relations), nor on tools or methodologies required.

Two central dimensions have already been investigated in the relation between language use and gesture (see [1] for a review), namely timing and meaning. Issues that have not been fully solved include the transition from pure manual gesture annotation to tools like automatic recognition of specific patterns, segmentation tools, and natural language processing.

2.2   Interaction with Other Fields

Technological innovation in multimodal communication research is relevant not only for understanding human communication but also for a number of other fields, such as communication of emotions, human-computer interaction (HCI), neuroscience, clinical research and animal communication (do specific gestures and vocalizations co-occur to convey novel meanings during communicative interactions [7]? A multimodal approach may be crucial to really understand the meaning entailed by animal communication). For example, principles such as the tight coupling of perception and expression between social agents not only underpin communication using language [145], but also extend to nonverbal facial [172] and auditory [52] communication and benefit from multimodal measurements (e.g., [64]).

The consideration of multimodality in neuroscience may foster theoretical and functional innovations: Brain systems mediating perception and expression in a modality are often overlapping both in humans and non-human animals (see, e.g., [52] for the auditory domain), yet higher-order regions processing abstract information that is not part of the signal (e.g., syntax and semantics) such as the language network seem to be organized in a modality-independent fashion [90,185,189]. Increasingly, "mobile friendly" neuroscience methods such as fNIRS (functional near-infrared spectroscopy) are used for the investigation of more than one person and more than one brain during interaction [126] to assess brain mechanisms and synchronization/coordination processes across brains [88]. Such approaches would greatly benefit from additional fine-grained assessment of multimodal data streams reflecting communicative behavior and integrated neurobehavioral analysis.

Multimodal communication researchers are often in the business of understanding time-varying bodily motions acting together in a referential or indicative way. While the tools and conceptual schemes to categorize these complex communicative objects have advanced, the analyses of the time-varying motion have as such been lacking. There is thereby relatively little integration with human movement science which focuses on non-referential bodily motions, and hitherto a general lack of application of concepts from kinematics or biomechanics, and a lack of integration of tools that deal with high-dimensional time-varying data. But this is changing too. For example, there is increasingly robust research on the kinematic information about intentions (e.g., [29,144,188]), application of kinematic-acoustic analyses in typical and non-typical populations (e.g., [39,104]), and new ways of compressing high-dimensional data for analyzing multimodal signaling (e.g., [5,149]).

Time-sensitive, kinematic studies can contribute to a debated but difficult to investigate phenomenon of multimodal communication, namely the cross-modal constitution of "ensembles" [79,118]. Such ensembles, *when used repetitively in conversation*, have a statistical effect (as assessed in information theoretic terms for speech–gesture pairs by [115]). A generalization of such ensembles has been suggested to be a cornerstone of multimodal communication in terms of multi-modal gestalts [67]; see also the challenges pointed out in Sect. 1 (the speed of producing and comprehending). However, recurrent ensembles or gestalts may lead to a simplification of form – on side of the gesture, on side of speech, or both [107]. It is suggestive to ascribe such simplifications to a balance between production effort and comprehension, facilitated by repetition of use. In order to quantify such recurrent phenomena, combined temporal and spatial measurements are needed. These may also feed into time-dependent, embedding-based approaches as employed, for instance, in semantic change detection [176].

Communicative movement is special and not simply guided by clearly testable performance variables [183]. Rather, for communicative movements "meaning is a performance variable" [95, p. 359]. Yet, meaning needs not always be such an elusive concept, and communicative movements may also have informative value qua movements, for example by deviating from how one usually moves [144] or making use of biomechanical stabilities [151].

Advancement in multimodal communication research may also provide strong benefits to clinical research, for example, to people with sensory impairments or users of a cochlear implant [8,45]. Moreover, many developmental and mental disorders are associated with problems in visual communication and social functioning. Disentangling the respective mechanisms for different disorders is important for advancing diagnostics (e.g., [171]) and intervention. For example, although perception, expression, and imitation of facial emotions are disturbed in the Autism Spectrum Disorder (ASD) [190], it is controversial whether facial motor mimicry is involved as a mechanism that drives such disturbance [41,172]. Research into cross-modal imitation (for instance, a reflexive facial expressive response that matches the emotion perceived in another's voice) [110] suggests a multimodal nature of emotion processing, but studies tackling this issue explicitly remain quite rare [200].

For clinical contexts and applications in real-world settings (i.e., when ecological validity is particularly important), methods are needed that are easy to apply, non-invasive, and flexible. For example, facial emotion expressions or speech were traditionally measured using electrodes or sensor coils (e.g., facial electromyography [172], real-time magnetic resonance imaging (MRI), or electromagnetic articulography [123], respectively). Although precise and well-established, such methods have the disadvantage of being bound to a lab than more recent contact-free approaches like video recordings for the analyses of facial expression, acoustic analysis for automatic speech recognition, and recognition of emotions in speech [40,170]. Video-based assessment of body pose is also increasingly used in clinical populations [111], however, developing efficient machine learning algorithms for semantic analysis of body pose and gestures remains a challenge. Ultimately, this depends on the exact definition of seman- tically interpretable body configurations for the respective situation (e.g., a ges- ture "vocabulary", categories of the emotional expression of movement). Fur- thermore, these new methods also allow studying other species during natural interactions, without having to recur to invasive research, which can be ethically problematic in some cases.

Overall, multimodal data acquisition poses both a challenge and an opportu- nity in this respect: richer data allows for more precise characterizations, but its mapping to meaningful communicative events requires stringent, theory-based descriptions and theoretical models. Theoretical questions (broadly understood) as well as empirical knowledge of previous studies should lay the foundation for the development of standard procedures and technological development of new tools. A step in the right direction would be, from our point of view, to estab- lish fruitful collaborations across researchers, labs, research institutions, etc. In this way, we could integrate our different needs, develop standard definitions of concepts (e.g., from semantics, prosody, and technology), achieve more system- aticity in terms of manual labeling and foster the development of technological tools for the benefit of theoretical and applied research in this field.

3   Available Tools, Methods and Databases

Having assessed the integration of multimodal communication research into cog- nitive science, in this section we provide a state-of-the-art on available tools, methods and databases for empirical multimodal research. The employment of automatic tools and methods for studying multimodal natural language use can be roughly distinguished in terms of an annotation ladder, sketched in Fig. 2. To give a brief, stepwise description: (i) First, the physical signals realizing the communicative behavior under observation need to be recorded. Therefore the specificities of the recording techniques and knowledge about previous stud- ies are key factors. Recording multiple signals with different devices imposes a synchronization problem (bottom row). (ii) Within the continuous recording stream, the actual units of observation have to be identified (segmentation). This may require mapping the recorded signals into a meaningful feature space first (e.g., mapping Cartesian movement coordinates onto a skeleton model). Seg- ments from different signals have to be aligned (middle row). (iii) The units of observation can then be classified (e.g., functionally, taxonomically). Note that the labels of annotation and how to use them should be defined in an annotation scheme. Multi-channel classification basically has to decide whether different sig- nals/segments belong to a single "ensemble" [80], bear a coherence relation, or remain unrelated. Along these lines, results of automatized processing finally feed into qualitative or quantitative theory building and testing (see Sect. 1).

The annotation ladder sketch is useful for assessing the subsequent survey of recording and annotation tools in the discussion in Sect. 4.

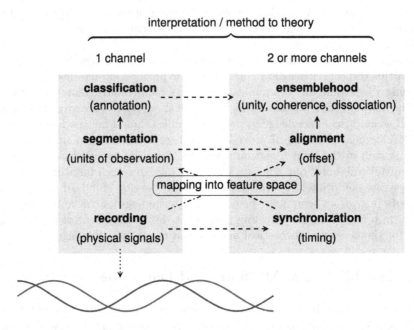

Fig. 2. The annotation ladder for multimodal signals on a single channel (left) gives rise to temporal or (dis-)integrative multi-channel relationships on each rung (right). The blue and red lines represent distinct modes of continuous signals. The unidirectionality of arrows indicates a step on the next rung. Depending on the study in question, however, knowledge from higher rungs may be used in the opposing direction (top-down) to contribute to solving annotations on lower rungs. Note that in multilogue the annotation ladder applies both within a single speaker and between different speakers. (Color figure online)

3.1   Motion Recording Techniques

Data recording is often a crucial step when doing research in multimodal communication and it offers a variety of technologically supported tools. In this section, we will review the main behavioral recording techniques. When multimodal communication research is carried out, human-to-human communication is usually recorded with one or more video cameras in *immobile* (cameras distributed in space [101]) or *mobile* (cameras move with the people recorded; e.g., to reflect the perspectives of the actors [72, 201]) recording setups. For good audio quality, it is advisable to use (external) condenser microphones. In the following, we describe different implementation options for data recording, which are not mutually exclusive but can be combined in various ways to balance out their individual advantages and disadvantages. Note, however, that overly complex setups may come at the expense of truly huge amounts of data, which also may need to be synchronized and processed in a complex fashion during analyses (see Sect. 3.3). The choice of a recording technique is often based on the research objectives, space, price, mobility, technical know-how, scalability, accuracy, frequency, feature, scenario, etc. [51, 206].

Recording scenarios can focus on the body as a whole or on specific body parts. Full body tracking can be carried out by *room-scale systems* (which statically record scenes; are very specialized and accurate; require specifications in advance, e.g., [22]), by *AI systems* (which are standalone cameras typically with depth sensors; natively track body motion using specific key points), or by *body trackers* (which are key points placed on the actor; can be either standalone or combined with external stations; typically 3–8 trackers are needed; e.g., [141, 204]). Recording strategies focusing on single body parts usually record the movement of the face, hands or eyes, using more specific key points (not allowing full body tracking), and they are usually implemented by using mobile *head-mounted systems*. Examples of these systems are *eye tracking glasses* (which are glasses-type devices indicating the exact point the recorded eye fixates; e.g., [75, 191]), *Virtual Reality (VR) glasses* (which usually measure head movements in space, but increasingly also provide direct hand tracking and gesture recognition, native eye tracking, and face tracking; they are inexpensive and widespread; can help to visualize stimuli/scenarios [136]; with the disadvantages that a portion of the face is covered and they do not allow for direct human interaction) or *Augmented Reality (AR) glasses* (which augment the real world for the user; and include hand and eye tracking).

Tracking technology provides versatile means and devices for recording body signals of various kinds. However, from the practical viewpoint of multimodal researchers, their productive use in empirical studies places some obstacles: (i) Special equipment is needed, which also needs to be operated by an expert. That is, many of the above-mentioned methods do not work out of the box for untrained researchers. (ii) The tracking data needs to be post-processed. However, in contrast to written and digitized text, there is a glaring lack of automatic annotation procedures (see Sect. 1). (iii) Even manual annotation poses problems: standard annotation tools are not prepared to handle data types other than digitized text, audio or video files - see Sect. 3.4. Furthermore, there are no agreed-upon annotation schemes or standards for many non-verbal kinematic communicative behaviors.

3.2   Neural and Physiological Methods

In contrast to motion recording techniques (Sect. 3.1) that capture spontaneous, behavioral data from the environment, neuroscientific methods are also used with a focus on a better understanding of the underlying control or processing components in multimodal communication. However, while there is relative robustness of e.g., eye-tracking data against artifacts that originate from freely moving participants – given careful and repeated calibration and firmly fitting eye-tracking glasses – recording and analysis of, for example, electrophysiological data in interactive settings are more complicated. A number of such methods are introduced in the following.

For example, *electroencephalography* (EEG) is a powerful tool to investigate the time-course of cognitive processes. The electrical brain activity is recorded from an electrode cap and any kind of movement generates artifacts – even eye-blinking. Most previous studies with freely-moving subjects used so-called dual-task experiments, in which participants have to perform a common task from experimental psychology (e.g., oddball detection) while performing a second task (e.g., [100,124]). This type of study compares the response to a target stimulus in different mobility conditions, for instance walking and sitting. Traditional averaging methods to compute event-related potentials (ERPs; i.e., electrophysiological signals time-locked to a stimulus event) have proven quite robust to movement-related artifacts after standard preprocessing [100]. However, the movements in these studies were temporarily and semantically unrelated to the experimental task. Thus, their influence on the ERPs of interest might be small and "canceled out" in the averaging process. In real-world experiments researchers are, for instance, interested in language use and co-speech gestures, however, the bodily movements (gestures) are related to another modality of the experimental stimuli of interest (speech). Therefore, they systematically occur in critical trials and thus overlap with each other and with the critical language input. As a consequence, the language-related ERPs usually overlap with gesture-related potentials, as well as fixation-related potentials (since participants are looking at gestures while listening to speech). Failing to account for this overlap might lead to a critical distortion of the results. Therefore, calculating traditional, averaged ERPs is not suited for this kind of data. Instead, it is advisable to use time-resolved regression (deconvolution) to calculate regression-based ERPs (rERPs) in real-world studies. There are toolboxes for EEGs that have the flexibility for multimodal analysis (cf. [166] or [44]).

Another common method to measure brain activity is *functional near-infrared spectroscopy* (fNIRS), which is increasingly used in interaction research (e.g., [152,177]) due to its ability to capture multimodal signals. fNIRS is a haemodynamic technique to assess functional activity based on the different optical properties of oxygenated and deoxygenated haemoglobin [169]. fNIRS devices are highly portable and relatively robust to motion artifacts (e.g., [9,147]). For example, accurate signals have been obtained even while dancing [127] or playing table tennis [10].

In addition, the emergence of *hyperscanning* studies [120] (i.e., measuring the activity of multiple brains simultaneously) has started to decipher the brain mechanisms underlying social interaction as a whole (rather than recording only the brain of one involved person e.g., [11,54,137]). Opening new ways to measure interaction, hyperscanning provides an experimental means that enables more ecological validity in neuroscientific studies of the social brain. More generally, we can also assess other physiological measures, such as individuals' heart rate or skin conductance, which should be sensitive to individuals' movement.

A challenge of working with multimodal data is to identify the point at which modality-specific information is accessible. For example, the intonational contour provides cues as the speech signal unfolds, and gestures or signs consist of various components. When we are considering time-sensitive data, it is thus crucial to consider the different signal components. ERP research on sign languages has for instance used different time-locking points (triggers) that vary in latency up to around 400 ms: *handshape change* (i.e. the neutral position of the hand between two signs), *target handshape* (point of complete access to target handshape) and *sign onset* (point at which target location is reached) [68].

3.3   Data Synchronization

A peculiarity of synchronization between audio and video is that these data streams tremendously differ in most experiments regarding their sampling rate, with audio having a much higher rate than video. For synchronization purposes, it is advisable that one sampling frequency is an integer multiple of the other (for further recommendations, see [130]). Otherwise, this can lead to a serious timing difference between the two streams (offset). This offset between two streams increases over time, i.e. the longer a recording, the more asynchronous the timing of the streams. In controlled, laboratory experiments, the synchronization of two data streams (e.g., eye-tracking and EEG) is straightforward and usually achieved via software trigger pulses which are simultaneously sent to the two recording devices by the stimulus presentation software (or during preprocessing). Alternatively, a generated audio beep can be recorded on two devices, allowing for synchronization during data post-processing. Synchronization based on image data is less common. In the future, another possibility, especially for non-specialists, might be to move forward with the synchronization of various data streams on multiple computers (which have different internal clocks that can result in delays between signals). Also, since these synchronization events are usually repeated trial by trial, the offset between two streams virtually never reaches a level that might be relevant for analysis. While a high-precision synchronization in the ms range for events between multiple participants or across multiple data streams is not necessary for every application, it is essential for applications such as time-locked neural responses (e.g. event-related potentials), neural synchronization, behavioral synchronization that uses analysis techniques for coherence in the frequency domain (such as wavelet coherence or lagged cross–correlation) and the temporal study of acoustic and visual cues.

In interactive experiments, researchers often do not depend on stationary, wired equipment, and they may even not present stimuli with specific presentation software. One way to facilitate synchronization is then to use a clapperboard like in the film industry, and later align the different streams manually, before processing. A shortcoming of this approach is that, as time unfolds, timing imprecision increases. Another powerful tool is *Lab Streaming Layer (LSL)*, an open source, platform-independent library to send, receive, and synchronize (neuro-)physiological and behavioral data from a large variety of devices[1]. LSL performs clock synchronization in regular intervals (default 5s), keeps track of the differences between recorded data streams, and stores the data and timing information in the extensible data format .xdf[2] via the app LabRecorder[3]. LSL also offers software for smartphones and is adaptable to specific recording situations.

3.4   Manual Annotation and Existing Multimodal Corpora

Annotation Tools. The manual annotation of multimodal data allows researchers to quantitatively analyze multimodal data, by using annotation software such as ELAN [197], EXMARaLDA [168], or Anvil [83]. These types of software allow for the creation of time-aligned annotations on various tiers or tracks, which can in turn be organized hierarchically to show relationship dependencies between different annotations. While these tools are open source, an actual system of coding methods has not been established in the field. As a result, individual researchers, labs, or funded projects develop coding schemes that may be disseminated through the publication of a coding manual.

While multimodal annotation software supports the annotation of both the acoustic signal and the visual signal, a more in-depth and potentially fine-grained annotation of the acoustic signal should preferably be done in Praat [21], for a tutorial on Praat see [20]. Two potential areas of application are conceivable for Praat. First, calculating precise time-aligned measures of gestures-speech interaction requires the accurate demarcation of corresponding domains in speech, e.g., phrase, word, or syllable boundaries which are connected to visually communicative events [102,113]. Second, investigating the prosody-gesture link (e.g., [48,102,175]) requires an analysis of prosodic categories like pitch accents and/or boundary tones. Usually, this type of analysis relies on annotating prosody according to a ToBI system [74] of a given language, which is most conveniently applied in a speech processing tool like Praat. In addition, Praat allows for many kinds of acoustic-phonetic analyses. For gesture research, the individual spectral or temporal parameters can be extracted and related to components of gestures such as the apex, the stroke, the gesture phase or phrase [79]. In particular, with respect to prosody, Praat allows for detailed phonetic analyses of pitch accentuation, concretely their f0-shape or f0-height relations. For instance, measuring the slope of falling pitch accents as a function of the presence or absence of focus can in turn be related to the degree of alignment between a gestures' apex and the pitch accent [59].

Manual annotation is a time-consuming, labor-intensive practice that can highly benefit from technological advances. In terms of gesture annotation, combining (automatic) motion-tracking data with manual annotation allows labelers to achieve consistent measures of time points when an individual gesture begins

---

[1] https://github.com/sccn/labstreaminglayer.
[2] https://github.com/sccn/xdf.
[3] https://github.com/labstreaminglayer/App-LabRecorder.git.

or ends. Recent effort has focused on using automatic annotation tools to speed up the annotation process (e.g., SPUDNIG [163]; the annotation tool from [71]). While such automatic systems have revealed high reliability with human coders identifying moments of movement (i.e., gesturing) and moments of rest, there is still much work to be done with regard to automatically assessing more nuanced aspects of individual gestures (in terms of type or function with regards to speech).

As previously mentioned, much gesture research accounts for the interaction between gesture and speech, consequently resulting in the need for annotation of multiple modes of communication (i.e., not only gestures but also textual transcriptions and further annotation including, e.g., prosodic annotation or part-of-speech annotation). While researchers have a multitude of automatic tools to facilitate such transcriptions and annotations, it is important that the resulting annotations capture the phenomena of interest. That is, they should maintain information such as hesitations, filled pauses, restarts, etc., as these aspects of speech may be of key interest to researchers who are working on speech fluency, for example.

Annotation Schemes. To achieve reliability, comparability, and ease of multimodal data processing, several coding schemes have been developed for (gesture) annotation. Today, an internet search will return dozens of proposed coding schemes, such as M3D [165], OTIM [19], LASG [24], NEUROGES [96], MUMIN [4]. While many of these coding systems were designed to establish and develop standard annotation procedures to assess the form and communicative function of co-speech gestures, the theoretical foundations underlying each system vary widely, as well as the aspects of gestures that the system proposes to annotate. For example, a recent review of 10 gesture annotation systems [164] showed how most systems largely agree on approaches to code gestural form (e.g., handshape, palm orientation); however, only about half of the reviewed systems included guidelines for articulators other than the hands (e.g., head movements or facial expressions). For these articulators, specific annotation schemes have been developed (e.g., for facial expressions [46], gesture timing [84], phonetics [93], turns [173]), also for species other than humans [26,140,192,194]. Methodological differences in assessing gestural meaning are even more pronounced. For example, in the field of gesture studies, McNeill's (1992) [113] conception of gestures being iconic, metaphoric, deictic, or beat types is widely accepted, yet only one of the reviewed annotation systems directly adopts McNeill's categorization of gestures, and only one system takes a "dimensional" approach to assess gestural meaning. Specifically, M3D labels a gesture's meaning in terms of degrees of iconicity, metaphoricity, or deixis as proposed by McNeill in 2006 [114]. Other systems either do not account for gestural meaning or develop their own taxonomies based on criteria stemming from form and/or function. Similar challenges apply to the annotation of sign languages. While the use of glosses to refer to (the meaning of) signs is consistent and signbanks (sign language resources) may link lemma collections to video corpora (e.g., [33]), there are several annotation systems for phonological parameters of manual cues (e.g., [35, 63, 182]) and separate systems for non-manual cues (eyes: [30]; mouth: [34]). In non-human animal research, additional strategies come into play to assess the meaning of a gesture: context and response of the recipients [7, 66, 99].

The availability of so many labeling options offers the advantage that researchers may choose to adopt a particular labeling system over another, as it may be particularly relevant to answer the types of questions the researcher aims to answer. For example, a researcher interested in the pragmatic functions of gestures may be interested in the CorpAGEst labeling scheme [23]. However, the field may also benefit from adopting more standardized terminology and approaches to the assessment of gestural data (e.g., gesture classification, the classification of the pragmatic meanings associated with gesture, gesture phasing schemes; cf. Sect. 1.2).

Any approach to labeling gestural data should be widely accessible to the general community and easily adaptable. Indeed most labeling systems merely publish a short manual that briefly describes the annotation values that are to be employed in ELAN. NEUROGES offers occasional training seminars to become official NEUROGES-Certified labelers. The manual for the M3D system offers more detailed examples, workflow tips, and solutions to ambiguous cases and the system will be soon supported by further online training materials. Thus, the community as a whole would benefit greatly from converging on a set terminology and key approaches to assessing gesture, and crucially to making this approach as openly accessible and reproducible as possible. Importantly, this should be taken into account when considering how we can advance in tandem with computer technology specialists.

In this context, it is also important to keep apart *annotation* (labeling an annotation unit) from *segmentation* (identifying an annotation unit) [180]. A well-known example from gesture studies is the individuation of gestures and the demarcation of gesture phases (preparation, stroke, retraction – see [78]). Since identifying annotation units is logically prior to annotation, differences in the identification of annotation units do not only affect labeling, but also impact any time-related analysis, from descriptive figures (e.g., number of gestures, mean stroke length) to time-series analysis (e.g. [150]). Moreover, they also affect the analysis of temporal relations between the relative timing of and some relationships between communicative events on different channels (see e.g., [135]). Different segmentations furthermore lead to different outputs of multimodal behavior-producing systems, where output behaviors are regimented in terms of the *Behavior Markup Language* [193], a representation format that captures the timing of various signals relative to each other. Note that segmentation poses a genuine problem for evaluating annotation schemes, which is usually carried out in terms of agreement studies (see the corresponding chapters in [70]). The reason is that widespread statistical coefficients like Kappa [31] work on different annotators' labels of a common set of items – whereas it is the very items that are in question in segmentation. To this end, researchers have developed unitizing [87] or segmentation agreement [180] approaches, the latter being also used within the video annotation software ELAN by means of *Staccato* [108].

Hence there are detailed annotation schemes only for a small subset of multimodal communication signals, and there are abstract markup languages for representing structured uni- or multimodal signals. There is still a need for a unified form- and function-based annotation system for the full range of communicative behaviors, a need already addressed but not satisfactorily solved in Birdwhistell's Kinesics [18], which might also be successfully applied in species other than humans.

Multimodal Corpora. Annotated multimodal corpora represent a crucial resource for gesture researchers, as a single corpus may be used to answer a whole host of research questions through different analyses or the addition of further annotation. However, in order to make the most of such resources, it is necessary that they be made openly accessible. Online repositories such as TalkBank[4], The Language Archive[5], or Ortolang[6] host a large number of multimodal corpora. A browse through the multimodal corpora available on these websites makes apparent the vast diversity of the types of corpora available. For example, the TalkBank repository hosts multiple subcomponents which host corpora specific to child development (e.g., CHILDES [109]), multilingualism (e.g., BilingBank), or clinical research (e.g., DementiaBank [16]).

In line with what has been previously mentioned for annotation schemes, the development of multimodal corpora has also often been carried out in order to answer very specific research questions or to reach particular objectives. As such, multimodal corpora often present a lot of variation. For instance, they may include spontaneous conversational speech or play (e.g., the Signes et Familles corpus, [121], or the EVA corpus [116]), recorded presentations (e.g., the M3D-TED corpus [165]) to structured task-based corpora (e.g., the SAGA corpus [106]) to a combination thereof (DGS [154]). For a discussion of the specificity of multimodal corpora, as well as a general overview of the goals of multimodal corpus linguistics, see [138]. Importantly, the multitude of diverse multimodal corpora which are openly available in different online repositories represents a rich resource (for research on humans but not other species) that can be exploited to foster joint advancement in technological and multimodal communication research.

3.5   Machine Learning

In addition to manual labeling, there is also the option of automated data processing by appropriately trained systems. The data generated in this way is much more error-prone than human-generated data, but can be used as a basis for the actual annotation so that the data only needs to be corrected (e.g. by filtering them so that only relevant data points are processed, or by extending them with features that are helpful but beyond the scope of the actual annotation; e.g., [117,202]).

---

[4] www.talkbank.org.
[5] https://archive.mpi.nl/tla/.
[6] https://www.ortolang.fr/.

Most tools are accessible if video footage of the communication is available. There are countless tools (for a review see: [122]) to recognize (communicating) persons and their pose based on these videos (e.g., OpenPose [28], MMPose [32], PaddleDetection [134], OpenFace [12], although the latter has been reported to require a non-negligible amount of manual verification [62]). Depending on the system and model, the general pose of the actor can be determined based on predefined key points such as the head, elbows, shoulders, or feet, but also the position and posture of the hands and fingers, facial movements, and gaze directions. These data can then be used to quantify a number of parameters such as the amount of motion of an actor or a particular body part [186]. In animal research, tools such as DeepLabCut [112] or SLEAP, revolutionized the ease with which researchers can track morphologically unique body poses in a wide range of animals. DeepLabCut also allows for flexible tracking of objects together with biological objects, e.g., in communicative contexts where there are also interactions of objects.

In addition to Pose Estimation, there are also systems that already perform appropriate classifications at a wide variety of levels. For instance, there are classifiers that determine the action and interactions that people perform [205], what type of hand gestures are performed [131], or the classification of emotions based on facial expressions [98], body language [3], or spoken language [81]. As a current limitation, these systems are usually trained on very specific training data and thus, the target classes are predefined. Further, the machine learning community is increasingly taking up the challenge to employ state-of-the art machine learning architectures for manual gesture detection (e.g., [91]), which thereby goes beyond the current tools that researchers might already use (e.g., Spudnig).

Such supporting Machine Learning tools are not limited to visual information but include also acoustic information. For most analyses, a conversion of spoken words to a text format seems necessary, providing a base for the normalization of spoken language which is needed to identify aspectual differences (e.g., in the intonation of otherwise identical words). Countless tools are available to convert spoken language to text (e.g., Whisper [158]). However, depending on the tool, a lot of information can be lost, because many tools may clean up the speech directly: For example, disfluencies, intonation pauses, and overlapping of speakers are usually lost.

Depending on the application, it might be important to use systems that translate from one modality to another, e.g., by reconstructing hand gestures from body movements [125] or facial movements from speech [161]. These models can then be used to analyze the correlation between modalities [27]). However, translations can also contribute to accessibility, e.g., through models that recognize words based on lip movements (lip reading) [49] or translate sign languages into spoken languages [73].

Not only pre-trained models need to be used, but one can train models by using simulations [196] or by understanding the annotation process itself as a bootstrapping approach (a model is trained with a small dataset, the human corrects and improves the model, which results in speeding up the annotation process [198]). Promising developments that increase flexibility are tools such as NOVA [15]. Using a principle of "collaborative machine learning", NOVA provides a general user interface tailored towards manual annotation, with further integration of supervised machine classification methods (such as Support Vector Machines or Neural Networks). These can be trained on initial manual annotations, in turn allowing the user to hand-correct and retrain the classifier. In general, a restriction is that many of these modern machine learning systems are not freely available or easy to set up and use, require expensive hardware (graphic cards), or require specialized programming effort, making these systems very inaccessible to researchers from disciplines other than computer science.

In addition, personal data often raise ethical issues. For example, models that reconstruct speech based on lip movements can be used for people who do not like to be overheard, or there are initial approaches that can track people and movements based on reflected Wi-Fi signals [53, 160]. The machine learning community generates many ongoing interdisciplinary implications that go beyond developing tools. A good example in this regard is the recent advance in the artificial recreation of believable human co-speech gestures, or gesture synthesis in short [128]. While it may seem that gesture synthesis might only have implications for human-computer interaction systems such as avatar design in games or other contexts, it also indirectly informs theories in cognitive science and linguistics. For example, machine learning models trained on associations of acoustic signal with body poses occurring as co-speech gestures, become very capable of synthesizing rhythmic beat-like gestures from novel acoustic signals alone [55, 128]. Therefore, such models show that there is information in speech sounds that can reliably predict the presence of a gesture [203], and they also allow identifying what features in speech are predictive for specific kinematic properties in gesture [50].

Exciting further research in this direction comes from work that makes use of joint multimodal embedding spaces. Neural networks (transformers) trained on detecting co-regularities between gesture poses and speech content (represented as text), for instance, can make reliable predictions about discourse markers, and can differentiate between the language spoken (Spanish vs. English) based on body poses alone [2]. These findings from the machine learning community thus forward theorizing in multimodal communication research about the information available in multimodal signals, and how they inform one another, and they will also further shape cognitive science research about what information humans use in practice during communication [187].

3.6 Factors that Can Accelerate Integration Between Disciplines

In order to promote interdisciplinarity in multimodality research and implement automatic tools and methods in the process, cooperation and mutual help are crucial. This entails understanding the other field's questions and mode of inquiry, to formulate joint research questions and possibly conduct studies in a

420 A. Gregori et al.

way that other modes of inquiry may become available. Moreover, this interoperability is a mutual endeavor, in that researchers need to become more literate about each other's core state-of-the-art and the key methods for investigating the same phenomenon.

Data Requirements, Metadata Practices, and Tools to Overcome Privacy Challenges to Open Data. If we are moving towards more integrated fields, rather than isolated pockets of specializations [129], bridges between disciplines need to be built. One such bridge is metadata maintenance, i.e. how we archive data so that it is maximally reusable later, possibly also in other fields with different conventions. The fast pace of algorithm development in computer science drives innovation, but may sometimes be at odds with requirements for empirical studies that try to use these algorithms as research tools. For example, replicability, evaluation of validity, and e.g., clinical utility require systematic investigation of larger data samples [85]. The resulting resources (e.g., stimulus databases, tests, algorithms, tutorials, workshops) should ideally be available to the scientific community according to open science principles (e.g., [165,184]).

Open science principles can be a challenge for the protection of privacy. Indeed, especially in multimodal communication research on humans, original data that support one's analyses are often not openly shared, because they often consist of audiovisual recordings of identifiable people. There is, however, an increasing number of tools that allow to partially mask the identities from video and audio automatically, while still extracting non-identifiable information that can support analyses, such as facial, hand, and body pose information [82,133,156]. It is important to note that these tools do not count as anonymization tools, because either the transformed sound is still re-transformable to its original (thereby allowing identification in principle) or is still present next to a bodily mask. Indeed, as the yearly voice privacy challenge[7] shows, the anonymization of voices while maintaining their rich transmission of information is still an unsolved problem. In any case, new computer vision and signal processing methods allow for decreasing privacy risks when sharing multimodal data, which is a positive development. Hopefully, these practices will be increasingly picked up by researchers working in different domains.

Community of Learners. We believe that an important way to become more literate as a community of researchers is to take up responsibilities that support a "community of learners". In the most general sense, this means that as researchers, we strive to provide the didactic means to facilitate becoming literate in the particular methods employed. Practically, this can mean a number of things. We need to write more transparent "computationally reproducible" manuscripts ensuring that data and code are well-annotated with additional documentation provided. There are many tools available now to fully integrate and write one's manuscript in a "computationally reproducible way",

---

[7] https://www.voiceprivacychallenge.org/.

enabling readers to follow the computation procedures step-by-step using tools like RMarkdown or Jupyter notebook [142] or more recent platform agnostic tools (Quarto[8]), which depict one strategy to make publications and tools easier to reuse.

Another practical implication of a community of learners is that new tools or terminologies are supported in the literature with hands-on tutorials that are written for either more or less informed audiences. The Huggingface platform[9], for example, offers a wide collection of pre-built and even fine-tuned machine learning models provided by the community, including sample code and "spaces" where they can be tried out directly. This may mean that a tutorial on machine learning or phonology will look very different depending on whether you are tailoring it toward readers in computer science or linguistics. Lastly, of course, there must be undergraduate and graduate curricular integration at universities that ensure that the different fields can, and do cooperate.

3.7 Summary

In this section, we provided insights into the currently available tools, methods, and databases for data collection, enrichment, and analysis in multimodal communication research. A non-exhaustive overview of these resources is given in Fig. 3. Focusing on the visual and acoustic modes of communication, we started by presenting possible recording techniques for the visual mode (Sect. 3.1) and communicative modes in general (Sect. 3.2). Before or after recording, the synchronization between different types of data needs to be ensured (Sect. 3.3). Subsequently, data can be enriched by manual segmentation and annotation (Sect. 3.4) or by using natural language processing (Sect. 3.5). Then, datasets can be analyzed, assembled to form multimodal corpora (Sect. 3.4) and used across research disciplines to move multimodal communication research forward (Sect. 3.6).

4 Discussion

This paper aimed to provide an overview of the currently available tools and methods in multimodal communication research. We presented state-of-the-art tools that can facilitate research in this field and expressed specific requirements to achieve feasible technological development that can be integrated into data collection, preparation, and analysis in the visual and acoustic domains. Multimodal data acquisition and digital data analysis are yet relatively new challenges in communication research (although they have been addressed with a different focus in semiotics [148, Part 2], Conversation Analysis [167], and human-computer interaction [132]). Therefore, we highlighted the need to introduce specific terminology and importantly, presented the availability of various kinds of systems. These are steps in establishing congruency within the fields of multimodal communication research on the one hand, but also computer science on the other hand.

---

[8] https://github.com/quarto-dev/quarto.
[9] https://huggingface.co/ (last visited 27.01.2023).

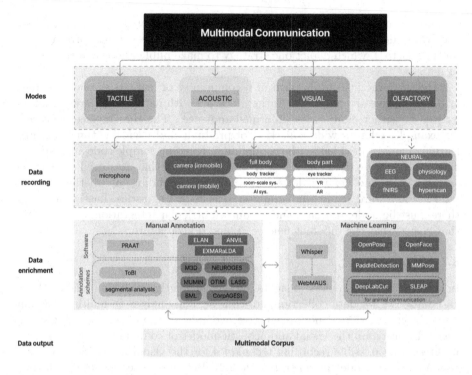

Fig. 3. Non-exhaustive overview over available tools for data recording and enrichment. (Color figure online)

We argue that increased interdisciplinarity in cognitive science and computer science with regard to multimodal communication will have important implications: On the one hand, increased literacy by linguists/cognitive scientists in computer science implies a better understanding of what machine learning algorithms actually do, and what they can do for multimodal communication in the future (e.g., better understandings of large language models like Lambda or GPT3 [181]). Similarly, while multimodal researchers might hope that annotating minimal meaningful units as metaphoric gesture strokes will soon be something of the past, it is also clear that machine learning systems cannot learn to classify linguistic categories if researchers do not first agree on the definition or application of those categories. On the other hand, computer scientists becoming more literate in aspects of multimodal communication will also prevent downright renderings of the object of study (e.g., sign languages being understood as incomplete languages; [199]) and minimally it will also combine what can be done with what a particular community of users benefits from (cf. [47,89]).

In short, mutually informed research communities can advance research in their own respective fields with crucial understandings from other disciplines. As a side benefit, interdisciplinarity also provides training data for machine learning for processing of increasingly complex linguistic and multimodal structures (manual annotations lead to the training of models which in turn can improve the underlying annotations; e.g., Multimodal Distributional Semantics [13,157]). Investigating the synchronization of acoustic and visual aspects of communication opens the way to investigate multimodal transfer learning in new ways[10]. One example is how data from one modality are technologically used to segment or disambiguate data in another modality or to reconstruct them in an expectation-driven manner when they have not been manifested or detected [14,139]. This approach would eventually allow us to study the diverse relationships and interdependencies of the modalities involved – whether on the level of signals or their higher-level representations. An application of multimodal interoperability allows the transfer and leveraging of annotations of one modality for the annotation or automatic processing of another modality.

We can imagine the analysis of communication to be broken down into different levels of observation, which can be visualized as follows (cf. Fig. 2): **signal → event → communicative behavior → [from quantitative to qualitative] meaning → embedding in utterance context**. From left to right, there is a tendency for an increased amount of interpretation, even from a human point of view. In terms of measurements, we are expecting an increase of nominal scale measurements (classifications; cf. the distinction between well-understood type-i measurements and less understood type-ii measurements as described by [61] – on the right-hand side it is even not obvious what the scales should be, indicated by the square bracket parenthesis ("from quantitative to qualitative"). With the raw signal as input to a machine learning algorithm, it is therefore an increasingly difficult task to automatically classify the respective units of observation: Acoustic and visual signals and communicative events can be identified more easily and automatically than the more complex communicative acts that involve meaning, unless there is a huge amount of data annotated for the various observational levels.

These considerations, against the backdrop of the overview given mainly in Sects. 2 and 3, point at a number of (near-) future challenges:

- The majority of tools focus on the initial – and fundamental – step of recording signals of various provenance, and in a synchronized way. In order to progress from tracking to parsing, tools for segmentation and classification are of course welcome. As above mentioned, this is not an obligation for computer science in the first place; rather communication researchers are in the need to agree on annotation schemes for individual signals as well as integrated ones for multiple signals (see Sect. 3.4), and provide annotated datasets.
- Computational linguistics has developed powerful algorithms and tools for processing text. However, these devices cannot readily be applied to spoken or signed languages: the speech or sign stream are signals that do not come in discrete units [159]. Hence, the acoustic or visual signal has to be transcribed first. In the acoustic domain, automatic transcription is brought about by Automatic Speech Recognition (ASR) systems.
  However, current ASR systems miss out on a couple of features of the audio file [103]. For instance, the sound string "bob are (.) uh is_sleeping"

---

[10] For a recent overview of transfer learning, see [195].

(using minimal notation following a conversation-analytic transcription system [173]) is transcribed as *Bob is sleeping*. While this output can be input to natural language processing tools, it lacks two peculiarities that are important for multimodal communication studies: the speech error [97] is ignored as is the hesitation marker *uh*, which may both trigger a lexical access-related gesturing [86]. In order to capture these features of spoken language, ASR systems have to be developed "more impurely" from a phonetic and incremental point of view, including that communication researchers agree on a useful transcription system (for humans *and* computers) – and provide big amounts of transcribed data.

- While temporal synchrony is an important aspect of multiple signals in face-to-face interactions, it yet does not fully determine coordination of semantic meaning of those signals [162]. While temporal alignment is an observable, measurable feature of multi-channel communication, semantic integration involves interpretation [94]. That is, with temporal alignment as with any signal, the meaning (also the grammar) is not in the signal but imposed by the one processing the signal. Hence, it remains to be seen how far automatic multi-signal classifications (the top-right node in Fig. 2) can be pushed.

- We observe a plurality of methods: there are VR-based tracking methods (see Sect. 3.1), methods that work on the basis of video recordings (currently the most widespread ones; Sects. 3.1 and 3.5), and physiological and neurological recordings (Sect. 3.2). This pluralism poses the questions (i) whether the approaches should be developed into enhanced stand-alone pipelines, or (ii) how they can be inter-operated despite their *prima facie* incommensurability. In either case, it would surely be beneficial to incorporate some of the advances from computer vision and machine learning (Sect. 3.5).

We believe that interoperability in multimodal communication will play an important role in the further development of multimodal annotation. Thus, we envision a system in which actions are generated by subjects in controlled environments to provide experimenters with controlled access to multimodal data. This can ground the communicative aspects involved in these actions and their manifestations in the form of gestures, gazes, body movements, etc., but also in equally controlled objects, their properties, and relations. One can see in this an alternative to independent approaches to multimodal research, an alternative that is integrating various views on multimodality.

Concretely, the wishes of our consortium towards the automatization of processes in multimodal research concern multiple steps in data acquisition. Starting with the facilitation of programming communication experiments (partly automated by functional software) and generating synchronized (acoustic and visual) stimuli, technical innovation can unburden research before data collection. As has been brought up in this paper, technical innovation can improve the processing of data for analysis. This may include the automatic identification of specific factors of visual data annotation e.g., (on-/offset and turning points of movements; temporal alignment between acoustic and visual cues; grouping and clustering of gestures; up to identification of smallest meaning bearing units).

Ideally, this can ultimately be achieved for gestures as well as signs and for human and non-human communication. Similarly, the automatic processing of acoustic signals could be facilitated by providing better segmentation of vocalized input or automated prosodic annotation. This can ideally lead to the training of neural networks (as mentioned in Sect. 3.5) which could largely support the annotation of big data sets.

This leads us to a final, self-reflective note: We started out by envisioning "a roadmap for technical innovation in multimodal communication research". On every path on this roadmap we observed, however, the need for well-worked out formats, standards and guidelines, *defining our units of analysis* in the first place. Addressing this, important roadmap ground will already be covered.

Table of contributions (contributions indicated by grey cell color)

Initials	Concept	Sec 1	Sec 2	Sec 3	Sec 4	Rev/Edit
AG	▓	▓	▓	▓	▓	▓
FA						▓
IB				▓		
AC	▓	▓				▓
LF				▓		
SF	▓	▓				
AH				▓		
OH		▓				
FK				▓		▓
JL		▓				
KL						▓
AL	▓			▓		▓
AM					▓	▓
KTN						▓
WP	▓					
PP			▓	▓		
PR			▓		▓	
PSR			▓			
MSR			▓	▓		
PS		▓	▓	▓		
SS			▓			
VS		▓	▓	▓	▓	
PT		▓		▓		▓
CvE			▓			

References

1. Abner, N., Cooperrider, K., Goldin-Meadow, S.: Gesture for linguists: a handy primer. Lang. Linguist. Compass **9**(11), 437–451 (2015). https://doi.org/10.1111/lnc3.12168
2. Abzaliev, A., Owens, A., Mihalcea, R.: Towards understanding the relation between gestures and language. In: Proceedings of the 29th International Conference on Computational Linguistics, pp. 5507–5520 (2022)
3. Ahmed, F., Bari, A.H., Gavrilova, M.L.: Emotion recognition from body movement. IEEE Access **8**, 11761–11781 (2019). https://doi.org/10.1109/ACCESS.2019.2963113
4. Allwood, J., Cerrato, L., Jokinen, K., Navarretta, C., Paggio, P.: The mumin coding scheme for the annotation of feedback, turn management and sequencing phenomena. Lang. Resour. Eval. **41**(3), 273–287 (2007). https://doi.org/10.1007/s10579-007-9061-5
5. Alviar, C., Dale, R., Dewitt, A., Kello, C.: Multimodal coordination of sound and movement in music and speech. Discourse Process. **57**(8), 682–702 (2020). https://doi.org/10.1080/0163853X.2020.1768500
6. Alviar, C., Kello, C.T., Dale, R.: Multimodal coordination and pragmatic modes in conversation. Language Sciences, p. 101524 (2023). https://doi.org/10.1016/j.langsci.2022.101524
7. Amici, F., Oña, L., Liebal, K.: Compositionality in primate gestural communication and multicomponent signal displays. Int. J. Primatol. (2022). https://doi.org/10.1007/s10764-022-00316-9
8. Anderson, C.A., Wiggins, I.M., Kitterick, P.T., Hartley, D.E.H.: Adaptive benefit of cross-modal plasticity following cochlear implantation in deaf adults. Proc. Natl. Acad. Sci. U.S.A. **114**(38), 10256–10261 (2017). https://doi.org/10.1073/pnas.1704785114
9. Aranyi, G., Pecune, F., Charles, F., Pelachaud, C., Cavazza, M.: Affective interaction with a virtual character through an fNIRS brain-computer interface. Front. Comput. Neurosci. **10**, 70 (Jul 2016). https://doi.org/10.3389/fncom.2016.00070
10. Baladrin, J.B., et al.: Imaging brain function with functional near-infrared spectroscopy in unconstrained environments. Front. Hum. Neurosci. **11**, 258 (2017). https://doi.org/10.3389/fnhum.2017.00258
11. Balconi, M., Fronda, G., Bartolo, A.: Affective, social, and informative gestures reproduction in human interaction: hyperscanning and brain connectivity. J. Mot. Behav. **53**(3), 296–315 (2021). https://doi.org/10.1080/00222895.2020.1774490
12. Baltrusaitis, T., Zadeh, A., Lim, Y.C., Morency, L.P.: Openface 2.0: Facial behavior analysis toolkit. In: 2018 13th IEEE International Conference On Automatic Face & Gesture Recognition (FG 2018), pp. 59–66. IEEE (2018). https://doi.org/10.1109/FG.2018.00019
13. Baroni, M.: Grounding distributional semantics in the visual world. Lang. Linguist. Compass **10**(1), 3–13 (2016). https://doi.org/10.1111/lnc3.12170
14. Barros, P., Parisi, G.I., Fu, D., Liu, X., Wermter, S.: Expectation learning for adaptive crossmodal stimuli association. In: EUCog Meeting Proceedings. EUCog, EUCog Meeting (Nov 2017). ARXIV:1801.07654
15. Baur, T., et al.: eXplainable cooperative machine learning with NOVA. KI - Künstliche Intelligenz **34**(2), 143–164 (2020). https://doi.org/10.1007/s13218-020-00632-3

16. Becker, J.T., Boller, F., Lopez, O.L., Saxton, J., McGonigle, K.L.: The natural history of Alzheimer's disease: description of study cohort and accuracy of diagnosis. Arch. Neurol. **51**(6), 585–594 (1994). https://doi.org/10.1001/archneur.1994.00540180063015

17. Bierman, A.K.: That there are no iconic signs. Res. **23**(2), 243–249 (1962). https://doi.org/10.2307/2104916

18. Birdwhistell, R.L.: Kinesics and Context. Conduct and Communication Series, University of Pennsylvania Press, Philadelphia (1970). https://doi.org/10.9783/9780812201284

19. Blache, P., Bertrand, R., Ferré, G., Pallaud, B., Prévot, L., Rauzy, S.: The corpus of interactional data: A large multimodal annotated resource. In: Handbook of linguistic annotation, pp. 1323–1356. Springer (2017). https://doi.org/10.1007/978-94-024-0881-2_51

20. Boersma, P.: The use of Praat in corpus research. In: Durand, J., Gut, U., Kristoffersen, G. (eds.) The Oxford handbook of corpus phonology, pp. 342–360. Oxford handbooks in linguistics, Oxford University Press, Oxford (2014). https://doi.org/10.1093/oxfordhb/9780199571932.013.016

21. Boersma, P., Weenink, D.: Praat: doing phonetics by computer [computer program] version 6.3.03. https://www.praat.org/ (2022)

22. Bohannon, R.W., Harrison, S., Kinsella-Shaw, J.: Reliability and validity of pendulum test measures of spasticity obtained with the polhemus tracking system from patients with chronic stroke. J. Neuroeng. Rehabil. **6**(1), 1–7 (2009). https://doi.org/10.1186/1743-0003-6-30

23. Bolly, C.T.: CorpAGEst annotation manual (ii. speech annotation guidelines) (2016). https://corpagest.wordpress.com/working-papers/

24. Bressem, J.: A linguistic perspective on the notation of form features in gestures. In: Müller, C., Cienki, A., Fricke, E., Ladewig, S.H., McNeill, David und Bressem, J. (eds.) Body - Language - Communication. An International Handbook on Multimodality in Human Interaction, Handbooks of Linguistics and Communication Science, vol. 1, chap. 70, pp. 1079–1089. De Gruyter Mouton, Berlin and Boston (2013). https://doi.org/10.1515/9783110261318.1079

25. Burks, A.W.: Icon, index, and symbol. Res. **9**(4), 673–689 (1949). https://doi.org/10.2307/2103298

26. Caeiro, C.C., Waller, B.M., Zimmermann, E., Burrows, A.M., Davila-Ross, M.: OrangFACS: A muscle-based facial movement coding system for orangutans (Pongo spp.). Int. J. Primatol. **34**(1), 115–129 (2013). https://doi.org/10.1007/s10764-012-9652-x

27. Caliskan, A., Bryson, J., Narayanan, A.: Semantics derived automatically from language corpora contain human-like biases. Science **356**(6334), 183–186 (2017). https://doi.org/10.1126/science.aal4230

28. Cao, Z., Hidalgo Martinez, G., Simon, T., Wei, S., Sheikh, Y.A.: OpenPose: real-time multi-person 2d pose estimation using part affinity fields. IEEE Trans. Pattern Anal. Mach. Intell. (2019). https://doi.org/10.1109/TPAMI.2019.2929257

29. Cavallo, A., Koul, A., Ansuini, C., Capozzi, F., Becchio, C.: Decoding intentions from movement kinematics. Sci. Rep. **6**(1), 1–8 (2016). https://doi.org/10.1038/srep37036

30. Chételat-Pelé, E., Braffort, A., Véronis, J.: Annotation of non manual gestures: Eyebrow movement description. In: sign-lang@ LREC 2008, pp. 28–32. European Language Resources Association (ELRA) (2008)

31. Cohen, J.: A coefficient of agreement for nominal scales. Educ. Psychol. Measur. **20**, 37–46 (1960). https://doi.org/10.1177/001316446002000104

32. Contributors, M.: Openmmlab pose estimation toolbox and benchmark. https:// github.com/open-mmlab/mmpose (2020)
33. Cormier, K., Crasborn, O., Bank, R.: Digging into signs: Emerging annotation standards for sign language corpora. In: Efthimiou, E., Fotinea, S.E., Hanke, T., Hochgesang, J.A., Kristoffersen, J., Mesch, J. (eds.) Proceedings of the LREC2016 7th Workshop on the Representation and Processing of Sign Languages: Corpus Mining, pp. 35–40. European Language Resources Association (ELRA), Portorož, Slovenia (May 2016)
34. Crasborn, O., Bank, R.: An annotation scheme for the linguistic study of mouth actions in sign languages (2014). https://hdl.handle.net/2066/132960
35. Crasborn, O., Zwitserlood, I., van der Kooij, E., Ormel, E.: Global SignBank manual, version 2 (11 2020). https://doi.org/10.13140/RG.2.2.16205.67045/1
36. Cutler, A., Dahan, D., Van Donselaar, W.: Prosody in the comprehension of spoken language: a literature review. Lang. Speech 40(2), 141–201 (1997)
37. Dale, R.: The possibility of a pluralist cognitive science. J. Exp. Theor. Artif. Intell. 20(3), 155–179 (2008). https://doi.org/10.1080/09528130802319078
38. Dale, R., Warlaumont, A., Johnson, K.: The fundamental importance of method to theory. Nature Rev. Psychol. 2, 55–66 (2022). https://doi.org/10.1038/s44159-022-00120-5
39. Danner, S.G., Barbosa, A.V., Goldstein, L.: Quantitative analysis of multimodal speech data. J. Phon. 71, 268–283 (2018). https://doi.org/10.1016/j.wocn.2018.09.007
40. Dogdu, C., Kessler, T., Schneider, D., Shadaydeh, M., Schweinberger, S.R.: A comparison of machine learning algorithms and feature sets for automatic vocal emotion recognition in speech. Sensors 22(19), (2022). https://doi.org/10.3390/s22197561
41. Drimalla, H., Baskow, I., Behnia, B., Roepke, S., Dziobek, I.: Imitation and recognition of facial emotions in autism: A computer vision approach. Molecular Autism 12(1) (2021). https://doi.org/10.1186/s13229-021-00430-0
42. Ebert, C., Ebert, C.: Gestures, demonstratives, and the attributive/referential distinction. Talk at Semantics and Philosophy in Europe 7, ZAS, Berlin (2014)
43. Ebert, C., Ebert, C., Hörnig, R.: Demonstratives as dimension shifters. Proc. Sinn und Bedeutung 24(1), 161–178 (2020)
44. Ehinger, B.V., Dimigen, O.: Unfold: an integrated toolbox for overlap correction, non-linear modeling, and regression-based EEG analysis. PeerJ 7, e7838 (2019). https://doi.org/10.7717/peerj.7838
45. von Eiff, C.I., Frühholz, S., Korth, D., Guntinas-Lichius, O., Schweinberger, S.R.: Crossmodal benefits to vocal emotion perception in cochlear implant users. iScience 25(12), 105711 (2022). https://doi.org/10.1016/j.isci.2022.105711
46. Ekman, P., Friesen, W.V.: Facial Action Coding System: A Technique for the Measurement of Facial Movement. Consulting Psychologists Press, Palo Alto, CA (1978). https://doi.org/10.1037/t27734-000
47. Erard, M.: Why sign-language gloves don't help deaf people. The Atlantic. https://www.theatlantic.com/technology/archive/2017/11/why-sign-language-gloves-dont-help-deaf-people/545441/ (2017)
48. Esteve-Gibert, N., Prieto, P.: Prosodic structure shapes the temporal realization of intonation and manual gesture movements. J. Speech Lang. Hear. Res. 56(3), 850–864 (2013). https://doi.org/10.1044/1092-4388(2012/12-0049)
49. Fernandez-Lopez, A., Sukno, F.M.: Survey on automatic lip-reading in the era of deep learning. Image Vis. Comput. 78, 53–72 (2018). https://doi.org/10.1016/j.imavis.2018.07.002

50. Ferstl, Y., Neff, M., McDonnell, R.: Understanding the predictability of gesture parameters from speech and their perceptual importance. In: Proceedings of the 20th ACM International Conference on Intelligent Virtual Agents, pp. 1–8 (2020). https://doi.org/10.1145/3383652.3423882

51. Filippeschi, A., Schmitz, N., Miezal, M., Bleser, G., Ruffaldi, E., Stricker, D.: Survey of motion tracking methods based on inertial sensors: a focus on upper limb human motion. Sensors **17**(6), 1257 (2017). https://doi.org/10.3390/s17061257

52. Frühholz, S., Schweinberger, S.R.: Nonverbal auditory communication - evidence for integrated neural systems for voice signal production and perception. Prog. Neurobiol. **199**, 101948 (2021). https://doi.org/10.1016/j.pneurobio.2020.101948

53. Geng, J., Huang, D., De la Torre, F.: Densepose from wifi. arXiv preprint arXiv:2301.00250 (2022)

54. Gerloff, C., Konrad, K., Kruppa, J., Schulte-Rüther, M., Reindl, V.: Autism Spectrum Disorder Classification Based on Interpersonal Neural Synchrony: Can Classification be Improved by Dyadic Neural Biomarkers Using Unsupervised Graph Representation Learning? In: Abdulkadir, A., et al. (eds.) Machine Learning in Clinical Neuroimaging, vol. 13596, pp. 147–157. Springer Nature Switzerland, Cham (2022). https://doi.org/10.1007/978-3-031-17899-3_15

55. Ginosar, S., Bar, A., Kohavi, G., Chan, C., Owens, A., Malik, J.: Learning individual styles of conversational gesture. In: Proceedings of the IEEE/CVF Conference on Computer Vision and Pattern Recognition, pp. 3497–3506 (2019)

56. Ginzburg, J., Poesio, M.: Grammar is a system that characterizes talk in interaction. Front. Psychol. **7**, 1938 (2016). https://doi.org/10.3389/fpsyg.2016.01938

57. Goodman, N.: Languages of Art, 2nd edn. An Approach to a Theory of Symbols. Hackett Publishing Company Inc, Idianapolis (1976)

58. Goodwin, C.: Pointing as situated practice. In: Kita, S. (ed.) Pointing: Where Language, Culture, and Cognition Meet, chap. 2, pp. 217–241. Lawrence Erlbaum Associates Inc, Mahwah, New Jersey (2003). https://doi.org/10.4324/9781410607744

59. Gregori, A., Kügler, F.: Multimodal marking of focus: Articulatory and visual hyperarticulation (submitted)

60. Gussenhoven, C.: The phonology of tone and intonation. Cambridge: Cambridge University Press (2004). https://doi.org/10.1017/CBO9780511616983

61. Gwet, K.: Handbook of Inter-Rater Reliability. STATAXIS Publishing Company, Gaithersburg, MD (2001)

62. Hammadi, Y., Grondin, F., Ferland, F., Lebel, K.: Evaluation of various state of the art head pose estimation algorithms for clinical scenarios. Sensors **22**(18), 6850 (2022). https://doi.org/10.3390/s22186850

63. Hanke, T.: HamNoSys - representing sign language data in language resources and language processing contexts. In: LREC. vol. 4, pp. 1–6 (2004)

64. Hartz, A., Guth, B., Jording, M., Vogeley, K., Schulte-Rüther, M.: Temporal behavioral parameters of on-going gaze encounters in a virtual environment. Front. Psychol. **12** (2021). https://doi.org/10.3389/fpsyg.2021.673982

65. Herrmann, A., Pendzich, N.K.: Nonmanual gestures in sign languages. In: Müller, C., Cienki, A., Fricke, E., Ladewig, S.H., McNeill, D., Bressem, J. (eds.) Handbook Body - Language - Communication, pp. 2147–2160. DeGruyter Mouton, Berlin, Boston (2014)

66. Hobaiter, C., Byrne, R.W.: The meanings of chimpanzee gestures. Curr. Biol. **24**, 1596–1600 (2014)

67. Holler, J., Levinson, S.C.: Multimodal language processing in human communication. Trends Cogn. Sci. **23**(8), 639–652 (2019). https://doi.org/10.1016/j.tics.2019.05.006

68. Hosemann, J., Herrmann, A., Steinbach, M., Bornkessel-Schlesewsky, I., Schlesewsky, M.: Lexical prediction via forward models: N400 evidence from German sign language. Neuropsychologia **51**(11), 2224–2237 (2013). https://doi.org/10.1016/j.neuropsychologia.2013.07.013

69. Höhle, T.N.: Über Komposition und Derivation: zur Konstituentenstruktur von Wortbildungsprodukten im Deutschen. Z. Sprachwiss. **1**(1), 76–112 (1982). https://doi.org/10.1515/zfsw.1982.1.1.76

70. Ide, N., Pustejovsky, J. (eds.): Handbook of Linguistic Annotation. Springer, Netherlands, Dordrecht (2017). https://doi.org/10.1007/978-94-024-0881-2_1

71. Ienaga, N., Cravotta, A., Terayama, K., Scotney, B.W., Saito, H., Busà, M.G.: Semi-automation of gesture annotation by machine learning and human collaboration. Language Resources and Evaluation, pp. 1–28 (2022). https://doi.org/10.1007/s10579-022-09586-4

72. Jaimes, A., Sebe, N.: Multimodal human-computer interaction: a survey. Comput. Vis. Image Underst. **108**(1), 116–134 (2007). https://doi.org/10.1016/j.cviu.2006.10.019

73. Jiang, Z., Moryossef, A., Müller, M., Ebling, S.: Machine translation between spoken languages and signed languages represented in signwriting. arXiv preprint arXiv:2210.05404 (2022). https://doi.org/10.48550/arXiv.2210.05404

74. Jun, S.A.: The ToBI transcription system: conventions, strengths, and challenges. In: Barnes, J., Shattuck-Hufnagel, S. (eds.) Prosodic Theory and Practice, pp. 151–181. MIT Press, Cambridge (2022)

75. Kano, F., Tomonaga, M.: How chimpanzees look at pictures: a comparative eye-tracking study. Proc. Royal Society B: Biol. Sci. **276**(1664), 1949–1955 (2009)

76. Kelly, S., Healey, M., Özyürek, A., Holler, J.: The processing of speech, gesture, and action during language comprehension. Psychonom. Bull. Rev. **22**(2), 517–523 (2014). https://doi.org/10.3758/s13423-014-0681-7

77. Kempson, R., Cann, R., Gregoromichelaki, E., Chatzikyriakidis, S.: Language as mechanisms for interaction. Theor. Linguist. **42**(3–4), 203–276 (2016). https://doi.org/10.1515/tl-2016-0011

78. Kendon, A.: Some relationships between body motion and speech. An analysis of an example. In: Siegman, A.W., Pope, B. (eds.) Studies in Dyadic Communication, chap. 9, pp. 177–210. Pergamon Press, Elmsford, NY (1972)

79. Kendon, A.: Gesticulation and speech: Two aspects of the process of utterance. In: Key, M.R. (ed.) The Relationship of Verbal and Nonverbal Communication, pp. 207–227. No. 25 in Contributions to the Sociology of Language, Mouton, The Hague (1980)

80. Kendon, A.: Gesture: Visible Action as Utterance. Cambridge University Press, Cambridge, MA (2004). https://doi.org/10.1017/CBO9780511807572

81. Khalil, R.A., Jones, E., Babar, M.I., Jan, T., Zafar, M.H., Alhussain, T.: Speech emotion recognition using deep learning techniques: a review. IEEE Access **7**, 117327–117345 (2019). https://doi.org/10.1109/ACCESS.2019.2936124

82. Khasbage, Y., et al.: The Red Hen Anonymizer and the Red Hen Protocol for de-identifying audiovisual recordings. Linguist. Vanguard (0) (2022). https://doi.org/10.1515/lingvan-2022-0017

83. Kipp, M.: Anvil-a generic annotation tool for multimodal dialogue. In: Seventh European Conference on Speech Communication and Technology, pp. 2001–354 (2001). https://doi.org/10.21437/Eurospeech.

84. Kipp, M., Neff, M., Albrecht, I.: An annotation scheme for conversational gestures: how to economically capture timing and form. J. Lang. Resour. Eval. - Special Issue Multimodal Corpora **41**(3–4), 325–339 (2007). https://doi.org/10.1007/s10579-007-9053-5

85. Kowallik, A.E., Schweinberger, S.R.: Sensor-based technology for social information processing in autism: a review. Sensors **19**(21), 4787 (2019). https://doi.org/10.3390/s19214787

86. Krauss, R.M., Hadar, U.: The role of speech-related arm/hand gestures in word retrieval. In: Campbell, R., Messing, L.S. (eds.) Gesture, speech, and sign, pp. 93–116. Oxford University Press, Oxford (1999). https://doi.org/10.1093/acprof:oso/9780198524519.003.0006

87. Krippendorff, K.: Content Analysis: An Introduction to Its Methodology, 4th edn. SAGE Publications, Thousand Oaks, CA (2018)

88. Kruppa, J.A., et al.: Brain and motor synchrony in children and adolescents with ASD-a fNIRS hyperscanning study. Social Cogn. Affect. Neurosci. **16**(1–2), 103–116 (07 2020). https://doi.org/10.1093/scan/nsaa092

89. Kubina, P., Abramov, O., Lücking, A.: Barrier-free communication. In: Mehler, A., Romary, L. (eds.) Handbook of Technical Communication, chap. 19, pp. 645–706. No. 8 in Handbooks of Applied Linguistics, De Gruyter Mouton, Berlin and Boston (2012)

90. Kuhnke, P., Beaupain, M.C., Arola, J., Kiefer, M., Hartwigsen, G.: Meta-analytic evidence for a novel hierarchical model of conceptual processing. Neurosci. Biobehav. Rev. **144**, 104994 (2023). https://doi.org/10.1016/j.neubiorev.2022.104994

91. Köpüklü, O., Gunduz, A., Kose, N., Rigoll, G.: Real-time hand gesture detection and classification using convolutional neural networks. In: Proceedings of the 14th IEEE International Conference on Automatic Face & Gesture Recognition, pp. 1–8. FG 2019 (2019). https://doi.org/10.1109/FG.2019.8756576

92. Ladd, D.: Intonational phonology. Cambridge: Cambridge University Press, 2 edn. (2012). https://doi.org/10.1017/CBO9780511808814

93. Ladefoged, P.: The revised international phonetic alphabet. Language **66**(3), 550–552 (1990). https://doi.org/10.2307/414611

94. Lascarides, A., Stone, M.: Discourse coherence and gesture interpretation. Gesture **9**(2), 147–180 (2009). https://doi.org/10.1075/gest.9.2.01las

95. Latash, M.L.: Synergy. Oxford University Press (2008). https://doi.org/10.1093/acprof:oso/9780195333169.001.0001

96. Lausberg, H., Sloetjes, H.: Coding gestural behavior with the neuroges-elan system. Behav. Res. Methods **41**(3), 841–849 (2009). https://doi.org/10.3758/BRM.41.3.841

97. Levelt, W.J.M.: Monitoring and self-repair in speech. Cognition **14**(1), 41–104 (1983). https://doi.org/10.1016/0010-0277(83)90026-4

98. Li, S., Deng, W.: Deep facial expression recognition: a survey. IEEE Trans. Affect. Comput. **13**(3), 1195–1215 (2020). https://doi.org/10.1109/TAFFC.2020.2981446

99. Liebal, K., Oña, L.: Different approaches to meaning in primate gestural and vocal communication. Front. Psychol. **9**, 478 (2018)

100. Liebherr, M., et al.: Eeg and behavioral correlates of attentional processing while walking and navigating naturalistic environments. Sci. Rep. **11**(1), 1–13 (2021). https://doi.org/10.1038/s41598-021-01772-8

101. Liszkowski, U., Brown, P., Callaghan, T., Takada, A., De Vos, C.: A prelinguistic gestural universal of human communication. Cogn. Sci. **36**(4), 698–713 (2012). https://doi.org/10.1111/j.1551-6709.2011.01228.x

102. Loehr, D.P.: Temporal, structural, and pragmatic synchrony between intonation and gesture. Lab. Phonol.: J. Assoc. Lab. Phonol. **3**(1), 71–89 (2012). https://doi.org/10.1515/lp-2012-0006
103. Lopez, A., Liesenfeld, A., Dingemanse, M.: Evaluation of automatic speech recognition for conversational speech in Dutch, English, and German: What goes missing? In: Proceedings of the 18th Conference on Natural Language Processing, pp. 135–143. KONVENS 2022 (2022)
104. Lozano-Goupil, J., Raffard, S., Capdevielle, D., Aigoin, E., Marin, L.: Gesture-speech synchrony in schizophrenia: a pilot study using a kinematic-acoustic analysis. Neuropsychologia **174**, 108347 (2022). https://doi.org/10.1016/j.neuropsychologia.2022.108347
105. Lücking, A.: Gesture. In: Müller, S., Abeillé, A., Borsley, R.D., Koenig, J.P. (eds.) Head Driven Phrase Structure Grammar: The handbook, chap. 27, pp. 1201–1250. No. 9 in Empirically Oriented Theoretical Morphology and Syntax, Language Science Press, Berlin (2021). https://doi.org/10.5281/zenodo.5543318
106. Lücking, A., Bergman, K., Hahn, F., Kopp, S., Rieser, H.: Data-based analysis of speech and gesture: the Bielefeld speech and gesture alignment corpus (SaGA) and its applications. J. Multimodal User Interfaces **7**(1), 5–18 (2013)
107. Lücking, A., Mehler, A., Menke, P.: Taking fingerprints of speech-and-gesture ensembles: Approaching empirical evidence of intrapersonal alignmnent in multimodal communication. In: Proceedings of the 12th Workshop on the Semantics and Pragmatics of Dialogue, pp. 157–164. LonDial'08, King's College London (2008)
108. Lücking, A., Ptock, S., Bergmann, K.: Assessing agreement on segmentations by means of Staccato, the Segmentation Agreement Calculator according to Thomann. In: Efthimiou, E., Kouroupetroglou, G., Fotina, S.E. (eds.) Gesture and Sign Language in Human-Computer Interaction and Embodied Communication, pp. 129–138. No. 7206 in LNAI, Springer, Berlin and Heidelberg (2012). https://doi.org/10.1007/978-3-642-34182-3_12
109. MacWhinney, B.: The CHILDES Project: Tools for Analyzing Talk, 3rd edn. Lawrence Erlbaum Associates, Mahwah, NJ (2000)
110. Magnee, M., Stekelenburg, J.J., Kemner, C., de Gelder, B.: Similar facial electromyographic responses to faces, voices, and body expressions. NeuroReport **18**(4), 369–372 (2007). https://doi.org/10.1097/WNR.0b013e32801776e6
111. Marschik, P.B., et al.: Open video data sharing in developmental and behavioural science (2022). 10.48550/ARXIV.2207.11020
112. Mathis, A., et al.: DeepLabCut: markerless pose estimation of user-defined body parts with deep learning. Nat. Neurosci. **21**(9), 1281–1289 (2018). https://doi.org/10.1038/s41593-018-0209-y
113. McNeill, D.: Hand and Mind - What Gestures Reveal about Thought. Chicago University Press, Chicago (1992). https://doi.org/10.2307/1576015
114. McNeill, D.: Gesture: A psycholinguistic approach. In: Brown, K. (ed.) The encyclopedia of language and linguistics, pp. 58–66. Elsevier (2006)
115. Mehler, A., Lücking, A.: Pathways of alignment between gesture and speech: Assessing information transmission in multimodal ensembles. In: Giorgolo, G., Alahverdzhieva, K. (eds.) Proceedings of the International Workshop on Formal and Computational Approaches to Multimodal Communication under the auspices of ESSLLI 2012, Opole, Poland, 6–10 August (2012)
116. Mlakar, I., Verdonik, D., Majhenič, S., Rojc, M.: Understanding conversational interaction in multiparty conversations: the EVA Corpus. Lang. Resour. Eval. (2022). https://doi.org/10.1007/s10579-022-09627-y

117. Monarch, R.M.: Human-in-the-Loop Machine Learning: Active learning and annotation for human-centered AI. Simon and Schuster (2021)
118. Mondada, L.: The local constitution of multimodal resources for social interaction. J. Pragmat. **65**, 137–156 (2014). https://doi.org/10.1016/j.pragma.2014.04.004
119. Mondada, L.: Challenges of multimodality: language and the body in social interaction. J. Socioling. **20**(3), 336–366 (2016). https://doi.org/10.1111/josl.1_12177
120. Montague, P.: Hyperscanning: simultaneous fMRI during linked social interactions. Neuroimage **16**(4), 1159–1164 (2002). https://doi.org/10.1006/nimg.2002.1150
121. Morgenstern, A., Caët, S.: Signes en famille [corpus] (2021)
122. Munea, T.L., Jembre, Y.Z., Weldegebriel, H.T., Chen, L., Huang, C., Yang, C.: The progress of human pose estimation: a survey and taxonomy of models applied in 2d human pose estimation. IEEE Access **8**, 133330–133348 (2020). https://doi.org/10.1109/ACCESS.2020.3010248
123. Narayanan, S., et al.: Real-time magnetic resonance imaging and electromagnetic articulography database for speech production research (TC). J. Acoust. Society Am. **136**, 1307 (2014). https://doi.org/10.1121/1.4890284
124. Nenna, F., Do, C.T., Protzak, J., Gramann, K.: Alteration of brain dynamics during dual-task overground walking. Eur. J. Neurosci. **54**(12), 8158–8174 (2021). https://doi.org/10.1111/ejn.14956
125. Ng, E., Ginosar, S., Darrell, T., Joo, H.: Body2hands: Learning to infer 3d hands from conversational gesture body dynamics. In: Proceedings of the IEEE/CVF Conference on Computer Vision and Pattern Recognition, pp. 11865–11874 (2021)
126. Nguyen, T., Schleihauf, H., Kayhan, E., Matthes, D., Vrtička, P., Hoehl, S.: The effects of interaction quality on neural synchrony during mother-child problem solving. Cortex **124**, 235–249 (2020). https://doi.org/10.1016/j.cortex.2019.11.020
127. Noah, J.A., et al.: fMRI Validation of fNIRS Measurements During a Naturalistic Task. J. Visualized Experiments **100**, 52116 (Jun 2015). https://doi.org/10.3791/52116
128. Nyatsanga, S., Kucherenko, T., Ahuja, C., Henter, G.E., Neff, M.: A comprehensive review of data-driven co-speech gesture generation. arXiv preprint 2301.05339 (2023). https://doi.org/10.48550/arXiv.2301.05339
129. Núñez, R., Allen, M., Gao, R., Miller Rigoli, C., Relaford-Doyle, J., Semenuks, A.: What happened to cognitive science? Nat. Hum. Behav. **3**(8), 782–791 (2019). https://doi.org/10.1038/s41562-019-0626-2
130. Offrede, T., Fuchs, S., Mooshammer, C.: Multi-speaker experimental designs: methodological considerations. Lang. Linguist. Compass **15**(12), e12443 (2021). https://doi.org/10.1111/lnc3.12443
131. Oudah, M., Al-Naji, A., Chahl, J.: Hand gesture recognition based on computer vision: a review of techniques. J. Imag. **6**(8), 73 (2020). https://doi.org/10.3390/jimaging6080073
132. Oviatt, S.: Ten myths of multimodal interaction. Commun. ACM **42**(11), 74–81 (1999). https://doi.org/10.1145/319382.319398
133. Owoyele, B., Trujillo, J., De Melo, G., Pouw, W.: Masked-Piper: masking personal identities in visual recordings while preserving multimodal information. SoftwareX **20**, 101236 (2022). https://doi.org/10.1016/j.softx.2022.101236
134. PaddlePaddle: PaddleDetection, object detection and instance segmentation toolkit based on PaddlePaddle. https://github.com/PaddlePaddle/PaddleDetection (2019)

135. Paggio, P., Navarretta, C.: Integration and representation issues in the annotation of multimodal data. In: Navarretta, C., Paggio, P., Allwood, J., Alsén, E., Katagiri, Y. (eds.) Proceedings of the NODALIDA 2009 workshop: Multimodal Communication - from Human Behaviour to Computational Models, pp. 25–31. Northern European Association for Language Technology (2009)

136. Pan, X.N., Hamilton, A.F.D.: Why and how to use virtual reality to study human social interaction: the challenges of exploring a new research landscape. Br. J. Psychol. **109**(3), 395–417 (2018). https://doi.org/10.1111/bjop.12290

137. Pan, Y., Cheng, X., Zhang, Z., Li, X., Hu, Y.: Cooperation in lovers: an fNIRS-based hyperscanning study: cooperation in lovers. Hum. Brain Mapp. **38**(2), 831–841 (2017). https://doi.org/10.1002/hbm.23421

138. Paquot, M., Gries, S.T.: A practical handbook of corpus linguistics. Springer Nature (2021)

139. Parisi, G.I., Kemker, R., Part, J.L., Kanan, C., Wermter, S.: Continual lifelong learning with neural networks: a review. Neural Netw. **113**, 54–71 (2019). https://doi.org/10.1016/j.neunet.2019.01.012

140. Parr, L., Waller, B., Burrows, A., Gothard, K., Vick, S.J.: Brief communication: MaqFACS: a muscle-based facial movement coding system for the rhesus macaque. Am. J. Phys. Anthropol. **143**(4), 625–630 (2010)

141. Peer, A., Ullich, P., Ponto, K.: Vive tracking alignment and correction made easy. In: 2018 IEEE conference on virtual reality and 3D user interfaces (VR), pp. 653–654. IEEE (2018). https://doi.org/10.1109/VR.2018.8446435

142. Peikert, A., Brandmaier, A.M.: A Reproducible Data Analysis Workflow With R Markdown, Git, Make, and Docker. Quantitative and Computational Methods in Behavioral Sciences, pp. 1–27 (2021). https://doi.org/10.5964/qcmb.3763

143. Perniss, P.: Why we should study multimodal language. Front. Psychol. **9**, 1109 (2018). https://doi.org/10.3389/fpsyg.2018.01109

144. Pezzulo, G., Donnarumma, F., Dindo, H., D'Ausilio, A., Konvalinka, I., Castelfranchi, C.: The body talks: sensorimotor communication and its brain and kinematic signatures. Phys. Life Rev. **28**, 1–21 (2019). https://doi.org/10.1016/j.plrev.2018.06.014

145. Pickering, M.J., Garrod, S.: An integrated theory of language production and comprehension. Behav. Brain Sci. **4**, 329–347 (2013). https://doi.org/10.1017/s0140525x12001495

146. Pierrehumbert, J.B.: The phonology and phonetics of English intonation. Ph.D. thesis, Massachusetts Institute of Technology (1980)

147. Pinti, P., et al.: The present and future use of functional near-infrared spectroscopy (fNIRS) for cognitive neuroscience. Ann. N. Y. Acad. Sci. **1464**(1), 5–29 (2020). https://doi.org/10.1111/nyas.13948

148. Posner, R., Robering, K., Sebeok, T.A., Wiegand, H.E. (eds.): Semiotik : ein Handbuch zu den zeichentheoretischen Grundlagen von Natur und Kultur = Semiotics. No. 13 in Handbücher zur Sprach- und Kommunikationswissenschaft, de Gruyter, Berlin (1997)

149. Pouw, W., Dingemanse, M., Motamedi, Y., Özyürek, A.: A systematic investigation of gesture kinematics in evolving manual languages in the lab. Cogn. Sci. **45**(7), e13014 (2021). https://doi.org/10.1111/cogs.13014

150. Pouw, W., Dixon, J.A.: Gesture networks: introducing dynamic time warping and network analysis for the kinematic study of gesture ensembles. Discourse Process. **57**(4), 301–319 (2020). https://doi.org/10.1080/0163853X.2019.1678967

151. Pouw, W., Fuchs, S.: Origins of vocal-entangled gesture. Neuroscience & Biobehavioral Reviews, p. 104836 (2022). https://doi.org/10.1016/j.neubiorev.2022.104836
152. Power, S.D., Falk, T.H., Chau, T.: Classification of prefrontal activity due to mental arithmetic and music imagery using hidden Markov models and frequency domain near-infrared spectroscopy. J. Neural Eng. **7**(2), 026002 (2010). https://doi.org/10.1088/1741-2560/7/2/026002
153. Prieto, P.: Intonational meaning. WIRES. Cogn. Sci. **6**(4), 371–381 (2015). https://doi.org/10.1002/wcs.1352
154. Prillwitz, S., Hanke, T., König, S., Konrad, R., Langer, G., Schwarz, A.: DGS corpus project-development of a corpus based electronic dictionary German Sign Language/German. In: sign-lang@ LREC 2008, pp. 159–164. European Language Resources Association (ELRA) (2008)
155. Quer, J., Pfau, R., Herrmann, A.: The Routledge Handbook of Theoretical and Experimental Sign Language Research. Routledge (2021)
156. Rachow, M., Karnowski, T., O'Toole, A.J.: Identity masking effectiveness and gesture recognition: Effects of eye enhancement in seeing through the mask. arXiv preprint 2301.08408 (2023). 10.48550/arXiv. 2301.08408
157. Radford, A., et al.: Learning transferable visual models from natural language supervision. In: International Conference on Machine Learning, pp. 8748–8763. PMLR (2021)
158. Radford, A., Kim, J.W., Xu, T., Brockman, G., McLeavey, C., Sutskever, I.: Robust speech recognition via large-scale weak supervision. arXiv preprint arXiv:2212.04356 (2022). 10.48550/arXiv. 2212.04356
159. Ramscar, M., Port, R.F.: How spoken languages work in the absence of an inventory of discrete units. Lang. Sci. **53**, 58–74 (2016). https://doi.org/10.1016/j.langsci.2015.08.002
160. Ren, Y., Wang, Z., Wang, Y., Tan, S., Chen, Y., Yang, J.: Gopose: 3d human pose estimation using wifi 6(2) (jul 2022). https://doi.org/10.1145/3534605
161. Richard, A., Zollhöfer, M., Wen, Y., de la Torre, F., Sheikh, Y.: Meshtalk: 3d face animation from speech using cross-modality disentanglement. In: Proceedings of the IEEE/CVF International Conference on Computer Vision (ICCV), pp. 1173–1182 (October 2021)
162. Rieser, H., Lawler, I.: Multi-modal meaning - an empirically-founded process algebra approach. Semantics Pragmatics **13**(8), 1–55 (2020). https://doi.org/10.3765/sp.13.8
163. Ripperda, J., Drijvers, L., Holler, J.: Speeding up the detection of non-iconic and iconic gestures (SPUDNIG): a toolkit for the automatic detection of hand movements and gestures in video data. Behav. Res. Methods **52**(4), 1783–1794 (2020). https://doi.org/10.3758/s13428-020-01350-2
164. Rohrer, P.: A temporal and pragmatic analysis of gesture-speech association: A corpus-based approach using the novel MultiModal MultiDimensional (M3D) labeling system. Ph.D. thesis (2022)
165. Rohrer, P.L., et al.: The multimodal multidimensional (m3d) labeling system (Jan 2023). https://doi.org/10.17605/OSF.IO/ANKDX
166. Sassenhagen, J.: How to analyse electrophysiological responses to naturalistic language with time-resolved multiple regression. Lang., Cogn. Neurosci. **34**(4), 474–490 (2019). https://doi.org/10.1080/23273798.2018.1502458
167. Schegloff, E.A.: On some gestures' relation to talk. In: Atkinson, J.M., Heritage, J. (eds.) Structures of Social Action. Studies in Conversational Analysis, chap.

12, pp. 266–296. Studies in Emotion and Social Interaction, Cambridge University Press, Cambridge, MA (1984)

168. Schmidt, T., Wörner, K.: EXMARaLDA - creating, analysing and sharing spoken language corpora for pragmatic research. Pragmatics **19**(4), 565–582 (2009)

169. Scholkmann, F., et al.: A review on continuous wave functional near-infrared spectroscopy and imaging instrumentation and methodology. NeuroImage **85**, 6–27 (2014). https://doi.org/10.1016/j.neuroimage.2013.05.004, https://linkinghub.elsevier.com/retrieve/pii/S1053811913004941

170. Schuller, B.W.: Speech emotion recognition: two decades in a nutshell, benchmarks, and ongoing trends. Commun. ACM **61**(5), 90–99 (2018). https://doi.org/10.1145/3129340

171. Schulte-Ruether, M., et al.: Using machine learning to improve diagnostic assessment of ASD in the light of specific differential and co-occurring diagnoses. J. Child Psychol. Psychiatry **64**(1), 16–26 (2023). https://doi.org/10.1111/jcpp.13650

172. Schulte-Ruether, M., et al.: Intact mirror mechanisms for automatic facial emotions in children and adolescents with autism spectrum disorder. Autism Res. **10**(2), 298–310 (2017). https://doi.org/10.1002/aur.1654

173. Selting, M., Auer, P., et al.: Gesprächsanalytisches Transkriptionssystem 2 (GAT 2). Gesprächsforschung - Online-Zeitschrift zur verbalen Interaktion 10, 353–402 (2009). https://www.gespraechsforschung-ozs.de

174. Shattuck-Hufnagel, S., Turk, A.E.: A prosody tutorial for investigators of auditory sentence processing. J. Psycholinguist. Res. **25**, 193–247 (1996)

175. Shattuck-Hufnagel, S., Yasinnik, Y., Veilleux, N., Renwick, M.: A method for studying the time-alignment of gestures and prosody in American English: 'Hits' and pitch accents in academic-lecture-style speech. In: Esposito, A., Bratanic, M., Keller, E., Marinaro, M. (eds.) Fundamentals of Verbal And Nonverbal Communication And The Biometric Issue, pp. 34–44. IOS Press, Amsterdam (2007)

176. Shoemark, P., Liza, F.F., Nguyen, D., Hale, S., McGillivray, B.: Room to Glo: A systematic comparison of semantic change detection approaches with word embeddings. In: Proceedings of the 2019 Conference on Empirical Methods in Natural Language Processing and the 9th International Joint Conference on Natural Language Processing, pp. 66–76. EMNLP-IJCNLP, Association for Computational Linguistics, Hong Kong, China (2019). https://doi.org/10.18653/v1/D19-1007

177. Sitaram, R., et al.: Temporal classification of multichannel near-infrared spectroscopy signals of motor imagery for developing a brain-computer interface. Neuroimage **34**(4), 1416–1427 (2007). https://doi.org/10.1016/j.neuroimage.2006.11.005

178. Streeck, J.: Gesture as communication I: its coordination with gaze and speech. Commun. Monogr. **60**(4), 275–299 (1993)

179. Struckmeier, V.: Attribute im Deutschen: Zu ihren Eigenschaften und ihrer Position im grammatischen System. No. 65 in studia grammatica, Akademie Verlag, Berlin (2007)

180. Thomann, B.: Oberservation and judgment in psychology: assessing agreement among markings of behavioral events. Behav. Res. Methods, Instruments, Comput. **33**(3), 248–339 (2001)

181. Tiku, N.: The Google engineer who thinks the company's AI has come to life (2022)

182. Tkachman, O., Hall, K.C., Xavier, A., Gick, B.: Sign language phonetic annotation meets phonological corpustools: Towards a sign language toolset for phonetic

notation and phonological analysis. In: Proceedings of the Annual Meetings on Phonology, vol. 3 (2016)

183. Torricelli, F., Tomassini, A., Pezzulo, G., Pozzo, T., Fadiga, L., D'Ausilio, A.: Motor invariants in action execution and perception. Physics of Life Reviews (2022)

184. Trettenbrein, P.C., Pendzich, N.-K., Cramer, J.-M., Steinbach, M., Zaccarella, E.: Psycholinguistic norms for more than 300 lexical signs in German Sign Language (DGS). Behav. Res. Methods **53**(5), 1817–1832 (2020). https://doi.org/10.3758/s13428-020-01524-y

185. Trettenbrein, P.C., Papitto, G., Friederici, A.D., Zaccarella, E.: Functional neuroanatomy of language without speech: an ale meta-analysis of sign language. Hum. Brain Mapp. **42**(3), 699–712 (2021). https://doi.org/10.1002/hbm.25254

186. Trettenbrein, P.C., Zaccarella, E.: Controlling video stimuli in sign language and gesture research: the openposer package for analyzing openpose motion-tracking data in r. Front. Psychol. **12** (2021). https://doi.org/10.3389/fpsyg.2021.628728

187. Trujillo, J.P., Holler, J.: Interactionally embedded gestalt principles of multimodal human communication. Perspectives on Psychological Science 17456916221141422 (2023)

188. Trujillo, J.P., Simanova, I., Bekkering, H., Özyürek, A.: Communicative intent modulates production and comprehension of actions and gestures: A Kinect study. Cognition **180**, 38–51 (2018)

189. Uddén, J.: Supramodal Sentence Processing in the Human Brain: fMRI Evidence for the Influence of Syntactic Complexity in More Than 200 Participants. Neurobiol. Lang. **3**(4), 575–598 (2022). https://doi.org/10.1162/nol_a_00076

190. Uljarevic, M., Hamilton, A.: Recognition of emotions in autism: a formal meta-analysis. J. Autism Dev. Disord. **43**(7), 1517–1526 (2013). https://doi.org/10.1007/s10803-012-1695-5

191. Valtakari, N.V., Hooge, I.T.C., Viktorsson, C., Nyström, P., Falck-Ytter, T., Hessels, R.S.: Eye tracking in human interaction: possibilities and limitations. Behav. Res. Methods **53**(4), 1592–1608 (2021). https://doi.org/10.3758/s13428-020-01517-x

192. Vick, S.J., Waller, B.M., Parr, L.A., Smith Pasqualini, M.C., Bard, K.A.: A cross-species comparison of facial morphology and movement in humans and chimpanzees using the facial action coding system (FACS). J. Nonverbal Behav. **31**(1), 1–20 (2007)

193. Vilhjálmsson, H., et al.: The behavior markup language: Recent developments and challenges. In: Pelachaud, C., Martin, J.C., André, E., Chollet, G., Karpouzis, K., Pelé, D. (eds.) Intelligent Virtual Agents. pp. 99–111. Springer, Berlin and Heidelberg (2007). https://doi.org/10.1007/978-3-540-74997-4_10

194. Waller, B.M., Lembeck, M., Kuchenbuch, P., Burrows, A.M., Liebal, K.: GibbonFACS: a muscle-based facial movement coding system for hylobatids. Int. J. Primatol. **33**(4), 809–821 (2012)

195. Weiss, K., Khoshgoftaar, T.M., Wang, D.D.: A survey of transfer learning. J. Big Data **3**(1), 1–40 (2016). https://doi.org/10.1186/s40537-016-0043-6

196. Winkler, A., Won, J., Ye, Y.: Questsim: Human motion tracking from sparse sensors with simulated avatars. In: SIGGRAPH Asia 2022 Conference Papers, pp. 1–8 (2022). https://doi.org/10.1145/3550469.3555411

197. Wittenburg, P., Brugman, H., Russel, A., Klassmann, A., Sloetjes, H.: Elan: A professional framework for multimodality research. In: 5th International Conference on Language Resources and Evaluation (LREC 2006), pp. 1556–1559 (2006), https://hdl.handle.net/11858/00-001M-0000-0013-1E7E-4

198. Wu, X., Xiao, L., Sun, Y., Zhang, J., Ma, T., He, L.: A survey of human-in-the-loop for machine learning. Futur. Gener. Comput. Syst. (2022). https://doi.org/10.1016/j.future.2022.05.014

199. Youmshajekian, L.: Springer nature retracts chapter on sign language deaf scholars called "extremely offensive". Retraction Watch. https://retractionwatch.com/2023/01/23/springer-nature-retracts-chapter-on-sign-language-deaf-scholars-called-extremely-offensive/ (2023)

200. Young, A.W., Frühholz, S., Schweinberger, S.R.: Face and voice perception: understanding commonalities and differences. Trends Cogn. Sci. **24**(5), 398–410 (2020). https://doi.org/10.1016/j.tics.2020.02.001

201. Yu, C., Ballard, D.H.: A multimodal learning interface for grounding spoken language in sensory perceptions. ACM Trans. Appl. Percept. **1**(1), 57–80 (2004). https://doi.org/10.1145/1008722.1008727

202. Yu, F., Seff, A., Zhang, Y., Song, S., Funkhouser, T., Xiao, J.: Lsun: Construction of a large-scale image dataset using deep learning with humans in the loop. arXiv preprint arXiv:1506.03365 (2015)

203. Yunus, F., Clavel, C., Pelachaud, C.: Sequence-to-sequence predictive model: From prosody to communicative gestures. In: Digital Human Modeling and Applications in Health, Safety, Ergonomics and Risk Management. Human Body, Motion and Behavior: 12th International Conference, DHM 2021, Held as Part of the 23rd HCI International Conference, HCII 2021, Virtual Event, July 24–29, 2021, Proceedings, Part I, pp. 355–374. Springer (2021). https://doi.org/10.1007/978-3-030-77817-0_25

204. Zeng, Q., Zheng, G., Liu, Q.: Pe-dls: a novel method for performing real-time full-body motion reconstruction in vr based on vive trackers. Virtual Reality, pp. 1–17 (2022). https://doi.org/10.1007/s10055-022-00635-5

205. Zhang, H.B., et al.: A comprehensive survey of vision-based human action recognition methods. Sensors **19**(5), 1005 (2019). https://doi.org/10.3390/s19051005

206. Zhou, H., Hu, H.: Human motion tracking for rehabilitation-a survey. Biomed. Signal Process. Control **3**(1), 1–18 (2008). https://doi.org/10.1016/j.bspc.2007.09.001

News Articles on Social Media: Showing Balanced Content Adds More Credibility Than Trust Badges or User Ratings

Patrick Halbach[1]●, Laura Burbach[1]●, Martina Ziefle[1]●,
and André Calero Valdez[2(✉)]●

[1] RWTH Aachen University, Campus Boulevard 57, 52076 Aachen, Germany
{halbach,burbach,ziefle}@comm.rwth-aachen.de
[2] Institute for Multimedia and Interactive Systems, University of Lübeck,
Ratzeburger Allee 160, Lübeck 23560, Germany
calerovaldez@imis.uni-luebeck.de

Abstract. Since digital media has become an important vehicle for news consumption, users are inevitably faced with a plethora of different news sources to choose from. Whether or not news is credible is often decided by recognition, intuition, and habits. However, it has become increasingly difficult for users to accurately assess the credibility of news articles. To understand how users evaluate credibility when seeing news on Facebook, we examine the interplay of the opinion of an article with additional credibility cues. To determine their utility, we use a novel conjoint-based research approach. In our experiment (n=178) we study four cues: Facebook reactions, a user rating, an institutional badge, and links to related content. In the last case, this content can either support or contradict the original news. We found that different cues have significantly different effects on credibility evaluation. We see that related content creates higher credibility than the other cues.

Keywords: user study · credibility cues · social media · trust badges · conspiracy theories · fake news

1 Introduction

The internet has tremendously changed the way how users get their information and how they select which news to read. The sheer amount of available news has increased, as events can be reported immediately from everyone and almost from everywhere in the world [18]. This leads to an amount of information that is no longer fully assessable for everyone.

As we have to limit our attention to a small fraction of the available information, we must decide how to do that. Some stick to a single news provider when reading news online, while others try to read news from both sides of the political spectrum [5]. Further, social media has become a major factor in online

V. G. Duffy (Ed.): HCII 2023, LNCS 14029, pp. 439–460, 2023.
https://doi.org/10.1007/978-3-031-35748-0_31

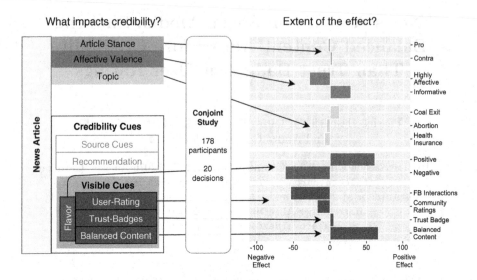

Fig. 1. Using a conjoint study we assess the impact of visible credibility cues on users' credibility assessment of news posts on Social Media.

news consumption [24], thus handing over the decision of what to read, to the different algorithms of social media providers.

Digital media has changed our habits of news consumption. Moreover, news are presented in novel contexts with other news and other users' opinions. Inevitably, this additional information or context leaves us with more opportunities to believe in or question the credibility of news sources. Users still have lower trust in news that they consume on social media platforms compared to other news sources [26]. Credibility cues are a plausible approach to tackle this trend and therewith make social media platforms more beneficial for political opinion formation and information exchange among users.

The fact that a large proportion of users now consumes news through social media—often incidentally [20]—has both benefits and drawbacks. One strong benefit is that people have discovered a new form of involvement with news [14,37] and may get empowered as opinion leaders [46]. Also, we see that especially younger adults who claim to be politically uninterested may profit from incidental exposure as they get more easily involved in political discussions and can not ignore awareness of the political content in their newsfeeds [16].

Through digital media, it has become easier for users to focus on content that fits their interests and confirms their opinions compared to traditional news sources [39]. Hereby some users may end up in confirmation loops, constantly narrowing their world view and losing touch with opinions that are contrary to their own. There is both confirmatory [53] and disproving [22] evidence for this assumption, which indicates a need for further research in this domain. Furthermore, users mainly focus on *distributing* their self-beliefs and ideologies [37].

At the same time, people's self-beliefs and ideologies shape their preferences in selecting content, causing them to rarely *read* opposing opinions [35].

Credibility cues can promote the positive effects of social media on news consumption and opinion formation. They also reduce selective exposure and confirmation bias. They can be utilized to help users overcome cognitive dissonances and to help deal with attitude-challenging information [40]. In addition, they may be able to enhance the users' trust in news articles in social media environments. However, even when the content is cross-cutting, it remains unclear how effective various types of visible cues are at determining the credibility of news sources.

Our Contribution. Addressing this gap, our research is the first to combine multiple cues for credibility and news selection on social media platofrms like Facebook. To measure the performance of different visible cues, we systematically address the most important factors for assessing credibility using a mixed method approach, i.e., focus groups and a conjoint user study (see Fig. 1).

2   Related Work

Following, we give a broad overview of the research addressing the credibility assessment of news articles in online environments. Therefore, we will introduce different existing credibility cues. In this way, we motivate our novel approach of research and the selection of the examined factors.

2.1   News Consumption in Digital Media

Digital media stimulates new ways of news consumption. News are consumed less regularly and as a less time-consuming activity. Today's users rely on a broad range of media platforms [64]. Younger adults show a trend towards consuming news in small quantities and from multiple platforms which also changes their potential for political participation [14]. The use of mobile devices reinforces this behavior as it enables users to access news throughout the day filling gaps of leisure time [42]. This allows users to use social media platforms as a feedback channel while consuming other media in parallel [38].

Social media platforms like Facebook simplified news sharing and opened up new ways for interacting with news which fosters positive effects by increasing the range of online news sources [20]. Users get more involved by sharing and discussing news on social media platforms and may get empowered as opinion leaders [46]. In general, users of social media platforms show a higher engagement in forming a political opinion [14].

2.2   How Do We Select the News Articles We Read?

First of all, the available choice of news in a social media feed is—in most cases—algorithmically filtered. Here, however, we solely focus on the decision task after presenting choices. The process of deciding whether or not to really read a news article depends on a variety of factors. Several concepts exist and have been empirically investigated, helping to understand this decision-making process. From a high-level perspective two major aspects play a role. First, the context of a *news article*. Several cues are evaluated before an article is read. Such cues are the recency of an article, source cues, expertise cues, but also recommendations by other users. Clearly visible cues play a large role. Second, the content of the article is evaluated. This includes topic, the stance and the affective valence portrayed in an article. Both play different roles in the credibility assessment. Here, processes such as confirmation bias and selective information seeking play a role in how the content is processed and selected. Next, we elaborate on these concepts.

Recency. When a user selects a news article, he considers several cues that originate from the content, the context, and additional information. In times of continuous and endless streams of news, the recency of an article has become a very important cue for news selection [65]. According to Westerman et al., it can even have an indirect effect on source credibility assessment. They compared different levels of update recency based on Twitter pages and found that more recent posts are positively related to cognitive elaboration, which is in turn positively related to source credibility [60].

Credibility Cues. The source credibility is naturally also primed through the user's prior knowledge and habits in news consumption. In this manner, most people rate the societal relevance of media coverage higher for established news outlets than for tabloids [25]. Sundar et al. compared this so-called source effect to the recency-effect and other visible cues and consider the source even as more relevant for the credibility assessment of a news article [55]. However, it is important to keep in mind that media outlets can be biased and users have a hard time detecting this bias. This makes it indispensable to include further factors to assess the credibility of news content [17]. One possibility to cope with this is to give additional information about the source as Liao et al. did by applying a source expertise indicator. This indicator led to a more frequent selection of sources that are marked to have high expertise compared to sources with lower indicated expertise [36]. If such additional cues are not available and users perceive a source as rather dubious, they will look for further cues that are given through the context such as user comments or ratings [61].

Content of the Article. Regarding the actual content of the news article, the topic and the choice of words can affect users in their credibility assessment. If the users are highly involved in a news topic, credibility judgments may get less precise, because users then rely on fewer cues for their judgment than they would do with lower involvement [45]. However, relying on all available cues can also be problematic. If users try to assess the public opinion through the stance of an article and its user comments, perception may be biased, as already a few comments may lead to a misguided perception of the public opinion [62].

The choice of words is also relevant for credibility ratings. In this regard, research often draws a line between tabloids and mainstream news as they use different approaches to attract their readers' interest [49]. For creating more sensational and eye-catching content, tabloids tend to use more emotional stories. Mainstream news in contrast mostly aim for maintaining a credible image and therefore rely more on informational writing styles.

Recommendations. Since social media platforms provide various possibilities to receive content through recommendations, the type and the source of such recommendations also has to be considered as a credibility cue. Research in this area shows that friends on such platforms are trusted and used as indicators for credible news articles. In this context closer relationships are more important than distant acquaintances [25]. If a news article is received from a close friend, this can even lead to bypassing other cues that would have prevented reading the article [3]. Besides, friends who are perceived as experts for a certain topic increase trust in the content they recommend [58]. Compared to other cues that are available in news feeds of social media platforms, Koroleva et al. found that Facebook users rely heavily on their social relationships for selecting news articles. They only take other information into account—such as likes and comments—if they assess a post that is not shared by a friend [32].

Community-Based Cues. Almost every social media platform allows its users not only to share and recommend content, but also to interact directly through liking or commenting on a news post. This introduces a cue based on the community and may lead social media users to assumptions about public opinion [62]. As Douglas et al. could show, social media users are aware of those cues and use them to evaluate political content [15]. Thereby, comments on a news post can already be a critical criterion for users [2]. Thinking one step further, it seems reasonable to give users more cues based on community evaluation. Investigating a community-based rating of source-reputation, Kim et al. revealed a unilateral influence on perceived credibility. Negative ratings lowered the source-reputation, while positive ratings did not have an influence. Also, the sheer existence of ratings on some articles reduces the value of content without ratings [28].

Besides cues that stem from active user interaction, cues from passive interaction exist as well. Solely a count of users who have read an article can serve as such a cue that—if provided—reduces the time users spend on selecting news articles [66].

Trust-Badges. Some websites pursue a more direct approach to support their users in credibility assessment. Big social media platforms like Facebook and Twitter provide verification badges that inform the user about the authenticity of a particular account. Although these badges are widely known, users do not seem to consider them in their assessment [59]. In contrast, badges that refer more directly to the content of a news article are more successful. Examining the effect of warning signs for misinformation, Pennycook et al. found that such warnings can help users with differentiating between true and false news. Interestingly, their study showed that the warnings were more effective for news that are in line with the users' political ideologies. They also found an effect which they named "implied truth": in an environment where some articles are marked as fake news, the credibility of other, unmarked articles increases implicitly [48].

Showing Related Content. Other lines of research have investigated how showing related news affects credibility of news articles. By reading content from other sources, users can actively look for confirming or contradicting evidence. Some platforms already provide directly related content next to an article. Examining the effect of correcting related news articles, Bode et al. found that they can help users to reflect their opinion. Even when they contradict pre-existing attitudes of the user, they lead to an change of attitude [6].

2.3 Confirmation Bias and Credibility Cues

The well studied confirmation bias refers to the phenomenon that human beings tend to process information differently, depending on whether or not it matches their presuppositions. Confirmatory evidence is trusted; contradictory evidence is rejected. When it comes to news articles, similar behavior occurs. Users prefer articles that match their opinion or have balanced confirming and contradicting arguments over news articles that only conflict with their opinion [63]. Considering an increasing polarization in societies, this poses a problem [21,44].

Credibility cues can help users to increase exposure towards opinion-contrasting content as Metzger et al. showed: Credibility cues have a motivational influence on the user to overcome cognitive dissonance and to deal with attitude-challenging information [40].

The confrontation with content that contradicts our views and beliefs shows further positive effects on political participation both on- and offline. However, according to the findings of Min and Wohn, it differs from cross-cutting exposure in a face-to-face environment. Min and Wohn argue that this difference stems from the more anonymous and comfortable interaction that social media platforms provide. Social media provides connections to "weak tie" relationships where no strong personal connection would prevent one from recklessly arguing against the others opinion [41]. Determining how these differences between on- and offline worlds can be bridged in a more civilized discourse poses a strong research desideratum.

2.4 Measuring Contextual Decision-Making Using Conjoint Studies

Normal psychometric survey studies aim to isolate interaction of effects when measuring individual concepts. This is achieved by creating and validating measurement scales than typically span several similar sounding items. While this method improves the measurement of the individual concept, it has several drawbacks. When decision making is involuntary or even subconscious, replicating this process in a survey is hindered by directly asking about it. Asking a person how much they are willing to share personal data on Facebook might elicit different responses than Facebook will tell you. Paradoxical behavior and behavior that is governed subconsciously eludes survey measurement.

A conjoint study is a study that utilizes a forced-choice paradigm. It achieves implicit measurement by combining different attributes on different levels into a set of scenarios and asking the user to pick the best option. Asking the user to pick the best option from a set of possible scenarios forces the user to evaluate options in a contextual holistic fashion, yielding better prediction for individual *importances* and *utilities* of the measured variables. By asking a user several of these forced-choice settings with randomized scenario options, a good within-subject and between subject coverage is achieved. Using a hierarchical Bayes' algorithm allows to determine the importance of individual attributes for the decision and even the utility of individual attribute levels [12,47].

2.5   Research Question

Previous research has shown that users have to overcome various pitfalls when assessing the credibility of a news article. While there is plenty of research on the individual influencing factors, there is no conjoint evaluation of those factors to examine their interplay and assess the effect of additional visible cues on a more realistic level. Looking at this as an holistic approach is the aim of the study presented in this article.

To keep the duration of the study acceptable for our participants, we will limit the investigation to a subset of the introduced factors. The *source effect* has high potential for distorting the results, because participants have different sets of preferred media outlets and rate media bias individually. Also *recommendation* through friends or systems was excluded, because their implementation into a conjoint-based research approach is not trivial and requires large groups of "friends" to partake in a study at the same time. We include contextual factors such as the *topic*, *stance*, and *affective valence* of an article as well as *visible cues* that derive from our literature review. As such, we look at *trust badges*, *community-based ratings*, *balanced content* and the well-known *community-based cues* that are available in a regular Facebook news post (i.e., number of likes and comments and positive or negative reactions). Overall, our study aims to answer the following research question:

RQ: How do the opinion of readers and additional credibility cues—and their interaction—affect the credibility of news articles on Social Media?

3   Method

As we are interested in understanding in how visible credibility cues may support users of social media platforms from a holistic perspective, we have decided to utilize a conjoint-study and analysis in this research. As the amount of possible factors that could be studied is too large for a single conjoint study, a typical approach is to reduce the set of factors using qualitative prestudies. In these studies, participants are asked to reflect on the context of the conjoint study and rate the relevance of factors after group-discussions. When high agreement relating relevance of factors between different groups is reached, these factors are then chosen for the conjoint-study.

Our goal was to simulate a realistic decision task between different news articles. For this purpose we conducted three focus groups to determine the most relevant factors and then used these as factors in a conjoint study.

We share all research artifacts (survey (German), raw data, cleaned data, analysis code) using the Open Science Framework.[1]

3.1 Online Questionnaire

We implemented an online questionnaire which was divided into two parts. In the first part of the questionnaire, we collected demographic information and user factors. Besides age, gender, and education, we wanted to know about the personality traits (BFI-10) [50] of our participants and their attitude towards education (6 items on a 6-point Likert scale) and politics (PEKS) [4]. We also asked for their sources of opinion formation, trust in media and media usage habits, as these might be confounding variables in the assessment on news article credibility.

Our Conjoint Study. Our conjoint study consists of **five attributes** that cover both content-related and visual credibility cues. We use news posts in the typical layout and style of Facebook to provide an authentic object of investigation. Regarding the content, we vary the topic, the stance, and the affective valence of a news article. We decided to include three topics that relate to distinct subject areas: Coal exit, the abolition of private health insurance, and a ban on advertising for abortions. All topics were picked due to their recency and their societal discourse in Germany during the survey period and to cover a breadth of possible pre-existing opinions.

News Topics. The topic of coal exit is part of the German energy transition, i.e., the ongoing switch to renewable energy. While this transition as a whole is supported by a majority of the population as well as most major political and economic forces, coal exit remains to be the subject of contemptuous debate [13, 34]. In the face of opposition by environmental activists, electricity providers assert that coal exit comes with the threat of blackouts [9].

The discussion about a possible abolition of private health insurance affects all German citizens. Germany has a two-tier health insurance system with statutory public health insurance and private health insurances, with private health

---

[1] https://osf.io/89mrw/.

insurance being a voluntary substitute for statutory health insurance. Only members of specific occupational groups and high earners are eligible for private health plans which often cover more diverse treatments and offer benefits in comparison to public health plans [27]. In an aging society, the private insurers are generally better prepared for health spendings increasing with the insured's age because of the way premiums are calculated [27]. Critics point out that the larger compensations physicians receive for treating privately insured patients lead to systematic disadvantages for the publicly insured [30,56].

Finally, the topic of advertising for abortions pertains to the difficult standing of abortions in Germany's society and legal system. Despite abortion technically being illegal, since 1995, terminating a pregnancy will not be punished if that pregnancy is the result of rape, if it poses a health risk or if it causes exceeding distress to the pregnant person [8]. What remains illegal as well as punishable, however, is advertising for abortions. In 2017, German courts convicted a doctor, arguing that her informing about abortions on her homepage constitutes advertisement [1]. This ruling refueled the debate around the ethics and legality of pregnancy terminations in Germany [33].

The articles for those topics were systematically varied in their stance resulting in respectively two supporting and two opposing articles per topic. One of each was formulated following a highly affective choice of words while the other one was based on an objective writing style. This way, we can examine the influence of both confirmation bias on the one hand and the perceived content credibility on the other hand towards the credibility judgment. Affective valence of texts was validated from six independent coders with high inter-rater reliability (Cohen's Kappa = .85).

Credibility Cues. Regarding the visual attributes, we investigate 4 kinds of visible credibility cues in 2 different "flavors" (more on flavors in the next paragraph): 1) Conventional *Facebook Interactions* (Like, Share, Comment), showing the count of interactions and either positive Like reactions (Like, Love, Wow) or negative Like reactions (Anger, Fear). 2) *Community Ratings* of content credibility, summarizing the credibility rating of Facebook users who already have read the article. Rating was set at either 80% or 20% credibility. 3) A *Trust Badge* which was introduced as a governmental credibility classification and rated a post either as trustworthy or as dubious. 4) *Related content*: showing two article headlines that are related to the main topic and either both consistent or contradictory in its stance towards the topic.

All visible cues come in 2 different flavors: either certifying *high or low credibility*. To allow direct comparisons of their impact, all types of credibility cues had the same number of possible flavors, although it would have been easy to vary for example the community-based credibility, e.g. providing an additional neutral level. We wanted to get a first broad insight into the effect of credibility cues and will continue our research for more detailed explanatory power in later studies.

All possible combinations of attribute levels and flavors produce 96 unique stimuli. Each participant performed a randomized set of 20 decision tasks. On each of them, three posts with differing variations of attribute levels were presented and the participant had to choose the one that is most credible from their opinion.

The research design was tested for robustness and for a simulation with 150 participants it showed standard errors below 0.05. Therewith it is suitable for our research purposes.

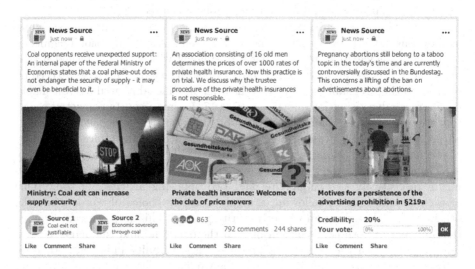

Fig. 2. The used Facebook News posts with the community-based and FBReactions visible cue. The left article contains related news headlines that are contrary to the article. The article in the middle show the trust badge in its negative flavor. The right article shows the Community Ratings in its negative flavor.

3.2   Sample Description

Participants for the conjoint study were recruited using snowball-sampling starting from the individual social networks of the authors. Participants were asked to share the study-link in their own social network to interested participants.

Participation was voluntary and participants were not not paid for taking part in the study.

The data of this study were collected in spring 2019 in Germany. Our sample consists of 178 participants in total of whom 112 are women and 66 are men. The average age is 31.5 years with a notably high share of participants within an age range of 20-30 years. Concerning the education level, the sample is higher than the mean of the German population [10].

Our participants follow the trend towards consuming their news most frequently in online environments ($M = 70\%, SD = 24\%$ on a semantic differential between $0\% =$ solely conventional media use and $100\% =$ solely digital media use). A total of 78% of the sample are Facebook users who state that their main purpose to use Facebook is to communicate with friends (scale: 1–6, $M = 4.26, SD = 1.33$) and to follow their activities and stories ($M = 3.95, SD = 1.36$). Reading ($M = 3.03, SD = 1.62$) and sharing ($M = 2.19, SD = 1.35$) of news or voicing their own opinion ($M = 1.86, SD = 1.23$) was less frequently reported as an intention to use Facebook. Looking at the age of the participants, we see that older adults rather reject digital media and stick with their familiar news sources ($r(178) = -.24, p < 0.01$). Also they use Facebook less often, but in line with previous research the usage motives are similar compared to younger users [67].

Sources of Credibility. We asked our participants to rate the importance of various sources they rely on for opinion formation. The majority reports that credible sources are related to personal experiences and people with close social ties, followed by sources that originate from everyday life such as university, school, or the workplace. Media and news play a subordinated role for opinion formation and especially social media platforms are reported as very unimportant. These findings provide initial insights into how our participants attempt to verify credibility of online news sources, as they show their commitment to different source types. We will consider these insights later on.

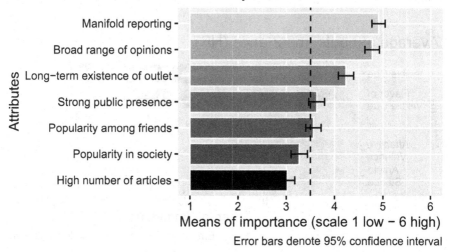

Fig. 3. Relevant attributes for assessing the credibility of a media outlet

Zooming in on the attributes for assessing the credibility of media outlets, we see a somehow different picture. Participants see *manifold reporting* as the most important cue, followed by a *broad range of opinions*. Also a *long-term existence* and a *strong public presence* were more important than the *popularity* of a news outlet among friends and the society in general (see Fig. 3).

In summary, our sample has a high affinity for digital media and consists mostly of regular Facebook users. However, they state to be not as active in distributing and receiving news via social media.

4   Results

Following, we give insight into the main findings of our research approach using a conjoint study.

4.1   Credibility Cues in Facebook News Posts

Conjoint analysis allows to rate the relative importance of individual attributes in a decision process. Importances range from 0 to 100. The more important an attribute is the stronger its influence in the decision making process. Different levels of an attribute may also have different influences in the decision making process; this influence is called utility in conjoint analyses. Utilities are a zero-sum for each attribute and take larger values when the respective importance is high. We use the Hierarchical Bayes analysis to derive the average importances of our examined attributes and respective average level utilities from the conjoint results.

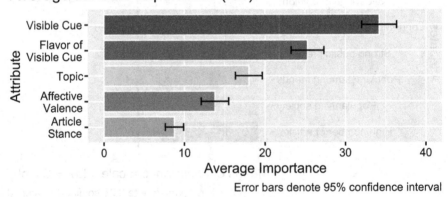

Fig. 4. The average attribute importance reveals visible cues as the most important attribute followed by their flavor and the topic.

Figure 4 shows, that the *visible cues* attained the highest importance ($M = 34.17, SD = 14.84$) followed by their *flavor* ($M = 25.29, SD = 13.90$). The *topic* of the news article shows mediocre importance compared to the other attributes

($M = 17.99, SD = 11.29$), followed by the *affective valence* ($M = 13.78, SD = 11.56$) and the *stance* of an article ($M = 8.77, SD = 7.78$) as the least important attribute. This shows that the validation of an article through visible cues and their flavor is more important than the actual content in our study.

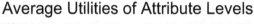

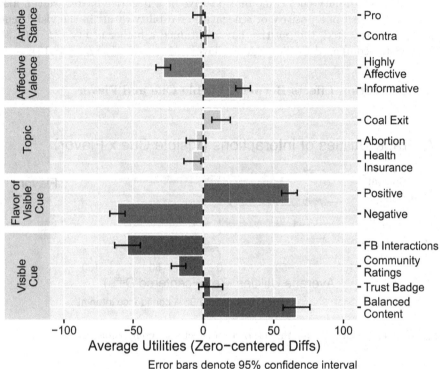

Error bars denote 95% confidence interval

Fig. 5. The average utility of the attribute levels.

After looking at the average importance of the attributes, we now look at the relative utility of the attribute levels. Figure 5) shows how individual attribute levels impact decision making. A positive flavor, i.e., the cue hints towards credibilty, increase the utility of an option, while a negative flavor decreases it. This is expected, as a positive credibility cue should increase credibility and vice versa.

Our results show that the levels for *visible cues* and their *flavor* differ more strongly in utility compared to the attributes related to the content of the articles—with one exception: Regarding *affective valence*, articles with an *informative* choice of words show higher utility ($M = 28.3, SD = 34.96$) than articles written *highly affectively* ($M = -28.3, SD = 34.96$). Concerning the article topic, *coal exit* reached a significant higher utility than the *advertising ban on abortion* and the *abolition of the private health insurance*. The *article stance* seems not to influence relative utility for the participants.

Through the conjoint-analysis we can determine that our participants value related content as the most *useful* visible cue for assessing credibility ($M = 66.31$, $SD = 65.69$). Less utility was credited to the trust badge ($M = 5.34$, $SD = 57.61$), followed by the user rating ($M = -17.57$, $SD = 35.17$), and Facebook Interactions ($M = -54.08$, $SD = 63.99$) with the least utility.

Since all credibility cues come in a positive or a negative flavor, we can also evaluate the effect of a positive or a negative credibility rating in the visible cue. As could be expected, the positive flavor obtained a higher utility ($M = 61.25$, $SD = 38.15$) compared to the negative flavor ($M = -61.25$, $SD = 38.15$).

4.2   Interaction Effects Between Visible Cue and Flavor

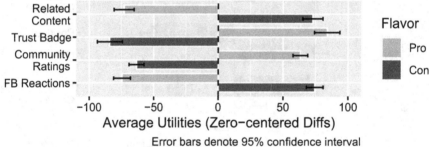

Fig. 6. Average Utilities for the interaction effects between visible cues and flavors.

Previous research indicates that the effect of a visible cue may depend on its rating [19, 28]. Therefore, we were also interested in the interaction effects between the visible cues and the flavors. Our results show that the flavor leads to different evaluations across our visible cues in terms of utility (see Fig. 6).

The *community ratings* were attributed with higher utility if they state a positive evaluation of credibility. Thus showing a summarized user rating is generally trusted and considered directly in evaluating the credibility of the article. This means that a summarized numerical rating of credibility even if provided by users seems trustworthy. In contrast, *Facebook Reactions* show the inverse effect. This means that when reactions are negative towards the content, users evaluated the article as more credible. This means that emotional cues, such as spontaneous affective reactions to an article are generally distrusted.

Trust badges received higher utility when they state a positive evaluation of credibility, showing an even stronger interaction with the flavor than community ratings. A positive trust badge thus increases credibility, while a negative one decreases credibility. The implication is that the badge itself is trusted, however, the impact on the evaluation is rather small (see Fig. 5).

Interestingly, *Related Content* also showed an inverse interaction with flavor. Here, average utilities were higher when combined with a negative flavor. In this case, showing contradicting information next to the news seems to lend credibility to the original post. Thus, when the context suggests an unbiased presentation it helps to improve the credibility evaluation of any news article.

5   Discussion

From our results, we see that credibility assessment is complex and depends on multiple interacting effects. Looking first at the credibility cues that already exist, we see that the *topic* plays a rather unimportant role. Most notably our participants value other credibility cues over the congruence of the **article stance** with their own opinions and beliefs. This contradicts previous findings [31,54,63] and could indicate that our participants have a higher need to access a broad spectrum of information rather than reading articles that confirm their own beliefs and views. But it is also possible, that our topics were perceived as rather inauthentic as the different versions of the same news articles were shown repeatedly in different combinations with other attributes. However, all topics were parts of the current discourse in Germany during the time of data collection. The high utility of the topic on coal exit could be related to a stronger relevance of this topic compared to the other two levels to the relatively young sample. Designing a conjoint-study always comes with repeated exposure to similar levels, as it needs these multiple data points as within-subject measurements. Some artificiality in experimentation is necessary to isolate the effects of individual levels. However, this does not necessarily mean that a conjoint study exchanges internal validity for external validity. On the contrary, during the experiment users develop a subconscious understanding of what each level means and make more natural and meaningful choices. This may contradict intuition, but results show more clearly how behavior is influenced. Our findings show that the integration of our credibility cues is a valuable approach to help the users.

The **affective valence** was less important than the *topic*. *Affective valence* was only implemented in the short teaser text of the Facebook post. Thus, participants could have overlooked the different *valence levels* as they had to make multiple decisions in a row. However, the experiment showed significant differences between the valence levels, indicating that differences did impact decision making. We see that the informatively written article outperformed the highly affective one which confirms findings of other studies [7].

The Hierarchical Bayes analysis revealed that the **visible cues are the most important attribute** of our conjoint-based study. Other researchers also found a dominating influence of such visible cues [66]. In particular, posts that do not have such cues receive lower credibility, when presented together with posts that have cues [48]. Participants carefully considered the visible cue in their credibility assessment, as the *flavor* turned out to be the second most important attribute.

Whereas Kim et al. found stronger effects for negative visible cues compared to positive cues [28], our study shows that the visible cues were utilized by our participants more often when cues had a positive flavor.

On a closer look at the different visible cues, we see that participants prefer the credibility cue that shows additional confirmatory or contradictory content over other cues. This preference clearly outperforms the effect of the other visible cues and seems to align with the participants' earlier self-report on credibility cues for media outlets. This indicates that they want to get an impression themselves rather than getting recommendations from the community or other organizations. This finding confirms the potential of related news that was already demonstrated by Bode et al. [6]. However, we cannot say whether participants changed their opinion as we did not explicitly ask for the initial opinions of our participants.

The **weak performance of trust badges and community ratings** seems to indicate that participants' have a desire for self-sufficiency with credibility assessment. Compared to previous research, this result is not surprising for trust badges [11], but still surprising for community ratings which performed even weaker. Another possible explanation for this result could be the missing number of users who have rated the credibility of the article. Winter et al. has shown that providing such an indication is valuable for increasing the perceived reliability of the rating. In their user study, the number of users who have read an article led users to include user ratings in their credibility perception [61]. Semaan et al. found that readers of news want to view, understand, and select the readership that they are dealing with. This allows readers to partake in a beneficial political deliberation and discourse [52]. In our study, we limited the complexity of community ratings and did not show information on readership to keep the overall study design feasible.

Lastly, the **conventional Facebook interactions performed weakest** in terms of conjoint utility. As mentioned above, this could be explained by contrasting effects that are created by the popularity of our other cues.

Regarding the **interactions between visible cue and flavor**, we see that for combinations with positive flavor the trust badge has the highest interaction utility followed by the community ratings. We assume that this stems from the ease of recognition of the positive and negative trust badges as well as different community ratings. Facebook interactions and related content performed best in combination with a negative flavor which gives food for thought. At least for the Facebook interactions one could hypothesize that this is due to the weak distinctiveness of attribute levels and also the low overall utility of this attribute. However, it is also possible that users have developed a general distrust in the affective low-involvement emotions of other users [29]. Theses signals are often directed at other social media friends and do not generally convey credibility. Especially in a polarized society, when other uses react with anger or fear, it could indicate that the article is worth reading for the opposite side.

For *related content* we see a similar direction. This entails that news posts on Facebook accompanied by contradicting news headlines show higher utilities than news headlines that are confirming the original post. Users seem to prefer a post with a broader viewpoint over a news post with solely confirmatory information. This finding is comparable to the study of Sülflow et al. who showed that a discrepancy between a news post and a user comment as a credibility cue led to a longer reading time of the content [54].

From our results, we conclude that the use of a *related content credibility cue* will offer the most added value for the credibility assessment—if implemented correctly. This in turn will also foster positive effects on political participation as the users will be exposed to more diverse content [41]. It has to be questioned though *how* such related articles should be selected and combined into a valuable broader spectrum. Munson et al. found that the interests of providers of social media platforms are to keep users online, which also poses as a limiting factor for the integration of such features [43].

Limitations of our study lay in its rather small and non-diverse sample and the static and limited set of examined factors. It would have been helpful to use real social media data for investigating users' behavior "in the wild". Although rather complex, the feasibility of such a study was shown by Saha et al. [51]. Nevertheless, our study helps to understand the interplay between different credibility cues and their efficacy which—until now—was examined in rather isolated settings. Furthermore, it would be an interesting extension to our study to include more attribute levels for the visible cues so that also effects like the aforementioned "implied truth" effect can be examined [48].

5.1   Implications for Design

Generally speaking, none of the credibility cues suggested in our study are easy fixes in a working system. Deciding on a specific cue requires to make other decisions early in the design process. The quality of the cues may be heavily dependent on available data, processes, and man-power. For example, trust-badges require the setup of a process to evaluate content. However, it must be asked: Evaluation by whom and by what standards? And how is the evaluation evaluated? On the other hand, providing related content for news articles requires an infrastructure that can identify content-relatedness, article stance, and quality. Thus, it makes sense to put significant effort into deciding which credibility cues to consider early in the design process (e.g., during prototyping), as to ensure supporting structures (data, processes, etc.) are available later in the development phase.

As participants in our study picked balanced content as the most credible option, we suggest providing news in a context that offers related content from different perspectives. However, this is easier said than done. Looking at this problem from an algorithmic point of view, it could be possible to include other news topics using a recommender system that suggests articles that address the same topic but produced higher levels of engagement from users that were dissimilar to the user of the system. Additionally, one must consider that simply providing"alternative facts" is not a viable solution. Additional metrics for picking high-quality content should be in place to prevent backfiring and accidentally spreading dis-/misinformation. How this is achieved is another problem on its own.

Some cues in our study are somewhat opaque in how credibility is established. And given the extensive research on explanations in recommender systems, it might make sense to help the user understand the rationale behind the credibility cue in a real-life system. The adjacent field of recommender systems has studied the impact of explanation for more than ten years [57] and has derived its own set of guidelines to consult when including explanations e.g.,[23]. These should be considered as well.

As a last thought, we would like to point out that engineering credibility cues from the platform perspective have the long-term danger of creating a social engineering toolbox. Once implemented, the truth could be crafted, by systematically selecting related content that either makes opposing views look weak or that makes confirming views look more credible. This could also happen by accident. The field of complex systems and opinion dynamics has rich research on how small changes can produce unintended consequences. Thus it is important to consult experts from these fields when designing such systems.

6   Conclusion

Looking at the "whole picture" is the key for harmonizing the findings on credibility assessment and news article selection in online environments so far. We were able to show that credibility assessment builds on the interplay of different attributes and that it can be supported very effectively by showing further options of evaluation to the users. As we have shown, providing a balanced content fulfills both the wish of the users to reaffirm themselves and the societal aim for an increased exposure to attitude-challenging content. However, it remains to be seen whether or not this leads to an decrease in political polarization.

Acknowledgement. We would like to thank our participants for taking part in the study. This work was supported by the Digital Society research program funded by the Ministry of Culture and Science of the German State of North Rhine-Westphalia under Grant 005-1709-0006.

References

1. Urt. v. 24.11.2017 507 Ds 501 Js 15031/15 AG Giessen. Informationen über Schwangerschaftsabbrüche auf der ärztlichen Website als strafbare Werbungi.S.d. §219a StGB. Medizinrecht, vol. 37(1), pp. 77–79 (2019). ISSN 1433–8629
2. Almoqbel, M.Y., Wohn, D.Y., Hayes, R.A., Cha, M.: Understanding facebook news post comment reading and reacting behavior through political extremism and cultural orientation. Comput. Hum. Behav. **100**, 118–126 (2019). ISSN 07475632
3. Anspach, N.M.: The new personal influence: How our facebook friends influence the news we read. Political Commun. **34**(4), 590–606 (2017). ISSN 1058–4609, 1091–7675
4. Beierlein, C., Kemper, C.J., Kovaleva, A., Rammstedt, B.: Ein Messinstrument zur Erfassung politischer Kompetenz- und Einflussüberzeugungen - Political Efficacy Kurzskala (PEKS). GESIS Working Papers **18**(2012) (2012)

5. Bentley, F., Quehl, K., Wirfs-Brock, J., Bica, M.: Understanding online news behaviors. In: Conference on Human Factors in Computing Systems - Proceedings. Association for Computing Machinery (2019). ISBN 9781450359702
6. Bode, L., Vraga, E.K.: In related news, that was wrong: The correction of misinformation through related stories functionality in social media. J. Commun. **65**(4), 619–638 (2015). ISSN 00219916
7. Borah, P.: Interactions of news frames and incivility in the political blogosphere: Examining perceptual outcomes. Political Commun. **30**(3), 456–473 (2013). ISSN 10584609
8. Braun, K.: From ethical exceptionalism to ethical exceptions: The rule and exception model and the changing meaning of ethics in german bioregulation. Dev. World Bioeth. **17**(3), 146–156 (2017)
9. Brock, A., Dunlap, A.: Normalising corporate counterinsurgency: engineering consent, managing resistance and greening destruction around the Hambach coal mine and beyond. Political Geogr. **62**, 33–47 (2018). ISSN 0962–6298
10. Bundesamt, S.: Bildungsstand der Bevölkerung - Ergebnisse des Mikrozensus 2017 -. Technical report, Statistisches Bundesamt (Destatis), Wiesbaden (2018)
11. Calero Valdez, A., Ziefle, M.: Believability of news. In: Bagnara, S., Tartaglia, R., Albolino, S., Alexander, T., Fujita, Y. (eds.) IEA 2018. AISC, vol. 822, pp. 469–477. Springer, Cham (2019). https://doi.org/10.1007/978-3-319-96077-7_50
12. Chrzan, K., Orme, B.: An overview and comparison of design strategies for choice-based conjoint analysis. Sawtooth Softw. Res. Paper Ser. **98382**(360), 1–22 (2002)
13. Coggio, T., Gustafson, T.: When the exit?: the difficult politics of german coal. German Politics Soc. **37**(1), 47–65 (2019). ISSN 1558–5441, 1045–0300
14. Diehl, I., Weeks, B.E., de Zúñiga, H.G.: Political persuasion on social media: tracing direct and indirect effects of news use and social interaction. New Media Soc. **18**(9), 1875–1895 (2016). ISSN 1461–4448
15. Douglas, S., Raine, R.B., Maruyama, M., Semaan, B., Robertson, S.P.: Community matters: how young adults use facebook to evaluate political candidates. Inform. Polity **20**(2–3), 135–150 (2015). ISSN 18758754
16. Douglas, S., Maruyama, M., Semaan, B., Robertson. S.P.: Politics and young adults: The effects of facebook on candidate evaluation. In: ACM International Conference Proceeding Series, pp. 196–204. Association for Computing Machinery, New York (2014). ISBN 9781450329019
17. Elejalde, E., Ferres, L., Herder, E.: On the nature of real and perceived bias in the mainstream media. PLoS ONE **13**(3) (2018). ISSN 19326203
18. Fang, I.: A History of Mass Communication. Routledge, New York (1997). 9780080508160
19. Flanagin, A.J., Metzger, M.J.: Trusting expert- versus user-generated ratings online: The role of information volume, valence, and consumer characteristics. Computers in Hum. Behav. **29**(4), 1626–1634 (2013). ISSN 0747–5632
20. Fletcher, R., Nielsen, R.S.: Are people incidentally exposed to news on social media? a comparative analysis. New Media Soc. **20**(7), 2450–2468 (2018). ISSN 1461–4448
21. Gao, M., Do, H.J., Fu, W.T.: Burst your bubble! an intelligent system for improving awareness of diverse social opinions. In: International Conference on Intelligent User Interfaces, Proceedings IUI, pp. 371–383. Association for Computing Machinery (2018). ISBN 9781450349451
22. Garrett, R.K., Carnahan, D., Lynch, E.K.: A turn toward avoidance? selective exposure to online political information, 2004–2008. Political Behav. **35**(1), 113–134 (2013). ISSN 01909320

23. Gedikli, F., Jannach, D., Ge, M.: How should i explain? a comparison of different explanation types for recommender systems. Int. J. Hum Comput Stud. **72**(4), 367–382 (2014)
24. Hermida, A., Fletcher, F., Korell, D., Logan, D.: Share, like, recommend: Decoding the social media news consumer. J. Stud. **13**(5–6), 815–824 (2012). ISSN 1461670X
25. Kaiser, J., Keller, T.R., Kleinen-von Königslöw, K.: Incidental news exposure on facebook as a social experience: The influence of recommender and media cues on news selection. Commun. Res., 009365021880352 (2018). ISSN 0093–6502
26. Kalogeropoulos, A., Suiter, J., Udris, L., Eisenegger, M.: News media trust and news consumption: factors related to trust in news in 35 countries. Int. J. Commun. **13**, 22 (2019). ISSN 1932–8036
27. Karlsson, M., Klein, T.J., Ziebarth, N.R.: Skewed, persistent and high before death: medical spending in germany: medical spending in Germany. Fiscal Studies **37**(3–4), 527–559 (2016). ISSN 01435671
28. Kim, A., Moravec, P., Dennis, A.R.: Behind the stars: The effects of news source ratings on fake news in social media. SSRN Elect. J. (2018). ISSN 1556–5068
29. Kim, C., Yang, S.-U.: Like, comment, and share on facebook: How each behavior differs from the other. Public Relat. Rev. **43**(2), 441–449 (2017). ISSN 0363–8111
30. Klein, J., von dem Knesebeck, O.: Social disparities in outpatient and inpatient care: An overview of current findings in Germany. Bundesgesundheitsblatt - Gesundheitsforschung - Gesundheitsschutz **59**(2), 238–244 (2016)
31. Knobloch-Westerwick, S., Meng, J.J.: Looking the other way. Commun. Res. **36**(3), 426–448 (2009). ISSN 0093–6502
32. Koroleva, K., Krasnova, H., Stimac, V., Kunze, D.: I like it because i('m) like you - measuring user attitudes towards information on facebook. In: International Conference on Information Systems 2011, ICIS 2011, vol. 2, pp. 1223–1241 (2011). ISBN 9781618394729
33. Krolzik-Matthei, K.: Abtreibungen in der Debatte in Deutschland und Europa. Aus Politik und Zeitgeschichte (20) (2019)
34. Leipprand, A., Flachsland, C.: Regime destabilization in energy transitions: The German debate on the future of coal. Energy Res. Soc. Sci. **40**, 190–204 (2018). ISSN: 22146296
35. Liao, Q.V., Fu, W.T.: Beyond the filter bubble: Interactive effects of perceived threat and topic involvement on selective exposure to information. In: Conference on Human Factors in Computing Systems - Proceedings, pp. 2359–2368 (2013). ISBN 9781450318990
36. Liao, Q.V., Fu, W.T.: Expert voices in echo chambers: Effects of source expertise indicators on exposure to diverse opinions. In: Conference on Human Factors in Computing Systems - Proceedings, pp. 2745–2754. Association for Computing Machinery (2014). ISBN 9781450324731
37. Lottridge, D., Bentley, F.R.: Let's hate together: How people share news in messaging, social, and public networks. In: Conference on Human Factors in Computing Systems - Proceedings, vol. 2018. Association for Computing Machinery (April 2018). ISBN 9781450356206
38. Maruyama, M., Robertson, S.P., Douglas, S., Semaan, B., Faucett, H.: Hybrid media consumption: How tweeting during atelevised political debate influences the vote decision. In: Proceedings of the ACM Conference on Computer Supported Cooperative Work, CSCW, pp. 1422–1432. Association for Computing Machinery, New York (2014). ISBN 9781450325400
39. Melican, D.B., Dixon, T.L.: News on the net: credibility, selective exposure, and racial prejudice. Commun. Res. **35**(2), 151–168 (2008). ISSN 00936502

40. Metzger, M.J., Hartsell, E.H., Flanagin, A.J.: Cognitive dissonance or credibility? Commun. Res., 009365021561313 (2015). ISSN 0093–6502

41. Min, S.J., Wohn, D.Y.: All the news that you don't like: Cross-cutting exposure and political participation in the age of social media. Comput. Hum. Behav. **83**, 24–31 (2018). ISSN 07475632

42. Molyneux, L.: Mobile news consumption: A habit of snacking. Digital J. **6**(5), 634–650 (2018). ISSN 2167082X

43. Munson, S.A., Resnick, P.: Presenting diverse political opinions: how and how much. In: Conference on Human Factors in Computing Systems - Proceedings, vol. 3, pp. 1457–1466. ACM Press, New York (2010). ISBN 9781605589299

44. Nelimarkka, M., Laaksonen, S.M., Semaan, B.: Social media is polarized, social media is polarized: Towards a new design agenda for mitigating polarization. In: DIS 2018 - Proceedings of the 2018 Designing Interactive Systems Conference, pp. 957–970. Association for Computing Machinery Inc. (2018). ISBN 9781450351980

45. Oeldorf-Hirsch, A., DeVoss, C.L.: Who posted that story? processing layered sources in facebook news posts. J. Mass Commun. Q., 107769901985767 (2019). ISSN 1077–6990

46. Oeldorf-Hirsch, A., Sundar, S.S.: Posting, commenting, and tagging: Effects of sharing news stories on facebook. Comput. Hum. Behav. **44**, 240–249 (2015). ISSN 07475632

47. Orme, B.: Interpreting the results of conjoint analysis. Getting Started with Conjoint Analysis: Strategies for Product Design and Pricing Research, pp. 77–88 (2010)

48. Pennycook, G., Rand, D.G., Collins, E., Rand, D.G.: Assessing the effect of 'disputed' warnings and source salience on perceptions of fake news accuracy. SSRN Electron. J. (2017). ISSN 1556–5068

49. Pieper, C.: Use your illusion: Televised discourse on journalistic ethics in the united states, 1992–1998. Soc. Semiotics **10**(1), 61–79 (2000). ISSN 10350330

50. Rammstedt, B., Kemper, C.S., Klein, M., Beierlein, C., Kovaleva, A.: A short scale for assessing the big five dimensions of personality: 10 item big five inventory (bfi-10). Methods Data Anal. **7**(2), 17 (2017). ISSN 2190–4936

51. Saha, K.: Social media as a passive sensor in longitudinal studies of human behavior and wellbeing. In: Conference on Human Factors in Computing Systems - Proceedings. Association for Computing Machinery (2019). ISBN 9781450359719

52. Semaan, B., Robertson, S.P., Douglas, S., Maruyama, N.: Social media supporting political deliberation across multiple public spheres: Towards depolarization. In: Proceedings of the ACM Conference on Computer Supported Cooperative Work, CSCW, pp. 1409–1421. Association for Computing Machinery, New York (2014). ISBN 9781450325400

53. Stroud, N.J.: Media use and political predispositions: Revisiting the concept of selective exposure. Political Behav. **30**(3), 341–366 (2008). ISSN 01909320

54. Sülflow, M., Schäfer, S., Winter, S.: Selective attention in the news feed: An eye-tracking study on the perception and selection of political news posts on facebook. New Media Soc. **21**(1), 168–190 (2019). ISSN 1461–4448

55. Shyam Sundar, S., Knobloch-Westerwick, S., Hastall, M.R.: News cues: Information scent and cognitive heuristics. J. Am. Soc. Inform. Sci. Technol. **58**(3), 366–378 (2007). ISSN 15322882

56. Sundmacher, L., Ozegowski, S.: Regional distribution of physicians: the role of comprehensive private health insurance in Germany. Europ. J. Health Econ. **17**(4), 443–451 (2016). ISSN 1618–7598, 1618–7601

57. Tintarev, N., Masthoff, J.: A survey of explanations in recommender systems. In: 2007 IEEE 23rd international conference on data engineering workshop, pp. 801–810. IEEE (2007)
58. Turcotte, J., York, C., Irving, J., Scholl, R.M., Pingree, R.J.: News recommendations from social media opinion leaders: Effects on media trust and information seeking **20**(5), 520–535 (2015). ISSN 10836101
59. Vaidya, T., Votipka, D., Mazurek, M.L., Sherr, M.: Does being verified make you more credible? In: Proceedings of the 2019 CHI Conference on Human Factors in Computing Systems - CHI 2019, pp. 1–13. ACM Press, New York (2019). ISBN 9781450359702
60. Westerman, D., Spence, P.R., Van Der Heide, B.: Social media as information source: Recency of updates and credibility of information. J. Comput.-Mediated Commun. **19**(2), 171–183 (2014). ISSN 10836101
61. Winter, S., Krämer, N.C.: A question of credibility - Effects of source cues and recommendations on information selection on news sites and blogs. Communications **39**(4), 435–456 (2014). ISSN 1613–4087
62. Winter, S., Krämer, N.C.: Who's right: The author or the audience? effects of user comments and ratings on the perception of online science articles. Communications **41**(3) (2016). ISSN 0341–2059
63. Winter, S., Metzger, M.J., Flanagin, A.J.: Selective use of news cues: A multiple-motive perspective on information selection in social media environments. J. Commun. **66**(4), 669–693 (2016). ISSN 00219916
64. Wolf, C., Schnauber, A.: News consumption in the mobile era: The role of mobile devices and traditional journalism's content within the user's information repertoire. Digital J. **3**(5), 759–776 (2015). ISSN 2167082X
65. Xu, Q.: Social recommendation, source credibility, and recency. J. Mass Commun. Q. **90**(4), 757–775 (2013). ISSN 1077–6990
66. Yang, J.: Effects of popularity-based news recommendations "most-viewed" on users' exposure to online news. Media Psychol. **19**(2), 243–271 (2016). ISSN 1521–3269
67. Yu, R.P., Ellison, N.B., Lampe, C.: Facebook use and its role in shaping access to social benefits among older adults. J. Broadcasting Electron. Media **62**(1), 71–90 (2018). ISSN 15506878

Semantic Scene Builder: Towards a Context Sensitive Text-to-3D Scene Framework

Alexander Henlein[(⊠)][iD], Attila Kett, Daniel Baumartz, Giuseppe Abrami[iD],
Alexander Mehler[iD], Johannes Bastian, Yannic Blecher, David Budgenhagen,
Roman Christof, Tim-Oliver Ewald, Tim Fauerbach, Patrick Masny, Julian Mende,
Paul Schnüre, and Marc Viel

Goethe University, Frankfurt, Germany
{henlein,abrami,mehler}@em.uni-frankfurt.de,
{attila.kett,baumartz,s0844411,s5746085,s8335023,s5562603,
s1835525,s8023823,s2152151,s7587383,s7647597,
s7362826}@stud.uni-frankfurt.de

Abstract. We introduce Semantic Scene Builder (SESB), a VR-based text-to-3D scene framework using SemAF (Semantic Annotation Framework) as a scheme for annotating discourse structures. SESB integrates a variety of tools and resources by using SemAF and UIMA as a unified data structure to generate 3D scenes from textual descriptions. Based on VR, SESB allows its users to change annotations through body movements instead of symbolic manipulations: from annotations in texts to corrections in editing steps to adjustments in generated scenes, all this is done by grabbing and moving objects. We evaluate SESB in comparison with a state-of-the-art open source text-to-scene method (the only one which is publicly available) and find that our approach not only performs better, but also allows for modeling a greater variety of scenes.

Keywords: Text-to-3D Scene Generation · Semantic Annotation Framework · Virtual Reality

1 Introduction

Humans are able to describe visual scenes linguistically and, conversely, to generate visual representations, e.g., in their mind's eye or on a sheet of paper, on the basis of linguistic descriptions [75,76]. These modality changes require mental capabilities in the area of multimodal fusion and fission [21]. From a computational point of view, the second of these capabilities is modeled in terms of text-to-scene systems (e.g. [88]), namely when it comes to generating 3D scenes from text descriptions (e.g. [16]).

While language-assisted image generation has received a lot of attention recently (e.g. [1,20,70,71,74,77]), 3D scene generation from language has not been explored that much [34,53,92]. Image-generating models benefit immensely from the advances in grounded language modeling (like CLIP; [69]) and the sheer amount of data available (cf. LAION-5b[1] which provides 5,85 billion image-text pairs). This amount of data is

---

[1] https://laion.ai/.

V. G. Duffy (Ed.): HCII 2023, LNCS 14029, pp. 461–479, 2023.
https://doi.org/10.1007/978-3-031-35748-0_32

currently unthinkable for text-to-3D scene applications. There are large-scale 3D object datasets like ShapeNet [8] or 3D-FUTURE [30], and large-scale 3D scene datasets, like Matterport3D [6], 3D-Front [28] or SUNCG ([85], which is currently not available due to license problems). But non of these datasets is annotated with textual descriptions. As a result, recent work increasingly emphasizes generating ever more realistic scenes (c.f., Scene Synthesis; [95]), where the use of language is increasingly reduced to imposing constraints on the generated scenes so that the alignment of natural language and scenes takes a back seat. This is exemplified by Ma et al. [53] where language processing does not go beyond pattern matching of dependency trees and keywords. That is, the quality of the generated scenes is primarily achieved via co-occurrence patterns of objects in already modeled scenes.

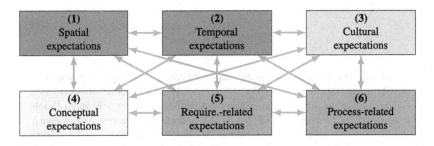

Fig. 1. Areas of contextual expectations that are relevant for scene generation.

Yet human language is so versatile and flexible in describing events, often based on elliptical or underspecified constructions, which, however, are perfectly understandable by exploring knowledge shared by speakers and listeners, i.e., their common ground [14,32]: Hearing, for example, a sentence like

"After eating my croissant, I read the newspaper."

the listener is likely to assume that the speaker is describing an event in which he ate a croissant in the kitchen or dining room, that the croissant was eaten with a coffee, that the event took place in the morning, etc. But none of these common ground-related expectations are expressed in the sentence – although they are relevant to the imagination of a sufficiently complete scene. The breadth and depth of such expectation-driven understanding of scene descriptions is contrasted with a lack of data that make them explicit and link them to image representations. Figure 1 lists ranges of such information implied by scene descriptions concerning

(1) expectations about **spatial** relations regarding, e.g., the placement of objects (e.g. piece of cake *on* a plate) [11],
(2) **temporal** relations and epoch-related expectations (e.g. a medieval kitchen compared to today) [3],
(3) **cultural** expectations (e.g. a classic German vs. a French breakfast) [33],
(4) expectations about **conceptual** relations and object affordances (e.g., chairs are for sitting) [66],

(5) **requirements-related** expectations (e.g. eggs are needed to make omelets) [79],
(6) and **process-related** expectations (in terms of what has been processed so far or will likely happen next) [64].

These domains are interrelated and give rise to complex expectations about, e.g., courses of events [2]. Thus, there is a large body of work dealing with descriptive models of contexts (e.g. [18,54,57,60,62,89]).

Much has been done to generate realistic scenes, but the range of linguistic descriptions of such scenes is far from exhausted. We argue that this is mainly due to the lack of available data and a computational framework for its generation, processing and maintenance. We present *Semantic Scene Builder* (SESB), a VR-based[2] text-to-3D scene framework to fill this gap. Its interactive approach, based on VR and a unified data model, allows the system to be used for every step of text-to-3D scene generation, from annotation of data to integration of individual specialized tools to complete end-to-end models. For each of its processing steps we implemented 1-3 modules based on state-of-the-art tools, including a self-trained BERT [19] model for extracting spatial entities and relations, and a dataset for processing associations between actions and objects. For evaluation, we generated scenes with SESB and with the system of Ma et al.[53] and compared them regarding two criteria: naturalness and plausibility.

The paper is structured as follows: Sect. 2 describes current text-to-3D scene systems and their limitations. We review the range of linguistic variants of scene descriptions and outline IsoSpace and SemAF. Section 3 presents the functionality of SESB and Sect. 4 its implementation. Section 5 evaluates SESB in comparison to a state-of-the-art text-to-3D scene system. Section 6 describes future work and Sect. 7 gives a conclusion.

2   Related Work

2.1   Text-to-3D Scene

One of the first successful text-to-3D scene systems is WordsEye [16]. To date, thanks to various additions, it is one of the linguistically most comprehensive systems [34]. The basic version already supported representations of actions, avatars, negations and of proverbs. This functionality was later extended by means of frame semantics (VigNet, [15]) and SpatialNet [90], a hand-annotated resource for spatial relations. These manually created and non-open-source resources allow to disambiguate and resolve ambiguous prepositions and verbs.

Another well known text-to-3D scene system is that of Chang et al. [9–11], meanwhile referred to as SceneSeer [7]. It creates a scene s given an utterance u using a conditional probability:

$$P(s|u) = P(t|u)P(t'|t,u)P(s|t',t,u)$$
$$= P(t|u)P(t'|t)P(s|t') \tag{1}$$

---

[2] *VR* here stands for *fully-immersive virtual reality*, supported by hand tracking and head-mounted displays [73].

That is, $P(s|u)$ is decomposed into the product of the parsing probability $P(t|u)$, the inference probability $P(t'|t)$ and the generation probability $P(s|t')$. t stands for the scene template given utterance u, while t' is the completed scene template. This model assumes that s is independent of t and u, and t' is assumed to be independent of u – a weakness that Chang et al. [7] already noted, but most systems retain to this day. There is also a transformer-based [91] end-to-end approach (SceneFormer; [92]), but the text-conditioned model has not been published yet.

In the *parsing* step, u is preprocessed and the objects and relations mentioned in u are mapped to elements of the scene template t. In the *inference* step, objects and constraints implied by t (and optimally from u) are inferred to generate the expanded template t'. This is done using coincidence probabilities learned *a priori* from spatial datasets. Finally, in the *generation* step, the output scene s is produced starting from t'. s can be adjusted by the user to allow the system to continue learning.

Few systems actively use external language resources in addition to pre-configured rooms to enable more diverse language inputs [34]. At first glance, these systems generate very realistic scenes from scene descriptions, but are rather application scenario specific. Thus, while they learn, e.g., from large 3D corpora (like, SUNCG [85] and 3D-FRONT [29]) how a kitchen is typically set up and that a pan is usually placed on the stove, the same is not true for expressions that express ambiguous linguistic relations [25, 36]. Take the following examples

(1) "I am *on* the wall."
(2) "The mirror is *on* the wall."
(3) "I am *on* the airplane."

which illustrate three different meanings of *on*[3]. WordsEye, for example, tries to resolve such ambiguities by means of SpatialNet. However, the underlying system is not open source and thus not extensible. Such problems can be solved with the help of IsoSpace (see below).

There are many other systems that address the creation of 3D scenes, which are based, e.g., on images [44], relation patterns [96] and scene categories [49]. Since we focus on text-based scene generation, we do not consider this approach. The same applies to text-based generations of avatar movements [63] or 3D objects [12].

2.2 SemAF and IsoSpace

IsoSpace [43, 67] is part of the *Semantic Annotation Framework* (SemAf [40, p. 128]), "an annotation scheme for the markup of spatial relations, both static and dynamic, as expressed in text and other media" ([40, p. 989]). SemAF is a further development of *Spatial Role Labeling* [46, 47] and consists of two main components: *entities* marked directly in the text and *links* that relate these entities to each other. According to IsoSpace, entities are divided into (i) spatial entities, such as objects, persons or places (ii) signal words, mostly prepositions (iii) events, mostly verbs, and (iv) measures. Entities can be provided with attributes (e.g., *type*, *dimensionality* and *cardinality*) and linked by (i) *Qualitative Spatial Links* (QSLinks, representing topological RCC8+ relations [72]; see Table 1), (ii) *Orientation Links* (OLinks, denoting all

---

[3] https://dictionary.cambridge.org/dictionary/english/on.

Table 1. The list of RCC8+ (*Region Connection Calculus*) relations [43].

Value	Description	Example
DC	disconnected	[Europe] - [America]
EC	externally connected	the [book] on the [table]
PO	partial overlap	the [light switch] on the [wall]
EQ	equal	[The White House] - [1600 Pennsylvania Avenue]
TPP	tangential proper part	the [windows] of the [house]
NTTP	non-tangential proper part	the [heart] of the [city]
IN	disjunction of TTP and NTTP	the [table] in the [room]

other spatial relations; e.g. *in front of, north, across*), (iii) *Movement Links* (MoveLinks regarding movements of entities in space), and (iv) *Measure Links* (MLinks, used to represent sizes and distances, e.g., *2m, 4l*).

We also use the SemAF specifications for semantic roles (SrLinks, [41]) and coreference annotation (MetaLinks, [42]). In the case of MetaLinks, we use the type value *Part* to indicate meronymy and holonymy relations, a relation not covered by IsoSpace by default. The links distinguished so far allow, for example, for resolving ambiguous prepositions:

(1) "**I** am *on* the **wall**."
    → QSLink(EC), OLink(ABOVE)
(2) "The **mirror** is *on* the **wall**."
    → QSLink(EC), OLink(FRONT)
(3) "**I** am *on* the **airplane**".
    → QSLink(IN)

For a second example of using SemAF for disambiguation see Fig. 2.

IsoSpace does not claim to cover all aspects of spatial language; however, it is still the most comprehensive annotation model of this sort. IsoSpace is not limited to spatial descriptions but can also be used for representing tasks such as [43]: (a) creating routes based on route descriptions; (b) tracking moving objects based on motion descriptions; (c) conversion of viewer-centered descriptions into other-oriented descriptions or descriptions based on absolute coordinates. Related work concerning the transfer of IsoSpace into VR environments is presented by Henlein et al. [35]. However, this work focuses primarily on annotations, while we focus on their application for text-to-3D scene systems.

3   Semantic Scene Builder

To date, there is no extensible open source system that integrates comprehensive SemAF-related annotations to generate data for training text-to-3D scene systems. We propose SESB, to fill this gap. SESB implements the following features:

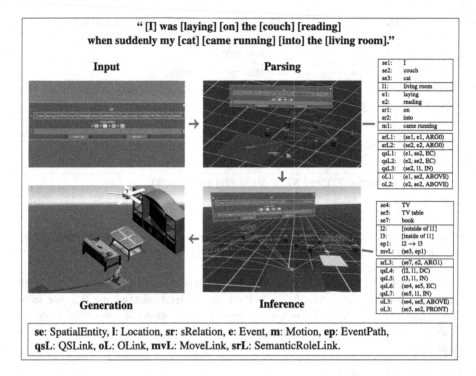

Fig. 2. Example of an IsoSpace-based, user-supported text-to-3D scene result generated with SESB (not all attributes are displayed as, e.g., trigger references to the sRelations for the IsoSpace links; the list of IsoSpace links is only displayed in part). The images show the complete text-to-3D scene process, from the initial scene description to the final scene. Start and end points of the *cat* were added manually by the user during the processing steps. In the last image (Generation), the links have been omitted for clarity. Main points: (1) Entities not explicitly mentioned in the text are added [e.g. se4 and se5]. (2) Implicit Semantic Role Labeling [srL3] is annotated. (3) Entity movements are also annotated. For this purpose, an EventPath is created that describes the path [ep1] and is linked to the moving entity via a MoveLink [mvL1]. (4) Beyond entities, events are linked using IsoSpace links. For dynamic scenes, this allows the acting entity to not be directly linked to objects and therefore perform actions in different areas [qsL1, oL1]. (5) Though not being shown in this example, SESB allows for annotating (sub-)coreferences and partonymy relations using MetaLinks.

1. Its SemAF-based data model allows for modeling a wide range of semantic relations. In this way, not only spatial objects but also events and movements can be represented.
2. SESB is not distributed across a number of heterogeneous, proprietary, barely interoperable systems. Rather, SESB integrates its functionality into a single system that is freely accessible and extensible.
3. Users maintain control at all times and can adjust scene generation according to their needs. Changes to data representations can be made in the course of scene generation, so that SESB can be used as an active learning environment [81].

SESB stores all data (e.g., input texts, entity labels, links, object placements) in a UIMA-based [26] XMI format based on SemAF. We now describe the modules of SESB by distinguishing four steps of generating text-to-3D scenes (for the first three steps cf. Sect. 2.1), that is, *parsing*, *inference*, *generation* and *annotation*. In this way, we stepwise generate a scene s starting from a given scene description u.

3.1 Parsing

For preprocessing of scene description u (including, e.g., tokenization, sentence splitting, POS tagging and lemmatization) we use the Stanza [68] interface to CoreNLP [55]. For semantic role labeling, we use the AllenNLP [31] implementation of Shi & Lin [82].

We use a two-step approach for detecting objects and their relations in u: first we extract entities and links with IsoSpaceSpERT (see below), and then augment and correct them with a rule-based model.

Rule-Based Model. As a baseline, we reimplemented the rule-based approach of Ma et al. [53]. That is, anything recognized as a noun by POS tagging is labeled as a spatial entity. Attributes and relations are assigned using hand-generated dependency rules, which we transferred to the QS-/OLink schema: e.g. "The cat is in front of the table." is mapped onto (cat, in_front_of, table) and OLink(cat, table, front).

Table 2. Evaluation of IsoSpaceSpERT. *: Evaluated on (figure, ground, trigger, rel_type) and MoveLinks.

	SpRL-CWW	S-BERT	Prec.	Rec.	F1
Place	74.7	86.8	81.4	82.6	82.0
Path	61.7	94.9	81.0	76.4	78.7
Spatial entity	80.8	89.9	79.7	87.6	83.5
Motion	76.9	94.3	79.2	87.4	83.1
Motion signal	78.6	90.7	84.4	88.8	86.6
Spatial signal	70.9	85.9	76.1	83.6	79.6
Measure	79.1	98.3	88.6	91.2	89.9
Non-motion	56.4	89.4	59.4	63.3	61.3
average	74.6	90.0	78.7	82.6	80.6
QSLink	–	–	58.2	40.8	48.0
OLink	–	–	35.5	32.4	33.9
average	3.0*	–	46.9	36.6	41.0

IsoSpaceSpERT. Since no open source models are yet available for IsoSpace tagging [22,61,78,83], we trained IsoSpaceSpERT based on SpERT [23], which in turn is based on BERT [19] using the data from SpaceEval [65]. We also conducted experiments with REBEL [38] and PL-Marker [93]. However, both models performed significantly worse – probably due to the limited amount of training data.

Since no link annotations were published for the SpaceEval test data, we added QSLink and OLink annotations, arriving at 92% of the data reported in the official statistics for each of these types (all these data are made publicly available via this publication). For annotation we used the Multi-purpose Annotation Environment [87] that was originally used for generating the SpaceEval data[4]. We deleted files in the test data that also appeared in the training data and did not consider empty entities and their links.

We trained IsoSpaceSpERT to detect the type of spatial relation that connects entities: e.g., for QSLinks RCC8+ relations are tagged. Note that S-BERT [83] and SpRL-CWW [61] focus on finding relation triples (figure, ground, trigger) and therefore do not predict relation types. In addition, S-BERT only considers relations manifested by prepositions. These differences make it difficult to directly compare our results with previous work on QSLink and OLink detection.

Table 2 shows the results of evaluating IsoSpaceSpERT. The results of hyperparameter optimization using wandb [4] are shown in Table 3 (appendix). We trained separate models for QSLinks and OLinks, as this resulted in significantly better link detection results, even though entity detection benefits from joint training. The results for entity detection are generated by the QSLink model. We achieve an F1-Score of 41% for QSLinks (48%) and OLinks (33.9%). There is one dominant error due to our model architecture: since the prediction of relations between two entities only takes into account the context that lies between them, the model has problems with statements like: "*On x is y*", where the preposition is to the left of x and y.

3.2   Inference

SESB contains two mechanisms for inferring contextual information for expectation-driven understanding (see Fig. 1). This relates to aspects of spatial and process-related expectations.

Spatial or Room-Related Inference. To exploit knowledge about rooms, we estimate the conditional probability $P(r \mid o)$ of a room r given an object o. $P(r \mid o)$ estimates, e.g., the probability of objects like bathtubs being typically located in bathrooms. To this end, we use the NYU Depth V2 dataset [84]. It contains 464 labeled real-world scenes and nearly 900 different object labels, and therefore significantly more than, e.g., COCO [50] with only 80 object categories. Using NYU Depth V2 to estimate $P(r \mid o)$, we add the five most strongly associated objects to the scene. Note that using $P(r \mid o)$ to determine these associations generated the better results, because of filtering out uninteresting objects (like ceiling or curtain), while selecting objects that

---

[4] http://jamespusto.com/wp-content/uploads/2014/07/SpaceEval-guidelines.pdf.

are interesting for a room type (e.g. bed → bedroom). This is done for each room label occurring in the input scene description u detected by the parsing module.

Process- Or Task-Related Inference. To insert objects inferred from described actions into the scene s, we use a version of HowToKB [13]. HowToKB represents task-related knowledge along with attributes for the parent task, the preceding and the succeeding subtask. This knowledge is extracted from WikiHow[5] articles by means of OpenIE [24]. HowToKB also contains information about tools and objects required to perform a task, if they are explicitly listed in a separate section of the original article.

We created a new crawl of WikiHow and updated the whole pipeline based on How-ToKB. We also performed WordNet-related [59] *Word Sense Disambiguation* (WSD) using LMMS [51,52] and updated task clustering to include disambiguation as well. Using WSD, we expanded the number of objects extracted from WikiHow articles and added to task-specific lists of required objects (increasing the amount of labeled *objects involved* from 1.4M to 2.2M). To to process queries, we imported HowToKB into Neo4J.[6]

For each event e described in the input description u, we then search our extended knowledge base for all object-event combinations that contain e. For each such entry, the corresponding object is finally inserted into the scene s if it is missing there.

In future work, we will experiment with systems such as COMET-ATOMIC 2020 [39], ConceptNet [86] or TransOMCS [94] to provide SESB as an application for evaluating commonsense systems.

3.3 Generation

The next step is to select 3D objects for all the objects detected so far and place them in the scene s in a meaningful way (taking into account constraints mentioned in u). For this purpose we use the scene generation tool of Ma et al. [53]. This tool creates a scene from all extracted objects and extends it with objects and relations that are still missing (e.g., a given plate implies a table on which it is placed). The models that [53] trained for this purpose were created using various annotated scene resources, that is, SUNCG [85], SceneSynth [27] and SceneNN [37]. This includes

(1) the **support model** for adding matching supports of objects (e.g. a plate as a support under a piece of cake),
(2) the **co-occurrence model** for adding relevant objects based on co-occurrence probabilities (e.g. a mouse next to keyboard),
(3) the **pairwise model** to predict the relative positioning between two objects,
(4) the **group model** for handling with group relations (e.g. "messy table");
(5) and the **relative model** to handle conflicts between explicit relations specified in the input record and implicit relations specified by existing objects.

This approach is originally based on Fisher et al. [27]. It shows that modules do not have to strictly adhere to the succession of parsing, inference, and generation, since objects and relations can also be inferred and added during generation.

---

[5] https://www.wikihow.com/.
[6] https://neo4j.com/.

3.4 Annotation

Based on VR, SESB allows users to make changes at each processing step. These can be changes to the final scene by grabbing objects and repositioning, rotating, or scaling them. It may also concern the placement of inferred objects into the scene or deleting them. Furthermore, it is possible to interact with the input text u by means of a text window to annotate entities, set their attributes or insert links between them. In this way, the user has full access to SESB's data structure. In this way, SESB provides a 3D, VR-based annotation environment for SemAF and 3D scenes.

4 Implementation

SESB is based on V-FRAMEWORK, which builds on A-FRAMEWORK[7]. SESB is implemented in Unity3D[8] and can be used by means of 3D glasses. V-FRAMEWORK creates a virtual 3D environment in which scenes can be visualized and modified, with both operations provided by A-FRAMEWORK. A-FRAMEWORK is a platform-independent, WebSocket-based multi-user annotation framework which enables collaborative, simultaneous annotations based on UIMA [26]. Thus, different users can annotate the same scene s at the same time. To this end, scenes are modeled as UIMA documents, which are annotated with A-FRAMEWORK. Any change to a scene (e.g., by creating, moving, scaling, texturing, or relating objects) is interpreted as an annotation instruction that is communicated to each annotator of the same scene to update her or his view. To this end, all representations of object, their attributes and relations are modeled as annotation objects.

Since the representation of 3D objects is an essential part of scene generation, we use ShapeNetSem [80], a sub-project of ShapeNet [8], to visualize 3D objects. Through ShapeNetSem, it is possible to access 12 000 semantically annotated objects, which allows SESB to create and annotate a wide range of concrete, visualizable objects in addition to abstract objects such as cubes, planes and spheres.

All tools from Sect. 3 are included into V-FRAMEWORK via a Python implementation of ML-FRAMEWORK and work directly on UIMA documents; this is enabled by means of dkpro-cassis [45].

5 Evaluation

We compare SESB with the system of Ma et al. [53], the only related system that is freely available. We used both systems to generate scenes from 21 different scene descriptions. These descriptions each contain 1-3 sentences from the following three categories: (a) original descriptions from the appendix of Ma et al. [53], (b) room name-based descriptions (e.g. "I ate an apple in the kitchen."), and (c) action-based descriptions (e.g. "I like to make music."). Examples of the generated scenes can be found in the appendix (Fig. 5).

---

[7] V-FRAMEWORK, A-FRAMEWORK are ML-FRAMEWORK are synonyms to comply with the guidelines for author anonymity.
[8] https://unity.com/.

The annotators employed for our comparative evaluation were assigned a three-part task: each annotator was asked to determine for each pair of images the better scene representation produced either by Ma's approach or by SESB. Furthermore, each of the images was to be assigned a value between 0 and 5 for *naturalness* and *plausibility*. This approach follows the evaluation method of Ma et al. [53]. Which image of which system was displayed on which side of the screen was randomly selected; however, the images shown always referred to the same input description. The results of our evaluation are shown in Fig. 3a and 3b; they are based on a total of 22 participants.

Figure 3a shows that SESB performs slightly worse for concrete spatial descriptions. But when the spatial description is tagged with a room label or an action is described, scenes generated by SESB are clearly preferred by annotators. We hypothesize that the initially poorer results are due to the integration of additional systems (such as SpERT in particular) that interfere with room generation, as these systems produce increased noise. However, this integration allows SESB to ultimately process more complex input texts (as Fig. 5 (appendix) shows). Our findings are also reflected in the naturalness and plausibility ratings (Fig. 3b), where we perform slightly worse regarding concrete descriptions, but better in the other two scenarios. We hypothesize that the plausibility of SESB was rated somewhat lower than the naturalness of its action representations because we do not yet have the data to place the objects involved appropriately. That is, although objects are generally placed meaningfully in a room according to the annotators' ratings, they are not necessarily always relevant to the action being described.

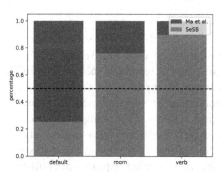

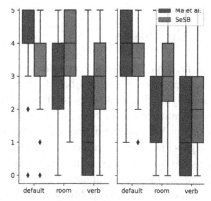

(a) Comparative evaluation of Ma et al. [53]'s approach and SESB.

(b) Rating of generated scenes regarding their naturalness (left) and plausibility (right).

Fig. 3. Evaluation results.

6   Discussion and Future Work

While it is possible to create 3D scenes from less constrained or more natural descriptions using SESB, the possibilities offered by natural languages for scene descriptions are far from exhausted. This becomes clear when looking at Fig. 1. While the system of Ma et al. [53] covers aspects (1) and (4), we extended aspect (4) by including additional spatial room concepts and partially consider aspect (5) as well. However, with the restriction that the positioning of objects is not conditioned by the described activity. Aspects (2) and (3) of Fig. 1 are still not considered. While considering these two aspects could generate a manageable amount of work, the true complexity comes from combinations of the aspects (1-6):

"A person listens to music in the 50 s."

Starting from the token "listens" (aspect 5) and the time expression "50 s" (aspect 2), a tube radio or a record player (aspect 4) seems more likely as the instrument involved. This instrument is then more likely to be found in a living room (aspect 1), while it can vary greatly in design (aspect 3) depending on the assumed region of the speaker (aspect 1). Obviously, text-image systems also have problems with such examples [56], regardless of the ever-increasing training datasets available to them. This is exemplified in the appendix (Fig. 4a and 4b) by means of DALL.E Mini [17][9]. Approaching this complexity will be part of future work and is unlikely to be realistically accomplished without active learning and far more sophisticated approaches to human computation [5,48,58].

7   Conclusion

We presented *Semantic Scene Builder* (SESB), a VR-based text-to-3D scene framework that generates 3D scenes based on scene descriptions. It uses SemAF and UIMA as underlying data structures and integrates a wide range of resources such as HowToKB and IsoSpaceSpERT to cover more complex scene descriptions. By enabling annotations in VR and the expressive power of SemAF that SESB covers, SESB is usable to generate training corpora for text-to-3D scene systems. This is important because this area of language understanding is still in its early stages and relevant data sets are therefore rare. We evaluated SESB against a state-of-the-art open-source text-to-scene method (the only one publicly available yet) and found that our approach not only performed better, but also allowed us to model a wider variety of scenes.

---

[9] https://huggingface.co/spaces/dalle-mini/dalle-mini.

A   Appendix

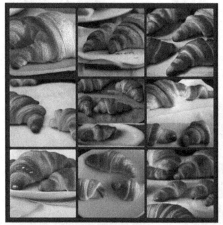 

(a) Images generated by DALL·E Mini for the sentence: "After eating my croissant, I read the newspaper". The model is fully fixed to the croissant.

(b) Images generated by DALL·E Mini for the sentence: "A person listens to music in the 50s". Only people who are making music are shown.

Fig. 4. DALL·E Mini results for different inputs.

Table 3. IsoSpaceSpERT Hyperparameter

Parameter	QSLink-SpERT	OLink-SpERT
BERT	bert-base-cased	
Epochs	30	
Batch size	10	
Negative entity count	300	320
Negative relation count	80	15
Learning rate	6.0e-5	6.3e-5
Weight decay	0.0082	0.0085
Relation filter threshold	0.44	0.23
Size embedding	60	45

Input Text   Ma et al. [53]   SESB

Fig. 5. Generated examples scenes from the evaluation.

References

1. Alayrac, J.B., et al.: Flamingo: a visual language model for few-shot learning. arXiv preprint arXiv:2204.14198 (2022)
2. Anderson, C.A.: Imagination and expectation: The effect of imagining. J. Pmonality Soc. Psychol. **4**(2), 293–330 (1983)
3. Baden-Powell, C.: Architect's pocket book of kitchen design. Routledge (2006)
4. Biewald, L.: Experiment tracking with weights and biases (2020). https://www.wandb.com/, software available from wandb.com

5. Bisk, Y., et al.: Experience grounds language. arXiv preprint arXiv:2004.10151 (2020)
6. Chang, A.X., et al.: Matterport3d: Learning from rgb-d data in indoor environments. In: International Conference on 3D Vision (3DV) (2017)
7. Chang, A.X., Eric, M., Savva, M., Manning, C.D.: SceneSeer: 3D scene design with natural language. arXiv preprint arXiv:1703.00050 (2017)
8. Chang, A.X., et al.: ShapeNet: An Information-Rich 3D Model Repository. Tech. Rep. arXiv:1512.03012 [cs.GR], Stanford University – Princeton University – Toyota Technological Institute at Chicago (2015)
9. Chang, A.X., Monroe, W., Savva, M., Potts, C., Manning, C.D.: Text to 3D scene generation with rich lexical grounding. In: Association for Computational Linguistics and International Joint Conference on Natural Language Processing (ACL-IJCNLP) (2015)
10. Chang, A.X., Savva, M., Manning, C.D.: Interactive learning of spatial knowledge for text to 3D scene generation. In: Association for Computational Linguistics (ACL) Workshop on Interactive Language Learning, Visualization, and Interfaces (ILLVI) (2014)
11. Chang, A.X., Savva, M., Manning, C.D.: Learning spatial knowledge for text to 3D scene generation. In: Empirical Methods in Natural Language Processing (EMNLP) (2014)
12. Chen, K., Choy, C.B., Savva, M., Chang, A.X., Funkhouser, T., Savarese, S.: Text2shape: Generating shapes from natural language by learning joint embeddings. arXiv preprint arXiv:1803.08495 (2018)
13. Chu, C.X., Tandon, N., Weikum, G.: Distilling task knowledge from how-to communities. In: Proceedings of the 26th International Conference on World Wide Web, pp. 805–814 (2017)
14. Clark, H.H.: Using Language. Cambridge University Press, Cambridge (1996)
15. Coyne, B., Bauer, D., Rambow, O.: VigNet: Grounding language in graphics using frame semantics. In: Proceedings of the ACL 2011 Workshop on Relational Models of Semantics, pp. 28–36. Association for Computational Linguistics, Portland, Oregon, USA (Jun 2011). https://www.aclweb.org/anthology/W11-0905
16. Coyne, B., Sproat, R.: Wordseye: an automatic text-to-scene conversion system. In: Proceedings of the 28th annual conference on Computer Graphics and Interactive Techniques, pp. 487–496 (2001)
17. Dayma, B., et al.: (July 2021). https://doi.org/10.5281/zenodo.5146400, https://github.com/borisdayma/dalle-mini
18. Dennerlein, K.: Narratologie des raumes. In: Narratologie des Raumes. de Gruyter (2009)
19. Devlin, J., Chang, M.W., Lee, K., Toutanova, K.: BERT: Pre-training of deep bidirectional transformers for language understanding. In: Proceedings of the 2019 Conference of the North American Chapter of the Association for Computational Linguistics: Human Language Technologies, vol. 1 (Long and Short Papers), pp. 4171–4186. Association for Computational Linguistics, Minneapolis, Minnesota (Jun 2019). https://doi.org/10.18653/v1/N19-1423, https://www.aclweb.org/anthology/N19-1423
20. Ding, M., Zheng, W., Hong, W., Tang, J.: Cogview2: Faster and better text-to-image generation via hierarchical transformers. arXiv preprint arXiv:2204.14217 (2022)
21. Dumas, B., Lalanne, D., Oviatt, S.: Multimodal interfaces: a survey of principles, models and frameworks. In: Lalanne, D., Kohlas, J. (eds.) Human Machine Interaction. LNCS, vol. 5440, pp. 3–26. Springer, Heidelberg (2009). https://doi.org/10.1007/978-3-642-00437-7_1
22. D'Souza, J., Ng, V.: Utd: Ensemble-based spatial relation extraction. In: Proceedings of the 9th International Workshop on Semantic Evaluation (SemEval 2015), pp. 862–869 (2015)
23. Eberts, M., Ulges, A.: Span-based joint entity and relation extraction with transformer pretraining. CoRR abs/ arXiv: 1909.07755 (2019). https://arxiv.org/abs/1909.07755
24. Etzioni, O., Fader, A., Christensen, J., Soderland, S., et al.: Open information extraction: The second generation. In: Twenty-Second International Joint Conference on Artificial Intelligence (2011)

25. Feist, M.I., Gentner, D.: On plates, bowls, and dishes: Factors in the use of english in and on. In: Proceedings of the Twentieth Annual Conference of the Cognitive Science Society, pp. 345–349. Routledge (1998)
26. Ferrucci, D., Lally, A.: Uima: an architectural approach to unstructured information processing in the corporate research environment. In: Natural Language Engineering, pp. 1–26 (2004)
27. Fisher, M., Ritchie, D., Savva, M., Funkhouser, T., Hanrahan, P.: Example-based synthesis of 3d object arrangements. In: ACM SIGGRAPH Asia 2012 papers, SIGGRAPH Asia 2012 (2012)
28. Fu, H., et al.: 3d-front: 3d furnished rooms with layouts and semantics. In: Proceedings of the IEEE/CVF International Conference on Computer Vision, pp. 10933–10942 (2021)
29. Fu, H., et al.: 3d-front: 3d furnished rooms with layouts and semantics. arXiv preprint arXiv:2011.09127 (2020)
30. Fu, H., et al.: 3d-future: 3d furniture shape with texture. Int. J. Comput. Vision **129**(12), 3313–3337 (2021)
31. Gardner, M., et al.: Allennlp: A deep semantic natural language processing platform (2017)
32. Garrod, S., Pickering, M.J.: Why is conversation so easy? Trends Cogn. Sci. **8**(1), 8–11 (2004)
33. Gibney, M.J., et al.: Breakfast in human nutrition: The international breakfast research initiative. Nutrients **10**(5), 559 (2018)
34. Hassani, K., Lee, W.S.: Visualizing natural language descriptions: A survey. ACM Comput. Surv. **49**(1) (June 2016). https://doi.org/10.1145/2932710, https://doi.org/10.1145/2932710
35. Henlein, A., Abrami, G., Kett, A., Mehler, A.: Transfer of isospace into a 3d environment for annotations and applications. In: Proceedings of the 16th Joint ACL - ISO Workshop on Interoperable Semantic Annotation, pp. 32–35. European Language Resources Association, Marseille (May 2020), https://www.aclweb.org/anthology/2020.isa-1.4
36. Herskovits, A.: Language and spatial cognition, vol. 12. Cambridge University Press Cambridge (1986)
37. Hua, B.S., Pham, Q.H., Nguyen, D.T., Tran, M.K., Yu, L.F., Yeung, S.K.: Scenenn: A scene meshes dataset with annotations. In: International Conference on 3D Vision (3DV) (2016)
38. Huguet Cabot, P.L., Navigli, R.: REBEL: Relation extraction by end-to-end language generation. In: Findings of the Association for Computational Linguistics: EMNLP 2021, pp. 2370–2381. Association for Computational Linguistics, Punta Cana, Dominican Republic (Nov 2021). https://aclanthology.org/2021.findings-emnlp.204
39. Hwang, J.D., et al.: Comet-atomic 2020: On symbolic and neural commonsense knowledge graphs. In: AAAI (2021)
40. Ide, N., Pustejovsky, J. (eds.): Handbook of Linguistic Annotation. Springer, Dordrecht (2017). https://doi.org/10.1007/978-94-024-0881-2
41. ISO: Language resource management - Semantic annotation framework (SemAF) - Part 4: Semantic roles (SemAF-SR). Standard ISO/IEC TR 24617–4:2014, International Organization for Standardization (2014). https://www.iso.org/standard/56866.html
42. ISO: Language resource management - Semantic annotation framework (SemAF) - Part 7: Spatial information (ISO-Space). Standard ISO/IEC TR 24617–7:2014, International Organization for Standardization (2014). https://www.iso.org/standard/60779.html
43. ISO: Language resource management - Semantic annotation framework (SemAF) - Part 7: Spatial information (ISO-Space). Standard ISO/IEC TR 24617–7:2019, International Organization for Standardization (2019). https://www.iso.org/standard/76442.html
44. Kermani, Z.S., Liao, Z., Tan, P., Zhang, H.: Learning 3d scene synthesis from annotated rgb-d images. In: Computer Graphics Forum, vol. 35, pp. 197–206. Wiley Online Library (2016)

45. Klie, J.C., de Castilho, R.E.: Dkpro cassis - reading and writing uima cas files in python (2020)
46. Kordjamshidi, P., Moens, M.F., van Otterlo, M.: Spatial role labeling: Task definition and annotation scheme. In: Proceedings of the Seventh conference on International Language Resources and Evaluation (LREC 2010), pp. 413–420. European Language Resources Association (ELRA) (2010)
47. Kordjamshidi, P., Van Otterlo, M., Moens, M.F.: Spatial role labeling: Towards extraction of spatial relations from natural language. ACM Trans. Speech Lang. Process. (TSLP) **8**(3), 1–36 (2011)
48. Kumar, A.A.: Semantic memory: A review of methods, models, and current challenges. Psychon. Bull. Rev. **28**(1), 40–80 (2021)
49. Li, M., et al.: Grains: Generative recursive autoencoders for indoor scenes. ACM Trans. Graph. (TOG) **38**(2), 1–16 (2019)
50. Lin, T.-Y., et al.: Microsoft COCO: common objects in context. In: Fleet, D., Pajdla, T., Schiele, B., Tuytelaars, T. (eds.) ECCV 2014. LNCS, vol. 8693, pp. 740–755. Springer, Cham (2014). https://doi.org/10.1007/978-3-319-10602-1_48
51. Loureiro, D., Camacho-Collados, J.: Don't neglect the obvious: On the role of unambiguous words in word sense disambiguation. In: Proceedings of the 2020 Conference on Empirical Methods in Natural Language Processing (EMNLP), pp. 3514–3520. Association for Computational Linguistics, Online (Nov 2020). https://doi.org/10.18653/v1/2020.emnlp-main. 283, https://www.aclweb.org/anthology/2020.emnlp-main.283
52. Loureiro, D., Jorge, A.: Language modelling makes sense: Propagating representations through WordNet for full-coverage word sense disambiguation. In: Proceedings of the 57th Annual Meeting of the Association for Computational Linguistics, pp. 5682–5691. Association for Computational Linguistics, Florence, Italy (Jul 2019). https://doi.org/10.18653/v1/ P19-1569, https://www.aclweb.org/anthology/P19-1569
53. Ma, R., et al.: Language-driven synthesis of 3d scenes from scene databases. ACM Trans. Graph. (TOG) **37**(6), 1–16 (2018)
54. Mainwaring, S.D., Tversky, B., Ohgishi, M., Schiano, D.J.: Descriptions of simple spatial scenes in english and japanese. Spat. Cogn. Comput. **3**(1), 3–42 (2003)
55. Manning, C.D., Surdeanu, M., Bauer, J., Finkel, J., Bethard, S.J., McClosky, D.: The Stanford CoreNLP natural language processing toolkit. In: Association for Computational Linguistics (ACL) System Demonstrations, pp. 55–60 (2014). https://www.aclweb.org/anthology/P/P14/ P14-5010
56. Marcus, G., Davis, E., Aaronson, S.: A very preliminary analysis of dall-e 2. arXiv preprint arXiv:2204.13807 (2022)
57. Marszalek, M., Laptev, I., Schmid, C.: Actions in context. In: 2009 IEEE Conference on Computer Vision and Pattern Recognition, pp. 2929–2936. IEEE (2009)
58. McClelland, J.L., Hill, F., Rudolph, M., Baldridge, J., Schütze, H.: Extending machine language models toward human-level language understanding. CoRR abs/ arXiv: 1912.05877 (2019), https://arxiv.org/abs/1912.05877
59. Miller, G.A.: Wordnet: a lexical database for English. Commun. ACM **38**(11), 39–41 (1995)
60. Neumann, B., Möller, R.: On scene interpretation with description logics. Image Vis. Comput. **26**(1), 82–101 (2008)
61. Nichols, E., Botros, F.: Sprl-cww: Spatial relation classification with independent multi-class models. In: Proceedings of the 9th International Workshop on Semantic Evaluation (SemEval 2015), pp. 895–901 (2015)
62. Oliva, A., Torralba, A.: The role of context in object recognition. Trends Cogn. Sci. **11**(12), 520–527 (2007)
63. Petrovich, M., Black, M.J., Varol, G.: Temos: Generating diverse human motions from textual descriptions. arXiv preprint arXiv:2204.14109 (2022)

64. Pustejovsky, J., et al.: The specification language timeml. (2005)
65. Pustejovsky, J., Kordjamshidi, P., Moens, M.F., Levine, A., Dworman, S., Yocum, Z.: SemEval-2015 task 8: SpaceEval. In: Proceedings of the 9th International Workshop on Semantic Evaluation (SemEval 2015), pp. 884–894. Association for Computational Linguistics, Denver, Colorado (Jun 2015). https://doi.org/10.18653/v1/S15-2149, https://www.aclweb.org/anthology/S15-2149
66. Pustejovsky, J., Krishnaswamy, N.: VoxML: A visualization modeling language. In: Proceedings of the Tenth International Conference on Language Resources and Evaluation (LREC 2016), pp. 4606–4613. European Language Resources Association (ELRA), Portorož, Slovenia (May 2016), https://aclanthology.org/L16-1730
67. Pustejovsky, J., Moszkowicz, J.L., Verhagen, M.: ISO-space: the annotation of spatial information in language. In: Proceedings of the Sixth Joint ISO-ACL SIGSEM Workshop on ISA, pp. 1–9 (2011)
68. Qi, P., Zhang, Y., Zhang, Y., Bolton, J., Manning, C.D.: Stanza: A Python natural language processing toolkit for many human languages. In: Proceedings of the 58th Annual Meeting of the Association for Computational Linguistics: System Demonstrations (2020). https://nlp.stanford.edu/pubs/qi2020stanza.pdf
69. Radford, A., et al.: Learning transferable visual models from natural language supervision. In: International Conference on Machine Learning, pp. 8748–8763. PMLR (2021)
70. Ramesh, A., Dhariwal, P., Nichol, A., Chu, C., Chen, M.: Hierarchical text-conditional image generation with clip latents. arXiv preprint arXiv:2204.06125 (2022)
71. Ramesh, A., et al.: Zero-shot text-to-image generation. In: Meila, M., Zhang, T. (eds.) Proceedings of the 38th International Conference on Machine Learning. Proceedings of Machine Learning Research, vol. 139, pp. 8821–8831. PMLR (18–24 Jul 2021)
72. Randell, D.A., Cui, Z., Cohn, A.G.: A spatial logic based on regions and connection. In: KR 1992, 165–176 (1992)
73. Riva, G.: Virtual reality. Wiley encyclopedia of biomedical engineering (2006)
74. Rombach, R., Blattmann, A., Lorenz, D., Esser, P., Ommer, B.: High-resolution image synthesis with latent diffusion models (2021)
75. Sadoski, M., Goetz, E.T., Olivarez, A., Jr., Lee, S., Roberts, N.M.: Imagination in story reading: The role of imagery, verbal recall, story analysis, and processing levels. J. Reading Behav. **22**(1), 55–70 (1990)
76. Sadoski, M., Paivio, A.: Imagery and text: A dual coding theory of reading and writing. Routledge (2013)
77. Saharia, C., et al.: Photorealistic text-to-image diffusion models with deep language understanding (2022). https://doi.org/10.48550/ARXIV.2205.11487, https://arxiv.org/abs/2205.11487
78. Salaberri, H., Arregi, O., Zapirain, B.: Ixagroupehuspaceeval:(x-space) a wordnet-based approach towards the automatic recognition of spatial information following the iso-space annotation scheme. In: Proceedings of the 9th International Workshop on Semantic Evaluation (SemEval 2015), pp. 856–861 (2015)
79. Sap, M., et al.: Atomic: An atlas of machine commonsense for if-then reasoning. In: Proceedings of the AAAI Conference on Artificial Intelligence, vol. 33, pp. 3027–3035 (2019)
80. Savva, M., Chang, A.X., Hanrahan, P.: Semantically-enriched 3D models for common-sense knowledge. In: CVPR 2015 Workshop on Functionality, Physics, Intentionality and Causality (2015)
81. Settles, B.: Active learning literature survey (2009)
82. Shi, P., Lin, J.: Simple BERT models for relation extraction and semantic role labeling. CoRR abs/ arXiv: 1904.05255 (2019). https://arxiv.org/abs/1904.05255

83. Shin, H.J., Park, J.Y., Yuk, D.B., Lee, J.S.: Bert-based spatial information extraction. In: Proceedings of the Third International Workshop on Spatial Language Understanding, pp. 10–17 (2020)
84. Silberman, N., Hoiem, D., Kohli, P., Fergus, R.: Indoor segmentation and support inference from RGBD Images. In: Fitzgibbon, A., Lazebnik, S., Perona, P., Sato, Y., Schmid, C. (eds.) ECCV 2012. LNCS, vol. 7576, pp. 746–760. Springer, Heidelberg (2012). https://doi.org/10.1007/978-3-642-33715-4_54
85. Song, S., Yu, F., Zeng, A., Chang, A.X., Savva, M., Funkhouser, T.: Semantic scene completion from a single depth image. In: Proceedings of 30th IEEE Conference on Computer Vision and Pattern Recognition (2017)
86. Speer, R., Chin, J., Havasi, C.: Conceptnet 5.5: An open multilingual graph of general knowledge (2017). https://aaai.org/ocs/index.php/AAAI/AAAI17/paper/view/14972
87. Stubbs, A.: Mae and mai: lightweight annotation and adjudication tools. In: Proceedings of the 5th Linguistic Annotation Workshop, pp. 129–133 (2011)
88. Tan, F., Feng, S., Ordonez, V.: Text2scene: Generating compositional scenes from textual descriptions. In: Proceedings of the IEEE/CVF Conference on Computer Vision and Pattern Recognition, pp. 6710–6719 (2019)
89. Tosi, A., Pickering, M.J., Branigan, H.P.: Speakers' use of agency and visual context in spatial descriptions. Cognition **194**, 104070 (2020)
90. Ulinski, M., Coyne, B., Hirschberg, J.: Spatialnet: A declarative resource for spatial relations. In: Proceedings of the Combined Workshop on Spatial Language Understanding (SpLU) and Grounded Communication for Robotics (RoboNLP), pp. 61–70 (2019)
91. Vaswani, A., et al.: Attention is all you need. In: Advances in Neural Information Processing Systems, pp. 5998–6008 (2017)
92. Wang, X., Yeshwanth, C., Nießner, M.: Sceneformer: Indoor scene generation with transformers. In: 2021 International Conference on 3D Vision (3DV), pp. 106–115. IEEE (2021)
93. Ye, D., Lin, Y., Li, P., Sun, M.: Packed levitated marker for entity and relation extraction. In: Muresan, S., Nakov, P., Villavicencio, A. (eds.) Proceedings of the 60th Annual Meeting of the Association for Computational Linguistics (Vol. 1: Long Papers), ACL 2022, Dublin, Ireland, 22–27 May 2022, pp. 4904–4917. Association for Computational Linguistics (2022). https://aclanthology.org/2022.acl-long.337
94. Zhang, H., Khashabi, D., Song, Y., Roth, D.: Transomcs: From linguistic graphs to commonsense knowledge. In: Proceedings of International Joint Conference on Artificial Intelligence (IJCAI) 2020 (2020)
95. Zhang, S.H., Zhang, S.K., Liang, Y., Hall, P.: A survey of 3d indoor scene synthesis. J. Comput. Sci. Technol. **34**(3), 594–608 (2019)
96. Zhao, X., Hu, R., Guerrero, P., Mitra, N., Komura, T.: Relationship templates for creating scene variations. ACM Trans. Graph. (TOG) **35**(6), 1–13 (2016)

A Digital Human Emotion Modeling Application Using Metaverse Technology in the Post-COVID-19 Era

Chutisant Kerdvibulvech[✉]

Graduate School of Communication Arts and Management Innovation, National Institute of Development Administration, 148 SeriThai Rd., Klong-Chan, Bangkok, Bangkapi 10240, Thailand
chutisant.ker@nida.ac.th

Abstract. The metaverse has the potential to revolutionize various industries recently by providing a more engaging and personalized experience. It includes mainly augmented reality (AR) technology—a quickly growing area that is an interactive experience of a real-world scene added by a virtual world using artificial intelligence (AI). This paper proposes a new digital human emotion modeling study that utilizes augmented reality technology in the post-COVID-19 stage. We conduct a study on how human emotions are recognized and what augmented reality applications these emotional responses are related to. Then, we explore augmented reality systems that provide an immersive and interactive virtual environment where users can experience and express their emotions. By leveraging the advancements in artificial intelligence and augmented reality, the application models and responds to human emotions in real-time, creating a more personalized and human-like experience. In this paper, we divide augmented reality systems with human emotion modeling into two main categories—(1) human emotions modeled and used for evaluating the performances of augmented reality systems, and (2) human emotions modeled and used for triggering augmented reality content. This study is expected to have a great impact on various fields such as human-computer interaction, medical healthcare, and mental health. The paper concludes by discussing the potential benefits and limitations of this technology and its implications for the future.

Keywords: Augmented Reality · Digital Human Modeling · Emotion Recognition · Human Emotions

1 Introduction

Speaking of augmented reality (AR), its primary goal is to create a seamless integration and smooth interaction between virtually generated digital content and the physical world. To create reasonable interaction with the physical world in real time, it is necessary that augmented reality systems must understand the physical world which usually involves an unknown environment containing unpredictable and dynamic objects, animals, or humans. Hence, it is crucial that such systems require some underlying technologies that will help the systems comprehend the physical world in order to interact with it in an intelligent manner; for example, location-based augmented reality systems in our previous works [1, 2] rely on technologies of positioning systems, and camera- or image-based augmented reality systems rely on technologies of computer vision, such as a real-time multi-target web augmented reality application [3] using computer vision presented by Al-Zoube, a real-time augmented reality platform for giving feedback to pharmacists while training in sterile pharmaceutical compounding training called SterileAR [4] using computer vision built by Babichenko et al., and a real-time mobile augmented reality 3D lighting estimation framework called Xihe [5] for precise omnidirectional lighting estimation using computer vision proposed by Zhao and Guo. However, in this paper, we focus on different purposes from the works of [1–5]. Focusing on augmented reality systems that involve modeling human emotions digitally, this paper conducts a study on how human emotions are recognized and what augmented reality applications these emotional responses are related to.

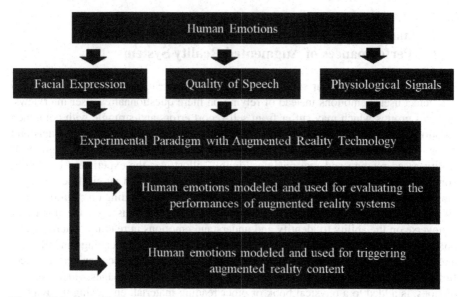

Fig. 1. This paper divides augmented reality systems with human emotion modeling into two categories—(1) human emotions modeled and used for evaluating the performances of augmented reality systems, and (2) human emotions modeled and used for triggering augmented reality content.

Emotions play a very important role in determining the user's overall experience with augmented reality systems. Understanding these emotions can help improve the design and functionality of augmented reality systems. Emotion detection approaches, such as facial expression recognition, can be used to quantify emotional responses to augmented reality systems, and these metrics can be used to measure the effectiveness of augmented reality system features and interfaces. Additionally, user surveys and interviews can also be used to gather subjective feedback on the emotional impact of augmented reality systems. According to the survey of [6] from Gayathri and Matilda, there are several techniques for digitally modeling and recognizing human emotions—facial expression, quality of speech, physiological signals (e.g., electrocardiogram (ECG), electromyogram (EMG), electroencephalogram (EEG)), and a combination of the techniques mentioned earlier. Among these techniques, facial emotion recognition is mentioned as the most widely used technique despite its limitation that people may act to deceive or conceal their real facial emotions. In this paper, we divide augmented reality systems with human emotion modeling into two main categories—(1) human emotions modeled and used for evaluating the performances of augmented reality systems, and (2) human emotions modeled and used for triggering augmented reality content. Figure 1 illustrates our study of how augmented reality technologies interact and connect with human emotions, including facial expression, quality of speech, and physiological signals. The purpose of our paper is to provide an overview of the current state of metaverse technology and its application to human emotion modeling and to highlight the potential for this technology to revolutionize the way people interact in the virtual world.

2 Human Emotions Modeled and Used for Evaluating the Performances of Augmented Reality Systems

For the first category of our study, existing augmented reality systems directly model and detect users' emotions instead of relying on mere questionnaires, user interviews, or focus groups which may suffer from self-report errors and struggle with combined emotions regarding a long continuous event. For example, Daşdemir [7] models and recognizes a reader's emotion with an electroencephalogram to compare augmented reality-based reading and real reading. Figure 2 illustrates the experiment of how to compare augmented reality-based reading and real reading with an electroencephalogram. Cognitive investigation on the role of metaverse-based reading on cognitive classification achievement emotionally is a research area that focuses on the impact of metaverse on the ability to identify and understand emotions in reading materials. The goal of the research is to understand how augmented reality-based reading can influence a reader's emotional responses and improve their emotional classification performance. In augmented reality-based reading, digital information, such as images, videos, or animations, is added to a physical book or other reading material, enhancing the reading experience and providing additional context and information to the reader. By incorporating augmented reality technology, they aim to understand how it affects the reader's emotional engagement with the reading material and their ability to classify emotions. In this way, their conclusion is that augmented reality-based reading with 3D models not only has a significant discriminatory effect but also achieves higher classification performance than real reading with texts and 2D pictures.

Also, the work of [8] conducted by Papakannu uses a deep neural network to model and recognize users' emotions from captured facial images. Estimating user engagement via facial expressions in metaverse technology with dynamic time warping is a technique

Fig. 2. A study for recognizing a reader's emotion with electroencephalogram to compare augmented reality-based reading and real reading during the experiment presented by Daşdemir. Please note that this figure comes from Daşdemir's work [7] for the use of academic purposes.

that aims to measure a user's engagement with an augmented reality system by analyzing their facial expressions. Dynamic time warping is an algorithm used to relatively compare and align time series data, and in this case, it is used to compare a user's facial expressions over time with a set of pre-defined expressions that indicate engagement, such as smiling or frowning. Facial expressions are a powerful indicator of a user's emotional state, and by analyzing these expressions in real-time during an augmented reality experience, researchers can gain insights into the user's level of engagement with the system. This information can be used to improve the design and functionality of augmented reality systems, making them more user-friendly and effective. In their research work, the result shows that augmented reality tasks encourage non-neutral emotion changes more than non-augmented reality tasks, confirming that user emotions in augmented reality environments are unique and not the same as in non-augmented reality environments. For this reason, in our view, estimating user engagement via facial expressions in metaverse technology with dynamic time warping is quite a promising technique that can provide valuable insights into the effectiveness of augmented reality systems. By using dynamic time warping to analyze facial expressions, researchers can gain a better understanding of the user's level of engagement and make improvements to the augmented reality experience. More recently, in 2023, the work of Zhao et al. [9] uses augmented reality to provide real-time photographic guidance to boost smartphone photography; the proposed system is called an augmented reality-based mobile photography application (ARMPA). To evaluate ARMPA, the authors use not only traditional pre/post-test and questionnaires, but also electroencephalogram to model four emotions (i.e., engagement, relaxation, interest, and focus). The use of electroencephalogram for digital human modeling here is to effectively explore and evaluate ARMPA from an emotional perspective. Experimental results reveal that participants using ARMPA have better emotional states than participants using a traditional two-dimension application.

3　Human Emotions Modeled and Used for Triggering Augmented Reality Content

For the second category, the popular facial emotion recognition has not only appeared in several end-user augmented reality applications but has also been featured in many augmented reality tools and platforms lately. For example, at the time of writing this paper, Meta's Spark AR Studio from https://sparkar.facebook.com/ar-studio/learn/patch-editor/interaction-patches is an augmented reality platform that provides a set of features for face gesture detection and tracking, including many facial gestures like a happy face, kissing face, smile, and surprised face. Also, according to https://www.deepar.ai/emotion-detection, Amazon's DeepAR is another software development kit (SDK) with 60 million monthly users that can add augmented reality infrastructure to any app. It is designed to forecast future values based on historical time series data utilizing a recurrent neural network with long short-term memory cells to capture the patterns and dependencies in the time series data and make accurate predictions. It is optimized for large-scale time series data, making it well-suited for use in real-world applications, such as demand forecasting for retail, energy demand forecasting, and web traffic forecasting. More specifically for human emotions, DeepAR uses deep neural networks to detect faces of five emotions (i.e., sad, happy, angry, surprised, and scared) in a video feed so that augmented reality creators can overlay augmented reality content corresponding to these emotions in an interactive manner. With support from these augmented reality tools/platforms, it has become a lot easier for augmented reality creators to trigger their augmented reality applications or services with facial emotions.

Another interesting usage scenario of facial emotion-triggered augmented reality applications is for enhancing human empathy and reducing social barriers for autistic people. According to the work of [10] done by Kar and the report of [11] explained by Hutson, modeling the inner mechanism of the brain with neural networks suggests that autistic adults may have noisy or inefficient sensory neural connections, causing them the problem of emotion recognition. Hence, a higher level of happiness in a face is necessary for autistic people to look at the face and recognize it as a happy face. While there exist augmented reality systems that assist autistic people in learning human emotions like the work of Miningrum [12] which is designed specifically for children with Autism Spectrum Disorders and uses emotional expression recognition to help them understand and recognize emotions in others, Hutson's report [11] suggests that using augmented reality goggles should further adapt or tweak these facial pixels so that the final image presented is optimal for autistic adults and children.

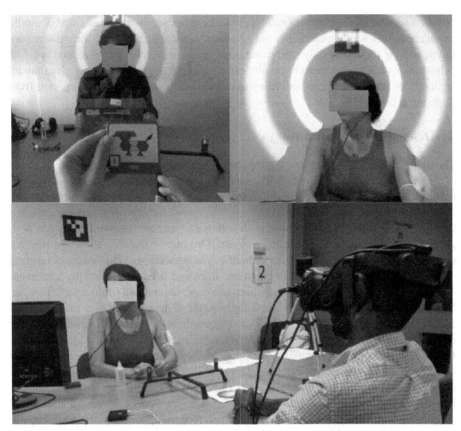

Fig. 3. An empathic augmented reality system that uses deep neural networks to model human emotions via electrocardiogram data called AuRea developed by Valente et al. in Portugal. Please note that this figure is adapted from Valente et al.'s system [13] for the use of academic purposes.

As for non-face emotion recognition used to trigger augmented reality content, AuRea [13] is introduced by Valente et al. from the University of Lisbon in Portugal as an empathic augmented reality work that uses deep neural networks to model human emotions via electrocardiogram data, as depicted in Fig. 3. In the context of face-to-face communication, AuRea draws a colorful representation of emotional cues and overlays it as augmented reality content. The results show a positive effect on emotional understanding. Another interesting system is AR Fidget [14] proposed by Ji and Isbister. AR Fidget is an interactive prototype that uses augmented reality glasses to feed interactive visual and audio feedback to a user. The purpose of doing so is to help a user shift their emotional state toward a calm state for mental well-being. This is done by facilitating emotion regulation that allows a user to regulate anxiety, boredom, and anger via swiping left and right, tapping, and free-form swiping upon augmented reality visual content respectively. As a proof-of-concept prototype, this work hasn't yet included experimental results that evaluate how well the proposed augmented reality system performs regarding emotion regulation. However, the authors state that a more polished version of the current prototype will be proposed in the future, and it should include not only augmented reality but also machine learning. Hence, their future prototype will be able to digitally model and detect emotional state change related to fidget behaviors, which, in our opinion, should lead to dynamic augmented reality visual/audio content that can be triggered according to current users' emotions as interpreted from fidgeting actions.

4 Discussion and Summary

The rapid advancement of technology has brought a new dimension to our lives in terms of communication, entertainment, and even education. With the advent of the COVID-19 outbreak, there has been a huge shift toward online activities and virtual experiences. In this context, the concept of a "metaverse" has become increasingly relevant, representing a virtual world where humans can interact with each other and with digital objects both partly and totally in an immersive environment. One interesting utilization of metaverse technology is in the realm of digital human emotion modeling. This involves creating realistic digital representations of human emotions and behaviors, allowing humans to emotionally interact with virtual characters in a more natural and lifelike way. This can be achieved through the use of advanced algorithms and machine learning techniques, as well as the integration of various sensors and wearable devices. In conclusion, due to the recent advances in artificial intelligence (AI), there are several cutting-edge techniques for modeling real-time human emotions digitally and effectively. However, we found that many augmented reality systems like [15–17] still rely on traditional methods of observing users' emotions manually or asking users to tell their emotions explicitly. For instance, the work of [17] proposed by Schaper and Parés explores an augmented reality case study of an immersive heritage experience to support the emotional learning of students, mainly primary students, in the related socio-cultural class. In their case study, an air-raid-shelter constructed in the 20th century during the Spanish Civil War is selected to evaluate. By examining the possibility of the interaction paradigm (World-as-Support: WaS), they suggest that the experience augmented learners' potentialities to mirror educationally upon importantly sensitive issues linked to the value of human rights and dignity. Their research study finds that it grasps the important qualities of the value of solidarity and connects past histories with current political Spanish issues. Apart from Instagram-like emotion-triggered augmented reality filters, it is still uncommon to find augmented reality systems that are fully equipped with digital human emotion modeling as their core features, allowing much room for future applications and services.

Despite the two different categories of how digital human modeling is incorporated into an augmented reality pipeline, we found some conclusions that are shared in both categories. Due to the unique nature of augmented reality applications that are real-time, interactive, and highly responsive, facial expression and physiological signals (e.g., electroencephalogram and electrocardiogram) seem to be two of the most popular underlying technologies used to digitally model human emotions. This is because they allow non-interrupt emotion modeling during a particular augmented reality session. To the best of our knowledge, we found very few works that use quality of speech to model human emotion regarding an augmented reality application. A possible reason is speech input for augmented reality applications.

The COVID-19 outbreak has dramatically changed the way people live, work, and interact with one another. With widespread lockdowns and social distancing measures, there has been a significant increase in the use of digital technologies for communication and entertainment. In this context, the concept of metaverse has gained attention as a potential solution for the limitations of traditional virtual environments. A metaverse refers to a shared, immersive, and interactive virtual world that can be accessed by multiple users from different locations. It is likely that digital human emotion modeling applications using metaverse technology, particularly augmented reality, will become more prevalent in the post-COVID-19 era. The outbreak has quickly accelerated the shift towards digital technologies, and metaverse technology has the potential to create immersive and interactive digital experiences that can replicate or even enhance human social interactions. By modeling human emotions, such applications can provide a more realistic and human-like experience for users, making them feel as though they are interacting with real people in a virtual environment. In the post-COVID-19 era, as remote work and virtual communication become more widespread, it is likely that metaverse technology will be used for a variety of purposes, such as online education, remote collaboration, and virtual events. Digital human emotion modeling has the potential to make these virtual experiences more engaging and effective by incorporating emotional intelligence into virtual interactions. Additionally, as virtual reality technology continues to improve, the realism of these digital human emotion models is likely to increase, further enhancing their effectiveness as communication tools. In summary, digital human emotion modeling applications using metaverse technology are likely to play an increasingly essential role in the post-COVID-19 era as society continues to embrace digital technologies and virtual interactions become more prevalent. Our future work for the digital human emotion modeling application using metaverse technology in the post-COVID-19 era includes several important areas for improvement and expansion. Some of the key areas for our future work are:

1. Improving Emotion Recognition Accuracy: The current emotion recognition algorithms can be improved by incorporating more data from diverse sources and training the model with a larger and more diverse dataset.
2. Enhancing the User Experience: Future work can focus on enhancing the overall user experience by integrating more advanced augmented reality and/or virtual reality technologies and incorporating user feedback to help and support the overall design and functionality of the application.
3. Integrating with Other Applications: The emotion modeling application can be integrated with other applications, such as gaming and education platforms, to provide a more comprehensive and interactive experience.
4. Enhancing Human-Computer Interactivity: Future work can focus on enhancing the interactivity between users in the metaverse environment by implementing more advanced communication tools and incorporating social elements, such as virtual multiclass sentiment analysis, and multi-label sentiment classification from a social media on the pandemic-related tweets [18].
5. Investigating the Psychological Impact: Further research can be conducted to investigate the psychological impact of the application, particularly in terms of the effects of immersive virtual environments on human emotions and behavior, such as the

psychological impact of social comparison and emotion regulation, psychological welfare, and passive social media utilization in the post-outbreak era [19].

In this way, the future work for the digital human emotion modeling application using metaverse technology in the post-outbreak era can lead to significant advancements in the field and provide more engaging and personalized experiences for users in the virtual world.

Acknowledgments. This research presented herein was partially supported by a research grant from the Research Center, NIDA (National Institute of Development Administration).

References

1. Kerdvibulvech, C.: Geo-based mixed reality gaming market analysis. Hum. Behav. Emerging Technol. **2022**, Article ID 1139475, 9 pages (2022). https://doi.org/10.1155/2022/1139475
2. Kerdvibulvech, C.: Location-based augmented reality games through immersive experiences. In: Schmorrow, D.D., Fidopiastis, C.M. (eds.) HCII 2021. LNCS (LNAI), vol. 12776, pp. 452–461. Springer, Cham (2021). https://doi.org/10.1007/978-3-030-78114-9_31
3. Al-Zoube, M.A.: Efficient vision-based multi-target augmented reality in the browser. Multimedia Tools Appli. **81**, 14303–14320 (2022). https://doi.org/10.1007/s11042-022-122 06-6
4. Babichenko, D.: SterileAR: Exploration of augmented reality and computer vision approaches for real-time feedback in sterile compounding training. In: 6th International Conference of the Immersive Learning Research Network (iLRN), San Luis Obispo, CA, USA, vol. 2020, pp. 62–69 (2020). https://doi.org/10.23919/iLRN47897.2020.9155164
5. Zhao, Y., Guo, T.: Xihe: a 3D vision-based lighting estimation framework for mobile augmented reality. In: MobiSys 2021, pp. 28–40 (2021)
6. Gayathrim P., Matilda, S.: Emotion recognition: a survey. Int. J. Adv. Res. Comput. Sci. Appli. **3**(1) (2015)
7. Daşdemir, Y.: Cognitive investigation on the effect of augmented reality-based reading on emotion classification performance: A new dataset. Biomed. Signal Process. Control **78**, 103942 (2022)
8. Papakannu, K.R.: Examining user engagement via facial expressions in augmented reality with dynamic time warping. Master thesis, Arizona State University (May 2021)
9. Zhao, G., et al.: An augmented reality based mobile photography application to improve learning gain, decrease cognitive load, and achieve better emotional state. Int. J. Hum.-Comput. Interact. **39**(3), 643–658 (2023). https://doi.org/10.1080/10447318.2022.2041911
10. Kar, K.: A computational probe into the behavioral and neural markers of atypical facial emotion processing in autism. J. Neurosci. **42**(25), 5115–5126 (2022)
11. Hutson, M.: Artificial neural networks model face processing in autism. MIT News (June 2022). https://news.mit.edu/2022/artificial-neural-networks-model-face-processing-in-autism-0616 (Accessed 19 October 2022)
12. Miningrum, T., Tolle, H., Bachtiar, F. A.: Augmented reality adapted book (AREmotion) design as emotional expression recognition media for children with autistic spectrum disorders (ASD). Int. J. Adv. Comput. Sci. Appli. (IJACSA) **12**(6) (2021)
13. Valente, A., Lopes, D.S., Nunes, N., Esteves, A.: Empathic AuRea: exploring the effects of an augmented reality cue for emotional sharing across three face-to-face tasks. In: IEEE Conference on Virtual Reality and 3D User Interfaces (VR) (2022)

14. Ji, C., Isbister, K.: AR fidget: augmented reality experiences that support emotion regulation through fidgeting. CHI Extended Abstracts **180**(1–180), 4 (2022)
15. Papalazaridis, G., Tzafilkou, K., Anastasios, A.: Economides: mobile augmented reality and consumer experience: a mixed-methods analysis on emotional responses and intention to buy household items. HCI (39), 527–536 (2022)
16. Rojas, J.: Towards an augmented reality based system for monitoring and handling of emotions. In: Intelligent Environments (Workshops), pp. 350–359 (2022)
17. Schaper, M.-M., Parés, N.: Enhancing students' social and emotional learning in educational virtual heritage through projective augmented reality. CHI Extended Abstracts **18**(1–18), 9 (2022)
18. Vernikou, S., Lyras, A., Kanavos, A.: Multiclass sentiment analysis on COVID-19-related tweets using deep learning models. Neural Comput. Appli. **34**, 19615–19627 (2022). https://doi.org/10.1007/s00521-022-07650-2
19. Yue, Z., Zhang, R., Xiao, J.: Passive social media use and psychological well-being during the COVID-19 pandemic: The role of social comparison and emotion regulation. Comput. Hum. Behav. **127**, 107050 (2022)

Bibliometric Analysis and Systematic Literature Review on Data Visualization

Byeongmok Kim[✉], Yonggab Kim, and Vincent G. Duffy

Purdue University, West Lafayette, IN 47907, USA
{kim3453,kim3233,duffy}@purdue.edu

Abstract. This study aims to investigate the literature review as a job and explore the research trend of data visualization. This study used various methods to perform a systematic literature review on data visualization. Metadata was abstracted from well-known research databases such as SCOPUS, Google Scholar, and Web of Science. The metadata was used for analysis by VOSviewer, MAXQDA, BibExcel, and Citespace. In conclusion, we discuss the research trend and anticipated future studies on data visualization.

Keywords: Data visualization · Job design · Human Factor · Human Computer Interaction

1 Introduction

Thanks to the advanced improvement of ICT and data storage technologies, we live in the Big Data era. Using Big Data properly, we can estimate the future more accurately and develop a more sophisticated decision-making process. However, because Big Data has a massive amount of data, researchers easily get daunted by the number of data and throw out a large portion of data just because they cannot find any information. Data visualization is the key to utilizing Big Data more efficiently and effectively. Among five sensor systems of the human body, visual is the most prioritized sensor of most humans. Therefore, we can find more insights from data and understand more about data using data visualization skills. Many researchers, especially IE engineers, are currently delving into the research on decision-making and future prediction based on Big Data. The necessity of these researches is to visualize the data. Therefore, many Big Data platforms are equipped with data visualization functions. For more advances in data utilization, research/industrial/government societies should emphasize research on data visualization.

Figure 1 shows the number of articles related to the data visualization based on the country. The top 10 countries are listed in Fig. 1, and the United States appears to be the most activating country in researching data visualization.

V. G. Duffy (Ed.): HCII 2023, LNCS 14029, pp. 490–502, 2023.
https://doi.org/10.1007/978-3-031-35748-0_34

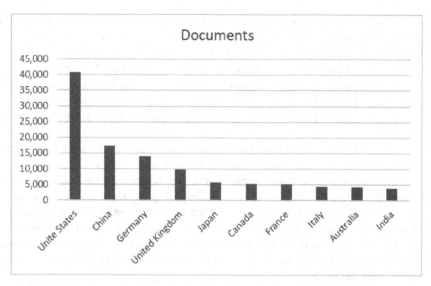

Fig. 1. The number of articles related to data visualization based on the country [15].

2 Purpose of Study

This study focuses on investigating the literature review as a job and exploring the research trend of data visualization. This study used various methods to perform a systematic literature review on data visualization. Metadata was abstracted from well-known research databases such as SCOPUS, Google Scholar, and Web of Science. The metadata was used for analysis by VOSviewer, MAXQDA, BibExcel, and Citespace. In conclusion, we discuss the research trend and anticipated future studies on data visualization.

3 Research Methodology

3.1 Steps of Systematic Review

Steps	Things to do
1	Search articles relevant to the topic on different database
2	Write Introduction and abstract
3	Select key articles and compare between the databases
4	Create trend analysis, world cloud
5	Create VOS viewer analysis and cite space analysis
6	Write Discussion and Conclusion
7	Create bibliography
8	Revise and format the report
9	Submit

Fig. 2. Steps of systematic review.

Figure 2 shows the steps taken for the data visualization systematic review. First, the articles were searched through Scopus, Google Scholar, and Web of Science. Based on the articles and the literature search, the big frame of the literature review was conceptualized. The introduction and the abstracts were written based on this survey. The critical articles were selected, and a comparison of the search results of databases was made. The trend analysis over the years and the word cloud is created to explain how the data visualization topic gained attention last year and what keywords were used in this research.

The VOS viewer and the CiteSpace analysis were created to see which pa-pers visually relate to the other. Several clusters were made from the analysis, and the names were labeled. By seeing the visualization, it could be understood what kind of subtopics in the data visualization were researched. Also, by seeing the size of the cluster, we could realize how big the research is being done. After conducting an analysis and creating a visualization to induce the insights, the discussion and conclusion are written. Based on the analysis, the result of the research and what could have been gained was discussed. The reference was created at the end and written in a uniform format. The report is finally submitted after this process.

3.2 Data Collection

We used the three research databases, Google Scholar, Scopus, and Web of science, to find data visualization-related literature. The number of articles from chosen databases was gathered using keyword data visualization. The number of papers from 2014 to 2021 is represented in Table 1..

Table 1. The number of papers on data visualization from Google Scholar, Scopus, and Web of Science.

Google Scholar ($\times 1,000$)				Web of Science ($\times 1,000$)				SCOPUS ($\times 1,000$)			
'14 ~ '15	'16 ~ '17	'18 ~ '19	'20 ~ '21	'14 ~ '15	'16 ~ '17	'18 ~ '19	'20 ~ '21	'14 ~ '15	'16 ~ '17	'18 ~ '19	'20 ~ '21
1,010	958	770	445	18.94	23.01	28.82	33.54	13.34	15.45	19.05	21.10

3.3 Statistical Analysis

The descriptive statistics of each database are represented in Table 2.. Since the search mechanism and paper retrieve policy are different among databases, the average number of articles does not become significantly important. However, we can see some gaps between the variances between different databases, which implies that each database may represent a different research trend. Therefore, we exploit statistical inference to analyze the differences between databases regarding research trends.

Table 3. indicates the F-test results under the 5% significance level settings. The null hypothesis was set that variances in increase/decrease in the number of articles over the

Table 2. The descriptive statistics of the number of papers on data visualization from Google Scholar, Scopus, and Web of Science.

Google Scholar ($\times 1,000$)			Web of Science ($\times 1,000$)			SCOPUS ($\times 1,000$)		
Avg.	Var.	Std. dev.	Avg.	Var.	Std. dev.	Avg.	Var.	Std. dev.
795.75	48,979.19	221.31	26.08	30.89	5.56	17.24	9.15	3.02

same periods are the same between two different databases. The results show that the null hypothesis was accepted when we ran F-test on Web of Science and SCOPUS. On the other hand, other two combinations of comparisons, such as Google Scholar vs. Web of Science and Google Scholar vs. SCOPUS, were rejected. Therefore, we concluded that the trend of increase/decrease in the number of articles on both Web of Science and SCOPUS are statistically the same.

Table 3. The statistical inferences (F-test) result on number of papers on data visualization from Google Scholar, Scopus, and Web of Science.

Google Scholar vs. Web of Science		Google Scholar vs. SCOPUS		Web of Science vs. SCOPUS	
P-value	Decision (5% significance level)	P-value	Decision (5% significance level)	P-value	Decision (5% significance level)
5.3717e-05	Reject	8.6629e-06	Reject	0.3442	Accept

3.4 Engagement Measure

We use Vicinitas to measure the engagement level of the topic and data visualization based on Twitter feeds. Hashtags and keywords in tweets are searched using the keyword as data visualization. The Results are depicted in Fig. 3. The result shows that the frequency of appearances of Data visualization in everyday people's conversations has increased as time goes by.

3.5 Trend Analysis

We analyze the research trend by using the metadata obtained from Scopus. We assume that the number of papers represents the research trend in academia. For instance, if the number of papers on a specific topic increases, then the research trend of that topic increases, and vice versa. We search for the data visualization at Scopus to analyze the research trend. The number of literature from 1990 to 2021 is represented in Fig. 4.

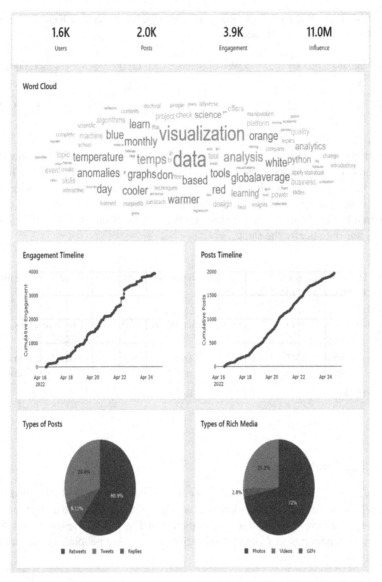

Fig. 3. Results from Vicinitas analysis on the Twitter feed for "Data visualization".

Figure 4 shows that the literature regarding data visualization steadily increases from 1990 to 2021, implying that the importance of data visualization has gained more popularity.

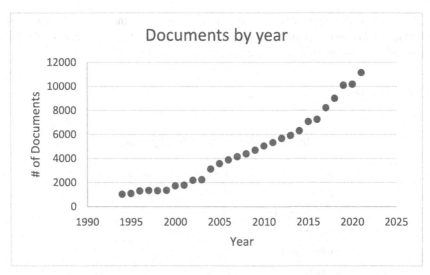

Fig. 4. Trend analysis of the number of documents from Scopus [15].

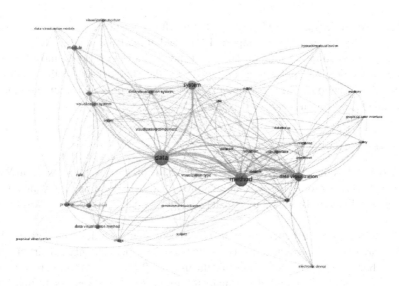

Fig. 5. Data visualization of VOS viewer result [10].

4   Results

4.1   Content Analysis

The VOS viewer result is created using the VOS viewer (see Fig. 5.) Multiple clusters were created, and the relationship between the keywords was identified. The search result from the Web of Science was used to create this image. The minimum number of frequencies of the word was set to 10 to exclude the data that does not show up often.

Of all the keywords, 60 words met the criteria. The top 36 most relevant words were chosen to display on the graph. The most frequent three key terms are data, method, and system. Most of the words are circled with these accessible terms.

4.2 Pivot Table

Table 4. Number of publications by authors.

Author	Number of publications
Heer J	17
Shneiderman B	15
Keim DA	13
Andrienko G	13
Stolte C	11

The pivot table was created based on the result of the BibExcel [13] (see Table 4.). The Web of science results was imported and used at the BibExcel [13] to analyze the number of publications by authors. The result shows that Heer J had the most significant number of publications, publishing 17 papers, and the Shneider-man followed the next, having 15 publications. These two authors were the most active and leading researchers in the data visualization area.

4.3 Cluster Analysis

Figure 6 was developed based on 4,000 search results of data visualization from Web of Science. According to Fig. 8, we can recognize that there are three most cited articles on data visualization. Based on the cluster's shape, we can conclude that most research papers are interrelated.

A citation burst was generated using CiteSpace. The two articles that are displayed in Fig. 7 are currently experiencing a citation burst. The fact that only two articles show up in the burst diagram demonstrates that the use of VR for safety training is a relatively new phenomenon. At the end of this analysis, all the articles chosen for further review were saved in Mendeley to generate a reference list [12]. The list included 5 articles from co-citation analysis which was performed using VOSviewer, 1 chapter from the handbook of human factors and ergonomics, 2 articles from citation burst, and 1 article from google scholar search.

Fig. 6. Cluster analysis with labels abstracted using keywords [14].

Top 2 References with the Strongest Citation Bursts

References	Year	Strength	Begin	End	2016 - 2019
Ware C, 2012, INFORM VISUALIZATION, V0, P0	2012	5.61	**2016**	2017	▬▬▬▬
Heer J, 2012, COMMUN ACM, V55, P45, DOI 10.1145/2133806.2133821, DOI	2012	2.3	**2016**	2017	▬▬▬▬

Fig. 7. Citation burst results [14].

Figure 7 was developed based on 4,000 search results of data visualization from Web of Science. According to Fig. 9, the top two references have the most powerful citation bursts.

Table 5. indicates the keywords of the top ten most cited articles related to data visualization. The keyword "visualization" is involved in most of the top ten cited articles. Other than visualization, the keywords vary by the domain of the articles, such as computer science, psychology, and human factors. For instance, the keyword memorable is frequently used in psychology and the keyword multifaceted is the jargon of computer science.

4.4 Content Analysis Using MAXQDA

The word cloud was created from 8 data visualization papers (see Fig. 8). The top 30 most frequent keywords were shown, and the minimum occurrence was set to 4 to avoid displaying unimportant words. The most frequent keyword from the papers was "data." The data is the most crucial part of the data visualization before making it into an image. According to its data type, whether it is categorical or numerical, and according to its implication and format, the data visualization is made differently [1]. Various research papers have been published, investigating what data visualization is suitable for their domain field data implications and the data type [2–4].

Table 5. Leading table on authors and keywords.

No.	Authors	Keywords
1	Munzner, Tamara [21]	Visualization, Analysis, and Design
2	Ware, Colin [24]	Information, Visualization, Perception, Design
3	Satyanarayan, Arvind, Dominik Moritz, Kanit Wongsuphasawat, and Jeffrey Heer [23]	Grammar, Interactive, Graphics
4	Wongsuphasawat, Kanit, Dominik Moritz, Anushka Anand, Jock Mackinlay, Bill Howe, and Jeffrey Heer [25]	Exploratory, Analysis, Visualization, Recommendations
5	Liu, Shixia, Weiwei Cui, Yingcai Wu, and Mengchen Liu [20]	Information, Visualization
6	Brehmer, Matthew, and Tamara Munzner [18]	Typology, Visualization
7	Bostock, Michael, Vadim Ogievetsky, and Jeffrey Heer [17]	D^3, Data-driven
8	Satyanarayan, Arvind, and Jeffrey Heer [22]	Interactive, Visualization, Design, Environment
9	Kehrer, Johannes, and Helwig Hauser [19]	Visualization, Multifaceted, Data
10	Borkin, Michelle A., Azalea A. Vo, Zoya Bylinskii, Phillip Isola, Shashank Sunkavalli, Aude Oliva, and Hanspeter Pfister [16]	Visualization, Memorable

Other noticeable keyword is "audience," "visualization," and "graph." Data visualization is the concept of converting the data into an image. It is to help the audience to understand the data or the analysis research result better [5, 6]. In this perspective, we need to think from the audience's perspective about what kind of trouble they would have. The audience might not have a technical background; therefore, the graph might need a brief jargon description. Alternatively, the audience might be color blind, and the usage of colors they could be identified by the color blind could be a consideration. This perspective is closely related to the human factor. To accommodate humans to understand the topic they do not understand. Other research has been done on data visualization from a human factor perspective [7–9].

Fig. 8. Word cloud from data visualization papers [11].

5 Discussion

Data visualization is an emerging technology in society. Since we live in the big data era, we have many chances to get access to data and find some insights from them. However, data itself cannot turn into meaningful information without visualizing the data. Since the big data era started, many researchers have studied the core technology of data visualization as well as its applications of it. This paper presented a systematic literature review on data visualization and presented some meaningful insights from it.

In addition, from the job design perspective, when we search for the articles from the research databases. We derive some insights about the user interface regarding three research databases: Google Scholar, Web of Science, and Scopus. First of all, in terms of accessibility, Google Scholar is the most accessible database compared to other databases. Google Scholar does not require users to sign in, so we can enter the Google Scholar website and find the articles we want to search. On the other hand, Web of Science and Scopus requires users to sign in, and only users with the right to access those databases can search the articles at those databases. Therefore, we need to access those websites via the Purdue library with a signed-in Purdue account. This difference in accessibility affects a lot to users. As graduate students, we searched many articles, and the highly accessible Google Scholar makes us prefer it to any other databases. Second, Google Scholar is easier to download the article than other databases. When we search for something on Google Scholar, we can find the download link beside the title. However, Scopus and Web of Science require several steps to download the article. Therefore, we have concluded that the usability of Google Scholar is the best among the three research databases.

6 Conclusion

This study is designed to investigate the literature review as a job and explore the research trend of data visualization. For analyzing the literature, we use various methods such as statistical inferences, trend analysis, data mining technique, citation analysis, VOS viewer, and emergence analysis on social media. Most conventional literature review studies only retrieve the data from the research databases such as Google Scholar, Web of Science, and Scopus. The conventional way to retrieve the data is limited because it only considers academia, not society, especially discussions on the Internet world. We retrieve the data from the research database and Twitter, so we believe our study reflects the more data that considers the societal discussion on our topic. Data visualization is a prevalent topic, especially in the significant data era. We find increased research trends in data visualization, and also data visualization is a hot topic on the website. From the literature review perspective as a job, we conclude that Google Scholar is the preferable database among other databases such as Web of Science and Scopus because the accessibility and user-friendliness are better than those databases. Lastly, we provide the most cited literature and the citation relationship between the literature on data visualization. We believe that the result of citation analysis helps readers to find the most impactful research paper.

7 Future Work

The emergence of big data and machine learning has increased the importance of data visualization. The trend graph and the statistical analysis mentioned in this article show the growing interest in data visualization. More data visualization tools are developed to customize and help users create their images easily. The data visualization should convey the analysis of the machine learning method. Also, it should satisfy the growing needs of different users and apply to any application. The human factor research on how the data visualization could increase usability can be a future research study.

Figure 9 shows the NSF award for data visualization research that has contributed to increasing public understanding of scientific data by using data visualization. Scientific data and its concept are complicated for a non-technical person to understand the research insights and process. Some breakthrough research is neglected because it is hard to understand. The visual image is a perfect tool to increase the interest and fund the research that might potentially impact a better future. This award indicates further future work for data visualization research to advance public understanding.

Fig. 9. The NSF award for increasing public understanding of scientific data by data visualization.

References

1. Cumming, G., Finch, S.: Inference by eye confidence intervals and how to read pictures of data. Am. Psychol. **60**, 170–180 (2005)
2. Harris, C.R., et al.: Array programming with NumPy. Nature **585**, 357–362 (2020)
3. Gorodov, E.Y.E., Gubarev, V.V.E.: Analytical review of data visualization methods in application to big data. J. Elect. Comput. Eng. (2013)
4. Hunter, J.D.: Matplotlib: A 2D graphics environment. Comput. Sci. Eng. **9**, 90–95 (2007)
5. McKinney, W.: Data structures for statistical computing in python. In: Proceedings of the 9th Python in Science Conference, pp. 56–61, SciPy (2010). https://doi.org/10.25080/majora-92bf1922-00a
6. Jebb, A.T., Parrigon, S., Woo, S.E.: Exploratory data analysis as a foundation of inductive research. Hum. Resour. Manag. Rev. **27**, 265–276 (2017)
7. Ginda, M., Richey, M.C., Cousino, M., Börner, K.: Visualizing learner engagement, performance, and trajectories to evaluate and optimize online course design. PLoS ONE **14** (2019)

8. Lopes, A.T., de Aguiar, E., De Souza, A.F., Oliveira-Santos, T.: Facial expression recognition with Convolutional Neural Networks: Coping with few data and the training sample order. Pattern Recogn. **61**, 610–628 (2017)
9. Tsarouchi, P., Makris, S., Chryssolouris, G.: Human–robot interaction review and challenges on task planning and programming. Int. J. Comput. Integr. Manuf. **29**, 916–931 (2016)
10. "VOSviewer." n.d. https://www.vosviewer.com/
11. "MAXQDA." n.d. https://www.maxqda.com/
12. "Mendeley." n.d. https://www.mendeley.com/
13. "BibExcel." n.d. https://homepage.univie.ac.at/juan.gorraiz/bibexcel/
14. "CiteSpace." n.d. http://cluster.cis.drexel.edu/~cchen/citespace/
15. "Scopus." n.d. https://www.scopus.com/search/form.uri?display=basic&zone=header&origin=#basic
16. Borkin, M.A., et al.: What makes a visualization memorable? IEEE Trans. Visual Comput. Graph. **19**(12), 2306–2315 (2013)
17. Bostock, M., Ogievetsky, V., Heer, J.: D^3 data-driven documents. IEEE Trans. Visual Comput. Graph. **17**(12), 2301–2309 (2011)
18. Brehmer, M., Munzner, T.: A multi-level typology of abstract visualization tasks. IEEE Trans. Visual Comput. Graph. **19**(12), 2376–2385 (2013)
19. Kehrer, J., Hauser, H.: Visualization and visual analysis of multifaceted scientific data: A survey. IEEE Trans. Visual Comput. Graph. **19**(3), 495–513 (2012)
20. Liu, S., Cui, W., Wu, Y., Liu, M.: A survey on information visualization: recent advances and challenges. Vis. Comput. **30**(12), 1373–1393 (2014). https://doi.org/10.1007/s00371-013-0892-3
21. Munzner, T.: Visualization analysis and design. CRC press (2014)
22. Satyanarayan, A., Heer, J.L.: An interactive visualization design environment. In: Computer Graphics Forum, vol. 33(3), pp. 351–360 (2014)
23. Satyanarayan, A., Moritz, D., Wongsuphasawat, K., Heer, J.: Vega-lite: A grammar of interactive graphics. IEEE Trans. Visual Comput. Graph. **23**(1), 341–350 (2016)
24. Ware, C. Information visualization: perception for design. Morgan Kaufmann (2019)
25. Wongsuphasawat, K., Moritz, D., Anand, A., Mackinlay, J., Howe, B., Heer, J.: Voyager: Exploratory analysis via faceted browsing of visualization recommendations. IEEE Trans. Visual Comput. Graph **22**(1), 649–658 (2015)

A Modular Framework for Modelling and Verification of Activities in Ambient Intelligent Systems

Alexandros Konios[1]([✉]), Yasir Imtiaz Khan[2], Matias Garcia-Constantino[3], and Irvin Hussein Lopez-Nava[4]

[1] Nottingham Trent University, Nottingham, UK
`alexandros.konios@ntu.ac.uk`
[2] HORIBA MIRA Ltd., Nuneaton, UK
[3] Ulster University, Belfast, UK
[4] CICESE (Centro de Investigación Científica y de Educación Superior de Ensenada), Ensenada, Mexico

Abstract. There is a growing need to introduce and develop formal techniques for computational models capable of faithfully modelling systems of high complexity and concurrent. Such systems are the ambient intelligent systems. This article proposes an efficient framework for the automated modelling and verification of the behavioural models capturing daily activities that occur in ambient intelligent systems based on the modularity and compositionality of Petri nets. This framework consists of different stages that incorporate Petri net techniques like composition, transformation, unfolding and slicing. All these techniques facilitate the modelling and verification of the system activities under consideration by allowing the modelling in different Petri net classes and the verification of the produced models either by using model checking directly or by applying Petri net slicing to alleviate the state explosion problem that may emerge in very complex behavioural models. Illustrative examples of ambient intelligent system applied to health and other sectors are provided to demonstrate the practicality and effectiveness of the proposed approach. Finally, to show the flexibility of the proposed framework in terms of verification, both an evaluation and comparison of the state space required for the property checking are conducted with respect to the typical model checking and slicing approach respectively.

Keywords: Petri nets · Slicing · Model-checking · Intelligent/Smart Systems · Assisted Activities

1 Introduction

Ambient intelligent systems were originally developed in the late 1990's and have already attracted the attention of the researchers. The tremendous advance of technology has contributed to the construction of such systems, which incorporate both ubiquitous and pervasive computing [2,37] resulting in their rapid

V. G. Duffy (Ed.): HCII 2023, LNCS 14029, pp. 503–530, 2023.
https://doi.org/10.1007/978-3-031-35748-0_35

proliferation. These systems aimed at the creation of intelligent environments that would interact with the users, facilitating their daily activities. Their inter-activity with the users is expressed through the embedded technology that governs their architecture [4]. Ambient intelligence is applied to a wide spectrum of different domains, such as public or private environments [3]. Examples of developed ambient intelligent systems are presented in [11,17], referring to ambient assisting living systems that have been applied to public or private environments.

To understand ambient intelligent systems, a deep and thorough study of their intricate architecture and behaviour is required, focusing on several different aspects, such as interactivity [14], mobility [9], fault-tolerance [16] and user's experience [35]. It is worth noting that there already exists a substantial literature on the role of formal methods in modelling and evaluation of interactive systems [13,14], but not on examining their interaction and context-awareness using Petri nets. Thus, this work introduces a framework that proposes a modular approach of representing and examining the interactive behaviour of such systems by capturing the system behaviour as a collection of actions/steps, which are composed using a repetitive composition process that is defined by two new composition operators.

This work pursues two main goals. The first one is to introduce a framework that will facilitate the modelling of assisted living activities in real ambient intelligent systems through the compositionality of a fundamental modular Ambient Petri Net, the *basic step net*, which captures a single interaction between the user and the environment [24,28]. This modular net can be repetitively composed to produce the behavioural model of the examined intelligent system, which can then be transformed into the respective low or high-level Petri net through the application of both construction and unfolding, allowing the use of further modelling and verification techniques (see Fig. 1). Due to the specific structure of the basic step nets, the modularity and compositionality of this modelling approach enable the predictability of some safety and liveness properties of the examined systems. The second goal is to enhance the analysis of ambient intelligent systems combining the qualitative reasoning of Petri nets and the analysis of system properties using of model checking or/and Petri net slicing.

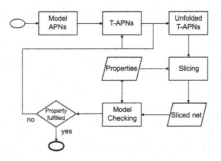

Fig. 1. An overview of the proposed modelling and verification framework.

The rest of the paper is structured as follows. Section 2 provides the definitions of Petri net classes used in the proposed framework, introducing the Ambient Petri Nets (APNs) and Transformed Ambient Petri Nets (T-APNs) classes. Section 3 presents a stepwise modelling approach and defines the two Petri net composition operators used for the development of the behavioural models of ambient intelligent systems. In Sect. 4, the definition of the construction algorithm that transforms the APN nets into the respective T-APN nets is described. This construction is used for verification purposes to convert a non-verifiable class of inhibitor nets like APNs into a verifiable class of non-inhibitor nets, the T-APNs. The unfolding process used in this framework is discussed in Section 4.2. In Sect. 5, the slicing algorithm used by the proposed approach is discussed. Section 6 evaluates the efficiency of the slicing technique by comparing the number of states required for the verification of properties in the sliced model with that required in the un-sliced models generated through the framework's different stages. Finally, Sect. 7 presents useful conclusions about the framework's applicability and efficiency.

2   Formal Definition of Petri Net Classes

This section presents the formalisms of the Ambient Petri Nets (APNs) and Transformed Ambient Petri Nets (T-APNs) classes used in the proposed method[1].

2.1   Ambient Petri Nets Class

The APN class presented below is required for the description of the step-modelling approach, which is used for the construction of the behavioural models of intelligent systems.

Definition 1 (Ambient Petri Net). *An APN is a tuple* $\mathcal{N} = (P, T, Pre, Post, I, Cl, C, K, M_0, G)$, *where:*

- *P is a finite set of places.*
- *T is a finite set of transitions disjoint from P.*
- *$Pre, Post : T \rightarrow \mu P$ are the pre and post mappings.*
- *$I \subseteq P \times T$ is a set of inhibitor arcs. Assume that:*
  $\forall\, p \in P \,\forall\, t \in T\colon (Pre(t)(p) > 0 \lor Post(t)(p) > 0) \Rightarrow (p,t) \notin I.$
- *Cl is a non-empty finite set of non-empty colour sets, called as the* structuring set.
- *$C : P \cup T \rightarrow Cl$ is a colour function used to structure places and transitions:*
  - *$\widetilde{P} = \{(p,g) \mid p \in P \land g \in C(p)\}$ is the set of structured places.*
  - *$\widetilde{T} = \{(t,c) \mid t \in T \land c \in C(t)\}$ is the set of structured transitions.*
- *K is a constant function that defines the capacities of places.*

---

[1] For further reading, the APN and T-APN semantics are provided in [25].

- $M_0 \in \mu\widetilde{P}$ is an initial marking satisfying $M_0 \le K$. Any $M \in \mu\widetilde{P}$ such that $M \le K$ is a marking.
- $G \subseteq P$ is a set of gluing (or interface) places.

The graphical representation of P (places) and T (transitions) is as in the standard net theory. The set of places, G, is used for the composition of APNs and the *Pre* and *Post* mappings give the direct arcs of the net. The set of inhibitor arcs introduced by Definition 1 are colour-sensitive inhibitor arcs that can be used to put firing restrictions on specific colours of tokens without disabling the execution of a transition for all the other colours of tokens. It should be mentioned that this element of the APN class differs from all the other types of inhibitor arcs that have been introduced in other existing Petri net classes since they do not disable the transition for all the tokens like the other inhibitor arcs do, but only for those tokens that reside in the respective inhibitor places. Finally, the introduction of the colour-sensitive inhibitor arcs makes the APN a Petri net class that can effectively capture the activities of an intelligent system reducing the model complexity and the number of elements required for the modelling process (i.e., places, transitions, arcs, etc.) compared to other Petri net classes that do not include the feature of the colour-sensitive inhibitor arc.

2.2   Transformed Ambient Petri Nets Class

The formalism of Transformed Ambient Petri Nets (T-APNs) is presented below defining its elements.

Definition 2 (Transformed Ambient Petri Net). *A T-APN is a tuple* $\mathcal{N} = (P, T, Pre, Post, Cl, \overline{Cl}, C_P, C_T, Ins, K, Gd, M_0, G)$, *where:*

- P is a finite set of places.
- T is a finite set of transitions disjoint from P.
- $Pre, Post : T \to \mu P$ are the pre and post mappings.
- $Cl, \overline{Cl}$ are non-empty finite sets of non-empty colour sets, such that $(\bigcup Cl) \cap (\bigcup \overline{Cl}) = \emptyset$ and there exists a bijection $f \colon (\bigcup Cl) \to (\bigcup \overline{Cl})$. Cl and $\overline{Cl}$ are called the structuring sets.
- $C_P : P \to CSets$ is a colour function used to structure places with $CSets \subseteq 2^{(\bigcup Cl) \cup (\bigcup \overline{Cl})}$ being a non-empty subset of non-empty colour sets from $2^{(\bigcup Cl) \cup (\bigcup \overline{Cl})}$:
    • $\widehat{P} = \{(p, g) \mid p \in P \land g \in C_P(p)\}$ is the set of structured places.
- $C_T : T \to Cl$ is a colour function used to structure transitions:
    • $\widetilde{T} = \{(t, c) \mid t \in T \land c \in C_T(t)\}$ is the set of structured transitions.
- $Ins : A \to Cl \cup \overline{Cl} \cup \{\emptyset\}$ is a colour function that assigns inscriptions[2] to the arcs, where:
    • $A = \bigcup_{t \in T} A^t_{in} \cup \bigcup_{t \in T} A^t_{out} \cup \{no - arc\}$ is the set of arcs of the net,
    • $A^t_{in} = \{(p, t) \mid p \in supp(Pre(t))\}$, the set of incoming arcs of transition t,

---

[2] The inscriptions are presented in terms of colour sets.

- $A_{out}^t = \{(t,p) \mid p \in supp(Post(t))\}$, the set of outgoing arcs of transition t,
- $no - arc$ is an 'empty' arc (no connection) for which $Ins(no - arc) = \emptyset$,
- $A^t = A_{in}^t \cup A_{out}^t$, the set of arcs connected to transition t,
- $\widehat{A} = \{(a, ins) \mid a \in A \wedge ins \in Ins(a)\}$ is the set of structured arcs.
- K is a constant function that defines the capacities of places.
- $Gd : \widetilde{T} \rightarrow \{true, false\}$, is a Boolean guard function defined as follows:

$$\forall t \in T_G: Gd((t,c)) = \begin{cases} true & if \ (c, f(c)) \in B_t \\ false & otherwise \end{cases} \quad and \ \forall \ t \in T_{NG}: Gd((t,c)) =$$

true where $B_t = \{(x, f(x)) \mid x \in C_T(t)\}$ is a set of binding pairs and $T = T_G \cup T_{NG}$, with T_G being a set of transitions with guards and T_{NG} being a set of transitions 'without' guards[3].
- $M_0 \in \mu\widehat{P}$ is an initial marking satisfying $M_0 \leq K$. Any $M \in \widehat{P}$ such that $M \leq K$ is a marking.
- $G \subseteq P$ is a set of gluing (or interface) places.

3 Modelling Ambient Intelligent Systems

In this work, the modelling focuses on the interactivity of ambient intelligent systems with the users considering assisted living activities. Thus, using APNs, we examine how the users' actions affect the system's operation and vice versa. The interactivity of these systems is usually expressed in terms of detection or prediction of users' actions and advices (notification or feedback) that the system returns to the users after those actions [23]. Another system feature that is examined through the modelling process is the context-awareness, which indicates the ability of these systems to interact with the users in respect of the information provided each time that an action occurs. For the modelling of the interactivity and context-awareness of these systems, components like sensors and output devices (private/public displays) are considered in the behavioural model to capture the user's activities and system's response (if any) using the *step-modelling* approach.

3.1 Step-Modelling Approach

The step-modelling approach is based on the logic that a user, as an entity, acts *step by step*, but he/she also executes tasks[4] concurrently with the system's or other users' activities. This approach relies on a fundamental building block, the *basic step net*; the repetitive composition of which results in the development of the behavioural APN models for ambient intelligent systems, being expressed as a collection of all the potential activities that can occur in those smart environments. Thus, a basic step net describes a single action/step of a user's activity and the way in which it leads to the state change (i.e., next step) for both the system and the user.

---

[3] Guards are applied to all the transitions, but it is considered that every $t \in T_{NG}$ is a transition with 'no guard' since as its enabledness is not affected by the guard value, which is constantly set to *true*.

[4] These tasks are usually parts/steps of assisted living activities.

Basic Step Nets A *basic step net* captures the structure of the introduced building block that is defined below. The general structure of which is presented in Fig. 2.

Definition 3 (Basic step net). *A basic step net is an APN net $\mathcal{N}_S = (P_S, T_S, Pre_S, Post_S, I_S, Cl, C_S, K_S, M_0^S, G_S)$ containing two parts, the step system and control system, that satisfy the structural conditions below:*

- $P_S = P_{ST} \uplus P_{CS}$, *where P_{ST} and P_{CS} are the sets of places of the step system and control system respectively. Explicitly, $P_{ST} = \{p_s, p_f\}$ contains the starting (p_s) and finishing (p_f) places of the unique step transition t_s, while $P_{CS} = P_r \uplus P_d \uplus \{p_c\}$ consists of three subsets such that (with $n \geq 1$): (1) $P_r = \{p_r^1, \ldots, p_r^n\}$ is a set of response places, (2) $P_d = \{p_d^1, \ldots, p_d^n\}$ is a set of database places and (3) p_c is a unique control place of the finishing place p_f associated with transition t_s (denoted by $p_c = cp^{t_s}(p_f)$).*
- $T_S = T_{ST} \uplus T_{CS}$, *where T_{ST} and T_{CS} are the set of transitions of the step system and control system respectively. Expressly, $T_{ST} = \{t_s\}$ contains a unique transition, called a step transition. $T_{CS} = T_r \uplus T_{em}$ is built out of two subsets such that (with $n \geq 1$): (1) $T_r = \{t_r^1, \ldots, t_r^n\}$ is a set of retrieve transitions and (2) $T_{em} = \{t_{em}^1, \ldots, t_{em}^n\}$ is a set of emptying transitions.*
- $Pre_S, Post_S : T_S \to \mu P_S$ *are such that:*
  1. $Pre_S(t_{em}^i) = \{p_c, p_d^i\}$ *and* $Post_S(t_{em}^i) = \{p_r^i\}$ *for $i = 1, \ldots, n$.*
  2. $Pre_S(t_r^i) = \{p_r^i\}$ *and* $Post_S(t_r^i) = \{p_d^i\}$ *for $i = 1, \ldots, n$.*
  3. $Pre_S(t_s) = \{p_s\}$ *and* $Post_S(t_s) = \{p_f, p_c\}$.
- $I_S = \emptyset$.
- *All the places except for the database places are unmarked. These places are marked by at least one token of some allowed colour.*
  1. $M_0^S(p, c) = 0$, *for every $p \in P_{ST} \cup P_r \cup \{p_c\}$ and $c \in C_S(p)$.*
  2. $M_0^S(p, c) \neq 0$, *for every $p \in P_d$ and some $c \in C_S(p)$.*
- $G_S = \{p_s\}$.

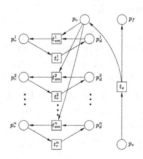

Fig. 2. General structure of an unmarked basic step net.

Explanation of Step and Control Systems: The *step* and *control* systems refer to the user's and system's actions respectively. Specifically, the places and transition of the step system describe the user's action and the state change that results from that action, while the places and transitions of the control system depict the system's response to the user's action returning feedback based on the data stored in the system database. The system's actions that provide the system's feedback and the update of the system database are represented by the *emptying* and *retrieve* transitions respectively. For instance, a step system could represent a single step of an activity or even the entire activity and the way that the smart environment detects or responds depending on the abstraction level of the modelling process [12].

To further explain the elements and functioning of the Control System (CS) of a step system, it could be described as a component of the building block (i.e. basic step net) that consists of:

- the *control place* (p_c),
- the *database places* (P_d),
- the *response places* (P_r) and
- transitions whose pre- and post-places are either *control, database* or *response* *places*.

The *control place* (p_c) is used to control the corresponding place of the step (i.e., the post-place of the transition of the step). In other words, there is a one-to-one correspondence between the control places and the post-places of transition of the steps. The control place is also used for depositing tokens reflecting in that way the detection of the user's action, which prompts the system to give the respective response to the user. Note that each control system has only one control place. The *database places* (P_d) store all the useful information about the configuration of the system in the form of tokens. For instance, after firing a transition that has as pre-places the control place and a database place, the system can respond to the user's action according to the information that is given through the token that resides in the control place. For example, in Fig. 4(c), if we assume that a black token is stored in the control place, in this example p_7, then the system will check the colour of the token, will also check its database places, and will then execute the transition that is enabled giving the proper advice to the user. In this case, the system realises that the colour of the token is black, checks the database place p_9 (where the information about the black token is located) and finds out that the user associated with the black token must be provided with the information that is indicated by the post-place p_{11} of the executed transition t_7. The *response places* (P_r) represent the advice that is given to the user through the output devices of the system (public or private displays, etc.). An example of a response place is place p_{11}, as was mentioned previously. It is noted that the number of the response and database places of a control system is determined by the number of different options or advices that a user can take after performing an action, which is described by the associated step systems. For instance, let's assume that the first step of Fig. 6 represents a user moving from an initial position p_1 (e.g., living room) to another position p_2 (e.g., kitchen). Let's also assume that when a user (represented by either a white or a black token) reaches p_2, he/she can go either forward or to the right (i.e. place p_6 and p_{13} respectively). If the final destination of both users is the same, then the system will provide only one advice to both users resulting in the presence of only one database place that will include all the users (i.e. tokens) and one response place that will show the same advice to both of them. Continuing with the second step of Fig. 6, we assume that at place p_6 each user has two options (go left or forward). Thus, if a (black) user is at place p_6, then the system should provide the correct advice regardless of what the user's choice will be after that advice. In this example, the system has linked the black and white users with an activity and depending on where this activity is carried out (according to the topology of the smart system), it gives directions to the respective user. Hence, being at place p_6, the system should advise the user to go towards the appropriate direction, executing transition t_7. However, in ambient intelligent systems, a user always has the initiative, which means that he/she is not obliged to follow the advice given. On the contrary, the system should always provide the correct information to the user. Regarding the advice given to the user through the response places of the control system, it should be noted that the labels of these places represent the nature of the advice (e.g. instructions like forward, backward, right or left are represented by the respective labels in case of a guidance system). Finally, the absence or presence of tokens in these places indicates if an advice has been given or not.

To complete the description of the control system, we explain the role of its transitions, i.e., the retrieve (T_r) and emptying (T_{em}) transitions. The retrieve transitions have as pre-places the response places and as post-places the database places, and are used to refill the database places with the tokens that have been removed from those places recently. The importance of refilling the database places lies in the fact that a user may want to repeat the same action in the future. The emptying transitions have as pre-places the database places and the control place and as post-places the response places. These transitions are responsible for the advice that is given to the user as their firing results in depositing tokens into the response places. Furthermore, the emptying transitions control the state of the control places, and by extension, the state of the next step transition. For example, if an advice has not been given to a user, due to the fact that the system has not responded to a user's action yet (i.e., the respective emptying transition has not been executed), the user is not allowed to proceed to another task (because a token still resides in the control place) until he/she receives the advice, 'controlling' in that way (via the colour-sensitive inhibitor arc) the interaction.

Root Net: A root net is used in the APNs' composition to indicate the 'starting/initial' state of the APN model of the examined system.

Definition 4 (Root net). *A root net is defined as an APN net that has two places: a place p that acts as both starting and finishing place of a 'collapsed' step* *and its control place* $p_c = cp^\epsilon(p)$, *where* ϵ *denotes the 'collapsed' transition of the collapsed step[5]. The root net is denoted by* $\mathcal{N}_{Rt} = (P_{Rt}, T_{Rt}, Pre_{Rt}, Post_{Rt}, I_{Rt}, Cl, C_{Rt}, K_{Rt}, M_0^{Rt}, G_{Rt})$, *where:*

- $P_{Rt} = \{p, p_c\}$,
- $T_{Rt} = \emptyset$,
- Pre_{Rt} *is an empty function,*

- $Post_{Rt}$ *is also an empty function,*
- $I_{Rt} = \emptyset$,
- $G_{Rt} = \{p\}$.

A root net provides the initial information of the system by marking each of its places with some chosen sets of tokens. The place p is marked with the set of initial system users/resources. For example, in Fig. 3(a, b), there are two users represented by black and white tokens. The control place, p_c, is provided to define the initial restrictions. The root net of Fig. 3(a) states no restrictions about any of the allowed users, while the root net of Fig. 3(b) states restrictions for the 'black' user: this user is not allowed to perform further activities or steps of an activity.

Fig. 3. Root nets (a, b).

The use of the root net will become apparent in the next section, where its composition with other APN nets is demonstrated to construct the APN models of ambient intelligent systems.

3.2   Composing Ambient Petri Nets (APNs)

Composition is a fundamental technique of Petri nets used for the construction of large system models out of simpler ones. Several approaches have been proposed in the past years based either on the composition of places or transitions of Petri nets [1,34]. In this section, two composition operators are introduced for the APNs based on the gluing of net places: the *forward* and *backward* composition operators. Explicitly, they describe how two APN nets are glued on the places of their *step systems*. Note that whenever any of these compositions is conducted between two nets, colour-sensitive inhibitor arcs are generated between the control places of the first net and the step transition of the second one.

Forward Composition (FC) of APNs: The forward composition operator enables the 'sequential' composition of two APN nets. 'Sequential' implies that the gluing of two APN nets is conducted only on one pair of gluing places creating in that way a sequence of glued nets.

---

[5] The notation can be extended to: $p \in {}^\bullet\epsilon$ and $p \in \epsilon^\bullet$.

Definition 5 (Forward composition). *Let's assume that* $\mathcal{N} = (P, T, Pre, Post, I, Cl, C, K, M_0, G)$ *is an Ambient Petri Net such that, for every place* $g \in G$ *and* $t \in {}^\bullet g$, *there is a control place in* $t^\bullet$ *denoted by* $cp^t(g)$. *Moreover, let* $\mathcal{N}_S = (P_S, T_S, Pre_S, Post_S, \emptyset, Cl, C_S, K_S, M_0^S, G_S)$ *be a basic step net (as in definition 3) such that* $P \cap P_S = T \cap T_S = \emptyset$, *and let* $g \in G$ *be a place satisfying:* $C(g) = C_S(p_s) = C_{SET}$ *and* $K(g, c) = K_S(p_s, c)$, *for every* $c \in C_{SET}$. *The forward composition of* $\mathcal{N}$ *and* $\mathcal{N}_S$ *w.r.t. the gluing pair* (g, p_s) *of places is an Ambient Petri net* $\mathcal{N} \oplus^g \mathcal{N}_S = \mathcal{N}' = (P', T', Pre', Post', I', Cl, C', K', M_0', G')$, *where the components are defined as follows:*

- $P' = P \cup (P_S \setminus \{p_s\})$ *and* $T' = T \cup T_S$.
- $Pre', Post' : T' \rightarrow \mu P'$ *are defined by:*

$$Pre'(t)(p) = \begin{cases} Pre(t)(p) & \text{for } t \in T \text{ & } p \in P, \\ Pre_S(t)(p) & \text{for } t \in T_S \text{ & } p \in P_S \setminus \{p_s\}, \\ Pre_S(t)(p_s) & \text{for } t \in T_S \text{ & } p = g, \\ 0 & \text{otherwise.} \end{cases} \quad Post'(t)(p) = \begin{cases} Post(t)(p) & \text{for } t \in T \text{ & } p \in P, \\ Post_S(t)(p) & \text{for } t \in T_S \text{ & } p \in P_S \setminus \{p_s\}, \\ Post(t)(p_s) & \text{for } t \in T \text{ & } p = g, \\ 0 & \text{otherwise.} \end{cases}$$

- $I' \subseteq P' \times T'$ *is defined by:* $I' = I \cup \{(cp^t(g), t_s) \mid t \in {}^\bullet g \text{ in } \mathcal{N}\}$, *where* $t_s \in T_S$ *is* $\mathcal{N}_S$*'s unique step transition.*
- $C' : P' \cup T' \rightarrow Cl$ *is defined by:* $C'|_{P \cup T} = C$ *and* $C'|_{(P_S \setminus \{p_s\}) \cup T_S} = C_S$.
- K' *is defined by:* $K'|_{\widetilde{P}} = K$ *and* $K'|_{\widetilde{P_S \setminus \{p_s\}}} = K_S|_{\widetilde{P_S \setminus \{p_s\}}}$.
- $M_0' \in \mu\widetilde{P'}$ *is defined by:* $M_0'|_{\widetilde{P}} = M_0$ *and* $M_0'|_{\widetilde{P_S \setminus \{p_s\}}} = M_0^S|_{\widetilde{P_S \setminus \{p_s\}}}$.
- $G' = G \cup \{p_f\}$.

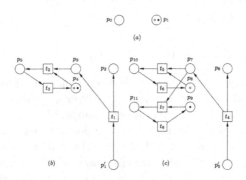

Fig. 4. $\mathcal{N}_1 \in X_{Root}$ (a), $\mathcal{N}_2 \in X_{Basic}$ (b) and $\mathcal{N}_3 \in X_{Basic}$ (c).

Although in the above definition $\mathcal{N}$ is a general Ambient Petri Net, for the composition operator to work as desired, $\mathcal{N}$ should have a specific structure. More precisely, it should be a *forward composite step net*. In what follows, X_{Basic} denotes all the basic step nets, and X_{Root} all the root nets.

Definition 6 (Forward composite step nets). *The set of* forward composite step nets X_{Com}^F *is defined inductively as follows:*

- $X_{Root} \subset X_{Com}^F$.
- If $\mathcal{N} \in X_{Com}^F$ and $\mathcal{N}_S \in X_{Basic}$, then $\mathcal{N} \oplus^g \mathcal{N}_S \in X_{Com}^F$.

Note that for every gluing place of a net $\mathcal{N} \in X_{Com}^F$ there will be at least one control place. Indeed, the only gluing place of a root net has its unique control place associated with collapsed transition ϵ, and this transition can be considered both as pre and post-transition of this gluing place. Also, the place added to the set of gluing places after a forward composite net is extended by a basic step net (p_f of the basic step net) comes with its control place as well. The forward composition can be applied on the same gluing place of a composite step net several times extending the net, from that gluing place, by a basic step net each time. In the forward composite step nets, there is always a unique control place for every gluing place of $\mathcal{N} \in X_{Com}^F$. As a result, the added set of colour-sensitive inhibitor arcs (in Definition 5) will be just a singleton set. Note that applying the forward composition, only directed tree graphs can be produced, such as path (or linear tree) graphs, caterpillar trees and star graphs.

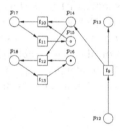

Fig. 5. $\mathcal{N}_4 \in X_{Basic}$, an example of a basic step net.

Example of Forward Composition: Let $\mathcal{N}_1 \in X_{Root}$ and $\mathcal{N}_2 \in X_{Basic}$ be two nets, as shown in Fig. 4(a, b). They are composed by choosing (p_1, p_1') as a gluing pair of places and constructing $\mathcal{N}_1 \oplus^{p_1} \mathcal{N}_2$. Composing them, a colour-sensitive inhibitor arc is inserted between place p_0 and transition t_1. The resulting net belongs to the set X_{Com}^F. This net is extended further by the step defined by the net $\mathcal{N}_3 \in X_{Basic}$ (see Fig. 4(c)), by gluing the places p_2 and p_5'. The resulting net contains an inserted colour-sensitive inhibitor arc between p_3 and t_4 and belongs to the set X_{Com}^F. Let's call it $\mathcal{N}$. At this point, the forward composite step net $\mathcal{N}$ has a set of gluing points with three elements: $\{p_1, p_2, p_6\}$. Any of these can be a starting point for future extensions. Assuming that place p_2 is selected as the next gluing point with the net $\mathcal{N}_4$ of Fig. 5 describing the next step. For this forward composition (p_2, p_{12}) will be used as the next gluing pair.

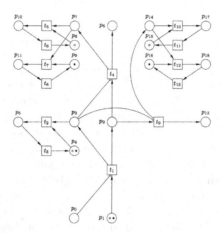

Fig. 6. A forward composition of a forward composite net $\mathcal{N}$ and a basic step net $\mathcal{N}_4$.

The resulting final net is shown in Fig. 6. The two component nets, $\mathcal{N}$ and $\mathcal{N}_4$, are composed according to Definition 5, and their composition fuses the places of the gluing pair removing the place p_{12}. A new colour-sensitive inhibitor arc is added between the control place $p_3 = cp^{t_1}(p_2)$ and the step transition t_9. Note that the set ${}^\bullet p_2$ has only one element, t_1, and so only one inhibitor arc is added. Finally, p_{13}, which is the p_f place of the net $\mathcal{N}_4$, is added to the gluing places of the new net.

Backward Composition (BC) of APNs: The forward composition of APNs does not allow a step to return to an already existing place. Therefore, the backward composition is introduced, which uses two gluing pairs of places enabling the creation of 'cyclic' APN nets. For this composition, the basic step net is extended, defining the one step net, which allows the net gluing on two different step places.

Definition 7 (One step net). *A one step net is defined as a basic step net, with the only difference that its set of gluing places contains both the starting and finishing places:* $G_S = \{p_s, p_f\}$. *The set of all one step nets is denoted by* X_{One}.

Definition 8 (Backward composition). *Let $\mathcal{N}$ be an Ambient Petri Net, and $\mathcal{N}_S$ be a one step net, as in Definitions 5 and 7, respectively (the two nets should have disjoint sets of places and transitions). Moreover, let $g_1, g_2 \in G$ be places satisfying:* $C(g_1) = C(p_s) = C^1_{SET}$, *and* $C_S(g_2) = C_S(p_f) = C^2_{SET}$ *as well as, for all* $c \in C^1_{SET}$ *and* $c' \in C^2_{SET}$, $K(g_1, c) = K_S(p_s, c)$, *and* $K(g_2, c') = K_S(p_f, c')$. *The backward composition of $\mathcal{N}$ and $\mathcal{N}_S$ w.r.t. the gluing pairs (g_1, p_s) and (g_2, p_f) of places is an Ambient Petri Net:* $\mathcal{N} \oplus^{g_1}_{g_2} \mathcal{N}_S = \mathcal{N}' = (P', T', Pre', Post', I', Cl, C', K', M'_0, G')$, *where the different components are defined as follows:*

- $P' = P \cup (P_S \setminus \{p_s, p_f\})$ and $T' = T \cup T_S$.
- Pre', $Post' : T' \to \mu P'$ are defined by:

$$Pre'(t)(p) = \begin{cases} Pre(t)(p) & \text{for } t \in T \ \& \ p \in P, \\ Pre_S(t)(p) & \text{for } t \in T_S \ \& \ p \in P_S \setminus \{p_s, p_f\}, \\ Pre_S(t)(p_s) & \text{for } t \in T_S \ a\& \ p = g_1, \\ Pre(t)(p_f) & \text{for } t \in T \ \& \ p = g_2, \\ 0 & \text{otherwise.} \end{cases}$$

$$Post'(t)(p) = \begin{cases} Post(t)(p) & \text{for } t \in T \ \& \ p \in P, \\ Post_S(t)(p) & \text{for } t \in T_S \ \& \ p \in P_S \setminus \{p_s, p_f\}, \\ Post(t)(p_s) & \text{for } t \in T \ \& \ p = g_1, \\ Post_S(t)(p_f) & \text{for } t \in T_S \ \& \ p = g_2, \\ 0 & \text{otherwise.} \end{cases}$$

- $I' \subseteq P' \times T'$ is defined by $I' = I \cup \{(cp^t(g_1), t_s) \mid t \in {}^\bullet g_1 \ in \ \mathcal{N}\} \cup \{(cp^{t_s}(p_f), t) \mid t \in g_2^\bullet \ in \ \mathcal{N}'\}$, where $t_s \in T_S$ is $\mathcal{N}_S$'s unique step transition.
- $C' : P' \cup T' \to Cl$ is defined by: $C'|_{P \cup T} = C$ and $C'|_{(P_S \setminus \{p_s, p_f\}) \cup T_S} = C_S$.
- K' is defined by: $K'|_{\widetilde{P}} = K$ and $K'|_{P_S \widetilde{\setminus \{p_s, p_f\}}} = K_S|_{P_S \widetilde{\setminus \{p_s, p_f\}}}$.
- $M_0' \in \mu\widetilde{P'}$ is defined by: $M_0'|_{\widetilde{P}} = M_0$ and $M_0'|_{P_S \widetilde{\setminus \{p_s, p_f\}}} = M_0^S|_{P_S \widetilde{\setminus \{p_s, p_f\}}}$.
- $G' = G$; moreover, the control places of the gluing places in G' are inherited from $\mathcal{N}$ except for g_2 that has an additional control place $cp^{t_s}(g_2)$ which was $cp^{t_s}(p_f)$ in $\mathcal{N}_S$[6].

In backward composition, more colour-sensitive inhibitor arcs are needed to ensure that the user takes the appropriate advice before executing the next action. This is because this composition introduces 'cycles' into the resulting net, and it is not only needed to consider execution sequences containing tt_s, but the execution sequences containing $t_s t$ as well. The gluing places of $\mathcal{N}'$ are simply the gluing places of $\mathcal{N}$[7]. The combination of the two composition operations can result in the creation of cyclic graphs, Directed Acyclic Graphs (DAGs) (e.g. rhombus graph) and polytree graphs (e.g. N-graph) considering an ordering in the way that these compositions are performed. As in Definition 5, the interest of this composition lies on nets which derive compositionally forming the set X_{Com} of composite step nets.

Definition 9 (Composite step nets). *The set of* composite step nets X_{Com} *is defined as follows:*

- $X_{Com}^F \subset X_{Com}$.
- *If $\mathcal{N} \in X_{Com}$ and $\mathcal{N}_S \in X_{Basic}$, then $\mathcal{N} \oplus^g \mathcal{N}_S \in X_{Com}$, conducting the forward composition.*
- *If $\mathcal{N} \in X_{Com}$ and $\mathcal{N}_S \in X_{One}$, then $\mathcal{N} \oplus_{g_2}^{g_1} \mathcal{N}_S \in X_{Com}$, conducting the backward composition.*

Example of Backward Composition: This example describes the creation of a *bidirectional step*, the simplest form of a 'circle', which is produced by composing two basic step nets backwards, as presented below. A bidirectional step allows the user to retrieve a previous state by 'undoing' the last activity step or action. The construction of bidirectional steps turned out to be a necessity

---

[6] So now the user executing some existing transition $t \in g_2^\bullet$ in $\mathcal{N}'$ will not be able to proceed without 'taking the instructions' from the system following the execution of transition t_s.

[7] In the definition of backward composition, as in Definition 5, $\mathcal{N}$ is a general APN net.

for the modelling of ambient intelligent systems. The simplest way to create a bidirectional step is by gluing two basic step nets w.r.t. the places of their step systems (see Fig. 7). This net is generated by following the definition of backward composition for the forward composite net $\mathcal{N} = \mathcal{N}_1 \oplus^{p_1} \mathcal{N}_2$ (see Fig. 4 for nets $\mathcal{N}_1$ and $\mathcal{N}_2$) and the net $\mathcal{N}_3$ from Fig. 4 treated as an one step net. For the composition of these two nets, $(g_1, p_s) = (p_2, p_5')$ and $(g_2, p_f) = (p_1, p_6)^8$ are chosen as the two gluing pairs $(\mathcal{N} \oplus_{p_1}^{p_2} \mathcal{N}_3 = \mathcal{N}')$. In this case, the places removed during the composition of the two nets are p_5' and p_6 respectively. Furthermore, the set of colour-sensitive inhibitor arcs of the resulting net consists of the colour-sensitive inhibitor arcs that connect the transitions t_4 and t_1 with the control places p_3 and p_7 respectively, together with the colour-sensitive inhibitor arc (between t_1 and p_0) that are added after $\mathcal{N}_1$ and $\mathcal{N}_2$ are composed. Indeed, knowing that p_f is glued with g_2, $p_f = p_6$, $t_s = t_4$, $g_1 = p_2$, $g_2 = p_1$ and $^\bullet p_2 = \{t_1\} = p_1^\bullet$ in $\mathcal{N}$ (and $\mathcal{N}'$), the following is obtained from Definition 8:
$$I' = I \cup \{(cp^t(g_1), t_s) \mid t \in {}^\bullet g_1 \text{ in } \mathcal{N}\} \cup \{(cp^{t_s}(p_f), t) \mid t \in g_2^\bullet \text{ in } \mathcal{N}'\}$$
$$= \{(p_0, t_1)\} \cup \{(cp^t(p_2), t_4) \mid t \in {}^\bullet p_2 \text{ in } \mathcal{N}\} \cup \{(cp^{t_4}(p_6), t) \mid t \in p_1^\bullet \text{ in } \mathcal{N}'\} =$$
$$\{(p_0, t_1)\} \cup \{(cp^{t_1}(p_2), t_4)\} \cup \{(cp^{t_4}(p_6), t_1)\} = \{(p_0, t_1)\} \cup \{(p_3, t_4)\} \cup \{(p_7, t_1)\}.$$

Note that p_1 of the resulting net has two associated control places: p_0 and p_7. Place p_0 'controls' the actions of the users starting from place p_1 after they get there by executing an empty transition ϵ ($p_0 = cp^\epsilon(p_1)$). Contrarily, place p_7 was a control place of the place p_6 in $\mathcal{N}_3$ (i.e., $cp^{t_4}(p_6)$). Now, after composing $\mathcal{N}$ and $\mathcal{N}_3$, where p_1 and p_6 were glued, p_7 'controls' the actions of the users starting from place p_1 after they get there by executing transition t_4 ($p_7 = cp^{t_4}(p_1)$). So, $p_7 = cp^{t_4}(p_6)$ in $\mathcal{N}_3$, but $p_7 = cp^{t_4}(p_1)$ in $\mathcal{N}'$.

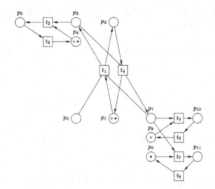

Fig. 7. A bidirectional step resulting from the composition of the basic step nets of Fig. 4.

4 Transforming and Unfolding Ambient Petri Nets

This section presents a construction of a T-APN net out of a given APN net showing the relation between the two classes. Demonstrating that these nets

---

8 p_s and p_f are the starting and finishing places of $\mathcal{N}_3$.

behave equivalently, a non-verifiable APN net could be 'verified' via the equivalent T-APN net.

4.1 Defining the Construction

Initially, the construction of a T-APN net is defined by describing the relation of the tuple elements of the given APN net with those of the constructed T-APN net.

Preliminaries of Construction: All the notions used for the definition of the construction are defined focusing on a particular sub-class of the APN nets, the composite step nets (see Definition 9). Therefore, for a given composite step net $\mathcal{N} = (P, T, Pre, Post, I, Cl, C, K, M_0, G)$, the constructed net is referred to as the T-APN net associated with $\mathcal{N}$ and is denoted by $\varphi(\mathcal{N}) = (P', T', Pre', Post', Cl', \overline{Cl}, C_P, C_T, Ins, K', Gd, M_0', G')$.

A given APN net in the following construction is a composite step net[9]. Then, $P = P_R \cup P_D \cup P_C \cup P_{SF}\star$ where $P_R = \bigcup\limits_{i=0}^{n} P_r^i, P_D = \bigcup\limits_{i=0}^{n} P_d^i, P_C = \bigcup\limits_{i=0}^{n} \{p_c^i\}, P_{SF} \subset \bigcup\limits_{i=0}^{n} P_{ST}^i$, with $P_r^i, P_d^i, \{p_c^i\}$ and P_{ST}^i being the sets of response, database, control and step places of the components of $\mathcal{N}$ respectively. P_{SF} is a subset of the step places used to specify the set of starting and finishing places of the given composite step net by removing the duplicates of the gluing places of the composed nets. The set of inhibitor places $P_I = \{p \in P \mid \exists_{t \in T} \, (p, t) \in I\}$ refers to a sub-set of the set of control places[10]. This set is necessary for the definition constructed T-APN net specifying the additional of the $Post'$ mapping of the constructed T-APN net specifying the additional arcs and their location. Also, the transitions of $\mathcal{N}$ are composed of retrieve, emptying and step transitions, i.e., $T = T_R \cup T_{EM} \cup T_{STEP}$ $(\star)$, where $T_R = \bigcup\limits_{i=1}^{n} T_r^i, T_{EM} = \bigcup\limits_{i=1}^{n} T_{em}^i$ and $T_{STEP} = \bigcup\limits_{i=1}^{n} T_{ST}^i \cup \{\epsilon\} = \bigcup\limits_{i=1}^{n} \{t_s^i\} \cup \{\epsilon\}$. Note that the root net does not contribute to T, though it has one 'collapsed' transition denoted by ϵ[11]. Also, for every $t \in T_{STEP}$, there exists exactly one post-place p of t such that $p \in P_{SF}$ (denoted by p_t). For the sake of simplicity, Cl_{ID} and Cl_{SPEC} are used in the construction of the sets of identity and special colours respectively, where $Cl_{ID} = \bigcup Cl$ and $Cl_{SPEC} = \bigcup \overline{Cl}$.

Definition 10 (Construction). *Let $\mathcal{N} = (P, T, Pre, Post, I, Cl, C, K, M_0, G)$ be a composite step APN net. A T-APN net $\varphi(\mathcal{N}) = (P', T', Pre', Post', Cl', \overline{Cl}, C_P, C_T, Ins, K', Gd, M_0', G')$ associated with $\mathcal{N}$ is defined as follows:*

---

[9] Composed out of n basic or one step nets and a root net.

[10] An inhibitor place is always a control place but not the other way around.

[11] If it is considered that its only step place, e.g., p^0, is both starting and finishing place of ϵ.

(i) $P' = P$ and $T' = T$.

(ii) Pre', $Post' : T' \to \mu P'$ are defined as follows:

$$Pre'(t)(p) = \begin{cases} 1 & \text{if } (p,t) \in I, \\ Pre(t)(p) & \text{otherwise.} \end{cases} \quad Post'(t)(p) = \begin{cases} 1 & \text{if } Post(t)(p) = 0 \wedge ((t \in T_{EM} \wedge p \in P_C \cap P_I \\ & \wedge\ Pre(t)(p) > 0) \vee (t \in T_{STEP} \wedge\ p = cp^{\hat{t}}(p_t) \\ & \wedge\ \hat{t} \in (T_{STEP} \setminus \{t\}))), \\ Post(t)(p) & \text{otherwise.} \end{cases}$$

(iii) $Cl' = Cl$ and $\overline{Cl}$ is a structuring set built as a complementary set to the structuring set Cl (given by bijection $f:(\bigcup Cl) \to (\bigcup \overline{Cl})$).

(iv)

$$\forall p \in P : C_P(p) = \begin{cases} C(p) & \text{if } p \in (P_D \cup P_R \cup P_{SF}), \\ C(p) \cup \{f(g) \mid g \in C(p)\} & \text{if } p \in P_C. \end{cases} \quad \text{and } \forall t \in T : \ C_T(t) = C(t).$$

(v) $Ins(a) = \begin{cases} \{f(col) \mid col \in Cl_{ID}\} & \text{if } a \in Pre_{REP} \vee a \in Post_{NEW}, \\ \{col \mid col \in Cl_{ID}\} & \text{otherwise.} \end{cases}$

where $Pre_{REP} = \{(p,t) \mid (p,t) \in I\}$ and $Post_{NEW} = \{(t,p) \mid Post(t)(p) = 0 \wedge Post'(t)(p) = 1\}$.

(vi) $K'((p,c)) = \begin{cases} K((p,c)) & \text{if } p \in P \wedge c \in Cl_{ID}, \\ 1 & \text{if } p \in P \wedge c \in Cl_{SPEC}. \end{cases}$

(vii) $Gd : \tilde{T}' \to \{true, false\}$, is a Boolean guard function defined as follows:

$$\forall t \in T_G : Gd((t,c)) = \begin{cases} true & \text{if}(c, f(c)) \in B_t, \\ false & \text{otherwise.} \end{cases} \quad \text{and } \forall t \in T_{NG} : \ Gd((t,c)) = true.$$

where $T' = T_G \cup T_{NG}$[12] and $B_t = \{(x, f(x)) \mid x \in C(t)\}$ is a set of binding pairs.

(viii) Initial marking M_0' is defined as follows:

$$M_0'((p,g)) = \begin{cases} M_0((p,g)) & \text{if } p \in P \setminus \{p_c^0\} \wedge g \in Cl_{ID}, \\ 1 - M_0((p,g)) & \text{if } p = p_c^0 \wedge g \in Cl_{ID}, \\ 1 - M_0((p, f^{-1}(g))) & \text{if } (p \in (P_C \cap P_I) \wedge (\exists_{t \in T_{STEP} \setminus \{t\}} : Post(t)(p) = 0 \wedge Post'(t)(p) = 1 \wedge \\ & M_0((p_t, f^{-1}(g))) > 0) \wedge g \in Cl_{SPEC}) \vee (p \in (P_C \cap P_I) \wedge (\exists_{t' \in T_{EM}} : \\ & Post(t')(p) = 0 \wedge Post'(t')(p) = 1) \wedge (\exists_{t \in T_{STEP} \setminus \{t\}} : p = cp^t(p_t) \wedge \\ & M_0((p_t, f^{-1}(g))) > 0) \wedge g \in Cl_{SPEC}) \vee (p = p_c^0 \wedge g \in Cl_{SPEC}), \\ 0 & \text{otherwise.} \end{cases}$$

where f^{-1} is the inverse function of bijection f.

(ix) $G' = G$.

(i) This relation shows that the number of places of the constructed T-APN is equal to the number of places in the APN net and that for every place of the APN net there exists a respective place in the T-APN net. The same remarks, like those of the places above, are applied to the transitions.

(ii) For the Pre' mapping of the constructed $\varphi(\mathcal{N})$ net, every colour-sensitive inhibitor arc of $\mathcal{N}$ is replaced by a direct arc and every direct arc of the Pre mapping of $\mathcal{N}$ remains structurally the same in the constructed $\varphi(\mathcal{N})$ net. For the $Post'$ mapping of the $\varphi(\mathcal{N})$ net, new direct arcs are added to the T-APN net. Firstly, new direct arcs are added starting from the step transitions

---

[12] T_G consists of all those transitions of the T-APN net that are associated with transitions of the APN net that have inhibitor places. The remaining transitions of the T-APN net belong to T_{NG}.

and ending at all the control places of the post-places of those transitions. These additional arcs are generated to maintain the functionality of the net when either a unidirectional step (i.e., basic step net) or a bidirectional step is followed by a bidirectional one. Secondly, new direct arcs are added between all the emptying transitions and the respective control places, starting from the emptying transitions and ending at those control places. Thirdly, new direct arcs are added between the step transitions that have as post-place the 'starting' place of the $\varphi(\mathcal{N})$ net and the control place of the root net when the 'starting' place is a place of one or more bidirectional steps or can be revisited[13]. Finally, regarding the rest of the post mapping of the constructed net $\varphi(\mathcal{N})$, all the other post-arcs remain the same as in $\mathcal{N}$.

(iii) The Cl' structuring set of the $\varphi(\mathcal{N})$ net that defines the set of the identity colours of the net is the same as the Cl structuring set of $\mathcal{N}$. On the contrary, the $\overline{Cl}$ structuring set provides the 'special/complementary' colours of tokens given by bijection f, which are used to maintain the functioning of the constructed $\varphi(\mathcal{N})$ net the same as that of the APN net $\mathcal{N}$.

(iv) The C_P function of the $\varphi(\mathcal{N})$ net is related to the colour function C of the APN net through the function above. If the places of $\varphi(\mathcal{N})$ to be structured are database, response or step places then in both nets these places will be structured taking colours that derive from function C. All the control places of $\varphi(\mathcal{N})$ will be structured taking colours that derive from both function C and the set of special colours. Finally, the transitions of both nets are structured taking colours from the same structuring set as defined above by the relation of the two colour functions C_T and C.

(v) The Ins function defines what type of coloured tokens can be carried by each arc of $\varphi(\mathcal{N})$. This function is not related with any colour function of the $\mathcal{N}$ as all the arcs of $\mathcal{N}$ are not considered as structured and can carry any colour of the set Cl, but it is related to the structuring set Cl showing how the colours of the arc inscriptions can derive from that set. In $\varphi(\mathcal{N})$ not all the arcs can carry the same colours of tokens, as the inscriptions are given by the disjoint structuring sets Cl and $\overline{Cl}$[14]. All the newly added direct arcs carry tokens of special colours only and all the other direct arcs carry tokens of identity colours as described by the function above.

(vi) The capacity of the places of $\mathcal{N}$ is maintained the same for the respective places of $\varphi(\mathcal{N})$ when the colours of the tokens belong to the identity set of colours. Otherwise, K' returns 1 for each place of $\varphi(\mathcal{N})$ when the colours of the tokens of that place belong to the special set of colours.

(vii) The APN net $\mathcal{N}$ has no guards. Guards are introduced in $\varphi(\mathcal{N})$ to replace in some sense the absence of the colour-sensitive inhibitor arcs, which are doing in $\mathcal{N}$ what the guards do in $\varphi(\mathcal{N})$. From the above relation, T_G transitions depend on the set of binding pairs B_t for the guard evaluation to either true or false, but the guards of the T_{NG} transitions are always set to true. The set of binding pairs B_t of $\varphi(\mathcal{N})$ is constructed through the colour function C of $\mathcal{N}$. It is noted that all $t \in T_G$ are defined as the transitions associated with

---

[13] The last case is a special case of the first one.
[14] This happens to maintain the behaviour of $\mathcal{N}$ in the T-APN net $\varphi(\mathcal{N})$.

those transitions in $\mathcal{N}$ that have at least one inhibitor place. All the other transitions of $\varphi(\mathcal{N})$ belong to the T_{NG} set of transitions[15].

(viii) The initial marking of $\varphi(\mathcal{N})$ is defined with respect to both the places that host the tokens and the colours of tokens that are held in each place of $\mathcal{N}$. If the examined place of $\varphi(\mathcal{N})$ is a database, response or step place or a control place of the same building block with that of the step place controlled by it and the colour of token in the place of $\mathcal{N}$ belongs to the 'identity' set of colours, then the marking of the examined place of $\varphi(\mathcal{N})$ remains the same as it is in the respective place of $\mathcal{N}$ (see first clause of the function). If the examined place is the root control place of $\varphi(\mathcal{N})$ and the colour of token in the respective place of $\mathcal{N}$ belongs to the 'identity' set, then the marking of that place is given by the second point of the marking function defining the presence or absence of 'identity' colour of tokens depending on the absense or presence of tokens in the respective place. Finally, if the examined place of $\varphi(\mathcal{N})$ is a control place of a step place that belongs to a different building block from that of the step place that is 'controlled' by it, then the marking of that place is given by the third clause of the marking function defining it as the complementary colours of tokens (i.e., 'special' colours) that reside in the respective step place of the $\mathcal{N}$ net.

(ix) All the gluing places of $\mathcal{N}$ are considered as gluing places of the constructed $\varphi(\mathcal{N})$ net. Expressly, the places of $\varphi(\mathcal{N})$ that correspond to the gluing places of $\mathcal{N}$, are the gluing places of $\varphi(\mathcal{N})$.

A Construction Example: The construction is illustrated using the APN net $\mathcal{N}$ presented in Fig. 7 in order to build the T-APN net $\varphi(\mathcal{N})$ that is associated with $\mathcal{N}$. In this example, the labelling of the elements is exactly the same for both nets referring to two respective elements. For instance, place p_1 of $\varphi(\mathcal{N})$ is the respective place of p_1 of $\mathcal{N}$.

The set of places of $\mathcal{N}$ is defined as $P = \{p_1, p_2, p_3, p_4, p_5, p_6, p_7, p_8, p_9, p_{10}, p_{11}\}$, where $P_R = \{p_5, p_{10}, p_{11}\}$, $P_D = \{p_4, p_8, p_9\}$, $P_C = \{p_0, p_3, p_7\}$ and $P_{SF} = \{p_1, p_2\}$ correspond to the response, database, control and step places of $\mathcal{N}$, as defined by the equation $P = P_R \cup P_D \cup P_C \cup P_{SF}$. The control places of the 'starting' place are also needed for the construction of the initial marking of the $\varphi(\mathcal{N})$ net, where $p_c^0 = \{p_0\}$ and $cp^{t_4}(p_1) = \{p_7\}$ implying that the 'starting' place p_1 gets places p_0 and p_7 as its control places. The set of inhibitor places P_I is the same as the set of control places P_C. Thus, $P_I = \{p_0, p_3, p_7\}$. Now, the construction of the places of the $\varphi(\mathcal{N})$ net is performed according to Definition 10(i), giving $P' = P = \{p_1, p_2, p_3, p_4, p_5, p_6, p_7, p_8, p_9, p_{10}, p_{11}\}$ and $P'_R = P_R = \{p_5, p_{10}, p_{11}\}$, $P'_D = P_D = \{p_4, p_8, p_9\}$, $P'_C = P_C = \{p_0, p_3, p_7\}$ and $P'_{SF} = P_{SF} = \{p_1, p_2, p_6\}$. For the transitions of $\mathcal{N}$, $T = T_R \cup T_{EM} \cup T_{STEP}$, with $T = \{t_1, t_2, t_3, t_4, t_5, t_6, t_7, t_8\}$, $T_R = \{t_3, t_6, t_8\}$, $T_{EM} = \{t_2, t_5, t_7\}$ and $T_{STEP} = \{t_1, t_4\}$. From the construction follows that $T' = T = \{t_1, t_2, t_3, t_4, t_5, t_6, t_7, t_8\}$. with $T'_R = T_R = \{t_3, t_6, t_8\}$, $T'_{EM} = T_{EM} = \{t_2, t_5, t_7\}$ and $T'_{STEP} = T_{STEP} =$

---

[15] From Definition 10(ii) and Equation ($\star$) follows that $T_{STEP} = T_G$ and $T_{EM} \cup T_R = T_{NG}$.

$\{t_1, t_4\}$. Also, Definition 10 $(i), (vii)$ imply that $T'_{STEP} = T_G$ and $T'_R \cup T'_{EM} = T_{NG}$

Next, all the pre and post-arcs of $\mathcal{N}$ are presented. The set of all the pre-arcs, denoted by Pre_{ALL} is divided into direct pre-arcs and inhibitor arcs, which are denoted by Pre_{DIR} and I respectively. Therefore, $Pre_{ALL} = Pre_{DIR} \cup I$, where $Pre_{DIR} = \{(p_1, t_1), (p_3, t_2), (p_5, t_3), (p_4, t_2), (p_2, t_4), (p_7, t_5), (p_7, t_7), (p_8, t_5), (p_9, t_7), (p_{10}, t_6), (p_{11}, t_8)\}$ and $I = \{(p_0, t_1), (p_3, t_4), (p_7, t_9)\}$. According to the construction of the pre-arcs for the $\varphi(\mathcal{N})$ net, $Pre'_{ALL} = Pre'_{DIR} \cup Pre_{REP}$ with $Pre'_{DIR} = Pre_{DIR} = \{(p_1, t_1), (p_3, t_2), (p_5, t_3), (p_4, t_2), (p_2, t_4), (p_7, t_5), (p_7, t_7), (p_8, t_5), (p_9, t_7), (p_{10}, t_6), (p_{11}, t_8)\}$ and $Pre_{REP} = \{(p_0, t_1), (p_3, t_4), (p_7, t_9)\}$, with Pre_{REP} being the set of direct arcs that replaces the respective set of inhibitor arcs. The post mapping of $\mathcal{N}$, denoted by $Post_{ALL}$, gives the post-arcs of $\mathcal{N}$, $Post_{ALL} = \{(t_1, p_2), (t_1, p_3), (t_2, p_5), (t_3, p_4), (t_4, p_1), (t_4, p_7), (t_5, p_{10}), (t_6, p_8), (t_7, p_{11}), (t_8, p_9)\}$. Now, the post mapping of $\varphi(\mathcal{N})$ is given considering the existing post-arcs of $\mathcal{N}$ and the new direct post-arcs added to $\varphi(\mathcal{N})$ between the emptying transitions and every inhibitor place and between the step transitions and the control places of those step places that are revisited. Thus, $Post_{NEW} = \{(t_2, p_3), (t_4, p_0), (t_5, p_7), (t_7, p_7)\}$ and $Post'_{ALL} = Post_{ALL} \cup Post_{NEW} = \{(t_1, p_2), (t_1, p_3), (t_2, p_5), (t_3, p_4), (t_4, p_1), (t_4, p_7), (t_5, p_{10}), (t_6, p_8), (t_7, p_{11}), (t_8, p_9)\} \cup \{(t_2, p_3), (t_4, p_0), (t_5, p_7), (t_7, p_7)\} = \{(t_1, p_2), (t_1, p_3), (t_2, p_5), (t_3, p_4), (t_4, p_1), (t_4, p_7), (t_5, p_{10}), (t_6, p_8), (t_7, p_{11}), (t_8, p_9), (t_2, p_3), (t_4, p_0), (t_5, p_7), (t_7, p_7)\}$.

The Cl in $\mathcal{N}$ is set to $\{b, w\}$ structuring both the places and transitions denoting that black and white colours are used for the tokens in $\mathcal{N}$. In Definition 10(iii), Cl' is equal to Cl signifying that the same structuring set is used in $\varphi(\mathcal{N})$. Moreover, for the construction of $\varphi(\mathcal{N})$, the complementary set of Cl is needed, i.e., the $\overline{Cl}$, taking its values from bijection f. Thus, $\overline{Cl} = \{g, l\}$ implying that the complementary colours used in $\varphi(\mathcal{N})$ are the grey (g) and light grey (l) respectively, with $f(b) = g$ and $f(w) = l$. In $\mathcal{N}$, the colour function C structures all the net places using the set Cl, which allows them to host either black or white tokens or both. The places in $\varphi(\mathcal{N})$ are structured by the function C_P, as stated in Definition 10(iv). Thus, for all the response, database and step places of $\varphi(\mathcal{N})$, it is set equal to C and for all the control places of $\varphi(\mathcal{N})$, C_P takes values both from C and the complementary set of colours. Hence, $P'_C = \{p_0, p_3, p_7\}$ host tokens of black, white, grey and light grey colour while $P'_R = \{p_5, p_{10}, p_{11}\}$, $P'_D = \{p_4, p_8, p_9\}$ and $P'_{SF} = \{p_1, p_2\}$ host only black and white tokens.

The transitions of $\varphi(\mathcal{N})$ are structured in the same way as those of $\mathcal{N}$, meaning that all the transitions of $\varphi(\mathcal{N})$ work under black and white modes, since they take their values from function C (i.e., $C_T = C$). The Ins function that structures the arcs of $\varphi(\mathcal{N})$ depends on the set where each arc belongs to. From Definition 10(v) follows that all the direct arcs apart from the newly added arcs and those arcs associated with the inhibitor arcs of $\mathcal{N}$ are 'inscribed' by the Cl set, which is $\{b, w\}$, carrying black and white tokens while all the other arcs carry grey and light grey tokens (complementary colours) and their inscription is $\{g, l\}$. The capacity of each place in $\varphi(\mathcal{N})$ is defined according to the capacity of the respective place in $\mathcal{N}$. If the examined place hosts a token of identity colour, then its capacity is the same as that of the respective place in $\mathcal{N}$, else it is set to 1 per special colour of token. Here, the capacity of the $\varphi(\mathcal{N})$ places is one for any colour of tokens.

Further, from Definition $10(vii)$ follows that the guards of the T_G transitions of $\varphi(\mathcal{N})$ evaluate to true for the set of *binding pairs* B_t and that the guards of the transition T_{NG} are always true. In this case, $B_t = \{(b,g),(w,l)\}$ with $f(b) = g$ and $f(w) = l$, implying that all the step transitions are equipped with guards that evaluate to true for any of these *binding pairs*. Now, regarding the initial marking of $\varphi(\mathcal{N})$, every place of $\varphi(\mathcal{N})$ retains the colours and the number of tokens that reside in the respective places of $\mathcal{N}$, except for the control places of the step places and the 'starting' place of the net, which take values from the second and third clause of the construction for the initial marking. This results in $M_0' = \{(p_0,g),(p_0,l),(p_1,b),(p_1,w),(p_4,b),(p_4,w),(p_7,g),(p_7,l),(p_8,b),(p_9, w)\}$. To complete the construction of the T-APN net $\varphi(\mathcal{N})$, the gluing places need to be defined. From Definition $10(ix)$ derives that $G' = G = \{p_1,p_2\}$ implying that the set of gluing places of $\varphi(\mathcal{N})$ is 'inherited' from $\mathcal{N}$. Finally, the constructed T-APN net $\varphi(\mathcal{N})$, associated with the given APN net $\mathcal{N}$, is shown in Fig. 8.

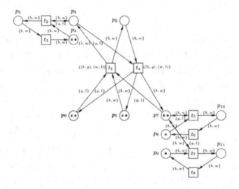

Fig. 8. The constructed T-APN net $\varphi(\mathcal{N})$ associated with the APN net $\mathcal{N}$ from Fig. 7.

Observing the two nets, their structure differs regarding the additional arcs and coloured tokens used in $\varphi(\mathcal{N})$. In terms of functioning, the two nets provide isomorphic reachability graphs showing that the transformation of APNs to T-APNs results in behaviourally equivalent nets [25].

4.2   Unfolding T-APNs into General Petri Nets

Considering that the T-APN class is a variant of the Coloured Petri Nets class, it provides a compact approach to model the intricate behaviour of ambient intelligent systems. But, many of the basic analysis techniques and tools that are used in the general Petri nets cannot be extended to this class. Therefore, the 'translation' of T-APNs into behaviourally equivalent general Petri nets is incorporated into the proposed framework by using a Coloured Petri Net unfolding technique [31]. For the past decades, Petri Net unfoldings have been widely studied regarding their construction, properties and use in different classes and system applications [5,8,15,22]. In this work, unfolding is used to facilitate the slicing of Petri nets and their model checking. The proposed framework adopts the *Liu et al* algorithm that is based on transition unfolding and is formally presented in [31].

Example of T-APNs Unfolding: The unfolding of the T-APNs is demonstrated below via the application of *Liu et al* algorithm to the T-APN net constructed out of an APN composite step net (see Fig. 8) resulting in the general Petri net of Fig. 9.

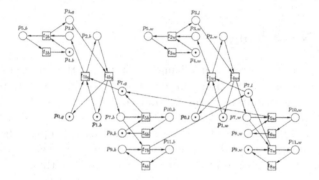

Fig. 9. The unfolded Petri net resulted from the T-APN net $\varphi(\mathcal{N})$ of Fig. 8.

The algorithm first computes all the valid bindings for each of the T-APN transitions and then a transition instance is created for each valid binding set. For example, two different instances have been created for t_1, one for the black and grey binding (i.e., $\{b,g\}$) and another for the white and light grey binding (i.e., $\{w,l\}$). In this way, all the instances of the T-APN transitions are created. Then, the pre-arcs are checked to construct the colour instances of the pre-places for the considered transitions. For instance, taking the pre-arc (p_4, t_2), the pre-place instances created are the places p_{4_b} and p_{4_w}, as the arc inscription is $\{b,w\}$ and its colours belong to the binding of the transition. This occurs since the transition has no guard, implying its evaluation to be true for any colour of the inscription. Then, the place instances are linked to the respective transitions. In this case, the places p_{4_b} and p_{4_w} are connected with the transitions t_{2b} and t_{2w} respectively. Now, considering the tokens distribution, tokens of the colours that belong to a valid transition binding are allocated to the respective place instances. For example, the marking of place p_4 in Fig. 8 shows that it hosts a black and a white token. Thus, a token is distributed to p_{4_b} and p_{4_w} of the unfolded net respectively, as shown in Fig. 9.

The same logic is followed for the post-arcs of the T-APN net to create the colour instances of the post-places of the transitions. For example, considering the post-arc (t_2, p_3), then the post-place instances created are the places p_{3_g} and p_{4_l} respectively, since the arc inscription of is $\{g, l\}$. This occurs because the transition has no guard, which means that evaluates to true for any of the colours of the inscription of the post-arc considering its colours as elements of a valid binding. Consequently, these place instances are linked to the transition instance that corresponds to the binding where each colour belongs to. The binding $\{b, g, w, l\}$ is a valid binding in this case, since transition t_2 consumes either black or white tokens from its pre-places and deposits into the post-places either grey or light grey tokens, depending on what colour token is consumed every time. Therefore, the place p_{3_g} is connected with the transition instance t_{2b} and the place p_{3_l} with t_{2w} via a post-arc each. Finally, the token allocation of the post-places follows exactly the same rationale as that used for the pre-places.

5   Petri Net Slicing

In [38], M. Weiser introduced slicing to improve the program debugging by removing non-essential program parts and keeping only those of interest (based on the examined variables and code lines). This technique gained great attention in the recent years motivating the creation of several slicing approaches [6,7,21,29]. Recently, Petri net community adopted slicing to alleviate the state explosion problem caused by the model checking of Petri net models. This resulted in the introduction of various algorithms for the efficient slicing of different Petri net classes, addressing the aforementioned problem [10,19,21,30,32,33]. Petri nets slicing is defined as a syntactic technique that slices a model based on given properties. It is worth noting that the slicing algorithm integrated in this framework is the *abstract slicing*, which is formally defined and described by Khan et al. in [20].

Abstract Slicing Algorithm: In general, the abstract slicing algorithm starts with a Petri net model and a slicing criterion $Q \subseteq P$ containing place(s) and builds a Petri net slice based on Q. In more detail, the algorithm takes as input an unfolded T-APN net and the slicing criterion place(s). Initially, the set of transitions that represent the slice transitions (i.e., T') are extracted including all the pre and post-transitions of the criterion place(s), which correspond to non-reading transitions only[16]. Also, the set of places that represents the slice places (i.e., P') contains all the pre-places of the transitions in T'. The algorithm then iteratively adds other preset transitions together with their preset places to

---

[16] Informally, *reading transitions* do not change the marking of a net place, while non-reading transitions can change it [33].

T' and P' respectively. Finally, the neutral transitions[17] are identified and their pre and post-places are merged to one place together with their markings.

To demonstrate its application to the unfolded T-APNs, the net of Fig. 9 is considered. The algorithm gets this net as input along with the criterion places, which are extracted from the properties examined. To support the application of the *abstract slicing algorithm,* a stand alone tool named *SLiM*[18] developed using a Java-based GUI to slice and represent unfolded T- APNs [18].

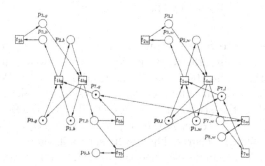

Fig. 10. Petri net Slice by *Abstract Slicing Algorithm*

The properties of interest for this example can be informally expressed as follows:

ϕ_1: *"The system always receives a detection signal after every user's action".*
ϕ_2: *"Eventually the system receives information after a user's action or the system's response".*

Formally, these two properties can be specified in the Computation Tree Logic (CTL) as:
$\phi_1 = \mathbf{AG}((p_{2\_b} \wedge \neg p_{1\_b} \wedge \neg p_{3\_g}) \implies p_{3\_b})$ and
$\phi_2 = \mathbf{EF}((p_{3\_b} \wedge p_{3\_w}) \mid (p_{3\_g} \wedge p_{3\_l}))$

Considering the generation of only one slice for these two properties, the slicing criterion $Q = \{p_{3\_b}, p_{3\_w}, p_{3\_g}, p_{3\_l}\}$ is chosen as all these places are concerned by both of them. The resultant sliced Petri net is observed in Fig. 10, which is smaller than the original T-APN net.

6   Evaluation

In this section, the size of the generated state space is examined in respect to the models produced by the different stages of this framework. Hence, four

---

[17] Neutral transitions remove and add the same no. of tokens from and to its incoming and outgoing place respectively [20].
[18] *SLiM* reads/exports unfolded nets using the Petri Net Markup Language (*PNML*) defined by the standard ISO/IEC 15909.

benchmark case studies are considered referring to ambient intelligent systems with different characteristics and behaviours. These systems are: 1) an *ambient garage*, 2) an *ambient conference room*, 3) a smart extra care home and 4) a smart kitchen, the specifications of which are described in [12,17,25,26]. To evaluate the state space required for the verification of each Petri net model, different CTL properties were examined against these models using model checking. These properties are divided into two classes i.e., 1) the *safety* properties and 2) the *liveness* properties, which are mainly expressed by the **G** and **F** temporal operator respectively followed by the propositions[19].

Comparing the State Space: Having checked CTL properties for each case study, we conduct a comparative evaluation of the created state space required for their verification. The state space construction for each Petri net model is based on both the single and maximal step analysis. The calculation of the state space also considers the stubborn and non-stubborn reduction. Moreover, the number of states required to verify the properties ϕ_1 and ϕ_2 of the four systems is presented in the following charts. The results shown in those charts are organised into two categories, the single step and the maximal step construction with and without stubborn reduction respectively.

The single step construction generates the state space of the different Petri net models considering only the single actions that are conducted throughout the operation of the observed systems. On the contrary, the maximal step construction takes into account only the actions that are performed exclusively under the maximum possible concurrency omitting any intermediate levels of it. Finally, in some cases, the notion of the stubborn sets, introduced in [36], is considered for the reduction of the state space in both the T-APNs and the general Petri nets. Informally, this state space reduction relies on the computation of stubborn sets for each state of the system, where the only transitions included are the enabled ones of the stubborn sets. This idea is based on the mutual interaction of transitions and the Petri net concurrency.

Interpreting the results of the single step construction for the state space of each model (shown in Fig. 11), a considerable reduction of the state space is observed when using the sliced unfolded model generated by the *abstract slicing algorithm*. It is also worth noting that the number of states required for the verification of the properties ϕ_1 and ϕ_2 for all the systems is significantly smaller in the sliced models regardless of considering the stubborn reduction or not for the generation of the state space.

For example, taking into account the chart of Fig. 11(a), the state space required for the verification of the examined ϕ_1 property for the ambient garage, ambient conference room, Extra Care Home and Smart Kitchen is 56336, 183707, 137057 and 75321 states for the T-APN model respectively. Similarly for the respective unfolded models of those systems, where the same number of states is required for the properties to be model checked; while their sliced models need only 144, 882, 324 and 512 states for the model checking, respectively. This

---

[19] The case studies and properties can be found in [27].

reveals that slicing can efficiently deal with the state space reduction dropping the number of states dramatically. The same observation occurs for the charts (b), (c) and (d) of Fig. 11, where the sliced models consist of the smaller number of states for all the examined systems, compared to the other two cases.

Now, analysing the results of Fig. 12, it is observed that even in the case of the maximal concurrency where the state space is already smaller than that of the single step construction (as the single actions are discarded), the abstract slicing algorithm improves further the size of the state space required for the properties' verification since it provides the smaller number of states according to the charts.

For instance, in chart (d) of Fig. 12, the state space required for the verification of the examined ϕ_2 property for the ambient garage, ambient conference room, Extra Care Home and Smart Kitchen is 52, 137, 144 and 92 states for the T-APN model respectively, while for the unfolded model, 52, 80, 138 and 88 states are required. Finally, the sliced models of the systems need 15, 37, 30 and 41 states for the property to be model checked, respectively. This indicates that even in the case that the state space is reasonably small, the slicing can reduce it further by generating a state space that is even smaller compared to the closest one. In terms of savings, this reduction can have a strong impact on the time and memory needed for the model checking of properties.

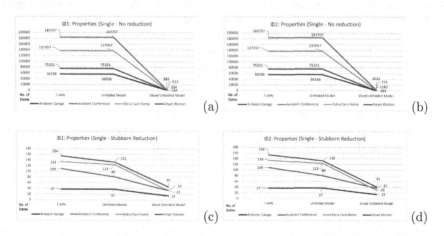

Fig. 11. Single step construction of state space with and without stubborn reduction for properties ϕ_1 & ϕ_2

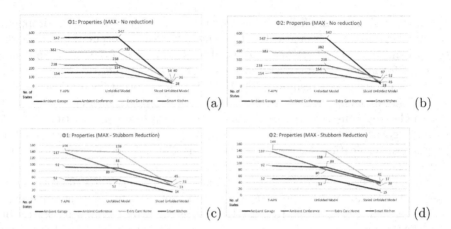

Fig. 12. Maximal step construction of state space with and without stubborn reduction for properties ϕ_1 & ϕ_2

7 Conclusion

This work introduced a modelling and verification framework that can be efficiently used for the formal analysis of the ambient intelligent systems. Specifically, it comprises several stages that combine the use of different Petri net classes. This approach enhances the behavioural analysis of the activities taking place at this kind of systems by incorporating the modelling features and verification techniques employed by these classes. Finally, the aim of this framework is to enable the use of several modelling and verification techniques that are applied to different classes of Petri nets offering the flexibility to use a wide range of tools to model and verify behaviourally equivalent nets. This implies that the user can follow the different stages of the proposed approach to the extent that is dictated by the system modelling and verification requirements.

References

1. Anisimov, N., Kovalenko. A.: Asynchronous composition of petri nets via places. In: Proceedings of 2nd AP Ershov International Memorial Conference on Perspectives of System Informatics, pp. 214–219 (1996)
2. Augusto, J.C.: Ambient intelligence: the confluence of ubiquitous/pervasive computing and artificial intelligence, pp. 213–234. Springer, London (2007). https://doi.org/10.1007/978-1-84628-943-9_11
3. Augusto, J.C.: Ambient intelligence: Basic concepts and applications. In Filipe, J., Shishkov, B., Helfert, M., (eds.) Software and Data Technologies, pp. 16–26 (2008)
4. Augusto, J.C.: Past, present and future of ambient intelligence and smart environments. In: Filipe, J., Fred, A., Sharp, B., (eds.) Agents and Artificial Intelligence, pp. 3–15 (2010)
5. Baldan, P., Haar, S., König, B.: Distributed unfolding of petri nets. In: Foundations of Software Science and Computation Structures, pp. 126–141 (2006)

6. Binkley, D.: The application of program slicing to regression testing. Inf. Softw. Technol. **40**(11), 583–594 (1998)
7. Binkley, D.W., Gallagher, K.B.: Program slicing, volume 43. Advances in Computers, pp. 1–50. Elsevier (1996)
8. Bonet, B., Haslum, P., Hickmott, S., Thiébaux, S.: Directed unfolding of petri nets. Trans. Petri Nets Other Mod. Concurrency **I**, 172–198 (2008)
9. Cardelli, L., Gordon, A.D.: Mobile ambients. Theoret. Comput. Sci. **240**(1), 177–213 (2000)
10. Chang, J., Richardson, D.: Static and dynamic specification slicing. In: Proceedings of the Fourth Irvine Software Symposium (1994)
11. Cook, D.J., Crandall, A.S., Thomas, B.L., Krishnan, N.C.: Casas: A smart home in a box. Computer **46**(7), 62–69 (2013)
12. Garcia-Constantino, M., Konios, A., Nugent, C.: Modelling activities of daily living with petri nets. In: 2018 IEEE International Conference on Pervasive Computing and Communications Workshops (PerCom Workshops), pp. 866–871 (March 2018)
13. Harrison, M.D., Kray, C., Sun, Z., Zhang, H.: Factoring user experience into the design of ambient and mobile systems. In: Engineering Interactive Systems, pp. 243–259 (2008)
14. Harrison, M.D., Massink, M.: Modelling interactive experience, function and performance in ubiquitous systems. Electron. Notes Theoret. Comput. Sci. **261**, 23–42 (2010)
15. Hayman, J., Winskel, G.: The unfolding of general Petri nets. In: IARCS Annual Conference on Foundations of Software Technology and Theoretical Computer Science, vol. 2. Leibniz International Proceedings in Informatics (LIPIcs), pp. 223–234 (2008)
16. Iliasov, A., Romanovsky, A., Arief, B., Laibinis, L., Troubitsyna, E.: On rigorous design and implementation of fault tolerant ambient systems. In: 10th IEEE International Symposium on Object and Component-Oriented Real-Time Distributed Computing, pp. 141–145 (2007)
17. Jing, Y., Eastwood, M., Tan, B., Konios, A., Hamid, A., Collinson, M.: An intelligent well-being monitoring system for residents in extra care homes. In: Proceedings of the 1st International Conference on Internet of Things and Machine Learning, IML 2017, pp. 8:1–8:6 (2017)
18. Khan, Y.: Slim - a slicing tool. https://bit.ly/2GAGwO1
19. Khan, Y.I.: Optimizing verification of structurally evolving algebraic petri nets. In: Gorbenko, A., Romanovsky, A., Kharchenko, V. (eds.) SERENE 2013. LNCS, vol. 8166, pp. 64–78. Springer, Heidelberg (2013). https://doi.org/10.1007/978-3-642-40894-6_6
20. Khan, Y., Guelfi, N.: Slicing high-level petri nets. In: International Workshop on Petri Nets and Software Engineering (PNSE 2014), pp. 201–220 (2014)
21. Khan, Y.I., Konios, A., Guelfi, N.: A survey of petri nets slicing. ACM Comput. Surv. **51**(5), 109:1–109:32 (2018)
22. Khomenko, V., Koutny, M.: Towards an efficient algorithm for unfolding petri nets. In: Larsen, K.G., Nielsen, M. (eds.) CONCUR 2001. LNCS, vol. 2154, pp. 366–380. Springer, Heidelberg (2001). https://doi.org/10.1007/3-540-44685-0_25
23. Konios, A.: Ambient systems and taxonomy approaches. Technical report, CS-TR-1281, School of Computing Science, Newcastle University (2011)
24. Konios, A.:Modelling ambient systems with petri nets. In: Proceedings of the 13th International Conference on Application of Concurrency to System Design (ACSD), pp. 247–251 (2013)

25. Konios, A.: Modelling and Verification of Ambient Systems using Petri Nets. PhD thesis (2015)
26. Konios, A., Jing, Y., Eastwood, M., Tan, B.: Unifying and analysing activities of daily living in extra care homes. In: 2018 IEEE 16th Intl Conf on Dependable, Autonomic and Secure Computing, 16th International Conference on Pervasive Intelligence and Computing, 4th International Conference on Big Data Intelligence and Computing and Cyber Science and Technology Congress(DASC/PiCom/DataCom/CyberSciTech), pp. 474–479 (2018)
27. Konios, A., Khan, Y.I.: Modelling and verification of activities in ambient intelligent systems. https://bit.ly/2O58iXg
28. Konios, A., Pietkiewicz-Koutny, M.: Modelling ambient systems with coloured petri nets. Technical report, School of Computing Science, Newcastle University (2013)
29. Korel, B., Laski, J.: Dynamic slicing of computer programs. J. Syst. Softw. **13**(3), 187–195 (1990)
30. Lee, W., Kim, H., Cha, S., Kwon, Y.: A slicing-based approach to enhance petri net reachability analysis. J. Res. Pract. Inform. Technol. **32**, 131–143 (2000)
31. Liu, F., Heiner, M., Yang, M.: An efficient method for unfolding colored petri nets. In: Proceedings of the 2012 Winter Simulation Conference (WSC), pp. 1–12 (2012)
32. Llorens, M., Oliver, J., Silva, J., Tamarit, S., Vidal, G.: Dynamic slicing techniques for petri nets. Electron. Notes Theor. Comput. Sci. **223**, 153–165 (2008)
33. Rakow, A.: Safety slicing petri nets. In: Haddad, S., Pomello, L. (eds.) PETRI NETS 2012. LNCS, vol. 7347, pp. 268–287. Springer, Heidelberg (2012). https://doi.org/10.1007/978-3-642-31131-4_15
34. Reisig, W.: Simple composition of nets. In: Proceedings of Applications and Theory of Petri Nets: 30th International Conference, PETRI NETS 2009, pp. 23–42 (2009)
35. Silva, Ó. J.L., Ribeiro, R., Fernandes, J.M., Campos, J.C., Harrison, M.D.: The apex framework: Prototyping of ubiquitous environments based on petri nets. In: Human-Centred Software Engineering, pp. 6–21 (2010)
36. Valmari, A.: Stubborn sets for reduced state space generation. Adv. Petri Nets **1990**, 491–515 (1991)
37. Want, R., Pering, T.: System challenges for ubiquitous & pervasive computing. In: Proceedings of the 27th International Conference on Software Engineering, ICSE 2005, pp. 9–14 (2005)
38. Weiser, M.: Program slicing. In: Proceedings of the 5th International Conference on Software Engineering, ICSE 1981, pp. 439–449 (1981)

An Analysis and Review of Maintenance-Related Commercial Aviation Accidents and Incidents

Neelakshi Majumdar[1]([✉]) [iD], Divya Bhargava[2] [iD], Tracy El Khoury[3],
Karen Marais[1] [iD], and Vincent G. Duffy[1]

[1] Purdue University, West Lafayette, IN 47907, USA
{nmajumda,kmarais,duffy}@purdue.edu
[2] Drexel University, Philadelphia, PA 19104, USA
db3493@drexel.edu
[3] Oliver Wyman CAVOK, Atlanta, GA 30354, USA

Abstract. Maintenance issues in commercial aviation are one of the major causes of flight delays and cancellations. Presently, there is a gap in our knowledge about the current state of aviation maintenance safety. Specifically, we do not know the following: (1) What is the status of maintenance errors in commercial aviation accidents? (2) What issues dominate, and has that changed? Are new issues arising, for example, as composites become more prevalent? (3) What proactive and reactive methods are used to identify aviation maintenance risks, maintainer errors, and conditions? We addressed these questions by reviewing the tools, programs, and methods developed in the past three decades to reduce aviation maintenance errors. Next, we analyzed the NTSB reports for six maintenance-related accidents and 25 serious incidents in U.S. commercial aviation from 2009–2018. Fourteen reports cited incorrect service of aircraft parts, and five reports cited inadequate inspection. We compared our findings with previously published findings from the 14 maintenance-related accidents in 1998–2008. We found new factors that were not cited in the 1998–2008 accidents, such as incorrect decision-making or judgment by maintenance personnel. Finally, we discussed the current regulatory approaches in the United States to address maintenance errors.

Keywords: Commercial aviation maintenance · Aviation maintenance risk · Aviation safety · Aviation maintenance human factors

1 Introduction

The aviation maintenance system aims to ensure safe and reliable air transportation. Safety is compromised when maintenance errors such as inadequate inspection, installation errors, or failure to follow procedures occur. Maintenance issues are one of the major causes of flight delays and cancellations. Marx (1998) estimated that maintenance issues cost the U.S. aviation industry over $1 billion annually. Hobbs (2008) estimated that the cancellation of a Boeing 747–400 flight may cost an airline around $140,000, while a delay at the gate costs an average of $17,000 per hour. Further, maintenance errors lay financial burdens on companies in case of accidents. Almost 27% of fatal commercial aviation accidents from 1998–2008 involved maintenance related errors (Marais & Robichaud, 2012). These accidents are 6.5 times more likely to be fatal than accidents in general, leading to 3.6 times more fatalities, on average.

Researchers have conducted studies in the past three decades to address safety issues in commercial aviation maintenance. Industries and researchers have developed and implemented various strategies to improve aviation maintenance safety using reactive and proactive measures. Reactive measures identify safety issues following unwanted outcomes such as accidents and incidents. Proactive measures identify unsafe conditions or hazards within an organization that may lead to accidents or incidents. For example, reactive measures involve analyzing historical events, such as identifying maintenance errors in accidents, and proactive measures include safety training and creating policies or procedures.

One approach to identifying maintenance errors is by analyzing historical accident reports. In the U.S., the National Transportation Safety Board (NTSB) investigates all civil aviation accidents and selected incidents. After concluding their investigation, the NTSB publishes a final report, which includes a summary analysis of the accident, a discussion of the probable cause and findings, and other related information on personnel and aircraft (NTSB, 2023). The NTSB also uses a coding system to record events that led to these accidents and incidents, and their causes and factors in their database.

Previously, researchers analyzed accident and incident reports recorded in the NTSB database. For example, researchers have applied the Human Factors Analysis and Classification System-Maintenance Extension (HFACS-ME) framework on accident narratives to identify human factors and incorrect maintainer acts. The HFACS-ME framework describes human error as four failure categories: (1) management conditions; (2) maintainer conditions; (3) working conditions; and (4) maintainer acts (Schmidt et al., 2003; Boquet et al., 2004; Rashid et al., 2010; Illankoon et al., 2019). Most of these studies found organizational issues (e.g., inadequate supervision) and maintainer acts (e.g., installation errors) as the primary contributing factors to maintenance accidents. The most recent U.S. commercial aviation accident analysis considered accidents up to 2008 (Marais & Robichaud, 2012). Further, very few literature surveys have been published to present the state of commercial aviation maintenance (Latorella et al., 2000; Shanmugam & Robert, 2015; Mendes et al., 2022).

Presently, there is a gap in our knowledge about the state of aviation maintenance safety. Specifically, we do not know the following: (1) What is the status of maintenance errors in commercial aviation accidents? (2) What issues dominate, and has that changed? Are new issues arising, for example, as composites become more prevalent? (3) What proactive and reactive methods are used to identify aviation maintenance risks, maintainer errors, and conditions? We address these questions by analyzing 31 commercial aviation accidents and incidents from 2009–2018. Then, we compare the findings from the accidents and incidents in 2009–2018 with those in 1998–2008 (from a previous study). Next, we review current efforts for identifying, reporting, and managing human errors in aviation maintenance. We conclude this paper by discussing other potential approaches, such as regulatory methods, and the existing approaches for addressing maintenance error causes.

2 Analysis of Maintenance-Related Accidents and Incidents

This section analyzes commercial aviation maintenance-related accidents and incidents in 2009–2018 from the NTSB database. Section 2.1 describes our method of identifying and analyzing maintenance-related accidents and incidents from the NTSB database. In Sect. 2.2, we discuss our results from the analysis.

2.1 Using the NTSB Coding System to Identify Maintenance-Related Accidents and Incidents

The FAA (49 CFR 830.2) defines an accident as an "occurrence associated with the operation of an aircraft that takes place between the time any person boards the aircraft with the intention of flight and all such persons have disembarked, and in which any person suffers death, or serious injury, or in which the aircraft receives substantial damage" (CFR, 2023). An incident is an occurrence other than an accident, associated with the operation of an aircraft, which affects or could affect the safety of operations (CFR, 2023). After completing an accident or incident investigation, the NTSB records them in its database using a set of codes for occurrences and findings. The occurrence codes describe major defining events, and the finding codes describe the contributing factors of the accidents and incidents. The NTSB uses modifier codes with the finding codes to further describe the findings.

Our dataset consists of accidents and incidents that involved fixed-wing aircraft operating under Part 121 of the Title 14, Code of Federal Regulations (CFR). Part 121 operations are "commercial, passenger-carrying operations limited to controlled, towered airports and airspace that provide radar, navigation, weather, ground, and maintenance support" (NTSB, 2009).

Identifying maintenance-related accidents and incidents. The NTSB database has a downloadable M.S. Access dataset. The access file has a "data dictionary" table that contains all the codes that the investigators use for reporting accidents. We sifted through the data dictionary to identify codes that described maintenance-related issues by searching for "maintenance," "service," and "inspection" and their derivatives (e.g., "maintain"). Table 1 shows all the codes we identified from the NTSB data dictionary. In Table 1, 'XX' in the finding code *010105XX: maintenance/inspections* represents five different errors under maintenance/inspections that range from *00: general* to *50: unscheduled maintenance checks*. Similarly, *020615XX: inspection* includes four types of inspection errors (from *00: general* to *20: scheduled/routine inspection*), and *020620XX: maintenance* includes eight types of maintenance errors (from *00: general* to *40: unauthorized maintenance/repair*). We identified all part 121 accidents and incidents in 2009–2018 that cited any of these listed codes in their reports.

From 2009–2018, the NTSB recorded 255 Part 121 accidents. Two of these accidents were fatal, with a total of 52 fatalities. The NTSB also investigated 96 incidents from 2009–2018. Six accidents (3.1%) and 25 incidents (26.1%) from 2009–2018 were maintenance-related. None of the maintenance-related accidents were fatal. Of the 25 maintenance incidents, 19 had minor aircraft damage, and six had no damage. Figures 1 and 2 show the contribution of maintenance related errors to the number of accidents and incidents in 2009–2018, respectively.

Table 1. List of NTSB Maintenance-related Codes with Descriptions

Finding Code	Description
010105XX	Maintenance/inspections
020615XX	Inspection
020620XX	Maintenance
02062515	Record-keeping-Aircraft/maintenance logs
04023025	Scheduling-Maintenance scheduling
04032020	Oversight-Oversight of maintenance
04033025	Documentation/record keeping-Maintenance records
Occurrence Code	**Description**
20	Aircraft servicing event
40	Aircraft maintenance event
50	Aircraft inspection event
Modifier Code	**Description**
13	Incorrect service/maintenance
14	Not serviced/maintained
15	Inadequate inspection
16	Not inspected
18	Related maintenance information
41	Maintenance personnel
65	Maintenance provider

2.2 Analyzing Accidents and Incidents Using the NTSB Codes

We determined how often the maintenance-related NTSB codes were cited in the accident and incident reports in 2009–2018, as shown in Figs. 3 and 4, respectively.

Two of the six maintenance-related accidents cited inadequate scheduled/routine maintenance by maintenance personnel, and one accident cited inadequate decision-making/judgment by maintenance personnel. One accident cited the occurrence code *40: aircraft maintenance event.* Two accidents cited inadequate inspection of aircraft parts (escape slide and main landing gear), and one accident cited incorrect service/maintenance of the main fuselage structure. There is not much information specified in the database codes that would differentiate between the meaning of inadequate inspection and incorrect service/maintenance. One accident cited the finding code *101052018: scheduled maintenance checks—related maintenance information.* This modifier code *related maintenance information* does not provide any specific information about the issues in the scheduled maintenance checks.

The NTSB coding system groups finding codes based on categories and sub-categories with similar issues. For example, in the finding code 0102321015, the first two digits, 01, stand for the *Aircraft* category, and the next two digits, 02, for the *aircraft*

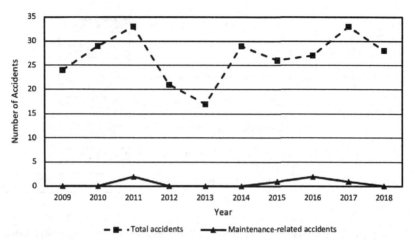

Fig. 1. Number of total Part 121 airplane accidents versus the number of maintenance-related accidents in 2009–2018.

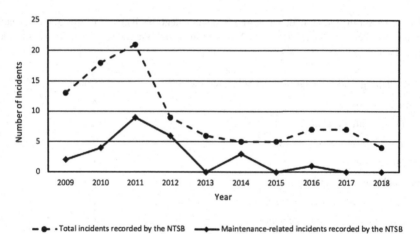

Fig. 2. Number of total Part 121 airplane incidents versus the number of maintenance-related accidents recorded in the NTSB database in 2009–2018. Note that this number does not represent the total number of incidents in that period. The NTSB investigates only a select few incidents each year.

systems sub-category. Table 2 shows the count of finding codes categories listed as causes and contributing factors in the six maintenance-related accidents from 2009–2018.

The NTSB mentioned issues such as fatigue, failure, and inadequate inspection with the code sub-categories of aircraft systems and structures in the accident reports. Sub-categories such as task performance issues, lack of experience, and improper action/decision were cited with personnel issues in the reports. We found one accident that cited the management issues of inadequate policy or procedures by the airline operator.

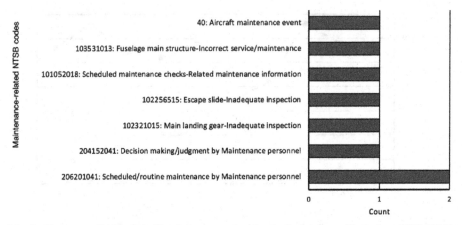

Fig. 3. Frequency distribution of maintenance-related codes in the six accidents from 2009–2018. Since multiple codes can be listed for each accident, the total count is not equal to the total number of accidents.

Table 2. Count of finding code categories and sub-categories listed as causes and contributing factors in maintenance-related accidents. Note that since multiple codes are cited for each accident, the total sum is not equal to six.

NTSB Finding Codes Categories and Sub-categories	Count
Aircraft-Aircraft systems	6
Aircraft-Aircraft structures	2
Personnel issues-Task performance	2
Aircraft-Aircraft handling/service	1
Personnel issues-Action/decision	1
Personnel issues-Experience/knowledge	1
Organizational issues-Management	1

Figure 4 shows the frequency distribution of maintenance-related codes in the 25 incidents from 2009–2018. The NTSB cited the modifier code *13: Incorrect service/maintenance* of various aircraft parts (such as brakes and main landing gear) most frequently. Similarly, *15: Inadequate inspection* was cited three times in the incidents. The NTSB used the modifier code *41: maintenance personnel* 12 times with different finding codes that describe maintainer conditions and acts. Installation errors by maintenance personnel were cited most frequently (in three incidents). One incident cited the code *402101565: Adequacy of policy/procedures by maintenance provider,* which conveys deficiencies in the organization. Further, four incidents listed the occurrence code *40: Aircraft maintenance event,* and one listed *20: Aircraft servicing event.*

Table 3 shows the count of finding code categories and sub-categories listed as causes and contributing factors in the 25 maintenance-related incidents. The NTSB

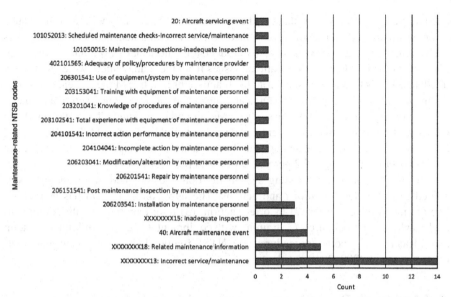

Fig. 4. Frequency distribution of maintenance-related codes in the 25 incidents from 2009–2018. The "XXXXXXXX" in the NTSB codes represents the first eight digits in the finding code used with the modifier codes 13, 15, and 18 that represent aircraft parts such as 1023210: Main landing gear. Since multiple codes can be listed for each accident, the total count is not equal to the total accidents.

Table 3. Count of finding code categories and sub-categories listed as causes and contributing factors in the 25 maintenance-related incidents. Note that since multiple codes are cited for each accident, the total sum is not equal to 25.

NTSB Finding Codes Categories and Sub-categories	Count
Aircraft-Aircraft systems	19
Aircraft-Aircraft powerplant	15
Aircraft-Aircraft structures	8
Personnel issues-Task performance	7
Organizational issues-Management	6
Personnel issues-Experience/knowledge	3
Aircraft-Fluid/miscellaneous hardware	5
Personnel issues-Action/decision	3
Organizational issues-Development	1
Organizational issues-Support/oversight/monitoring	1
Aircraft-Aircraft handling/service	1

cited aircraft systems, powerplant, and structures most frequently with modifiers such as failure, damaged, malfunction, and incorrect service/maintenance. Personnel issues such as improper task performance, action/decision, and lack of experience were cited 13 times in the incidents. Organizational issues from the management were cited in six incidents. The NTSB cited issues from the manufacturer in five of these incidents where the management's policy or procedures and the design of documents were inadequate.

Comparing our results with the study by Marais and Robichaud (2012), we found that the proportion of maintenance accidents decreased slightly from 4.11% in 1999–2008 to 2.35% in 2009–2018. The average number of fatalities also significantly decreased in 2009–2018 to, on average, 5.2 per year from 18.8 per year in 1999–2008.

The NTSB changed its coding system in 2008 and included more finding codes related to personnel conditions and actions. The new coding system has new codes like (1) incomplete action; (2) incorrect action; (3) total experience with equipment; (4) knowledge of procedures; (5) training with equipment; (6) use of equipment/system; and (7) adequacy of policy/procedures. The NTSB frequently used these new personnel-related codes in 2009–2018 accidents.

3   Methods to Detect Human Error in Maintenance

In 2009–2018, the NTSB cited only codes describing the maintainer's experience/knowledge and action/decision. Although the NTSB has unique codes to describe maintainer conditions (e.g., mental state and alertness) and working conditions (e.g., workspace lighting), those codes do not appear in the accident reports. The absence of citing maintainer and their working conditions in accident and incident reports does not necessarily indicate that accidents and incidents rarely involve these conditions. Researchers have argued that these underlying conditions often lead to improper maintainer acts (Drury, 1991; Latorella & Prabhu, 2000).

Recently, Mendes et al. (2022) conducted a literature review on risk management in aviation maintenance. They discussed proactive and predictive measures (using artificial intelligence and machine learning tools) to mitigate aviation maintenance risks. They found that although researchers mostly use reactive measures, there has been a growing emphasis on proactive and predictive analysis methods to mitigate aviation risks. Latorella and Prabhu (2000) conducted a review of reactive measures. In this section, we review methods that aim to detect human error and the causes of those errors using reactive measures. We discuss the applicability of the methods explained by Latorella and Prabhu (2000) and any modifications to these methods. Additionally, we extend their review by adding new methods developed since their paper was published.

Figure 5 summarizes the methods that we discuss in this section.

3.1   Accident and Incident Investigations

Despite being a major contributor to improving aviation safety, accident data on maintenance-related errors usually reveals few details on underlying conditions such as maintainer and working conditions (Schmidt et al., 2003). The International Civil Aviation Organization's (ICAO) accident investigation manual recommends delving into

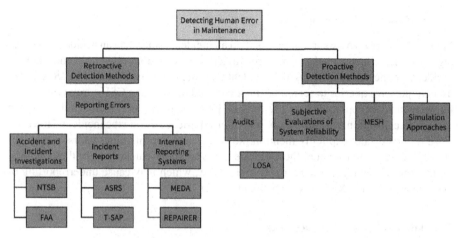

Fig. 5. Different methods for detecting human error in maintenance

these underlying factors when investigating maintenance-related accidents and incidents (ICAO, 2011). Although the manual provides a detailed list of potential issues in maintainer and working conditions, it is often challenging for investigators to detect these underlying factors. While pilot or controller errors, if left uncorrected, usually propagate rapidly, maintainer errors may occur and remain undetected for days, months, or even years before the resulting accident (Kanki, 2010). For example, Japan Airlines Flight 123 experienced a sudden cabin decompression due to a fatigue failure of the Boeing 747's aft pressure bulkhead (Aircraft Accident Investigation Commission, 1987). The fatigue failure happened due to the faulty repair of the pressure bulkhead in Tokyo seven years before the accident. In other words, maintenance errors exhibit latency with respect to incidents and accidents. This latency means that a maintainer's memory of events during servicing of the accident aircraft may start fading, and some of the underlying factors contributing to the human error may get lost in the investigation process (Latorella & Prabhu, 2000; ICAO, 2011).

Additionally, maintenance tasks may not be limited to one technician or even one geographical location. When maintenance occurs over multiple days, shifts, and locations, it may be difficult for investigators to find and isolate the specific personnel conditions that caused those errors (Latorella & Prabhu, 2000; Johnston et al., 1994).

Given the time delay between the occurrence of an error and its detection, it may be difficult for investigators to track the personnel who made the error. Further, personnel may not even be aware that they made an error. As a result, they do not report their error, making it challenging to identify the underlying causes of these errors using reports from self-reporting programs such as NASA's Aviation Safety Reporting System (ASRS) (Johnston et al., 1994). Additionally, a lack of recorded data sources, such as voice recorders in aircraft maintenance, does not provide more insight into personnel or working conditions (Johnston et al., 1994). These challenges limit the information available regarding personnel-related underlying conditions involved with maintenance errors.

3.2 FAA Incident Reports

Maintenance errors may sometimes result in an incident rather than an accident. Analyzing these incidents may help identify the underlying conditions that could contribute to accidents in the future. The FAA's Accident and Incident Data System (AIDS) enables users to perform queries to search for incidents and download a CSV format of the preliminary incident reports (FAA, 2023). Each FAA incident report includes information such as date, location, aircraft details, and pilot experience during the incident. However, these reports do not explicitly mention the causes and contributing factors in the incidents. The freeform format of these reports limits an empirical analysis of these reports. Further, not all incidents are reported to the FAA, which may cause underreporting of maintenance events (Marais & Robichaud, 2012).

3.3 Anonymous Incident Reports

Confidential reporting systems such as NASA's Aviation Safety Reporting System (ASRS) and Technical Operations Safety Action Program (T-SAP) allow aviation personnel to report unsafe conditions. Analyses of the ASRS self-reports revealed patterns of errors and conditions among maintainers that are otherwise difficult to detect from the NTSB reports (Patankar & Taylor, 2008; Bao & Ding, 2014; Hobbs & Kanki, 2008). For example, in a study of 939 ASRS reports, the top underlying conditions were lack of awareness, complacency, time constraints, lack of knowledge or experience, and workplace distractions (Patankar & Taylor, 2008).

Although there is a mechanism for maintenance personnel to report incidents in the ASRS, pilots are this system's primary and major users. Aircraft maintenance technicians (AMTs) reports are much less frequent than pilot reports (Latorella & Prabhu, 2000). However, since maintenance/inspection issues may also arise from pilot-initiated reports, analyzing the ASRS database can provide meaningful insights into the role of human factors and underlying causes that contribute to maintenance-related incidents.

Researchers have suggested that a system specifically for aviation inspection and maintenance technicians might be more efficient in detecting maintenance-related errors (Latorella & Prabhu, 2000). Other reporting systems, such as T-SAP, Aviation Safety Action Program (ASAP), and the Voluntary Disclosure Reporting Program (VDRP), allow technicians and repair stations to report potential safety hazards voluntarily. The FAA has made T-SAP available in some areas of the U.S. since 2011. In the first three years of implementing the program, T-SAP reports contributed to over a hundred safety improvements (FAA, 2012).

3.4 Internal Reporting Systems

One way to identify the underlying causes of aviation maintenance errors is to collect data directly from maintainers by creating questionnaires. Previous studies focus on questionnaires for aircraft maintenance technicians (AMTs) from different airlines to include cases and questions about personnel-related underlying conditions (Chiu & Hseih, 2016; Signal et al., 2019; Watson & Johnson, 2001; Hobbs & Williamson, 2003). The studies helped to identify factors such as AMTs' adverse psychological conditions and fatigue. According to AMTs at a Taiwanese airline, maintenance capabilities such as lack of experience and physical/mental limitations are the most significant factors for rule-based mistakes (Chiu & Hseih, 2016). Hobbs and Williamson (2003) found that most maintenance incidents happen due to personnel-related factors such as unusual time pressure, inadequate training, and fatigue. Fatigue has been identified as a significant contributing factor in many studies. For example, 22% of 966 AMTs at one airline indicated making work errors due to tiredness in the last month (Signal et al., 2019).

Similarly, 30% of 499 AMTs in another study showed that fatigue negatively impacts job performance (Watson & Johnson, 2001). Half of these AMTs felt they worked under inadequate lighting conditions for much of their working time. Additionally, the AMTs indicated that inadequate light conditions and high temperatures at the workplace negatively impacted their job performance. Moreover, 70% AMTs at a large airline reported receiving no education from their maintenance sites on personal strategies for coping with the effects of shift work (Signal et al., 2019).

Literature suggests that studies such as questionnaires and self-generated reports that get maintainers' perspectives facilitate a more in-depth understanding of personnel conditions than analyses that rely only on historical investigation data. One way to get maintainers' perspectives is by directly interacting with them and using a no-blame approach, such as the maintenance Aviation Safety Action Program (ASAP), which is meant to permit maintenance personnel to report errors without fear of discipline. Another approach is to survey and interview maintainers where they can share their experiences related to maintenance issues and errors. Majumdar & Marais (2022) conducted a similar study where they surveyed pilots using the Human Factors Analysis and Classification System (HFACS) framework to identify the role of human factors in General Aviation loss of control incidents. The findings from the investigations may be valuable in providing more context to the maintenance errors. By investigating maintenance errors in context, it may be possible to better understand their origins and facilitate the development of interventions (Hobbs & Kanki, 2008).

4 How Can We Prevent the Causes and Maintenance Errors?

Companies have designed investigation tools and modeling techniques to better understand and address the human factors that lead to maintenance errors to ensure safer maintenance practices in their facilities. In 1990, Pan American World Airways addressed its aging aircraft agenda by training its maintenance management in assertive and open communication techniques that had proven effective on the flight deck (Taylor, 2000). This initiative was the first case of training for open communication in maintenance. Boeing published guidance documents and organizational procedures in their Maintenance Error Decision Aid (MEDA), which later became a widely used tool in the airline industry (Rankin et al., 2000). The industry also started shifting away from a blame culture. In 1992, the International Association of Machinists and Aerospace Workers (IAM/AW) worked with the FAA and the U.S. Airways Management to eliminate maintenance paperwork error sources in a way that did not punish workers (Taylor, 2000). The organizations identified the most critical paperwork error sources by conducting focus groups with technicians. They provided recommendations to eliminate them, which paved the way for the development of maintenance resource management (MRM) training in 2000 by the FAA. MRM is a program that aims to foster collaboration and communication for maintenance safety (Taylor, 2000).

Hobbs and Williamson (2002) stated, "if safety interventions are to be appropriately targeted [...], it is important to identify the tasks that are most likely to be subject to error and to predict the error forms that may occur in those situations." Comprehensive investigation and analysis of large sets of past incidents and accidents often reveal patterns and allow the identification of tasks that are particularly prone to error. Understanding how a system or a procedure will most likely fail is key to designing and implementing effective and targeted prevention methods.

Some recent efforts to prevent human error in aviation maintenance have focused on specific errors. The studies identified the most prevalent types of errors and suggested prevention measures targeting these specific errors. For example, Chang and Wang (2008) categorized and examined 77 preliminary and 46 primary risk factors and found the nine most significant risk factors related to labor contracts and work culture (e.g., safety attitude, horizontal communications, salary, and reward). To improve AMTs' performance and reduce human errors, they recommended a series of measures that protect and value employee professionalism: increasing salaries, establishing a safe and rewarding reporting culture, improving the safety of the work environment, examining the demands of manpower, strengthening the selection of AMTs, and enforcing the long-term recurrent safety training that provides AMTs with better safety attitudes, knowledge, and skills.

Liang et al. (2009) surveyed 40 maintenance events and their causality relative to human errors at a specific airline maintenance company. They used MEDA's three categories for reporting error occurrences: event, maintenance error, and contributing factors. They concluded that prevention of maintenance errors should focus on repetitive or monotonous jobs and tasks, complacency, and cases where work processes or procedures are not followed. They developed an online maintenance assistance platform (on-line MAP) for technicians and assessed its effectiveness relative to the traditional paper-based work card. The tool increased the teams' risk cognition, situational awareness, and technicians' performance and job satisfaction.

Liang et al. (2009) also identified other issues that might be contributing to errors in aviation maintenance, most of which were consistent with the findings from other studies. For example, Liang et al. (2009) found evidence that technicians' language abilities were hindering task satisfaction and suggested native language assistance for maintenance procedures to improve technicians' comprehension ability and, therefore, task satisfaction. This finding echoes a recommendation made four years earlier by the Secretary of Transportation: "The FAA should establish a method for determining whether language barriers result in maintenance deficiencies" and the findings from Drury et al. (2005) to address the FAA's recommendation. This growing concern about the effect of language on maintenance errors is justified by the fastest-growing segment of the worldwide Maintenance, Repair, and Operations (MRO) market being outside the U.S., in countries where the native language is not necessarily English. Drury et al. (2005) found that these technicians may have to use English manuals because even airlines with low reported levels of English ability did not translate documents into their native language (Drury et al., 2005).

Liang et al. also found that work card design did not conform to existing human factors guidelines for information design and that experts with more experience had more errors. Both the findings are consistent with previous studies: Gramopadhye et al. (2000) found similar design issues for aircraft inspection, while other researchers found evidence of complacency in experts not following work procedures (Latorella and Prabhu, 2000 and Rankin et al., 2000).

Safety Management System (SMS) has been a standard throughout the aviation industry worldwide. The International Civil Aviation Organization (ICAO) defines SMS as an organized approach to managing safety, including the necessary organizational structures, accountability, policies, and procedures (ICAO, 2013). Earlier, SMS were primarily applied in the context of flight crew management, flight safety, and air traffic management. SMS practices are now becoming increasingly popular in aviation maintenance operations. Zimmermann & Duffy (2022) identified factors such as communication, teamwork, organizational efforts, oversight agencies, and human factors, that impact the effective development and implementation of SMS into aviation maintenance operations.

5 Discussion

The aviation industry has mostly focused on reactive measures in the form of accident analysis for safety analysis. Lessons learned from accident and incident investigations have significantly improved aviation safety (Oster et al., 2013). However, the literature suggests that the reactive measures do not provide a complete picture of the safety level (Herrera et al., 2009).

In aviation maintenance, the accident and incident reports provide information about mechanical defects, organizational malfunction, and maintainer acts but provide limited data for personnel-related underlying conditions that cause maintainer errors in the first place. Maintenance error differs from pilot error or controller error. While pilot or controller errors are evident immediately, maintenance errors can remain latent for days or even years before they result in an accident or incident. It may be challenging for the investigator to trace back to identify working and maintainer conditions when an accident or incident happens. Additionally, unlike pilots in flight, maintainers are not subjected to data or voice recording, making it difficult to investigate the context of maintainer errors.

Proactive measures may help predict maintenance issues even before they happen, therefore preventing accidents and incidents, and the associated costs. Designing activities in a way that hazards are eliminated, introducing safety and warning devices, and furthering existing safety provisions and training are some of the proactive approaches to reduce human error in aviation maintenance. Traditional maintenance operations, such as inspections and repairs, heavily rely on manual work. Automation may help to assist AMTs in tasks, such as (1) providing up-to-date maintenance information (e.g., maintenance task cards with instructions and job scheduling); (2) troubleshooting and testing of aircraft systems and components (Zimmermann & Duffy, 2022).

However, automation may also lead to new threats to safety. For example, methods to safely integrate automation to ensure human-automation interaction are needed (Billings, 2018).

6   Conclusion

In this study, we addressed the following questions: (1) What is the status of mainte-nance errors in commercial aviation accidents? (2) What issues dominate, and has that changed? Are new issues arising, for example, as composites become more prevalent? (3) What proactive and reactive methods are used to identify aviation maintenance risks, maintainer errors, and conditions?

We found that compared to 1999–2008, the total aviation accidents and maintenance-related accidents in 2009–2018 decreased slightly, though we caution that since the total number of accidents is low (~200–360), this decrease should not be taken too seriously. Aircraft systems issues were most frequently cited in the 2009–2018 maintenance acci-dents and incidents (25 out of 31 incidents and accidents). In 2008, the NTSB included personnel-related codes in its new coding system and cited maintainer-related codes, such as maintenance personnel's incorrect decision-making or judgment, in 17 out of 31 accidents and incidents. Organizational issues, such as oversight and management, were cited in eight incidents and one accident.

Next, we reviewed reactive and proactive methods to identify aviation maintenance risks, maintainer errors, and conditions. Although current risk tools and models are reactive, there has been a significant recent effort to use proactive methods. In avia-tion maintenance, reactive methods such as accident and incident reports provide infor-mation about mechanical defects, organizational malfunction, and maintainer acts but provide limited information about underlying conditions that cause maintainer errors in the first place. For maintenance-related accidents and incidents, most investigations stop when errors are identified. Just as errors are often precursors of improper mainte-nance, personnel-related conditions can be precursors of errors. Previous studies suggest that proactive measures such as questionnaires, workshops, and focus groups provide a more in-depth understanding of various personnel and working conditions. Therefore, using proactive and reactive methods where maintainers could share their incidents and perspectives on their conditions may provide rich insights into the role of personnel con-ditions in maintenance errors. One way to get maintainers' perspectives is by directly interacting with them and using a no-blame approach so that maintenance personnel can report errors without fear of discipline. Another recommendation is to regularly document maintenance errors and working conditions in aircraft maintenance facilities. Further, using predictive measures, such as artificial intelligence and machine learning tools, may help to predict aviation maintenance risks and mitigate them in the future.

References

1. Marx, D.: Learning from our mistakes: a review of maintenance error investigation and anal-ysis systems. Report prepared for FAA. Galaxy Scientific Corporation (1998). https://www.faa.gov/about/initiatives/maintenance_hf/library/documents/media/mx_faa_(formerly_hfs kyway)/other_research_program_reports/1998_reports_learning_from_our_mistakes.pdf. Accessed Jan 2023
2. Alan, H.: An overview of human factors in aviation maintenance. ATSB Safety Report, Aviation Research and Analysis Report AR 55 (2008). https://www.atsb.gov.au/media/27818/hf_ar-2008-055.pdf. Accessed Feb 2023

3. Marais, K.B., Robichaud, M.R.: Analysis of trends in aviation maintenance risk: an empirical approach. Reliab. Eng. Syst. Saf. **106**, 104–118 (2012). https://doi.org/10.1016/j.ress.2012.06.003

4. National Transportation Safety Board (NTSB). Government Information Locator Service (GILS): Aviation accident database (2023). https://www.ntsb.gov/GILS/Pages/AviationAccident.aspx. Accessed Jan 2023

5. Schmidt, J. K., Lawson, D., Figlock, R.: Human Factors Analysis & Classification System Maintenance Extension (HFACS-ME) Review of Select NTSB Maintenance Mishaps: An Update" (2003). Retrieved from: https://www.faa.gov/about/initiatives/maintenance_hf/library/documents/media/hfacs/ntsb_hfacs-me_updated_study_report.pdf

6. Boquet, A., Detwiler, C., Roberts, C., Jack, D., Shappell, S., Wiegmann, D.A.: General aviation maintenance accidents: an analysis using HFACS and focus groups (2004). https://pdfs.semanticscholar.org/d347/19c437532d29b5c650790f757ca8fe9cc57c.pdf

7. Rashid, H.S.J., Place, C.S., Braithwaite, G.R.: Helicopter maintenance error analysis: beyond the third order of the HFACS-ME. Int. J. Ind. Ergon. **40**(6), 636–647 (2010). https://doi.org/10.1016/j.ergon.2010.04.005

8. Illankoon, P., Tretten, P., Kumar, U.: A prospective study of maintenance deviations using HFACS-ME. Int. J. Ind. Ergon. **74**, 102852 (2019)

9. Kara, A.L., Prabhu, P.V.: A review of human error in aviation maintenance and inspection. Hum Error Aviat. **26**, 521–549 (2017). https://doi.org/10.1016/S0169-8141(99)00063-3

10. Shanmugam, A., Robert, T.P.: Human factors engineering in aircraft maintenance: a review. J. Quality Maintenance Eng. **21**(4), 478–505 (2015). https://doi.org/10.1108/JQME-05-2013-0030

11. Naila, M., Vieira, J.G.V.V., Mano, A.P.: Risk management in aviation maintenance: a systematic literature review. Saf. Sci. **153**, 105810 (2022). https://doi.org/10.1016/j.ssci.2022.105810

12. Electronic Code of Federal Regulations. Title 49, Subtitle B, Chapter VIII, Part 830 (2023). https://www.ecfr.gov/cgi-bin/text-idx?SID=20fdfa0045448f0ac86bf239a78e9c0c&mc=true&node=pt49.7.830&rgn=div5#se49.7.830_12. Accessed Feb 2023

13. NTSB. "Annual review of aircraft accident data—2006" (NTSB/ARC-10/01). Washington, DC: National Transportation Safety Board (2009). Online: http://libraryonline.erau.edu/online-full-text/ntsb/aircraft-accident-data/ARC10-01.pdf. Accessed Jan 2023

14. Drury, Colin, D.G.: Errors in aviation maintenance: taxonomy and control. In: Proceedings of the Human Factors Society Annual Meeting, vol. 35, no. 2, pp. 42–46. Sage CA: Los Angeles, CA: SAGE Publications (1991). https://doi.org/10.1518/1071181917867558

15. ICAO. "Manual of Aircraft Accident and Incident Investigation. 1st ed. Montréal, Québec, Canada: International Civil Aviation Organization. Part III. Investigation" (2011). https://www.skybrary.aero/sites/default/files/bookshelf/3282.pdf

16. Kanki, Barbara, K.G.: Maintenance human factors: A brief history. In: Human Factors in Aviation, pp. 659–697. Academic Press (2010). https://doi.org/10.1016/B978-0-12-374518-7.00021-3

17. Aircraft Accident Investigation Commission. Ministry of Transport. Aircraft Accident Investigation Report (1985). http://www.air-accidents.com/event/3487120885.pdf

18. Johnston, N., McDonald, N., Fuller, R.: Aviation psychology in practice Farnham: Ashgate Pulishing. (1994). https://books.google.com/books?id=scg3DwAAQBAJ&lpg=PT103&ots=9TgCyPuqQN&dq=aviation%20psychologist%20maintenance&lr&pg=PT104#v=onepage&q=aviation%20psychologist%20maintenance&f=false. Accessed Jan 2023

19. FAA Accident and Incident Data System (AIDS) (2023). https://www.asias.faa.gov/apex/f?p=100:12:::NO. Accessed Feb 2023

20. Patankar, M.S., Taylor, J.C.: MRM training, evaluation, and safety management. Int. J. Aviat. Psychol. **18**(1), 61–71 (2008). https://doi.org/10.1080/10508410701749449
21. Bao, M., Ding, S.: Individual-related factors and management-related factors in aviation maintenance. Procedia Eng. **80**, 293–302 (2014). https://doi.org/10.1016/j.proeng.2014.09.088
22. Hobbs, A., Kanki, B.G.: Patterns of error in confidential maintenance incident reports. Int. J. Aviat. Psychol. **18**(1), 5–16 (2008). https://doi.org/10.1080/10508410701749365
23. Federal Aviation Administration (FAA). Notice U.S. Department of Transportation. Technical Operations Safety Action Program (T-SAP) (2012). https://www.faa.gov/documentLibrary/media/Notice/2012-03-28%20Signed%20N%20JO%207210.807%20TSAP.pdf
24. Chiu, M.-C., Hsieh, M.-C.: Latent human error analysis and efficient improvement strategies by fuzzy TOPSIS in aviation maintenance tasks. Appl. Ergon. **54**, 136–147 (2016). https://doi.org/10.1016/j.apergo.2015.11.017
25. Leigh, S.T., van den Berg, M.J., Mulrine, H.M.: Personal and work factors that predict fatigue-related errors in aircraft maintenance engineering. Aerospace Med. Hum. Perf. **90**(10), 860–866 (2019). https://doi.org/10.3357/AMHP.5000.2019
26. Jean, W., Johnson, W.B.: Assessing aviation maintenance work environments and worker rest. In: Proceedings of the 15th Symposium on Human Factors in Aviation Maintenance (2001). https://citeseerx.ist.psu.edu/document?repid=rep1&type=pdf&doi=7b9e69a1d539d1a738187aa4d9689ff7c9735dcb
27. Hobbs, A., Williamson, A.: Associations between errors and contributing factors in aircraft maintenance. Hum. Factors **45**(2), 186–201 (2003). https://doi.org/10.1518/hfes.45.2.186.272
28. Neelakshi, M., Marais, M.: A Survey of Pilots' Experiences of Inflight Loss of Control Incidents and Training. In: AIAA AVIATION 2022 Forum, p. 3778 (2022). https://doi.org/10.2514/6.2022-3778
29. James, C.T.J.: A new model for measuring return on investment (ROI) for safety programs in aviation: an example from airline maintenance resource management (MRM). No. 2000-01-2090. SAE Technical Paper (2000). https://doi.org/10.4271/2000-01-2090
30. Rankin, W., Hibit, R., Allen, J., Sargent, R.: Development and evaluation of the maintenance error decision aid (MEDA) process. Int. J. Ind. Ergon. **26**(2), 261–276 (2000). https://doi.org/10.1016/S0169-8141(99)00070-0
31. Chang, Y.-H., Wang, Y.-C.: Significant human risk factors in aircraft maintenance technicians. Saf. Sci. **48**(1), 54–62 (2010). https://doi.org/10.1016/j.ssci.2009.05.004
32. Liang, G.-F., Lin, J.-T., Hwang, S.-L., Wang, E.-Y., Patterson, P.: Preventing human errors in aviation maintenance using an on-line maintenance assistance platform. Int. J. Ind. Ergon. **40**(3), 356–367 (2010). https://doi.org/10.1016/j.ergon.2010.01.001
33. Drury, C. G., Jiaqi Ma, and C. Marin. "Language error in Aviation maintenance." University at Buffalo The state university of New York. W. Hughes technical center 10 (2005). Retrieved from: http://www.tc.faa.gov/LOGISTICS/grants/pdf/2002/02-G-025.pdf
34. Gramopadhye, A.K., Drury, C.G.: Human factors in aviation maintenance: how we got to where we are. Int. J. Ind. Ergon. **26**(2), 125–131 (2000). https://doi.org/10.1016/S0169-8141(99)00062-1
35. ICAO. Safety Management Manual (SMM) (Doc 9859) (2013). https://www.icao.int/SAM/Documents/2017-SSP-GUY/Doc%209859%20SMM%20Third%20edition%20en.pdf
36. Zimmermann, N., Duffy, V.G.: Systematic Literature Review of Safety Management Systems in Aviation Maintenance Operations. In: Duffy, V.G., Landry, S.J., Lee, J.D., Stanton, N. (eds) Human-Automation Interaction. Automation, Collaboration, & E-Services, vol 11. Springer, Cham (2023). https://doi.org/10.1007/978-3-031-10784-9_19
37. Oster, C.V., Strong, J.S., Zorn, C.K.: Analyzing aviation safety: Problems, challenges, opportunities. Res. Trans. Econ. **43**(1), 148–164 (2013). https://doi.org/10.1016/j.retrec.2012.12.001

38. Ivonne A.H., Nordskag, A.O., Myhre, G., Halvorsen, K.: Aviation safety and maintenance under major organizational changes, investigating non-existing accidents. Accid. Anal. Prev. **41**(6), 1155-1163 (2009). https://doi.org/10.1016/j.aap.2008.06.007
39. Charles E.B.: Aviation automation: The search for a human-centered approach. CRC Press, (2018). https://trid.trb.org/view/572335. Accessed Feb 2023
40. Yeun, R., Bates, P., Murray, P.: Aviation safety management systems. World Rev. Intermodal Trans. Res.**5**(2), 168–196 (2014). https://doi.org/10.1504/WRITR.2014.067234

Analysis of Human Factors and Resilience Competences in ASRS Data Using Natural Language Processing

Mako Ono[✉] and Miwa Nakanishi

Keio University, Yokohama 223-8522, Kanagawa, Japan
makoono@keio.jp

Abstract. In safety-related fields, analysis on accidents which are instances of failure to maintain safety has been conducted. Today, however, as accidents have decreased, there is a need to analyze not only accidents but also resilient behavior that flexibly responds to changing circumstances in daily successful operations. However, it is difficult to collect daily successful operations as data for analysis. In this study, we analyzed incident reports, which were considered as describing events where an accident or a disaster had been successfully avoided or overcome. The Aviation Safety Reporting System (ASRS), which collects a wide range of aviation incidents, was used as the data, and the efforts or actions practiced at the field to make things go right (Resilience Competence) were extracted. Furthermore, using the extracted Resilience Competences and the Human Factors analyzed by ASRS staffs, the incidents were organized to identify Human Factors that are likely to lead to worse situation and the Resilience Competences needed to prevent them.

Keywords: ASRS · Resilience · Human Factor · NLP · Text mining

1 Introduction

Research in the field of safety has focused its analysis on accidents. Today, however, as technology has developed and accidents have decreased, analysis on incidents and daily successful operations, in addition to accidents, are being promoted from a safety perspective.

The importance of incidents has long been recognized, especially in the aviation sector, and a system for collecting incidents has been established. In the U.S. aviation industry, a voluntary reporting system called the Aviation Safety Reporting System (ASRS) has been established. This system is operated by NASA, and reports on aviation safety are made by various people involved in aviation, including pilots, air traffic controllers, flight attendants, mechanics, etc. The data reported in 2021 amounted to 7,128 reports/month on average. The reports include the date, weather, metadata such as Human Factors analyzed by the staff, and free descriptions (Narrative) from the reporter [1].

© The Author(s), under exclusive license to Springer Nature Switzerland AG 2023
V. G. Duffy (Ed.): HCII 2023, LNCS 14029, pp. 548–561, 2023.
https://doi.org/10.1007/978-3-031-35748-0_37

Resilience engineering, which focuses on flexible response and adjustment to changing circumstances, has been highlighted as an analysis of daily successful operations from a safety perspective. Hollnagel (2017) states that resilience is an expression of how people, alone or together, cope with everyday situations---large and small--- by adjusting their performance to the conditions [2].

However, the application of resilience to the field has not yet progressed, and more concrete explanations that are more relevant to the field are desired [3]. Therefore, research is being conducted in various fields [4–6] to identify specific behaviors that demonstrate resilience, and to grasp the characteristics of resilience from on-site behaviors.

Although interviews with experts and observation of daily operations are necessary to analyze resilience demonstrated in daily cases, it is difficult to conduct such interviews and observations in the field. Therefore, attempts are being made to consider incidents not as "failures that almost lead to accidents" but as "successes that prevented accidents" and to explore resilient behavior [7].

The number of incidents is large, and they are being collected by systems such as ASRS. However, it takes a lot of time and cost to have an expert analyze each incident, making it difficult to take advantage of this system. Therefore, to reduce the time and cost required for analysis, analysis using natural language processing has been attracting attention [8–10].

In this study, we analyzed the ASRS Narrative using natural language processing to extract specific behaviors (Resilience Competences) necessary to demonstrate resilience. In addition, by topic modeling the Narrative, we organized the situations in which incidents are more frequent in the aviation field. We then attempted to identify the Human Factors that lead to a worsening of the situation and the Resilience Competences necessary to prevent such situations from occurring.

2 Construction of Resilience Competence Extraction Model from ASRS Data

First, we attempted to extract a comprehensive list of specific actions taken to demonstrate resilience in the airline industry. We analyzed each sentence in the Narrative to see if each sentence contained resilient behavior, and created a model of natural language processing technology using this as training data.

2.1 Data

Incident data published in ASRS was downloaded [11] and the Narratives were analyzed. Considering that the system and rules for older data differ significantly from those in use today, and in order to minimize the bias of cases by year and ensure sufficient data volume, we decided to use reports for the five-year period from 2016 to 2020 (26,891 reports). From this data, we constructed training data consists of one sentence each using 5,013 sentences from 289 reports (329 Narratives), which were selected so that there was no bias in job types and time periods. Examples of the reported data are shown in Table 1.

Table 1. Examples of ASRS reports (Narrative).

	Examples
①	We were returning from a local flight. We were using Runway XXL & R which is not our normal pattern. Therefore, instead of flying closer to the airport, we were maneuvering to a XX landing pattern. We had called the tower 15 miles Southeast to obtain a clearance to enter the D space. We were given a squawk code and told by the tower operator we were observed now at 8 miles Southeast and told to 'fly present heading to avoid traffic'. We were doing so and a minute or two later saw what appeared to be Aircraft Y at our 12:00 position lightly lower and noticed a rapid close rate. He initiated a rapid turn to his left, east. We turned rapidly to our left, west, and avoided contact. The tower called at about that time and instructed us to dive immediately. It was a close call. The tower asked me to call him after we landed. We discussed the event from the point at which he gave us the beacon code. I am not sure if he was talking to Aircraft Y traffic or not. We were able to see and avoid the traffic so it worked out. The operator and I agreed we were closer than we would have liked to be.
②	On preflight of crew O2 masks the only available means of sanitizing the masks was SaniWipes. SaniWipes have been determined not to be effective against COVID-19 virus. CFR 135.89 requires use of O2 mask if one pilot leaves flight station above 25,000 feet MSL. Adequate means of sanitizing the masks is required.Adequate means of sanitizing masks is required ASAP.

2.2 Annotating Sentences with Resilience Behavior

ASRS reports include: ① reports of incidents (Table 1, ①); ② reports of unsafe conditions (Table 1, ②). An overview of reports such as ① reveals that they often consist of a description of the case background, what the reporter and others involved saw or heard, the actions taken in response, along with the results and reflections on the event. It was also confirmed that the reports included actions for resilience and flexibility to changing circumstances, such as "We turned rapidly to our left, west, and avoided contact."

Therefore, we separated the reports into sentence units and annotated each sentence as to whether or not it contained behaviors for resilience, and if so, whether or not it demonstrated the four resilience abilities (anticipating, monitoring, responding, and learning) (with/without each ability applicable). Anticipating was defined as the ability to predict the future and consider necessary actions for responding; monitoring was defined as the ability to recognize situations and changes correctly and to identify threats; responding was defined as the ability to respond to threats correctly at the right time; and learning was defined as the ability to learn. Learning is applicable when it includes actions to reflect on and learn from the event that occurred.

Referring to the procedure used by Osawa et al. (2018) in their study that attempted to identify Resilience Competences and extract behaviors practiced to make things go well in aviation using text mining on Japanese aviation incidents data [7], the training data for resilience behavior extraction in this study were annotated as shown in Fig. 1.

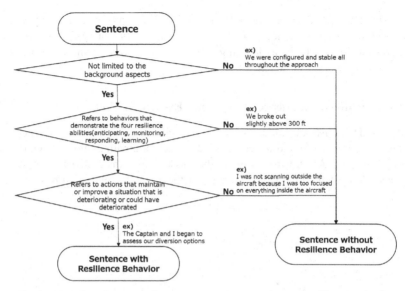

Fig. 1. Flowchart for annotating sentences with and without Resilience Behavior.

Table 2. Annotation results for the training data.

Annotations		Examples	Number of sentences
Sentence without Resilience Behavior		Yesterday I was contacted by the FOQA Gatekeeper in respect to my landing [recently] at JFK.	3,888
Sentence with Resilience Behavior (1,125 sentences)	Anticipating	Up to this point, we were considering diverting to DTW or continuing to ORD.	243
	Monitoring	Level in cruise at FL340 I felt a slight yaw in the aircraft, and noted a roll on the flight director.	266
	Responding	I moved passengers that were within 3 rows away from the mom and child.	626
	Learning	My realization is that not many people are able to recognize, nor take seriously, time sensitive critical medical conditions.	135

The annotation results identified 1,125 of the 5,013 sentences as containing resilience behaviors. Of the 1,125 sentences, 243 were annotated as anticipating, 266 as monitoring, 626 as responding, and 135 as learning. The annotation results and examples of the annotated sentences are shown in Table 2.

2.3   Construction of Resilience Competence Extraction Model

We attempted to construct a model to extract the behaviors that include resilience and to estimate the presence of the four resilience abilities (anticipating, monitoring, responding, and learning). As shown in Fig. 2, the model was constructed in two stages: a Resilience Competence extraction model and the four resilience abilities estimation model.

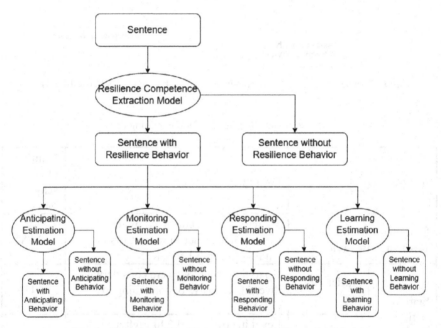

Fig. 2. Overview of Resilience Competence Extraction Model

In the Resilience Competence Extraction Model, the sentences obtained from the segmented reports were used as input, and the output was whether or not they contain resilience behavior. The 5,013 annotated sentences were divided into 4,010 training sentences and 1,003 test sentences to avoid bias. This model was constructed using BERT (Bidirectional Encoder from Transformers), a model that learns the context in a bidirectional manner by considering the meaning of words in context. After preprocessing, bert-base-uncased was used as the pre-trained model and fine-tuned with the training data. The accuracy is shown in Table 3. Although the precision of the test data is rather low at 65.34%, the recall indicates that 74.55% of the annotated sentences with resilience behavior could be extracted.

Table 3. Accuracy of Resilience Competence Extraction Model

	Training data	Test data
Accuracy	92.33%	85.74%
Precision	77.39%	65.34%
Recall	92.41%	74.55%

The Four Resilience Abilities Estimation Model was preprocessed in the same way as the Resilience Competence Extraction Model and constructed individually for anticipating, monitoring, responding, and learning. Sentences containing resilience behaviors were used as input, and the presence/absence of each ability was estimated for each sentence. From the 1,125 sentences identified as containing resilience behaviors at the time of annotating, we constructed models using 900 sentences as training data and 225 sentences as test data.

The highest accuracy is shown in Table 4, and the parameter combinations are shown in Table 5. Even for the least accurate prediction, a recall of over 60% was obtained with the test data. This accuracy is considered to be sufficient to grasp the characteristics of the behaviors that demonstrate the four resilience abilities.

Table 4. Accuracy of Four Resilience Abilities Estimation Model

		Anticipating	Monitoring	Responding	Learning
Training data	Accuracy	94.44%	99.31%	97.64%	100.00%
	Precision	80.66%	98.17%	97.82%	100.00%
	Recall	96.69%	98.77%	98.06%	100.00%
Test data	Accuracy	81.78%	87.56%	79.11%	98.67%
	Precision	61.11%	87.23%	78.51%	96.15%
	Recall	62.26%	65.08%	81.90%	92.59%

3   Application of the Model to ASRS Data and Embodying Resilience Competence

The model constructed was applied to the unannotated data, and the sentences that were estimated to contain each ability were clustered using the k-means method to analyze what characteristics of the behavior appeared.

3.1 Data

The model was applied to 26,602 unannotated reports from 2016–2020 (30,795 Narrative counts, 464,686 sentences); 113,466 sentences were extracted as demonstrating Resilience Competence, among which 32,990 sentences were estimated with anticipating, 17,943 sentences with monitoring, 61,956 sentences with responding, and 11,949 sentences with learning (Table 5).

Table 5. Results of Resilience Competence Extraction Model application

		Examples	Number of sentences
Estimated Sentence without Resilience Behavior		A county mobile vehicle got on the runway about 5 minutes later to do a daily routine inspection.	351,220
Estimate Sentence with Resilience Behavior (113,466 sentences)	Anticipating	We agreed that only the critical surfaces needed to be anti-iced but the whole aircraft had to be deiced.	32,990
	Monitoring	I realized that the tow bar had become disconnected and began to make efforts to stop the airplane gently.	17,943
	Responding	I immediately entered auto-rotation and made a [priority request] radio call.	61,956
	Learning	It would have been safer if he'd instructed our aircraft to begin our missed approach two miles before the missed approach.	11,949

3.2 Embodying Resilience Competence

Characteristic Extraction of Four Resilience Abilities. Characteristic verbs were extracted from the sentences estimated with each ability, and the characteristics of the demonstrated actions and behaviors were captured (Table 6).

In anticipating, verbs such as "tell" and "say" were extracted, suggesting that communication is important; in monitoring, verbs related to auditory information and noticing were extracted, indicating that auditory information is demonstrated in addition to visual information; in responding, verbs such as "continue" were extracted, indicating that continuing the current action is one of the options; and in learning, verbs such as suggestion and recommendation were extracted, indicating that improvement is often mentioned.

Clustering of Each Resilience Ability. Clustering was performed to examine in more detail what kind of behavior is exhibited by each ability. Sentences in which each ability

Table 6. Examples of Characteristic Verbs

Ability	Examples
Anticipating	tell, say, explain, advise, discuss, agree, brief, send, decide, determine
Monitoring	see, look, observe, glance, monitor, hear, notify, realize, check, find
Responding	turn, climb, run, land, go, start, begin, continue, stop, proceed, complete, maintain
Learning	recommend, suggest, learn, think, consider, prevent, avoid, focus

was estimated to be exhibited by the model were clustered by the k-means method after creating feature vectors in doc2vec. The number of clusters was determined using the elbow method and silhouette diagram, and it was determined that 7 clusters were optimal for anticipating, monitoring, and responding, and 6 clusters were optimal for learning.

Cluster names were determined by interpreting the meaning of the clusters from the sentences classified into each cluster. The proportion of verbs characteristic of each ability included in each cluster was also used as a reference. Table 7 shows the cluster names and the examples of sentences included in the clusters. The cluster names manifest the characteristics of each of the clustered abilities. Therefore, we decided to regard the cluster names as Resilience Competences, which are specific behavioral characteristics necessary to demonstrate resilience.

4 Application of the Structural Topic Modeling to ASRS Data

Using Structural Topic Modeling (STM), the situations in which incidents are likely to occur in aviation were organized and analyzed to determine what Human Factors are likely to cause incidents in each situation and what Resilience Competences are necessary for each situation. STM is one of the methods of topic modeling [12], a model that estimates effect of metadata on a topic, and is often used in incident analysis [9].

4.1 Data

For each Narrative, STM was performed with whether the Human Factor was related to the worsening of the situation and whether it included behaviors that demonstrated Resilience Competence as the covariates. The data used were 30,398 Narratives with 20 or more words out of the Narratives applied to the Resilience Competence extraction model and stemming, etc., was performed as preprocessing.

4.2 Estimating Topics

Based on Semantic Coherence and other indices, the number of topics was determined to be optimal at 17 topics. Topic characteristics were found from words with the highest

Table 7. Embodying Resilience Competence

	No.	Name of cluster	Examples
Anticipating	1	Confirming and sharing the recognition of self and others	I told him that we were only 400 miles from ZYHB and that time was critical for planning the fuel stop.
	2	Checking for possible situations and response to them	We discussed this and felt with the additional speed we were OK, but briefed what to do in the event of a wind-shear warning or caution.
	3	Recognizing and sharing information regarding delayed tasks as hazards	The captain and I had a short discussion about the fact that we had not been handed over to PHX approach yet, which seemed to be late.
	4	Recognizing and sharing situational and environmental changes as hazards	As we circled over the field, we informed operations that we were a return and requested that they contact [Company] as we felt we were too low to attempt this.
	5	Recognizing and sharing situational and environmental changes as chances	We could not confirm the actual fuel leak and we all agreed it was the best option to continue on to our destination with [nearby airports] as alternates.
	6	Checking for situations in which hazards increase	I indicated that I was not sure that pulling the aileron disconnect handle would improve our situation, and could in fact make the situation more dangerous than it was.
	7	Checking for situations in which chances increase	The Captain and I briefly discussed our best course of action and both determined that the safest, most conservative response was to divert.
Monitoring	1	Detecting damages and objects in abnormal conditions	We monitored brake temps and returned to the gate where Maintenance very quickly ascertained that the rod connecting the gear to the gear door had failed and was no longer attached.
	2	Paying attention to information from the auditory	As we rotated and climbed out, I could hear 'Fire, fire, fire' from the Passengers in the cabin.
	3	Paying attention to information from the sensed of smell and touch	I smelt odd fumes for about twenty to thirty minutes and also after confirming the smell with the other working flight attendants, after the 'B' flight attendant reported the odor to the flight deck, I reported it also.
	4	Paying attention to the individual's internal conditions	However, after being in the air for about a hour and half, I could feel fatigue starting to set in.
	5	Checking for the external factors	I was looking to the right and back at the wingtip to make sure we had proper clearance for the right hand turn.
	6	Detecting the movements and changes of others	During pushback, I noticed the wing walker sprinting back towards the aircraft with his wands set in an 'X' orientation indicating that we should stop.
	7	Detecting objects in unnatural conditions	It was at this time we realized that we didn't have all the parts we needed.
Responding	1	Cooperating with other departments and staff	The other helicopter was unaware of my location (he hadn't seen me at all) and so I made another radio call to make it clear I was to the south of his position heading west
	2	Change plans in the short term	I took evasive action turning 45 degrees to the left and dropping an additional 100 feet of altitude.
	3	Change plans in the long term	We notified ATC of our issue and following a discussion and crew inputs, the decision was made to return to ZZZZ.
	4	Prioritizing the continuation of tasks	We decided to continue to [destination] as we were only about 20 mins out and it was going to be quicker.
	5	Stopping or delaying tasks	I immediately assessed the catastrophic event that was about to happen, and I stopped Aircraft X's altitude at 030 and issued him a 320 heading.
	6	Restarting tasks	I reviewed the checklist again and completed another full run-up check with the boost pumps set to 'low'.
	7	Replacing priorities in the plan	We further decided to lower the gear and configure flaps before initiating a call to dispatch/maintenance.
Learning	1	Coming up with specific procedures, plans, or tips that wpuld enhance future operations	In the future, I will request a two minute delay from the tower prior to accepting a takeoff clearance behind a B757, unless I am light enough to be sure I can rotate and climb above their path.
	2	Reflecting on the indivisual's internal conditions	We both learned immensely from this situation that when an abnormal condition arises, that we both need to be more methodical, focus entirely on addressing the situation, and do not become distracted with other, less important tasks.
	3	Reflecting on the influence of external factors	I would propose that this situation could be corrected by changing the LOA to exclude [this aircraft type] departures from the provision allowing the use of pilot provided visual separation between successive departures.
	4	Reflecting with others and sharing the lessons learned	As of this writing, I have spoken to two Assistant Chief Pilots about the situation and we discussed the flight, its procedures, and decisions and outcomes.
	5	Gaining knowledge about hazardous situations such as high-workload situations	Had he made the right turn to 120 as originally instructed, he would've gone even deeper into a higher MVA, posing a substantial safety risk.
	6	Adding options and responses	I should have stayed higher on the visual approach until on the localizer to guarantee the altitudes.

Table 8. Estimating Topic Name.

Fuel	Highest Prob	fuel	zzz [airport name]	flight	dispatch	system
	Narrative	[I was] unable to contact flight released was not amended for new destination. [The flight] diverted due to a possible fuel leak. Diversion was noticed on...				
Work Rule	Highest Prob	flight	time	pilot	oper	day
	Narrative	This flight canceled due to duty limitations. Management is impeding the Part 117 rules by punishment of its pilots. The company has implemented a policy...				
Taxing	Highest Prob	runway	taxi	takeoff	aircraft	taxiway
	Narrative	We received taxi instructions to cross Runway 22R at K, Taxiway P to cross the active Runway 29 hold short Runway 22R. Once we crossed Runway 29 and...				
Ground	Highest Prob	aircraft	gate	ramp	ground	push
	Narrative	During pushback normal pushback procedures were in use. After the pushback was complete I was asked to set the brakes. I could tell that the ground crew...				
Low Altitude Traffic	Highest Prob	approach	system	altitud	navig	land
	Narrative	While on Visual Approach received Terrain Caution. Because it was at night, I disconnected the automation and adjusted flight path to correct error. We...				
Weather	Highest Prob	weather	turbul	condit	wind	aircraft
	Narrative	At FL300, [we] encountered a severe mountain wave event with moderate turbulence. Autopilot was engaged at the time and remained engaged...				
Runway-Communication	Highest Prob	runway	land	tower	approach	final
	Narrative	Wind calm/variable at 04 knots according to ASOS. I approached ZZZ from 10 miles to the north. Started making radio calls on UNICOM [CTAF] that I would...				
Passenger & Flight Attendant	Highest Prob	flight	passeng	attend	captain	call
	Narrative	Passenger moved from his original seat to seat XXC. Right after we leveled off Mrs. X (XXB) rang her FA call button and asked to be reseated, as her...				
Airspace	Highest Prob	aircraft	control	sector	time	coordin
	Narrative	I was working BEARZ and noticed two aircraft flashing in conflict alert, one was an aircraft that CRIBB (sector 81) had PVDed (displaying an aircraft data tag...				
Cargo	Highest Prob	door	load	cargo	bag	batteri
	Narrative	Issue was brought to my attention today by management....While working as the Lead RSE (Ramp Service Employee) on Aircraft X, the [Load Plan] was showing 96 bags, 124 pieces of Mail, 4 pieces of [small parcel], 1 piece of...				
Maintenance	Highest Prob	mainten	aircraft	equip	list	minimum
	Narrative	During Track and balance of Aircraft X, it was determined a Main Rotor (M/R) blade was needed. Mechanic I was working with and I removed blade and...				
Cruising-Communication	Highest Prob	control	traffic	air	clearanc	departur
	Narrative	In cruise flight at 45,000 feet we were given a shortcut on the route. We had 2 similar sounding and spelling fixes on our flight plan. I was pilot monitoring...				
Engine	Highest Prob	engin	land	checklist	refer	air
	Narrative	Climbing through the mid-20s we began receiving multiple intermittent Left Engine Oil Pressure High CAS messages. The oil pressure indication confirmed the CAS. We leveled at 29,000 ft. and executed the single step QRH...				
Traffic	Highest Prob	flight	traffic	foot	rule	visual
	Narrative	After a VFR departure, tower approved a right turn on course for departure eastbound. Shortly after departing the class D airspace during level cruise...				
Landing	Highest Prob	gear	land	aircraft	left	right
	Narrative	During a routine training flight, while practicing wheel landings, the student failed to maintain longitudinal control during touchdown. This act caused the airplane to yaw to the left towards the edge of the runway. The student...				
Takeoff	Highest Prob	first	offic	speed	flap	captain
	Narrative	It was a configuration 2 takeoff out of ZZZ and I was the PF. After passing 1,000 feet AFE, I selected climb power and the FO verified climb power. After...				
Light	Highest Prob	light	see	look	posit	switch
	Narrative	I experienced an issue using Foreflight that I thought I'd share. On a VFR flight I noticed the Foreflight app on my iPad mini froze shortly after turning on my Stratus device. I then attempted to reset the app by canceling the program...				

appearance probability within each topic and some Narrative likely to belong to each topic, and topic names were given. Top 5 words with the highest appearance probability and the most representative Narrative for each topic are shown in Table 8 and the change in Semantic Coherence values with the number of topics is shown in Fig. 3.

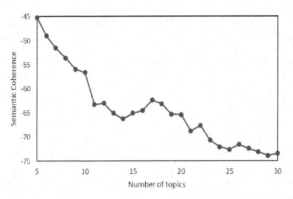

Fig. 3. The Change in Semantic Coherence Values with the Number of Topics

4.3 Human Factor and Resilience Competence Closely Related to the Topic

For each topic, the presence of Human Factor and Resilience Competence were used as covariates for the topic, and regressions were estimated with Human Factor and Resilience Competence as explanatory variables and the proportion of each Narrative about a topic in the STM model as the objective variable. Covariates were considered to have effect on the topic at a significance level of 5% or less.

When looking at Resilience Competences that have an effect on a topic, we found that within a single topic, competences of the same ability were similar in the direction of effect (positive or negative slope of regression). Therefore, we considered that if many of the Resilience Competences of each ability had an effect on the topic (5 competencies for anticipating, monitoring, and responding, and 4 or more for learning), and if the direction of effect (sign of the coefficient of the slope of the regression equation) was the same, the ability was closely related to the topic and had a similar effect on the topic. For Human Factor, we focused on those with particularly large effects (|t value|>8.0) as being closely related. The relationship between the Human Factor, topic and the effect of four Resilience abilities is shown in Fig. 4.

For example, in the fuel incident, it can be seen that the Human Factor during Troubleshooting is often involved in the worsening of the incident situation, and that Situational Awareness is less often involved. In addition, Anticipating ability is especially prevalent in this incident. In other words, when a fuel-related event occurs, the Human Factor during Troubleshooting often leads to a worsening of the situation, and in order to avoid this, it is necessary to take actions that demonstrate Anticipating, as shown in Table 7.

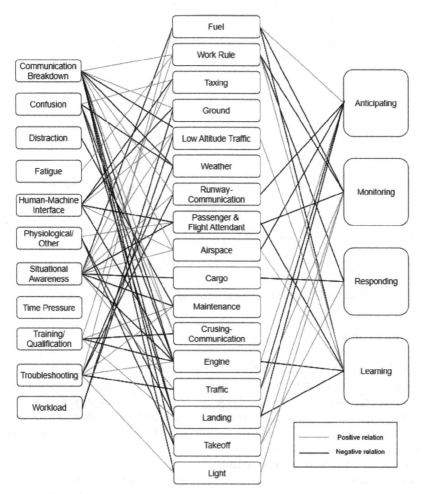

Fig. 4. Relationship between Topic, Human Factor, and Four Resilience Abilities

Although the resilience ability did not show a close relationship with the topic, there were some Resilience Competences that had significant effect to the topic (|t value|>8.0), as shown in Fig. 5. The Resilience Competence numbers correspond to those in Table 7.

For example, Fig. 5 shows that topics related to incidents during Taxing often exhibit Monitoring6 (Detecting the movements and changes of others) and Responding5 (Stopping or delaying tasks). Figure 4 also shows that Human Factors such as Confusion and Situational Awareness are often responsible for worsening the situation during Taxing incidents. In other words, Human Factors such as Confusion and Situational Awareness often cause the situation to deteriorate during Taxing, and actions such as Monitoring6 and Responding5 are considered useful to avoid such deterioration.

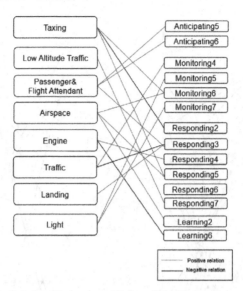

Fig. 5. Relationship between Topic and Resilience Competences

5 Conclusion

In this study, the ASRS was analyzed using natural language processing. A model was constructed to extract behaviors that demonstrated resilience, and the results of applying the model were used for further analysis. Resilience Competence was embodied by clustering the behaviors that demonstrated resilience, and the situation in aviation was organized by applying topic modeling to the Narrative. The Human Factors that are likely to worsen the situation and the Resilience Competences necessary to prevent them were then identified for each situation in aviation.

Since the accuracy of the model is not very high, some of the results are difficult to interpret. However, by organizing the results by situation, we were able to clarify points to be aware of and actions to take in each situation, and we believe we were able to present the results in a form that is easier to put into practice in the field.

References

1. ASRS Program Briefing, https://asrs.arc.nasa.gov/docs/ASRS_ProgramBriefing.pdf. Accessed 07 July 2023
2. Hollnagel, E.: Safety-II in practice: developing the resilience potentials. Routledge (2017)
3. Nemeth, C. P., Hollnagel, E.: Resilience engineering in practice, Volume 2: Becoming resilient. CRC Press (2016)
4. Holbrook, J., Prinzel III, L.J., Stewart, M.J., Kiggins, D.: How Do Pilots and Controllers Manage Routine Contingencies During RNAV Arrivals? In: Arezes, P.M., Boring, R.L. (eds.) AHFE 2020. AISC, vol. 1204, pp. 331–338. Springer, Cham (2020). https://doi.org/10.1007/978-3-030-50946-0_44

5. Wachs, P., Saurin, T.A., Righi, A.W., Wears, R.L.: Resilience skills as emergent phenomena: a study of emergency departments in Brazil and the United States. Appl. Ergon. **56**, 227–237 (2016)
6. Wachs, P., Righi, A.W., Saurin, T.A.: Identification of non-technical skills from the resilience engineering perspective: a case study of an electricity distributor. Work **41**(Supplement 1), 3069–3076 (2012)
7. Osawa, A., Takagi, T., Nakanishi, M.: An attempt to extract good jobs from safety reports using text mining -analysis of voluntary information contributory to enhancement of the safety (VOICES) Data-. Human Factors in Japan, 25(2) (in press) (2021)
8. Rose, R. L., Puranik, T. G., Mavris, D. N.: Natural language processing based method for clustering and analysis of aviation safety narratives. Aerospace **7**(10), 143 (2020)
9. Kuhn, K.D.: Using structural topic modeling to identify latent topics and trends in aviation incident reports. Transp. Res. Part C Emerg. Technol. **87**, 105–122 (2018)
10. Dong, T., Yang, Q., Ebadi, N., Luo, X. R., Rad, P.: Identifying incident causal factors to improve aviation transportation safety: Proposing a deep learning approach. J. Adv. Transp. **2021** 1–15 (2021)
11. ASRS Database Online, https://asrs.arc.nasa.gov/search/database.html. Accessed 02 July 2023
12. Roberts, M.E., Stewart, B.M., Tingley, D.: Stm: An R package for structural topic models. J. Stat. Softw. **91**, 1–40 (2019)

Non-immersive vs. Immersive: The Difference in Empathy, User Engagement, and User Experience When Simulating the Daily Life of Rheumatoid Arthritis Patients

Alexicia Richardson[✉], Cheryl D. Seals, Kimberly B. Garza, Gary Hawkins, Sathish Akula, Sean Kim, Adam Biggs, Lily McGuckin, Ravindra Joshi, and Majdi Lusta

Auburn University, Auburn, AL 36849, USA
{adr0021,sealscd,kbl0005,hawkigs,sza0096,szk0131,ajb0217,lily.mcguckin,
rzj0038,mal0087}@auburn.edu

Abstract. This research focuses on developing and testing an application that simulates some of the difficulties rheumatoid arthritis (RA) patients encounter through daily experience. Rheumatoid arthritis can limit one's joint mobility and cause discomfort. It can be challenging to understand what someone is experiencing if they never experience it themselves. This research aims to show college students what it is like for an RA patient who is trying to do activities that most people do every day, but their disease makes it more difficult than it would generally be. The simulation will occur in a non-immersive and immersive setting. In this research, we investigate and compare the difference in empathy, user experience, and user engagement of college students when participating in an immersive and non-immersive experience.

Keywords: e-Learning and Distant Learning · User Survey · UX (User Experience) · VR · AR · MR · XR and Metaverse · immersion · healthcare

1 Introduction

Virtual reality's use has increased in many areas and expanded in the discipline of medical education. Virtual Reality (VR) has been used as a tool to educate students medicine, conduct medical training exercises, and potentially impact the empathy of medical professionals for their patients. The literature describes the potential of VR and its impact on empathy, as illustrated in the work of Schutte and Stilinovic [12], where the authors used a VR experiment in an effort to observe how it impacts empathy and user engagement of its users. In terms of medical education, we've seen a range of work done by researchers, from

V. G. Duffy (Ed.): HCII 2023, LNCS 14029, pp. 562–575, 2023.
https://doi.org/10.1007/978-3-031-35748-0_38

investigating VR's impact on cancer patients who need to undergo radiotherapy [14] to observing the decision-making skills of users in a VR application [6].

Our research compares VR to a non-immersive experiment simulating a day in the life of a patient with Rheumatoid Arthritis (RA). RA is a disease that impacts the joints and can be painful. Although RA affects many different joints within the human body, our focus is on the hands. By limiting the joint mobility of the users in each experiment, our objective is to investigate the difference in their empathy, user experience, and user engagement.

2 Experimental Design

Each subject participated in both non-immersive and immersive experiences. The first half of our experimental group completed the non-immersive trial first, followed by the immersive trial, and vice versa for the second half of the experimental group. In an effort to simulate joint mobility difficulties that RA patients endure, a pair of simulation gloves purchased from the University of Cambridge [7] was employed for both of our experiences. These gloves were designed to demonstrate the struggles of someone with limited joint mobility. In each of the experiences, We simulate three daily activities to illustrate a glimpse into typical day for an RA patient. For the immersive experience, the Oculus Quest 2 [13] was used along with our VR application. The immersive experience used the hand-tracking features of the headset for the activities.

In an effort to compare the different impacts that the non-immersive and immersive experiences have, we used a survey to measure their empathy [3,4,12], user experience [11], and user engagement [8]. Students who participated in the study were required to complete three surveys. The students completed demographic questions as a pre-survey, followed by RA and VR experience questions, and an empathy questionnaire. Students also were required to complete a survey after each experience. The post-experience surveys included an empathy questionnaire, a user experience questionnaire, and a user engagement questionnaire. We aim to investigate the differences between empathy, user experience, and user engagement in a non-immersive versus immersive setting to decide whether the immersive experience has a more significant impact than the non-immersive experience. If not, how can we enhance the VR application to have a more significant effect than the non-immersive experience?

2.1 Non-immersive Set Up

For the non-immersive experience, the participants had three tasks to complete while wearing the simulation gloves. The three tasks were a hygiene task (teeth brush preparation and simulation), a pill sorting task, and making a cup of coffee. In the non-immersive setting, these tasks were completed using real-world objects and simulation gloves. These three activities were chosen based on [1] that mention RA patients' limitations throughout their daily activities. This research focuses on hand joint mobility of RA patients and the application centered on grasping. These three activities were specifically chosen using the Activities of Daily Living (ADL) from [5]. Basic ADL includes hygiene (brushing teeth), instrumental ADL includes managing medications (pill sorting), and making a cup of coffee can be considered basic (feeding oneself) or instrumental (preparing a meal). The participants were given approximately one minute and thirty seconds for each task from the perspective of an RA patient. Once all three activities were completed, the participants were removed from the gloves and asked to complete the post-non-immersive survey.

2.2   Immersive Set Up

When entering the immersive experience station, the participants were seated and assisted in putting on the headset because they had the simulation and beige gloves on. The participants were required to wear both the simulation gloves and a pair of beige gloves because the Oculus' hand-tracking features could not consistently track the hands while wearing the simulation gloves alone. Both pairs of gloves were worn for the non-immersive and immersive experiments to retain consistency. The participants were seated for this experiment due to an effort to limit motion sickness. The participant also was not allowed to move around in the virtual environment to limit the effect of limit motion sickness. Once the headset was on, the user was tasked with completing the activities from the perspective of an RA patient and navigating through the application that way. In the immersive experience, the participants were asked to complete the same tasks as the non-immersive experience, but virtually. The participants were limited to one minute and thirty seconds per activity. At the end of the immersive experience, the users received feedback on their performance in each activity. After their immersive experience, the gloves and headset were removed, and the participant was asked to complete a post-VR experience survey. Each post-survey questionnaire took approximately 10 minutes to complete and included questions on empathy, user experience, and user engagement.

3   Application Development

The following section shows our final application development results before conducting our experiment. Figure 1 shows the beginning scene with the user's perspective of the main menu. The main menu has three options: About Disorders, Tutorial, and Get Started. When a user chooses About Disorders, the application transitions to a scene where they can select which disorder to get more information about. In our case, the focus of our study was RA. In Fig. 2, the image shows the About Disorders information for RA. The information about the disease was displayed on the left panel, while on the right panel, an image that represents the disease was shown.

Fig. 1. Main Menu Scene [9]

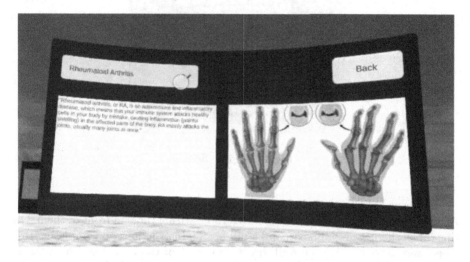

Fig. 2. RA Selection Display [2,10]

Once the user selects Get Started and chooses Rheumatoid Arthritis as their disease to experience, the application transitioned to the RA experiment. The first task the user completed was the hygiene task, as shown in Fig. 3. In this scene, the participant was placed in front of a "mirror" with the objects they needed to complete the activity. The scene was inside a bathroom that contained a toothbrush and toothpaste lying on the sink in front of the user. The instructions were along the "mirror" to guide them through the task. It offered step-by-step instructions on what to do to fully complete this task and receive a perfect score (100 points). The participants were instructed to press start to begin the task and the timer. Once they start, they should pick up the toothpaste and remove the top. Once the top is off, the user should pick up the toothbrush and connect the toothpaste and toothbrush together to put toothpaste on the toothbrush. Once completed, they were asked to mimic brushing their teeth until the toothpaste disappeared from the brush and select done to move on to the next activity.

Fig. 3. Hygiene Scene

The next activity that the user was tasked with completing was pill sorting. As seen in Fig. 4, the user was moved to a room with a table in front of them. On this table, there were pill boxes and a pill bottle. Instructions on completing this scene were displayed on the wall directly in front of the user. Like the hygiene scene, the user must press start to begin the activity and start the timer. The user's next instruction was to pick up the pill bottle and remove the lid. Once the lid was removed, the user had to tilt the pill bottle until the pills were displayed on the table, as seen in Fig. 5. Once the pills were shown, the user released the pill bottle and began sorting the pills into each pill box. For the sorting to be deemed successful, the user was required to place one pill of each color in each of the pill boxes on the table. Once pill sorting was complete, the user pressed done and moved on to their last activity.

Fig. 4. Pill Sorting Scene

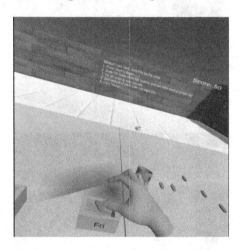

Fig. 5. Pill Sorting

The final activity the user was tasked to complete involved making a cup of coffee. As seen in Fig. 6, the user was placed in front of a table containing what was needed to make a cup of coffee. A coffee machine and a tray containing a coffee mug, a jug of milk, a plate with sugar cubes, and a spoon were on the table. Much like the pill sorting scene, the instructions for this scene were displayed on the back wall in front of the user. Similar to the other activities in this application, the user must press start to begin the activity and the timer. The user was asked to pour coffee into the mug by grabbing the coffee pot from the machine. Once the user poured some coffee into the mug, they placed the coffee pot back and then were instructed to add a sugar cube into the mug. The next step of making the cup of coffee requires the user to grab the jug of milk and add milk into the mug. An example of this scenario is shown in Fig. 7, where a user can be seen pouring coffee into a coffee mug. Once this activity was complete, the user pressed done to transition to the game over scene.

Fig. 6. Pouring Coffee Scene

Fig. 7. Pouring Coffee

In Fig. 8, the Game Over scene is displayed. Once the user completed all their tasks, they were transitioned to the final scene to see their success. At the top of the user interaction panel, the text was shown, letting the user know the game has ended. Below the home button and game over text, images were shown to represent each activity from the experiment. Underneath each activity, the user could see their score for that activity along with the time it took for them to complete it. The highest score that a user could achieve on any scene was 100. Once the user is done observing the results from their experience, the home button returns the application to its main menu.

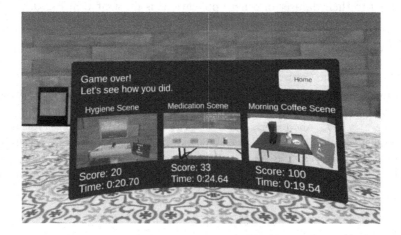

Fig. 8. Game Over Scene

4 Results

Using the non-immersive experiment and the application we developed, as seen in Sect. 3, we investigated the impact that each had on the students who participated. During our recruitment at Auburn University, we initially had 44 students sign up for the pre-survey to participate. During the experiment, 22 students participated in sessions to complete the non-immersive and immersive experiences. In our results, we investigated the impact on the user experience, empathy, and user engagement of our participants.

4.1 User Experience

In this section, we focus on the differences between non-immersive and immersive experiences regarding user experience. To measure the participants' user experience, we utilized the User Experience Questionnaire (UEQ) [11]. This survey came equipped with a Data Analysis Tool that analyzes and compares the results to the benchmark results of other applications within their dataset. The data analysis tool also provides a visual representation (i.e., chart) indicating how we compare to a dataset of other experiments. In Table 1, the results of our non-immersive experience are shown. Compared to the benchmark, the non-immersive experience was considered below average (mean = 0.92) compared to other experiments. However, our non-immersive experience was considered good in terms of perspicuity (mean = 1.81), dependability (mean = 1.19), stimulation (mean = 1.38), and novelty (mean = 0.67). In terms of efficiency, we were above average (mean 1.36). The visual representation of our non-immersive results compared to their dataset of other applications is illustrated in Fig. 9.

Table 1. UEQ Data Analysis Tool Benchmark Results - Non-immersive

Scale	Mean	Comparison to benchmark	Interpretation
Attractiveness	0.92	Below average	50% of results better, 25% of results worse
Perspicuity	1.81	Good	10% of results better, 75% of results worse
Efficiency	1.36	Above average	25% of results better, 50% of results worse
Dependability	1.19	Good	25% of results better, 50% of results worse
Stimulation	1.38	Good	10% of results better, 75% of results worse
Novelty	0.67	Good	50% of results better, 25% of results worse

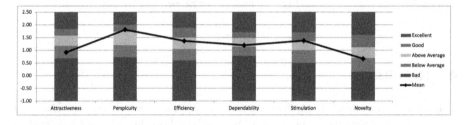

Fig. 9. UEQ Data Analysis Tool Benchmark Chart Results - Non-Immersive

Table 2 shows the results from the Data Analysis Tool for our VR (immersive) experience. Compared to the benchmark, the VR experience was below average in the efficiency (mean = 0.89) and dependability categories (1.00). However, our VR application was considered good in terms of novelty (mean = 1.42) and above average in attractiveness (1.41) and perspicuity (mean = 1.40). The VR application received its best ratings with respect to stimulation, ranging in the top 10% of the best results in stimulation (mean = 1.73). The chart to show our immersive results compared to their dataset is shown in Fig. 10.

Table 2. UEQ Data Analysis Tool Benchmark Results - VR

Scale	Mean	Comparison to benchmark	Interpretation
Attractiveness	1.41	Above average	25% of results better, 50% of results worse
Perspicuity	1.40	Above average	25% of results better, 50% of results worse
Efficiency	0.89	Below average	50% of results better, 25% of results worse
Dependability	1.00	Below average	50% of results better, 25% of results worse
Stimulation	1.73	Excellent	In the range of the 10% best results
Novelty	1.42	Good	10% of results better, 75% of results worse

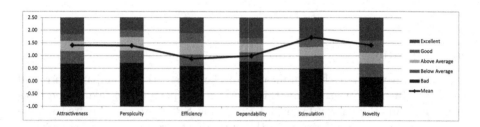

Fig. 10. UEQ Data Analysis Tool Benchmark Chart Results - VR

In an effort to compare the differences in attractiveness, perspicuity, efficiency, dependability, stimulation, and novelty between the non-immersive and VR (immersive) experiences, we used SPSS to run a statistical analysis on the data that was transformed via the Data Analysis Tool. The results from that analysis can be seen in Table 3. Based on the paired t-test results, there is no significant difference in attractiveness ($p = 0.054$), perspicuity ($p = 0.094$), or dependability ($p = 0.359$). However, there is a significant difference in efficiency, stimulation, and novelty. In terms of efficiency, there was a significant difference between the non-immersive and immersive experiences ($p = 0.023$, $p < 0.05$), with the non-immersive experience being more efficient than the immersive experience. There were also significant differences between the stimulation ($p = 0.020$, $p < 0.05$) and novelty ($p = 0.010$, $p < 0.05$) of the non-immersive and immersive experiences. However, in terms of stimulation and novelty, the immersive experience outperformed the non-immersive.

Table 3. SPSS UEQ Results - Paired Sample t Test

Pair	NI Mean	I Mean	t	Two-sided p
NI Attractiveness v. I Attractiveness	0.917	1.409	-2.045	0.054
NI Perspicuity v. I Perspicuity	1.807	1.398	1.756	0.094
NI Efficiency v. I Efficiency	1.364	0.886	2.444	0.023
NI Dependability v. I Dependability	1.193	1.000	0.938	0.359
NI Stimulation v. I Stimulation	1.375	1.727	-2.512	0.020
NI Novelty v. I Novelty	0.671	1.421	-2.796	0.011

NI = Non-Immersive, I = Immersive

4.2 Empathy

Next, we investigated the significance of the differences in empathy pre and post-experiment. We used empathic concern and perspective-taking questions from our empathy survey from [3,4,12]. Using SPSS, we ran a paired sample t-test to analyze the differences in the participants' responses after completing each experiment. To do this, each user's responses in their pre-survey and post-surveys to empathic concern were summed to get a score between 0 and 28, and the same with perspective-taking.

Table 4 shows the mean responses for each empathy category for each survey. In terms of empathic concern and perspective-taking, the larger mean values are considered better in terms of responses. The largest mean for empathic concern occurred in the pre-survey, while the largest mean for perspective-taking came after the non-immersive experience. In Table 5, we used a paired sample t-test to compare the pre-survey responses to each post-survey. There were no significant differences in the users' responses between the pre-survey and each post-survey. We calculated the change score to evaluate the impact that each non-immersive and immersive experience had on empathy. To calculate the change score, we

Table 4. SPSS Empathy Results - Mean

Survey-Type	Mean
PS Empathic Concern	20.45
NI Empathic Concern	20.23
I Empathic Concern	20.32
PS Perspective-Taking	18.64
NI Perspective-Taking	19.00
I Perspective-Taking	18.73

NI = Non-Immersive, I = Immersive, PS = Pre-Survey

took the pre-survey responses and subtracted them from each of the post-survey responses for both empathic concern and perspective-taking. Using those differences, we compared the change scores in SPSS. In Table 6, the results from that paired-sample t-test are shown. The table shows no significant difference in the change scores between the non-immersive and immersive experiences regarding empathic concern ($p = 0.853$) or perspective taking ($p = 0.618$).

Table 5. SPSS Empathy Results - Paired Sample t Test

Pair	t	Two-sided p
PS Empathic Concern v. NI Empathic Concern	0.533	0.599
PS Empathic Concern v. I Empathic Concern	0.335	0.741
PS Perspective-Taking v. NI Perspective-Taking	−0.508	0.617
PS Perspective-Taking v. I Perspective-Taking	−0.134	0.895
NI = Non-Immersive, I = Immersive, PS = Pre-Survey		

Table 6. SPSS Empathy Change Score Results - Paired Sample t Test

Pair	NI - PS Mean	I - PS Mean	t	Two-sided p
NI - PS v. I - PS Empathic Concern	−0.23	−0.14	−0.188	0.853
NI - PS v. I - PS Perspective-Taking	0.36	0.09	0.506	0.618
NI = Non-Immersive, I = Immersive, PS = Pre-Survey				

4.3   User Engagement

Finally, we investigated the user engagement differences between non-immersive and immersive experiences. To measure user engagement of the users, they were given the User Engagement Scale short form from [8]. The scale is broken up into four categories: Focused Attention, Perceived Usability, Aesthetic Appeal, and Rewarding. The results are shown in Table 7. As seen in the table, there is no significant difference in the Perceived Usability or Rewarding categories. However, there are significant differences in the Focused Attention ($p = 0.009$, $p < 0.05$) and Aesthetic Appeal ($p = 0.027$, $p < 0.05$) categories. In both cases, the immersive experience had better results than the non-immersive experience. We also found no significant difference in the overall scores of the experiences.

Table 7. SPSS User Engagement Results - Paired Sample t Test

Pair	NI Mean	I Mean	t	Two-sided p
NI Focused Attention v. I Focused Attention	2.864	3.561	−2.878	0.009
NI Perceived Usability v. I Perceived Usability	3.652	3.576	0.435	0.668
NI Aesthetic Appeal v. I Aesthetic Appeal	3.576	4.061	−2.374	0.027
NI Rewarding v. I Rewarding	4.212	4.349	−0.798	0.434
NI Overall v. I Overall	3.576	3.886	−1.967	0.062

NI = Non-Immersive, I = Immersive

5   Conclusion and Future Work

In this paper, we show the development and test results from our VR application created to simulate the daily activities of someone with RA. Our results show that in terms of user experience, there were significant differences in efficiency, stimulation, and novelty, with the non-immersive being better in terms of efficiency and the immersive being better in stimulation and novelty. Regarding empathy, we found no significant difference in the empathic concern or perspective-taking change scores between the pre-survey and each post-experience survey. It is possible that we did not find the statistically significant difference in empathy that we anticipated because we did not have enough power to detect a difference. For user engagement, we found significant differences between the non-immersive and immersive experiences regarding focused attention and aesthetic appeal, with the immersive experience being the better of the two. We also found that there is no significant difference in the overall engagement of the two experiences.

We can break down the future work of this research into two areas: (1) enhance technology integration for the RA portion of the application and (2) expand this application to support other scenarios for RA, other diseases, and disorders like Parkinson's disease, Multiple Sclerosis, and more. Refinement of the RA VR scenario entails adding more technology to the experience. We currently utilize the Cambridge simulation glove [7], and a VR headset [13]. In the future, we plan to use a high-tech glove that can be connected to the headset with haptic capabilities to broaden the immersive experience with more realism and a higher sense of touch. The haptic gloves will enhance the experience with plans to incorporate the full-body haptic suit so that we can expand to more than just the impact of RA on the hands. These additions will help to increase the immersive experience's effect on empathy, user engagement, and user experience, which is a goal of this research.

References

1. Barbour, K.E., Helmick, C.G., Boring, M., Brady, T.J.: Prevalence of doctor-diagnosed arthritis and arthritis-attributable activity limitation - united States, 2013–2015. MMWR. Morb. Mortal. Wkly Rep. **66**(9), 246–253 (2017). https://doi.org/10.15585/mmwr.mm6609e1
2. Centers for Disease Control and Prevention. Rheumatoid arthritis (RA). Centers for Disease Control and Prevention from https://www.cdc.gov/arthritis/basics/rheumatoid-arthritis.html. Accessed 24 Feb 2023
3. Davis, M.H.: A multidimensional approach to individual differences in empathy. JSAS Catalog Sel. Doc. Psychol. **10**, 85 (1980)
4. Davis, M.H.: Measuring individual differences in empathy: evidence for a multi-dimensional approach. J. Pers. Soc. Psychol. **44**(1), 113–126 (1983). https://doi.org/10.1037/0022-3514.44.1.113
5. Edemekong, P.F., Bomgaars, D.L., Sukumaran, S., et al.: Activities of daily living. [Updated 2022 Feb 17]. In: StatPearls [Internet]. Treasure Island (FL): StatPearls Publishing; 2022 Jan-. https://www.ncbi.nlm.nih.gov/books/NBK470404/?report=classic
6. Harrington, C.M., et al.: Development and evaluation of a trauma decisionmaking simulator in Oculus virtual reality. Am. J. Surg. **215**(1), 42–47 (2018). https://doi.org/10.1016/j.amjsurg.2017.02.011
7. Inclusive design toolkit. Cambridge Simulation Gloves. (n.d.). from https://www.inclusivedesigntoolkit.com/gloves/gloves.htm. Accessed 9 Mar 2022
8. O'Brien, H.L., Cairns, P. Hall, M.: A practical approach to measuring user engagement with the refined user engagement scale (UES) and new UES short form. Int. J. Hum. Comput. Stud. **112**, 28–39 (2018)
9. Perez, J.: Medical Consultation/Practice Room in Unreal Engine Marketplace Retrieved from: https://www.unrealengine.com/marketplace/en-US/item/09d9c5fe334c441987d478abacb320dd. Accessed 9 Mar 2022
10. Rheumatoid inflammatory disease - joints health. joints. (n.d.). https://joints-health.co.uk/rheumatoid-inflammatory-disease. Accessed 24 Feb 2023
11. Schrepp, M., Hinderks, A., Thomaschewski, J.: Construction of a benchmark for the User Experience Questionnaire (UEQ). Int. J. Interact. Multimedia Artif. Intell. **4**(4), 40–44 (2017)
12. Schutte, N.S., Stilinović, E.J.: Facilitating empathy through virtual reality. Motiv. Emot. **41**(6), 708–712 (2017). https://doi.org/10.1007/s11031-017-9641-7
13. VR headsets, Games & Equipment. Oculus., https://www.oculus.com/. Accessed 28 Mar 2022
14. Wang, L.J., Casto, B., Luh, J.Y., Wang, S.J.: Virtual Reality-Based Education for Patients Undergoing Radiation Therapy. J. Cancer Educ. **6**, 1–7 (2020). https://doi.org/10.1007/s13187-020-01870-7

Trend Analysis on Experience Evaluation of Intelligent Automobile Cockpit Based on Bibliometrics

Lei Wu[(⊠)] and Qinqin Sheng

School of Mechanical Science and Engineering, Huazhong University of Science and Technology, Wuhan 430074, People's Republic of China
lei.wu@hust.edu.cn

Abstract. With the advancement of automated driving systems, intelligent automobile cockpits have received increased attention. This study comprehended the global characteristics of international research on intelligent automobile cockpit experience evaluation and investigated new future development trends based on current research hotspots. Based on the relevant literature collected by Web of Science and bibliometrics, the publication trends, high-frequency keywords, high-frequency authors, high-frequency areas, organizations, main publications, and highly cited papers were sorted out and analyzed visually. The findings show that in the field of intelligent automobile cockpit experience evaluation research, Germany is the first in the number of publications, followed by the United States, and China ranks fourth. The top three productive authors are Burnett G, Bengler K, and Krems JF; the top three important research institutions are Technical University of Munich, BMW AG and VOLVO; the main research hotspots are HMI, human factors engineering, design and trust. This paper visualizes and analyzes the current research status, development trend, and research hotspots in the field of intelligent automobile cockpit experience evaluation research, which has corresponding guidance significance for relevant researchers.

Keywords: Intelligent automobile cockpit · Experience evaluation · Bibliometrics · VOSviewer

1 Introduction

The term 'intelligent automobile' describes a new generation of vehicles equipped with the ability to partially or automate driving, progressively transforming them from basic modes of transportation into intelligent mobile spaces [1]. The term 'intelligent automobile cockpit' refers to a new trend of digital and intelligent development in the automotive industry. It primarily refers to the integration and innovation in the fields of automotive cockpit interior and electronics. It aims to enhance the safety, comfort, and operability of the intelligent automobile cockpit by developing a novel human-computer interaction system from the perspective of customer needs and application scenarios [2].

V. G. Duffy (Ed.): HCII 2023, LNCS 14029, pp. 576–589, 2023.
https://doi.org/10.1007/978-3-031-35748-0_39

Currently, the key elements of intelligent automobile cockpits can be divided into three categories: hardware (cockpit chip, HUD, electronic rearview mirror, and other hardware), software (operating system, remote online upgrade technology), and interaction (voice recognition, face recognition, touch recognition, biometrics). The development history of the vehicle cockpit can be loosely split into three stages: mechanical, electrical, and intelligent. Intelligent automobile cockpit research is still in the emerging development stage [3]. When it comes to cockpit products from the mechanical era, the 1960s to the 1990s, the only information available is speed, engine speed, water temperature, fuel consumption, and other simple information. Mechanical instrument panels and simple audio playback equipment make up the majority of the cockpit products. In the electronic era, 2000–2016, with the advancement of automotive electronics, cockpit products into the electronic era, the device still primarily mechanical instruments, but some small size center LCDs began to use, in addition to enhancing the navigation system, audio, and video functions, to provide more information for the driver. The central control screen and instrument panel integrated design program started to appear, some models added HUD head-up display, streaming media rearview mirror, etc., diversified human-computer interaction, the degree to which the large size center LCDs screen as the representative of the first to replace the traditional central control, full LCDs instrumentation began to gradually replace the traditional instrumentation, and the degree to which the integrated design program for the central control screen and instrument panel appeared.

The liberation of humans brought about by autonomous driving necessitates intelligent improvements in intelligent automobile cockpit operations from five dimensions: interaction, environment, control, space, and data [4]. Digitalization has become the center of automotive intelligence. In the present time of continuous scientific and technological advancement, as well as the use of a wide range of technological equipment, the single attribute of the car as a mode of transportation is gradually giving way to the multiple attributes of 'transportation + intelligent terminal equipment'. The industry has not provided a clear definition for intelligent automobile cockpits; however, this paper believes that intelligent automobile cockpits are achieved through a variety of intelligent means, and the user's sensory interaction, emotional interaction, action interaction, natural interaction, more intelligent, and humane to meet the various needs of different people in the car. In the future, personalized and naturalized interaction experience research will be an important development direction for intelligent automobile cockpits. How to make the scientific and effective evaluation of the user experience of intelligent car cockpit becomes a key issue for research.

2 Experiment Method

2.1 Experiment Methodology Selection

The bibliometric method is currently one of the most widely used methods of conducting literature research. The scientific knowledge map obtained by visualization means by VOS viewer software is both a visual knowledge graph and a serialized knowledge genealogy, which can visually and accurately show the evolutionary history and trend trends of a discipline or knowledge field developed in a certain period, and it has become an important tool widely used in bibliometric research.

In this paper, VOSviewer was used as the research tool platform to download and export the txt format file of literature information from the Web of Science database and import the text into VOSviewer according to the needs of the research content, and then perform data analysis.

2.2 Experiment Data Source

To ensure the quality and academic value of the research, the Web of Science database core data collection was selected as the literature data source for this paper. In the process of literature data collection, the Web of Science database core data collection was selected as the literature source, and the search criteria were 'Topic:(vehicle HMI OR automotive human-machine interface OR smart cabin OR smart cockpit OR intelligent vehicle cockpit OR intelligent automobile cockpit) AND Topic:(user experience OR interactive experience OR test or evaluation OR ergonomic design evaluation OR usability test OR user preference OR evaluation OR assessment OR evaluate)', and the discipline scope was limited to related disciplines. A total of 351 papers were selected as the research sample after strict screening and elimination of papers that did not fit the topic of HMI evaluation of intelligent automobile cockpits.

3 Experiment Results

3.1 Publication Trends

As shown in Fig. 1, the number of publications on intelligent automobile cockpit experience evaluation in WOS from 2000–2022 showed a rapid growth trend over time: 5 papers in 2001, 10 papers in 2016, 20 papers in 2017, and 46 papers in 2019. This

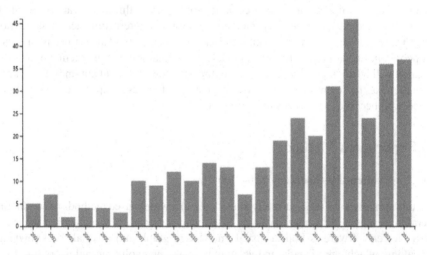

Fig. 1. Publication trends of intelligent automobile cockpit experience evaluation

indicates that the academic community is paying more and more attention to intelligent automobile cockpit experience evaluation research, which has rapidly become a research hotspot.

3.2 High-Frequency Keywords

Based on the previous data acquisition method, the keywords and word frequencies of the research literature on intelligent automobile cockpit experience evaluation in WOS from 2000–2022 were ranked as shown in Table 1 and Fig. 2. The keyword frequencies from

Table 1. High-frequency co-occurrences keywords

No	Keyword	Freq	No	Keyword	Freq
1	HMI	42	11	Model	13
2	Human-machine interface	34	12	Acceptance	13
3	Design	23	13	Systems	13
4	Trust	15	14	Behavior	9
5	Drivers	15	15	Safety	15
6	Performance	18	16	Workload	12
7	Driving simulator	17	17	Information	9
8	Automated driving	19	18	Task	8
9	Automated vehicles	13	19	Usability	10
10	Human factors	15	20	Automated vehicles	13

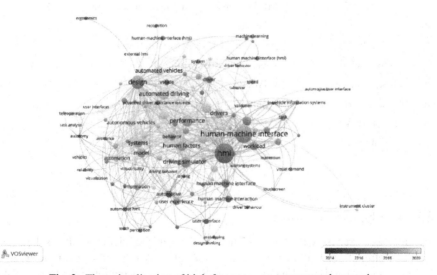

Fig. 2. Time visualization of high-frequency co-occurrence keywords

highest to lowest are HMI, human factors engineering, design, trust, driver, behavior, driving simulator, and autonomous driving.

3.3 High-Frequency Authors

The analysis of authors facilitates the identification of high-output researchers in the field, and important authors could be found by their number of publications and frequency of citations. A total of 1919 authors were involved in research papers in this field. The authors and citations of intelligent automobile cockpit experience evaluation research in Web of Science from 2000 to 2022 were ranked, and the authors with the TOP 10 publications were shown in Table 2. The authors in descending order of publication are Burnett G of the University of Nottingham, Bengler K of Technische Universität München, Krems JF of IMC University of Applied Sciences Krems, Naujoks F of BMW AG, the Queensland University of Technology Rakotonirainy A, Skrypchuk L of Jaguar Land Rover Limited, etc.

Figure 3 represents the graph of collaborations between important authors in this field, from which direct or indirect collaboration between various scholars. Different colors represent different clusters, and the strength of the different clusters and their interaction relationships were interpreted by the color, size, and clustering results of the nodes.

Table 2. The top 10 most high-frequency authors

No	Author	Affiliation	Amount
1	Burnett G	University of Nottingham	11
2	Bengler K	Technical University of Munich	10
3	Krems JF	IMC University of Applied Sciences Krems	8
4	Naujoks F	BMW AG	8
5	Rakotonirainy A	Queensland University of Technology	8
6	Skrypchuk L	Jaguar Land Rover Limited	8
7	Keinath A	BMW AG	7
8	Zhao XH	Beijing University of Technology	7
9	Forster Y	BMW AG	6
10	Gabbard J	Atrium Hlth Wake Forest Baptist	6

3.4 High-Frequency Areas

The number of papers included in SCI and the frequency of citations reflects the overall scientific strength and influence of a country/region. A total of 47 countries/regions, including Germany, USA, England, China, Sweden, etc., were retrieved from the Web of Science core collection database to publish research papers on intelligent automobile

Fig. 3. Time visualization of co-occurrence of author keywords

cockpit evaluation. The top 10 countries/regions in terms of the number of publications were shown in Table 3.

The distance between countries/regions indicates the closeness of cooperation between countries/regions, and the smaller the distance, the closer the cooperation between countries/regions. The smaller the distance, the closer the cooperation between countries/regions. The smaller the distance, the closer the cooperation between the countries/regions. As can be seen from Fig. 4, each country/region cooperates closely with each other and contributes to the research on intelligent automobile cockpit evaluation.

Table 3. The top 10 most high-frequency areas

No	Country / Region	Amount
1	Germany	87
2	USA	52
3	England	38
4	China	33
5	Sweden	26
6	Italy	25
7	France	24
8	Australia	16
9	Japan	15
10	Spain	15

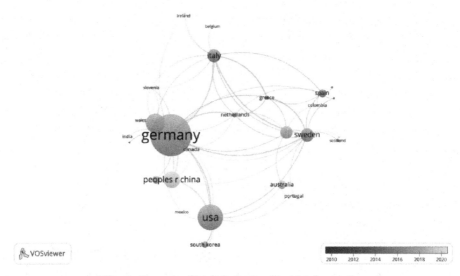

Fig. 4. Time visualization of co-authorship of countries

3.5 Organizations

Through analysis, there are 456 research institutions involved in research papers in this field, and the top 10 research institutions were shown in Table 4. 18 articles were published by the Technical University of Munich in the field of intelligent automobile cockpit evaluation research from 2000 to 2022, which is higher than the second-ranked BMW AG (14 articles) and the third-ranked VOLVO (13 articles).

Figure 5 showed the cooperation relationship between important research institutions in this field, from which we could see the cooperation relationship between each research institution, among which Technical University of Munich has cooperation with BMW AG and Delft University of Technology.

3.6 Main Publications

An analysis of journals in a particular field of study identifies the core journals that were SCI sources in that field. The impact factor is a method of calculating the impact of a journal, which is the total number of citations of papers published by a journal in the previous two years divided by the total number of papers published by the journal in the previous two years. There are 262 journals participating in this field, and the top 10 journals in terms of the number of publications are shown in Table 5. The impact factor of Transportation Research Part F: Traffic Psychology and Behaviour, the first journal in terms of the number of articles published, is 4.595, and the impact factor of Applied Ergonomics, the second journal in terms of the number of articles published, is 4.641.

3.7 Highly Cited Papers

The citation frequency of an article reflects to a certain extent, the degree of attention paid to research work, and could indicate the extent to which scientific papers were

Table 4. The top 10 most productive organizations

No	Organization	Amount
1	Technical University of Munich	18
2	BMW AG	14
3	VOLVO	13
4	Jaguar Land Rover	12
5	Technische Universitat Chemnitz	11
6	Helmholtz Association	10
7	Université Gustave Eiffel	10
8	University of Warwick	10
9	Queensland University of Technology	8
10	Beijing University of Technology	7

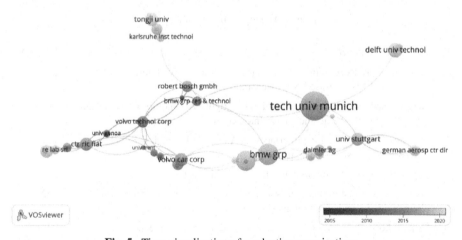

Fig. 5. Time visualization of productive organizations

used and valued in the research process, as well as their role and status in academic communication. The frequency of citations is increasingly used as an indicator of the importance of papers in current research evaluations. The top 10 most cited papers in this field were shown in Table 6.

4 Discussion

4.1 The Trend of Experience Evaluation Platforms

There are currently two types of test platforms available for evaluating the design of intelligent automobile cockpits: real vehicle tests and traffic driving simulator tests [5]. Real vehicle tests have the advantage of producing accurate results; however, they are

Table 5. The top 10 most productive publications

No	Main publications	Amount
1	Transportation Research Part F: Traffic Psychology and Behaviour	20
2	Applied Ergonomics	17
3	IEEE Transactions on Intelligent Transportation Systems	15
4	Lecture Notes in Computer Science	12
5	Accident Analysis and Prevention	9
6	IEEE Intelligent Vehicles Symposium	9
7	Information	7
8	Sensors	6
9	Advances in Intelligent Systems and Computing	5
10	Applied Sciences Basel	5

Table 6. The top 10 highly cited papers

No	Highly cited papers	Citations
1	Hand Gesture Recognition in Real Time for Automotive Interfaces: A Multimodal Vision-Based Approach and Evaluations	225
2	Maneuver-Based Trajectory Planning for Highly Autonomous Vehicles on Real Road with Traffic and Driver Interaction	191
3	External Human-Machine Interfaces on Automated Vehicles: Effects on Pedestrian Crossing Decisions	117
4	Extensive Tests of Autonomous Driving Technologies	116
5	A fuel economy optimization system with applications in vehicles with human drivers and autonomous vehicles	102
6	Smartphone-Based Vehicle Telematics: A Ten-Year Anniversary	97
7	Human-machine interfaces based on EMG and EEG applied to robotic systems	92
8	An experimental study to investigate design and assessment criteria: What is important for communication between pedestrians and automated vehicles?	90
9	A Modular CACC System Integration and Design	90
10	What externally presented information do VRUs require when interacting with fully Automated Road Transport Systems in shared space?	80

more dangerous, and repeatability is difficult to control, increasing development costs and time. The advantages of traffic driving simulator tests include a broad evaluation range, easy control of evaluation conditions, good repeatability of working conditions, high test efficiency, low test risk [6]. The current design and development of the initial stage of the driving simulator test to evaluate the intelligent automobile cockpit.

Riera, B [7] proposed a method to test and evaluate the human-computer interaction interface using a driving simulator, and through the analysis of the human-computer interaction interface evaluation method, a test platform based on the driving simulator was built and the relevant measurement parameters were determined. Li, L [8] proposed a method to evaluate the HCI interface in the cockpit and built a simple simulated driving environment. In the evaluation process, it was verified that the line-of-sight offset time could be used to reflect the difficulty of human-computer interaction. Xie, J.Y [9] compared the differences between intelligent automotive active safety technology and traditional automotive safety technology, elaborated the design concept of intelligent active safety technology, and also designed and verified a simply fixed driving simulator, which can be used and guided the evaluation and optimization of HMI of intelligent active safety products. Yin, C.Q [10] used distributed theory to establish a joint platform for automotive simulation and build an in-vehicle human factor co-simulation system. The feasibility of the simulation test was verified by simulating and analyzing the case of switching between non-driving and driving tasks and obtaining the same results as in the real vehicle environment.

4.2 The Trend of Experience Evaluation Method

The evaluation method of intelligent automobile cockpit experience has not been regulated yet, and the evaluation methods of scholars include the 'formula method' and 'experimental method'. The formula method uses mathematical models, such as the fuzzy rough set evaluation method, and hierarchical analysis method [11], which can quantify human psychological feelings, but is more subjective; the experimental method measures the physiological responses of subjects during the experience through instruments, such as EEG test [12, 13], eye movement test [14, 15], functional MRI test [16].

Trapanese, S [17] characterized the comfort level in the cockpit by analyzing the relaxation level of human muscles. Liu, X [18] proposed a "mission-oriented human-machine-loop evaluation model", analyzed the mission task of the evaluation object in a hierarchical objective, and established a four-level mission-oriented human-machine ergonomics assessment index system for the cockpit of a fighter aircraft. Liu, Y.J [19] analyzed the application scenarios of the LDW function in an advanced driver assistance system, taking the intelligent and networked functions of automobiles as an example, and applied the HMI design to the driving simulator for usability testing. Wang, R [20] studied the characteristics of the multi-channel interface interaction mode of intelligent vehicles. Through user behavior analysis, the high-frequency behavior during interface interaction, the average system response time, and the learning mastery time of interface interaction methods was studied, and the characteristics of different HMI interaction methods were summarized.

Yang, T.H [21] investigated the special requirements of the brake pedal in terms of ergonomic user experience by using the brake pedal as the main display control component. Using the eye-tracking analysis module to complete the extraction of effective eye-tracking data, the division of AOI interest area and visualization analysis. Sun, G.L [22] filtered and analyzed the difference in automotive dashboards based on eye-tracking data, and found that the reasonable layout and color scheme design of the dashboard influenced the recognition speed and efficiency of the measured object, and the speedometer should be placed on the right side, and the color scheme should not be more than three. Wang, J.M [23] analyzed the information on AR-HUD and W-HUD in ACC function based on three levels of situational awareness: perception, understanding, and prediction, with the entry scenario of intelligent vehicle automatic cruise control function as the main research object. Based on the theoretical model of driving trust, You, F [24] designed the human-computer interaction interface in typical driving scenarios to increase the driver's trust in the takeover system, improve the safety and comfort of using Level 3 autonomous driving, and validated the design on a simulated driver. Wang, J.M [25] selected the forward car cut-in as a typical scenario for the adaptive cruise control function, an important component of the advanced driver assistance system, combined the driver's operation and cognitive tasks when using ACC, classified the HMI information, and summarized the information architecture and corresponding design elements of ACC in different stages under the cut-in scenario. Yu, S.C [26] subdivided the cockpit function points based on the car use scenario, combined the multi-dimensional index system such as subjective index, vehicle index and eye-movement index according to the function points, built a comprehensive evaluation model of cockpit interaction experience based on the combination of subjective and objective measurement methods. Guo, X [27] took "user experience" as the core, explored the user preferences of intelligent seats, established the use scenario system, extracted the cockpit evaluation dimensions of user perception, established a subjective test system for user evaluation of the intelligent automobile cockpit of vehicles, and conducted subjective evaluation tests on the intelligent automobile cockpit of current representative models. Conduct subjective evaluation tests on the intelligent automobile cockpit of representative models.

4.3   The Trend of Experience Evaluation Index

Before the era of the intelligent automobile, research on car interaction experience design was primarily focused on the basic operation of the steering wheel, gas pedal, and brake [28] and instrument panel [29], the safety and comfort of car seats [30], the functional layout of the central control area [31], and driver fatigue [32]. New research on automotive interaction experience design in the transition to the intelligent automobile tends to focus on interaction technology and tools [33], a user-driving pleasure experience, integrated touch panel research, multi-channel interaction mode, and feedback.

Zhao, X.H [34] designed 13 traffic situations for various road conditions, traffic states, special events, and evaluated the driver adaptability of the vehicle-road coordination system in two dimensions, subjective and objective, including subjective perception, efficiency, safety, ecology, comfort, and effectiveness, and found that using the vehicle-road coordination technology-based design of HMI can effectively improve the driver's speed control ability. Jin, X [35] used a literature research method to establish automotive HMI evaluation indexes, collected subjective and objective data on safety and user experience dimensions through experiments based on a driving simulation system, tested and evaluated different sizes of buttons, and found that there is the correlation between button size and click button position, visual subjective rating, workload, and usability. You, F [36] constructed a multidimensional evaluation system containing driving indicators, behavioral indicators, and subjective indicators based on team situational awareness theory and user experience elements, and analyzed the correlation between situational awareness and user experience elements through pre-experimental analysis of task stages and channels.

5   Conclusion

Based on bibliometric data, this study examines the pertinent literature from 2000 to 2022 that was part of the WOS database for research on intelligent automobile cockpit evaluation. According to the survey, China comes fourth in terms of the number of articles published, with Germany coming in top place overall. Burnett G., Bengler K., and Krems J.F. are the top three greatest productive authors, Technical University of Munich, BMW AG, and VOLVO are the top three most significant research institutions, and the main journals are Transportation Research Part F: Traffic Psychology and Behaviour, Applied Ergonomics, and IEEE Transactions on Intelligent Transportation Systems, among others. HMI, human aspects of engineering, design, and trust are the key areas of research interest.

The following conclusions are obtained. The intelligent automobile cockpit is entering a time of rapid development, while in the future, the study of individualized and naturalistic interaction will be a key area for development. The study of user-driving pleasure and multi-channel interaction mode has replaced function as the focus of research on the cognitive load and task complexity of in-vehicle human-computer interaction. Examining task scenarios of varying complexity is important for assessing the intelligent automobile cockpit experience. Vehicle simulation tests are currently used the majority of the time to review intelligent car cockpit design. The "formula technique" and "experimental method" are the two basic ways to evaluate the cockpit experience in intelligent automobiles. The user's driven experience, interaction mode, and feedback are frequently highlighted in the assessment indices of intelligent automobile cockpits.

The platform, method, and index for evaluating user experience in intelligent automobile cockpits have yet to be standardized. Existing research attempts to establish a prediction system of intelligent automobile cockpit human-computer interaction, to apply this model to a design concept, user experience perception, and prediction of intelligent automobile cockpit products. However, the system cannot handle problems that require the driver to regain control of the vehicle in provisional autonomous driving (L3), and research on the experience evaluation of intelligent automobile cockpits has not been conducted systematically in L3-level autonomous driving conditions. Less researchers have currently looked into user experience evaluation in L3-level autonomous driving scenarios. The handover between humans and machines is a component of L3 autonomous driving, and how well it goes will have a significant effect on road safety.

Acknowledgments. This work was supported by the Key Research and Development Project of Hubei Province (2022BAA071).

References

1. Popovich, V.: Space theory for intelligent GIS. In: Popovich, V., Schrenk, M., Thill, J.-C., Claramunt, C., Wang, T. (eds.) Information Fusion and Intelligent Geographic Information Systems (IF&IGIS'17). LNGC, pp. 3–13. Springer, Cham (2018). https://doi.org/10.1007/978-3-319-59539-9_1
2. Yu, S.C., Meng, J., Zhang, B.: Discussion about the development status and future trend of automobile intelligent cockpit. Auto Time **05**, 10–11 (2021)
3. Lina, D., Ou, X.G., Deng, H., Wu, F.: Status and prospect of intelligent cockpit interactive experience. Automobile Appl. Technol. **16**, 48–50 (2022)
4. Zhou, Y., Zhu, L.J.: Research on the development trend of HMI design in smart cockpit. Auto Time **10**, 113–114+117 (2021)
5. Auckland, R.A., Manning, W.J., Carsten, O., et al.: Advanced driver assistance systems: objective and subjective performance evaluation. Veh. Syst. Dyn. **46**(S1), 883–897 (2008)
6. Weir, D.H.:Application of a driving simulator to the development of in-vehicle human-machine-interfaces. IATSS Res. **34**(1),16–21 (2010)
7. Riera, B., Grislin, M., Millot, P.: Methodology to evaluate man-car interfaces. IFAC Proc. Volumes **27**(12), 425–430 (1994)
8. Li, L., He, J.P., Liu, W.G et al.: Evaluation method study of human-machine-interface of advanced driver assistance systems. Automobile Technol. **02**, 58–62 (2014)
9. Xie, J.Y., Zhang, S.: Research on the design concept of intelligent vehicle active safety human-computer interaction interface evaluation method. Qual. Stand. **07**, 53–56 (2016)
10. Yin, C.Q., Tan, T.R., Wang, J.M et al.: Research and implementation of on-board human factors collaborative simulation system. J. Syst. Simul. **34**(01),134–144 (2022)
11. Hsiao, S.W., Hsu, C.F., Lee, Y.T.: An online affordance evaluation model for product design. Des. Stud. **33**(2), 126–159 (2012)
12. Khushaba, R.N., Greenacre, L., Kodagoda, S., et al.: Choice modeling and the brain: a study on the electroencephalogram (EEG) of preferences. Expert Syst. Appl. **39**(16), 12378–12388 (2012)
13. Khushaba, R.N., Wise, C., Kodagoda, S., et al.: Consumer neuroscience: assessing the brain response to marketing stimuli using electroencephalogram (EEG) and eye tracking. Expert Syst. Appl. **40**(9), 3803–3812 (2013)
14. Ramakrisnan, P., Jaafar, A., Razak, F.H.A., et al.: Evaluation of user interface design for lean-ing management system (LMS): investigating student's eye tracking pattern and experiences. Procedia-Soc. Behav. Sci. **67**(0), 527–537 (2012)
15. Peng, Y., Zhou, T., Wang, S., et al.: Design and implementation of a real-time eye tracking system. J. China Univ. Posts Telecommun. **1**, 1–5 (2013)
16. Soltysik, D.A., Thomasson, D., Rajan, S., et al.: Improving the use of principal component analysis to reduce physiological noise and motion artifacts to increase the sensitivity of task-based FMRI. J. Neurosci. Methods **241**, 18–29 (2015)
17. Trapanese, S., Naddeo, A., Cappetti, N.: A preventive evaluation of perceived postural comfort in car-cockpit design: differences between the postural approach and the accurate muscular simulation under different load conditions in the case of steering-wheel usage. SAE Tech. Paper 2016–01–1434 (2016)
18. Liu, X.: Task-oriented indicator system for human factor assessment of fighter cockpit. Mech. Eng. **06**, 88–90 (2018)

19. Liu, Y.J., Wang, J.M., Wang, W.J.: Experiment research on HMI usability test environment based on driving simulator. Trans. Beijing Inst. Technol. **40**(09), 949–955 (2020)
20. Wang, R., Dong, S.Y., Xiao, J.H.: Research on human-machine natural interaction of intelligent vehicle interface design. J. Mach. Des. **36**(02), 132–136 (2019)
21. Yang, T.H., Hei, Y.F.: Subjective evaluation of the efficacy of automobile display control interface brake pedal. Automob. Ind. **12**, 32–34 (2020)
22. Sun, G.L., Li, Q., Meng, Y.H., et al.: Design of car dashboard based on eye movement analysis. Packag. Eng. **41**(02), 148–153+160 (2020)
23. Wang, J.M., Liu, Y.J., Li, Y., et al.: Vehicle human-machine interface design based on situational awareness. Packag. Eng. **42**(06), 29–36 (2021)
24. You, F., Zhang, J.H., Zhang, J., et al.: Interaction design for trust-based takeover systems in smart cars. Packag. Eng. **42**(06), 20–28 (2021)
25. Wang, J.M., Wang, W.J., You, F., et al.: HMI design in ACC cut-in scenario based on control strategy data. Packag. Eng. **42**(18), 9–17 (2021)
26. Yu, S.C., Meng, J., Hao, B.: Research on ergonomic evaluation of driver-based intelligent cabin. Automot. Eng. **44**(01), 36–43 (2022)
27. Guo, X., Sun, L., Yang, J.: Research on subjective test scheme of intelligent cockpit. Intern. Combust. Eng. Parts **01**, 174–177 (2022)
28. Zhang, X.N., Zhao, J., Wang, G.W., et al.: Coordinated throttle and brake switching control for intelligent vehicle. Mach. Des. Manuf. **10**, 112–115 (2014)
29. Feng, F.J.: Comparison design of virtual operating of dashboard and steering wheels. J. Mach. Des. **30**(01), 107–110 (2013)
30. Yuan, Z., Wang, D.: Safety reviews of car seat. Automobile Parts **1**, 87–88 (2016)
31. Bhise, V.D., Dowd, J.D.: Driving with the traditional viewed-through-the-steering wheel cluster vs. the forward-center mounted instrument cluster. In: Proceedings of the Human Factors and Ergonomics Society Annual Meeting, pp. 2256–2260. SAGE Publications, Los Angeles (2004)
32. Li, Z.Y., Wang, C.T.: Research on driver fatigue and ergonomics design of automobile. Mach. Des. Manufact. Eng. **05**, 12–14 (2001)
33. Schmidt, A., Spiessl, W., Kern, D.: Driving automotive user interface research. IEEE Pervasive Comput. **9**(1), 85–88 (2009)
34. Zhao, X.H., Chen, Y.F., Li, H.Y., et al.: Comprehensive test and impact assessment for human factors of connected vehicle system. China J. Highw. Transport **32**(06), 248–261 (2019)
35. Jin, X., Li, L.P., Yang, Y.F., et al.: Touch key of in-vehicle display and control screen based on vehicle HMI evaluation. Packag. Eng. **42**(18), 151–158 (2021)
36. You, F., Xie, Y.K., Yue, T.Y., et al.: A team situation awareness-based approach to automotive HMI evaluation and design. J. Graph. **42**(06),1027–1034 (2021)

Intelligent Human-Computer Interaction Interface: A Bibliometric Analysis of 2010–2022

Yi Zhang, Yaqin Cao$^{(\boxtimes)}$, Yu Liu, and Xiangjun Hu

School of Economics and Management, Anhui Polytechnic University, Wuhu 241000, People's Republic of China
caoyaqin.2007@163.com

Abstract. Intelligent interfaces play an important role in the harmony and naturalness of human-computer interaction. The purpose of this paper is to investigate the hot spots and trends in the field of intelligent human-computer interaction interfaces (IHCII) from 2010 to 2022 by bibliometric analysis. Author, citation, co-citation, and keyword co-occurrence networks were visualized using bibliometrics. The analysis included 1,784 articles and 80,964 cited references. The results showed that emotion recognition and EEG are at the forefront of IHCII research. China leads in publications (359), but the US dominates in citations (7,007 times). The Centre National de la Recherche Scient fique is the most productive organization. IEEE Access is the journal with the most papers on IHCII. The keyword co-occurrence analysis shows that "user experience", "virtual reality", "eye tracking", "emotion recognition", "big data", and "mental workload" may be the research hotspots in this field. For researchers, this paper proposes that interface design features are a research gap in the field of IHCII.

Keywords: Intelligent human-computer interaction interfaces (IHCII) · Bibliometric analysis · VOSviewer · CiteSpace

1 Introduction

With the deep development of artificial intelligence and the Internet of Things, the interaction interface is gradually changing from simple to intelligent. The consensus among academics, as represented by Nielsen, is that the upcoming generation of new interfaces should achieve greater personalization and customization [1]. This new interface, also known as an intelligent human-computer interaction interface (IHCII), is built around user perception. IHCII is not only widely used in people's daily life, but also has irreplaceable applications in the military, aviation, education, and other industrial fields. An adaptive interface was created by Zhu et al. [2] to satisfy the demands of HCI tasks in military command and control modules. Laureano et al. [3] established an intelligent interface related to teaching-learning processes based on affective-cognitive structures. Lim et al. [4] gave IHCII the ability to assess the environmental state and operator state in the Manned and Unmanned Aircraft study.

IHCII refers to adaptively adjusting the elements, layout, and structure of the interface based on the user's cognitive state to better serve specific user needs [5]. It is important to understand how IHCII contributes to lower user cognitive load, fewer human errors, and better user experience.

In recent years, more and more scholars are interested in the field of IHCII. Some scholars have focused more on the study of intelligent interfaces to improve the efficiency of professional operators [6], while others believe that intelligent interactive interfaces should be designed for inexperienced novice users and people with limited sensory abilities [7, 8]. Overall, The main object of those studies was to explore how to integrate visual, auditory, tactile, and other design elements to achieve the user's requirements [9].

Although there are some review articles in this field, such as [8, 10], they mainly focus on studying one aspect or development of IHCII. In particular, they do not propose a systematic framework for the IHCII research. To pinpoint the factors that have influenced IHCII's evolution over time, the following research objectives are proposed in this paper:

RQ1. What are the influential research trends, influential researchers, and publications on IHCII?

RQ2. What have been the hot issues in IHCII research in the last decade?

RQ3. What are the main research areas and research framework of IHCII?

2   Methodologies

In this paper, we adopted the databases from WoS core. Considering IHCII embodies patterns of intelligence, such as emotion recognition or detection of user cognition. Therefore, the search code used is "TS = (human-computer interaction interface) AND TS = (intelligent OR emotion OR affective OR cognitive)". The investigation mainly concentrates on the last ten years, which could reflect the frontier research on the IHCII. There were 1,784 articles from 2010 to 2022 downloaded and recorded in the database, including journal articles, reviews, and conference proceedings.

Utilizing VOSviewer 1.6.18, CiteSpace 6.1.3, and Excel 2021 as the main bibliometric analysis tools, we primarily focused on citation analysis and co-occurring keyword analysis. Firstly, Excel was used to analyze the performance of journals, papers, authors, countries, and institutions. Secondly, VOSviewer is our go-to tool for co-occurring keyword analysis due to its clarity and simplicity. The current research hotspots for IHCII can be objectively found by co-occurring keyword analysis. Finally, CiteSpace has richer functions, so we use it to analyze the reference co-citation and reference burst.

3   Results and Discussion

3.1   Performance Analysis

After reviewing and filtering the bibliographic records, we exported the records as an Excel file to analyze the performance of the nation, journals, and institutions. Figure 1 shows the general trend in the number of papers published from 2010 to 2022 (black solid line) and the contribution of each country (colored dotted line).

What can be observed in Fig. 1 is that there is an overall ascending trend of research on IHCII. In particular, there is an explosive upward trend after 2018. It further indicates that scholars are becoming more and more interested in researching IHCII. The research trends in each country can be shown in the colored dotted lines in Fig. 1. China, the USA, Spain, Germany, and England have made the largest contributions to the field of intelligent HCI interfaces research, and the number of publications in these nations has generally followed the global trend. In terms of details, the USA started researching this subject first and has produced more articles than any other nation before 2017. Since 2018, the number of documents published by Chinese scholars has increased rapidly, surpassing that of other countries.

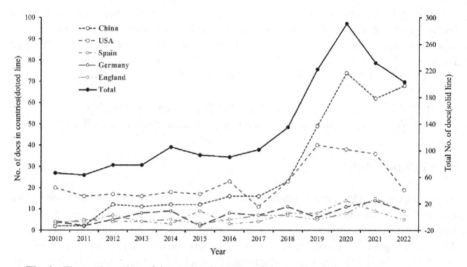

Fig. 1. The total number of documents by year and the number of documents by country.

Next, we sorted the journals by the number of publications and summarized the number of times each journal was cited. Table 1 shows the top ten journals ranked in descending order by the number of publications in academic research related to intelligent HCI interfaces.

These journals account for 27.6% of the 1,784 sub-papers, indicating that they have a high level of attention to IHCII. Located in the second column of the table is the total number of scholarly documents in their journals, and the third column represents the number of times these journals have been cited in the WoS core. Research publicized in these journals has focused on smart sensor research (e.g., EEG sensors, electrodermal sensors, and wearable devices) and on the physiological signals measured by these sensors. Through these studies, research on affective computing as well as human-computer interaction has been developed. It is worth noting that research on multimodal tools is also included in Table 1, which suggests that for intelligent interactive interfaces, it may be necessary to link human-computer interaction through multimodal recognition methods and multichannel output methods.

A statistical analysis of research institutions can help us understand where research on IHCII is mainly done. Table 2 lists the 10 research institutions that produced the most papers, accounting for 13.6% of the total number of papers.

Table 1. The top 10 contributing journals.

Journal Title	No. of docs	No. of citations
IEEE Access	96	1112
Sensors	66	928
International Journal of Human-Computer Studies	57	1227
Multimedia Tools and Applications	50	449
IEEE Transactions on Affective Computing	47	1554
International Journal of Human-Computer Interaction	44	337
Computers & Education	40	1761
Interacting With Computers	36	867
Behaviour & Information Technology	30	182
ACM Transactions on Computer-Human Interaction	26	516

Table 2. The top 10 contributing institutions.

Institutions	Location	No. of docs	No. of citations
Centre National de la Recherche Scient fique (CNRS)	France	37	694
UDICE French Research Universities	France	35	692
Chinese Academy of Sciences	China	29	525
University of California System	USA	27	858
State University System of Florida	USA	24	459
University of London	England	24	949
Tsinghua University	China	19	374
Aalto University	Finland	17	279
Nanyang Technological University	Singapore	15	1115
University College London	England	15	270

In Table 2, the two research institutions that produced the most output were in France, followed by the Chinese Academy of Sciences. From a citation perspective, the University of London in the UK and Nanyang Technological University in Singapore have a clear advantage. It is worth mentioning that Nanyang Technological University, which produced only 15 papers but received 1115 cited numbers, has gained a good reputation in affective computing.

3.2 Keyword Co-occurrence Analysis

We used the VOSviewer_1.6.18 to analyze keywords in co-occurrence analysis. Based on the co-occurrence analysis, we selected all keywords as the analysis unit and created a synonym dictionary for them. For all keywords, the threshold facility was set to 7, i.e., a keyword was included in the co-occurrence analysis only when it appeared 7 times in the literature. In total, we got 285 keywords in the co-occurrence analysis. The keyword co-occurrence map obtained is shown in Fig. 2.

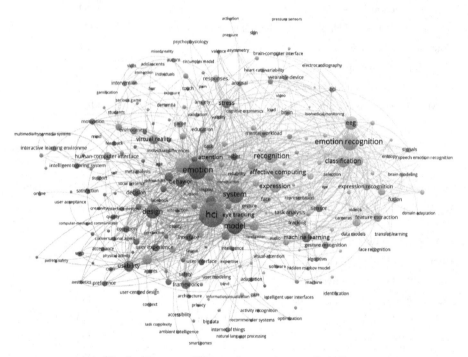

Fig. 2. The map of Keyword co-occurrence clustering.

The six clusters are shown in Fig. 2. The first cluster is in the red portion. Words like "emotion", "cognition", "decision", "user experience", "satisfaction", "trust", "design", "user interface", and "interface design" can be found in this cluster. These keywords capture both human-related and machine-related variables that influence interactions at the interface between humans and computers. It is possible to build user-adaptive inter-action interfaces by measuring these human-related aspects. The machine-related factors are mainly reflected in the main carriers of interaction interfaces, such as robots and web pages, etc. For example, [11] reviewed the impact of user experience on driving safety and user acceptance in the context of autonomous driving. [12] argued that satisfying universal psychological needs, such as competence, relatedness, popularity, or auton-omy, are the main sources of positive experiences with interactive technologies. [13] focused on the study of conveying emotions through complex and rich touch and found that the information conveyed by touch seems to outweigh the information displayed by visual and textual signals. Each of the above research can be categorized as a user experience study, regardless of whether they focus directly on user experience or user emotion because emotion is a crucial cue for user experience.

The green portion is the second cluster. These clusters show the traits of the two sides of an interaction interface that interact, i.e., the presentation or environment of the interface and the traits of the interface's intended users. These interactive interfaces are supported by platforms like "virtual reality", "games", "augmented reality", "mixed reality", "interactive learning environments", etc. Users of the interactive interface are described as "children", "adults", and "students", along with details about each of their characteristics, such as "stress", "anxiety", and "depression". For this clustering of keywords, in general, researchers seem to have focused their studies in the direction of particular interactive environments, as well as exploring the adaptations of the target users supported by such environments. For example, [14] investigated the differences between active interactive and passive guided interactions in the context of virtual reality and the impact of these two types of interactions on teaching and learning activities. [7] defined for the first time user-centered AR instructions (UCAI), which are more beneficial than traditional AR instructions for improving users' spatial cognitive abilities. [15] explored the possibility of using chatbots equipped with AI technology as book conversation companions to improve students' reading experiences. The above literature mainly focused on whether a certain interaction approach employed in different interactive interface environments (e.g., virtual reality environments, instructional interactive environments, book exchange environments, etc.) can have a positive impact on the target users (e.g., teenagers [14], assemblers [7], children [15], etc.).

The first two clusters highlight the HCI's fundamental composition. In other words, the human-computer interface's pertinent elements and entity traits are displayed. The third cluster, which is displayed in the orange area of the diagram, highlights the visual perception of an intelligent interactive interface. Specifically, the keywords in this category are mainly related to the specific method of eye tracking, which is usually used to measure visual perception. This clustering can be further divided into two categories: one related to visual perception, such as "eye tracking", "gaze tracking", "movement", "vision", etc. The other category is related to interactive interfaces, such as "navigation", "computer vision", "visualization", "real-time systems", "data visualization", etc. Scholars have extensively investigated the application of eye-tracking techniques in human-machine interfaces. [6] used eye-tracking techniques to classify the information usage of drivers of partially autonomous vehicles to inform the design of an adaptive interface. [16] investigated the performance of eye-tracking-only data, interaction-only data, and combined data for predicting users' cognitive abilities in the context of a traffic visualization decision interface. What can be found is that in most of these types of studies, researchers have applied techniques such as eye-tracking to task-specific analysis. It is the reason that many of the keywords in this section fall into the red area, as eye-tracking technology is also an important way to measure user experience.

The fourth major category is the yellow part. The intrinsic connection of this cluster is that they are all related to recognition and classification. For example, the keywords "speech emotion recognition", "expression recognition", "emotion recognition", "face recognition", etc., represent different types of recognition. Most of the related studies are about the recognition of emotion and expression. Another set of keywords in this cluster, "support vector machine", "convolutional neural network", "feature extraction", "accuracy", and "deep learning", show the algorithmic models of the recognition process. "EEG (Electroencephalogram)", "physiological signals", "database", and other keywords reflect the input of the emotion recognition model. For example, [17] used both text and audio modalities for sentiment recognition to improve the robustness of the recognition system. [18] proposed emotional context recognition, which refers to the recognition of a user's emotions considering the context in which they are placed, bridging the gap between data-driven techniques that are highly dependent on learning data.

The purple part represents the fifth cluster. In general, most of the terms in this cluster are about IHCII based on big data. The keywords "internet", "internet of things (IoT)", "big data", "machine learning", "algorithm", etc., reflect the source of data and the analysis method. The other category of keywords reflects the main form of intelligent HCI, such as the keywords "artificial intelligence", "ambient intelligence", "intelligent agent", "smart homes", "gesture recognition", "sentiment analysis", etc. For example, [19] designed and functionally validated a smart home environment based on IoT data, as well as robotic assistance that uses homework activities as a support tool for children with or without attention deficit disorders. [20] investigated a comprehensive technology that combines high-tech achievements from multiple fields in the context of the IoT to achieve human-computer interaction naturally and intelligently, improving the user experience and efficiency of human-computer interaction in virtual reality technology.

Cluster 6 is shown in the blue part. This section in general appears with keywords regarding human cognition load. Words such as "attention", "cognitive load", "mental workload", "pressure", "heart-rate-variability", etc. describe the terminology of human brain cognitive load. The terms "wearable device", "BCI (Brain Computer Interface)", "situation awareness" and "cognitive ergonomics" show the methods for measuring cognitive load. [21] examined eye-tracking of website complexity from a cognitive load perspective. To improve the estimation of cognitive load in automated driving systems, various eye gaze metrics were studied and evaluated as measures of cognitive load [22].

3.3 Research Areas Analysis

An overview of the research directions can help us to more easily understand the overall lineage of this research as well as the application areas. Figure 3 shows the top ten areas for research on IHCII and the top research directions.

Sorting by the number of documents, we found that the top ten research directions were Computer Science (1195 articles, 66.9% of total documents), Engineering (842 articles, 47.2%), Telecommunications (194 articles, 10.9%), Psychology (123 articles, 6.9%), Chemistry (121 articles, 6.7%), Instruments Instrumentation (108 articles, 6%), Physics (83 articles, 4.6%), Neurosciences Neurology (72 articles, 4%), and Science Technology Other Topics (67 articles, 3.7%), Materials Science (65 articles, 3.6%). The top four research domains with a cumulative 80% representation are Computer Science, Engineering, Telecommunications, and Psychology. It can be said that these domains and the combined domains among them cover most of the research on intelligent HCI interfaces. Among the computer science fields, [23] is the most representative with 426

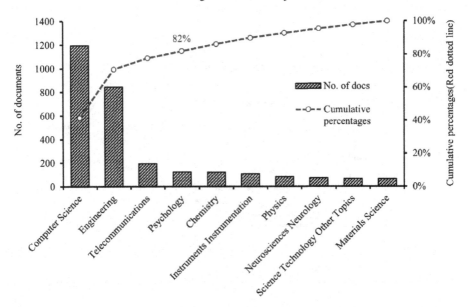

Fig. 3. The top 10 research areas.

cited times. Robert Jenke et al. have made important contributions to feature extraction methods, emotion recognition, and electrode selection, concluding that multivariate feature selection techniques perform better than univariate methods. The most cited in the combined field of computer science and engineering is [24] with 701 citations. Cambria et al. have done a systematic analysis of sentiment computing, which provides an important reference for a wide range of scholars. The most contributed in the intersection areas of telecommunications, computer science, and engineering is [25], cited 179 times. Barbara Rita Barricelli et al. used literature analysis to provide a reference for the definition, characterization, and application of the digital twin. In the combined areas of psychology, engineering, and behavioral sciences, [26] is cited 421 times. Raja Parasuraman et al. provide an integrated theoretical model of empirical research on complacency and bias in human interaction with automation and decision support systems.

3.4 Co-citation Network

The frequency with which two documents are co-cited by other documents is known as co-citation [27]. In the co-citation analysis, two perspectives can be analyzed: the citing reference and the cited reference. The analysis of citing references, which are the 1784 articles in our dataset, can help us understand the frontiers of a certain cluster. The cited literature may not be too relevant to the clusters, but it is the basis for the study of a certain cluster. Among the 1784 articles, there are 80980 references, and the final co-citation network constructed with CiteSpace 6.1.3 has 695 nodes and 1892 edges, with 80964 valid references (99.98%). Figure 4 shows the constructed co-citation network. The most highly cited paper was written by Zeng ZH in 2009 [28], and the second and third papers were [29] and [30], respectively.

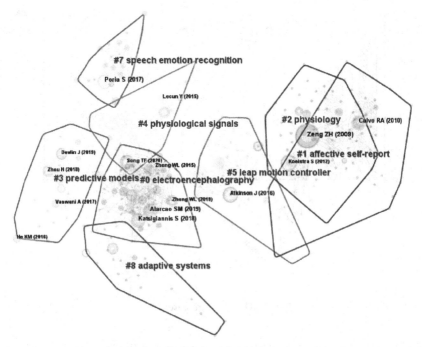

Fig. 4. Co-citation and cluster analysis.

Table 3 gives specific information on the most dominant 7 of the 11 clusters. The quality of the clusters can be evaluated by the "silhouette" score, which reflects the homogeneity or consistency of the clusters [31].

Table 3. Specific information on the 7 major clusters.

Cluster ID	No. of docs	Silhouette	Mean year	Cluster term	Leading citing reference	Leading cited reference
#0	65	0.876	2018	Electroencephalography	[32]	[29]
#1	61	0.979	1992	Affective self-report	[33]	[28]
#2	42	0.942	1963	Physiology	[34]	[35]
#3	39	0.978	2017	Predictive models	[36]	–
#4	34	0.916	2016	Physiological signals	[37]	[38]
#5	33	0.972	2014	Leap motion controller	[39]	[40]
#7	22	0.986	2018	Speech emotion recognition	[41]	[30]

[32] summarized and reviewed the EEG-based approach to Transfer Learning in BCI (Brin Computer Interface) and pointed out future research directions. [29] investigated the continuum of emotions and guided possible future directions. [34] introduced a new toolbox for brain-computer interface design, providing experimental scientists and method developers with efficient tools for brain data analysis. [36] investigated intelligent open-domain dialogue systems in terms of semantics, coherence, and interactivity. [37] provides a detailed discussion and summary of the current state of development of multichannel sentiment datasets, multichannel feature extraction, and multichannel fusion strategies and recognition methods. [39] effectively identify emotional states by analyzing the features of the electroencephalographic (EEG) signal and selecting the best combination of these features. [41] explored speech emotion recognition, proposing a two-stream deep convolutional neural network.

3.5 Research Trends Analysis

The academic dynamics of a particular field can be characterized to some extent by citation bursts. A citation burst indicates the possibility that the scientific community has paid or is paying special attention to relevant contributions [42]. Table 4 shows the top 20 most bursts articles out of the 26 references. Here are a few articles to focus on that feature the earliest bursts, the longest duration, and the most frontiers.

Zeng et al.'s [28], which received the earliest attention from scholars (2010–2014), investigated the progress of audio, visual, and spontaneous expression-based emotion recognition methods. [43] by Andrea Kleinsmith et al. had the most sustained outburst (2014- 2018), who did a detailed investigation and study of body expression perception and recognition. Literature such as [38, 40, 44, 45] has generated a larger response in the last two years (2020–2022), indicating that the discussion on the topic of emotion recognition is ongoing and cutting-edge.

3.6 Research Framework

Based on the above analysis, we derive a basic logical framework of intelligent interactive interface research, as shown in Fig. 5.

Figure 5 shows the three main parts of the IHCII study. The first part focuses on the human physiological signal or behavioral signal measurement aspect. This part mainly focused on how to select physiological or behavioral signal combinations to enhance the accuracy of IHCII in identifying human perceptual states. The second part is about the research on machine learning algorithms for emotion recognition, cognitive recognition, etc. The third part takes user experience as the focus and aims to find out which elements of smart interface design can give the user a positive perceptual experience.

Table 4. Top 20 References with the Strongest Citation Bursts.

Author	Year	Strength	Begin	End	2010 - 2022
Zeng ZH	2009	9.68	2011	2014	
Fairclough SH	2009	3.01	2011	2012	
Calvo RA	2010	7.17	2012	2015	
Kim J	2008	3.4	2012	2013	
El AYADIM	2011	3.09	2012	2014	
Chang CC	2011	4.01	2013	2014	
Zander TO	2011	3.73	2013	2015	
Koelstra S	2012	5.85	2014	2017	
Kleinsmith A	2013	3.27	2014	2018	
Jenke R	2014	4.46	2017	2019	
Soleymani M	2016	2.86	2018	2020	
Poria S	2017	4.67	2019	2020	
Lecun Y	2015	4.64	2019	2020	
Zheng WL	2015	4.64	2019	2020	
Pu XJ	2017	3.37	2019	2020	
Zhou H	2018	3.37	2020	2022	
Atkinson J	2016	3.34	2020	2022	
Liu W	2016	3.04	2020	2022	
Dzedzickis A	2020	3.04	2020	2022	
Huang G	2017	3.04	2020	2022	

3.7 Limitations

Although the current research was reviewed systematically in this paper, admittedly, the main limitation is that specific aspects of IHCII have not been studied in depth, due to the overly broad scope of the study. On the other hand, since only the WoS Core database was used in this paper, there may be some literature that has not been covered. Therefore, there is still a need to expand the database and screen references based on particular rules for in-depth research in subsequent work. For example, select papers that include the topic of intelligent interaction interface design features for detailed study, and achieve precise research by reducing the amount of literature data.

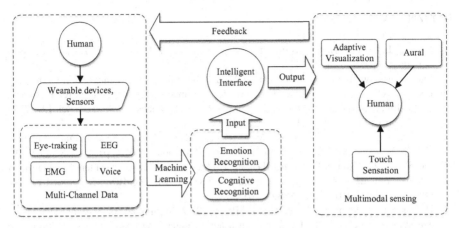

Fig. 5. The logical framework of IHCII studies.

4   Conclusion

Firstly, by gathering all pertinent papers published between 2010 and 2022 in the WoS Core database, a thorough scientific review of the IHCII field is demonstrated. Through the co-citation network and reference burst, we can conclude that emotion recognition and EEG are at the forefront of IHCII research. China leads in publications (359), but the US dominates in citations (7,007 times). The Centre National de la Recherche Scient fique is the most productive organization. IEEE Access is the journal with the most papers on IHCII. The paper by Zeng ZH (2009) is the most co-cited.

Secondly, the keyword co-occurrence analysis helps us find that "user experience", "virtual reality", "eye tracking", "emotion recognition", "big data", and "mental work-load" may be the research hotspots of the past decade in this field. These frontiers or hot topics build a framework for IHCII. We suggest that research on IHCII should focus on building user models through multimodal sentiment or cognitive recognition, decreasing user cognitive workload through optimal interface design, and improving user experience.

Finally, from the research area survey, we can find that IHCII is a multidisciplinary subject, which mainly combines computer science, engineering, telecommunications, and psychology. This finding reminds researchers of the need for multidisciplinary integration to make studies fuller and more adequate. We also propose a research framework for IHCII through the complete assessment, which outlines the logical progression of the study from the input side of smart wearable devices, physiological signal measurement, and emotion recognition, to the output side of multimodal interface features.

Acknowledgments. This work was supported by National Natural Science Foundation of Anhui Province (grant number 2208085MG183), the Key Project for Natural Science Fund of Colleges in Anhui Province (grant numbers KJ2021A0502), and the Project for Social Science Innovation and Development in Anhui Province (grant numbers 2021CX075). Further, we thank the editor and anonymous reviewers for their valuable comments and advice.

References

1. Nielsen, J.: User interface directions for the Web. Commun. ACM. **42**, 65–72 (1999). https://doi.org/10.1145/291469.291470
2. Interface Design for the Command-control Module Based on Adaptive Interaction Technology
3. Laureano-Cruces, A.L., Sánchez-Guerrero, L., Ramírez-Rodríguez, J., Ramírez-Laureano, E.: Intelligent interfaces: pedagogical agents and virtual humans. Int. J. Intell. Sci. **12**, 57–78 (2022). https://doi.org/10.4236/ijis.2022.123005
4. Lim, Y., et al.: Avionics human-machine interfaces and interactions for manned and unmanned aircraft. Prog. Aeosp. Sci. **102**, 1–46 (2018). https://doi.org/10.1016/j.paerosci.2018.05.002
5. Van Velsen, L., Van Der Geest, T., Klaassen, R., Steehouder, M.: User-centered evaluation of adaptive and adaptable systems: a literature review. Knowl. Eng. Rev. **23**, 261–281 (2008). https://doi.org/10.1017/S0269888908001379
6. Ulahannan, A., Jennings, P., Oliveira, L., Birrell, S.: Designing an adaptive interface: using eye tracking to classify how information usage changes over time in partially automated vehicles. IEEE Access **8**, 16865–16875 (2020). https://doi.org/10.1109/ACCESS.2020.2966928
7. Wang, Z., et al.: The role of user-centered AR instruction in improving novice spatial cognition in a high-precision procedural task. Adv. Eng. Inform. **47**, 101250 (2021). https://doi.org/10.1016/j.aei.2021.101250
8. Karpov, A.A., Yusupov, R.M.: Multimodal interfaces of human-computer interaction. Her. Russ. Acad. Sci. **88**, 67–74 (2018). https://doi.org/10.1134/S1019331618010094
9. Dibeklioğlu, H., Surer, E., Salah, A.A., Dutoit, T.: Behavior and usability analysis for multimodal user interfaces. J. Multimodal User Interfaces **15**(4), 335–336 (2021). https://doi.org/10.1007/s12193-021-00372-0
10. Wang, M., et al.: Fusing stretchable sensing technology with machine learning for human-machine interfaces. Adv. Funct. Mater. **31**, 2008807 (2021). https://doi.org/10.1002/adfm.202008807
11. Tan, H., Sun, J., Wenjia, W., Zhu, C.: User experience & usability of driving: a bibliometric analysis of 2000–2019. Int. J. Hum. Comput. Interact. **37**, 297–307 (2021). https://doi.org/10.1080/10447318.2020.1860516
12. Hassenzahl, M., Diefenbach, S., Göritz, A.: Needs, affect, and interactive products – facets of user experience. Interact. Comput. **22**, 353–362 (2010). https://doi.org/10.1016/j.intcom.2010.04.002
13. Teyssier, M., Bailly, G., Pelachaud, C., Lecolinet, E.: Conveying emotions through device-initiated touch. IEEE Trans. Affect. Comput. **13**, 1477–1488 (2022). https://doi.org/10.1109/TAFFC.2020.3008693
14. Ferguson, C., van den Broek, E.L., van Oostendorp, H.: On the role of interaction mode and story structure in virtual reality serious games. Comput. Educ. **143**, 103671 (2020). https://doi.org/10.1016/j.compedu.2019.103671
15. Liu, C.-C., Liao, M.-G., Chang, C.-H., Lin, H.-M.: An analysis of children' interaction with an AI chatbot and its impact on their interest in reading. Comput. Educ. **189**, 104576 (2022). https://doi.org/10.1016/j.compedu.2022.104576
16. Conati, C., Lallé, S., Rahman, M.A., Toker, D.: Comparing and combining interaction data and eye-tracking data for the real-time prediction of user cognitive abilities in visualization tasks. ACM Trans. Interact. Intell. Syst. **10**, 12:1–12:41 (2020). https://doi.org/10.1145/3301400
17. Zhang, T., Li, S., Chen, B., Yuan, H., Chen, C.L.P.: AIA-Net: adaptive interactive attention network for text–audio emotion recognition. IEEE Trans. Cybern. 1–13 (2022). https://doi.org/10.1109/TCYB.2022.3195739

18. Ayari, N., Abdelkawy, H., Chibani, A., Amirat, Y.: Hybrid model-based emotion contextual recognition for cognitive assistance services. IEEE Trans. Cybern. **52**, 3567–3576 (2022). https://doi.org/10.1109/TCYB.2020.3013112
19. Berrezueta-Guzman, J., Pau, I., Martín-Ruiz, M.-L., Máximo-Bocanegra, N.: Smart-home environment to support homework activities for children. IEEE Access **8**, 160251–160267 (2020). https://doi.org/10.1109/ACCESS.2020.3020734
20. Lv, Z.: Virtual reality in the context of Internet of Things. Neural Comput. Appl. **32**(13), 9593–9602 (2019). https://doi.org/10.1007/s00521-019-04472-7
21. Wang, Q., Yang, S., Liu, M., Cao, Z., Ma, Q.: An eye-tracking study of website complexity from cognitive load perspective. Decis. Support Syst. **62**, 1 (2014). https://doi.org/10.1016/j.dss.2014.02.007
22. Pillai, P., Balasingam, B., Kim, Y.H., Lee, C., Biondi, F.: Eye-gaze metrics for cognitive load detection on a driving simulator. IEEE-ASME Trans. Mechatron. **27**, 2134–2141 (2022). https://doi.org/10.1109/TMECH.2022.3175774
23. Jenke, R., Peer, A., Buss, M.: Feature extraction and selection for emotion recognition from EEG. IEEE Trans. Affective Comput. **5**, 327–339 (2014). https://doi.org/10.1109/TAFFC.2014.2339834
24. Cambria, E.: Affective computing and sentiment analysis. IEEE Intell. Syst. **6** (2016)
25. Barricelli, B.R., Casiraghi, E., Fogli, D.: A survey on digital twin: definitions, characteristics, applications, and design implications. IEEE Access **7**, 167653–167671 (2019). https://doi.org/10.1109/ACCESS.2019.2953499
26. Parasuraman, R., Manzey, D.H.: Complacency and bias in human use of automation: an attentional integration. Hum Factors **52**, 381–410 (2010). https://doi.org/10.1177/0018720810376055
27. Small, H.: Co-citation in the scientific literature: a new measure of the relationship between two documents. J. Am. Soc. Inf. Sci. **24**, 265–269 (1973). https://doi.org/10.1002/asi.4630240406
28. Zeng, Z., Pantic, M., Roisman, G.I., Huang, T.S.: A survey of affect recognition methods: audio, visual, and spontaneous expressions. IEEE Trans. Pattern Anal. Mach. Intell. **31**, 39–58 (2009). https://doi.org/10.1109/TPAMI.2008.52
29. Katsigiannis, S., Ramzan, N.: DREAMER: a database for emotion recognition through EEG and ECG signals from wireless low-cost off-the-shelf devices. IEEE J. Biomed. Health Inform. **22**, 98–107 (2018). https://doi.org/10.1109/JBHI.2017.2688239
30. Poria, S., Cambria, E., Bajpai, R., Hussain, A.: A review of affective computing: from uni-modal analysis to multimodal fusion. Information Fusion. **37**, 98–125 (2017). https://doi.org/10.1016/j.inffus.2017.02.003
31. Guo, F., Li, F., Lv, W., Liu, L., Duffy, V.G.: Bibliometric analysis of affective computing researches during 1999–2018. Int. J. Hum. Comput. Interact. **36**, 801–814 (2020). https://doi.org/10.1080/10447318.2019.1688985
32. Wu, D., Xu, Y., Lu, B.-L.: Transfer learning for EEG-based brain-computer interfaces: a review of progress made since 2016. IEEE Trans. Cogn. Dev. Syst. **14**, 4–19 (2022). https://doi.org/10.1109/TCDS.2020.3007453
33. Gunes, H., Schuller, B.: Categorical and dimensional affect analysis in continuous input: current trends and future directions. Image Vis. Comput. **31**, 120–136 (2013). https://doi.org/10.1016/j.imavis.2012.06.016
34. Kothe, C.A., Makeig, S.: BCILAB: a platform for brain–computer interface development. J. Neural Eng. **10**, 056014 (2013). https://doi.org/10.1088/1741-2560/10/5/056014
35. Koelstra, S., et al.: DEAP: a database for emotion analysis; using physiological signals. IEEE Trans. Affect. Comput. **3**, 18–31 (2012). https://doi.org/10.1109/T-AFFC.2011.15
36. Huang, M., Zhu, X., Gao, J.: Challenges in building intelligent open-domain dialog systems. ACM Trans. Inf. Syst. **38**, 21 (2020). https://doi.org/10.1145/3383123

37. Jiang, Y., Li, W., Hossain, M.S., Chen, M., Alelaiwi, A., Al-Hammadi, M.: A snapshot research and implementation of multimodal information fusion for data-driven emotion recognition. Inf. Fusion. **53**, 209–221 (2020). https://doi.org/10.1016/j.inffus.2019.06.019

38. Huang, G., Liu, Z., Van Der Maaten, L., Weinberger, K.Q.: Densely connected convolutional networks. In: 2017 IEEE Conference on Computer Vision and Pattern Recognition (CVPR), pp. 2261–2269 (2017). https://doi.org/10.1109/CVPR.2017.243

39. Mehmood, R.M., Du, R., Lee, H.J.: Optimal feature selection and deep learning ensembles method for emotion recognition from human brain EEG sensors. IEEE Access **5**, 14797–14806 (2017). https://doi.org/10.1109/ACCESS.2017.2724555

40. Atkinson, J., Campos, D.: Improving BCI-based emotion recognition by combining EEG feature selection and kernel classifiers. Expert Syst. Appl. **47**, 35–41 (2016). https://doi.org/10.1016/j.eswa.2015.10.049

41. Mustaqeem, K.S.: Optimal feature selection based speech emotion recognition using two-stream deep convolutional neural network. Int. J. Intell. Syst. **36**, 5116–5135 (2021). https://doi.org/10.1002/int.22505

42. Chen, C.: Searching for intellectual turning points: progressive knowledge domain visualization. Proc. Natl. Acad. Sci. **101**, 5303–5310 (2004). https://doi.org/10.1073/pnas.0307513100

43. Kleinsmith, A., Bianchi-Berthouze, N.: Affective body expression perception and recognition: a survey. IEEE Trans. Affect. Comput. **4**, 15–33 (2013). https://doi.org/10.1109/T-AFFC.2012.16

44. Liu, W., Zheng, W.-L., Lu, B.-L.: Emotion Recognition Using Multimodal Deep Learning. In: Hirose, A., Ozawa, S., Doya, K., Ikeda, K., Lee, M., Liu, D. (eds.) ICONIP 2016. LNCS, vol. 9948, pp. 521–529. Springer, Cham (2016). https://doi.org/10.1007/978-3-319-46672-9_58

45. Dzedzickis, A., Kaklauskas, A., Bucinskas, V.: Human emotion recognition: review of sensors and methods. Sensors **20**, 592 (2020). https://doi.org/10.3390/s20030592

Author Index

A

Abele, Nils Darwin I-317
Abrami, Giuseppe I-539, II-461
Adam, Stella I-162
Afisa II-357
Aguilar, Chloe I-330
Akula, Sathish II-562
Alapati, Sreejan I-3
Alkawarit, Mahmood I-162
Amici, Federica II-402
Amith, Muhammad I-330
An, Kai I-14
André, Rafael de Pinho I-24
Andreoni, Giuseppe I-35, I-205, I-566
Aoustin, Yannick I-3
Arias, Kika II-88
Arredondo, María Teresa II-260
Arroyo, Peña II-260
Auster-Gussman, Lisa II-88
Avanzini, Pietro I-205

B

Bagci, Mevlüt I-539
Balasankar, Santhosh Kumar I-429
Bassi, Marta I-444
Bastian, Johannes II-461
Baumartz, Daniel II-461
Berckmans, Daniel I-444
Bhargava, Divya II-531
Bian, Yishan II-154
Bier, Marina I-609
Biffi, Emilia I-35
Biggs, Adam II-562
Binu, Marlyn I-102
Blanchard, Nathaniel I-592
Blecher, Yannic II-461
Borges, Adriano Mendes II-3
Bosani, Enrica I-242
Braun, Christopher I-48
Brilmayer, Ingmar II-402

B (continued)

Brukamp, Kirsten II-225
Brutti, Richard I-578
Budgenhagen, David II-461
Burbach, Laura II-20, II-439

C

Cabrera, María Fernanda II-260
Calero Valdez, André II-20, II-368, II-439
Campis, Leonardo II-236
Campis-Freyle, Leonardo I-395, II-104
Cao, Yaqin II-590
Carissoli, Claudia I-444
Castro-Camargo, Zahiry II-272
Casu, Giulia I-194
Cavatorta, Maria Pia I-242
Celani-De Souza, Helder Jose II-104
Chablat, D. I-497
Charris-Maldonado, Cindy II-272
Chen, Jing II-65
Chen, Qi II-65
Chen, Yuerong II-154
Cheng, Hong I-642
Chevallereau, C. I-497
Christof, Roman II-461
Cibrario, Valerio I-242
Ciccone, Nicholas II-260
Cipric, Ana II-260
Cong, Ruichen II-154
Cullen-Smith, Suzanne II-123
Cunha Monteiro, Walbert II-3
Ćwiek, Aleksandra II-402

D

De Marco, Doriana I-205
de Oliveira Vargas, Vitor I-344
de Souza, Marcelo I-24
Dei, Carla I-35, I-444
Deng, Ou II-378
Despins, Laurel I-344
Delle Fave, Antonella I-444

Ding, Lin   I-14
Ding, Lv   II-77
Dong, Ziyan   I-290, II-169
Doyle, Julie   II-123
Du, Hongyu   II-392
Duan, Runlin   I-70
Duffy, Vincent G.   I-58, I-70, I-87, I-102,
    II-490, II-531

E

El Khoury, Tracy   II-531
Ellegast, Rolf   I-48, II-298
Engel, Juliane   I-539
Escorcia-Charris, Sulay   II-272
Espeleta-Aris, Andrea   II-104
Ewald, Tim-Oliver   II-461

F

Fabbri Destro, Maddalena   I-205
Fauerbach, Tim   II-461
Favacho Queiroz, Vinicius   II-3
Feng, Yuan   I-632
Fico, Giuseppe   II-260
Folkvord, Frans   II-260
Fonseca, Almir   I-24
Frank, Carolin   I-609
Franke, Thomas   I-368, II-306
Friemert, Daniel   I-48, I-162
Fritzsche, Lennart   II-402
Fruhling, Ann   II-138
Fuchs, Susanne   II-402

G

Gaikwad, Nandini   I-58
Ganser, Rachel   II-20
García-Constantino, Matías   II-272, II-503
Garofalo, Fabio   I-355
Garza, Kimberly B.   II-562
Ge, Chang   I-525
George, Micah Wilson   I-58
Gilbert, Kristin   I-383
Graham, Sarah   II-88
Greenwood, Allen G.   I-58
Gregori, Alina   II-402
Gruner, Marthe   I-368, II-306
Gruppioni, Emanuele   I-566
Guda, V. K   I-497
Guo, Wenbin   I-632

H

Haase, Germaine   I-383
Hafner, Florian   I-609
Halbach, Patrick   II-439
Hamilton, Jane   I-330
Hanning, Nina   I-609
Harth, Volker   I-48
Hartmann, Ulrich   I-48, II-298
Hashimoto, Nagisa   I-175
Hawkins, Gary   II-562
Hebri, Aref   I-120
Henlein, Alexander   I-539, II-402, II-461
Herbort, Oliver   I-510, II-402
Hernández Palma, Hugo   II-236
Hernandez, Leonel   II-236
Hernández-Palma, Hugo   I-395
Hoffmann, Sven   I-317
Hou, Jingming   I-642
Hu, Xiangjun   II-590
Hu, Xiuying   I-642
Hu, Xiyun   I-70
Hu, Zhe   II-38
Huang, Xu   I-632
Huang, Yingjie   II-77
Hussain, Muzammil   II-49

I

Islam, Md Tariqul   I-87
Iyer, Krittika J.   I-102
Izdebski, Krzysztof   I-162

J

Jacobs, An   II-123
Jaiswal, Ashish   I-120
Jiang, Yue   II-65
Jiménez-Delgado, Genett   I-395, II-104
Jin, Kevin   I-135
Jin, Qun   II-154, II-378
Jonnalagadda, Soundarya   II-138
Joshi, Ravindra   II-562

K

Kahl, Anke   I-609
Kasaie Sharifi, Alireza   I-344
Karamanidis, Kiros   I-48, II-298
Kaufmann, Mirko   II-298
Kaufman-Ortiz, Kevin J.   I-413
Kerdvibulvech, Chutisant   II-480
Kett, Attila   II-461

Khan, Tazrin   I-330
Khan, Yasir Imtiaz   II-503
Kim, Byeongmok   II-490
Kim, Jung Hyup   I-344
Kim, Mingyeong   II-185
Kim, Sean   II-562
Kim, Yonggab   II-490
Kluge, Annette   II-298
Kluth, Karsten   I-317
Konca, Maxim   I-539
Konios, Alexandros   II-104, II-503
Krause, Lisa-Marie   I-510
Krishnaswamy, Nikhil   I-592
Kügler, Frank   II-402

L
Laguardia, Luis   I-24
Lai, Kenneth   I-578
Laohakangvalvit, Tipporn   II-211
Laun, Martin   I-48
Leban, Bruno   I-194
Lee, Kevin   I-135
Lemanski, Jens   II-402
Leuthner, Nicolai   I-48
Li, Qingchen   I-147
Li, Tiantian   I-413
Li, Yi   II-38
Li, Yuxi   II-154
Liebal, Katja   II-402
Liu, Long   II-65
Liu, Qing   I-303
Liu, Weilin   II-392
Liu, Xiangyu   I-290, II-77, II-169
Liu, Xinran   I-290, II-169
Liu, Yang   I-525
Liu, Yu   II-590
Liu, Ziyi   I-70
Loitsch, Claudia   II-341
Londoño-Lara, Luz   I-395
López-Meza, Pedro   II-272
Lopez-Nava, Irvin Hussein   II-503
Lopomo, Nicola Francesco   I-35, I-205
Lu, Jiayuan   II-77
Lücking, Andy   I-539, II-402
Luebke, Andre   I-87
Lungfiel, Andy   I-276
Luo, Jing   II-197
Lupiáñez-Villanueva, Francisco   II-260
Lusta, Majdi   II-562

M
Ma, Liang   I-478
Majumdar, Neelakshi   II-531
Makedon, Fillia   I-120
Maletz, Lucia   I-609
Marais, Karen   II-531
Mashika, Mpho   II-250
Masny, Patrick   II-461
Mayat, Nils   I-162
McGuckin, Lily   II-562
Meenakshi, Sindhu   I-429
Mehler, Alexander   I-539, II-402, II-461
Meixner, Gerrit   I-256
Mekata, Yuki   I-175
Mende, Julian   II-461
Merino-Barbancho, Beatriz   II-260
Miao, Chongchong   I-14
Miao, Ke   II-77
Misran,   II-357
Molinares-Ramirez, Estefany   II-272
Molina-Romero, Jainer Enrique   II-236
Montero-Bula, Carlos   I-395
Mugisha, S.   I-497

N
Nakanishi, Miwa   I-175, II-548
Nakayama, Johannes   II-368
Narula, Nandini   I-102
Navarro-Jimenez, Eduardo   II-104
Negri, Luca   I-444
Nguyen, Kim Tien   II-402
Nickel, Peter   I-184, I-276
Nishimura, Shoji   II-154
Nunner, Hendrik   II-368
Nurmandi, Achmad   II-357

O
Ogihara, Atsushi   II-154
Oh, Yunmin   II-88
Ono, Mako   II-548
Orrante-Weber-Burque, Fernando   II-284
Ortiz-Barrios, Miguel   II-104, II-272, II-284

P
Pancardo, Pablo   II-284
Pannasch, Sebastian   II-341
Pau, Massimiliano   I-194
Perego, Paolo   I-35, I-566
Pérez-Aguilar, Armando   II-272, II-284

Peuscher, Heiko II-306
Peña Fernández, Alberto I-444
Pietrzyk, Ulrike I-383
Pinatti De Carvalho, Aparecido Fabiano
    I-317
Polak, Sara II-123
Porta, Micaela I-194
Pouw, Wim II-402
Prasetya, Aji II-236
Prieto, Pilar II-402
Puangseree, Passawit I-355
Pustejovsky, James I-578

Q
Qiu, Jing I-642
Quintero-Ariza, Iván I-395
Quintino, Marc I-539

R
Ramesh Babu, Ashwin I-120
Reisher, Elizabeth II-138
Rhee, Danniel I-330
Richards, Mackenzie I-135
Richardson, Alexicia II-562
Roca-Umbert Würth, Ana II-260
Rohrer, Patrick Louis II-402
Rojas-Castro, Edgar I-395
Romero-Gómez, Jeremy I-395
Ruiz Ariza, Jose II-236
Rujas, Miguel II-260

S
Sá, José Carlos I-395
Sánchez-Ramón, Paula G. II-402
Santana-de Oliveira, Jonas II-104
Santos, Gilberto I-395
Sarfraz, Isra II-49
Saukel, Kevin I-539
Savas, Lara S. I-330
Scalona, Emilia I-205
Schaub, Meike I-242
Schiefer, Christoph I-48
Schlenz, Anna I-215
Schmidt, Kerstin I-215
Schmidt, Paul I-215
Schneider, Moritz II-298
Schnüre, Paul II-461
Schreiber, Jakob I-539

Schrills, Tim I-368, II-306
Schrottenbacher, Patrick I-539
Schüler, Thomas I-162
Schulte-Rüther, Martin II-402
Schumacher, Petra B. II-402
Schwarz, Mario I-256
Schweinberger, Stefan R. II-402
Schweitzer, Marcus I-317
Seals, Cheryl D. II-562
Sepanloo, Kamelia I-87
Serique Meiguins, Bianchi II-3
Seth, Deep I-3
Sharma, Abhishek II-49
Sheng, Qinqin II-576
Shi, Bin II-77
Shi, Liangliang I-303
Sierra-Urbina, Gisell II-272
Sillevis Smitt, Myriam II-123
Siriborvornratanakul, Thitirat II-329
Sironi, Roberto I-566
Soares de Sousa, Thiago Augusto II-3
Spiekermann, Christian I-539
Sripian, Peeraya II-211
Stevanoni, Giulia I-35
Storm, Fabio Alexander I-444
Storm, Fabio I-35
Striegl, Julian II-341
Struckmeier, Volker II-402
Subekti, Dimas II-357
Sugaya, Midori II-211
Sun, Guoqiang I-14
Sun, Xiang II-392

T
Tago, Kiichi II-154
Tam, Christopher I-578
Tang, Hao II-77
Tang, Lu I-330
Tao, Cui I-330
Tegtmeier, Patricia I-459
Terhoeven, Jan I-459
Terschüren, Claudia I-48
Torres-Mercado, Alina II-272
Trettenbrein, Patrick C. II-402

V
Vale Pinheiro, Kelly II-3
van der Haar, Dustin II-250

van Leeuwen, Cora II-123
VanderHoeven, Hannah I-592
Vargas, Manuela I-242
Vásquez Avendaño, Emilse María II-236
Velluvakkandy, Ronak I-87
Vervier, Luisa II-20, II-368
Vicente, Diego I-256
Viel, Marc II-461
von Eiff, Celina I. II-402
Vox, Jan P. I-162

W

Waldorf, Julia I-609
Walther, Alexander II-341
Wang, Chen I-478
Wang, Hong I-632
Wang, Peicheng II-392
Wang, Yilin I-642
Weber, Anika I-162, II-298
Weber, Gerhard II-341
Westfal, Lucas I-24
Wetzel, Christoph I-276
Wischniewski, Sascha I-459
Wolf, Karen Insa I-162
Wu, Jianlun II-154
Wu, Lei II-576
Wu, Xiang I-290, II-169
Wu, Xu I-14
Wu, Yeqi I-290, II-169

Wu, Yongxin I-147
Wulf, Volker I-317

X

Xie, Hongqin I-642
Xiong, Wei I-478
Xu, Li I-290, II-169
Xu, Peng I-642
Xu, Tianfeng I-290, II-169
Xue, Yanmin I-303, I-525

Y

Yan, Wen I-525
Yan, Yuqing II-197
Ye, Yaping II-154
Yi, Jae Sun II-185
Yokoyama, Kayo I-24
Yu, Suihuai I-303

Z

Zaki Zadeh, Mohammad I-120
Zhang, Di II-77
Zhang, Wenping II-392
Zhang, Yi II-590
Zheng, Kaiqiao II-197
Zhou, Yihui I-525
Ziaratnia, Sayyedjavad II-211
Ziefle, Martina II-20, II-368, II-439
Zlatkin-Troitschanskaia, Olga I-539

Printed in the United States
by Baker & Taylor Publisher Services